M000105410

The laws of Shabbos

An English compilation of the laws of Shabbos from the Alter Rebbe's Shulchan Aruch, in accordance to topic.

Volume 3
This Volume includes the Laws of:
Chapters 322-325
Bathing
Medicine and First Aid
Shearing
Writing and Erasing
Meameir
Sewing and Gluing
Reading
Music
Home Cleaning
Games
Plants and trees
Shabbos Bris
International Dateline

Includes summaries and hundreds of practical Q&A.

Compiled by Rabbi Yaakov Goldstein

A Semicha aid for learning the Laws of Shabbos Vol. 3

Second Edition
Published and copyrighted © by
Yaakov Goldstein
Bar Yochaiy Safed, Israel
For orders, questions, comments, contact:
Tel: 050-695-2866
E-mail: rabbiygoldstein@gmail.com
www.shulchanaruchharav.com
Available on Amazon.com

5781 • 2021

Shulchanaruchharav.com is a state-of-the-art Halacha website that contains the largest English database of detailed Halacha available on the web. A Halacha database has been established to help the learner research a Halacha and have it available on his fingertips. For further information visit our site at
www.shulchanaruchharav.com
Please support us!
Our website is available free of charge and is dependent on subscription of our site members! Please see our website for member options!

ב"ה

RABBI MENACHEM M. GLUCKOWSKY
CHABAD RECHOVOT
12 HAGANA ST. RECHOVOT ISRAEL
Tel: 08-9493176 **Fax**:08-9457620 **Cel**: 050-4145770

מנחם מענדל גלוכובסקי
רב קהילת חב"ד ברחובות
מען : רח' ההגנה 12/1 רחובות 76214
משרד 08-9493176 פקס. 08-9457620 נייד 050-4145770

Elul 577

I have seen the valuable Sefer "A Semicha Aid for Learning The Laws of Shabbos" written by Rabbi Yaakov Goldstein. The purpose of this Sefer is to assist students learning Semicha in learning the material from the Alter Rebbe's Shulchan Aruch, as well as for them to come out with a valuable and large database of knowledge in practical Halachic questions dealt with in contemporary authorities. It excels in its clear presentation, concise language and thorough summaries in all the relevant laws covered in the Shulchan Aruch of Admur.

It can also serve the general English public in giving them the opportunity to learn the Laws of Shabbos faithful to the opinion of the Alter Rebbe.

Mention must be made, as writes the author in his foreword, that one is not to use this Sefer, amongst all Sefarim of Melaktim, to Pasken for himself. One must rather address all matters which require clarification to a qualified Rav.

I bless the author for his work and wish him much success.

Menachem Mendel Gluckowsky.

בס"ד

RABBI B. YURKOWICZ
CHABAD LOD

ברוך בועז יורקוביץ
רב ומד"א דשיכון חב"ד לוד
אה"ק ת"ו

The book "The laws of Shabbos" written by Rabbi Yaakov Goldstein is a comprehensive compilation of the laws and customs of Shabbos, up until the many Poskim of today's time, which discuss the practical applications of the laws. Sefarim of this nature are very important and will certainly strengthen the proper observance of Shabbos.

I thus come here with words of blessing and praise to my dear acquaintance, the author, who brings merits to the masses through this important work.

As the author himself has mentioned in his foreword I reiterate that which is known that the layman cannot use this Sefer to Pasken for himself even after learning it in whole, but must rather address all their questions to a qualified Rav.

I am confident that in the merit of this spreading of the laws of Shabbos, on which the Sages state "If the Jews guarded Shabbos they would be redeemed", it will hasten the coming of our righteous Moshiach speedily in our days.

Rabbi Baruch Jurkavitch

הרב ב... בועז יורקוביץ'
רב מרא דאתרא שיכון חב"ד לוד
08-9256070, 054-7977042

Notice

The Halachas provided in this book are intended to serve as an aid in understanding Halacha, and as a resource of practical Halachic questions. It is not meant at all to take the place of a competent Rav, Moreh Horaah. Hence one should not Pasken based on this book without either discussing the matter with a Rav or verifying the matter in the many resources provided by author.

Foreword

Acknowledgement:

First and foremost, I give thanks to the Almighty which has blessed me to be able to compile this work. I thank my wife, My Eishes Chayil, Shayna, which if not for her support this book would have been impossible to accomplish. I thank all the Rabbanim and Rosheiy Yeshivas which have given me advice and support regarding the project, and of course my students in which through teaching them many insights have been added to the laws written here, following the dictum of the Sages "And from my students more than all". A special thanks to Rabbi Roberto Szerer and his wife who have graciously given their support throughout the course of the writing of this Sefer, The merit of the masses rests on their shoulders. I also thank each and every member of shulchanaruchharav.com who with their monthly support throughout the course of the writing of this Sefer fulfill the dictum of the Sages "If there is flour [$] there is Torah" and allowed me the time to write this book.

The importance of learning Halacha:

It is known and evident the importance that the study and knowledge of Halacha plays in the role of the life of a Jewish man and woman. As is known, the Rebbe lived and preached that one must be a Shulchan Aruch Yid, a Jew which every movement of his life is dictated by the directives of the Shulchan Aruch. To such extent was the knowledge of Halacha in the forefront of the Rebbe's eyes, that he pleaded and suggested in a talk of Yud Shvat 1955 that in today's times the Yeshivas are not to begin the accustomed deep analytical studies in Talmud until the students have been taught the fundamental principles of Jewish belief and the laws which are written in Shulchan Aruch. The Rebbe continued, "If the situation continues the way it is, then in a number of years from now there will not be a Rabbi which will know a simple law regarding a Jew's daily life, such as a law in the laws of Muktzah. Yes, he will know maybe a law in Nezikin or Choshen Mishpat from the Talmud which he learned, but he will be ignorant of the simplest of laws brought down in Shulchan Aruch".

Ruling of Shulchan Aruch:[1] In the laws of Talmud Torah the following ruling is given: The learning of practical Halacha takes precedence over learning other fields of Torah. Only after one is clearly well versed in practical Halacha and knows the detailed laws relevant to his daily life, is he to study other parts of Torah in depth. One is to learn majority of Orach Chaim and selected sections of Yoreh Deah, Even Haezer and Choshen Mishpat.

The opinion of the Chassidic Rabbeim: The Baal Shem Tov and Maggid state that the evil inclination tries to persuade a Jew not to learn practical Halacha and tells him to spend all of his days learning the Talmud and its commentaries. This is done in order so the person does not serve G-d properly according to His will.[2] The Alter Rebbe distanced people from learning Torah simply for the sake of Pilpul and emphasized the necessity of learning in depth for the sake of practical Halacha.[3] The Mittler Rebbe decreed that every community is to set a study session to learn the entire Alter Rebbe's Shulchan Aruch on the section of Orach Chaim.[4] The Rebbe Rashab writes that every Chassid is obligated to learn the Alter Rebbe's Shulchan Aruch Orach Chaim from beginning to end and that every person is to establish a daily learning session to learn and review these Halachos.[5] In today's generations one must especially have Mesirus Nefesh not to swerve from even one letter of Shulchan Aruch.[6] The Rebbe Rayatz reiterates this by saying that every Jew must establish a daily Torah session in Halacha, each person on his level; Shulchan Aruch or Kitzur Shulchan Aruch.[7]

---

[1] Hilchos Talmud Torah 2:9-10; Shach Yoreh Deah 246; Hakdama of Mishneh Berurah; Toras Menachem 13 p. 236
[2] Tzivas Harivash 117; Or Torah of the Maggid 221
[3] Beis Rebbe p. 32
[4] Hakdama of Mittler Rebbe in Shulchan Aruch Harav
[5] Kuntrus Hatefilah 17
[6] Sefer Hamamarim "Ein Hakadosh Baruch Hu Ba Betrunya" 1888
[7] Sefer Hamamarim 1926 p. 263

The directives of the Rebbe:[8]

<u>Learning Halacha as part of the Yeshiva schedule</u>: The Rebbe stated that a revolution is to be made in the learning curriculum of the Yeshivas, for it to include the section of Orach Chaim and practical Halacha. The Rebbe stated that if the Yeshivas don't desire to change the curriculum of the regular study hours, it should at least be encouraged when the students are on break.[9] The Yeshivas are not to begin the accustomed deep analytical studies in Talmud until the students have been taught the fundamental principles of Jewish belief and the laws which are written in Shulchan Aruch.[10] This applies even to the Yeshivos Gedolos, as we see that the knowledge of the Yeshiva students is very minute amongst the laws found in Orach Chaim.[11] If I had the power I would establish that every Mosad, beginning from the kindergartens and through the Yeshivos and Klalim, establish a Shiur in these practical laws.[12]

<u>The importance of being an expert on the laws in Orach Chaim</u>: Elsewhere the Rebbe stated: Unfortunately, we see amongst many students that the more they expand their knowledge in Talmud and its commentaries the less they know the laws relevant to their practical life. The laws in Orach Chaim are extremely necessary for one to be constantly well versed in them, as the questions that arise in these subjects in many instances do not give one the time to ask a Rabbi or look in a Sefer for the answer.[13] This especially applies to the laws of Birchas Hanehnin; Hefsek in Tefilah; Muktzah, and laws of the like of which the ignorance in these topics is appalling.[14]

<u>Establishing Shiurim in practical Halacha in all communities</u>: If I had the power I would establish that every community has a Shiur in these practical laws.[15] These Shiurim should take place in the local Shul.[16] Thus, each community, and even each individual, is to include within his Torah Shiurim a set time for learning and reviewing practical Halacha.[17] One is to have a Shiur in these Halachas every single day, even for a few minutes.[18] For this purpose it is not necessary to learn specifically from the Shulchan Aruch [which can take much time] but rather to learn from compilations of Halachas such as those found in Derech Hachaim, Kitzur Shulchan Aruch and other compilations.[19] The Rav giving the Shiur is to then give over any extra information that the listeners need to know, that is not included in the compiled Halachas.[20]

Summary:
Every Jew is to have a set learning session every day in practical Halacha, even for a few minutes a day. One is to use this time to learn practical laws from available Halacha compilations, and not necessarily from the actual Shulchan Aruch.

---

[8] See Shulchan Menachem 4 p. 238-244 for a compilation of letters and Sichos on this topic.
[9] Sichas Tzav 13th Nissan printed in Toras Menachem 13 p. 236
[10] Sichas Yud Shvat 1955
[11] Igros Kodesh 16 p. 116
[12] Igros Kodesh 10 p. 270
[13] Igros Kodesh 10 p. 130
[14] Igros Kodesh 10 p. p. 130; p. 192; p. 270; p. 355
[15] Igros Kodesh 10 p. 143
[16] Igros Kodesh ibid based on the saying of Chazal [Brachos 8a] "Hashem loves the gates of Jewish law more than the Shul and Batei Midrash."
[17] Igros Kodesh 7 p. 238
[18] Toras Menachem 7 p. 114; Learning the Halachas every single day will help one remember also the Halachas he learned the day before. [ibid]
[19] Igros Kodesh 7 p. 238; Igros Kodesh 10 p. 144; Igros Kodesh 11 p. 281; Igros Kodesh 13 p. 24; Toras Menachem 7 p. 114; "This does not refer to Tur and Beis Yosef, but rather to Shulchan Aruch and Beir Heiytiv. However one who has time for more is praised." [ibid]
[20] Igros Kodesh 13 p. 24

The intended audience for this project:
Although the project is intended as an aid for Semicha learning students, it however is not limited for this usage. As advised by Rabbanim, the practical Q&A, which features here following the compilation and summarization of each subject in Shulchan Aruch, can be of use and help for even Rabbanim and Morei Horaah, as a providence of resources within the sea of Poskim. Regarding the use of this book as an aid for Semicha, mention must be made that in no way does this book replace the necessity of learning the laws within the original Hebrew text written by the holy hand of the Alter Rebbe. A proper and honest grasp of any Halachic topic may only be received after learning and properly comprehending the source of that Halacha, and in our case this refers to learning the text inside the Shulchan Aruch of the Alter Rebbe. Nonetheless, the compilation of this book is meant to assist the learner in a number of areas so at the conclusion of his study he comes to a full grasp of the final Halachic rulings of Admur, and their practical application in today's times.

The following are many useful features provided within:
Part 1- Free Translation:
Most of the subjects discussed in the book is split to two parts; the Translation section and the Compilation section. The Translation section is a free translation of each Halacha in Admur in accordance to their order in the Shulchan Aruch of Admur. This can assist the learner of the Hebrew text in understanding the statements made, as well as finding the definition of an unknown Hebrew word. However, it should be noted that leading Mashpiim which had compiled a similar project, received directives from the Rebbe that it is not possible to properly translate the Alter Rebbe's "golden tongue". **It is thus needless to say that no inferences can be made from the current translation**. This is an addition to the fact that one cannot make an inference from a translated work.

Part 2-Compilation:
➢ *Compilation of the laws in accordance to topic*: Many times the full details regarding a specific law being learnt in the Shulchan Aruch of Admur is not fully dealt with in that law, and is rather expounded on in later laws or chapters and at times even in another subject all together. Thus, we took upon ourselves to compile all the details of a law mentioned by Admur under the topic of that law. Thus, the learner can come to a proper conclusion of the topic of the Halacha being learned.
➢ *Translation*: The compiled Halachas have been given a free translation from their original Hebrew text in Admur. **The Halachas brought in this section are not a translation in the order which was written by Admur** but rather a translation of the compiled Halachas which has been done by the author. **It is thus needless to say that no inferences can be made from the current translation** being that it at many times does not contain the entire Halacha and not to mention previous Halachas, which exist in the original and shed light onto the current topic. This is an addition to the fact that one cannot make an inference from a translated work.
Note: All the references by the translated material [i.e. *as is explained in Chapter 308 Halacha 7*] refer to the Alter Rebbe's Shulchan Aruch and not to the chapters of the book!
➢ *Explanation*: Many times, we have added words into the translation to help the reader flow through the text, and add proper understanding to the law being read. **All words added by the translator within a translated Halacha have been placed in brackets so the reader can differ between the translated words used by Admur, and that added by the author.** We have also taken the liberty of explaining difficult laws within the many footnotes added into the translation.
➢ *Summary*: Without doubt, one of the major features of the book is its concise summary which follows each and every law which is learned. In the Shulchan Aruch there are at times many opinions, many details and reasons mentioned in a given law which effect one's understanding of the outcome of the final ruling. The summary sifts through all the details mentioned in a given Halacha and brings out a clear final Halachic ruling which results from the above.

➢ *The Q&A:* The Q&A which follow each summary lend the learner a greatly needed base knowledge for practical application of the resulting law learned within a topic. Many times, even after one has sifted and comprehended the final ruling of Admur, its influence within practical cases remain obscure. This is besides for the fact that researching a question amongst the sea of Poskim is both time comprising as well as not always practical. We therefore have compiled many major practical Halachic questions which connect with a given Halacha that was learned. The answers given have been compiled from various sources, including Shabbos Kehalacha, Piskeiy Teshuvos, Shemiras Shabbos Kehilchasa as well as the many resources of Poskim brought within these Sefarim. Mention must be made that effort was placed in verifying the sources of the rulings found within these Sefarim by looking into their sources and verifying their ruling. In cases where a dispute amongst Poskim is recorded we have not given final rulings, being that we are not in a position to rule for the public like which Posek one is to follow. In these cases, one is to consult with his personal Rav and receive guidance for what he is to do. **It is of importance to note that the ruling of one's personal Rav takes precedence over any dissenting opinion brought in the book, whether or not this opinion is known to the Rav. Furthermore, even those which are in Rabbinical position of giving rulings are not to base their rulings on opinions brought in this book without first studying and verifying its source.** As is known that one may not base a ruling on summarized Halachas [Melaktim a compiler of opinions] but is rather to discern this for himself in the sources that are brought. [See Piskeiy Teshuvos Vo. 3 in the approbations of Gedolei Yisrael, and the introduction there.]

Suggested method in how to use this book

1. *Step 1: Learn the original*
   One should learn each chapter in the original Hebrew text of the Alter Rebbe's Shulchan Aruch. One is to refer to the Translation section offered in the book to help in understanding the meaning of words and content of Halachas from the Hebrew original.

2. *Step 2: Study the compilation*
   After completing each subject inside the Hebrew original one should learn the subject inside the Compilation section offered in the book to help organize, summarize and receive practical application of the knowledge he has learned in Admur.

3. *Step 3: Review the summaries*
   Approaching review for the Semicha test one should mainly focus on the summaries offered in the book after each Halacha, and when necessary refer to the inside compilation or Hebrew original.

INTRODUCTION TO SHULCHAN ARUCH HARAV

Historical background:[21]

The Shulchan Aruch Harav, also known as the Alter Rebbe's Shulchan Aruch, or Shulchan Aruch Admur Hazakein; was written by Rav Schneur Zalman of Liadi.

Its initiation: The Maggid of Mezritch was encouraged by the heavenly courts to search amongst his students for a proper candidate to compile a new Shulchan Aruch.[22] The Maggid of Mezritch chose the Alter Rebbe to write this compilation.[23]

When was it written: It was written anywhere between the years 1765-1775.[24] Some[25] prove that the section of Orach Chaim was written in the years 1771-1772. The Rebbe Rayatz writes[26] that the Maggid asked Admur to write the Shulchan Aruch when he was 21 years old.[27] The other sections of the Shulchan Aruch were written at a later time. An exact date has not been historically proven.[28]

How long did it take to write?[29] The section of Orach Chaim was written by Admur in a span of two years.

When was it printed? The Shulchan Aruch was first printed in its entirety a few years after the Alter Rebbe passed away, in the year 1816.[30] Certain sections of the Shulchan Aruch were printed beforehand. Hilchos Talmud Torah was printed in Shklov in the year 1794.[31]

The name "Shulchan Aruch Harav": The source for this name "Shulchan Aruch Harav" is seemingly based on the title of "Rav" that was given to Admur by the students of the Maggid and the Maggid himself. The following is the story related to the giving of this title:[32] The Maggid once told Reb Zusha "write to our Gaon Reb Zalmana Litvak to come here". Upon the students hearing that the Maggid referred to the Alter Rebbe as our Gaon, they gave him the title "Rav". When Reb Avraham Hamalach told this over to his father the Maggid, the Maggid replied: *"The Chevraya Kadisha have projected the truth in this statement. A name has meaning, and the Halacha is like Rav. The **Shulchan Aruch of the Rav** will be accepted within all of Jewry."*

---

[21] See the following resources for historical background of the Shulchan Aruch Harav: Hakdama of Shulchan Aruch Harav, written by the children of Admur; Sifrei Halacha Shel Admur Hazakein; Sefer Hatoldos.

[22] To note that the Gr"a also intended on writing a Shulchan Aruch with all of his final rulings, bringing only one opinion. However this did not come into fruition being the Gr"a testified that he did not have heavenly permission to do so. [Hakdama of Biur Hagr"a written by his children] However the Maggid received Divine consent and motivation to write a new Shulchan Aruch. [Sifrei Halacha Shel Admur Hazakein p. 7 footnote 1; Talpiyos 4:1-2 p. 184 in name of the Admur of Radzin]

[23] Igros Kodesh Admur Hazakein [printed in Maggid Dvarav Leyaakov Hosafos p.47]; Hakdama on Shulchan Aruch Harav, written by the children of Admur. The Maggid stated that the four cubits of Halacha are dependent on the Alter Rebbe and that even the first thought of the Alter Rebbe in a given topic is a glimmer of Divine spirit [Ruach Hakodesh]. [Letter of Maggid printed in Sefer Hatoldos p. 36]

[24] It is unclear as to exactly which year Admur began writing the Shulchan Aruch. The above years are the estimated years of when it was written. [See Sifrei Halacha Shel Admur Hazakein p. 9] Many say that the writing of the Shulchan Aruch was begun by Admur at the age of 25. Accordingly, the beginning of the writing of the Shulchan Aruch would have begun in 1770. This is five years after the Alter Rebbe arrived in Mezritch. [He arrived in Mezritch for the first time at the age of 20 -Hakdama of Shulchan Aruch written by the children of Admur; Igros Kodesh Admur Hazakein 2:32; See also Beis Rebbe 2:1; Likutei Dibburim 3:483.] The year that the Alter Rebbe arrived in Mezritch was 1764. [Rebbe in Hagada Shel Pesach "Bedikas Chameitz"]

[25] Footnote 16-17 in Hakdama of new Kehos printing.

[26] Sefer Hasichos 1929 Sukkos brought in Sefer Hatoldos 3 p. 161

[27] Accordingly, it was written in the year 1765-1767. Vetzaruch Iyun

[28] See Sifrei Halacha Shel Admur Hazakein p. 9-10

[29] Hakdama of Shulchan Aruch Harav, written by the children of Admur.

[30] Prior to that time the Chassidim had many handwritten copies of the Shulchan Aruch. However, it was not printed in a formal book. [Piskeiy Hassidur introduction]

[31] Sefer Hatoldos p. 33

[32] Likkutei Dibburim 1 p. 100-101

The purpose of its compilation and its necessity over the Shulchan Aruch of Rav Yosef Caro [i.e. Michaber]:

The compilation of the new Shulchan Aruch was to serve a dual purpose:

1. To arbitrate between the many Halachic opinions that developed since the printing of the Shulchan Aruch of the Michaber.[33]
2. To explain the reasons behind the Halachas, hence lending the learner the ability to compare the reason to similar cases and later come to a proper Rabbinical decision.[34]

The burning of the manuscripts:[35]

In the year 1810 the original manuscripts of the entire Alter Rebbe's Shulchan Aruch were destroyed in a fire that broke out in Liadi.[36] The Alter Rebbe cried bitterly over this loss, and did not imagine he would get such Divine retribution. It is for this reason that many chapters, and selected laws within chapters, are missing from the available print, as the Shulchan Aruch was never formally printed until after the Alter Rebbe passed away, and by that time only copies, of parts of the original, remained.

The second version of the Shulchan Aruch [Mahadurah Basra] and the rulings of the Siddur:[37]

As stated above the first version of the Shulchan Aruch was written in the years 1765-1775 while Admur was by his teacher the Maggid of Mezritch. Years later Admur began writing a second version of the Shulchan Aruch with various changes in his conclusive rulings.[38] The second version was lost in the fire together with sections of the first version. To date only the first four chapters of the second version have been found.

The Siddur: The Siddur was first published in the year 1803.[39] It includes various Halachas written by Admur. These Halachas are split into two sections. 1) Halachas that are relevant to the different areas of prayer and 2) a summary of topics of Halacha called "Seder".

The general difference between the Siddur/Basra and Shulchan Aruch Kama:[40] The Siddur is not merely a summary of practical laws and directives that are needed at the worshipper's fingertips. It includes many Halachic novelties of Admur which he did not enter in his Shulchan Aruch. In many instances the rulings in his Siddur and Basra differ from his rulings in the Shulchan Aruch [Kama]. Various reasons have been attributed to this change of ruling. The general difference between the form of arbitration of the Shulchan Aruch [Kama] and that written in the Siddur and Basra is that the Shulchan Aruch [Kama] was written based on the opinions of the Talmudists and Codifiers and did not take into account the opinion of the

---

[33] Hakdama of Shulchan Aruch Harav, written by the children of Admur.
After the compilation of the Shulchan Aruch of the Michaber a number of dissenting opinions over various Halachas were voiced and later compiled as part of the Shulchan Aruch. These commentaries include the Magen Avraham; Taz; Elya Raba; Levush; Chok Yaakov; Shvus Yaakov; Olas Tamid; Bach; Ateres Zekeinim; Soles Belula; Peri Chadash; Tevuos Shur; Beir Heiytiv; Kreisy Upleisiy. This left the reader with an inability of knowing how he should practically follow. Thus the Alter Rebbe was given the great task of sifting through all the opinions, learning all the laws in extreme depth from their Talmudic sources and then handing down an authoritative decision regarding which opinion to follow. [ibid]

[34] Hakdama of Shulchan Aruch Harav; Sifrei Halacha Shel Admur Hazakein p. 31-32; Likutei Sichos 6 p. 40; Hilchos Talmud Torah Admur 1:6; 2:1.

[35] See Sifrei Halacha Shel Admur Hazakein p. 28

[36] Mittler Rebbe in Igros Kodesh p. 225; Hakdama of Shulchan Aruch Harav by the sons of Admur mentions two fires that destroyed the manuscripts. Perhaps this refers to the fire that broke out in 1813 when Admur was running away from Napoleon.
The Shulchan Aruch of the Mittler Rebbe: To note that the Mittler Rebbe, the son of the Alter Rebbe, likewise wrote a Shulchan Aruch on all four sections of the Tur. Likewise he wrote a lengthy commentary on the Shulchan Aruch of his father. Nevertheless, these manuscripts never made it to print and were lost over the years. [Migdal Oz p. 80 as told by the son of the Rebbe Maharash, Rebbe Menachem Mendal]

[37] See Shaar Hakolel 1:1; Piskeiy Hassidur Hakdama

[38] Hakdama of sons on the Shulchan Aruch: "After many years when he became aged in wisdom he began to edit and novelize his rulings in Orach Chaim, beginning with the laws of Netilas Yadayim."

[39] See Likkutei Sichos 11 p. 246; However, there were some that thought the Siddur of Admur was written earlier than the Shulchan Aruch. [See Shulchan Hatahor 8:2]

[40] See Shaar Hakolel 1:1; Piskeiy Hassidur Hakdama
Negation of saying the Siddur is only for Chassidim: Many were accustomed to say that the Shulchan Aruch was written for all the Jewish people while the Siddur was written for Chassidim. [see Minchas Elazar 1:23] The Piskeiy Hassidur ibid strongly disproves this claim saying it is completely unfounded and defies logic.

Mekubalim. However, in the Siddur and Basra, Admur took the opinion of the Kabbalists into account and in many instances follows their ruling as opposed to the Talmudists and Codifiers.[41] This however does not attribute for all the changes of ruling between the Shulchan Aruch [Kama] and Siddur and Basra.[42] In many instances the change in ruling is simply a change of arbitration in a dispute amongst the codifiers. It is known that in the Shulchan Aruch Kama, Admur refrained from writing any personal novelties that were not sourced in previous Codifiers. Likewise, he gave a lot of weight to the opinions of certain Poskim and hence followed their ruling in many instances.[43] However, in the Siddur and Basra, which was written much later in his life, Admur wrote his own personal understanding and arbitrations, giving less weight to the rulings of his predecessors which don't have support in the Talmud and Rishonim.[44] In majority of cases Admur was more stringent in his Siddur [and Basra] than his Shulchan Aruch, and in very few places was he lenient against his Shulchan Aruch.[45]

Who does one follow, the Siddur or the Shulchan Aruch?[46] Whenever there is a difference in ruling between the Siddur and the Shulchan Aruch one is to follow the rulings of the Siddur. The reason for this is because the Siddur was written later than the Shulchan Aruch and hence represents the final ruling of Admur in the given subject. [The same rule applies regarding the Kama and the Basra.]

Following the rulings of Shulchan Aruch Harav versus other Poskim:[47]
Chabad Chassidim have accepted the rulings of the Shulchan Aruch Harav for all matters, whether for leniency or stringency. This applies even if majority of codifiers argue on his opinion. This is similar to those who follow the opinion of the Rambam [or Michaber] and do not divert from his opinion. The Maggid stated that the four cubits of Halacha are dependent on the Alter Rebbe and that even the first thought of the Alter Rebbe in a given topic is a glimmer of Divine spirit [Ruach Hakodesh].[48] His rulings and arbitrations are considered as if they were given on Sinai.49 The Tzaddik, Reb Levi Yitzchak of Berditchiv writes50 as follows: *"I testify heaven and earth that if the Alter Rebbe were alive in the times of the Rif and Rambam he would be considered like one of their contemporaries etc. His "words of gold" is literally like the words of the Rif and Rambam of blessed memory."*

---

[41] In 25:28 Admur rules that when there is a dispute between the Talmudists and Codifiers and the Kabbalists one is to follow the Codifiers. However, if the Kabalists are stringent, one is to likewise be stringent like them, although this is not obligatory. Reb Hillel of Paritch related to Harav Avraham David Lavut [brought in his Sefer Shaar Hakolel 1:1; Likkutei Sichos 33 p. 95] that one time they asked the Alter Rebbe how to rule in a dispute between the codifiers and Kabalists and Admur answered that in general one is to follow the Kabalists. They then asked him that he himself ruled in his Shulchan Aruch that one is to follow the Poskim. Admur then replied: "That ruling that I wrote in the Shulchan Aruch follows the ruling of the Poskim in a case that there is a dispute between them and the Mekubalim. However, the Mekubalim write that in a case of dispute one is to follow the Kabala. It is not possible that the Mekubalim will rule against the Talmud or the Poskim that ruled based on the Talmud, as all Jews must abide by all the Talmudic rulings."
[42] The Shaar Hakolel ibid concludes that this is the main difference between the Kama and Siddur:Basra as in the later versions Admur follows the rulings of the Mekubalim. However, the Piskeiy Hassidur of Rav Avraham Chaim Naah adds that although this is true this does not attribute for all the Halachic differences.
[43] See Hakdama on the Shulchan Aruch: "The Shulchan Aruch is based on the opinion of all the Poskim, Rishonim and Achronim, with the M"A at their head. The Alter Rebbe did not argue on them but rather merely arbitrated between their opinions."; See Likkutei Sichos Vol. 32 p. 145 footnote 43
[44] Hakdama of sons on the Shulchan Aruch; Tzemach Tzedek 18:4; Divrei Nechemia 21; Minchas Elazar 1:23; Piskeiy Hassidur ibid
Hakdama of sons on the Shulchan Aruch: "The Shulchan Aruch is based on the opinion of all the Poskim, Rishonim and Achronim, with the M"A at their head. The Alter Rebbe did not argue on them but rather merely arbitrated between their opinions. However, after many years when he became aged in wisdom he began to edit and novelize his rulings in Orach Chaim, beginning with the laws of Netilas Yadayim."
Divrei Nechemia 21: "In the Shulchan Aruch the Alter Rebbe was very careful not to negate the rulings of the previous Poskim, especially the M"A. However, in his later years when he became exceedingly advanced in his wisdom he argued on the previous codifiers [Achronim] even in matters that they were stringent, and codified the laws in accordance to his own personal opinion even to be lenient. It was explicitly heard from Admur that he has retracted his original method of arbitration which gave a lot of weight to the opinion of the M"A. This especially applies by those rulings that the Achronim wrote without support from any of the Rishonim."
Tzemach Tzedek 18:4: "I heard from the Alter Rebbe himself that there are matters which he retracted from his rulings in Shulchan Aruch as he relied too much on the M"A."
[45] Piskeiy Hassidur ibid
[46] Shaar Hakolel 1:1; Likkutei Sichos 11 p. 246; Introduction of the Rebbe to the Shulchan Aruch Harav; See Divrei Nechemia 21
[47] Hakdama of Ketzos Hashulchan; See Divrei Nechemia Yoreh Deah 1
[48] Letter of Maggid printed in Sefer Hatoldos p. 36
[49] Letter of Maggid printed in Maggid Dvarav Leyaakov Hosafos p. 100
[50] Brought in Piskeiy Hassidur ibid

Our State-of-the-Art Shabbos Online course
Shulchanaruchharav.com

Shabbos Part 2
Shabbos 2

The Shabbos 3 course consists of the study of chapters 322-343 in Shulchan Aruch Orach Chaim

Content:
The course modules contain tests and assignment, per topic or chapter. The student works his way through each section until completion of the course. The students' progress and assignments are directly overseen by Semicha aid author Rabbi Yaakov Goldstein, dean of HSSP and director of Shulchanaruchharav.com

Intended Audience:
You may choose to take this course as part of our Semicha program [pending prior acceptance], or for personal knowledge.

Online Home Study Semicha Program
Under the Auspices of
Rabbi Yaakov Goldstein, Director of Shulchanaruchharav.com & Author of the "Semicha Aid" and
"Halacha Aid" series

About
Shulchanaruchharav.com runs an international Home Study Semicha Program, H.S.S.P., catered for those who desire to study the Semicha curriculum and receive Semicha certification although do not have the ability to do so in a Yeshiva setting. A home study program is hence available for students of all ages to become efficient in Halacha and receive Semicha certification from the comfort of their home, in accordance to their time and leisure. For more information on this program please see our website shulchanaruchharav.com.

The purpose of our Semicha program:
The purpose of our Semicha program is to provide Jewish men throughout the world the opportunity of learning practical Halacha within a Semicha curriculum. The entire idea behind today's Semicha is, as explained by the Lubavitcher Rebbe, to increase one's knowledge of practical Halacha in order to be aware of possible Halachic issues involving day to day occurrences. Often one is unable to turn to a Rav to verify the answer for a Shaala and hence prior knowledge is necessary. Through this program one will gain knowledge in various topics of practical Halacha. The student will be tested and receive certification for his accomplishments. We provide learning text books for each subject. These textbooks are meant to accompany the student throughout his home learning and afterwards whenever a question comes up. This allows students who are unable to learn in an actual Semicha institute to also learn the curriculum, gain the knowledge, and receive certification.

What is the difference between your Semicha program and other online Semicha programs that already exist?
Baruch Hashem, we have seen the sprout of many different Semicha programs which cater to different types of students and a variety of settings. Some online Semicha programs currently available, offers the student an online Yeshiva setting of learning Semicha with live online classes. Other programs do not provide set online classes by a teacher, but rather allow the student to learn the material on his own or with a Chavrusa at his own pace, with assistance from the Rabbinical staff. Our program offers both tracks. One can choose the **self-study track**, in which he follows the course module and completes the study of material, and assignments on his own, using the literature that we provide. A second track, the **Yeshiva track**, allows students to join an online classroom platform which includes live Shiurim by Rabbi Goldstein, who will escort the student in his learning throughout the course. Another aspect of our program which has not yet been seen in other Semicha programs is that we offer a large variety of practical Halachic topics for study within the Semicha curriculum. Another novelty of our program is that it caters also to those who do not have background in Hebrew and are unable to learn from the original text. We offer our own Semicha text which is made available in English.

For further details visit shulchanaruchharav.com!

HEBREW STATE-OF-THE-ART SHIURIM BY RABBI GOLDSTEIN ON THE LAWS OF SHABBOS

*Deep, clear, & comprehensive **Hebrew** language classes on the laws of Shabbos, corresponding to volume 2 and 3 [up until chapter 328] are available for purchase.*

סימן רנב' - מלאכה בערב שבת	⊘ ⋮
שבוע א-מראי מקומות .pdf	⊘ ⋮
1 Hakdama-הקדמה.mp3	⊘ ⋮
2-רנב.mp3	⊘ ⋮
3 רנב.mp3	⊘ ⋮
4 רנב.mp3	⊘ ⋮
5 רנב.mp3	⊘ ⋮

Includes over 130 Hebrew classes.

The classes originally featured as part of a renowned college course in Talmudic and Halachic studies which attracted thousands of students, including many renowned scholars who have all sung the praise of the clear and comprehensive lessons given by Rabbi Goldstein.

Access to the classes is available through download, for all annual subscribers to our website, or through individual purchase. See this link for details: https://shulchanaruchharav.com/store/

ABOUT THE AUTHOR

Rabbi Yaakov Goldstein currently lives with his wife Shayna, and eleven children K"H, in Tzfas, Israel. Rabbi Goldstein received Semicha from Rabbi Schneur Zalman Labkowski of the Tomchei Temimim headquarters in 2005 and served as a chaplain in the Lotar/Kalatz and K9 unit of the IDF from years 2005-2008. He is also a certified Shochet, and has performed Hashgacha work in slaughterhouses. Rabbi Goldstein is the director of Shulchanaruchharav.com, the world's leading web-based Halacha database, and is the director of the Home Study Semicha Program, a self-study web-based Semicha program. He is a prolific author of over 30 Sefarim studied by a wide range of readers throughout the world, which is used regularly in Semicha programs around the globe. He is a world renowned Posek, answering questions to a web-based market, and serves as a local Posek, Rav, and Lecturer, in the Tzemach Tzedek community Shul in Tzefas, Israel. His many classes can be heard both from his website, Vimeo and YouTube channel. Students can join live to classes given in the Tzemach Tzedek Shul, through the " בית צפת חבד Chabad Tsfat" YouTube channel.

Other works by the Author

The present author has written books on various subjects in Shulchan Aruch. Some of these sections are not yet available to the public in a published format although all currently available **free of charge** on our website Shulchanaruchharav.com. In order for these subjects to become available on the bookshelf, and in order to add more subjects to the website, we are in need of funding. If you or anyone you know would like to sponsor a Halachic section to become available in print or on the web, please contact the author and the merit of spreading Halacha, and the merit of the Alter Rebbe, will certainly stand in your favor!

The following is a list of other subjects currently available in print:

*All books are available for purchase on Shulchanaruchharav.com & Amazon.com

1. *The Chassidishe Parsha-Torah Or-Likkutei Torah*
2. *The Weekly Parsha Summary*
3. *The Tanach summary series-Sefer Yehoshua-Shoftim*
4. *Topics in Practical Halacha Vol. 1*
5. *Topics in Practical Halacha Vol. 2*
6. *Topics in Practical Halacha Vol. 3*
7. *Topics in Practical Halacha Vol. 4*
8. *Awaking like a Jew*
9. *The Laws of Tzitzis*
10. *The Laws of Tefillin*
11. *The Laws of Tefillin-Summary Edition*
12. *The Laws & Customs of Kerias Hatorah*
13. *Kedushas Habayis-A comprehensive guide on Siman Reish Mem*
14. *The laws & Customs of Rosh Chodesh*
15. *The laws & Customs of Pesach*
16. *The Pesach Seder*
17. *The Pesach Seder--Summary Edition*
18. *Between Pesach & Shavuos*
19. *The laws & Customs of Shavuos*
20. *The Laws & Customs of the Three Weeks*
21. *The Laws of Rosh Hashanah*
22. *The Laws & Customs of Yom Kippur*
23. *The Laws of Sukkos-Summary edition*
24. *The Laws & Customs of Chanukah*
25. *The Laws of Purim*
26. *A Semicha Aid for Learning the Laws of Shabbos Vol. 1*
27. *A Semicha Aid for Learning the Laws of Shabbos Vol. 2*
28. *The Laws of Shabbos Volume 3*
29. *The Practical Laws of Meat & Milk*
30. *The Laws and Customs of Erev Shabbos and Motzei Shabbos*
    a. *The laws of Shabbos-Workbook*
31. *A Semicha aid for learning the laws of Basar Bechalav*
    a. *Basar Bechalav-Workbook*
32. *A Semicha aid for learning the laws of Taaruvos*
    a. *Taaruvos-Workbook*
33. *A Semicha aid for learning the laws of Melicha*
    a. *Melicha-Workbook*
34. *The Laws & Customs of Mourning Vol. 1*
35. *The Laws & Customs of Mourning Vol. 2*
36. *The Laws & Customs of Mourning-Summary Edition*

Daily Halacha Subscription:

To subscribe to our websites mailing list please visit www.shulchanaruchharav.com **on your desktop** or tablet [not available on phone webpage] and look for the subscription bar on the right side of the page to enter your email to subscribe.

The subscription is free and includes a daily Halacha topic sent to you via email and/or WhatsApp, and a weekly Parsha email with a Parsha summary, Chassidic insights, and more. Likewise, you will be kept updated on all of our future publications.

TABLE OF CONTENTS

THE LAWS OF TAKING MEDICINE, TREATING THE SICK, AND APPLYING FIRST AID ON SHABBOS

123

CHAPTER 3: LIST OF MEDICAL SYMPTOMS AND THEIR RESPECTIVE LAWS REGARDING THEIR TREATMENT ON SHABBOS

CHAPTER 4: THE LAW OF A YOLEDES/WOMEN DURING AND AFTER CHILDBIRTH

List of Topics included in Volume 1:
- The Laws of Shehiyah
- The Laws of Chazara
- The Laws of Hatmanah
- The Laws of Bishul
- The Laws of Muktzah

List of Topics included in Volume 2:
- The Laws of Building and Destroying
- The Laws of Cutting and Tearing
- The Laws of Smearing
- The Laws of Ohel
- The Laws of Trapping/Killing
- The Laws of Tying and Untying
- The Laws of Borer
- The Laws of Winnowing
- The Laws of Squeezing
- The Laws of Melting
- The Laws of Molid Reiach
- The Laws of Dyeing
- The Laws of Salting
- The Laws of Grinding
- The Laws of Kneading

SUMMARY-SHULCHAN ARUCH CHAPTER 322

1. An egg laid on Shabbos:[1]

An egg which has been laid on Shabbos is forbidden to be eaten[2] and is therefore Muktzah.[3] It is even forbidden to merely touch the egg.[4] Nevertheless, it is permitted to place a vessel over the egg to protect it. However, it is forbidden for the vessel to touch the egg in the process.

If the egg became mixed with other eggs that were laid before Shabbos, then all the eggs are forbidden to be eaten and they are all Muktzah. This applies even if the ratio of the mixture is 1:1000.[5]

If an egg which was laid on Shabbos and the next day is Yom Tov or vice versa, then the egg remains Muktzah also the next day.[6]

All the above applies even if there is a doubt as to when the egg was laid, in which case we are nevertheless stringent to forbid eating the egg and its entire mixture.[7]

2. Fruits which fell off a tree:[8]

All fruits which have fallen off a tree on Shabbos are forbidden to be eaten until after Shabbos[9] and are therefore Muktzah[10]. [Furthermore, even if there is doubt as to if the fruits fell on Shabbos or beforehand it is forbidden.[11]]

Q&A

Are vegetables which have become detached from the ground on Shabbos forbidden?[12]

Yes. Hence, they are Muktzah.

Halacha 4
Tikkun Keli by foods:

Animal food [which includes all foods which are edible to animals[13]] does not contain within it [the

---

[1] Michaber 322:1; Admur 513:1-3

[2] The reason for this is because an egg which has been laid on a Shabbos which followed a Yom Tov [i.e. Yom Tov was on Friday], or on a Yom Tov which followed Shabbos [i.e. Yom Tov was on Sunday] then that egg is Biblically forbidden to be eaten. The reason for this is because the egg was already prepared to be laid the day before it was actually laid. Thus, it ends up that Yom Tov or Shabbos prepared the laying of the egg of Shabbos/Yom Tov, and the Torah states "And on the 6th day prepare [for the Sabbath]". From here it learned that only a weekday may prepare for Shabbos while a Holiday may not prepare for Shabbos. Likewise, Shabbos may not prepare for Yom Tov, as Yom Tov is also called Shabbos. [513:1] Now, although Biblically an egg which was laid on Shabbos that did not follow a Yom Tov is permitted, nevertheless the Sages made a decree against eating any egg laid on Shabbos or Yom Tov, as a safeguard around the Biblical prohibition. [513:2]

An egg laid on Motzei Shabbos: May be eaten as only an egg which is being eaten on Shabbos or Yom Tov is forbidden to be prepared on Shabbos or Yom Tov. [513:1]

Other preparations done on Shabbos: Only matters which are prepared from Heaven are forbidden when done on a Shabbos before Yom Tov, however preparations done through the hands of man are not Biblically forbidden. [ibid]

[3] Since the egg is forbidden to be eaten it serves no purpose and is therefore Muktzah. [513:3]

[4] Admur 513:3; Now although all Muktzah is allowed to be touched if one does not shake it in the process, nevertheless by an egg it is forbidden as an egg is oval and even mere touching will cause it to move in the process. [ibid]

[5] As the egg laid on Shabbos is a forbidden food which will eventually become permitted, of which the ruling is that it is never nullified even in 1000x. [513:4]

[6] Michaber 322:2

This is due to a Rabbinical decree, as it ends up that the day before prepared the egg, as it is better to eat an egg which has been out of the chicken for some while then an egg which has just emerged. Nevertheless, this is only a Rabbinical prohibition, as Biblically the egg was already prepared before Shabbos, and it is only when it was prepared to be hatched on Shabbos that it is forbidden the next day. [513:9]

[7] Admur 513:4

[8] Michaber 322:3

[9] The reason for this is due to a decree one may come to pluck a fruit from the tree on Shabbos. Alternatively, it is because the fruit is Muktzah as one did not have it in mind from before Shabbos. [M"B 322:7]

[10] Ketzos Hashulchan 146:23 from Peri Megadim, Upashut.

[11] M"B 322:5; brought in Ketzos Hashulchan 146:23

[12] M"B 322:6 in name of Peri Megadim

[13] M"B 9

prohibition of] fixing a vessel [and is permitted to be moved being that it is edible[14]].

Using straw or hay as a tooth pick: Therefore it is permitted to cut even with a knife [even into a particular measurement[15]] straw or hay and [use it] to pick at his teeth [i.e. to use as a toothpick].

Using a twig as a tooth pick: However a twig which is not animal food, even to take it in order to pick at his teeth is forbidden [due to it being Muktzah, and to cut a piece off is forbidden also due to the fixing a vessel prohibition[16]].

---

[14] M"B 10

[15] In which case it would normally contain the cutting prohibition, although here it is allowed being that it is a food, and by foods the cutting prohibition is not applicable. [M"B 12]

[16] If done with one's hand it is Rabbinically forbidden, and if done with a vessel is Biblically forbidden. [M"B 13]

SUMMARY-SHULCHAN ARUCH CHAPTER 323

1. Buying items on credit on Shabbos:
Coming up in a future Volume

2. Borrowing items on Shabbos:
Coming up in a future Volume

3. Measuring on Shabbos:
Coming up in a future Volume

4. Transporting items from one area to another on Shabbos:[1]
From a public area with an Eiruv: It is forbidden to carry from a public area [even if it has an Eiruv] four bottles of wine in a basket or box.[2] Rather one is to carry the bottles in his hands, carrying either one or two in each hand.[3] Nevertheless if one has many guests [even if they are not from out of town[4]] which are waiting for him to begin the meal, he may bring all the bottles in a box.[5]

From a closed area: If one needs to transport the bottles from a private area, such as from one apartment to another in the same building, or from one room to another room in the house, then one is to carry as many bottles as possible, even in a basket, in order to diminish the amount of trips made.

Summary:
When transporting items on Shabbos from a public area that has an Eiruv one may only transfer a small amount at a time, using one's hands rather than a box. If, however, one has to hurry home for his many guests, then there is no limitation.
When transporting from a private area, one is to transport as many items as possible in each trip that he makes.

---

5. Washing dishes on Shabbos:[6]
All dishes/cutlery needed to be used on Shabbos may be washed anytime on Shabbos, even much time prior to the meal.[7] Thus one may wash the Friday night dishes immediately after the meal on Friday night and does not need to wait until the morning. Furthermore, so long as there still remains one meal which he will eat on Shabbos one may wash as many number of dishes and cutlery as he wants, even if he only needs to use one of those dishes for the meal.[8] If however one will not be eating any more Shabbos meals, such as after Shalosh Seudos [or after the 2nd meal in those homes which do not eat Shalosh Seudos] then

---

[1] 323:4-5

[2] As doing so appears like a mundane act, as it appears as if one is carrying loads. It is therefore belittling of Shabbos to do so in an area that he can be seen by the public. Likewise, people may come to think one is doing so for a weekday purpose, which is forbidden to be done on Shabbos. [ibid

[3] As when carrying with one's hands he is doing so in a way different than that of the regular week. [ibid]

[4] Admur 510:20 regarding Yom Tov; Ketzos Hashulchan 146 footnote 41 regarding Shabbos.

[5] As having him make many trips will delay the start of the meal. If, however, one is able to bring the bottles in an irregular way without delaying the meal, then he must do so.

[6] 323:6-7

[7] Such as immediately after the previous meal. [ibid] Vetzaruch Iyun why doing so does not transgress the Borer restrictions?

[8] So rules Admur 323:6 regarding cups and the same applies for all eating utensils. The reason for this is because once the Sages allowed washing a dish for the meal, they no longer restricted how many dishes one may wash as every dish washed can possibly be used on Shabbos. Thus, this is allowed even if one is certain that he will not need to use all the dishes washed. [Ketzos Hashulchan 146 footnote 30 in name of Machatzis Hashekel and Peri Megadim]

it is forbidden to wash any dishes or cutlery.[9] [If however one decides to eat more past the 2nd/3rd meal then he may wash the dishes for the meal.[10]]

Washing cups: It is permitted to wash cups throughout the entire day of Shabbos, even after the final meal[11], unless one is certain that he will no longer need the cup, in which case it is forbidden to wash it.

Scrubbing, Shining and Polishing dishes and silverware:[12] One may scrub down, shine and polish all dishes and cutlery needed to be used on Shabbos, even if they are made of silver. It is however forbidden to clean or shine silver using a material which will inevitably remove a layer of the silver from it.[13]

Washing dishes with salt water:[14] One may not use salty water to scrub the vessels as by doing so one actively dissolves the salt which is forbidden due to the Nolad prohibition.[15] One may however rinse them using salty water [so long as he does not rub his hands in the process.[16] Likewise one may place salt in water initially on Shabbos for this purpose even if the water ratio will be less than 1/3 of the mixture.[17]]

Washing one's dishes with soap:[18] It is forbidden to wash one's dishes using a bar of soap.[19] [One may however use liquid soap as will be explained in the Q&A]

Washing off non-Kosher food from a utensil: See the end of the next Halacha!

Summary:

One may wash as many dishes as he wishes if there is still one remaining meal left to be eaten on Shabbos. After the final meal, dishes may not be washed with exception to cups, unless one knows for certain he will not be needing the cups until after Shabbos, in which case even cups may not be washed.

Q&A On washing Dishes

May one wash dirty dishes even if he has more clean dishes available?

Some Poskim[20] rule it is better not to wash the dishes if there are clean dishes available. Others[21] rule it is completely forbidden. Others[22] rule it is even initially permitted to wash dirty dishes for the meal even if one has clean dishes available to use. Practically the custom is to be lenient.

May one wash the dishes after his last meal if they are tarnishing the cleanliness of the house?[23]

Yes. One may do so according to all opinions, even if he does not need them to eat another meal on Shabbos.[24]

---

[9] As by doing so one is preparing for after Shabbos, and it is forbidden for one to trouble himself on Shabbos for the sake of after Shabbos. [ibid]

[10] Ketzos Hashulchan 146:16

[11] As there is no set time for drinking. [ibid]

[12] 323:11

[13] Silver is soft and can have layers of it rubbed off during polish. Doing so is forbidden due to the Memacheik:Smoothening prohibition. Now although one has no intention to remove a layer of the silver and smoothen it, but rather simply to shine it, nevertheless this is an inevitable occurrence and is hence forbidden. It is however permitted to polish the silver using soap and the like which do not inevitably remove the silver, as even if it happens to do so, since this is not inevitable and one did not intend to do so, it is therefore permitted. [ibid]

[14] 323:12

[15] See 320:19 which brings a dispute in this matter. Practically, Admur rules to be stringent.

[16] 320:19

[17] Ketzos Hashulchan 146 footnote 33, based on fact Admur omits the opinion of the Taz which rules making more than 2:3 ratio of salt to water is forbidden.

[18] 326:10

[19] As by doing so one dissolves the soap which is forbidden due to the Molid [creating new substance] prohibition. Now although there are opinions which rule that there is no prohibition against creating a new substance and the reason behind the prohibition for dissolving ice is due to a decree of fruit juices, which has no relevance to dissolving soaps and the like, and hence according to them it is permitted to dissolve soap. Nevertheless, Admur concludes one is to be stringent like the first opinion. [ibid]

[20] Minchas Shabbos 80:154; Tosefes Shabbos 323:8, Betzeil Hachachmah 4:130; see Sheivet Halevy 6:42

[21] Beir Moshe 6:82

[22] Bris Olam Ofah 90; Mishneh Halachos 6:80

[23] See Beir Moshe ibid; Piskeiy Teshuvos 323:1

[24] This is similar to the allowance to make the beds on Shabbos morning even though they will not be used until the after Shabbos.

May one wash dishes on Shabbos if he will only be using them the next Shabbos?
No.[25] However there are Poskim[26] which rule this is allowed.

May one soak the dishes in water after his last Shabbos meal?[27]
If one is doing so merely so the food does not stick to the dishes, then soaking it is allowed. If, however, food is already stuck on and one desires to soak it in order to remove the food, then doing so is forbidden. It is however permitted to place the dishes in the sink as normal, and then proceed to wash one's hands over it.[28]

May one wash his food pots on Shabbos?
No[29], unless one plans on using the pot on Shabbos for a certain usage.

May one enter water into his food pot in order to let the pot soak?
If there is food stuck to the bottom of the pot, doing so is forbidden, as explained above.

May one wash his Kiddush cup out after Kiddush of the day meal?
If one is particular to only use the cup for Kiddush and Havdala then it may not be washed after the daytime Kiddush unless one plans on using it. If, however, one is not particular in this respect then it may be washed without throughout the day as is the law by other cups.
In all cases one may rinse out the wine and then drink some water out from the cup and place it on the drying rack.

Q&A on Soaps
Which soaps may be used to wash dishes?[30]
- It is forbidden to use a bar of soap.
- Liquid soap: Liquid soap may be used on Shabbos.[31] This includes even if the soap is slightly thick to the point that it cannot be poured like actual liquid but is rather more like a pasty substance. [However, there is an opinion[32] which is stringent against using liquid soap even when the soap is thin like water due to the smoothening prohibition. However, if one added water to the soap and it has thus already been melted down with water then it is permitted to be used according to all[33].] Practically the custom is to avoid using thick liquid soap.[34] *Regarding using scented liquid soaps, see Volume 2 "The Laws of Molid Reiach"*
- Dish detergent:[35] May be used with a large amount of water, so as not to transgress the kneading prohibition. Likewise, one may rub it onto the dishes using wet hands and then wash it off.

May one place soap into a cup of liquid and have it dissolve and then use that to wash dishes? [36]
Yes, as doing so is similar to placing ice in one's drink which is allowed. Furthermore, one may even mix the soap into the water through shaking the vessel.[37]
However, some are stringent to only place in the bar of soap from before Shabbos.[38]

---

[25] Tehila Ledavid 302:6
[26] See Piskeiy Teshuvos 323:1
[27] SSH"K 12:3
[28] Az Nidbaru 5:36
[29] As pots are not a meal utensil and are rather used for the cooking. Hence cleaning them serves no benefit for the meal.
[30] SSH"K 14:16 footnote 49, based on Ketzos Hashulchan 138 footnote 31 with regards to using toothpaste. So rules also Ketzos Hashulchan explicitly in 146 footnote 32
[31] As it is already a liquid and the bubbles that it creates have no significance.
[32] Igros Moshe 1:113
[33] So rules Az Nidbaru 1:16 brought in Piskeiy Teshuvos 326:8
[34] Shabbos Kehalacha Vol. 3 17:73
[35] Piskeiy Teshuvos 323:5
[36] Ketzos Hashulchan 127 footnote 13
[37] As explained above in Halacha 2 Q&A there, based on Ketzos Hashulchan 127 Footnote 2. So also rules SSH"K 14:16
[38] Ketzos Hashulchan 146 footnote 32

Q&A on Sponges
Which forms of sponges may be used to wash the dishes?

<u>Regular sponge</u>: It is forbidden to use a sponge[39] on Shabbos due to the squeezing prohibition.[40] This applies even if the sponge has a handle.[41]

<u>Synthetic sponges and steel wool</u>[42]: Some Poskim[43] rule all forms of synthetic or steel wool sponges are forbidden to be used due to it being a mundane act, and due to the squeezing prohibition.

Others[44] however permit using synthetic [or metal[45]] sponges which have their threads visibly spread apart from each other, and thus does not involve squeezing. However, they forbid using steel wool[46], and any sponge which has its threads close to each other. Others[47] question that perhaps it is permitted in all cases[48], although they rule one is not to be lenient by closely knitted sponges. Others[49] rule that even by those sponges which are permitted one may only use it if it is designated specifically for Shabbos.

Q&A on Polishing

---

[39]

[40] 320:23

[41] As a sponge with a handle may only be used to clean spills, as in such a case it is not inevitable one will come to squeeze. When doing dishes however it is impossible not to come to squeeze, and the squeezed liquid does not go to waste as one uses it to help clean the dishes. [Regarding the sources for this conclusion: See Previous Halacha regarding cleaning spills with a sponge that has a handle and the footnotes there. Vetzaruch Iyun as explained there. See M"B 320:55; SSH"K 12 footnote 37; Minchas Yitzchak 3:50]

[42] There are three possible issues discussed in Poskim regarding these forms of sponges:
Squeezing, Uvdin Dechol, may apply by all sponges and Mimacheik may also apply by steel wool.

[43] Ketzos Hashulchan 146 footnote 33; Minchas Yitzchak 3:49; Beir Moshe 1:34
The Ketzos Hashulchan ibid prohibits it due to both reasons. The Minchas Yitzchak states that steel wool is forbidden being that it contains a Rabbinical squeezing prohibition similar to hair. Beir Moshe 1:34 states that although doing so does not involve a squeezing prohibition [certainly not by the thick stranded steel wool] it is perhaps forbidden due to Uvdin Dechol. Nevertheless, he does not rule this way conclusively and hence leaves room for it being allowed.

[44] SSH"K 122:10; Cheishev Haeifod 2:149-however see below that he rules the sponge must be designated.
Beir Moshe ibid in previous footnote rules that possibly no prohibition of squeezing is involved even by closely netted sponges of synthetic or metal materials, although it may be forbidden by all sponges due to Uvdin Dechol. Practically he concludes that by closely knitted sponges it is forbidden, while by others it is unclear due to Uvdin Dechol. SSH"K argues that there is no precedence to claim that there is an issue of Uvdin Dechol involved.

[45] According to this opinion if this metal sponge visibly has its strands not so close together then it is permitted to be used. [Piskeiy Teshuvos 323:4]

[46] Due to the Mimacheik prohibition, as ruled similarly regarding silver in 323:11 [SSH"K ibid] However it is clear from Beir Moshe:Ketzos Hashulchan that he does not hold of this. Nevertheless the Beir Moshe concludes not to use the steel wool on plates which involve lots of scrubbing.

[47] Beir Moshe ibid

[48] Even with steel wool [so long as one does not rub very thoroughly], and even if the strands are close together. [ibid]

[49] Cheishev Haeifod 2:149; Minchas Yitzchak 3:50 regarding a sponge with a handle.

May one polish glass dishes?
Yes.[50] This may be done if one plans to use the dishes on Shabbos. Nevertheless, there are Poskim[51] which forbid this in all cases.

May one polish silverware, copperware and other silver vessels?
Some Poskim[52] rule this is forbidden in all cases, even with a dry cloth. Seemingly however according to Admur[53] this is permitted to be done[54] so long as one is not using an item which will inevitably remove a layer of silver or copper from the vessel, such as to simply shine it and not remove tarnish. According to all it is forbidden to rub off tarnish from metal or silver.[55]

May one remove rust from metal, such as from the blades of a knife?[56]
No.[57]

6. *Immersing vessels in a Mikveh:[58]*

It is forbidden to immerse a vessel[59] in a Mikveh on Shabbos if the vessel requires immersion in order to be used.[60] Thus any vessel bought from a gentile and has not yet been immersed may not be immersed on Shabbos. This applies even if one did not have the ability to immerse the vessels before Shabbos.
Giving the vessel to a gentile: Being that one may not immerse the vessel on Shabbos, and it is forbidden to use a vessel without immersion, one's only option is to give the vessel to a gentile as a present and then borrow it back from the gentile. This however may only be done if one needs to use the vessel on

---

[50] SSH"K 12:24, and so is implied clearly from Admur 323:11 regarding polishing silver that it is only a problem if it inevitably will remove a layer of the silver, hence implying that plain polishing is not forbidden.
Background: The Mahril rules it is forbidden to polish glass dishes using oats. The M"A 323:15 questions as to why this should be forbidden and suggests that perhaps only washing dishes from dirt did the Sages allow, however to polish is forbidden. He concludes with a Tzaruch Iyun. Admur completely omitted this ruling of the Mahril hence implying it is allowed [in addition to the previously mentioned implication]. SSH"K 12:24 in name of Rav SZ"A rules it is allowed, as even according to Mahril it was only prohibited to polish using oats. Tehila Ledavid 323:17 however explains it is forbidden to polish the vessels due to Tikkun Keli.
[51] Mahril; Tehila Ledavid brought in previous footnote; Toras Shabbos 323:9
[52] SSH"K ibid, Vetzaruch Iyun Gadol as to the basis of his ruling!
[53] So is implied clearly from Admur 323:11 regarding polishing silver that it is only a problem if it inevitably will remove a layer of the silver, hence implying that plain polishing is not forbidden.
[54] However a cream may not be used due to the smearing prohibition. Likewise, if using water one must be careful to use only a permitted type of sponge, as explained above.
[55] As tarnish is an actual layer of the metal which has corroded, and its only form of cleansing is removal.
[56] Tehila Ledavid 323:17
[57] This is forbidden possibly due to the Mimacheik and Tochein prohibition. [ibid]
[58] 323:5
[59] Whether made of glass, metal or any other materials which requires immersion. [See M"B 323:32 and so is implied from Admur which does not differentiate between the two]
[60] So concludes Admur in 323:5 ["and if one is unable to do the above, don't immerse the vessels" and "if one transgressed and immersed the vessels" and so summarizes the Ketzos Hashulchan 146:3 that doing so is forbidden.]
Background: Admur brings a dispute regarding this matter:
1. The first [stam] opinion rules that new vessels may be immersed on Shabbos even if one was able to immerse them before Shabbos. Their reasoning is because according to them immersion is only Rabbinically required for new vessels, while Biblically the vessels may be used without immersion. Hence immersing the vessel is not considered like one is fixing the vessel, as Biblically the vessel is already useable.
2. Others however rule that immersing new vessels is forbidden due to it being considered like one is fixing the vessel. According to them this applies even if one did not have the ability to immerse the vessels before Shabbos.
3. It goes without saying that immersing vessels is forbidden according to the opinion which rules that immersing new vessels is Biblically required. As on this premises by immersing the vessel one is doing it a significant fixture according to all, of which the Sages forbade being that it is exactly similar to fixing a vessel which is a Biblical prohibition.
4. The practical ramification between the 2nd and 3rd opinion is regarding glass vessels, which according to all is only Rabbinically required to be immersed.
5. Practically: One may not immerse vessels in a Mikveh on Shabbos as the main opinion follows the opinion which rules that immersing new vessels is Biblically required. [so concludes Admur in 323:5 and so summarizes the Ketzos Hashulchan 146:3. Vetzaruch Iyun from the wording of Admur prior to this ruling that "A G-d fearing Jew will fulfill his obligation according to all and give the vessel to a gentile..." Hence implying that from the letter of the law one may be lenient like the first opinion and immerse the vessel. So also implies the M"B [323:33] from this similar wording of Michaber, that the Michaber rules mainly like the first opinion that it is permitted. Thus, how can Admur say that one who immersed the vessel has transgressed. Vetzaruch Iyun Gadol!!]

Shabbos.[61] In such a case, after borrowing the vessel back from the gentile one may use the vessel without immersion, as it now legally belongs to the gentile. Nevertheless, after Shabbos one must immerse the vessel without a blessing[62] [or immerse it together with a vessel that requires a blessing[63]]. [Alternatively, one should ask the gentile after Shabbos to acquire the vessel back to him as a complete present, or buy it back with a few coins, in which case one can make a blessing on the immersion of that vessel according to all.[64]]

Immersing the vessel in an inconspicuous manner: It is permitted to immerse the vessel in waters that are Kosher for a Mikveh if it is unnoticeable to the onlooker that he is doing so to purify the vessel. Hence a pitcher and other vessel meant to draw water may be entered into the Mikveh waters to draw out water, therefore purifying the vessel in the process.[65] In such a case one may not say a blessing on the immersion, as if he were to do so it would be evident that his intents are in truth to purify the vessel.[66] [Thus one who has other vessels available may not immerse the vessel in this method, as by doing so one is causing it to lose its blessing.[67] Likewise only pitchers and cups may be immersed, as only they are capable of drawing water and hence fooling the onlooker. One however may not immerse cutlery and china in a Mikveh under the disguise that he is simply washing off the dirt from the vessels, as it is not common at all to do so in a Mikveh, and one's true intent is hence evident to all.[68] Based on this **today** that it is no longer common to draw water at all from a Mikveh or any body of water other than one's sink, it would hence be **forbidden to immerse vessels in a Mikveh under all circumstances**, as doing so is always apparent of one's true intention.[69]]

The law if one transgressed and immersed the vessel: If one transgressed [even advertently[70]] and immersed a vessel on Shabbos it nevertheless may be used on Shabbos.[71]

The law on Yom Tov: It is forbidden to immerse vessels on Yom Tov just as is forbidden to be done on Shabbos. If however one did not have the ability to immerse the vessel at any time prior to Yom Tov and on Yom Tov he received his first opportunity, then one may immerse the vessel.[72] Nevertheless one may not rule this way for one who asks him if he may immerse these vessels, [and is rather to tell him that

---

[61] As it is only permitted to give a present to a gentile on Shabbos if it is being done for the sake of Shabbos. [ibid]

[62] Being that this vessel will now remain in the hands of the Jew forever, and is thus similar to him having bought it. Alternatively, it is similar to a borrowed Tallis which required Tzitzis after 30 days even though it is not his. Based on this it should be immersed even with a blessing. Nevertheless, since I have not found the matter explicitly ruled in Poskim I am hesitant to rule this way, and rather one should immerse another vessel that requires a blessing together with it. [Yoreh Deah Taz 120:18]

[63] Taz in previous footnote. This applies even according to Admur, and the reason Admur did not state this explicitly is because he is dealing with a case that one only has this vessel to immerse. [Ketzos Hashulchan 146 footnote 6]

[64] Ketzos Hashulchan 146 footnote 6

[65] This does not appear like one is fixing the vessel, as it is not evident at all that one is intending to purify the vessel. This is because not everyone knows that this vessel has not yet been immersed hence causing the onlooker to say he is doing so in order to use the drawn water. [ibid]

[66] As for why a woman who immerses on Shabbos may say a blessing, this is because the Sages never originally decreed against women immersing on Shabbos. The reason for this is because at the times of the Sages it was not recognizable as to for what purpose the woman is immersing, and hence the Tikkun was never recognizable. Alternatively, this is because the decree against immersing vessels is because one may come to actually fix a vessel which is Biblically forbidden. The Sages however were not this suspicious regarding a person immersing. [Ketzos Hashulchan 146 footnote 8]

[67] M"B 323:36

[68] Ketzos Hashulchan 146 footnote 7

Other opinions: However the Kaf Hachaim rules one may immerse all vessels in the Mikveh under the disguise that one is doing so to clean the vessel. The Ketzos Hashulchan argues on this saying that it is never common to wash dirt off vessels in a Mikveh, and hence all will know one's true intents.

[69] So is clearly implied from Ketzos Hashulchan ibid regarding his argument against the Kaf Hachayim, and so is evident from the fact he writes that drawing water with the vessel is allowed because "at times today people do draw water from the Mikveh". Now, although this may have been true in the 1950's, the time of the publishing of this Sefer, today this is certainly not the case, and hence the Halacha likewise changes.

[70] As if Admur is referring to one who did so by mistake, then his ruling carries no novelty, as it is already ruled in 339:7 that no fine was enacted against Rabbinical decrees done inadvertently. Hence one must conclude that Admur includes even the advertent sinner in this ruling, that no fine was applied even to him.

[71] Although in general the Sages fined all transgressors against benefiting from their forbidden actions until after Shabbos, even by a Rabbinical transgression, nevertheless in this case no fine was given being that there are opinions which allow doing so even initially. [ibid]

[72] Admur 323:8; 509:15

immersing is forbidden in all cases].[73] Likewise one may not immerse the vessels in front of other people.[74]

Washing off non-Kosher food from a utensil:[75] It is permitted to rinse off a vessel that was used to eat non-Kosher food if one plans to use the vessel that day.[76] This applies even if there is remnant of the non-kosher food on the vessel.[77]

Summary:
It is forbidden to immerse vessels on Shabbos in a Mikveh in all cases. If one needs this vessel for Shabbos and cannot do without it, then he may give the vessel to a gentile as a present and then borrow it back from him and use it without immersion. After Shabbos he is to immerse it without a blessing.

Q&A

May one immerse a vessel on Shabbos if there is a doubt as to whether it even requires immersion?

Some Poskim[78] rule that if there are no other vessels available, and one is unable to give it to a gentile, as explained above, then one may be lenient to immerse the questionable vessel whether it is made of glass or metal.

Others[79] rule that if the vessel in question is made of glass then it may be used on Shabbos without being immersed[80] and if made of metal may be immersed.

Others[81] however rule it is forbidden to immerse the vessel in all circumstances, and it is likewise forbidden to use the vessel even if made of glass, being that it still requires immersion.[82]

---

7. Issur which fell into one's food on Shabbos:[83]
See "The Laws of Cooking" Chapter 1 Halacha 16

---

[73] Admur 509:1

Thus for oneself to do so is allowed, if he knows this Halacha, while for another, it is not allowed if he does not know this Halacha, and hence one may not tell him that it is allowed. The reason for this is because if they are told it is allowed, they may come to also immerse vessels that could have been immersed before Yom Tov. [ibid]

[74] As this itself is considered as if one is ruling to them that immersing vessels is allowed, and they may come to immerse vessels even in cases that are not allowed. [ibid]

[75] 323:9

[76] According to all this is not considered as if one is fixing the vessel as the actual vessel is permitted to be used and it is just that the non-Kosher food prohibits its use. Hence rinsing it off is similar to rinsing off feces from it. [ibid]

[77] Although non-Kosher food is Muktzah, nevertheless its remains are nullified completely to the vessel and do not have the ability to prohibit moving it at all. [ibid]

[78] M"B 323:33

[79] Kaf Hachaim 323

[80] As this is a doubt in a Rabbinical case in which the rule allows one to be lenient.

[81] Ketzos Hashulchan 146 footnote 5

[82] As even in a case of doubt we rule all vessels need to be immersed, even if made of glass, as one may not actively enter himself into a Rabbinical doubt by avoiding the immersion. Thus, since the vessel is forbidden to be used until immersed even in a case of doubt, we return to the same debate in whether this it is allowed to be done or is forbidden because it appears as if one is fixing the vessel. [ibid]

[83] 323:10

SUMMARY[84] SHULCHAN ARUCH CHAPTER 324
Feeding animals on Shabbos

1. *Feeding animals:*[85]

It is permitted for one to feed home and farm animals, food and drink, if they are dependent on him for their food. It is however forbidden to feed home and farm creatures if they are not dependent on him for their food, such as bees, or pigeons.[86] It is forbidden to even simply place food in front of them.[87] It goes without saying that it is forbidden to feed wild animals or birds.

Dogs: It is permitted to feed dogs, even if they are wild and not owned[88] and are hence not dependent on oneself for their food. Furthermore, it is even a slight Mitzvah to do so.[89]

Pigs: It is forbidden to feed a pig on Shabbos [even if one owns it and it is dependent on oneself for food].[90]

Shabbos Shira:[91] Some are accustomed to place food in front of animals on Shabbos Shira, [even if the animals are not dependent on people for their food]. However, based on above doing so is incorrect being that these animals are not dependent on people for their food.[92] [Practically one is not do so, or even allow children above Chinuch to do so.[93] Rather one who wants to honor the custom is to set up food for the animals from before Shabbos. Likewise, one is to explain to children the importance of being merciful to animals.[94]]

Feeding insects:[95] It is permitted to feed worms [and other creatures] that one owns if they are dependent on oneself for their food.

Q&A

May one feed someone else's animal?[96]

All animals which are dependent on humans for food may be fed by any person, even if they are not the owner.

May one throw away leftovers in an area that animals will be able to eat them?[97]

Yes.[98] Hence one may shake breadcrumbs off one's table cloth onto ones porch for birds to eat.

May one feed a hungry wild animal from outside?

Some Poskim[99] rule one may feed any animal which appears famished and unable to find food for itself even if the animal is not owned.

---

[84] This section is not fully translated. It consists mostly of a summary of the rulings of Admur

[85] 324:7

[86] As they eat food from the field and are not dependent on the owner for food. [ibid]

[87] As the Sages only permitted troubling oneself on Shabbos for animals if the animals are dependent on oneself for their food. [ibid]

[88] Other Opinions: The Machatzis Hashekel understands the M"A to rule that if the dog is not owned it may not be fed.

[89] As G-d had mercy on the dog which finds little food, and made its food last in its abdomen for three days. [ibid]

[90] As it is forbidden to raise pigs, as the Sages said "Cursed is the man which raises pigs". [ibid]

[91] 324:8

[92] So rules M"A.
Nevertheless some justify the custom on the claim that since their intent is for a Mitzvah, in order to repay the birds which sang Shirah by Kerias Yam Suf, therefore they may do so. [Tosefes Shabbos 117; Minchas Shabbos; brought in Ketzos Hashulchan 131 footnote 5; Aruch Hashulchan 324:3; Nemukei Orach Chaim 324 states it is an accepted custom from the Holy Tzadik Reb M"M of Rimnav, to give the birds crumbs on Shabbos Shira in reward for them having eaten the leftover Man which Dasan and Aviram cunningly spread out on Shabbos night to make it appear as if the Man fell on Shabbos. He then goes on to defend the custom based on Halacha.]

[93] Shaar Halacha Uminhag 1:149
Other Opinions: Ashel Avraham Butchatch 167:6 allows children to do so being that it is not a complete Shvus.

[94] Shaar Halacha Uminhag 1:149

[95] 324:9

[96] Minchas Shabbos 87:114 brought in Ketzos Hashulchan 131:1

[97] Ashel Avraham Butschach 324

[98] Being that one in any event needs to trouble himself throw them out, it is not considered a superfluous act.

[99] Aruch Hashulchan 324:2

May one chase an animal outside if it has food in his mouth?[100]
It is forbidden to chase an animal which one owns from a private domain to an area without an Eiruv if the animal has food in his mouth.

---

2. Preparing food for one's animals:[101]

It is permitted to prepare foods on Shabbos for one's animals, in a non-forbidden way, in order to make the food fit to be eaten. It is however forbidden to trouble oneself to make the food more pleasurable for the animal if the food is edible for the animal in its current state. This applies even if enhancing the food does not contain any prohibition.[102] It is forbidden in all cases to prepare food for an animal if doing involves a Shabbos prohibition.

Cutting meat for a dog:[103] One may cut a [hard[104]] carcass and throw its meat to dogs [which one owns[105]] even if the animal died that day. It is not Muktzah even if one was not at all sick from before Shabbos and thus did not have in mind at all to feed its meat to dogs from before Shabbos.[106]

Measuring food for animals:[107] It is forbidden to measure food for his animals.[108] Rather one is to give the animal food based on a rough estimation.

Q&A
May one do Borer for the sake of one's animal?[109]
Doing Borer for an animal which one owns has the same laws as Borer for humans. Hence it is permitted to remove good from bad with one's hand to feed one's animal right away. It is forbidden to do Borer for an animal which one does not own.[110]

---

3. Gavage: Force-feeding animals that are dependent on oneself for food:[111]

It is forbidden to gorge an animal on Shabbos by stuffing food into his stomach, even if it is dependent on one for its food.[112] One may however stuff the food in his esophagus in a way which still allows the animal to spit the food back out and chew it. [Nevertheless, one must beware not to move the animal in the process due to the Muktzah prohibition. This applies to lifting the animal's legs off the ground. It is however permitted to move a limb to help it eat.[113]] [Even during the week it is strongly discouraged to force feed animals, as doing so can lead to one transgressing a number of prohibitions, besides for the fact that at times it punctures the trachea or esophagus and renders the animal a Treifa.[114]]

---

[100] Ketzos Hashulchan 131:2
[101] 324:4
[102] As it is forbidden to trouble oneself on Shabbos for the sake of animals unnecessarily.
[103] 324:5
[104] As if it is soft then the dogs do not need one top cut the meat for them and they rather are to do so on their own. It is only by a hard carcass in which the dogs are unable to eat without having it cut that the Sages allowed one to trouble himself to cut it. [ibid]
[105] If however one does not own the dog, then although it is permitted to feed him, it is forbidden to do any food preparations for it. [Ketzos Hashulchan 131 footnote 19]
[106] The reason for this is because an item which one removed his mind from is only considered Muktzah if one pushed it away with his hands, as was explained in chapter 310 [Halacha 6].
[107] 324:2
[108] As measuring even for non-business related matters is forbidden due to it being a mundane act. [ibid]
[109] Peri Megadim M"Z 319:5, brought in Ketzos Hashulchan 131:8
[110] Ketzos Hashulchan ibid footnote 19
[111] 324:6
[112] As this is considered a troubling oneself for the week, as there is no Shabbos need in gorging the animal on Shabbos. [ibid]
[113] Ketzos Hashulchan 131 footnote 8
[114] Shiyurei Bracha brought in Biur Halacha and Ketzos Hashulchan 131 footnote 7

May one force feed an animal if it cannot eat on its own?[115] It is permitted to have a gentile place food into an animal's stomach if it cannot eat on its own. If no gentile is available, then a child may do so. If there is no child available, then one may do so himself [although taking care to avoid the Muktzah prohibition as explained above].

4. Allowing one's animal to graze:[116]
It is permitted to allow one's animal to graze grass on Shabbos.[117] Furthermore, it is even permitted to lead one's animal there. It is however forbidden to lead one's animal to Muktzah produce [such as fruits which fell on Shabbos] due to suspicion one may come to lift the Muktzah with his hands in order to feed the animal.

5. Giving an animal another animals leftovers:[118]
It is forbidden to give the leftover food of one species to another species if it is close to certain that the animal will not eat it.[119] Furthermore, some are stringent to avoid switching the foods of any animal and place it in front of another species, however those which are lenient are not to be protested.

Halacha 3 Translation
Kneading course flour for animals on Shabbos:
A. First Opinion:
Biblically: It was already explained in chapter 321 [Halacha 16] that coarse grain is not a knead-able product and if it is kneaded on Shabbos there are opinions which say that he is Biblically exempt [from the transgression].

Rabbinically: Nevertheless, it is Rabbinically forbidden to knead coarse grain for an animal or chickens as is done during the week, and rather one must implore in irregularity [in the kneading process].

The definition of an irregularity is: Such as to knead it little by little as was explained there, or even a lot at a time although taking care to not mix it with one's hands after placing the water in it as is the usual way that one mixes it during the week. Rather one is to mix it with a large serving spoon or a stick which contains a horizontal piece of wood on it, even many times until it mixes well. This is considered an irregularity since he is not mixing it with his hands and is not circling the spoon or wooden stick in its usual form as done during the week, but rather is mixing it by pushing it horizontally and vertically; therefore, this is considered a complete irregularity.

It is as well permitted to pour it from vessel to vessel until it mixes well.

Mixing a lot at a time: It is permitted to mix the course flour in this method even a lot at a time, in accordance to the amount that his animals need, and separates the mixture into many different vessels and places it in front of each animal.

B. Second Opinion:
[However] according to the opinion which holds that one who kneads course flour is Biblically liable even by simply placing water into it, without kneading it, as [they hold] that the placing of the water is defined as kneading, as was explained there, then it is forbidden to place water into course flour on Shabbos even using an irregularity, unless the water was placed in from before Shabbos in which case kneading it on Shabbos does not contain a Biblical prohibition but rather a Rabbinical prohibition, which was permitted through making it with an irregularity in this form explained above.

---

[115] 305:27

[116] 324:10

[117] As the command of having one's animals rest does not refer to preventing it from eating from the ground. On the contrary this is its rest. We do not suspect one may come to uproot the grass to feed the animal, as it is known to all the severity of this prohibition. [ibid]

[118] 324:11

[119] As it is forbidden to trouble oneself on Shabbos for no need, and it is close to certain that the animal will not eat this food. [ibid]

C. Final Ruling

It was already explained there that one is to be stringent like the latter opinion and so is the custom.

Halacha 5 Translation

Cutting meat for a dog: One may cut a [hard[120]] carcass and throw its meat to dogs even if the animal died that day. It is not Muktzah even if one was not at all sick from before Shabbos and thus did not have in mind at all to feed its meat to dogs from before Shabbos.

The reason for this is because an item which one removed his mind from is only considered Muktzah if one pushed it away with his hands, as was explained in chapter 310 [Halacha 6].

---

[120] As if it is soft then the dogs do not need one top cut the meat for them and they rather are to do so on their own. It is only by a hard carcass in which the dogs are unable to eat without having it cut that the Sages allowed one to trouble himself to cut it. [ibid]

TRANSLATION & SUMMARY-SHULCHAN ARUCH CHAPTER 325
Chapter 325
A gentile which did forbidden work for a Jew
Contains 22 Halachas

Giving food and other items to a gentile on Shabbos:

Introduction:
The following chapter will discuss the laws regarding giving food and items to a gentile in a scenario that the gentile will carry it out to a different domain. At times doing so involves a Rabbinical prohibition and at times is completely allowed.

Halacha 1
Inviting him for the meal:
It is permitted to invite a gentile to one's house to join him to eat [the meal] on Shabbos.

The reason why on Shabbos this is allowed as opposed to Yom Tov: Now, although this is forbidden to do on Yom Tov due to a decree that one may come to cook more food on his behalf, as will be explained in chapter 512 [Halacha 1] [nevertheless on Shabbos it is allowed as] on Shabbos we are not worried [that one may come to cook food].

Giving him food: It is even allowed to place food in front of a lone gentile as since we sustain [also] gentile paupers it is considered that their sustenance depends on us [Jews].

Halacha 2
Giving him food to carry into a public domain:
Placing it in the courtyard: It is permitted to place food in front of [a gentile] in one's courtyard even though one knows that [the gentile] will take it outside [into a public domain] as long as [the gentile] has permission to eat [the food] there [in the courtyard] if he so wishes.

Placing it in the gentile's hand: In any event one may not actually place [the food] into his hands in order so he [the Jew] not be the one to extract the [food] from within the private domain[1], rather the gentile should take it from his hand as then the gentile is the one doing the actual extraction. It goes without saying that it is allowed [for the gentile to take it] if one places it on top of the ground or on a table and the gentile takes it from there.

Placing down the food in a scenario that is evident that it will have to be taken out: However if [the gentile] does not have permission to eat it there or there is a lot of food and it is impossible to eat it [all] there and it is [thus] evident that he [must] take it outside, as well as if the gentile is standing on the outside and he sticks his hand inside in which it is obvious and evident that he will take [the food that he is given] outside, then it is forbidden to place [the food] in front of him being that it appears like one is giving it to him on condition [that he] take it out.

Now, although he is taking it out for his benefit and not for the Jew, nevertheless since this item that he is taking out was given to him by the Jew from his own personal belongings, [therefore] it is forbidden for the reason explained in chapter 307 [Halacha 35].

Halacha 3
Giving objects to a Gentile on Shabbos:
Giving the gentile objects of a Jew: [Furthermore] even when [the gentile] is standing inside [the courtyard, the Sages] only permitted to give him food being that it is possible that he will eat it in the courtyard, however [he may] not [be given] other objects being that they are commonly taken out [from

---
[1] The prohibition of carrying from a private to public domain includes lifting up the object in the private domain and bringing it into the public domain and then putting it down. Thus, here we do not want the Jew to do the first part of the carrying which is the lifting up in the private domain.

the courtyard] and it thus appears as if one is giving it to him in order for him to take it outside.
Giving the gentile his own objects : However the above only refers to objects of a Jew, however the objects of a gentile are permitted to be given to him.

The reason: Now, although it appears like one is giving it to him in order to take outside, this does not pose a problem being that the [gentile] is not taking it on the behalf of the Jew, but rather on behalf of himself and the object does not belong to the Jew. [Furthermore] even to explicitly tell [the gentile] to do work with his own personal objects is allowed as was explained there [in Chapter 307 Halacha 35-36] thus certainly here it is allowed to give the gentile an object of his that he will carry to the outside].

If the gentile is standing outside and sticks his hand in: Nevertheless, if the gentile is standing on the outside and he sticks his hand inside it is forbidden to place [the object] in front of him even if it belongs to him.

The reason for this is: because it appears like wrongdoing being that one that sees the Jew giving it to him thinks [to himself] that the object belongs to that Jew. This is opposed to when one places [the gentiles object] in front of him in the courtyard [which is allowed] because people [from the outside] do not see [the Jew placing the object] there, and [rather all they see is a gentile] exiting from the domain of the Jew with something in his hand, of which [the bystander] thinks [to himself] that the [gentile] is taking his own belongings and not that of the Jews.

(Nevertheless, if in truth the object [being given to the gentile] does belong to the Jew, then it is forbidden [to give it to him] as perhaps the bystanders will [eventually] know the truth [that this object belonged to the Jew] and they will suspect the Jew of giving it to [the gentile] in order to take it out for him. However, when the object belongs to the gentile if the truth becomes known to the bystanders [that the object belongs to the gentile] then there is no suspicion [of wrongdoing at all])

Halacha 4
Returning a collateral to a gentile on Shabbos
Even if the object belongs to the gentile but [was given as] collateral to the Jew, then it has the status of an object owned by a Jew even if the gentile redeemed it before Shabbos.

[Furthermore] even if [the Jew] had designated a space, from before Shabbos, within his property for the gentile to place the collateral until the next day [Shabbos] in which he will then come and take it from there, it is forbidden to allow the [gentile] to take it from there on Shabbos being that this appears [to the onlookers] as wrongdoing.

Exceptions to all the above restrictions:
An aggressive Gentile: However, if the gentile has an aggressive personality [and thus refraining him from taking the collateral will cause friction] then one may be lenient [and allow him to take it] even if he [the Jew] had not designated a space [in his property] for the [collateral].

Sake of Peace: As well in any situation in which [giving the gentile an object] involves [common actions done for] the sake of peace [with other nations], such as [in a case that] an ill gentile sent a messenger to bring him food from a Jew, then it is permitted to give it to [the messenger] or to even [personally] send a gentile [messenger] to bring it to him.

Need of a Mitzvah: The same law applies when [giving the item to the gentile who will take it outside] is needed to be done for the sake of a Mitzvah, such as to remove Chameitz from ones house on Pesach, as will be explained in chapter 444 [Halacha 10-11].

The reason for all the above allowances is: because having a gentile do a forbidden labor on ones behalf is only a Rabbinical prohibition, and being that today there are opinions which say that public domains no longer exist and rather it is all defined as a Karmalis [which is only Rabbinically forbidden in carrying] as will be explained in chapter 345 [Halacha 11], thereby [asking a gentile to carry out the objects] is [asking him to do] a Rabbinical prohibition [which itself is] of [only a guard against] a Rabbinical prohibition which was permitted [to be done] in a case that involves a Mitzvah as was explained in chapter 307 [Halacha 12]. This same allowance [given] also applies in a situation that involves the making of peace [with the gentiles], as well as a situation which involves an aggressive gentile.

Not to ever place the objects into the gentile's hand: Nevertheless, one must beware not to place [the item] into the actual hand of the gentile being that one is able to avoid doing so [and still accomplish what is needed]. Even with objects that belong to the gentile one must beware against doing this.

Halacha 5
Giving back a collateral of clothing:

To a Gentile: It is allowed to exchange a collateral with a gentile on Shabbos if [the collateral being given to the gentile] is clothing and the gentile will wear it to the outside, being that [doing so] is not considered doing business.

To a Jew: As well [switching a collateral] in this fashion is permitted to be done [even] with a Jew, if the Jew needs the clothing to wear for Shabbos.

[Furthermore,] even if the gentile brings the money and takes the collateral it is allowed as long as [the Jew] does not calculate with him [how much of the loan was paid].

Not to touch the collateral: It is proper[2] that the gentile take the collateral himself rather than have the Jew touch it in order so it not appear like they are doing a business transaction. If [the gentile] gives [the Jew] a different collateral, then one should likewise not touch it.

Summary

Giving one's food to a gentile on Shabbos while in one's property:[3]

In a scenario that it is not evident or incumbent that the gentile will carry the item into a public domain: such as that the gentile has permission, and is physically able to eat the amount of food given to him in the property of the Jew, then it is permitted to place the food in front of the gentile, although not in his hands.

In a scenario that it is evident or incumbent that the gentile will carry the food outside: Such as if it is too large an amount of food to be eaten in the Jews house, or the Jew did not give him permission to eat it in his property, then it is forbidden to give it to him, even by placing it down on the floor.

Food that belongs to the gentile: See next scenario.

Giving objects to the gentile:

Objects that belong to the Jew:[4] Is forbidden in all cases.

Objects [including food] that belong to the gentile: Is permitted in all cases to place in front of the gentile, with exception to if the gentile is standing outside the property and places his hand inside, in which case one may not place the objects in front of him.[5] One may never place the object in his hand, even when the gentile is inside.[6]

A collateral which belongs to the gentile: Has the same laws as an item which belongs to a Jew, with exception that by an aggressive gentile which will cause one harm if not given the collateral one may allow him to take it.[7] As well as collateral of clothing is allowed for the gentile to take on condition that he will wear it to the outside. However, one is not to touch the collateral and rather is to have the gentile take it himself.[8]

---

[2] lit. good
[3] Admur 325:2
[4] Admur 325:3
[5] Admur 325:3
[6] Admur 325:4
[7] Admur 325:4
[8] Admur 325:5

Exceptions to all the above restrictions, both by food and by objects:[9]
In the following two cases one may always place food/object in front of the gentile, even if it belongs to the Jew, although may not place it in the gentile's hands.
1) One needs to give the food/object to the gentile for the sake of peace.
or
2) One needs to give the food/object to the gentile for the need of a Mitzvah:

Benefiting from items which a gentile did labor to on Shabbos for his own behalf

Introduction:
The following section will deal with the laws of foods and other items which had forbidden labor done to them on Shabbos by a gentile not on behalf of a Jew. At times the foods and other items are permitted and at times are forbidden as will be explained. When the labor to the item was done on behalf of a Jew the item is always prohibited as will be discussed in the next section.

Halacha 6
Taking Bakery bread from a gentile baker on Shabbos:
In places where it is accustomed to [allow] eating bread of a gentile bakery there are those opinions which permit to take from him on Shabbos even bread which was baked that day (on Shabbos) if it is a city which is majority of gentile population.
The reason for why this does not involve a prohibition of benefiting from a gentiles actions: because [when the majority of the population is gentile] one can assume that [the bakery] is baking it for the gentiles and not for the Jews, and thus there is no reason to prohibit [the bread] in consistency with the law regarding a gentile who does labor for a Jew [in which case the item that the work is done to is forbidden in benefit.]
The reason for why the bread is not Muktzah: As well it is not forbidden due to the laws of Muktzah even if it was flour or dough during twilight [of before Shabbos] which are [materials that are] Muktzah, as explained in chapter 308 [Halacha 8], [as] we do not apply here [the rule] that since [the "bread"] was Muktzah during twilight [of the entrance of Shabbos] it is therefore Muktzah for the entire Shabbos, as this rule is only said by an item which became ready and fit [to be used] on its own after dark [meaning after twilight was over], such as a candle which extinguished on its own after dark, however anything which was finished through a person, meaning that he finished preparing it on Shabbos and it becomes ready through a person, then it does not involve [the prohibition of] Muktzah at all, even during twilight when it is still not ready being that one does not remove his mind away from it at all during twilight from benefiting from it on Shabbos since it is within his ability to prepare it and make it ready for that day.
For example flour which is in the hands of a gentile does not have the status of Muktzah at all on Shabbos because he has the ability to bake and make it ready for that day, and since it is readily useable for the gentile which is the owner it is therefore considered readily useable for everyone.
Other Opinions-If was flour or dough by twilight then is Muktzah : [However] there are other opinions which say that [the Sages] only said that an item which was completed through the hands of a person does not have the law of Muktzah by an item which its action that is needed to prepare it to make it useable was already begun from before Shabbos and was then finished on Shabbos, such as for example a gentile which started to make a vessel before Yom Tov and finished it on Yom Tov [the vessel] does not contain the [Muktzah] status of "Nolad" [a new existence] since it was finished through the handiwork of a person as was explained in chapter 252 [Halacha 12]. (Similarly bread which started to bake [from before Shabbos], meaning that it was placed in the oven before Shabbos, then even though during twilight it was not yet ready [nevertheless] it still does not contain [the] Muktzah [prohibition])

---

[9] Admur 325:4

However, bread which its action that is needed to prepare it to make it useable, which is its baking, began on Shabbos then it does contain the problem of Muktzah if it was flour or dough during twilight.

However if it was grain during twilight and it was ground and baked on Shabbos then it does not contain a problem of Muktzah and neither of "Nolad" on Yom Tov, as will be explained in chapter 517 [Halacha 3].

The Final Ruling: Regarding the final ruling: One is to be strict like the latter opinion unless it is a pressing situation, such as one is the sole Jew who lives in certain settlement and thus it is impossible to ask for bread from [Jewish] acquaintances. [As well one may be lenient when done] for the need of a Mitzvah, such as by the festive meal of a Bris Mila or in order to make the blessing over bread [for the Shabbos meal], in which cases one may then rely on those that permit [using bread that was baked on Shabbos by a gentile bakery].

In any event it is forbidden to give money to a gentile baker from before Shabbos in exchange for the bread that he will give him on Shabbos as [in such a case] it ends up that [the gentile] baked [on Shabbos] for the need of the Jew of which [the law is that] it is forbidden to eat [from that bread] until enough time has passed after Shabbos to have been able to bake it, as will be explained [in Halacha 9].

Halacha 7
Food cooked by a gentile on Shabbos which is not Bishul Akum

(All the above [discussion] is with regards to bread, however a gentile which cooked for himself foods that do not have applicable to them the prohibition of "Bishul Akum" [food cooked by a gentile] then they do not have the status of Muktzah according to all opinions even if they are fruits which are not edible raw and were not at all fit [to be eaten] during twilight. [The reason for this is] because we only apply [the rule] of "since it was Muktzah during twilight it is Muktzah for the entire Shabbos" by things which were set aside from the mind of a person and was pushed away with his hands, such as by grains that were ground into flour, however not by something which was forcibly set aside from [the mind of the] person as was explained in chapter 310 [Halacha 6]).[10]

Halacha 8
Juices squeezed by a gentile on Shabbos:

All the above [allowances to benefit from a gentiles labor on Shabbos] only applies to baking and the like of actions which are done with [foods] detached from the ground, with exception to squeezing fruits in which case even if a gentile squeezed it for himself it is forbidden for a Jew [to drink it] until after Shabbos if it is a scenario that it would [also] be forbidden if [the juice] were to have oozed out [of the fruit] on its own as was explained in chapter 320 [Halacha 3].

The reason for this is because: as also these juices which arrive to a Jew through the squeezing of a gentile were included within the decree [that the Sages] decreed against juices that flowed out on their own, being that also these [juices that were squeezed by the gentile] have arrived to the Jew on their own just like [juice that] had flowed out by themselves.

Fruits picked by a gentile on Shabbos:

As well, a gentile that picked fruit which was attached [to the ground] for his own self use, then even if it is a scenario where there is no prohibition of Muktzah involved, such as for example when one heard the gentile saying from before Shabbos that "tomorrow (Shabbos) I will pick these fruits" and they are fruits which have fully ripened of which case preparing them [before Shabbos] helps [remove their Muktzah status] from them even if they are attached, as explained in chapter 318 [Halacha 6], nevertheless it is forbidden for a Jew [to eat] until after Shabbos.

The reason for this is: because [these fruits] are included in the decree against fruits that fell off a tree on their own [on Shabbos] as explained in chapter 322 [Halacha 3 in the Michaber[11]] being that also these

---

[10] Q. According to this explanation then why by whole grains did we need to resort, in the latter opinion brought in the previous Halacha, that it is only permitted because of the reasons explained in chapter 517, when in essence the reason is explained here in this Halacha?!

[11] This chapter of the Alter Rebbe is not in print.

fruits have arrived to the Jew on their own just like those which have fallen off [the tree] on their own.

Inedible items that were picked by a gentile: The above does not only apply to fruits but rather to any item connected [to the ground] which became detached on their own or through a gentile, even if [the item] is not food for a person, [nevertheless] it is included in this decree.

For example a gentile which picked grass that was attached [to the ground], then even if it is a case that there is no problem of Muktzah, such as [in a case] that the Jew has animals which are able to graze from this grass and these [grasses] are thus designated to him [for this use], nevertheless they are forbidden [to move] due to the decree against fruits that have fallen off of a tree [on their own] and therefore it is forbidden for a Jew to use these [grasses] for any purpose just like it is forbidden to use fruits that fell off a tree [for any purpose]. Therefore they are also forbidden to be moved being that they are not fit for him to use that day [on Shabbos] for any purpose and are thereby Muktzah just like fruits that have fallen off [a tree] are Muktzah for this reason.

[Furthermore] even wood [which is not used for food but for fuel] that a gentile cut for himself or that fell off on its own on Yom Tov are included in this decree as explained in chapter 507 [in Kuntrus Achron 7].

Creatures trapped by a gentile: Similarly a gentile which trapped fish or wild animals or birds for himself [on Yom Tov] is forbidden on Yom Tov as explained in chapter 515 [Halacha 4-8].

Summary[12]

Definition of an action done for a gentile's behalf:

This includes any case that either a) the gentile did so for himself or for a gentile friend or b) did so in order to sell and the majority his clients are gentiles.[13]

When not done for selling purposes then we always assume that the gentile did so for himself unless there is reason to believe otherwise, in which case even if one is in doubt if in truth it was done for a Jew one must be stringent as if he knows for certain that it was done for a Jews behalf.[14]

Bread baked on Shabbos for gentiles:[15]

The following today is not relevant for Chabad Chassidim as well as many Chareidi Jews being that our custom is to avoid eating Pas Akum all year round.

For those which do not avoid doing so, the following is the ruling:

If the bread was kneaded on Shabbos by the gentile, then it is permitted to eat it on Shabbos.

If it was kneaded before Shabbos and then entered into the oven on Shabbos, it may only be eaten in a pressing situation, such as there are no other Jews to borrow bread from, or for the need of a Mitzvah, such as for a Bris Milah or for the Shabbos Seudah [and only if the Jew is not an acquaintance of the gentile who baked it[16]].

Foods cooked on Shabbos for gentiles:

If the food does not contain a Bishul Akum prohibition then it may be eaten in all cases[17] unless one is an acquaintance of the gentile, in which case he may not eat it until after Shabbos[18].

The Mishneh Berurah [322:8] explains that the reason why fruits which have fallen, or even questionably have fallen from their tree on Shabbos is Muktzah is because a) The sages forbade them from being eaten lest one come to actually pick the fruits from the tree. B) Since they were attached to the ground before Shabbos one has removed his mind from them and they are thus Muktzah.

[12] Includes summary of Halacha brought later on that are relevant to this subject.

[13] Admur 325:6

[14] Admur 325:10

[15] Admur 325:6

[16] Admur 325:18

[17] Admur 325:7

[18] Admur 325:18

Juices squeezed on Shabbos by a gentile on behalf of gentiles:[19]
Is forbidden in all cases to be drunk by a Jew on Shabbos [and is thus Muktzah].

Fruits/vegetables/herbs and all other vegetation picked by a gentile on Shabbos on behalf of gentiles:
Is forbidden in all cases to be eaten by a Jew on Shabbos and is thus Muktzah.[20] Although one may lead his animal to eat from these foods, unless one is an acquaintance of the gentile, in which case it is forbidden to lead the animal to eat from that produce until after Shabbos[21], although one does not need to protest against the gentile feeding it on his own accord to one's animal[22].

Items carried from a private domain to a public domain on behalf of gentiles:
Are permitted to be used by all Jews other than the acquaintances of the gentile.[23] The acquaintances may benefit from it immediately after Shabbos.[24]

The general rule of an acquaintance of a gentile:[25]
An acquaintance of a gentile may not benefit from any labor done on Shabbos by the gentile, [even in the permitted cases mentioned above] unless the labor that was done is a type of labor in which even if the gentile would have also intended to do so for the acquaintance's behalf, he would not have had to increase the amount of labor done, such as to turn the light on in a room that both he and the acquaintance is in.
Nevertheless, after Shabbos the item is always permitted to be benefited from immediately.

Coffins and graves prepared by gentiles on Shabbos on behalf of gentiles:[26]
Is permitted to be used to bury immediately after Shabbos, [even by an acquaintance[27]].

Q&A
Are other actions which occurred on their own on Shabbos also forbidden to be benefited from?[28]
No. Only the above-mentioned items are forbidden on Shabbos. Thus, one may leave his hot water faucet open from Erev Shabbos even though this will cause the cold water entering into it to heat up on Shabbos. [However, one may not use this hot water which was heated on Shabbos to wash his hands as it is forbidden to wash with water heated on Shabbos even in a permitted way. It is forbidden to wash even a single limb even if the [water] was only slightly heated and is not Yad Soledes.[29]]

Benefiting from items which a gentile did labor to on Shabbos for a Jews behalf

Halacha 9
The law regarding the person for whom the work was done: If [a gentile] picked or trapped or baked or cooked or did any of the other forbidden actions for a Jew or for a Jew and a gentile then one must wait [from benefiting from the item] until enough time has passed after Shabbos for that action to have been done.
The Reason for why it is forbidden until the above amount of time passes after Shabbos: This is due to a

---

[19] Admur 325:8
[20] Admur 325:8
[21] Admur 325:17
[22] Admur 325:20
[23] Admur 325:16
[24] Admur 325:17
[25] Admur 325:18
[26] Admur 325:21
[27] As stated above.
[28] Shabbos Kihalacha Vol 1 p. 126
[29] Admur 325:4

decree that one may come to tell a gentile to do [forbidden] work [for him] on Shabbos in order so [the item] be available [to use] immediately after Shabbos.

The law regarding others: [Furthermore] even other [people] for whom the action had not been done, need to wait this amount [of time after Shabbos prior to benefiting from the action], as in any case a Biblically forbidden action was done on behalf of a Jew the Sages were strict to not differentiate between those for whom the action was done on their behalf and others.

However, if a Rabbinical prohibition was done on behalf of a Jew, it is permitted for others [to benefit from it] immediately as will be explained [in Halacha 11].

The definition of "Kdei Sheyasu": The definition of the measurement of "the amount of time it takes to have prepared the item" will be explained in chapter 515 [Halacha 4-8].

Halacha 10
The law in a case of doubt in whether or not the item had work done on Shabbos for a Jews behalf:
If there is a doubt if the [fruit] was picked on behalf of a Jew or [even] if one knows for certain that it was picked on behalf of a Jew but does not know if it was picked today [on Shabbos] or not, then it is forbidden on that day [Shabbos] as well as after Shabbos until enough time passes to have done that action.

The reason: Now, although this doubt is in regards to a Rabbinical prohibition nevertheless we do not rule leniently since it is an item which will eventually become permitted.

Other Opinions: [However] there are opinions which say that after Shabbos the item is immediately permitted.

Their Reasoning is because: since this prohibition [of benefiting] is only like a fine so that one not come to tell a gentile to do it for him on Shabbos, [therefore the Sages] were not so strict in a case of doubt even though it is something that will eventually become permitted regardless.

The Final Ruling: The main [Halachic] opinion is like the first opinion.

The law by a case that the gentile brought over fruits as a present or to sell: Even according to the latter opinion [the Sages] were only lenient [to allow one to eat the food immediately after Shabbos] in a case such as this, that the gentile had told the Jew before Shabbos that he would give him fruits on Shabbos and the [Jew] then went to the house of the gentile and received the fruits. As in such a case there is a doubt whether perhaps [the gentile] picked these fruits on Shabbos on behalf of the Jew, and he had his mind from before Shabbos on these fruits to pick them for him [the Jew] on Shabbos, or perhaps he had in mind to pick for him other fruits and these fruits he had picked for himself or on behalf of another gentile and afterwards he changed his mind and gave it to the Jew when he came over to him, and so too by all similar scenarios.

However if the gentile brought a present to a Jew or brought [fruits] to sell in a city that is majority of Jewish population then we are not inclined towards leniency to say that perhaps he had originally picked them for himself and afterwards changed his mind to bring them here [to sell or as a present], and rather we assume that he had picked it for this purpose [to sell or give as a present to a Jew].

Similarly, we are not inclined towards leniency [to say] that perhaps he picked them from before Shabbos being that a gentile which brings [fruits as] a present or for selling most likely intends to bring the best quality [fruits] and thus brings those [fruits] which he had picked today.

Trapped creatures: The same applies regarding [creatures] trapped [by a gentile] on Yom Tov.

See Summary at end of chapter.

Halacha 11

Brought for a gentile: An item which does not have suspicion of having been trapped or detached [from the ground] but was brought from outside the Shabbos city limit[30] then if it was brought on behalf of himself or for another gentile it is permitted for a Jew [to benefit from it] even on that day [i.e. Shabbos].

Brought for a Jew: [However] if it was brought for a Jew then it is forbidden to be eaten that day [Shabbos] for whoever it was brought for and they must wait until enough time has passed after Shabbos to have been able to bring it.

The reason: This is due to decree that one may come to tell a gentile to bring him items from outside the city limit on Shabbos in order so he could eat from it that day or immediately upon the entrance of evening [leave of Shabbos].

Others: However, for others [the food] is permitted [to be eaten] even on that day [if it was not carried through a public domain[31]] being that the prohibition of carrying from past the city limits is only Rabbinical [in origin] and thus they were not strict by a Rabbinical prohibition to also prohibit [the food] for even those that it was not brought on their behalf.

Moving the food: Therefore, even regarding the people who [the food] was brought for they are permitted to move it as it does not have the status of Muktzah being that it is fit to be eaten by others on that day.

Not to carry the food past a four-cubit radius: However, one does need to beware to not carry the item outside of the 4 cubit radius from the place that the gentile placed down [the food] if he placed it in an area which is not surrounded [by walls or a fence] for purposes of dwelling, such as by a field or by a city which does not have an Eiruv. Thus, this means that if one carried it 2 cubits then another may not carry it further, more than 2 cubits as will be explained in chapter 401 [Halacha 2] with regards to all items that a gentile carried past the city limits.

Items brought by ship: If the [food] was brought [by the gentile] on a ship from past the city limits then it is permitted to be eaten even for those [Jews] that it had been brought on behalf of in a case that the ship had traveled above 10 handbreadths [80cm.] [from the seabed] being that there is no [prohibition of] carrying past the city limits [when doing so] above ten handbreadths [from the ground] as will be explained in chapter 404 [Halacha 1].

However, one must [still] beware to not carry it past 4 cubits unless it was on the ship from before Shabbos and it had not been below ten handbreadths [from the ground] from when Shabbos arrived until it entered into the city limits of this particular place that he is now in as will be explained there.

Halacha 12
Those that the food was brought on their behalf may not switch the packages

Although [food] brought from outside the city limits is permitted [to be eaten] by those that the food had not been brought on their behalf nevertheless if [the gentiles] brought two items for two people [these two people] are forbidden to switch their [packages] as [when doing so] he nevertheless still benefits from the fact that [the package] was brought from outside the city limits, as through doing so his colleague is able to switch with him and give it to him.

Halacha 13
The definition of waiting "Kdie Sheyasu" after Shabbos when brought from outside the Techum

If one knows from where the food was brought: In any scenario [above] that one is required to wait [after Shabbos] the amount of time it had taken to do [the forbidden action on Shabbos] one only has to wait the amount of time it took the importer to bring it on Shabbos.

---

[30] On Shabbos one may not walk over 2000 cubits past the area that he is in when Shabbos begun. Thus, one has 2000 cubits from outside the city until which he may walk on Shabbos. These 2000 cubits are referred to as the city limits and should be taken in this context in wherever the term is mentioned in this book. An object which was outside the city limits before Shabbos may not be brought into the city.

[31] However, if the food was carried by the gentile through a public domain then it is forbidden for even others until enough time has passed after Shabbos to have been able to bring it through the public domain, as rules Admur in Halacha 16 and 22.

For example, if [the gentile] brought [the food] from a distant place, three daytime hours away, on Shabbos through riding on a horse and therefore arrived quicker [then he would have arrived on foot], then one does not have to wait after Shabbos the amount of time it would have taken [to travel that distance] on foot and rather it suffices to wait 3 hours.

One does not need to worry that perhaps [the gentile] did not ride so fast and rather traveled throughout Friday night because one can assume [that he did not do so being] that it is not common to ride at night.

If one does not now from where the food was brought: However this only refers to if one knew which place [the gentile] brought [the food] from, however if one does not know at all [the place from where the food was brought] and it is possible that it was brought from a close place, then it suffices to wait after Shabbos the amount of time it takes to bring it from outside the city limit besides for the amount of time he needs to wait for [the amount of time it took the gentile to] pick [the food] or trap [the animal] if it is a species of food which is attached [to the ground] or requires trapping, as explained in chapter 515 [Halacha 1].

Other Opinions: [However] there are opinions which say that any scenario where one needs to wait the amount of time it took to bring [the food] from outside the city limit, and it goes without saying if one needs to wait the amount of time it took to bring it from more distant place, then the night after Shabbos is not included in this amount [needed to wait] and rather one must wait this amount of time starting the next day from Sunday morning.

Their reasoning is: because it is not common to bring something at night from a distant place which is outside the city limit and there is thus suspicion that [if one were allowed to wait this time on the night after Shabbos that] one may come to tell a gentile to bring [the food] for him on Shabbos in order so it be ready to be used after Shabbos after waiting the amount of time it took for it to be brought.

The Final Ruling: One is to suspect for this latter opinion regarding Shabbos, although regarding Yom Tov one may be lenient like the first opinion. As well, even regarding Shabbos one may be lenient for the sake of guests or other *Seudos Mitzvah* [a meal which is being celebrated over the performance of a certain Mitzvah].

By other scenarios of "Kdei Sheyasu" one may wait from the night after Shabbos: However in a scenario where one must wait the amount of time [it took the gentile to do forbidden action to the food] when [the food was brought] from within the city limits, such as for example the gentile picked fruits or trapped fish from within the city limits, and one thus must wait the amount of the time [it took him] to pick [the fruit] or trap and [the amount of time it took him] to bring [the food] from that place that he had picked or trapped [the food] from within the city limit [until the Jew], then the night is included in the calculation according to all opinions.

Halacha 14
Food which is questionable as to whether or not was brought from outside the city limits:
If there is doubt as to whether [the food] was brought from outside the city limits, then the [food] is forbidden [to be eaten] by whoever it was brought for until enough time passes after Shabbos to have been able to bring it to him from outside the city limits.

The reason for this stringency despite it being a case of doubt in a Rabbinical prohibition is: because the [food] [will eventually become permitted and thus] has the status of a Davar Sheyeish Lo Matirin.

Other Opinions: [However] according to those opinions [above in Halacha 10] which hold that by this type of prohibition which is merely like a fine, so one not come to tell the gentile to do so for him on Shabbos, [the Sages] were not stringent in a case of doubt even though it is something which will eventually become permitted as written above [in Halacha 10], then here too it is permitted to be eaten by even the person for whom [the food] was brought for, and even on that day [on Shabbos].[32]

---

[32] Vetzaruch Iyun as there Admur explained that even the lenient opinion is stringent in a case that the food was brought specifically for the Jew, and only when there is doubt as to whom it was brought for are we lenient. Although in truth this is no question being that here there is true doubt as to whether any work was done on Shabbos by the gentile, while there we assume for certain that it was done on Shabbos and thus when brought to a Jew we assume also that it was done for the Jew. However still Tzaruch Iyun why here it is permitted on Shabbos itself while there

Final Ruling: It was already explained that the main Halachic opinion is like the former opinion.

Halacha 15
Food that was brought by a gentile that lives within one's city:
All the above refers to a gentile which does not reside with one in the same city, however if the gentile resides in one's city then and the fruits [that were brought] are commonly found in the city then we do not hold questionable that perhaps the gentile brought it from outside the city limits, and rather we say that [in the city] they were found and [in the city] they remained.

If he also has one house outside the city limit: [Furthermore] even if the gentile has two houses one within the city limits and one past the city limits, we incline towards leniency [and assume] that the [food] was brought from within the city limit, as it can be assumed that one will not ignore [bringing the fruits] from a closer home and travel to bring them from a more distanced home[33].

If he has two houses outside the city limit: However, if he has two houses which are outside the city limits and one house within the city limits then we do take into account the majority of homes that he has outside the city limits [and assume that the fruits were brought from those house].

Summary:
Food [as well as other items] brought from outside the Shabbos city limit:
In all cases it is only allowed if the food does not have suspicion of having been trapped or detached from the ground. If it was brought from outside the Shabbos city limit, then the following is the law: If it was.....

Brought for a gentile[34]: Then it is permitted for any Jew to benefit from it even on Shabbos [with exception to the acquaintances of the gentile[35]].

Brought for a Jew: Then it is forbidden to eaten on Shabbos for whomever it was brought for[36] and they must wait until enough time has passed after Sunday morning to have been able to bring it.

For others the food is permitted to be eaten even on Shabbos being that the prohibition of carrying from past the city limits is only Rabbinical[37]. [Although if the food was carried by the gentile through a public domain then it is forbidden for even others until enough time has passed after Shabbos to have been able to bring it through the public domain.[38]]

The food is not Muktzah even for those for whom it was brought for, although it may not be moved more than 4 cubits from where it was delivered, even by others, unless it was delivered into an enclosed area, in which case it may be moved anywhere within that enclosed area.

---

they were only lenient to permit it after Shabbos? Perhaps though here since it is a doubt in only a Rabbinical prohibition therefore, we are more lenient according to that opinion to permit it even on Shabbos itself. However, Tzaruch Iyun why the above should not be prohibited on Shabbos at the very least for having been brought from a Karmalis, as is ruled in Halacha 22?

[33] Meaning that when a closer home is available certainly, he will bring it from there rather than to travel far.
[34] Admur 325:11
[35] As explained below in Halacha 18
[36] Admur 325:11
[37] Admur 325:11
[38] Admur 325:16 and 22.

Items brought by ship:[39] Then if the ship traveled 80 cm above the seabed it is permitted for all to benefit from the food, however one may not move it more than 4 cubits as explained above, unless it was on the ship before Shabbos began and never entered within 80 cm until it entered the city limits.

Those that the food was brought on behalf of may not switch the foods:[40] Two people which had food brought for them from outside the city limits, even though each person delivery is permitted for others, nevertheless these two may not switch their packages with each other.

A case of doubt as to whether it was brought from outside the city limits: Has the same laws as if it were for certain brought from outside the city limits.[41] Although if the gentile lives in one's city then we always assume that it was brought from within the city limits, even if he has another home outside the city limits, unless he has two homes outside the city limits.[42]

Items brought from within the city limits but in areas forbidden to carry in: See next section.

Other cases of works of a gentile done on Shabbos

Halacha 16
Water filled by a gentile and carried from a private to public domain:

On behalf of a gentile: A gentile which filled [a bucket of] water on behalf of his animal from a well which was ten handbreadths deep and 4 handbreadths wide which was positioned within a public domain, and thus it ends up that he had carried [the water] from a private domain [the well] to a public domain [nevertheless] it is permitted for a Jew to give his animal to drink from this water.

The reason for this is: because since the gentile did not at all intend [to draw the water] for [the Jew].

If the gentile is an acquaintance of the Jew: However this only applies if the gentile does not know [the Jew], however if the gentile is acquainted with him then it is forbidden [for the Jew to benefit from this water on Shabbos[43]] due to a decree that perhaps the gentile will increase the amount of water that he is drawing in order so there be also enough for [the Jew] if [we were to allow] also the Jew to give [his animals] to drink from [the gentiles] water.

On behalf of a Jew: Even if the gentile is not acquainted with him, [nevertheless] if it was drawn on behalf of the animal of the Jew then it is forbidden for even others [for whom the water was not drawn on behalf of] to benefit from these waters, even for a different use [then that intended by the gentile], such as for bathing or for washing dishes.

The reason for this is: because any time that a Biblical prohibition was done by a gentile on behalf of a Jew the Sages did not differentiate between those that the labor was done on behalf of and others.

From or into a Karmalis: However if [the gentile] draw [water] from a well that was located in a Karmalis, or he brought the water into a public domain from a river which is a Karmalis, then the [water] is permitted [in benefit] for whomever it had not been brought on behalf of, being that the [carrying into or from a] Karmalis is only a Rabbinical prohibition, [of which the rule is that we are lenient for others, as explained above in Halacha 9].

The custom today: Asking a gentile to bring items from a Karmalis on Shabbos: [Furthermore] today, the world has accustomed themselves to allow to even initially ask a gentile to bring them beer or other items which are needed for Shabbos through a Karmalis.

The reason: There are opinions which have justified their behavior saying that Shabbos necessities are considered like a need for a Mitzvah in which the [Sages] permitted [to be done] in a case of a Rabbinical prohibition [i.e. asking a Gentile] which itself is only a Rabbinical prohibition [i.e. Shvus Deshvus] as was explained in Chapter 307 [Halacha 12].

Restrictions to the above allowance: [Nevertheless] those that do so must beware to not place the vessel

---

[39] Admur 325:11
[40] Admur 325:12
[41] Admur 325:14
[42] Admur 325:15
[43] However after Shabbos it is permitted immediately as will be explained in Halacha 17.

into the hand of the gentile as well as to not take it from his hand as was explained there [in chapter 307], as well as to not give money to the gentile as will be explained in chapter 517 [Halacha 4].

([Furthermore] nevertheless one may only be lenient regarding [asking the gentile to bring him] beer and the like of items which are a complete Shabbos necessity in which it is impossible to do without them and not be left in a slightly pressing situation. However, items which one does not have much need for such as fruits and varieties of extra dishes and the like, then they are not considered needed for a Mitzvah as explained in chapter 261, and one thus may not ask a gentile to bring them].

Halacha 17
If a gentile picked grass for his own behalf:
If a gentile picked grass which was attached [to the ground] for the need of [feeding] his animal then a Jew may afterwards feed his animal from it. Meaning that he may stand in front of his animal in a way that it can only turn to the area of the [picked] grasses as was explained in chapter 324 with regards to all items that are forbidden to be moved [i.e. are Muktzah] as these grasses are also forbidden to be moved as explained above [in Halacha 8].

If the gentile is an acquaintance of the Jew: However this only applies if the gentile does not know [the Jew], however if the gentile is acquainted with him then it is forbidden [for the Jew] to even stand before [the animal] in order so it eat from it on Shabbos due to a decree that perhaps the gentile will increase the amount [that he is picking] on behalf of the [Jew's] animal if he were to be allowed to feed his animal from it.

However, after Shabbos there is no need to wait the amount of time it took the gentile to pick it being that the gentile picked it for his own behalf and [even] on Shabbos the decree is only because perhaps the gentile will come to increase [the amount picked] also for [the Jew].

Halacha 18
The rule by Jewish acquaintances of a gentile who did work for himself:
Suspicion of increased work: The same law applies in all cases [of work done by a gentile for his own behalf] that there is suspicion that perhaps the gentile will increase on behalf of the Jew if [the gentile] is an acquaintance [of the Jew].

For example, a gentile which roasted or cooked for himself foods which are not prohibited due to "Bishul Akum" as well as all other cases in which when done for two people the amount must be increased more than if it were to be done for one person.

No suspicion of increased work: However, by matters in which there is no suspicion that perhaps [the gentile] will increase in the labor on behalf of the Jew, such as if [the gentile] lit a candle for himself [to use] or made a ramp to use to descend from a ship of which one candle and one ramp will suffice for many, then it is permitted to be benefited from even by his Jewish acquaintances.

Halacha 19
Work done which is evident that it was done for a Jew
Even if the gentile is not acquainted with a certain Jew, [nevertheless] if he says explicitly that he is doing [the labor] on behalf of the Jew or even if he does not say this [explicitly] although from his actions it is evident that he is doing it on behalf of the Jew, such as in a case that [the gentile] lit a candle in the house of a Jew and then the gentile left and did not benefit from it at all, then it is forbidden to benefit from its light.

Halacha 20
Allowing a gentile to feed herbs to ones animal if the gentile picked the herbs for that purpose:
If a gentile picked grasses (for his animal) and fed them (also) to the Jews animal, then one does not need to protest against him doing so.

The reason why one does not have to protest the picking of the grass: Now, although most probably [the gentile] had picked [the grasses] also on behalf of the Jew, [nevertheless] there is no prohibition at all involved in [allowing the gentile to] pick the grasses being that every gentile which does an action on his own accord certainly intends on doing so for his own self-interest, knowing that he will not lose anything out by doing so, as was explained in chapter 252 [Halacha 10].

If the grass belongs to the Jew: However [this is only allowed] so long as the grasses do not belong to the Jew but rather to the gentile or are un-owned, due to the reason explained there [in chapter 252].

The reason why one need not protest letting his animal eat it: (As well there is no prohibition in the fact that he is feeding the Jews animal from grasses which he had picked on [the Jews] behalf, as although it is forbidden for the Jew to get benefit from the action that the gentile had done for him even though the gentile intended in doing so for his own self-interest as was explained there [in chapter 252] nevertheless [since] here the actual physical body of the Jew is not benefiting from it, [therefore] the Sages did not decree [against the animal getting benefit] unless [the Jew] himself stands before the animal in order to lead it to eat from it, however [they did] not [decree] against letting the gentile feed [the animal] being that he intends in doing so for his own personal benefit.

Halacha 21
Coffins and graves prepared by gentiles on Shabbos:
On behalf of gentiles: A gentile which constructed on Shabbos a coffin or grave in order to bury a dead [relative] of his or in order to sell (in a city which has a majority gentile population) then it is permitted for a Jew to bury [a corpse] in it immediately after Shabbos.

On behalf of Jews: [However] if the gentile constructed [the above] on behalf of a Jew then he must wait until enough time has passed [after Shabbos] to have been able to construct it. This [restriction applies] whether to [use the coffin or grave] to bury the Jew for whom it was constructed on behalf of and whether to bury another Jew.

Made in a public area on behalf of a Jew: However [when made on behalf of a Jew it is only allowed to bury in it after Shabbos when] the [construction of the] grave or coffin [was done] in an isolated area and [thus] was not publicized to all that it had been constructed on Shabbos on behalf this specific Jew. However a grave [which was constructed] in a public location, as well as a coffin which was constructed near a grave which is located in a public area, in a way that is evident to all that this grave or coffin was made on Shabbos on behalf of this specific Jew, then it is forbidden to ever bury that Jew in it even after the set amount of time has passed [after Shabbos].

This [prohibition] is a fine over the fact that Shabbos was desecrated in public through a gentile on his behalf.

However, it is permitted to bury other Jews [in this grave or coffin] after waiting [after Shabbos] the amount of time it took to construct it.

Other actions done in public: The same law applies [by all other actions, that] if Shabbos was desecrated in public by a gentile on behalf of a living Jew it is forever forbidden for that Jew [to benefit from it] even if [the Jew] had not commanded the gentile to do so [for him].

Other Opinions: [However] there are opinions which say that [the Sages] did not forbid one from ever benefiting [from a public desecration done on behalf of] a corpse due to it being a fine but rather due to that it is a belittlement to the corpse for it to be buried in a grave which is publicized to have been [made through] desecrating Shabbos on his behalf. Thus, accordingly a [public desecration done on behalf of a] live person is permitted even for him [to benefit from] after enough time has passed after Shabbos for the action to have been done.

The Final Ruling: At a time of need one may rely on the latter opinion to be lenient in this [controversy over a] Rabbinical prohibition.

If one hired the gentile to do the work for him: Even according to the former opinion the Sages were only stringent when the gentile decided on his own to do the action, however if [the gentile] had been ordered before Shabbos to do so and the Jew had agreed to pay him a set price and no time frame was set as for when the work must be done and the gentile then on his own decided to do it on Shabbos, there is no prohibition from the letter of the law [from benefiting from it] after enough time has passed after Shabbos to have been able to do it even though the gentile did so in public.

[Furthermore] even if the gentile was hired to be paid per day but the Jew did not set with him which days [the work is to be done] and the [gentile went ahead] did so on his own on Shabbos, [it is allowed to benefit from it].

Even with regards to a corpse it is permitted from the letter of the law for him to benefit from it in such a situation.

Nevertheless, according to all opinions it is proper to be stringent even regarding [work done for] a live person, that no Jew ever get benefit from any action that had been done through a gentile publicly desecrating Shabbos on the command of a Jew even if the gentile was paid by the job [as opposed to by hour or day] in which case there is no prohibition from the letter of the law as will be explained in chapter 664. This is with exception to if [the Jew] protested the gentiles actions done [on Shabbos] and was ignored out of the gentiles own self interest, as was explained in chapter 244 [Halacha 7].

Halacha 22
A eulogy cymbal that was brought to a Jew on Shabbos through a public domain:

Brought from an actual public domain: A gentile which had brought on Shabbos through a public domain flutes to eulogize a Jew, then since he did with them a Biblical prohibition [of carrying] [therefore] one may not eulogize with them, not that Jew [that it was brought on behalf of] nor for any other Jew until one waits after Shabbos the amount of time that it took to bring it from the place that the gentile brought it from on Shabbos.

This applies whether the place was outside the city limits or whether it was inside the city limits.

If one does not know from where it was brought then it suffices to wait the amount of time it takes to bring it from outside the city limits.

Brought in a publicized manner: However [this allowance only applies] when he brought it in a discreet fashion., however if he brought it openly in a way that everyone knows that he brought it through a public domain on Shabbos for this specific person, then it is forbidden to ever eulogize with it that Jew.

Brought from a Karmalis: [However] all these [restrictions] apply when brought from an actual public domain, however if [the gentile] brought it through a *Karmalis,* then if it was brought from within the city limits one does not need to wait at all [after Shabbos] even for the person that it was brought on behalf of.

The reason for this leniency is: because the [Sages] were only strict against the person whom the [item] was brought on behalf of, through a *Karmalis,* that he may not benefit from it on Shabbos, however not that he should have to wait after Shabbos the amount of time it took to bring it, unless it is a case that it was brought from outside the city limits, as in such a case he benefits from [the gentile] having brought it on Shabbos. However when brought from within the city limits he does not benefit much from it having been brought on Shabbos (being that the Jew himself could have walked there on Shabbos and bring it back immediately after Shabbos, and the small amount of time that he would have delayed in bringing it after Shabbos from where it was to where he is now [we do not make issue of] being that there is no suspicion that he may come to tell the gentile to bring it from there on Shabbos [in order to save him this short delay after Shabbos]).

If there is doubt from where it was brought: In a case of doubt as to whether it was brought from outside the city limits or from within the city limits, it is forbidden for whomever it was brought on behalf of.

Others: However, for other people it is permitted even if one knows for certain that it was brought from outside the city limits.

If it was brought from outside the city limits through a *Karmalis* and afterwards it passed through a public domain then [other people] only need to wait after Shabbos the amount of time it took to bring it from the start of the public domain and after this [time is waited] it is permitted for others or even for the person whom it was brought on behalf of in a case that it was brought from within the city limits.

Supplement Chapter 226 Halacha 13
A bathhouse which was heated on Shabbos by a gentile:

Majority gentile population: A city with a Jewish and gentile population which has a bathhouse that is bathed in on Shabbos, then if [the city] has a majority gentile population then it is permitted to bathe in it immediately after Shabbos being that one can assume that it was heated up on Shabbos for the gentiles which are the majority.

Majority Jewish population: [However] if majority of the population are Jews then one must wait [after Shabbos] the amount of time it takes to heat [the water].[44]

Half-Half: Furthermore] even if the population is [exactly] half [Jewish] and half [gentile] one must wait the above amount of time because it can be assumed that it was up on Shabbos for both [Jew and gentile].

Summary

The general rule[45] by a forbidden action done by a gentile on Shabbos on behalf of a Jew:

A Biblical action: The food is forbidden for all until enough time has passed after Shabbos to have been able to do the action.

A Rabbinical action: For the person for whom the action was done the food is forbidden until enough time has passed after Shabbos to have been able to do the action.

For others the food is permitted even on Shabbos. [46]

An action done in public by the gentile[47]: Then if it is evident to the public that it was done on behalf of a Jew it is forbidden for that Jew to <u>ever</u> benefit from that object even if one had never hired the gentile to do so for him, unless it is a pressing scenario. However, others may benefit from it after enough time has passed after Shabbos to have been able to make it.

If one had hired the gentile from before Shabbos and agreed to pay him for the job, without specifying a date for when it must be done by and thus it was done on Shabbos by the gentiles own accord then although that from the letter of the law all may benefit from it after enough time has passed after Shabbos to be able to make it, nevertheless <u>all</u> Jews are to be stringent to not benefit from it unless the Jew had protested against the gentile doing so on Shabbos.

The definition of work done for a Jews behalf:[48]

Any work that is evident that it was done for a Jew, even if the Jew never asked him to do so and is not an acquaintance of the gentile, [and certainly if the gentile did so upon the request of a Jew].

The law in a case of doubt in whether or not the item had work done on Shabbos for a Jews behalf:[49]

If it was not done for selling purposes, we always assume that the gentile did so for himself unless there is reason to believe otherwise, in which case even if one is in doubt if in truth it was done for a Jew he must be stringent as if he knows for certain that it was done for a Jews behalf.[50]

When done for selling purposes then if majority of the city, [or even 50% of the city is Jewish[51]], then one must be stringent.

If the gentile carried through a Karmalis on behalf of a Jew:

Then it is permitted on Shabbos only for those whom the item was not brought on behalf of, unless the

---

[44] As although on Shabbos itself only gentiles bathe in it, nevertheless the main intention of heating it was so that the water be heated for the Jews to be able to use immediately after Shabbos. [Mishneh Berurah 37]

[45] There are exceptions to this rule which are mentioned in the cases below it.

[46] Admur 325:9 and 7

[47] Admur 325:21

[48] Admur 325:19

[49] Admur 325:10, as the stringent opinion is the main Halachic opinion.

[50] Admur 325:10

[51] See Supplement

item is needed for a Mitzvah, such as foods which are a complete Shabbos necessity which will impair ones Shabbos if not available, in which case it is permitted for all on Shabbos and one may even initially ask a gentile to bring it.[52]

Even when forbidden for the person for him it was brought for, if it was brought from within the city limits then it is permitted immediately after Shabbos.[53]

Allowing a gentile to feed herbs to one's animal which the gentile had picked for that purpose:[54]
Is allowed unless the herbs were the property of the Jew.

Coffins and graves prepared by gentiles on Shabbos on behalf of a Jew:[55]
Done in private: If what was done was not done in a publicized way then it is permitted to be used for all after enough time has passed after Shabbos to have done that work.
Done in public: It is forbidden for that Jew to ever benefit from it. Although others may benefit from it [unless the gentile had been hired by the Jew to make it, in which case it is proper that no Jew ever benefit from it].

Instruments carried for a Jews funeral by a gentile on Shabbos:[56]
In a public domain: Have the same law as the above case.
In a Karmalis: Is permitted for all immediately after Shabbos if brought from within the city limits.

---

[52] Admur 325:16
[53] Admur 325:22
[54] Admur 325:20
[55] Admur 325:21
[56] Admur 325:22

THE LAWS OF BATHING, SHOWERING, AND SWIMMING ON SHABBOS

Shulchan Aruch chapter 326

Translation
Shulchan Aruch Chapter 326

TRANSLATION CHAPTER 326
The laws of bathing on Shabbos
Includes 13 Halachos

Introduction:
The following chapter will discuss the laws of bathing and showering on Shabbos. There is a difference between hot and cold water, as well as to the amount of one's body that is being bathed. At times it is Rabbinically forbidden and at times it is completely permitted, as will be explained.

Halacha 1
The prohibition of bathing on Shabbos
Bathing: The Sages forbade bathing ones entire body or majority of it with hot water whether [the water] is within a vessel [or] whether it is in the ground, [and] even if it was heated form before Shabbos.
The reason for this prohibition is: because [back then] the people in charge of the bathhouses would heat up [the water] on Shabbos and claim that they heated it before Shabbos.
Now, although the Jewish people are not [to be] suspected to advertently desecrate Shabbos, nevertheless these [people in charge of the bathhouse] would place wood [in the fire that is] under the cold water before Shabbos, close to dark, and the woods would burn throughout the entire Shabbos thus heating up the water that is above it. Now [placing the wood so close to Shabbos] is forbidden because of a decree that one may come to forget and stoke the coals after Shabbos has begun. Therefore [the Sages] forbade anyone from bathing in hot water even if it is not [being done] in a public bathhouse [which is run by caretakers].
Showering: [Furthermore] even to pour water on one's body to rinse off [is forbidden] even though this is not the usual way of bathing in a bathhouse in which one enters his body and limbs into the water.
Washing each limb individually: Even to bathe each limb individually and not majority of his body at once [is forbidden].
The reason for this is: because the Sages did not differentiate within their decree [regarding different forms of washing] since [all the forms] slightly resemble bathing in a bathhouse in which one bathes his entire body or majority of it.
Bathing minority of one's body: However, it is permitted to bathe in hot water [that was permissibly heated from before Shabbos] one's face, hands and feet or other limbs so long as one does not [in total] wash majority of his body.
Doing Hefsek Taharah on Shabbos: Therefore, in a place where there is no [accepted] custom [otherwise], a woman is allowed to begin her seven clean days on Shabbos[1], being that [to do so] she only needs to wash her private part and between her thighs. However, she must be careful not to wash with a cloth so she not come to squeeze it.
Hot Springs: All the above is with regards to water heated through fire, however the hot water [from the] springs of Tiberius are permitted for one to even dip his entire body inside of.
Cold Water: It thus goes without saying that [this allowance applies with] cold water.
Hot water of Tiberius that is in a vessel: However it was only permitted [to bathe] in the hot waters of Tiberius when [the water] is in the ground, however when it is in a vessel then it has the same laws as water heated over fire being that all water that is in a vessel is not recognizable if it was [heated] from a fire or if it is from the hot springs of Tiberius, and there is thus [reason] to decree on these [hot waters of Tiberius] because of the hot waters [heated through fire].

---

[1] After a married woman menstruates, she must separate from her husband until she has counted seven clean days, meaning days that she has not seen any blood. To begin the count, she must wash herself the afternoon prior to her wanting to begin the seven-day count and then check herself to verify that the blood has stopped flowing. Thus, this washing may be done on Shabbos in order to have the first of the seven days begin after Shabbos.

Halacha 2
A roofed spring:

First opinion: [However] there are opinions which say that [the Sages] only permitted [washing oneself in] the hot springs of Tiberius when the area is not roofed, however if the area is roofed then it is forbidden.

Their reason is: because [a roofed spring] causes one to sweat and sweating is forbidden on Shabbos as will be explained.

Second opinion: [However] there are opinions which say that it is permitted to sweat in the hot waters of Tiberius.

Their reasoning is: because [the Sages] only forbade one from [actively causing himself to] sweat due to the decree made against bathing, as will be explained and thus since it is permitted to bathe in the hot springs of Tiberius then certainly it is permitted to sweat in them.

The Final Ruling: Regarding the final ruling, in [a controversy over] a Rabbinical prohibition one may follow the lenient opinion.

Supplement from Mahadurah Basra chapter 259[2]
May one bathe in warm water?

It is certainly permitted to bathe in warm water heated from before Shabbos as even the waters of a river in the summer are considered warm, or [waters] that are in a [heated] house in the winter [are considered warm, and nevertheless are permitted to bathe in on Shabbos].

Supplement from Chapter 328 Halacha 48
Bathing for healing purposes:

Waters that are commonly bathed in [on Shabbos]: One may bathe for healing purposes in waters of Gerar and waters of Chamson and waters of Tiberius and in the pure waters of the Mediterranean Sea even though that they are salty [and thus have a greater healing affect[3]].[4]

The reason for this allowance is: because it is common to bath in them even not for healing purposes and it is thus not evident that [one is bathing in them] with intent for healing.

Waters that are not commonly bathed in: However [one may not bathe for healing purposes] in foul water of the Mediterranean Sea, and not in flax water[5] being that they are repugnant, and it is [thus] uncommon to bathe in them for non-medical purposes.

To dip and leave: However, this restriction only applies if one remains in the water [for some time], however if one does not remain in them [and rather dips and leaves] then it is permitted [even in the foul waters] being that it simply appears as if he is cooling himself off [in it].

Tiberius hot springs: In places that it is common to only bathe in Tiberius hot springs for healing purposes, then it is forbidden to bathe in them on Shabbos for healing even if he does not remain in the waters [a long time].

Halacha 3
Insulating within the Tiberius hot springs

A channel of water from the hot springs of Tiberius is forbidden to place through it, even from before Shabbos, a tube of cold water which its opening [of the tube] extends past the channel and its [cold] waters spill into a ditch in the ground. This is done in order in order so the [cold] water that is in the tube heat up upon going through the channel of hot water.

---

[2] Page 884 in the new Shulchan Aruch. So rules also the Sefer Tehila Ledavid, and Minchas Shabbos, brought in Ketzos Hashulchan 133 footnote 1, and in SS"K chapter 14 footnote 3.

[3] Mishneh Berurah 138

[4] Seemingly although the custom is not to bathe even in cold water on Shabbos, nevertheless for healing it is allowed. Vetzaruch Iyun.

[5] Lit. Water that had material soaking in it

The Reason: Doing the above is considered similar to insulating with material that increases heat being that these [cold] waters [that are in the tube] are being insulated within the channel of the Tiberius hot springs which are considered a material that increases heat, and it was already explained in chapter 257 [Halacha 1] that it is forbidden to insulate with material that increases heat even from before Shabbos.

If one transgressed and placed the tube in the spring: [There too it was explained that] if one transgressed and insulated [in material that increases heat] it is forbidden [to benefit on Shabbos from that food]. Therefore, if one transgressed and placed the tube of cold water through the channel of [hot water] then the waters which are spilling from it into the ditch are forbidden either to use for bathing or for drinking just as is the law regarding if it were heated on Shabbos in which case it is forbidden to wash in them even one's face, hands and feet, and even [to wash] only a single limb [is forbidden].

On Erev Yom Tov: If one placed this tube [in the channel] before Yom Tov then it has the same laws as water heated on Yom Tov of which it is forbidden to bathe with it ones entire body or majority of it, although it is permitted to drink it or to wash in it ones face, hands and feet as is written in Chapter 511 [Halacha 1].

Having cold water flow into the hot spring:
However, all the above [restrictions] is only with regards to when the actual tube is encompassed from all sides [by the hot water] and it opens to outside the channel however if one has the [cold] water poured into the channel then this is not considered insulation at all being that the cold-water mixes into the hot water and is not insulated within it. Therefore, it is permitted before Shabbos to have cold water flow into there and have the flow continue throughout the entire Shabbos.

Doing so does not contain [a prohibition of] cooking because the action was begun from before Shabbos and finishes on its own on Shabbos as was explained in chapter 252 [Halacha 1].

Bathing in this channel: It is permitted to even bathe one's entire body simultaneously within this channel [that had cold water mixed into it] just like [is allowed] by other hot springs of Tiberius.

Halacha 4
Warming up ones wet body near a fire:
Majority of one's body: A person may not rinse his entire body in cold water and heat himself opposite a fire because by doing so he warms up the water that is on him and it is considered as if he has washed his entire body in hot water.

However, one is allowed to rinse himself off with cold water after having heated up [his body] near a fire because the [cold] water that [will be poured] on him will not get so hot [to be considered that he has bathed in hot water].

Warming up one's wet hands: [Furthermore] there are opinions which that even one who washes his hands needs to be careful not to heat it up opposite a fire even from an area where [the water on him will] not [reach] Yad Soledes, if one did not previously dry himself very well.

Their reasoning is: because by doing so he warms up the water that is on [his hands] and it is thus like he has bathed in hot water that was heated on Shabbos and hot water which was heated on Shabbos even in a permitted way is forbidden to wash in even one limb and even if the [water] was only slightly heated that it is not Yad Soledes.

The Final Ruling: One is to be strict like this latter opinion.

Halacha 5
Treating stomach pains with a vessel of hot water
A large amount of water: One who has a stomach pains is forbidden to place on his stomach a vessel that contains hot water because he may come to spill it on majority of his body, and it will thus be considered as if he has washed majority of his body in hot water.

A small amount: [Furthermore] even if there is only a small amount of hot water [in the vessel] which is not enough to wash majority of one's body [if it were to spill], nevertheless if it were heated on Shabbos even a little, [even if this were] to the point that it is not [yet] Yad Soledes, it is forbidden [to place it in a vessel on one's body for the reason] explained [in the previous Halacha, that one may not bathe even minority of one's body in water heated on Shabbos].

On a weekday: [Furthermore] even on a weekday this is not allowed to be done because of the possible danger [that it involves] as at times the water is very hot [and may come to spill on one's body and give him a serious burn].

Placing hot clothing on it: However, it is permitted to heat up clothing and place them on ones stomach even on Shabbos.

Halacha 6
Bathing in a river on Shabbos:
Must fully dry oneself upon leaving: One who bathes in a river [on Shabbos] needs to dry his body very well when he comes up from the river so that no water remains on him and have him carry it 4 cubits in a *Karmalis* as explained in chapter 301 [Halacha].

Not to swim and not to splash items away: As well one may not swim in the river and may not cause any item to swim [flow], such as twigs which are floating on the water it is forbidden for him to splash them away in order to clear up the water as will be explained in chapter 339.

Not to squeeze one's hair: As well every bather needs to beware not to squeeze his hair.

The Reason: Now, although there is the prohibition of squeezing is not applicable with hair, being that hair is hard and does not actually absorb water inside it [and rather the water is absorbed between each individual hair], nevertheless it is Rabbinically forbidden [to squeeze it].

The custom today: Due to that not everyone knows to beware in all the above therefore the custom spread in these provinces to not bathe at all on Shabbos, not even with cold water even though there is no prohibition involved from the letter of the law [in doing so].

Halacha 7
Going to Mikvah on Shabbos:
A person is allowed to purify himself of his impurities by immersing in a *Mikvah* on Shabbos even if this immersing is Biblically required [to be done], such as a *nidda* and the like, being that doing so does not appear like one is rectifying [something on Shabbos which is forbidden] but rather like one who is going [in the water in order] to cool himself off.

Dipping in reeky water, and dipping in the winter: [Furthermore] even to immerse in reeky water which is not commonly used to cool off in, and even [to immerse] in the winter when it is not at all common to [immerse in water to] cool oneself off, nevertheless [it is allowed as] at times when a person is dirty from mud and feces he washes himself even in the winter and even in reeky water in order to remove the mud and feces that are on him.

The custom regarding a woman's immersion: [However] in our provinces the custom is to forbid the immersing of a woman on Shabbos unless her husband is in the city as well as that it was not possible for her to immerse before Shabbos or [she was able to but] her husband was not in the city and only arrived on Erev Shabbos in which case she did no negligence in not having immersed prior to Shabbos. However, in any case that her husband was in the city and she was able to immerse [before Shabbos and did not immerse then she may not immerse on Shabbos.

The reason behind this custom: There are authorities which have given [the following] rational behind this custom [saying] that since the custom has spread to not bathe on Shabbos therefore when an impure person immerses to purify himself it appears as if he is rectifying [an item which is forbidden to do on Shabbos] and not like he is going in [the water] to cool off, being that it is not at all common to bath in order to cool off due to the reason explained [above in Halacha 6] even though that there is no prohibition in doing so.

The custom regarding immersing for purification of nocturnal emission: Nevertheless a man is allowed to immerse [to purify himself] from a seminal discharge.

The reason is because: since this immersion is not Biblically required (and is not even a complete Rabbinical obligation [therefore] it does not appear like one is rectifying [himself].)

The immersion of a penitent: (As well an apostate that repented is allowed to immerse on Shabbos because this immersion is not Biblically required as opposed to the immersion of a convert (as well as that there is not even a complete Rabbinical obligation [for the penitent to do so])).

A woman who needs to re-immerse on Shabbos due to a stringency: As well any woman which needs to re-immerse due to a mere stringency is permitted to immerse on Shabbos as explained in Yorah Deah chapter 197 [Halacha 1 in Shach].

Halacha 8
Washing oneself with liquid that also contains hair removal liquid on Shabbos:
It is permitted to wash one's face, hands and feet with liquids that do not remove hair which are mixed with hair removal substances so long as the majority of the mixture is not made up of hair removal substance in a way that [washing with this mixture] will inevitably [remove hair].

Halacha 9
Washing oneself with bran:
It is permitted to wash one's hands with bran on Shabbos being that [although] doing so involves kneading [it is considered done] with an irregularity.

The reason this is allowed: Now, although one is to be stringent not to knead on Shabbos [a thick mixture even] with an irregularity unless one placed the water in the mixture from before Shabbos as was explained in chapter 321 [Halacha 16], nevertheless here since he is not actually placing water into the bran and rather is merely taking the bran with wet hands it is permitted according to all [opinions].

Halacha 10
Washing one's hands in salt or soap:
It is forbidden to wash one's hands in salt and certainly with soap or other fats.

The reason for this is: because [the material] dissolves in one's hand and is as if one has created a new substance on Shabbos which resembles a forbidden action as was explained in chapter 320 [Halacha 16] that it is forbidden to crush snow and hail for this reason.

Other Opinions: [However] according to those which [held there] that the reason for the prohibition of crushing snow and hail is because of a decree made [to safeguard one from coming to] squeeze fruits which are designated for their juices as snow and hail are likewise designated for their liquids as was explained there [in Halacha 19], [then according to them] soap and other fat which are not designated as liquids are permitted to be [even] initially crushed [when washed in water].

The Final Ruling: One is to be stringent like the former opinion.

Halacha 11
The water of a bathhouse that got heated on its own on Shabbos:
A bathhouse which its fire is fueled from the outside, under [the bathhouse], if one closed before Shabbos those holes through which the [water in the] bathhouse heats up from then it is permitted to bathe in its water immediately after Shabbos being that [the water] had not been heated at all on Shabbos.

However, if its holes had not been plugged from before Shabbos then even though it heated up on its own on Shabbos [through one having stoked the fire right before Shabbos] nevertheless in the evening one must wait the amount of time it takes to heat it being that it was heated in a prohibited way. As it is forbidden for its holes to be left open on Shabbos when there is fire under it due to a decree that one may come to stoke the coals on Shabbos.[6]

---

[6] Seemingly this is referring to a case that the water was not heated to its halfway point from before Shabbos. However even then Tzaruch Iyun from chapter 254 Q&A there.

Halacha 12
Perspiring on Shabbos in a bathhouse:
Entering a steam room: The Sages forbade one to enter a bathhouse in order to even merely perspire due to the transgressors who would bathe themselves in hot water and claim that they were just perspiring.

To pass by a steam room: [Furthermore] there are opinions which say that even to walk past a bathhouse by an area where one is able to perspire is forbidden even though he has no intention to perspire.

Halacha 13
A bathhouse which was heated on Shabbos by a gentile:
Majority gentile population: A city with a Jewish and gentile population which has a bathhouse that is bathed in on Shabbos, if [the city] has a majority gentile population it is permitted to bathe in the water immediately after Shabbos being that one can assume that it was heated on Shabbos on behalf of gentiles which are the majority of the population.

Majority Jewish population: [However] if majority of the population are Jews then one must wait [after Shabbos] the amount of time it takes to heat [the water].[7]

Half-Half: Furthermore] even if the population is [exactly] half [Jewish] and half [gentile] one must wait the above amount of time because it can be assumed that it was heated on Shabbos for both [Jew and gentile].

---

[7] As although on Shabbos itself only gentiles bathe in it, nevertheless the main intention of heating it was so that the water be heated for the Jews to be able to use immediately after Shabbos. [Mishneh Berurah 37]

COMPILATION OF HALACHOS SUMMARIES AND Q&A

Introduction:
The following chapter will discuss the laws of bathing and showering on Shabbos. There is a difference between hot and cold water, as well as to the amount of one's body that is being bathed. At times it is Rabbinically forbidden and at times it is completely permitted, as will be explained.

Important note: In all cases mentioned that it is permitted to bathe in hot water heated from before Shabbos one must beware not to transgress the cooking prohibition through turning on the hot water faucet. See "The Laws of Cooking" Halacha 9 Q&A!

1. The prohibition of bathing/showering on Shabbos in hot water:
A. Bathing in hot water heated through fire:[8]
The Sages forbade bathing one's entire body or majority[9] of it with hot water whether [the water] is within a vessel [or] whether it is in the ground, [and] even if it was heated from before Shabbos.
The reason for this prohibition is:[10] because [back then] the people in charge of the bathhouses would heat up [the water] on Shabbos and claim that they heated it before Shabbos. Now, although the Jewish people are not [to be] suspected to advertently desecrate Shabbos, nevertheless these [people in charge of the bathhouse] would place wood [in the fire that is] under the cold water before Shabbos, close to dark, and the woods would burn throughout the entire Shabbos thus heating up the water that is above it. Now, [placing the wood so close to Shabbos] is forbidden because of a decree that one may come to forget and stoke the coals after Shabbos has begun.
Not in bathhouse:[11] Therefore [the Sages] forbade anyone from bathing in hot water even if it is not [being done] in a public bathhouse [which is run by caretakers].

B. Showering in hot water heated through fire:[12]
[Furthermore] even to pour water on one's body to rinse off [is forbidden] even though this is not the usual way of bathing in a bathhouse in which one enters his body and limbs into the water. [This applies even to water that was heated on Erev Shabbos, and even to water that is in the ground.[13]]

---

[8] Admur 326:1; Michaber 326:1; Shabbos 39b
[9] Admur ibid; M"A 326:2 in name of Kneses Hagedola; M"B 321:2
[10] Admur ibid [however see Admur 616:1 in parentheses]; Ran 40a, Rashba 40a in explanation of Gemara Shabbos 40a; Yerushalmi 3:3; See Tehila Ledavid 326:1
Other opinions: Some Poskim rule the reason behind this prohibition is because one may come to heat up the water on Shabbos and transgress a Biblical prohibition of Sekila. [Implication of Admur 616:1 in parentheses; M"A 326:1; Olas Shabbos 326:1; Tosefes Shabbos 326:1; M"B 326:1; Kaf Hachaim 326:1] As the Balanim [caretakers of the bathhouse] in previous times would heat up the water on Shabbos claiming it was heated before Shabbos. [Gemara ibid] They would place cold water into a Keli Rishon that is Yad Soledes which is Biblically forbidden on Shabbos. [P"M 326 A"A 4; Menorah Hatehorah 326:1; See Shabbos Kehalacha 18 footnote 56]
Why does this not constitute a Gzeira Legzeira: It is learned from a verse that the Sages may not make a decree upon a decree. [Rashi Beitza 2b; See Admur 511:1] The explanation of Admur and Ran in the above decree form a decree upon a decree, and thus the question is asked as to how this was permitted to be done by the Sages. The following answers can be used to explain this matter: 1) It is permitted to make a decree upon a decree if the original decree will not be fulfilled without the second decree. [Tosafus Brachos 53a] 2) It is permitted to make a decree upon a decree when the original decree is due to a suspicion that involves the item to which the action is being done, such as insulating with items that add heat is forbidden because one may come to insulate with ember which can lead one to stoke the ember. Since the decree against ember involves stoking itself, therefore making a further decree against all material that adds heat is not defined as a decree upon a decree. [Tosafus Rid Shabbos 31a] 3) Any matter which is commonly transgressed the Sages may make a decree upon a decree. [Chacham Tzvi 75; Gra 252]
[11] Admur ibid; implication of Rambam 26:2
[12] Admur ibid; Michaber ibid; Shabbos ibid
[13] M"B 326:4

C. Bathing in hot water heated through fire one limb at a time or minority of one's body:
The Sages forbade bathing one's entire body or majority[14] of it with hot water.
Washing each limb individually:[15] Even to bathe each limb individually and not majority of his body at once [is forbidden].
The reason for this is: because the Sages did not differentiate within their decree [regarding different forms of washing] since [all the forms] slightly resemble bathing in a bathhouse in which one bathes his entire body or majority of it.
Bathing minority of one's body:[16] However it is permitted to bathe in hot water [that was permissibly heated from before Shabbos] one's face, hands and feet[17] or other limbs[18] so long as one does not [in total] wash majority of his body. [**Regarding washing limbs that contain hair see Halacha 7 Q&A there!**]
Washing in a bathhouse:[19] It is forbidden to bathe in a bathhouse[20], even [minority of one's body including] one's face, legs and hands.[21] [This applies towards the Beis Hapenimi of the bathhouse, which is the area of the showers and Mikvaos. In the changing room one may shower these areas but not bathe them.[22]]
Hot water heated on Shabbos: See next!

Q&A
May one wash minority of his body in hot water heated before Shabbos inside a home bathtub or shower?[23]
Yes. A home bathtub is not defined as a Bathhouse.

D. Bathing in hot water heated on Shabbos:[24]
Hot water which was heated on Shabbos even in a permitted way is forbidden to be used to wash even one limb on Shabbos, even if the [water] was only slightly heated and is not Yad Soledes.

Examples of waters heated on Shabbos in a permitted way:
- Water heated to below Yad Soledes.
- A gentile warmed water on behalf of himself.[25]
- One heated water on behalf of a sick person.[26]

The law if the water was heated in a forbidden way:
It is forbidden in any benefit until Motzei Shabbos. It is forbidden to use such water even for washing dishes or washing hands for Netilas Yadayim.

---

[14] Admur ibid; M"A 326:2; M"B 321:2
[15] Admur ibid; Michaber ibid; Shmuel Shabos 40a
[16] 326:1; Michaber and Rama ibid; Shabbos 40a
[17] Admur ibid; Michaber ibid; Shmuel in Shabbos ibid
[18] Admur ibid; Rama ibid; Beis Yosef in name of Rosh; Taz 326:1
[19] Admur 511:1; Michaber 511:2
[20] Admur ibid; Michaber ibid; implication of Gemara in Shabbos 40a
The reason: As the main prohibition against bathing was in the actual bathhouse. [M"B 511:16]
[21] Admur ibid; Orchos Chaim Yom Tov 14; Beis Yosef 511; Levush 511:2
[22] M"B 511:16
[23] Piskeiy Teshuvos 511:4
[24] Admur 326:4; M"A 326:6; M"B 326:5 and 17; Reason of opinion in Michaber 326:5 and perhaps this applies even according to Michaber 326:4 [as explained in Shaar Hatziyon 326:8]; See Halacha 11! Shabbos 134b
[25] Aruch Hashulchan 326:2; Shevisas Hashabbos Mivasheil 127
Other opinions: Some Poskim rule that such water has the same law as water heated on Erev Shabbos. [Tehila Leadavid 326:10]
[26] Ketzos Hashulchan 133 footnote 3

Q&A

If one placed cold water onto his blech right before Shabbos, and it was thus only heated on Shabbos, may one bathe minority of his limbs in such water?[27]

Some Poskim[28] rule that such water is considered as if it was heated before Shabbos and is hence permitted to be used to bathe minority of the body on Shabbos.[29] However other Poskim[30] consider such water to have been heated on Shabbos and it is hence prohibited to wash even minority of one's body with this water. Furthermore some[31] say that even if the water was warmed before Shabbos but retained its heat due to its remaining over a flame and the like, then it is considered as if it were heated on Shabbos. Practically, we rule like the first opinion.[32]

If one mixed hot water that was heated from before Shabbos with cold water [in a way permitted to be done, such as cold pouring water into a Keli Sheiyni], may one bathe minority of his body with this water on Shabbos?[33]

Yes.[34]

May one use water heated on Shabbos for washing dishes?

Some[35] write it is permitted to do so. Vetzaruch Iyun, as why is this any different than drying the hands near a fire.

May one use water heated on Shabbos for washing hands to eat bread and the like?

Some[36] write it is permitted to do so, according to those that allow immersing in a hot Mikveh on Shabbos.

May one sit next to a heater after immersing in a Mikveh if his body is still wet?

No, due to the reason explained above. See Halacha 13!

Summary-Bathing/Showering on Shabbos in hot water

Water that was heated before Shabbos:

Bathing majority of one's body: Is Rabbinically forbidden even if the water was heated from before Shabbos, and even if one washes each limb individually.

Bathing minority of one's body: Is permitted to be bathed/washed with water that was permissibly heated from before Shabbos.

In hot water heated on Shabbos:[37]

Even if the water was heated in a permitted way [such as in the sun, or to less than Yad Soledes] it is forbidden to wash even one limb in that water. Thus, one may not dry his hands near a source of heat as doing so heats up the water on his hands.

---

[27] See Piskeiy Teshuvos 326:2; See Shabbos Kehalacha 18 Biurim 5

[28] Rav Akiva Eiger on M"A 326:4; Setimas Harishonim; SSH"K 14:3 in name of Rav SZ"A; Final position of Shevet Halevi 3:33; 4:31; 7:32; Shabbos Kehalacha 18:34; Piskeiy Teshuvos 326:2; See Shabbos Kehalacha 18 Biurim 5

[29] The reason: As since no action was done to the water on Shabbos it is considered heated from before Shabbos. [Rav Akiva Eiger]

[30] Tosafus Yisehinim Shabbos 39; original opinion of Sheivet Halevy 1:58; Shevisas Hashabbos Mivashel 126 in name of Mahariy Engel 72; Minchas Yitzchak 4:44; Or Letziyon 2:35-1; Betzeil Hachachma 4:136, brought in Piskeiy Teshuvah 226:2 and footnote 27 and 29

[31] Tosafus Yisehinim Shabbos 39; Sheivet Halevy ibid; See Poskim in Piskeiy Teshuvos 326 footnote 27

[32] SSH"K 14:3 in name of Rav SZ"A; Final position of Shevet Halevi 3:33; 4:31; 7:32; Shabbos Kehalacha 18:34; Piskeiy Teshuvos 326:2

[33] Iglei Tal Ofeh 66; Tehila Ledavid 326:10; Ketzos Hashulchan 133 footnote 2; Shabbos Kehalacha 18:36; Piskeiy Teshuvos 326:2

[34] Minchas Shabbos

[35] Piskeiy Teshuvos 326:1 and footnote 7

[36] Shabbos Kehalacha 18:31 based on Karban Nesanel that "Immersion is not bathing"; Piskeiy Teshuvos 326 footnote 7

[37] Admur 326:4

E. Bathing Children in hot water:[38]

It is forbidden for an adult to bathe a child [of any age, including a newborn[39]] with hot water on Shabbos, just as it is forbidden for the adult himself.[40] Thus, one may only wash a child using hot water if the water was heated before Shabbos and one is washing minority of his body. [If, however, the child is in pain or is dirty, then it is permitted to bathe him in hot water.[41]]

See Halacha 3 Q&A there regarding if bathing is allowed for healing purposes!

2. Bathing in water that was not heated through fire:[42]
A. Hot Springs:[43]

All the above is with regards to water heated through fire, however the hot water [from the] springs of Tiberius [and all other springs[44]] are permitted for one to even dip his entire[45] body inside of. *[See Halacha 3 regarding if this is allowed when done for healing purposes!]*

Hot water of Tiberius that is in a vessel:[46] However it was only permitted [to bathe] in the hot waters of Tiberius when [the water] is in the ground, however when it is in a vessel then it has the same laws as water heated over fire being that all water that is in a vessel is not recognizable if it was [heated] from a fire or if it is from the hot springs of Tiberius, and there is thus [reason] to decree on these [hot waters of Tiberius] because of the hot waters [heated through fire]. *[See Q&A regarding water heated through the sun!]*

B. A roofed spring:[47]

First opinion: [However] there are opinions[48] which say that [the Sages] only permitted [washing oneself in] the hot springs of Tiberius when the area is not roofed, however if the area is roofed then it is forbidden.

Their reason is:[49] because [a roofed spring] causes one to sweat and sweating is forbidden on Shabbos as will be explained later on.

Second opinion: [However] there are opinions[50] which say that it is permitted to sweat in the hot waters of Tiberius.

Their reasoning is:[51] because [the Sages] only forbade one from [actively causing himself to] sweat due to

---

[38] Admur 331:11; 616:1 regarding Yom Kippur; Michaber 331:9; M"A 616:1

Admur 331:11 *"Today that it is no longer viewed as a medical necessity to bathe a circumcised child, it remains forbidden to do so to the child the same way as is forbidden for an adult. Hence only one's face, hands and feet [i.e. minority of his limbs] may be bathed in hot water, and only if the water was heated before Shabbos."* **Admur 616:1** *"Although the oppressions of Yom Kippur do not apply to children, nevertheless they may only be bathed in cold water. However, one may not bathe his entire body in hot water, even if the water was heated before Shabbos, as bathing in hot water on Yom Kippur is not forbidden only due to oppression, but due to the prohibition applicable on every Shabbos of the year in which it is forbidden to bathe in hot water due to the decree against the bathhouses."*

Other opinions: Some Poskim rule it is permitted to bathe a child in hot water on Shabbos/Yom Kippur. [Bach, brought in M"A ibid] The M"A ibid negates his opinion and so rules Admur. See however Shevet Halevi 5:31 and Piskeiy Teshuvos 326 footnote 10 that one may bathe a child in hot water as this decree does not apply against a child. Vetzaruch Iyun from the Poskim above. Perhaps however they refer only to a case that the child needs it, such as he is dirty or sick and the like.

The law on Yom Tov: Admur records two opinions regarding if one may bathe a child entire body in hot water on Yom Tov-see 511:1!

[39] Admur and Michaber ibid which are discussing a child after Mila

[40] Being that bathing [majority of the body] in hot water is forbidden on Shabbos, it is likewise forbidden to do so to a child just as it is forbidden to feed a child any Rabbinically prohibited food, as explained in 343:1. [Admur 616:1

[41] As even an adult may bathe in hot water in a case of pain. See also Shevet Halevi and Piskeiy Teshuvos ibid

[42] 326:1

[43] Admur ibid; Michaber 326:1; Shabbos 40a

Previous times: In previous times the Sages decreed even against bathing in hot spring water, however they later retracted their decrees when they saw the people were unable to uphold it. [Admur 301:60 as edited by Kuntrus Hashulchan 58; Shabbos ibid]

[44] M"B 326:8

[45] Admur ibid; Michaber ibid; Sefer Hateruma 233

[46] Admur ibid; Michaber ibid; Tur; Sefer Hateruma ibid; Semag L.S. 65

[47] 326:2; Michaber 326:2

[48] First opinion in Admur and Michaber ibid; Rif Shabbos 62b; Geonim brought in Maggid Mishneh 22:2; Rambam ibid

[49] Admur ibid; Michaber ibid

[50] second opinion in Admur and Michaber ibid; Tosafus 147a; Rosh 22:12; Ramban; Rashba; Ran

[51] Admur ibid

the decree made against bathing, as will be explained later on, and thus since it is permitted to bathe in the hot springs of Tiberius then certainly it is permitted to sweat in them.

The Final Ruling:[52] Regarding the final ruling, in [a controversy over] a Rabbinical prohibition one may follow the lenient opinion.

C. The custom today by all springs:[53]
Due to that not everyone knows to beware in all the Halachic matters involved in bathing [as brought in 2B], therefore the custom spread in these provinces to not bathe at all on Shabbos, not even with cold water [and certainly not by hot springs of Tiberius] even though there is no prohibition involved from the letter of the law [in doing so].

Summary-Hot Springs:
From the letter of the law, one may bathe even his entire body in a natural hot spring, as long as the water is not in a vessel.[54] One may be lenient to bathe in it even if the spring is under a roof.[55] However the custom is to avoid bathing even in cold water.

Q&A

May one bathe in water that was heated by sun, such as in one's solar boiler?[56]
Heated from before Shabbos: It is forbidden to bathe majority of one's body in such water even if it was heated before Shabbos.[57] However one may wash minority of one's limbs in such water if the water became heated by the sun before Shabbos. However, one must beware not to transgress the cooking prohibition in doing so, as cold water enters into the boiler upon opening it. It is thus only allowed to be opened if either a) The water in the boiler is below Yad Soledes [110 F.] or b) One shut off the water pipe which adds more cold water to the boiler.

Heated on Shabbos: If the water was heated by the sun on Shabbos, even if it is merely warm, then it is implied from Admur that it is forbidden to wash even minority of one's body with it.[58] However, there are Poskim[59] who rule that even when heated on Shabbos it is allowed to bathe in such water minority of one's body. Practically, we are stringent like Admur.[60] Thus, if one brought a bottle of water outside into the sun and it became heated, one may not bathe even minority of his limbs in this water on Shabbos. However, if a cold bottle became room temperature, seemingly there is no need to

---

[52] Admur ibid; M"B 326:11 in name of Elya Raba

[53] Admur 326:6

[54] Admur 326:1

[55] Admur 326:2

[56] See Piskeiy Teshuvos 326:2; Shabbos Kehalacha 18:35

[57] Implication of Admur in Mahdurah Basra chapter 259 Page 884 in the new Shulchan Aruch; SSH"K 14:3 in name of RSZ"A based on the stringency of Admur regarding sun heated water.

The reason: Since the water is within the boiler it has the same status as spring water that is in a vessel and is hence forbidden. [so is implied from SSH"K ibid] However from Admur ibid it is implied that even if the water is not in a vessel, if it was heated from the sun it is forbidden, even if it was heated before Shabbos and it is hence much more stringent than spring water. This is implied from the fact that Admur ibid uses the allowance to bathe in warm river water as a proof that it is permitted to bathe in warm water. This implies that if the river water were to be hot it would be forbidden. Now, the river water of Friday night was heated by the sun before Shabbos, hence implying the prohibition applies even with water heated by the sun before Shabbos, even if it is not in a vessel.

Other Opinions: Some Poskim rule that water warmed through the sun is even more lenient than spring water that is within a vessel, and is permitted to be fully bathed in on Shabbos even if it is in a vessel. The reason for this is because people do not become confused between warm water in a vessel and hot water heated by fire. [Tehila Ledavid 326:3]

[58] So is implied from the next Halacha [E] regarding warm water in which Admur rules in the Mahdurah Basra that if the river water was warmed by the sun before Shabbos it is allowed, as proven from the fact that one may bathe in a warm river on Shabbos, thus implying that if the water got heated on Shabbos through the sun then this would not be allowed. So understands also Tehila Ledavid 326:3 and SSH"K 14 footnote 17 and so concludes Piskeiy Teshuvos 326:2

[59] Tehila Ledavid 326:3, thus arguing on his understanding of Admur;

[60] Piskeiy Teshuvos 326:2

be stringent.[61] Likewise, one may wash minority of his body with water from the solar boiler even if it became heated through the sun on Shabbos.[62]

3. May one bathe in warm water?[63]

The letter of the law: It is certainly permitted to bathe in warm water heated from <u>before</u> Shabbos as even the waters of a river in the summer are considered warm, or [waters] that are in a [heated] house in the winter [are considered warm, and nevertheless are permitted to wash with on Shabbos].[64] *[See Q&A regarding the definition of warm water.]* However hot [or even warm] water which was heated <u>on</u> Shabbos even in a permitted way is forbidden to use to wash even one limb, even if the [water] was only slightly heated that it is not Yad Soledes.[65]

The custom today[66]: Due to that not everyone knows to beware in all the Halachic matters involved in bathing [as brought in 2B], therefore the custom spread in these provinces to not bathe at all on Shabbos, not even with cold water even though there is no prohibition involved from the letter of the law [in doing so].

Summary:
From the letter of the law, it is permitted to bathe in warm water that was heated from before Shabbos, although the custom is to avoid doing so. However, water which was heated on Shabbos [whether by fire or by the sun[67]] is forbidden to bathe in even if only warm.

Q&A
What is defined as warm water as opposed to hot water?[68]
There is room to learn from Admur and the Poskim[69] that so long as the water is less than Yad Soledes then it is not considered hot and is thus allowed. Practically however, the Poskim[70] rule that even less than Yad Soledes is considered hot[71], and so long as the water is warmer than body temperate [37 celsius; 98.6 F], or its heat is felt in it, then it is forbidden just like hot water. Others[72] however write that since the measurement of hot water is not recorded, it most likely refers to all waters that people call hot, [and not necessarily to water that is above or below body temperature].

---

[61] See Tehila Ledavid ibid

[62] SSH"K 14:3; Piskeiy teshuvos ibid; Vetzaruch Iyun from Admur ibid
The reason: As since one did no action to heat the water it is considered as if it were to be heated before Shabbos, similar to water placed on a Blech before Shabbos. [SSH"K 14:3]

[63] See Piskeiy Teshuvos 326:1; Shabbos Kehalacha 18:19 Tosefes Biur 1 for all the opinions on this matter

[64] Supplement from Mahadurah Basra chapter 259 Page 884 in the new Shulchan Aruch; Chacham Tzevi 11 which forbids for women to immerse in water on Shabbos that is called hot, rather it must be cold or slightly warm; Nodah Beyehudah Tenyana Orach Chayim 24 that women may bathe in warm Mikvaos but not hot Mikvaos; Aruch Hashulchan 326:3; P"M 511 M"Z 5; Ashel Avraham Butchach 326; Tehila Ledavid 326:3; Minchas Shabbos, brought in Ketzos Hashulchan 133 footnote 1; Shevisas Hashabbos Mivaehseil 125; M"B 326:7; Igros Moshe 1:126; SS"K chapter 14 footnote 3; Piskeiy Teshuvos ibid; Shabbbos Kehalacha ibid;
Other Poskim: Some Poskim rule that warm water is forbidden to bathe in just like hot water [Beis Meir Y.D. 197:3; Rambam brought in Biur Halacha; However the M"B himself 326:7 writes that bathing in warm water is allowed [for Mikveh]. Some however write that in truth the M"B holds that only water in which some coldness is felt is allowed, and it is by this warmth that he allows to bathe, however water which its heat is felt is forbidden as writes the Rambam, as he brings in Biur Halacha. [Az Nidbaru, brought in Piskeiy Teshuvos 326:2].

[65] Admur 326:4; Supplement from Mahadurah Basra chapter 259 Page 884 in the new Shulchan Aruch; M"B 326:17; Igros Moshe 1:126; Piskeiy Teshuvos ibid; Shabbbos Kehalacha ibid

[66] Admur 326:6

[67] See Previous Halacha Q&A there!

[68] See Shabbos Kehalacha 18:29; Piskeiy Teshuvos 326:1 and footnote 14

[69] In Halacha 4 [brought above in Halacha 1C] regarding water heated on Shabbos Admur mentions "even if it will not be heated to Yad Soledes", implying that before Shabbos only water that is heated to Yad Soledes is forbidden. [Ketzos Hashulchan ibid] See Shabbos Kehalacha ibid 18 Tosefes Biur 1

[70] Tehila Ledavid 326:3; Ketzos Hashulchan 133 footnote 1 in name of Minchas Shabbos; Minchas Yitzchak 4:44; Or Letziyon 2:35-3; See SS"K chapter 14 footnote 3

[71] As the Rashba explicitly writes that people do not generally bathe in hot water that is above Yad Soledes.

[72] Aruch Hashulchan 326:3; This ruling is also found in the Chacham Tzevi 11 which forbids for women to immerse in water on Shabbos that is called hot, rather it must be cold or slightly warm; Zera Emes 71

4. Bathing/Showering with cold water:

A. The law and custom:

The letter of the law:[73] Being that hot water [from the] springs of Tiberius are permitted for one to even dip his entire body inside of, as the decree was only made against water heated through fire [as explained in above Halacha], it thus goes without saying that [this allowance applies with] cold water. It is permitted to do so even if the cold water is within a vessel.[74]]

The custom today:[75] Due to that not everyone knows to beware in all[76] the below mentioned matters, therefore the custom spread in these provinces to not bathe at all on Shabbos, not even with cold water even though there is no prohibition involved from the letter of the law [in doing so]. [This prohibition applies even against bathing in an enclosed area, such as inside a house and the like, and is not limited only to a river.[77] This applies even against showering[78], although in a time of need one may be lenient to shower as explained in the Q&A below. This custom has been around for many generations dating back hundreds of years, and one who comes to break the decree of the Rishonim on him it says "Yashchenu Nachash", as we have accepted this custom as a complete prohibition not to bathe in rivers, lakes and ponds at all on Shabbos.[79]]

B. Halachic matters which need to be followed when bathing in a river:[80]

Must fully dry oneself upon leaving:[81] One who bathes in a river [on Shabbos] needs to dry his body well when he comes up from the river so that no water remains on him and have him carry it 4 cubits in a *karmelis* as explained in chapter 301 [Halacha 61]. [He may not walk at all with the water on him, even less than four cubits.[82] Thus one is to prepare a towel, or place his clothing, near the shoreline and dry himself there prior to walking.[83] *See Q&A regarding if one may walk 4 cubits with water still in his beard! See Halacha 7 regarding if one is allowed to dry one's beard on Shabbos using a cloth!]*

Not to swim and not to splash items away: As well one may not swim in the river and may not cause any item to swim [flow], such as twigs which are floating on the water is forbidden for him to splash away in order to clear up the water [for him] as will be explained in chapter 339. [As will be explained in 2E]

---

[73] 326:1; Michaber 326:1; Shabbos 40a

[74] Setimas Hapoksim that only prohibit the hot springs that are within a vessel and not cold water; Implication of M"A 326:8

Other opinion: Some Poskim rule it is forbidden to bathe in cold water that is in a vessel. [Mordechai, brought in M"A ibid]

[75] 326:6; M"A 326:8; Bach; Maharil 139; Terumos Hadeshen 255; Beis Yosef Y.D. 199; M"B 326:21

Other opinions and Sephardic custom: Some Poskim rule that today the custom has spread to allow bathing in cold water. [Olas Shabbos 326:16] Accordingly, some Sephardi Poskim rule it is permitted to bathe in cold water. [Or Letziyon 2:35-2; Implication of Rav Poalim 4:12 and Y.D. 15 regarding a shower, however, see Yaskil Avdi 6:1 who is stringent] Practically, each community is to follow his custom. [Kaf Hachaim 326:25 and 31] This custom is omitted by the Michaber and Rama, although is mentioned by the Beis Yosef ibid

[76] From this wording it is implied that only when all these suspicions are applicable are we accustomed to avoid bathing, however from the concluding wording of Admur "therefore the custom spread in these provinces to not bathe at all on Shabbos, not even with cold water" it is implied that the custom spread to all items. Perhaps this is because the main worry which brought about this custom is that one may come to squeeze the hair, and so writes Beis Yosef and M"B ibid; However see Ketzos Hashulchan 133 footnote 8 that the decree only applies when all the suspicions are applicable.

[77] Implication of Admur ibid "therefore the custom spread in these provinces to not bathe at all on Shabbos, not even with cold water"; M"A ibid in name of Maharil, Mordechai and Beis Yosef which states that only a Mikveh is not used for this reason, and a Mikveh is usually in an enclosed area; M"B 326:7 "In a river or Mikveh due to squeezing of hair"; Minchas Yitzchak 6:32; See Shabbos Kehalacha 18 Biurim 7; See previous footnote that the main suspicion is the squeezing of the hair which is applicable in all cases.

Other opinions: Some Poskim write that the custom to avoid bathing in cold water does not apply to an enclosed area, as only one of the worries are applicable, nevertheless he concludes that one may not be lenient unless he is doing so for the sake of a Mitzvah [Tevila] or if one is in great pain. [Ketzos Hashulchan 133 footnote 8; See there that he brings the Beis Yosef as a proof for his statement unlike the M"A ibid who brings the Beis Yosef]

[78] Conclusion of all Poskim mentioned in Q&A that only permit doing so in a case of a very hot day; Mishneh Sachir 69; Poskim in Piskeiy Teshuvos 326 footnote 112; See Igros Moshe 4:74 and 75 that the Poskim do not discuss this issue and one can infer from Admur and Michaber 326:4 that showering is allowed and seemingly the custom in previous times was to allow showering, however in today's times the custom has become to prohibit even showering on Shabbos; See Shabbos Kehalacha 18 footnote 91

[79] Aruch Hashulchan 326:9

[80] 326:6; M"A 326:8 in name of Maharil 150

[81] Admur ibid; 301:61; Michaber 326:7; Rav Yehuda 141a

[82] M"B 326:22; However see Admur 301:61 and 326:6 who implies that it is permitted to be done, so long as he does not carry it four Amos

The reason: Although we rule [in 349:1] that one may carry within his four Amos, nonetheless here we suspect that one may come to carry the water that is on him even more than four Amos, and hence we require him to dry himself right away. [M"B ibid]

[83] M"B 326:22

Not to squeeze one's hair: As well every bather needs to beware not to squeeze his hair. [As will be explained in more detail in Halacha 7-See There!]

The Reason: Now, although there is the prohibition of squeezing is not applicable with hair, being that hair is hard and does not actually absorb water inside it [and rather the water is absorbed between each individual hair], nevertheless it is Rabbinically forbidden [to squeeze it].

Bathing/Showering in cold water:

The Sages did not decree against bathing in cold water on Shabbos and it is thus permitted to do so from the letter of the law.[84] Nevertheless, the custom in the Ashkenazi provinces is to avoid doing so being that there are many bathing restriction involved which people are not aware of.[85] [This custom has been around for many generations dating back hundreds of years, and one who comes to break the decree of the Rishonim on him it says "Yashchenu Nachash", as we have accepted this custom as a complete prohibition not to bathe in rivers, lakes and ponds at all on Shabbos.[86] This prohibition applies even against bathing in an enclosed area, such as inside a house and the like, and is not limited only to a river.[87] This applies even against showering[88], although in a time of need one may be lenient to shower as explained in the Q&A below.]

The bathing restrictions:
1. To dry oneself so no water is carried outside [in a place without an Eiruv].
2. Not to swim in the water.
3. Not to splash away debris.
4. Not to squeeze one's hair.[89] **Regarding details of this restriction-See Halacha 5 Q&A there!**

---

[84] Admur 326:1 and 6; Michaber 326:1; Shabbos 40a

Water in a vessel: It is permitted to do so even if the cold water is within a vessel. [Setimas Haposkim that only prohibit the hot springs that are within a vessel and not cold water; Implication of M"A 326:8]

Other opinion: Some Poskim rule it is forbidden to bathe in cold water that is in a vessel. [Mordechai, brought in M"A ibid]

[85] Admur 326:6; M"A 326:8; Bach; Maharil 139; Terumos Hadeshen 255; Beis Yosef Y.D. 199; M"B 326:21

Other opinions and Sephardic custom: Some Poskim rule that today the custom has spread to allow bathing in cold water. [Olas Shabbos 326:16] Accordingly, some Sephardi Poskim rule it is permitted to bathe in cold water. [Or Letziyon 2:35-2; Implication of Rav Poalim 4:12 and Y.D. 15 regarding a shower, however, see Yaskil Avdi 6:1 who is stringent] Practically, each community is to follow his custom. [Kaf Hachaim 326:25 and 31] This custom is omitted by the Michaber and Rama, although is mentioned by the Beis Yosef ibid

When does the custom apply? Admur ibid writes "Due to that not everyone knows to beware in all the below mentioned matters, therefore the custom spread in these provinces to not bathe at all on Shabbos." From this wording it is implied that only when all these suspicions are applicable are we accustomed to avoid bathing, however from the concluding wording of Admur "therefore the custom spread in these provinces to not bathe at all on Shabbos, not even with cold water" it is implied that the custom spread to all items. Perhaps this is because the main worry which brought about this custom is that one may come to squeeze the hair, and so writes Beis Yosef and M"B ibid; However see Ketzos Hashulchan 133 footnote 8 that the decree only applies when all the suspicions are applicable.

[86] Aruch Hashulchan 326:9

[87] Implication of Admur ibid "therefore the custom spread in these provinces to not bathe at all on Shabbos, not even with cold water"; M"A ibid in name of Maharil, Mordechai and Beis Yosef which states that even a Mikveh is not used for this reason, and a Mikveh is usually in an enclosed area; M"B 326:7 "In a river or Mikveh due to squeezing of hair"; Minchas Yitzchak 6:32; See Shabbos Kehalacha 18 Biurim 7; See previous footnote that the main suspicion is the squeezing of the hair which is applicable in all cases.

Other opinions: Some Poskim write that the custom to avoid bathing in cold water does not apply to an enclosed area, as only one of the worries are applicable, nevertheless he concludes that one may not be lenient unless he is doing so for the sake of a Mitzvah [Tevila] or if one is in great pain. [Ketzos Hashulchan 133 footnote 8; See there that he brings the Beis Yosef as a proof for his statement unlike the M"A ibid who brings the Beis Yosef]

[88] Conclusion of all Poskim mentioned in Q&A that only permit doing so in a case of a very hot day; Mishneh Sachir 69; Poskim in Piskeiy Teshuvos 326 footnote 112; See Igros Moshe 4:74 and 75 that the Poskim do not discuss this issue and one can infer from Admur and Michaber 326:4 that showering is allowed and seemingly the custom in previous times was to allow showering, however in today's times the custom has become to prohibit even showering on Shabbos; See Shabbos Kehalacha 18 footnote 91

[89] 326:6

Q&A on bathing in cold water

May one take a cold shower on a very hot day?[90]

If one is bothered by the heat or the perspiration, then he is allowed to shower in cold water [or warm water that was heated before Shabbos[91]].[92]

Hot water: To shower in hot water heated from before Shabbos is only allowed if one is in pain, as will be explained in Halacha 3 Q&A there. As well as one must take care not to transgress the cooking prohibition through turning on the hot water tab, as explained in "The Laws of Cooking" Halacha 9 Q&A there.

May one enter into a pool or river to cool off on a very hot day?

Some Poskim[93] imply that one may enter into a swimming pool if he is very hot, although he may not swim.[94] Other Poskim[95], however, rule that one may never enter a pool or river on a hot day, and the allowance is only to allow taking a shower on a hot day.

According to today's custom may one nevertheless bathe part of his body in cold water?

Yes.[96]

Areas which contain hair: Regarding washing the areas of hair which contain the squeezing prohibition [See Halacha 7 Q&A there] some Poskim[97] rule that that one should only be lenient to do so in case of discomfort or pain. Others[98] rule one may wash his head and beard even initially. According to all one may always wash his face despite the fact that water will inevitably get in his beard and be squeezed, as the Sages did not uphold their decree in such a case.[99]

According to today's custom may one nevertheless immerse in a Mikveh on Shabbos?[100]

Yes, as will be explained in Halacha 5-See there!

May one who has just awoken from sleep pour cold water on his head to awaken him?[101]

If not doing so gives one pain then it is allowed [see Halacha 3] being that in any event from the letter of the law it is permitted.

---

[90] Ketzos Hashulchan 133 footnote 8 [towards end]; Igros Moshe 4:74; Beir Moshe 6:73; Dvar Yehoshua 2:54; Az Nidbaru 1:61; SSH"K 14:1; Piskeiy Teshuvos 326:8; Shabbos Kehalacha 18:40; Minchas Yitzchak 6:32 implies that one may not bathe in cold water even to cool off, and may only do so for the sake of a Mitzvah, such as to use a Mikveh, however he then concludes by bringing the Ketzos Hashulchan ibid which is lenient.

[91] As explained above in Halacha 1 that warm water has the same status as cold water. See above Halacha 1 Q&A there regarding the definition of warm water.

[92] The reason: Being that in any event from the letter of the law it is allowed, and it is only a custom to be stringent, and in a case of pain this stringency need not be kept. [Poskim ibid]

[93] Ketzos Hashulchan 133 footnote 8 and 146 footnote 34:16; See below "Swimming on Shabbos"

[94] Being that in any event from the letter of the law it is allowed, and it is only a custom to be stringent, and in a case of pain this stringency need not be kept. [Ketzos Hashulchan 133 footnote 8]

[95] Implication of Igros Moshe 4:75; Piskeiy Teshuvos 326:8 which prohibits entering a pool even on a hot day.

[96] The Ketzos Hashulchan [133:4] adds into the quote of the Halacha of Admur that the custom pertains to bathing one's entire body in cold water, thus implying that minority of one's body is allowed to be bathed even according to the custom.

[97] Ketzos Hashulchan 133 footnote 8 [end] regarding pouring water over head; SSH"K; See Ashel Avraham 320:17; Avnei Nezer 157:14

[98] SSH"K 14 footnote 1 in name of Rav SZ"A; Igros Moshe 1:133; Piskeiy Teshuvos 326:11; See Shabbos Kehalacha 18 footnote 68 and Biurim 10

[99] Ketzos Hashulchan 133 footnote 8

[100] Ketzos Hashulchan 133 footnote 8

[101] Ketzos Hashulchan 133 footnote 8

Q&A on carrying water Four Amos

If one entered a river or sea on Shabbos [such as for Tevila] may he walk to shore with the drops of water on him and then dry himself on the shore, or must he dry himself as soon as he lifts his body above water?[102]

Some Poskim[103] rule one may not carry the water that is on him even while he is still prior to reaching shore.[104] Other Poskim[105], however, rule that so long as one's feet are in the water he may walk with his body carrying the water.[106] Practically, one is to shake the water from his body upon him lifting it out of the water, and stop every four Amos before continuing to walk.[107]

May one walk four cubits in a public domain if there are still drops of water in one's beard?[108]
Yes.[109]

C. Washing one's hands in a river:[110]

It is permitted to stand on the bed of the river and wash one's hands in its water. There is no prohibition involved in the removal of the water which is on his hands from the river onto the bed being that the river is a Karmalis and the bed of the river is likewise a Karmalis and it is permitted to remove [items] from one Karmalis to another Karmalis within the distance of four handbreadths. However, one must beware to dry his hands well immediately after removing them from the river prior to walking four cubits. [Seemingly doing so is allowed even according to the custom stated above.[111]]

Summary-Washing hands in a river:
Despite the custom to avoid bathing in even cold water it is permitted to wash one's hands at the bed of a river and dry them prior to walking four cubits.

D. Walking outside while it is raining:[112]

One who is walking through a public area and rain falls on him and on his clothes, the Sages[113] were not stringent on [his walking of four cubits with the drops of water on him]. [This applies even if he has a

---

[102] See Piskeiy teshuvos 326:7; Shabbos Kehalacha 18 Biurim 9

[103] Peri Megadim 326 M"Z 2; M"B 326:22; Kitzur SHU"A 86:4; Ketzos Hashulchan 133 footnote 7; Kaf Hachaim 326:26; Rishonim brought in Tehila Ledavid 326:12 and Shabbos Kehalacha ibid

[104] Thus, one is to not distance himself more than 4 Amos from the shoreline where his towel iis found. [M"B ibid] Alternatively, either go [without swimming] all the way to the shore having his body remain mainly underwater, or is to prepare a towel for himself on a rock or the like which is near the shoreline and dry himself there and then walk to the shore. [M"B ibid]

[105] Setimas Haposkim of Shulchan Aruch; See leniencies mentioned in Daas Torah 326:7; Tehila Ledavid 326:12; Eretz Tzevi 1:72; Tzur Yaakov 1:172; Or Meir 54; Rishonim brought in Tehila Ledavid 326:12 and Shabbos Kehalacha ibid; Shabbos Kehalacha ibid concludes like the lenient opinion after brining many

[106] The reason: As so long as one's feet is in the water it is considered as if all the water is in the river, as rules the Mishneh in Mikvaos 7:7; Michaber 201. [Daas Torah ibid; Tehila Ledavid ibid]

[107] Tehila Ledavid ibid; Piskeiy teshuvos ibid; Shabbos Kehalacha ibid; See M"B 349: that the Taz and Elya Raba rule one may even initially carry in a Karmalis through stopping every four Amos in a

[108] P"M 326 M"Z 2; Teshuvos Vehanhagos 2:178; 4:90; Eretz Tzevi 1:73; Har Tzevi 1:197; Kinyan Torah 4:32; Bris Olam Rechitza 18; Az Nidbaru 2:43; Divrei Moshe 1:16; Beir Moshe, Divrei Malkiel, Piskeiy Teshuvos 301:22 [66 in new]
Other opinions: Some were careful to dry the beard prior to walking 4 cubits [or leaving the Mikveh to a public domain which does not have an Eiruv]. [Steipler brought in Teshuvos Vehanhagos ibid; Piskeiy Teshuvos ibid footnote 465]

[109] The reason: It is allowed being the water does not contain Shiur Hotzaah, and is likewise not the common way of carrying and hence the Sages did not decree against it even in a Reshus Harabaim. [P"M ibid] Likewise, the drops of water being that the drops are nullified to ones beard, as is the law regarding water absorbed in a cloth.

[110] 301:61; Michaber 301:49; Tashbatz 34; Rabbeinu Yerucham 17

[111] So is implied from Ketzos Hashulchan 133:4

[112] 301:61; Michaber 326:7; Rosh Shabbos 20:13

[113] There is no Biblical prohibition involved in carrying the water as it is less than Shiur Hotzaah, and is likewise not the common way of carrying. [Beis Yosef, brought in Taz 326:2; P"M 326 M"Z 2; M"B 326:23]

large amount of rainwater on him.[114]]

The reason for this is:[115] because this is a matter which is impossible to avoid, as at times a person is walking in a public area [with clear skies] and it suddenly begins to rain on him.

To initially walk outside when it is already raining:[116] Therefore the Sages permitted [him to walk with the rainwater on him] in all cases (and he may walk outside even in a case that he sees that it is already raining outside, as we do not prohibit matters partially.) [See **Q&A regarding snowing!**]

Summary:
It is allowed to walk in the rain, and one may even initially go outside when it is raining despite the fact that he will inevitably carry the water that is pouring onto him.

Q&A

May one walk outside while it is snowing even though he will inevitably carry the snow?[117]
Yes.[118]

---

5. Bathing for healing purposes:[119]

Introduction: The bathing prohibition which applies when bathing in hot water, as well as the custom to prohibit bathing even in cold water, does not apply in a case that one is bathing for healing purposes.[120] Thus, the only matter which needs to be dealt with here is if doing so contains a "Medical treatment" prohibition, being that in general the Sages prohibited doing medical treatments on Shabbos, as will be explained in "The Laws of Medicine" Chapter 2 Halacha 7.

Waters that are commonly bathed in [on Shabbos]: One may bathe for healing purposes in waters of Gerar and waters of Chamson and waters of Tiberius and in the pure waters of the Mediterranean Sea even though that they are salty [and thus have a greater healing affect[121]].[122] *[See Q&A regarding water heated from before Shabbos]*

The reason for this allowance is: because it is common to bathe in them even not for healing purposes and it is thus not evident that [one is bathing in them] with intent for healing. *[See Footnote regarding if this allowance applies today[123]]*

Waters that are not commonly bathed in: However [one may not bathe for healing purposes] in foul water of the Mediterranean Sea, and not in flax water[124] being that they are repugnant, and it is [thus] uncommon to bathe in them for non-medical purposes.

To dip and leave: However, this restriction only applies if one remains in the water [for some time], however if one does not remain in them [and rather dips and leaves] then [even in the foul waters] it is permitted being that it simply appears as if he is cooling himself off [in it]. *[See Footnote regarding is*

---

[114] M"B 326:23 in name of Gr"a
[115] Admur ibid; Taz 326:2
[116] Admur ibid
[117] Piskeiy Teshuvos 326:3
[118] So rules SSH"K 15 footnote 123
[119] Supplement from Chapter 328 Halacha 48
[120] So is evident from the fact that hot water heated from before Shabbos is allowed to bathe in for healing, as explained in Q&A below, as well as that it was explained in Halacha 2 that in a case of discomfort one may shower and bathe in cold water and forgo the custom. Thus, certainly here in a case of pain the prohibition and custom do not apply. Vetzaruch Iyun from Ketzos Hashulchan 138 footnote 22 where he states that the allowance to bathe for healing is not in accordance to the custom that we no longer bathe today in even cold water. However, one must say that he was not referring to the aspect of not bathing due to the custom, but due to that since no one bathes due to the custom then it appears like healing which is forbidden. However, see footnote 53 where in his conclusion he rules that one may be lenient.
[121] Mishneh Berurah 326:138
[122] Seemingly although the custom is not to bathe even in cold water on Shabbos, nevertheless for healing it is allowed. Vetzaruch Iyun.
[123] Although today based on the custom to not bathe in even cold water one no longer bathes in these waters on Shabbos for non-healing purposes, and it is thus evident that one is doing so for healing, nevertheless today too it remains permitted as today even according to the custom one is allowed to immerse in the water to use as a Mikveh, as well as when one feels very hot and sweaty, it is thus is once again not recognizable that one is doing so for healing. [Based on Ketzos Hashulchan 138:22]
[124] Lit. Water that had material soaking in it

this allowance applies today[125]]

Tiberius hot springs:[126] In places that it is common to only bathe in Tiberius hot springs for healing purposes, then it is forbidden to bathe in them on Shabbos for healing even if he does not remain in the waters [a long time][127]. [**See Q&A**]

Bathing in hot water to relieve pain:[128] One may tell [a gentile] to bring him hot water on Shabbos from one courtyard to [another] courtyard of which do not have a Eiruv between them (or through a Karmalis, see what was written in chapter 325 [Halacha 16[129]]) in order to bathe one who is in pain.

Summary-Bathing for healing purposes:[130]

Bathing for healing purposes is only permitted to be done in waters which are commonly bathed in for mere pleasure or to cool off. However, waters in which bathing is only done for healing purposes, is forbidden to be bathed in for healing purposes. However, one may bathe in them for non-healing purpose, such as for Mikveh. [When permitted, it may be done even according to the custom today to avoid bathing in even cold water.[131]]

Q&A

May a person who is in pain bathe in hot water on Shabbos?[132]

Yes, one may bathe in hot water that was heated before Shabbos[133] even if his entire body does not feel sick.[134]

May one who showers daily and avoiding so on Shabbos will cause him extreme discomfort, shower with hot water heated from before Shabbos?[135]

Yes, as this is similar to one who is in pain.

May one today bathes in Tiberius springs for healing purposes?[136]

No, as today one only bathes in them for healing purposes. However, if in truth it has become accustomed to bathe in it even for non-healing purposes then it is allowed.

---

[125] Although today the custom is not to bathe in these waters for cleanliness, and it is thus evident that one is doing so for healing, nevertheless today too it remains permitted as today even according to the custom one is allowed to immerse in the water to use as a Mikveh, and it is thus once again not recognizable that one is doing so for healing. However, this would only work to allow men to bathe in it as opposed to women. [Ketzos Hashulchan 138 :22]

[126] Admur ibid; M"A 328:49

[127] However the M"B writes that it is only forbidden if one remains in the waters a long time. See Ketzos Hashulchan 138:22.

[128] Admur 307:12; Michaber 307:5

[129] There it is explained that many are accustomed to be lenient to ask gentiles to bring foods through a non-Eiruved courtyard as the foods are also for the need of a Mitzvah, which is Oneg Shabbos.

[130] Admur 328:48

[131] See Introduction.

[132] Rav Akivah Eiger 307:5 and 326:1 based on Michaber in 307:5 and Admur in 307:12; Teshuvos Radach 22; Biur Halacha 326:1 "Bemayim"; Kaf Hachaim 326:4; Ketzos Hashulchan 133 footnote 1; Shabbos Kehalacha 18:38; Lehoros Nasan 6:10; Piskeiy Teshuvos 326:1

Background:

As the Michaber in 307:5 and Admur in 307:12 rule that one may ask a gentile to carry hot water for oneself if he is pain so he can bathe in it. We thus see that it is permitted to wash in hot water to remove pain. [Rav Akivah Eiger 307:5] Now although the Michaber here does not mention **hot** water, it is mentioned in Admur and in the Rambam. However perhaps one can say the Michaber and Admur refer to washing minority of one's body with this water and not majority of the body, and hence there is no proof from this halacha. [See Tehila Ledavid 326:1; Shabbos Kehalacha ibid Biurim 6] However the Teshuvos Radach ibid interprets this Halacha of the Michaber to refer to the entire body, and so is proven to be the understanding of all the Poskim above. [See Tehila Ledavid and Shabbos Kehalacha ibid]

[133] Rebbe Akiva Eiger in 307:5; Shabbos Kehalacha ibid; Vetzaruch Iyun as to why water heated on Shabbos is forbidden in a case of pain, and what is the source for saying this.

[134] The reason: As not bathing in hot water on Shabbos is a weaker Shevus than other Shevusim and is hence permitted in a case of pain. [Rav Akivah Eiger 307:5] Alternatively the reason is because one is Now, regarding why here in the above Halacha no mention is made of water heated from before Shabbos, simply the reason for this is because this Halacha is addressing the issue of healing on Shabbos, which is only problematic by springs and other bodies of water as opposed to hot water found within a vessel. Thus, regarding the bathing prohibition, in truth it does not apply at all when a person is in pain, and one may bathe in water heated before Shabbos to release pain.

[135] SSH"K 14:1

[136] Ketzos Hashulchan 138 footnote 22

6. Doing Hefsek Taharah on Shabbos:[137]

[Being that washing only minority of one's limbs with water heated before Shabbos is permitted,] therefore in a place where there is no [accepted] custom [otherwise], a woman is allowed to begin her seven clean days on Shabbos[138], being that [to do so] she only needs to wash her private part[139] and between her thighs[140]. However, she must be careful not to wash with a cloth, so she not come to squeeze it. [She may use either cold water or hot water that was heated before Shabbos for the purpose of this wash.[141] Those areas however that are accustomed to being stringent not to do Hefsek Taharah on Shabbos are to be stringent.[142] Practically, the custom is to perform a Hefsek Taharah even on Shabbos.[143]]

Summary:
A woman may clean her area for a Hefsek Taharah as doing so is only washing minority of one's body.

How to use the hot water to do the Hefsek Taharah:[144]
Place the water that was heated from before Shabbos into a clean and dry vessel, add cold water to it to cool it down, and you may then use it on the body for the Hefsek Taharah.

---

7. Going to Mikvah on Shabbos:[145]

A person is allowed to purify himself of his impurities by immersing in a *mikvah* on Shabbos[146] even if this immersing is Biblically required [to be done], such as a *nidda* and the like.[147] [It is permitted to do so even if one was able to immerse before Shabbos.[148]]

The reason that this is allowed is:[149] being that doing so does not appear like one is rectifying [something on Shabbos which is forbidden] but rather like one who is going [in the water in order] to cool himself off.

Dipping in putrid water, and dipping in the winter:[150] [Furthermore] even to immerse in putrid water which is not commonly used to cool off in, and even [to immerse] in the winter when it is not at all common to [immerse in water to] cool oneself off, nevertheless [it is allowed as] at times when a person is dirty from mud and feces he washes himself even in the winter and even in putrid water in order to remove the mud and feces that are on him.

The custom regarding a woman's immersion:[151] [However] in our provinces the custom[152] is to forbid the immersing of a woman on Shabbos unless her husband is in the city[153] as well as that it was not possible

---

[137] Admur 326:1; Masas Binyamin 5; M"A 326:3; Michaber Y.D. 199:6 regarding Yom Tov and the same applies towards Shabbos; Shach 199:12; M"B 326:6

[138] After a married woman menstruates, she must separate from her husband until she has counted seven clean days, meaning days that she has not seen any blood. To begin the count, she must wash herself the afternoon prior to her wanting to begin the seven-day count and then check herself to verify that the blood has stopped flowing. Thus, this washing may be done on Shabbos in order to have the first of the seven days begin after Shabbos.

[139] Admur ibid; Rama ibid

[140] Admur ibid; Masaas Binyamin ibid, brought in Shach ibid

[141] Maasas Binyamin ibid, brought in Shach ibid and Machatzis Hashekel ibid; Kitzur Dinei Taharah 4:7

[142] Brought in Maasas Binyamin ibid; M"A ibid; Shach ibid; M"B ibid; implied from Admur ibid

The reason for this custom: As women do not know how to properly wash themselves without transgression, as they may come to use water heated on Shabbos, and they may come to squeeze the cloth. [Maasas Binyamin ibid, brought in Shach ibid] Alternatively, the reason is because they do not want their Tevila to fall on Motzei Shabbos and thus have the Chafifa pushed to Friday. [Shach ibid; Machatzis Hashekel ibid]

[143] Taharas Yisrael 197:14; Darkei Teshuvah 197:14; Aruch Hashulchan 199:19

[144] See Piskeiy Teshuvos 326 footnote 44

[145] Admur 326:7; See Shabbos Kehalacha p. 196-210

[146] Admur ibid; Michaber 326:8; Beitza 17b

[147] Admur ibid as implied from Gemara ibid; Rama 197:2 in name of Rishonim

[148] M"B 326:24; Gemara ibid

[149] Admur ibid; M"B 326:24; Rava Beitza 18a

[150] Admur ibid; M"B 326:24

[151] Admur ibid; M"A 326:8; Terumos Hadeshen 255; Maharil 139; Rama Yoreh Deah 197:2; Bach 197; Shach 197:3; M"B 326:25

for her to immerse before Shabbos[154] or [she was able to but] her husband was not in the city and only arrived on Erev Shabbos[155] in which case she was not negligent in not having immersed prior to Shabbos.[156] However in any case that her husband was in the city and she was able to immerse [before Shabbos] and did not immerse then she may not immerse on Shabbos.[157]

The reason behind this custom:[158] There are authorities[159] which have given [the following] rational behind this custom [saying] that since the custom has spread to not bathe on Shabbos therefore when an impure person immerses to purify himself it appears as if he is rectifying [an item which is forbidden to do on Shabbos] and not like he is going in [the water] to cool off, being that it is not at all common to bath in order to cool off due to the reason explained [above in Halacha 2] even though that there is no prohibition in doing so.

The custom regarding immersing for purification of nocturnal emission:[160] Nevertheless a man is allowed

---

Other opinions: The Beis Yosef [brought in Shach 197:3] rules that there is never a prohibition to immerse on Shabbos in any situation. [Vetzaruch Iyun if this is even if she could have immersed beforehand? Seemingly yes, as so is implied from the fact that the Michaber never rules anywhere regarding any restrictions in immersing on Shabbos, and rather wrote simply that one may immerse on Shabbos.] Others rule that it is forbidden to immerse on Shabbos even if [she had holy reasons to avoid doing so beforehand, such as that] her husband did not arrive until Erev Shabbos. [stringent opinion in Rama ibid; Taz 197:4 based on his understanding of the Terumas Hadeshen] However he too agrees that in a case that she could not immerse due to a physical impracticality [Oness], such as that she is after birth and did not have the strength to immerse beforehand, then it is allowed. Thus, the Taz argues on Rama which holds that it is dependent on the custom and rather rules that it is always forbidden unless it was physically impossible for her to do so. In the Nekudos Hakesef the Shach debates against the ruling of the Taz and supports the ruling of the Rama and Bach.

Custom of Sephardim: The Sefaradim are accustomed to be lenient in this matter and immerse on Friday nights. [Beis Yosef ibid; Rav Poalim O.C. 4:12; Mizbeiach Adam 199; Kneses Hagedola 197:5; Shulchan Gavoa 197:4; Taharas Habayis 2:454; However, see Darkei Taharah p. 170 that writes to be stringent in this matter as rule Admur here and Rama ibid.]

[152] See Rama Yoreh Deah 197:2 which implies that it is forbidden from the letter of the law. However, to note that in Orach Chayim 326:8 the Rama does not make any mention against bathing in a river or against immersing on Shabbos, of which the Michaber rules there that it is permitted. Vetzaruch Iyun as to why no gloss was written by the Rama being that he in truth holds that it is forbidden, as he writes in Yoreh Deah. Perhaps then one can say that the Rama too agrees that it is permitted from the letter of the law and that just due to the custom it is forbidden, as is the common explanation in other contradictory rulings. Vetzaruch Iyun.

[153] Admur ibid; 613:20; Rama 197:3 based on Terumos Hadesehn 195; This follows Michaber ibid and Rabbeinu Tam in Tosafus Niddah 36a and Yuma 8a that there is no Mitzvah unless the husband is in city.

Other rulings of Admur and other Poskim: However see Admur Y.D. 187:8 that it is forbidden for a woman to delay her Tuma even if her husband is not in the city, and so rules Shevet Hamussar 24; Darkei Teshuvah 184:64. [See Likkutei Sichos 14:27 footnote 58 that leaves this in Tzaruch Iyun; See Taharah Kehalacha 21:1; See there Biurim 1 for explanation of Admur ibid however practically, the custom is not to immerse when the husband is not in the city, even during the week. [See Piskeiy Teshuvos 240 footnote 45; Shiureiy Shevet Halevi 197:1; Taharah Kehalacha ibid]

[154] Admur ibid; Rama ibid in Yoreh Deah 197:2; M"A ibid; M"B ibid

[155] Admur ibid; lenient opinion in Rama Yoreh Deah 197:2; Bach and Shach 197:3, based on their understanding of the Terumas Hadeshen ibid; Mahrshag 2:55; Shevet Halevi 4:107; Piskeiy Teshuvos 326:9

Other opinions: Some Poskim rule it is forbidden to immerse on Shabbos if it is not the night after the seven clean days, even if the husband was not in town. [stringent opinion in Rama ibid; Taz 197:4 based on his understanding of Terumos Hadeshen ibid; Maryu 48] The Rama ibid concludes and rules that "so is the custom in certain places, however in a community where there is no custom then one is not to be stringent." As rules Rama, so rules also the Bach and Shach [Shach 197:3, based on their understanding of the Terumas Hadeshen] that the main opinion is like the lenient opinion and thus in a place where there is no custom one may be lenient. However, Admur rules simply like the lenient opinion that she may immerse in such a case and does not make any mention of customs. However, the Taz [197:4] rules [based on his understanding of the Terumas Hadeshen] like the stringent opinion in Rama that it is forbidden to immerse on Shabbos even if [she had holy reasons to avoid doing so beforehand, such as that] her husband did not arrive until Erev Shabbos. However, he too agrees that in a case that she could not immerse due to a physical impracticality [Oness], such as that she is after birth and did not have the strength to immerse beforehand, then it is allowed. Thus, the Taz argues on Rama which holds that it is dependent on the custom and rather rules that it is always forbidden unless it was physically impossible for her to do so. In the Nekudos Hakesef the Shach debates against the ruling of the Taz and supports the ruling of the Rama and Bach.

[156] Admur ibid; Shach ibid; Piskeiy Teshuvos ibid

[157] Admur ibid; M"A ibid; Implication of Rama ibid; Shach ibid; Terumos Hadeshen ibid;

[158] Admur ibid

[159] Terumos Hadeshen 255; Maharil 139; M"A 326:8; Taz Yoreh Deah 197:4; M"B 326:24

[160] Admur ibid; M"A 326:8; Olas Shabbos; Elya Raba Tosefes Shabbos; Shulchan Atzei Shitim; Aruch Hashulchan 326:10; M"B 326:24; Poskim in Piskeiy Teshuvos 326:9 footnote 118

Other opinions: Some Poskim rule a Baal Keri may not immerse in a Mikveh on Shabbos as it appears like fixing [Biur Hagr"a 326:8, brought Biur Halacha 326:8 "Adam Mutar"; See M"A 128:70 and Admur 128:57] Even according to this opinion however one may immerse if he became a Baal Keri on Shabbos. [M"B ibid; Biur Halacha ibid] However some were accustomed to be stringent even in such a case. [M"A and Admur ibid] The Gr"a, brought in Biur Halacha ibid rules that since today we are accustomed not to bathe even in cold water it therefore appears like one is fixing and one may thus not immerse for nocturnal emission. The Ketzos Hashulchan 133 footnote 8 however adds that today since many are accustomed to immerse for the sake of additional purity [which does not involve a fixing prohibition according to all] it therefore once again is unnoticeable that one is immersing for nocturnal emission and thus even according to the GR"A it would be allowed. See also Poskim in Piskeiy Teshuvos ibid who bring this ruling.

to immerse [to purify himself] from a seminal discharge. [**See Q&A regarding immersing for prayer**]

The reason is because:[161] since this immersion is not Biblically required (and is not even a complete Rabbinical obligation [therefore] it does not appear like one is rectifying [himself].[162])

The immersion of a penitent:[163] (As well an apostate that repented is allowed to immerse on Shabbos because this immersion is not Biblically required as opposed to the immersion of a convert[164] (as well as that there is not even a complete Rabbinical obligation[165] [for the penitent to do so])).

A woman who needs to re-immerse on Shabbos due to a stringency: As well any woman which needs to re-immerse due to a mere stringency is permitted to immerse on Shabbos as explained in Yorah Deah chapter 197 [Halacha 1 in Shach].

Summary-Going to Mikvah on Shabbos:[166]

For penitence or for Keri: Is permitted to be done in cold water, even if the water is murky, and even in the winter.

A Nidah: Is from the letter of the law permitted to immerse, although the custom is to only allow her to immerse if her husband is in town and she did not have a chance to immerse prior to Shabbos, or had a chance but her husband only arrived on Erev Shabbos. A woman may always immerse if she is only required to do so as a mere stringency. [According to all, a woman may immerse on Shabbos if she was unable to do so due to a physical impalement, such as being after birth.[167]]

Q&A on a women's Immersion [Yoreh Deah 197]

If the wife knows that her husband is arriving on Erev Shabbos is she to immerse on Friday night or Thursday night?[168]

She is to immerse on Thursday night. This applies even during other days of the week; that if her husband is arriving the next day, she should immerse the night before. She is to sleep that night with a knife under her pillow[169], or is to spread a clothing of her husband over her[170]. [Nevertheless, if she did not immerse on Thursday night, she may nevertheless immerse on Friday night being her husband was not in the city.[171]]

What is the definition of negligence that we prohibit her to immerse on the night of Shabbos?

Example: Wedding on Thursday night; Busy on Thursday; Purim on Thursday night etc

Some[172] say so long as there is a valid reason for pushing it off, it is valid, and only when absolute negligence and carelessness are we Machmir.

Ruling of Admur and M"A regarding Kohanim: In 128 the M"A 128:70 and Admur 128:57 explain that the Kohanim were accustomed not to do Nesias Kapayim on Shabbos due to the prohibition against immersing on Shabbos. See Nimukei Orach Chaim 326:1

[161] Admur ibid; M"A ibid

[162] Admur ibid; Machatzis Hashekel ibid; M"B ibid; Seemingly Admur here is coming to answer why be a Baal Keri we permit the immersion even though by Keilim we are stringent even though some rule that Tevilas Keilim is only Rabbinical.

[163] Admur ibid; M"A 326:8; Pischeiy Teshuvah Y.D. 268:10

[164] See Rama Y.D. 268:12

[165] Admur ibid

[166] Admur 326:7

[167] Taz 197:4

[168] Shiureiy Sheivet Halevi 107:2-1; Taharah Kehalach 21:5Nitei Gavriel 30:3 in name of Kinaas Sofrim 64; Taharas Yisrael 198:48; Implication of Darkei Taharah ibid; and so I heard from Rav Asher Lemel Hakohen

[169] Shvus Yaakov 3:77

[170] Kaf Hachaim 240:14-15

[171] See Shiureiy Sheivet Halevi p. 304; Taharah Kehalacha 21:11; Piskeiy Teshuvos 326:9; Nitei Gavriel vol. 3 31:8-11

[172] Piskeiy Teshuvos 326:9; Nitei Gavriel vol. 3 31:8-11

If the couple had a fight and she did not immerse on Thursday night, may she immerse on Friday night?[173]
Yes.

If ones Mikveh night fell on the night of her Veses which is Thursday night, when is she to Tovel?[174]
On Thursday night. They may not have Tashmish and she is to sleep with a knife and Beged. If, however, she did not do so, she may Tovel on Friday night.

What is the law if one transgressed and immersed in a case that she was not allowed to do so, is she considered pure?[175]
If this was done advertently, despite knowledge of the prohibition, then she remains prohibited to her husband until after Shabbos. If, however, this was done inadvertently, without prior knowledge of the prohibition, then she is permitted to her husband.

Does the above prohibition apply also on Yom Tov?[176]
Some opinions[177] say that Yom Tov initially maintains the same laws as do Shabbos in this regard, however stating that Bedieved, after the fact, she is considered pure even if she immersed advertently despite knowing of the prohibition. Other Poskim[178] however argue on this saying that there is no prohibition at all to immerse on Yom Tov in any circumstance and she may do so even initially.

If one was not required to wait 5 days in those cases in which it is explained that there is no need to do so, but did so anyways, may she immerse on Shabbos if that's when her 7th clean day falls on?[179]
Some Poskim[180] rule this is forbidden to be done, and if one did so she may not immerse on Friday night. Others[181] however rule it is permitted to be done and she may therefore immerse on Friday night.

If by mistake a woman did not do her Hefsek Taharah on time [before Sunset], and this thus caused her Mikvah night to be pushed off a day later which is Friday night, may she immerse?
Yes.[182]

May a woman after birth push off her Hefsek Taharah to Friday which may cause her to go to Mikveh on Shabbos?
She may do so according to all if she does not feel physically ready to go to Mikveh until that time. If she does feel ready beforehand and pushed it off for other reasons, then this matter is disputed as mentioned above.

[173] Nitei Gavriel 31:6 in name of Daas Torah
[174] Taharah Kehalacha 21:10 in name of Vayan Yosef 29
[175] Toras Hashelamim 197:3; Pischeiy Teshuvah 5 in name of Shut Chut Hashani
[176] Toras Hashelamim 197:3
[177] Shut Chut Hashani
[178] Toras Hashelamim 197:3; Sidrei Taharah 197:2; Chochmas Adam 118:8; Lechem Vesimla 197:10; Levushei Mordechai 93; Shaareiy Tohar 17:4; Divrei Yatziv 104; Nitei Gavriel 31:13
[179] Shiureiy Sheivet Halevi p. 305; Taharah Kehalacha 21:10
[180] Nodeh Beyehuda 131; Pischeiy Teshuvah 197:4
[181] Daas Kedoshim in Daas Torah Mahrsham; Avnei Nezer Yoreh Deah 246
[182] Nodeh Beyehudah, brought in Pischeiy Teshuvah 197:2

Q&A on Men immersing in Mikveh on Shabbos

According to today's custom to not bathe at all on Shabbos may one nevertheless immerse in a Mikveh on Shabbos?[183]

Yes, not only is it allowed[184] but it is even a Mitzvah[185] to immerse for the sake of purification from nocturnal emission or even for additional purity as is customarily[186] done on Shabbos morning prior to prayer. However, one must nevertheless take caution not to squeeze any of his hair.

How many times is one to immerse in the Mikveh on Shabbos day?[187]

It suffices to immerse one time.[188] [Although if one is a Baal Keri] he is to immerse twice.

May one do a Nine Kavim shower on Shabbos if a Mikveh is not available?

Yes. Upashut!

May one who desires to immerse in a Mikveh do so even in a river or sea?[189]

Yes. One who needs to immerse due to nocturnal emission [or Tosefes Kedusha, and a regular Mikveh is not available[190]] may do so even in a river or ocean[191], although taking care to avoid transgressing any of the matters mentioned in Halacha 2. However, there are Poskim[192] which prohibit immersing in any water that is not within a private domain. From Admur, it is implied like the former opinion.[193]

---

[183] Ketzos Hashulchan 133:4 footnote 8; Aruch Hashulchan 326:10; All Poskim in Piskeiy Teshuvos 326:9 footnote 118

Opinion of Mishneh Berurah: The Biur Halacha 326:8 "Adam Mutar" rules that one is to avoid immersing for purposes of additional purity being that one may come to squeeze his hair, and it suffices that we already allow to be lenient to immerse for nocturnal emission. [Biur Halacha 326:8 "Adam Mutar"] The Ketzos Hashulchan 133 footnote 8 however takes to par this ruling of the M"B being that a) The source of the M"B is in the Mahril which sates with regards to women that would avoid immersing on Shabbos if that is not their Halachic date of immersing. Now the Mahril states that the reason for this stringency is to avoid any carrying of the water, swimming, squeezing hair. Now, regarding men immersing in an indoor Mikveh only the squeezing of hair is relevant and thus there is no source from the Mahril to be stringent when only one suspicion is relevant. Furthermore, the suspicion of squeezing hair is a lot more relevant by women than men, and thus there is no support from the ruling regarding women at all. b) The Arizal writes that it is a Mitzvah to immerse on Shabbos morning and it is thus considered its right time, as opposed to the ruling by women which involves a date which is not their correct time. c) The custom of not bathing in cold waters is itself a stringency and it thus suffices to be stringent to not bathe for pleasure, and not to extend this to even Mitzvah purposes. [ibid]

[184] The reason: The reason for this is a) As the Mahril states that the reason for the stringency against immersing is to avoid any carrying of the water, swimming, squeezing hair. Now, regarding men immersing in an indoor Mikveh only the squeezing of hair is relevant, which is easily avoidable, while the carrying and swimming issues are not relevant. Thus, one may be more lenient. Now although Admur wrote that "the custom is to not bathe at all on Shabbos ", nevertheless it is evident from the fact that later on Admur states the permission to immerse that this custom only applies to pleasure baths and not to baths motivated for other purposes. b) The Arizal writes that it is a Mitzvah to immerse on Shabbos morning and it is thus considered its right time, as opposed to the ruling by women which involves a date which is not their correct time. c) The custom of not bathing in cold waters is itself a stringency and it thus suffices to be stringent to not bathe for pleasure, and not to extend this to even Mitzvah purposes. [ibid]
[Ketzos Hashulchan 133 footnote 8]

[185] As writes the Arizal and other Mekubalim that one is to immerse on Shabbos. [ibid] The Arizal writes that if one is a Baal Keri or had Tashmish on Friday night then he is obligated to immerse on Shabbos day. Furthermore, he writes, even if the above did not occur one must still immerse on Shabbos day in order to garb his soul with the new revelations of Shabbos day, which one did not yet receive with his immersion done on Erev Shabbos. [Kaf Hachaim 260:6]

[186] So is the custom of majority of the Torah sages in Jerusalem of all sects, including the Sephardim and Perushim. [ibid]

[187] Kaf Hachayim 260:6

[188] So writes Arizal, in order to garb his soul with the holiness of Shabbos day. [ibid]

[189] Tosefes Shabbos; Ketzos Hashulchan 133 footnote 8; Piskeiy Teshuvos 326:7

[190] Pashut, as otherwise one enters himself into many worries of Shabbos transgressions, as explained above.

[191] The reason: As we did not accept this custom in the place of a Mitzvah such as Tevila. This is seemingly no different than women immersing on the night of their Mikveh.

[192] Minchas Yitzchak 6:32, Piskeiy Teshuvos 339:1

[193] So is implied from Admur 326:7 which does not differentiate between bodies of water, despite having brought the custom in 326:6.

May one immerse in a hot Mikveh[194] on Shabbos?

Warm: It is permitted to immerse in a warm Mikveh without question, just as is the law regarding a cold Mikveh. Regarding the definition of warm versus hot: The Poskim define warm as "no longer called hot" or below 98.6 Fahrenheit, and thus it must be below this temperature to be allowed without question, otherwise it has the status of hot water. See however Halacha 1D that according to Admur there is room to learn that so long as it is below Yad Soledes it is considered warm and not hot.

Hot:[195] Some Poskim[196] prohibit immersing in a hot water Mikveh on Shabbos, based on the prohibition against bathing the majority of one's body in hot water on Shabbos. This applies even to women who have a Mitzvah to immerse, and certainly applies to men. Other Poskim[197], however, permit immersing in even hot water for the sake of a Mitzvah[198] [such as women immersing for Nida, or even men who immerse for Taharah or Baal Keri purposes[199]]. Practically, the widespread custom is like this approach.[200] However, some are initially stringent like the former opinion and immerse in only warm or cold water.[201] Nevertheless, one may not remain in the water for pure pleasure purposes and is rather to immerse and immediately leave. Those who stay in the water more than necessary transgress the bathing prohibition according to all, and must be protested and told to leave.[202] However, one may immerse in the water as many times as he is used to doing during the week.[203]

Custom of the Sephardim:[204] The custom of Sephardi women is to immerse in hot water during Bein Hashmashos of Friday night. After Bein Hashmashos, they may only immerse in warm water. [Accordingly, Sephardi men are certainly to avoid immersing in hot water on Shabbos.]

If the water was heated on Shabbos through a timer or gentile?[205] Some are accustomed to be lenient to allow immersing in such water however many have written against doing so. The Igros Moshe[206]

---

[194] Regarding the Kashrus of a Hot Mikveh from the aspect of the laws of Mikvaos see Yoreh Deah 201:75 that Michaber forbids this even during the week [due to people coming to think that a bathhouse is also a Kosher Mikveh-Taz] while the Rama rules that in those places that are lenient may do so, although one is to be stringent. See as well Tikunei Mikvaos where Admur writes that hot water is placed into the Mikveh.

[195] See Pischeiy Teshuvah Yorah Deah 197:1 for a compilation of different opinions.; Shabbos Kehalacha 18:47; Piskeiy Teshuvos 326:5

[196] Chacham Tzevi 11; Nodah Beyehudah Tinyana Orach Chayim 24 [so writes Pischeiy Teshuvah as well as Divrei Chayim, however Tzitz Eliezer argues on their opinion in Nodah Beyehudah.]; Chayeh Adam 70:1; Chochmas Adam 122:22; Aruch Hashulchan 326:10; Rav Poalim O.C. 4:15; M"B 326:7 in name of Chayeh Adam; Igros Moshe 4:74; Or Letziyon 2:35-3; The Sheivet Halevy [5:44] rules that it is best to immerse in a warm Mikveh if he is able to, despite the fact that the custom is to be lenient.; See Poskim in Piskeiy Teshuvos 326:5 footnote 58

[197] Karban Nesanel [Perek Bameh Madlikin 22:11] says that this is not included in the decree against bathing; Bircheiy Yosef Yoreh Deah 197:2; Divrei Yosef 64, although he concludes with a Tzaruch Iyun [so says Pischeiy Teshuvah, however Tzitz Eliezer differs that he does allow it and so learns others as well]; Sidrei Taharah Y.D. 197:16; Chesed Lealafim 326:7; Divrei Chayim 2:26, Avnei Nezer 1:526; Darkei Teshuvah 197:7; Levushei Mordechai 1:1; Maharshag 2:127; M"B 326:7 brings the Karban Nesanel and in Shaar Hatziyon 326:5 writes one may be lenient in a time of need; Kaf Hachaim 326:33; Minchas Yitzchak 5:32; Tzitz Eliezer 6:22 brings many opinions which permit it; Divrei Yatziv 160-161; Orchos Rabbeinu 1:152 writes that Steipler would immerse in hot Mikveh if nothing else available; Sheivet Halevy 5:44 rules that it is best to immerse in a warm Mikveh if he is able to, despite the fact that the custom is to be lenient; See many Poskim in Piskeiy Teshuvos 326:5 footnote 54

[198] The Karban Nisanel ibid does not explicitly state why a Mikveh is not included in the decree of bathing, however the other Poskim who discuss his ruling record several reasons: 1) As many people are there and one will not come to transgress; 2) As it is done for the sake of a Mitzvah. 3) A mere dip is not considered bathing. Practically, the second reason is the main reason recorded behind the basis of this custom. [See Noda Beyehuda ibid; Avnei Nezer ibid; Divrei Yatziv ibid; Igros Moshe 1:126; Piskeiy Teshuvos 326 footnote 51]

[199] While many of the above Poskim discuss specifically a woman's immersion it is evident that this would apply likewise to a man. Furthermore, some of the above Poskim explicitly write that this extends also to the immersion of a man. [See Chesed Lealafim ibid; Aveni Nezer ibid who permits but says Lechatchila is best for man to avoid if just for Tosefes Taharah; Divrei Yatziv ibid; Piskeiy Teshuvos 326 footnote 54 and 58]

[200] Divrei Chaim ibid

[201] See Piskeiy Teshuvos 326:5

[202] Avnei Nezer 1:526 *"To sit in the hot Mikveh after immersing is certainly forbidden, however to enter, immerse and immediately leave has room for Halachic leniency"* [However, based on reason 1 and 3 recorded above, even this would be allowed. However, practically the main reason is reason 2, and it is hence only permitted for the sake of a Mitzvah.]

Does this apply even if the Mikveh is warm? Seemingly, even if the Mikveh is not hot, but warm or cold, one is to leave right away, as it is nevertheless forbidden to bathe in even cold water due to custom. [See Lehoros Nasan 4:30; Piskeiy Teshuvos 326:5] However, perhaps we say that once one has entered with permission, there is no longer a custom to prohibit remaining a little longer. Vetzaruch Iyun

[203] See Piskeiy Teshuvos 326 footnote 56

[204] See Zera Emes 1:71; Rav Poalim 4:21; Or Letziyon 2:35-3; Yabia Omer 10:55; Darkei Halacha p. 169; Piskeiy Teshuvos 326 footnote 54

[205] Piskeiy Teshuvos 326:2

[206] 1:126

allows one to Bedieved use such a Mikveh even if it was heated by a Jew on Shabbos. [Opinion of Admur: Seemingly according to the ruling of Admur above in Halacha 1 that even water warmed on Shabbos in a permitted way may not be placed on one's body, this would be forbidden.[207]]

Does the water of a hot Mikveh need to be heated to its halfway point before Shabbos?[208]
Night Mikveh: If the Mikveh is to be used at the night of Shabbos [such as a women's Mikveh], then it is to be pre-heated before Shabbos to its halfway point.[209] If this is not able to be done, one should lock the room that has the temperature settings, and this is considered as if he covered the fire [under a pot of food].[210]
Day Mikveh: If the Mikveh is heated for the day [such as a men's Mikveh] one is likewise to verify that the Mikveh reach its halfway point before Shabbos, or at the very least lock the thermostat area.[211] However there are opinions[212] which say that there is no need to verify that the water be preheated halfway before Shabbos.[213]

May one swim in a Mikveh on Shabbos?
Depends on the Mikveh. See Halacha 8 Q&A there!

May one splash away the dirt that floats on the surface of a Mikvah?[214]
Yes. See Halacha 9 Q&A there.

May one take a cold shower after the Mikveh to wash off the Mikveh water?
Seemingly yes, just as one may stay in the cold or warm Mikveh water for an extended period of time, if the water is cold.

May one remove the stopper which attaches the Mikveh to the pit of rainwater?[215]
Yes[216], doing so does not pose a problem of Tikkun Keli[217] or of removing a pit cover[218].

---

[207] Vetzaruch Iyun as perhaps since it's not being done for purposes of bathing it is permitted even if the water is heated on Shabbos, as from the aspect of bathing the entire body it is equally forbidden to be done whether with water heated before or on Shabbos.
[208] Shabbos Kehalacha Vol. 1 page 332-333
[209] Admur 326:1 [There Admur explains like the Ran that it was due to this reason that the Sages forbade bathing on Shabbos in hot water as the Balanim were not careful to heat the water to the halfway point before Shabbos.]
[210] Rav Shlomo Zalman Aurbach brought in Shabbos Kehalacha ibid
[211] As is the simple understanding of the Admur 253:29; 254:14-15, and is clearly ruled in 326:1 as rules the Ran [regarding the reason for the Issur of bathing on Shabbos] and 326:11 [regarding the Issur of bathing in hot water heated in a way that transgressed the Shehiyah restrictions]. So is also the custom of Rav Wosner to be stringent in the Mikveh under his ruling.
[212] Mahrsham 229; Sheivet Haleivi 7:32
[213] Mahrsham rules it is allowed being that one does not plan to use the water until the next morning and is thus similar to raw meat, and because in any event it is forbidden to heat the Mikveh too much due to the prohibition of bathing in hot water. These arguments however are not relevant today being that we are accustomed to immersing in hot water. Furthermore, Admur clearly rules that we suspect for stoking the coals even one leaves the food for the next day, and why should we differentiate between food and water of the Mikveh. Just like one may come to change his mind and decide to eat the food at night, perhaps one will desire to immerse in the Mikveh at night, past sunset on Shabbos. In any event the Mahrsham concludes that the fire [or area of raising the temperature] is to be covered.
[214] Ketzos Hashulchan 146 footnote 34:17 and 35; Shabbos Kihalacha Vol. 2 p. 242.
Splashing away dirt may involve the "Swimming" prohibition as well as the Borer prohibition .
[215] Piskeiy Teshuvos 226:5 [24 in new]
[216] So rules Darkeiy Teshuvah Yoreh Deah 201:27 which brings many opinions which allow this as to opposed to the Mahrshik which writes that its forbidden; So rules also that it is allowed: Igros Moshe [did not find source], Dvar Moshe, Mishneh Halachos.
[217] As purifying impure waters is allowed to be done on Shabbos through pouring them into a Mikveh. [Rambam Shabbos 23:8]
[218] Removing a pit cover may contain two prohibitions: Muktzah if it does not have a handle [308:37] and Setirah [if it is not made to constantly remove]. In this case neither prohibition applies as it is made to constantly open and close, as well as that it appears that it is made for doing so despite the fact that it does not contain a handle. [Sheivet Hakehasi 3:132]

8. The allowance to dry oneself on Shabbos:[219]

One who washes his face hands and feet in hot water which was heated from before Shabbos, or even [one] who bathes his entire body in the Tiberius springs, or in cold water, the [Sages] permitted him to dry himself with a towel or sheet and the like, even if one is particular during the week to squeeze these clothes from their absorbed liquid.[220] Nevertheless, it is best to dry oneself with an item which one is not particular to squeeze even during the week.[221] [Likewise, it is best to shake the water off one's body prior to drying himself, even though from the letter of the law there is no need to do so, and the custom is to be lenient.[222] This applies even when using a towel designated for drying.[223]]

The reason that this does not involve a Rabbinical laundering prohibition:[224] The Sages did not suspect that one may forget and come to squeeze the towel on Shabbos being that this decree would be a decree which is impossible to implement, as being that all bathers need to dry themselves, if they were to prohibit drying in essence they would be prohibiting people to bathe, which is a matter that is impossible to prevent people from doing. [This inability to withstand the decree is known from past experience as] one time the Sages decreed not to bathe [even in water heated by fire before Shabbos] due to the bath house attendees which would heat up the water on Shabbos while claiming that it was heated before Shabbos, and afterwards [they decreed against even bathing in the Tiberius springs being that people would bathe in fire heated water claiming that it was Tiberius spring water, and afterwards] the Sages saw that the public is unable to uphold the decree and they thus retracted and rescinded it. Now, although today in which it is possible to abstain from bathing on Shabbos [and thus the decree is now one which can be kept by the public], and thus it is possible to decree against drying oneself, nevertheless drying oneself contains no prohibition being that it was never prohibited by the council of Sages [which are the only authority to make such decrees].

The allowance to carry the towel back home in an area with an Eiruv:[225] It is permitted for the bather to hold the towel in his hand and bring it from the bathhouse to his home so long as there is an Eiruv [in his community] and the Sages did not suspect that he may forget and come to squeeze the towel during his return home (as if they were to suspect for this and would thus forbid against bringing the towel back home, this would in essence be prohibiting drying oneself on Shabbos, as it is not possible for one to disown his towel and leave it in the bathhouse.[226])

Giving the towel to the house attendees:[227] In any event it is forbidden to give over the towel to the bath house attendees being that the attendees are suspected to squeeze [the towel] with their hands.

Regarding drying wet hair see next Halacha!

Summary:
It is permitted to dry oneself with a cloth on Shabbos, although it is best to use a towel to do so rather than using clothing which one is particular to squeeze out their water upon them getting wet. Likewise, it is best to shake the water off one's body prior to drying himself, even though from the letter of the law there is no need to do so, and the custom is to be lenient.]

---

[219] 301:60; Michaber 3021:48; Shabbos 147b
[220] Admur ibid; Implication of M"A 301:58; however see M"A 302:22
[221] Admur ibid; M"A 301:58; However regarding drying hands on a cloth the M"A 302:22 rules it is forbidden to use a garment that one is particular not to get wet. However see M"B 302:51 in name of Peri Megadim that argues one may be lenient by a small amount of water.
[222] Admur 302:21; Michaber 302:10; See Rama there; Piskeiy Teshuvos 302:24; Shabbos Kehalacha 18:56
The reason: As there are opinions [Yireim; Maharam; Mordechai] that rule there is a laundering prohibition involved in wetting a clothing even in a form of drying and only when a small amount of water is used is it allowed. [See Admur ibid and Kuntrus Achron 302:1; M"B 302:50]
[223] Shabbos Kehalacha 18:55-56; Piskeiy Teshuvos 302:24
[224] Admur ibid; M"A 301:58
The reason it does not contain a laundering prohibition? As it is Derech Lichluch and not Derech Kibbus. It is therefore permitted to dry oneself with a garment after bathing even if he has a lot of water on his body. [Admur 302:21; Rama 302:10]
[225] Admur ibid; Michaber ibid; Rebbe Yochanon in Shabbos ibid
[226] Admur ibid; Implication of M"A ibid; M"B 301:175
[227] Admur ibid; Michaber ibid; Shabbos ibid

> ### *Q&A*
> **Is a towel considered a clothing that one is not particular to squeeze?[228]**
> Yes.
>
> **Should one dry himself with a towel on Shabbos rather than wear his clothing while still wet?**
> Yes. It is better to use a towel, as one's clothing is not designated for drying with and he may therefore come to squeeze the water from it.

9. The prohibition of squeezing liquid from hair on Shabbos:[229]

Every bather needs to beware not to squeeze his hair.

The Reason: Now, although there is no applicable [Biblical] prohibition of squeezing hair[230] being that hair is hard and does not actually absorb water inside of it[231] [and rather the water is absorbed between each individual hair], nevertheless it is Rabbinically forbidden [to squeeze it due to the Mifarek prohibition].[232]

> ### *Q&A on squeezing and drying hair on Shabbos*
> **What areas of hair contain the squeezing prohibition?[233]**
> Only those areas which have hair growing in close proximity to each other such as the hair of the head, beard [underarms and pubic area]. However, the hair of the arms, [legs] and eyelashes are distanced from each other and thus do not contain a squeezing prohibition.
> *Eyelashes*: Some Poskim[234] rule the eyelashes do not contain a squeezing prohibition. Other Poskim[235] rule it contains a squeezing prohibition.
> *Eyebrows*: Some Poskim[236] rule it contains a squeezing prohibition. Practically, this depends on the amount of hair each person's eyebrows contain.[237]
>
> **May one squeeze the water out from his eyelids after leaving the Mikveh?[238]**
> This matter is dependent on the dispute mentioned above. Practically, one may be lenient to do so as otherwise there is pain involved in having the water get into one's eyes[239], as well as that since the hair of the eyelids are not close together, they most probably do not contain a squeezing prohibition at all.

---

[228] M"B 301:173 in name of Gr"a

[229] Admur 326:6; M"A 326:8; M"B 326:21

Opinions who rule there is a Rabbinical prohibition in squeezing hair: Admur ibid and in 330:1; M"A ibid and 320:23; Beis Yosef 330; Kesef Mishneh 2:11; Implication of Rambam 9:11; Kol Bo and Maharil 139 brought in M"A ibid and Beis Yosef Y.D. 199; M"B ibid and 326:24, 25, 320:55; Biur Halacha 302 "Assur"; Aruch Hashulchan 320:35; Kaf Hachaim 320:110

Other opinions: Some Poskim rule there is no prohibition involved in squeezing hair. [Implication of Gemara Shabbos 128b and Meiri Nidah 67b; Rashi and Rabbeinu Tam according to Avnei Nezer 157:14; Chida in Shiyurei Bracha 199:3 based on Beis Yosef Y.D. ibid; See Imros Moshe p. 332 for a lengthy discussion on the opinions on this matter.]

Does the laundering prohibition apply to hair? No. [Avnei Nezer ibid]

[230] Admur ibid; Raba and Rav Yosef in Shabbos 128b

[231] Admur ibid; Rashi ibid

[232] Poskim ibid; See previous footnotes

[233] Ketzos Hashulchan 133 footnote 8; Piskeiy Teshuvah 326:7; Shabbos Kehalacha 18:53

[234] Ketzos Hashulchan ibid; Minchas Shabbos 86:6; Rav SZ"A in Maor Hashabbos 4:44; Shabbos Kehalacha ibid

[235] Yeshuos Chochmah brought in Ketzos Hashulchan ibid; Az Nidbaru 13:10

[236] Yeshuos Chochmah brought in Minchas Shabbos ibid; Az Nidbaru 13:10; Rav SZ"A in Maor Hashabbos 4:44;

[237] Piskeiy Teshuvos 326 footnote 133

[238] Ketzos Hashulchan 133 footnote 8

[239] And in a case of pain the Sages did not uphold their decree.

If while drinking one wet his mustache, may he squeeze the water out?[240]

One is to be careful to only do so using a towel as opposed to one's hands.

May one scratch his hair when it is wet?[241]

Yes. Although doing so will inevitably cause water to get squeezed out it is nevertheless permitted to be done.[242] Nevertheless, it is best to do so using one's hat or the like.

May one wash one's beard/head and the like on Shabbos?

Some Poskim[243] rule it is forbidden to wash the hair on Shabbos, due to that in doing so one causes the water to be squeezed from his hair. Other Poskim[244] however rule it is permitted to wash one's hair on Shabbos, even if one will squeeze the water in the process of washing.[245] Practically, although doing so in it of itself is not prohibited from the letter of the law, the custom is to avoid doing so being that one may come to squeeze his hair in a way that is prohibited.[246]

In case of Discomfort:[247] In a case of discomfort one may wash his head.

In case of dirt:[248] If his head or beard have dirt in them, they may be washed.

Inside the Mikveh-under water:[249] It is permitted to wash and scrub one's beard/head while underwater, even though its causes water to squeeze out.[250]

Washing ones bearded face when no intent to wash the beard:[251] As well one may always wash and dry his face despite the fact that water will inevitably get in his beard and be squeezed, as the Sages did not uphold their decree in such a case.

May one use soap: From the letter of the law some[252] write that it is permitted to even use liquid soap to wash the hair, so long as one is careful not to squeeze the hair in the process. Nevertheless, practically one is not to do so, and so is the custom.[253]

Q&A on using a towel

May one dry his head or beard or other hairy area with a towel?[254]

Yes.[255] Nevertheless, one is to only do so gently, without force.[256] However, there are those which are

---

[240] Ben Ish Chaiy Pekudei 2:8; Ketzos Hashulchan 133 footnote 8

[241] Minchas Shabbos 86:6

[242] The reason: As a) One does not desire the water to get squeezed and it is thus a Pesik Reishei which is not Nicha Lei. As well b) In a case of pain the Sages did not apply their decree.

[243] Avnei Nezer 157:14; Sheivet Halevy 5:45; Mishneh Halachos 5:51; They are stringent to avoid washing the beard individually with ones hands [as opposed to when using a shower head or entering into a Mikveh] due to that it will inevitably cause hair to get squeezed out.

[244] M"B 326:25; Implication of Michaber 326:9 and Admur 326:8; Ashel Avraham Butchach 320:17; Ketzos Hashulchan ibid; Igros Moshe 1:133; Piskeiy Teshuvos 326:11; Rav SZ"A in his final ruling in SSH"K 14 footnote 1; See Shabbos Kehalach 18 footnote 70; Implication of Ben Ish Chaiy, Minchas Shabbos, Ketzos Hashulchan, as they allow to dry the hair. Furthermore, from the fact that Admur never mentions not to wash the beard or head when mentioning the ruling that one may wash minority of the body itself proves that according to Admur washing these areas contain no prohibition and it is only their squeezing that is problematic. Vetzaruch Iyun from SSH"K 14:11 which plainly rules that one is not to wash these areas, thus contradicting the ruling that he brought earlier in footnote 1 in the name of Rav SZ"A.

[245] The reason: As in addition to the reason he mentions there [that the water gets squeezed towards the body] the water squeezed goes to waste. Likewise, the Sages did notwe ant to decree against one washing his face on Shabbos. [See Ketzos Hashulchan ibid]

[246] Ashel Avraham Butchach 320:17; Sheivet Halevy 5:45; Mishneh Halachos 5:51; Piskeiy Teshuvos 326:11; See Keztos Hashulchan 133 footnote 8

[247] Piskeiy Teshuvos ibid

[248] Piskeiy Teshuvos ibid; Igros Moshe 1:133; Peri Megadim M"Z 320:12. However there are opinions [Sheivet Halevy 5:45; Mishneh Halachos 5:51] which are stringent in this.

[249] Rav SZ"A 14 footnote 9; Piskeiy Teshuvos 326 footnote 132; Shabbos Kehalacha 18:54

[250] The reason: As although water is squeezed out. Nonetheless other water comes right back in. [ibid]

[251] Ketzos Hashulchan 133 footnote 8

[252] Piskeiy Teshuvos 326:11 based on Michaber 326:9 and Admur 326:8 and M"B 326:25 and 28 which allows using Morson on the beard

[253] Sheivet Halevi 5:45; Piskeiy Teshuvos ibid

[254] See Shabbos Kehalacha 18:57; Piskeiy Teshuvos 326:12

[255] Ben Ish Chaiy Pekudei 2:8; Minchas Shabbos 8:6; Ashel Avraham Butchach 320:17; Ketzos Hashulchan 133 footnote 8; Kaf Hachaim 320:111; Shabbos Kehalacha ibid

Other opinions: Some Poskim[255] prohibit using a towel to dry one's hair even lightly. [Az Nidbaru 1:55; Beir Moshe 1:31]

Practically, one may rely on the great Poskim listed above which permit doing so, especially being the entire prohibition is of Rabbinical nature, scrupulous not to dry the hair of the beard and rather shake out the water and let it dry on its own.[257]

May one leave a towel over his wet hair letting the water get absorbed into the towel on its own?[258]

Yes, doing so is permitted even according to the stringent opinions mentioned above.

10. *Swimming on Shabbos:[259]*

Introduction: Although bathing in cold water is customarily forbidden on Shabbos, as explained in the previous Halachos, nevertheless it may be done in certain scenarios, such as for the sake of Mikveh, or to relieve pain and the like. [See Halacha 4] Although it is permitted to enter the body of water in these cases, it is nevertheless forbidden from the letter of the law to swim in certain areas. Thus, in all cases mentioned that bathing in cold water is allowed one may not swim in those waters in the cases mentioned here to which the swimming prohibition applies. Furthermore, as will be explained in the Q&A, even in those areas where swimming is allowed from the letter of the law, it is forbidden to swim today due to the custom against bathing even in cold water. This applies even if one entered the water to use as a Mikveh.

The law:[260] One may not swim [**See Q&A on the definition of swimming**] on the surface of water [that is in a river or certain pools as will be explained].

The reason for this is:[261] due to a decree that one may come to make a barrel [that is normally used by] swimmers. This [instrument] refers to a vessel made from reeds which are woven and are made like an elongated barrel of which one learns to swim with.

A river: However, when does the above [suspicion and stringency] apply? [when swimming] in a river.

Swimming in a vessel:[262] However when [swimming] in a vessel [this suspicion does not apply and] it is [thus] allowed [to swim in it] being that it is not common to make a barrel to swim with inside of a vessel.

A Pool without an external rim:[263] However [to swim] in a pool in one's courtyard is forbidden. [**See Q&A if one may enter the pool if he will not swim in it**]

The reason for this is:[264] because when the water overflows upon one swimming, [the waters] leave the pool and this is similar to a river.

A pool with an external rim:[265] [However] if the pool has an [external] rim around it [**See Q&A regarding the definition**], it is permitted to swim in it as even if the water overflows the rim returns the water to its place [in the pool] and it is thus similar to [swimming in] a vessel [as opposed to a river]. [**See Q&A regarding of this ruling applies even if the pool is in a public area, and regarding if this leniency at all applies today when the custom is to never bathe in cold water!**]

and one has no intent to squeeze the hair, and Admur never mentions in the laws of drying the body [in 301 and 302] any need to be careful in the above.

The reason: Now although one will inevitably squeeze out some water in the process, nevertheless it is allowed as the squeezing is done in an irregular fashion [using the towel], as well as that the water squeezed goes to waste. As well as regarding the beard, since one who does not dry his face it can break out in a skin problem, it was never decreed against drying it, even though it is inevitable that one will not squeeze out some of the water from his beard in the process. [Ketzos Hashulchan Ibid] Likewise it is permitted because the squeezed liquid is not recognizable and enters straight into the towel. [See Shabbos Kehalacha ibid footnote 133]

[256] Ben Ish Chaiy ibid; Kaf Hachaim 320:111; Ketzos Hashulchan ibid; Shabbos Kehalacha ibid
[257] Ben Ish Chaiy ibid; Keztos Hashulchan ibid
[258] Az Nidbaru ibid; Piskeiy Teshuvos ibid; Shabbos Kehalacha ibid
[259] Admur 339:1
[260] Admur ibid and 248:9 regarding the prohibition of entering a ship and 326:6; Michaber 339:2; Mishneh Beitza 36b

Other opinions: Some Poskim suggest that the decree against swimming in pools does not apply at all today being that we no longer make the swimming rafts. [Nodah Beyehuda Tinyana 49 that so would be the law according to Tosafus Beitza 30a regarding clapping on Shabbos] Practically however, this is not agreed upon by all Poskim. [Noda Beyehuda ibid; Ketzos Hashulchan 146 footnote 34:17] Nonetheless, one may use this lenient opinion as joint reason to allow one to splash away twigs in a Mikveh as will be explained in next Halacha.
[261] Admur ibid and 248:9; Gemara ibid and Rashi ibid; M"B 339:2
[262] Admur ibid; Michaber ibid; Shabbos 41a as explained by Rashi ibid; Razah; Ramban; Ran
[263] Admur ibid; Michaber ibid; Shabbos 40b
[264] Admur ibid; Michaber ibid; Rishonim ibid
[265] Admur ibid; Michaber ibif; Shabbos ibid

Summary:

It is forbidden from the letter of the law to swim in a river or a pool which does not contain a slanted rim. A pool with a slanted rim, or a vessel which contains water, does not contain a swimming prohibition, [although based on the custom today not to bathe in cold water, it remains forbidden to swim in it due to this custom. This includes even a case that one was allowed to enter the pool even based on the custom, such as he entered to use it as a Mikveh or due to it being very hot, even so one is not to swim in it. However, in all cases where bathing in cold water is allowed even according to the custom, it is allowed to enter into any swimming pool, even without a rim, or even into a river, so long as one does not swim in it or tread water.[266]]

Q&A

What is the definition of swimming?[267]

The lifting of both of one's feet off the floor of the pool/river and to thus tread the water or swim it with ones hands is defined as swimming.

May one enter into a non–rimmed pool if he will not swim in it?[268]

So long as one is allowed to do so even according to the custom to avoid bathing in cold water, [such as for Mikveh or on hot day] it is permitted to enter into a pool even if it is not rimmed, so long as one does not swim in it or tread water.

Q&A on rimmed pool

What is defined as a rim for the pool/What is the law if a pool is not filled to the top?[269]

A rim refers to a walled area which surrounds the pool and prevents any water from leaving the pool[270], as even if it leaves, the rimmed area will cause the water to come back in. However, those pools which do not have this rimmed area surrounding the pool, are considered to be "rimless" in this regard, even if they are not filled to their top and thus no water will splash out.[271] Thus most pools today do not carry the allowance to swim in them being that they do not contain an external rim.

If a rimmed pool is in a public area may one swim in it in cases that one is allowed to bathe in cold water?[272]

Some Poskim[273] rule that doing so is forbidden due to a suspicion that perhaps some of the water will splash outside of the 4 cubit radius of the pool and he will thus transgress the carrying prohibition.[274] Other Poskim[275] however rule that we do not suspect for this occurrence and it is thus allowed to swim in such a pool from the letter of the law. Nevertheless, even according to them, since today we are accustomed not to bathe even in cold water, and one who swims in the water appears as if he is

---

[266] Ketzos Hashulchan 146 footnote 34 number 16

[267] Mishneh Berurah 339:2; Ketzos Hashulchan 146:18; Rashi

[268] Ketzos Hashulchan 146 footnote 34 number 16.

[269] Ketzos Hashulchan 146 footnote 34 number 13 and 15.

[270] M"B 339:6

[271] The Ketzos Hashulchan ibid analyzed this scenario and although leans to be lenient from the letter of the law, he rules that one may not do so being that the scenario is not discussed in the Poskim. The following is the reason to be stringent: Since if this pool were to be filled to the top then the waters would leave the pool, therefore we are stringent to consider them similar to a river. However, by a pool with an external rim it is not common at all to fill the external rim with water, and thus this comparison to a river is not relevant. [Ketzos Hashulchan ibid 13]

[272] Ketzos Hashulchan 146 footnote 34

[273] M"B 339:4, based on his understanding of the opinion of Rashi Shabbos ibid and Rambam as he explains in Biur Halacha 339:1 "Veim"; Minchas Yitzchak 6:32

[274] The reason for forbidding pools is because perhaps the waters will splash past 4 cubits.

[275] Ketzos Hashulchan 146 footnote 34 based on the opinion of Rif and others [brought in Biur Halacha ibid] which hold the reason for forbidding pools is due to it being similar to a river of which swimming is prohibited, and thus if the pool has a rim it is permitted since it is no longer similar. Furthermore the Ketzos Hashulchan argues on the M"B understanding of Rashi and says that even according to Rashi a rimmed pool is not suspected for splashing out of 4 cubits. He concludes that in any event since the SHU"A clearly rules like the Rif and not Rashi there is no need to suspect for the M"B from the letter of the law.

contradicting the custom [even though in truth he was allowed to enter the water, such as he needed a Mikveh] therefore one is not allowed to do so.[276] Furthermore, if the pool has a depth of ten Tefachim and is four by four Amos wide then seemingly it has the status of a Reshus Hayachid, while outside the pool has a status of a Karmalis, and it hence should be forbidden according to all to enter and leave the pool with the water on one's body as one is carrying the water from a Reshus Hayachid to a Karmalis.[277]

May one who entered a rimmed pool to immerse in, or to cool off in, swim in that pool?[278]

One who has entered a pool in order to immerse in or to cool off in is not allowed to swim in that pool, even if it is rimmed, as to others it will appear that he is breaking the custom to not bathe in cold water on Shabbos. Furthermore, swimming may involve the same prohibition as does exercising on Shabbos if one intends to swim for exercising purposes.[279] [However it is permitted for him to tread in the pool, and he thus does not have to be careful not to lift his feet while immersing in the pool water.]

May one swim or tread inside a Mikveh?[280]

One is forbidden to do so even if the Mikveh is not filled to its top, unless it has an external rim which will flow back any water that splashes out.[281]

Final Summary:
Today one may never swim in a pool or river even in cases that he is allowed to bathe in it even according to the custom, such as to cool off or to do Tevilah.

11. Splashing twigs away while in a body of water:[282]

The rule: It is forbidden for a person in a river to splash an item away from oneself or towards oneself.
The reason for this is because:[283] doing so is also included in the decree against swimming on Shabbos.
Twigs: Therefore, twigs which are on the surface of water are forbidden to be splashed away to the sides in order to clean up the water that it be clear.
To which bodies of water does the prohibition apply?[284] [However] all the above applies to a river, however in a vessel or a pool with an [external] rim this decree was not made at all, as was explained above.

Summary:
Whenever it remains permitted to enter into a body of water on Shabbos [such as for Mikveh or on hot day], it remains forbidden to splash away from oneself, or towards oneself, dirt or other objects, unless it is a pool which contains an external rim, as explained above by swimming, in which case doing so is permitted.

---

[276] Ketzos Hashulchan ibid 16
[277] Piskeiy Teshuvos 326:7 based on 358, M"B 358:89
[278] Ketzos Hashulchan 146 footnote 34; Minchas Yitzchak 5:32; Igros Moshe Y.D. 2:13; Beir Moshe 3:56; Shraga Hameir 6:151; Teshuvos Vehanhagos 1:222; Piskeiy Teshuvos 339:1
[279] Piskeiy Teshuvos 326
[280] Ketzos Hashulchan 146 footnote 34:17; See also Piskeiy Teshuvos 339:1 footnote 1
[281] So is implied from Ketzos Hashulchan 146 footnote 34:17 which begins saying that it is forbidden to swim in the Mikveh and then goes on to explain that ideally splashing twigs away is as well forbidden, but the custom of the world is to be lenient in splashing away twigs. He then gives 5 different reasons for why one may be lenient in splashing away the twigs. Now although most of the reasons mentioned apply equally to allowing one to swim in the Mikveh, nevertheless he clearly states that the reasons are to allow splashing away the twigs and not to swim, as well as that some of the reasons only apply to splashing away twigs.
[282] Admur 339:9 and 326:6; Michaber 339:6; Yerushalmi Beitza 5:2; Mordechai Beitza 695 in name of Yerushalmi ibid; Hagahos Ashri Beitza 5:2 in name of Or Zarua
[283] Admur ibid; M"B 339:33; Implication of Yerushalmi ibid and Karban Heida ibid
[284] Admur ibid; M"A 339:12; M"B 339:34

Q&A

May kids who reached the age of Chinuch push away floating toys in water?
It depends on the body of water. If the water is in a vessel, such as a bucket, or bathtub, it is permitted to do so. If the water is a pond and the like, it is forbidden to do so.

May one splash away the dirt that floats on the surface of a Mikvah?[285]
One may splash the dirt to the sides even with his hands[286], even if the Mikveh is filled to the top[287]. Doing so does not involve a Borer prohibition [even if the dirt covers over the entire Mikveh and one thus would not desire to immerse without splashing the dirt away[288]] being that nothing is being removed from the Mikveh but is rather being moved to the sides.[289] Some[290] however write that it is nevertheless proper to take care to splash the dirt away to the sides together with a lot of water. [One however is not allowed to splash the dirt outside of the Mikveh, as explained next.]

May one remove the dirt from the Mikveh using with his hands?
No.[291] However some[292] suggest that one may be lenient to remove the dirt from the Mikveh using his hands. Practically, it is forbidden to do so.[293]

May one use a vessel to discard the dirt from the Mikveh, if he does so together with some of the water?
No.[294] However some[295] rule one may be lenient to do so if he respells part of that water back into the Mikveh.

May one use a net to remove dirt from a Mikveh on Shabbos?[296]
No. Doing is forbidden due to the Borer prohibition.

---

[285] Ketzos Hashulchan 146 footnote 34:17 and 35; Shabbos Kehalacha Vol. 2 p. 242; Piskeiy Teshuvos 319:45; Splashing away dirt may involve the "Swimming" prohibition as well as the Borer prohibition.

[286] And certainly, with ones legs and elbow in which one is doing so with an irregularity. [Ketzos Hashulchan ibid 35]

[287] In which case there is no room to say that it is considered to have a rim. This does not involve the swimming prohibition mentioned above as a) Perhaps the decree only applied to pools with an earth floor and not to a tiled floor, which is not exchangeable with a river, as well b) The Nodah Beyehuda rules that the decree against swimming in pools does not apply at all today being that we no longer make the swimming rafts, as well as c) The prohibition against splashing twigs is less severe than the swimming prohibition. Thus, with a joint of all the above one may be lenient to splash dirt away in a Mikveh, however not to swim or tread in. [Ketzos Hashulchan ibid 34:17]

[288] So is implied from Ketzos Hashulchan and so rules Shabbos Kehalacha ibid.
Other Poskim: Some Poskim rule that if there is a lot of filth blocking the entire water then it is considered Borer even to splash the water to another side. [P"M 339 A"A 14] See however Ketzos Hashulchan ibid that brings many reasons why in this case one may be lenient even according to the P"M ibid

[289] Ketzos Hashulchan ibid 35; Chelkas Yaakov 136

[290] Chelkas Yaakov ibid, brought in the Ketzos Hashulchan ibid, and so rules Shabbos Kehalacha ibid that it is proper to do so as this strengthens the allowance even more, although it is not required from the letter of the law. However, the Ketzos Hashulchan himself sides that there is no need at all to do so.

[291] P"M 339 A"A 14

[292] Piskeiy Teshuvos ibid footnote 359 based on that a) Some Poskim rule there is no Borer by floating objects. [Mahriytiz brought in Beir Heiytiv 319; Tal Oros 31; Iglei Tal Borer 6:5; Ketzos Hashulchan ibid] And b) The water is useable even with the dirt. Furthermore, another reason for allowance is because it is similar to peeling an item which is Derech Achila, so too removing the dirt from the water is Derech Achila, as there is no other way to clean the water. [This is in contrast to a fly in a cup in which one has the option to remove the liquid or the fly.]

[293] As all Poskim ibid that do not record this option and we do not rule like the Maharititz, and people are initially Makpid against the dirt.

[294] Based on Siddur Admur

[295] Vayaan Yosef 139; Piskeiy Teshuvos 319:45

[296] See Ketzos Hashulchan 146 footnote 35; Piskeiy Teshuvos 319:45 footnote 359

12. Perspiring on Shabbos in a bathhouse:[297]

Entering a steam room: The Sages forbade one to enter a bathhouse even in order to merely perspire [one's body].

The reason for this is:[298] due to the transgressors who would bathe themselves in hot water and claim that they were just perspiring.

To pass by a steam room: [Furthermore] there are opinions[299] which say that even to walk past a bathhouse by an area where one is able[300] to perspire is forbidden even though he has no intention to perspire.

Summary- Perspiring on Shabbos in a bathhouse:[301]

Is forbidden. Some even forbid walking by an area that will cause one to perspire even if he has no intention to do so.

Q&A

May one enter a Mikveh in which he knows that its heat will cause him to perspire?[302]

No. Thus, if due to the heat of the Mikveh room one will perspire upon staying there for a long time, he must dress quick enough after leaving the Mikveh water to prevent perspiration. Nonetheless, women who go to Mikveh on Friday night may be lenient in this matter if necessary.

May one enter a bathhouse in which he will sweat if he is wearing his clothing?

Some Poskim[303] rule it is permitted to do so.

May one enter an area in order to sweat if it is not a bathhouse?[304]

Yes.[305]

May one use a Sauna on Shabbos?

If the sauna is in a bathing area, then it is certainly forbidden to use it. If, however, it is not in a bathing area then this matter requires further analysis.[306] Practically, one is not to enter a sauna on Shabbos, even a dry sauna.[307]

May one take a suntan on Shabbos?

Doing so does not contain a sweating prohibition being that the sweating prohibition is only relevant when it is caused by hot water, as in that case the Sages feared that one may bathe and merely claim that he is sweating. However, if there is no water involved then mere sweating is permitted, as Admur ruled earlier regarding sweating in the Tiberius springs which is allowed.[308] Nevertheless there are other possible prohibitions involved in sun tanning and practically it is disputed amongst Poskim if it is allowed. See the next section "The Laws of Smearing Oil"!

---

[297] Admur 326:12; 616:1 in parentheses; Michaber 326:12; Shabbos 40a

[298] Admur ibid; M"B 326:35; Gemara ibid

[299] Rama 326:12; Rashi Shabbos ibid; Rosh 3:7; Ran ibid; Tur

Other opinions: According to the first opinion mentioned above [of Michaber ibid] it is permitted to do so. [M"B 326:35 in name of Beis Yosef]

[300] This means that one will for certain perspire, as if it is not a Pesik Resihsei, then it is permitted if one has no intent to do so. [Olas Shabbos 326:23; Kaf Hachaim 326:54]

[301] Admur 326:12

[302] M"B 326:36; Ketzos Hashulchan 133 footnote 13

[303] Ashel Avraham Butchach 326; Piskeiy Teshuvos 326:16

[304] Ashel Avraham Butchach 326; Piskeiy Teshuvos 326:16 based on Admur 326:2 and M"B 326:11

[305] The reason: As the prohibition is only applicable in an area that contains water in which it is forbidden to bathe, as rules Admur 326:2 regarding the Tiveria springs, and perhaps in this case the stringent opinion would also be lenient.

[306] As in the previous Q&A we stated that a non-bathing area does not carry a sweating prohibition. On the other hand, however, a Sauna is a room specifically associated for sweating simialr to a bathhouse.

[307] SSH"K 14 Footnote 68; Piskeiy Teshuvos ibid footnote 180

[308] See Minchas Yitzchak 5:32

May one leave a humidifier on in his room throughout Shabbos in order to sweat?[309]
Yes, as stated in the previous Q&A!

May one wear many layers of clothing in order to sweat?[310]
Yes.

---

13. Warming up one's wet body near a fire:[311]

Pouring cold water on one's body and heating it near a fire:[312] A person may not rinse his entire body in cold water and heat himself opposite a fire because by doing so he warms up the water that is on him and it is considered as if he has washed his entire body in hot water.[313] [This applies even if the water will not reach Yad Soledes. However, according to this opinion, one may rinse minority of his body in cold water and then heat it near a fire to below Yad Soledes, as this is not considered a complete form of bathing.[314] However, even according to this opinion, one may not bathe minority of his body with water that was heated on Shabbos to even below Yad Soledes, as this is considered a complete form of bathing which is completely prohibited on Shabbos according to all.[315] However, other Poskim[316] rule that according to this opinion, one may bathe minority of his body in hot water heated on Shabbos in a permitted way.]

Pouring cold water on ones hot body:[317] However one is allowed to rinse himself off with cold water after having heated up [his body] near a fire because the [cold] water that [will be poured] on him will not get so hot [to be considered that he has bathed in hot water].

Warming up ones wet hands:[318] There are opinions[319] which say that even one who washes his hands needs to be careful not to heat it up opposite a fire [or any source of heat[320]] even from an area where [the water on him will] not [reach] Yad Soledes[321], if one did not previously dry himself very well.

Their reasoning is:[322] because by doing so he warms up the water that is on [his hands] and it is thus like he has bathed in hot water that was heated on Shabbos and hot water which was heated on Shabbos even in a permitted way is forbidden to wash even one limb and even if the [water] was only slightly heated that it is not Yad Soledes.

The Final Ruling: One is to be strict like this latter opinion.

Summary:
One may not dry his hands near a source of heat as doing so heats up the water on his hands and transgresses the Bathing prohibition.

Q&A

May one warm his wet hands near a heater on Shabbos?
No. This applies even if the water on his hands will not reach Yad Soledes.

---

[309] Piskeiy Teshuvos 326:16
[310] Piskeiy Teshuvos 326:16 footnote 184
[311] Admur 326:4; Michaber 326:4-5; Shabbos 40b
[312] Admur ibid; Michaber 326:4; Rambam 22:3
[313] This means to say that the prohibition is not due to the cooking prohibition, but rather due to the bathing prohibition, and is hence forbidden even to warm it below Yad Soledes. [M"B 326:17]
[314] M"A ibid; M"B ibid
[315] M"B ibid and Shaar Hatziyon 326:8 based on implication of M"A ibid and reason of Admur ibid brought below
[316] Shaar Hatziyon 326:8 based on implication of Gr"a
[317] Admur 326:4; Michaber 326:4; Shabbos 40b
[318] Admur ibid; Michaber 326:5
[319] Tur; Rosh 3:9; Mordechai 305
[320] Biur Halacha 326:5 "Etzel Haeish"
[321] Admur ibid; M"A 326:6; M"B 326:17; Biur Halacha 326:5 "Yeish Omrim"
[322] Admur ibid; M"A 326:6; M"B 326:17

14. Treating stomach pains with a vessel of hot water:[323]

A large amount of water: One who has a stomach pains is forbidden to place on his stomach a vessel that has hot water.

The reason for this is:[324] because he may come to spill it on majority of his body and it will thus be considered as if he has washed majority of his body in hot water.

A small amount:[325] [Furthermore] even if there is only a small amount of hot water [in the vessel] which is not enough to wash majority of one's body [if it were to spill], nevertheless if it were heated on Shabbos even a little, [even if this were] to the point that it is not [yet] Yad Soledes, it is forbidden [to place in a vessel on one's body for the reason] explained [in the previous Halacha, that one may not bathe even minority of one's body in water heated on Shabbos]. [However, if the water was heated before Shabbos, then there is no Shabbos prohibition involved in placing the hot water on him if it not enough of an amount to bathe majority of his body.[326] Furthermore, even if the there is enough water to cover majority of the body, if it was heated before Shabbos and is now merely warm, there is no Shabbos prohibition involved in placing it on the body.[327]]

On a weekday:[328] [Furthermore] even on a weekday this is not allowed to be done because of the possible danger [that it involves] as at times the water is very hot [and may come to spill on one's body and give him a serious burn]. [This applies even if the water is merely warm, and even a small amount, as at times the water is boiling.[329] However some Poskim[330] are lenient in this matter, so long as the water is not Yad Soledes.]

Placing hot clothing on it:[331] However it is permitted to heat up clothing and place them on ones stomach even on Shabbos.

Summary:
It is forbidden to place an [open] vessel of hot water on one's stomach even during the week due to fear that it may spill and cause a burn. On Shabbos this is forbidden also due to the bathing prohibition, unless it were heated before Shabbos and is not wet enough to wet majority of one's body if it were to spill. [However, nevertheless it would remain forbidden due to danger.]

Q&A

If the water is placed in a closed bottle may one place it on his stomach?
Yes. This applies both on Shabbos and during the week.[332] However some Poskim[333] rule one may only be lenient on Shabbos in a time of great need or pain.[334]

---

[323] Admur 326:5; Michaber 326:6; Shabbos 40b

[324] Admur ibid; based on M"A 326:7; Rashi Gemara ibid

Other reasons: Some say the reason it is forbidden to do so on Shabbos is due to it being a medical treatment. [Tosafus in Shabbos ibid, brought in M"A ibid] The practical ramifications between these reasons is regarding the amount of water that is prohibited to be placed, and the law if the bottle is closed.

[325] Admur ibid; M"A ibid

[326] Implication of Admur and M"A ibid based on Rashi

Other opinions: According to the reason of Tosafus, even a small amount is forbidden to be placed on, as it is considered Refua.

[327] Implication of Admur and M"A ibid based on Rashi

Other opinions: According to the reason of Tosafus, even a warm amount is forbidden to be placed on, as it is considered Refua.

[328] Admur ibid; Michaber ibid; Gemara ibid

Other opinions: Some Poskim rule that if the water is less than Yad Soledes it is permitted to place on the stomach during the week. [Biur Halacha 326:6 "Shepiamim"

[329] Implication of Admur and M"A ibid; P"M 326 A"A 6

[330] Biur Halacha 326:6 "Shepiamim"

[331] Admur ibid; Rama ibid; Gemara ibid

[332] M"B 326:6 in opinion of Rashi and Admur ibid which only records Rashi's opinion

The reason: As there is now no suspicion that it will spill. As well, there is no medication prohibition involved here as is seen from the fact that Admur makes no mention of it.

Other opinions: According to the reason of Tosafus, even a closed bottle is forbidden to be placed on the body, as it is considred Refua. [M"B 326:19 in name of Karban Nesaanel]

[333] M"B 326:19; Beir Moshe 1:33-15

[334] The reason: To suspect for the opinion of Tosafus.

15. Washing oneself with liquid that also contains hair removal liquid on Shabbos:[335]

It is permitted to wash one's face, hands and feet with liquids that do not remove hair which are mixed with hair removal substances so long as the majority of the mixture is not made up of hair removal substance in a way that [washing with this mixture] will inevitably [remove hair].

Summary-Hair removal tonic:[336]
Is forbidden to use on Shabbos due to the sheering prohibition.

---

16. Washing one's hands in salt or soap:[337]

It is forbidden to wash one's hands in salt and certainly with soap or other fats.

The reason for this is: because [the material] dissolves in ones hand and is as if one has created a new substance on Shabbos which resembles a forbidden action, as was explained in "The Laws of melting snow and ice" [Halacha 4] that it is forbidden to crush snow and hail for this reason. [This prohibition is referred to as Molid.]

Other Opinions: [However] according to those which [held there] that the reason for the prohibition of crushing snow and hail is because of a decree made [to safeguard one from coming to] squeeze fruits which are designated for their juices as snow and hail are likewise designated for their liquids as was explained there [in Halacha 19], [then according to them] soap and other fat which are not designated as liquids are permitted to be [even] initially crushed [when washed in water].

The Final Ruling: One is to be stringent like the former opinion.

Summary of using soap:[338]
It may not be dissolved with one's hands. Thus, it is forbidden to wash one's hands or other body parts with a block of soap.

Q&A

Does washing one's hands with a bar of soap contain the smoothening prohibition [Mimachek] and would thus be prohibited according to all?
See "The Laws of Crushing and Melting Ice" Halacha 4 Q&A!

Does washing one's hands with a bar of soap which contains engraved lettering contain the "erasing" prohibition?[339]
See "The Laws of Crushing and Melting Ice" Halacha 4 Q&A!

May one place soap into a cup of liquid and have it dissolve and then use that to wash ones hands?[340]
See "The Laws of Crushing and Melting Ice" Halacha 4 Q&A!

May one wash his hands with liquid soap?[341]
See "The Laws of Crushing and Melting Ice" Halacha 4 Q&A!

---

[335] Admur 326:8
[336] Admur 326:8
[337] Admur 326:10
[338] Admur 318:19 and chapter 326 Halacha 10
[339] Ketzos Hashulchan 146 footnote 32
[340] Ketzos Hashulchan 127 footnote 13
[341] SSH"K 14:16 footnote 49, based on Ketzos Hashulchan 138 footnote 31 with regards to using toothpaste. So rules also Ketzos Hashulchan explicitly in 146 footnote 32

May one wash his hands with scented soaps?
See "The Laws of Crushing and Melting Ice" Halacha 4 Q&A!

May one place a bar of scented soap into his toilet?
See "The Laws of Crushing and Melting Ice" Halacha 4 Q&A!

17. Sponges and other cleaning and itching materials?[342]

Designated for use during the week: One may not rub with a vessel that is designated for rubbing with during the week, unless one's hands or feet are dirty with mud or feces [and he wants to scrape it off with the vessel, and the vessel is **dry**[343]].[344]

Designated for use on Shabbos:[345] If one has a scratching instrument which is designated for use only on Shabbos then it is allowed [to be used if it is **dry**[346]], and for this reason it is customary for single girls to have a vessel made of swine hair which is designated for Shabbos as written in chapter 303 [Halacha 27 in Michaber and Magen Avraham].

Summary:
A sponge may never be used when wet. If the sponge is dry it may be used if either a) It is designated to be used only on Shabbos or is not but b) one is using it to remove dirt from one's body and the like.

Q&A
May one scratch his body using his hands on Shabbos?[347]
Yes, so long as one is careful not to cause any bleeding through doing so.

May one use a back scratcher on Shabbos?
No, unless it is designated to be used only on Shabbos.

May one use a pen and the like to scratch his back on Shabbos?
Yes, as the pen is not designated for this purpose.

May one rub himself with a dry sponge designated for Shabbos if his body is wet?[348]
Yes.[349]

May one scrub himself with a wet sponge made of synthetic hairs?[350]
If the hairs are not very close together and the sponge is designated for only Shabbos use, it may be used.

---

[342] Admur 327:3; Michaber 327:3; Mishneh Shabbos 147a and Gemara 147b

[343] As if it is wet one transgresses the squeezing prohibition, Upashut. [Ketzos Hashulchan 133 footnote 16]

[344] The reason: This is forbidden to being a mundane act. [M"B 327:8; Rashi ibid]

[345] Admur ibid; M"A 327:1; Olas Tamid; Bach; M"B 327:10; Shabbos 147b
Other opinions: Some Poskim learn that according to the Gemara one may not use even a Shabbos designated instrument to scratch himself. [Elya Raba, brought in Shaar Hatziyon 327:9] We do not rule like this opinion. [Shaar Hatziyon ibid]

[346] As if it is wet one transgresses the squeezing prohibition, Upashut. [Ketzos Hashulchan 133 footnote 16]

[347] M"B 327:9

[348] Ketzos Hashulchan 133 footnote 16

[349] This does not involve a laundering prohibition as the absorbing of the moisture that is on one's body by the sponge is in a way of dirtying and not cleaning. [Ketzos Hashulchan ibid.]

[350] SSH"K 14:13

May one wash his body using a glove?[351]

Made of plastic: Yes, as the plastic does not absorb and thus no liquid is being squeezed.

Made of cloth: Is forbidden even if designated for only Shabbos use.

---

18. Bathing after Shabbos in water that was heated on Shabbos:

A. The water of a bathhouse that got heated on its own on Shabbos:[352]

A bathhouse which its fire is fueled from the outside, under [the bathhouse], if one closed before Shabbos those holes through which the [water in the] bathhouse heats up from, then it is permitted to bathe in its water immediately after Shabbos being that [the water] had not been heated at all on Shabbos. However, if its holes had not been plugged from before Shabbos then even though it heated up on its own on Shabbos [through one having stoked the fire right before Shabbos] nevertheless in the evening one must wait the amount of time it takes to heat it being that it was heated in a prohibited way. As it is forbidden for its holes to be left open on Shabbos when there is fire under it due to a decree that one may come to stoke the coals on Shabbos.[353]

B. A bathhouse which was heated on Shabbos by a gentile:[354]

Majority gentile population: A city with a Jewish and gentile population which has a bathhouse that is bathed in on Shabbos, if [the city] has a majority gentile population it is permitted to bathe in the water immediately after Shabbos being that one can assume that it was heated on Shabbos on behalf of gentiles which are the majority of the population.

Majority Jewish population: [However] if majority of the population are Jews then one must wait [after Shabbos] the amount of time it takes to heat [the water].[355]

Half-Half: Furthermore] even if the population is [exactly] half [Jewish] and half [gentile] one must wait the above amount of time because it can be assumed that it was heated on Shabbos for both [Jew and gentile].

Summary:

If one began heating the water before Shabbos and it did not reach its halfway point by the commencement of Shabbos, it is forbidden for all Jews to benefit from it until enough time passes after Shabbos for the water to heat. If a gentile heated it on Shabbos, then if majority of the customers are Jews one must wait until enough time passes after Shabbos for it to be able to heat up.

Q&A

Does one follow majority of the city's population or majority of the cliental?[356]
Majority of the cliental.

If the water was heated by a Jew on Shabbos what is the law?
It is permitted to be used by all other Jews immediately after Shabbos.[357]

---

[351] SSH"K 14:13
[352] Admur 326:11; Michaber 326:11; Shabbos 40a
[353] Seemingly this is referring to a case that the water was not heated to its half way point from before Shabbos. However even then Tzaruch Iyun from chapter 254 Q&A there.
[354] Admur 326:13; Michaber 336:13; Mishneh Machshirin 2:5
[355] As although on Shabbos itself only gentiles bathe in it, nevertheless the main intention of heating it was so that the water be heated for the Jews to be able to use immediately after Shabbos. [Mishneh Berurah 326:37]
[356] M"B 326:36
[357] See The laws of Cooking chapter 2 Halacha 1

If one visits a country club which heats their water on Shabbos may one bathe in that water after Shabbos?

If it was heated by a Jew, then yes. If it was heated by a gentile then one may only enter the heated water if enough time passes after Shabbos for the pool to have been heated, if majority of its customers are Jewish.

THE LAWS OF OILING ONE'S SKIN, AND OILING LEATHER ON SHABBOS

Based on: Shulchan Aruch Chapter 327

TRANSLATION- CHAPTER 327
The laws of smearing on Shabbos
Contains 5 Halachas

Introduction:

The following chapter will discuss the laws of smearing oil on one's body. The problem with doing so at times is that it falls under the decree made against healing. In continuation of this the laws of oiling leather will also be discussed.

Halacha 1
Smearing oil for medical treatment:

Applying a liquid ointment: One that has a pain in his hips is not allowed to smear (a mixture of) oil and vinegar [on it] because it is only common to smear it for healing purposes and any action done which is recognizable that one's intent [in doing so] is for healing, is forbidden [to be done on Shabbos] for the reason to be explained in chapter 328 [Halacha 1].

Plain oil: However, one is allowed to smear (plain) oil, although not rose oil because it is very expensive and is not commonly found and [thus] it is only common to oil [one's body] with it for healing [purposes]. [Although] if one is found in a place where rose oil is commonly available and it is common for people to smear it not for healing [purposes] then it is permitted to smear it for even healing [purposes].

Places which never smear oil: Those places that are not accustomed to smear oil with exception to when done for healing, it is forbidden [for them] to smear any oil for healing because it is recognizable that the [person is doing so] for healing.

Smearing on one's head: Therefore, it is forbidden to smear [oil] on [ones] head which has sores.

Halacha 2
Giving an oil massage on Shabbos:

It is permitted to smear [oil] and massage [it] with one's hand over one's entire body for pleasure so long as it is done differently than how it is done during the week. Meaning that he is to oil and massage simultaneously [as opposed to first smearing the oil and then massaging it], [as well as that] he is to not apply force [with his hands] but rather is to do it with his hands gently.

[However, it is forbidden to massage one's body with force even for mere pleasure and it goes without saying that this is forbidden to be done in order to exercise and sweat.[1]]

Halacha 3
Using a scratching instrument on Shabbos:

Designated for use during the week: One may not itch with a vessel that is designated for this use as is done during the week unless one's hands or feet are dirty with mud or feces [and he wants to scrape it off with the vessel].

Designated for use on Shabbos: If one has a scratching instrument which is designated for Shabbos then it is allowed, and for this reason it is customary for single girls to have a vessel made of swine hair which is designated for Shabbos as written in chapter 303 [Halacha 27 in Michaber and Magen Avraham].

Halacha 4
Oiling leather on Shabbos:

One may not smear his feet with oil when it is inside a new shoe or sandal because the leather softens through the oil residue and resembles [the prohibition of] tanning [leather].

However, one may smear his feet [with oil] and then afterwards place his feet into his shoes.

As well one may smear his entire body [with oil] and roll on top of leather without any worry [of a

---

[1] 328:47

prohibition] as long as the oil which drips from his body is not enough of the amount needed to tan the leather. [Although] even if it contains enough oil to polish it the leather it is permitted [to be done] as long as that he does not intend [on rolling on the leather] in order to polish it, [as if he does intend then it is forbidden] due to a decree against [coming to] tan.

Halacha 5
Softening and hardening leather on Shabbos:
One who tramples on leather until it becomes hard or one who softens it with his hands and stretches and flattens it the way it is done by professionals is liable for the tanning prohibition.

COMPILATION OF HALACHAS, SUMMARIES AND Q&A

Introduction
The following chapter will discuss the laws of smearing oil on one's body. The problem with doing so at times is that it falls under the decree made against healing. In continuation of this, the laws of oiling leather will also be discussed.
<u>Important note</u>: **Regarding using scented oils- See Halacha 1 Q&A 1 below. This law applies to all cases mentioned in this chapter.**

1. Smearing oil on the body on Shabbos for pleasure:[2]
It is permitted to smear oil one one's body for pleasure purposes.

Summary-Smearing oil on one's body for pleasure purposes:
Is always permitted.

Q&A

May one smear scented oils for pleasure?
Seemingly, if one intends to also create a new smell on his skin in addition to the smearing of oil, then it is forbidden to apply it on Shabbos as was explained in length in "The Laws of Molid Reiach".[3] However if one has no intent at all to create a new smell on him, then this is allowed.[4]

---

[2] Admur 327:1-2; Michaber 372:1-2; Mishneh Shabbos 111a and 147a

[3] Admur 511:7; Taz 511:8; Halachos Ketanos 1:19; Ben Ish Chaiy 2 Tetzaveh 11; Rav Poalim 2:51; Shoel Umeishiv Tinyana 2:7; Minchas Yitzchak 6:26 [see below in opinion of M"B]; Poskim in Kaf Hachaim 128:44 and 511:44 and so concludes the Kaf Hachaim ibid; Magen Avraham 511:11; 128:8 prohibits placing the scent into the water, although he does not mention if this prohibition applies even if the scent was placed from before Shabbos.
The reason: As this case is no different than the case mentioned there of washing one's hands with scented water in which although the main intent is not for the scent, nevertheless since one does also intend in absorbing it, it is thereby forbidden.
Other Opinions: Some Poskim rule the prohibition of Molid Reiach does not to one's skin being the smell does not last, and it is hence permitted to place perfume/cologne on the body on Shabbos. Thus, if one placed the perfume in the water from before Yom Tov it may be used. [Chacham Tzevi 92; Elya Raba 128:8; Ginas Veradim 3:16; Nechpah Bakesef 4; Shaareiy Teshuvah 511:4; Mishneh Berurah 128:23 and so is implied from 511:28; Beir Moshe 1:34 rules one may be lenient by skin, although one who is stringent is blessed; SSH"K 14:32 rules leniently that perfume may be applied anywhere on one's body, as learns the Chacham Tzevi, as brought in M"B] These opinions can draw proof for their ruling from Michaber 327:1 and 328:36 in which the Michaber allows smearing rose oil on the body, and chewing scented gum in the mouth. Admur and the Poskim ibid however learn that the scented oil is permitted because one has no intent for the scent, while the gum is permitted because its intent is only to remove the bad smell.
According to the M"B may one add smells to other parts of one's body other than the hands? In M"B 128:23 he rules that one may be lenient like the Chacham Tzevi and Elyah Raba that one may wash hands with perfume water. However the Minchas Yitzchak 6:26 explains that the M"B himself only allows this to be done to ones hands and not to the rest of one's body, as perfume on ones hands rubs off quicker than on the rest of the body. To note however that the Minchas Yitzchak himself there leans to be stringent like Admur and the other Gedolei Haposkim which prohibit perfume on any part of the body. However Rav SZ"A [brought in SSH"K 14 footnote 92, and so they rule in Halacha 32] learns that the M"B permits applying perfume to any part of one's body.
Placing oil on one's hair: Is forbidden according to all opinions being that hair is considered like clothing to which all agree there is a prohibition of Molid Reiach. [Piskeiy Teshuvah 127:1, Beir Moshe ibid, see Minchas Yitzchak ibid.]

[4] 511:7; Rashal Beitza 2:34; Taz 511:8; implication of M"A 511:10; Kuntrus Achron 511:1 based on proof from many Rishonim [Ramban; Ran; Rosh; Rif]; Neziros Shimshon; Mamar Mordechai; So also brings Piskeiy Teshuvos 327:1 in his understanding of Admur in this Halacha.
The reason: As Holadas Reiach is a light prohibition and is hence permitted if one does not have intent to do so. [Machatzis Hashekel 658:2 in explanation of Rashal; Implication of Admur in Kuntrus Achron ibid] Others however explain the reason is because these Poskim rule one may be lenient by a Pesik Reishei of a Rabbinical prohibition, and especially if Lo Nicha Lei. [P"M 321 M"Z 7 and 511 M"Z 8; Chemed Moshe; Nehar Shalom; Shaar Hatziyon 658:6; as rules Terumos Hadeshen, brought in M"A 314:5; Shaar Hatziyon 316:21; See Beis Yosef brought in Taz 316:3; Admur 314:3 regarding bees] This however is incorrect as Admur rules stringently regarding Pesik Resihei Delo Nicha Lei even by a Rabbinical prohibition, as brought in 316:4 and 320:24]
The ruling of the Gemara and Rama in 511:4: The Gemara Beitza 23a rules one may not place a cup of incense on clothing due to the prohibition of Molid Reiach, and so rules Rama ibid. They do not differentiate between whether one intended to do so or not.
Other opinions: Some Poskim rule it is forbidden to create a smell in clothing even if one does not intend to do so, and it is hence forbidden to place spices on clothing. [Implication of Rama 658:2; Maharil; Rokeiach 219 as explains M"A 658:2 and Admur in Kuntrus Achron 511:1; Implication of Rashi Beitza 23a as brings Admur ibid; and so rules M"A 658:2; Elya Raba 658:3; P"M 511 A"A 11; Chayeh Adam 141:20; Kitzur SHU"A 137:7; Moed Lekol Chaiy 23:46; M"B 658:7 and Kaf Hachaim 658:8 are lenient in a time of need] The reason this opinion is

May one smear thick oil on one's body?[5]
No, the above allowance only applies to liquidly oil, as in such a case there is no smearing prohibition applicable.

May one take a suntan on Shabbos?
Some Poskim[6] rule it is forbidden to suntan even when done for mere pleasure.[7] Other Poskim[8], however, rule that it is allowed when done for mere pleasure[9], and is done in private, and one has no intent to tan his skin. However according to others[10] it is even allowed if he intends to tan the skin being that he himself is not adding any dye.

Compilation-May one rub oil onto his body on Shabbos?

It used to be widely practiced in previous times for people to smear oil on their body for purposes of enjoyment and pleasure. While today this is not as common, people occasionally wish to rub oil on their body for medicinal purposes, or to pamper their skin. Smearing oil on one's body on Shabbos touches upon the following possible prohibitions, that need to be analyzed and negated, in order for it to be allowed.

1. The smearing prohibition.
2. The medicine prohibition
3. The prohibition to apply good scents to the skin.

A. Unscented oils:

For pleasure purposes:[11] It is permitted to smear oil one one's body for pleasure purposes. [Unlike a common misconception, there indeed is no smearing prohibition at all involved in rubbing liquid oil on one's body, as this prohibition is limited only to thick substances that need to be evened when on top of a surface, such as melted wax, lard, and various creams.]

For medicinal purposes:[12] It is forbidden to apply medicine to one's body on Shabbos, if it is recognizable that one is doing so for the medicinal purposes. Accordingly, it is forbidden to smear oil on one's body for medicinal purposes if it is uncommon in one's area to smear oil on the body for pleasure purposes [as is the case today[13]], as it is hence clearly evident that he is intending to apply medicine to his skin on Shabbos. It goes without saying that it is forbidden to apply special medicinal oil to one's skin on Shabbos.[14] However, one may place [even medicinal oils[15]] on his skin by the side of his wound and have it flow and drip onto the wound, as when this is done it is not recognizable that one's intention is for healing.[16]

---

stringent is because we hold that Pesik Reishei is forbidden even by a Rabbinical prohibition. [Chemed Moshe; Nehar Shalom; Shaar Hatziyon 658:6; As rules Admur 316:4; M"A 314:5; 316:9; Taz 315:3; M"B 316:17 regarding bees]

[5] SSH"K 14:27

[6] Minchas Yitzchak 5:32

[7] Due to a dyeing prohibition, and a possible pain afflicting prohibition [if it is very hot], and it being a degrading act which does not keep with the spirit of Shabbos, and it may cometo cause one to smear creams on him, and if done for healing, then due to a healing prohibition as one may come to try to heal himself with herbs. [Minchas Yitzchak ibid-Vetzaruch Iyun Gadol as since people sunbathes for mere pleasure the healing is not recognizable and should be allowed.]

[8] Az Nidbaru 2:30

[9] As if done for healing it is questionable whether it contains the healing prohibition.

[10] SSH"K 18 footnote 70

[11] Admur 327:1-2; Michaber 327:1-2; 328:22; Mishneh Shabbos 111a and 134b and 147a

[12] Admur 327:1 and 328:28; Michaber 327:1; Mishneh Shabbos 111a

[13] See Q&A!

[14] Admur and Poskim ibid regarding rose oil

[15] So is evident from the Halacha there in Admur, and so rules M"B 328:77; Ketzos Hashulchan 136:13, and footnote 20

[16] Admur 328:28; Michaber 328:22; Shabbos 134b

B. Scented oils:

It is forbidden to apply scented oils onto one's skin on Shabbos if one intends to create a new smell on his body through doing so.[17] However, if one has no intent at all to create a new smell on his body and is simply smearing it on his skin for pleasure, then this is allowed.[18] If it is smeared for medicinal purposes, then it follows the same law as above in A.

2. *Giving an oil massage for pleasure purposes on Shabbos:*[19]

It is permitted to smear [oil] *[See Q&A regarding using scented oils]* and massage [it] with one's hand over ones entire body for pleasure so long as it is done differently than how it is done during the week. Meaning that he is to oil and massage simultaneously [as opposed to first smearing the oil and then massaging it], [as well as that] he is to not apply force [with his hands] but rather is to do it with his hands gently.

Without oil-for pleasure:[20] It is forbidden to massage one's body with force even for mere pleasure, and even if oil is not being used.[21] One may however give a gentle massage throughout the entire body.

---

[17] Admur 511:7; Taz 511:8; Halachos Ketanos 1:19; Ben Ish Chaiy 2 Tetzaveh 11; Rav Poalim 2:51; Shoel Umeishiv Tinyana 2:7; Minchas Yitzchak 6:26 [see below in opinion of M"B]; Poskim in Kaf Hachaim 128:44 and 511:44 and so concludes the Kaf Hachaim ibid; Magen Avraham 511:11; 128:8 prohibits placing the scent into the water, although he does not mention if this prohibition applies even if the scent was placed from before Shabbos.

The reason: As this case is no different than the case mentioned there of washing one's hands with scented water in which although the main intent is not for the scent, nevertheless since one does also intend in absorbing it, it is thereby forbidden.

Other Opinions: Some Poskim rule the prohibition of Molid Reiach does not to one's skin being the smell does not last, and it is hence permitted to place perfume/cologne on the body on Shabbos. Thus, if one placed the perfume in the water from before Yom Tov it may be used. [Chacham Tzevi 92; Elya Raba 128:8; Ginas Veradim 3:16; Nechpah Bakesef 4; Shaareiy Teshuvah 511:4; Mishneh Berurah 128:23 and so is implied from 511:28; Beir Moshe 1:34 rules one may be lenient by skin, although one who is stringent is blessed; SSH"K 14:32 rules leniently that perfume may be applied anywhere on one's body, as learns the Chacham Tzevi, as brought in M"B] These opinions can draw proof for their ruling from Michaber 327:1 and 328:36 in which the Michaber allows smearing rose oil on the body, and chewing scented gum in the mouth. Admur and the Poskim ibid however learn that the scented oil is permitted because one has no intent for the scent, while the gum is permitted because its intent is only to remove the bad smell.

According to the M"B may one add fragrance to other parts of one's body other than the hands? In M"B 128:23 he rules that one may be lenient like the Chacham Tzevi and Elyah Raba that one may wash hands with perfume water. However the Minchas Yitzchak 6:26 explains that the M"B himself only allows this to be done to ones hands and not to the rest of one's body, as perfume on ones hands rubs off quicker than on the rest of the body. To note however that the Minchas Yitzchak himself there leans to be stringent like Admur and the other Gedolei Haposkim which prohibit perfume on any part of the body. However Rav SZ"A [brought in SSH"K 14 footnote 92, and so they rule in Halacha 32] learns that the M"B permits applying perfume to any part of one's body.

Placing oil on one's hair: Is forbidden according to all opinions being that hair is considered like clothing to which all agree there is a prohibition of Molid Reiach. [Piskeiy Teshuvah 127:1, Beir Moshe ibid, see Minchas Yitzchak ibid.]

[18] Admur 511:7; Rashal Beitza 2:34; Taz 511:8; Implication of M"A 511:10; Kuntrus Achron 511:1 based on proof from many Rishonim [Ramban; Ran; Rosh; Rif]; Neziros Shimshon; Mamar Mordechai; So rule regarding rose oil, that it may be smeared for pleasure purposes, thus proving that it does not contain a prohibition of creating a new smell if that is not one's intent: Admur 327:1; Michaber 327:1; Mishneh Shabbos 111; So also brings Piskeiy Teshuvos 327:1 in his understanding of Admur in this Halacha

The reason: As Holadas Reiach is a light prohibition and is hence permitted if one does not have intent to do so. [Machatzis Hashekel 658:2 in explanation of Rashal; Implication of Admur in Kuntrus Achron ibid] Others however explain the reason is because these Poskim rule one may be lenient by a Pesik Reishei of a Rabbinical prohibition, and especially if Lo Nicha Lei. [P"M 321 M"Z 7 and 511 M"Z 8; Chemed Moshe; Nehar Shalom; Shaar Hatziyon 658:6; as rules Terumos Hadeshen, brought in M"A 314:5; Shaar Hatziyon 316:21; See Beis Yosef brought in Taz 316:3; Admur 314:3 regarding bees] This however is incorrect as Admur rules stringently regarding Pesik Reishei Delo Nicha Lei even by a Rabbinical prohibition, as brought in 316:4 and 320:24]

The ruling of the Gemara and Rama in 511:4: The Gemara Beitza 23a rules one may not place a cup of incense on clothing due to the prohibition of Molid Reiach, and so rules Rama ibid. They do not differentiate between whether one intended to do so or not.

Other opinions: Some Poskim rule it is forbidden to create a smell in clothing even if one does not intend to do so, and it is hence forbidden to place spices on clothing. [Implication of Rama 658:2; Maharil; Rokeiach 219 as explains M"A 658:2 and Admur in Kuntrus Achron 511:1; Implication of Rashi Beitza 23a as brings Admur ibid; and so rules M"A 658:2; Elya Raba 658:3; P"M 511 A"A 11; Chayeh Adam 141:20; Kitzur SHU"A 137:7; Moed Lekol Chaiy 23:46; M"B 658:7 and Kaf Hachaim 658:8 are lenient in a time of need] The reason this opinion is stringent is because we hold that Pesik Reishei is forbidden even by a Rabbinical prohibition. [Chemed Moshe; Nehar Shalom; Shaar Hatziyon 658:6; As rules Admur 316:4; M"A 314:5; 316:9; Taz 315:3; M"B 316:17 regarding bees]

[19] Admur 327:2; Michaber 327:2; Mishneh Shabbos 147a and Gemara 147b

[20] Admur 328:47 and 327:2; Michaber 327:2; Shabbos 147a as explains Rashi

Other opinions: Some Poskim rule it is permitted to massage the body regularly for mere pleasure, even strongly. [Rambam 21:28 as brought in Shiltei Giborim and M"A 328:46; Rabbeinu Chananael on Gemara ibid; Elya Raba ibid; M"B 327:7 and Biur Halacha 328:42 "Kdei"] Some Poskim rule one may be lenient like this opinion, as this is the main opinion in the Gemara. [Elya Raba ibid; Harav Hamaggid on Rambam ibid; Biur Halacha ibid]

[21] The reason: This is forbidden due to Uvdin Dechol. [M"B 327:7; Tosafus Yom Tov]

For sweat:[22] It goes without saying that this is forbidden to be done in order to exercise and sweat. [See Q&A regarding if one may do so gently for sweat or healing]

Giving a massage:
Is only allowed to be done gently, and not with force. This applies whether it is being done for the purpose of pleasure or sweating. If oil is being used one may only do so by smearing the oil while simultaneously giving the massage.

Q&A
May one give a gentle massage for healing purposes?
Seemingly it is permitted to do so gently, without force.[23] Practically, some[24] write that one may not do so at all, even gently.

May one who feels weak and stressed out receive a gentle massage to give him strength?
It is questionable whether this is considered for healing or for pleasure.[25] Even if this is considered healing, seemingly it is permitted to do so gently, without force.[26] However some[27] write that doing so is considered healing and hence may not be done at all, even gently.

---

3. Smearing oil for medical purposes:[28]
A. Applying oil mixtures for treatment:
Applying oil with vinegar to treat hip pain:[29] One that has a pain in his hips is not allowed to smear (a mixture[30] of) oil[31] and vinegar [on it] because it is only common to smear it for healing purposes[32] and any action done which is recognizable that one's intent [in doing so] is for healing, is forbidden [to be done on Shabbos] for the reason to be explained in chapter 328 [Halacha 1].
Applying an oil and water mixture over a wound:[33] One may not apply a mixture of oil and hot water over a wound, and not over a bandage which is to be placed over the wound being that doing so is evident that it is being done for healing purposes.

B. Applying plain oil for treatment:
Applying plain oil and rose oil to relieve hip pain:[134] One is allowed to smear (plain[35]) oil [on ones hip][36],

---

[22] Admur 328:47; Michaber 328:42; Shabbos 147a as explains Rambam and Rabbeinu Chananael on Gemara ibid and certainly this would apply according to Rashi
[23] Implication of Michaber 328:42 "One is not to step on the body **with force** in order to sweat" and M"A 328:46 that even when done for healing, such as for sweating, it may be done gently; It is unclear from Admur 328:47 if even when done for healing, such as for sweating, it may be done gently. A reason to permit doing so gently is because any matter that is done by majority of healthy people may be done for purposes of healing being it does not appear like healing. [P"M 328 A"A 46] Vetzaruch Iyun
[24] Piskeiy Teshuvos 327:2; See M"B 328:130 in which it is not clear if he means to forbid it completely or only forbids doing so with force
[25] Shiltei Giborim brought in M"A 328:46; M"B 328:130
[26] See previous Q&A!
[27] Piskeiy Teshuvos 327:2; See M"B 328:130 in which it is not clear if he means to forbid it completely or only forbids doing so with force
[28] Admur 327:1 and 328:28
[29] Admur 327:1; Michaber 327:1; Mishneh Shabbos 111a
[30] Admur ibid; Levush 327:1; See Tehila Ledavid 327:1
[31] Admur ibid; Michaber ibid
Other opinions: Some Poskim read the Nussach in the Mishneh that one is not to place wine or vinegar on the area. [Rif; Rambam; Rabbeinu Chananeil; our Girsa in Mishenh; brought in M"B 327:1]
[32] Admur ibid; Levush ibid; M"B 327:1; Rashi ibid
[33] Admur 328:28; Michaber 328:22; Shabbos 134b
[34] Admur 327:1; Michaber 327:1; Mishneh Shabbos 111
[35] Admur ibid; Michaber ibid; Vetzrauch Iyun why Admur placed this in parentheses-see Admur 328:28
[36] The reason: As it is common to smear oil on the body even for pleasure, and it is hence not recognizeable that it is being done for healing. [M"B 327:2]

although not rose oil[37] because it is very expensive and is not commonly found and [thus] it is only common to oil [one's body] with it for healing [purposes].[38] [Although] if one is found in a place where rose oil is commonly available and it is common for people to smear it not for healing [purposes] then it is permitted to smear it for even healing [purposes].[39] [The rose oil however may only be smeared if one has no intent to create a smell on his skin through doing so, as explained in the previous Q&A regarding using scented oils.]

Places which never smear oil for mere pleasure:[40] In these places in which they are not accustomed to smear oil with exception to when done for healing, it is forbidden [for them] to smear any oil for healing because it is recognizable that the [person is doing so] for healing.

Smearing oil on one's head which has sores:[41] It is forbidden to smear [oil] on [ones] head which has sores.

Smearing a wound with oil:[42] One may remove the scab of a wound [with ones hands[43]] and may smear the wound with oil in places that it is common to smear oil also when there is no healing intended as explained above [i.e. for pleasure].

Smearing it with fat:[44] However one may not smear it with fat because it [causes it to] melt and is forbidden for the reason explained in chapter 326 [Halacha 10]

Final stage of the wound:[45] Even in the final stage of the wound, which is defined as when it has already healed and one feels no pain from it, it is permitted to remove the scab and to smear it with oil for mere pleasure [even in places that oil is never smeared for mere pleasure[46]].

Applying oil or water to a bandage:[47] (As well it is permitted to place plain oil) over a pad which will be placed on [the wound]. (However hot water even plain, may not be placed (if the pad is not designated for this purpose) due to a decree that one may come to squeeze it [and be liable for the laundering prohibition], although by oil there is no decree made that one may come to squeeze it as was explained in chapter 320 [Halacha 21].

C. Applying oil or an oil mixture near the wound, having it flow onto it:[48]
One may place [even an oil mixture, even in places that the custom is to only use oil for healing[49]] on his skin that is on the side of the wound and have it flow and drip onto the wound, as when this is done it is not recognizable that one's intention is for healing.

---

[37] Rose oil, is the essential oil extracted from the petals of various types of rose. *Rose ottos* are extracted through steam distillation, while *rose absolutes* are obtained through solvent extraction or supercritical carbon dioxide extraction, with the absolute being used more commonly in perfumery. Even with their high price and the advent of organic synthesis, rose oils are still perhaps the most widely used essential oil in perfumery.
[38] Admur ibid; M"B 327:3; Rashi ibid
[39] Admur ibid; Michaber ibid; Gemara Shabbos 111b
Vetzaruch Iyun Gadol how using rose oil does not transgress a prohibition of "creating a smell" on Shabbos, as explained in "Molid Reiach". One must thus conclude that using such oil is only allowed if one does not intend at all to create a new smell on his body, in which case it is allowed to be smeared, as explained there. However, if one also intends on creating the smell on his body, then doing this would be forbidden. Vetzaruch Iyun why Admur who holds of the prohibition of creating new smells does not make issue of this here in this Halacha. Furthermore, to note there are those [see Piskeiy Teshuvos 327:1] which use this ruling regarding rose oil [which is sourced in the Michaber] to say that there is no prohibition at all to create scents on one's skin. [So rules Chacham Tzevi 92, as opposed to the Taz, Magen Avraham and Admur in chapter 511 which prohibit.] It is thus on the one hand not understood why Admur here did not emphasize the limitation to that it is only allowed when not intended at all for smell, as well as on the other hand one cannot infer from this ruling here the opinion of the Michaber, the same way one cannot infer from here the ruling of Admur of which he makes clear in 511 that he does hold of a prohibition.
[40] Admur 327:1; Rama 327:1; Beis Yosef
[41] Admur 327:1; Taz 327:2; M"B 327:4
[42] Admur 328:28; Michaber 328:22; Shabbos 53b
[43] However, with a vessel is forbidden [Ketzos Hashulchan 136 footnote 22]
[44] Admur 328:28; Michaber ibid; M"B 327:4
[45] Admur 328:28
[46] M"B 328:70; Ketzos Hashulchan 136 footnote 20
[47] Admur 328:28
[48] Admur 328:28; Michaber 328:22; Shabbos 134b
[49] So is evident from the Halacha there in Admur, and so rules M"B 328:77; Ketzos Hashulchan 136:13, and footnote 20

Summary-Smearing oil for healing purposes:

<u>To place the oil directly on the wound</u>: Is only permitted in cases that it is commonly done for pleasure purposes and thus is not evident that one is doing so for healing.

<u>To place the oil near the wound</u> and have it flow onto the wound is permitted in all cases, even in places that oil is not applied for pleasure purposes.

Q&A

May one use medicinal oil for pleasure?[50]

Yes. This may be done even in places in which oil is only smeared for healing purposes.

May one smear oil over itchy skin [however the skin is not cracked or dry]?[51]

Yes.[52]

In our provinces is oil considered something that is only smeared for healing purposes?[53]

Yes. It thus may never be smeared for healing purposes unless done away from the wound, having it flow there, as explained above.

May one smear oil on cracked or dry skin, such as chapped lips?[54]

No as this is clearly evident that it is being done for healing. However, one may smear the oil near the dried skin and have it flow onto the dry area, as explained above. [Thus, for dried lips one may eat a vegetable dipped in oil and thus consequently oil his lips.]

May one smear oil on a baby for healing purposes [such as he has a rash and the like]?[55]

Yes.[56] [However regarding a cream see "The Laws of Medicine" Chapter 2 Halacha 6 if at times doing so may involve the Biblical prohibition of smearing.]

---

[50] See M"B 328:70; Ketzos Hashulchan 136 footnote 20; Piskeiy Teshuvos 327:1

[51] Ketzos Hashulchan 136 footnote 20, and Piskeiy Teshuvos 327:2, SSH"K 34:12, however there he brings Rav SZ"A which rules that this may not be done as he says it is not similar to the final healing process of a wound in which the smearing is merely done for pleasure and not to remove itching.

[52] As this is similar to applying oil to a wound which is in its final stage of healing, which is allowed even though that there too it normally still itches, as explained above.

[53] Ketzos Hashulchan 136:13 and footnote 20

[54] Piskeiy Teshuvos 327:2, and so is implied from Ketzos Hashulchan 136:20 where he doubts whether one is allowed to apply oil to one's feet which have peeled skin in order to prevent the socks from sticking onto his skin and thus causing him to get a virus. [Thus, if even then there is doubt, certainly when ones intent is to heal the skin it is not allowed.]

[55] Beir Moshe 1:36, brought in Piskeiy Teshuvos 327:1

[56] As a child is considered like an ill patient of which it is permitted for one to give them medication on Shabbos.

4. Treating leather on Shabbos:[57]

Introduction: It is Biblically forbidden to tan leather on Shabbos, as stated in Admur 321/2. Softening the leather and oiling leather in order to soften it is part of the Biblical tanning prohibition, and one who does so is liable.[58] If one oils the leather without intent to soften it but with intent to polish it, it is Rabbinically forbidden due to a decree that one may come to oil it in order to soften it and tan it.[59] If one does not have intent either to soften or to polish the leather then it is permitted to do so if he does not oil the leather directly but rather first oils himself and then places the leather on him.[60]

A. Oiling leather:

One may not smear his feet with oil when it is inside a new[61] shoe or sandal because the leather softens through the oil residue and resembles [the prohibition of] tanning [leather].[62] [This applies even if one has no intention to soften it, or even to polish it, nevertheless it is forbidden due to it appearing like softening.[63] If however one intends to soften it or polish it then it is a complete Biblical or Rabbinical prohibition, as explained next.]

Smearing feet with oil: However, one may smear his feet [with oil] and then afterwards place his feet into his shoes [if one has no intention to soften it, or even to polish it[64]]. As well one may smear his entire body [with oil] and roll on top of leather without any worry [of a prohibition] as long as the oil which drips from his body is not enough of the amount needed to tan the leather. [Although] even if it contains enough oil to polish it the leather it is permitted [to be done] as long as that he does not intend [on rolling on the leather] in order to polish it, [as if he does intend then it is forbidden] due to a decree against [coming to] tan.[65]

Summary:
It is forbidden to oil new leather on Shabbos unless one fulfills the following three conditions:
1. One first oils his body and then brings it into contact with the leather
2. One is not doing so with intent to soften the leather
3. One is not doing so with intent to polish the leather.

Q&A
Does the tanning prohibition apply to an already tanned leather item?[66]
Yes.

What is the definition of new shoes?
Some Poskim[67] rule that so long as the shoe has been worn one time it is now considered old.

---

[57] 327:4; Michaber 327:4; Shabbos 141b
[58] Implication of Admur 327:5; M"B 327:12
[59] Admur ibid; M"B 327:16; Shabbos ibid and Rashi ibid
[60] Admur ibid; Michaber ibid; Shabbos ibid
[61] Admur ibid; Rama ibid; Rambam 23:10; See Q&A regarding what actions are permitted to be done to new leather!
The reason: New leather carries the tanning prohibition while old leather does not contain the tanning prohibition. [M"B 327:13] As new leather is commonly softened and hence carries the tanning prohibition while old leather is not commonly tanned. [Olas Tamid 327:6; Tehila Ledavid 327:3]
Other opinions: Some Poskim rule it is forbidden to oil even old shoes. [Raavad, in opinion of Kalkeles Shabbos and M"B 327:12] Practically, it is forbidden to oil even old leather shoes as there are people that are ignorant of Halacha and will come to do so even to new leather. [M"B ibid in name of Chayeh Adam]
[62] Admur ibid; Rama ibid
[63] See M"B 327:15
[64] M"B 327:16
[65] From here we learn that oiling the leather in order to tan it is a Biblical prohibiotion, while oiling the elather in order to polish it is a Rabbinical prohibition.
[66] Tehila Ledavid 327:3 based on Rambam
[67] Tehila Ledavid 327:3 based on Bahag 20 Shabbos

May one oil old shoes on Shabbos with intent to polish it or soften it?
Some Poskim[68] rule that old leather may have any of the above actions performed to it, such as oiling for polishing purposes or softening purposes. However, from Admur ibid it is possible to learn that the softening prohibition applies in all cases[69], and the leniency awarded to old leather is only that one may oil his skin while wearing it, and not that one may intend to do so to soften it or polish it. Practically, one is to be stringent in this matter and not oil any shoe on Shabbos in order to polish it, and certainly in order to soften it, even if the shoe is defined as old.[70]

May one polish shoes on Shabbos?
It is forbidden to polish shoes on Shabbos using shoe polish.[71] Furthermore, it is forbidden to polish it even using oil or other non-colored material.[72] This applies to both new and old shoes, as stated above.
Shining the show with a brush or cloth-no liquid: Some Poskim[73] rule it is forbidden to shine the shoe even without using any liquid, but through rubbing on it a cloth or brush, or even through rubbing one's hands over it.
Cleaning a shoe without intent to shine:[74] It is permitted to clean a shoe on Shabbos if one does not have any intent to shine it. It is permitted to use even a cloth to lightly remove the dust. Some Poskim[75] however write that the custom is to only allow doing so using one's hands or through banging the shoe on the floor, and not through using a cloth.

What is the law if a gentile polished one's shoes on Shabbos?
It is forbidden to wear the shoes until after Shabbos Kdei Sheyaasu.[76] However this applies only if the shoe was not wearable without the polish. If however the shoe was wearable without the polish then it may be used.[77]

B. Softening and hardening leather on Shabbos:[78]
One who tramples on leather until it becomes hard or one who softens it with his hands and stretches and flattens it the way it is done by professionals is liable for the tanning prohibition. [Practically one is to be stringent even by old leather.[79]]

Q&A
May one fold and stretch his leather shoes on Shabbos in order to soften them?[80]
No, doing so contains the tanning prohibition.

---

[68] Tehila Ledavid 327:3; Implication of M"B 327:12 and 13 in the lenient opinion
[69] So is implied from 327:5 in which Admur does not limit the prohibition to new leather.
[70] Conclusion of Chayeh Adam and M"B 327:12
The reason: As a) Perhaps the Rama and Admur ibid did not intend to allow oiling old leather in order to soften it or polish it. B) There are Poskim who rule the prohibition applies equally to old leather. [brought in M"B ibid] C) There are people that are ignorant of Halacha and will come to do so even to new leather. [M"B ibid in name of Chayeh Adam]
[71] M"B 327:12
The reason: This is forbidden due to the dyeing prohibition [M"B 327:12] as well as due to the tanning prohibition. [M"B 327:16] being it is forbidden to polish the shoe due to that one may come to tan it.
[72] This is forbidden due to due to the tanning prohibition [M"B 327:16] and possibly even due to the dyeing prohibition, if by doing so it brings out the color of the shoe. [M"B 327:12; See Sheveut Halevi 7:43]
[73] Zichro Toras Moshe [of Chayeh Adam] 39:2; Bris Olam Miabeid 3; Piskeiy Teshuvos 327:5
[74] Aruch Hashulchan 327:4; Shut Rav Chaim Zonenfeld 38; Shevet Halevi 5:37; Ateres Moshe 1:108; Bris Olam Miabed 3; Piskeiy Teshuvos 327:5 and 302:3 footnote 43 in name of Poskim
[75] Shevet Halevi ibid; Ateres Moshe ibid; Bris Olam ibid; Piskeiy Teshuvos ibid
[76] M"B 327:16 in name of Tiferes Yisrael
[77] Teshuras Shaiy 2:152; Meorer Yesheinim 112; Piskeiy Teshuvos 327:5
[78] 327:5; M"A 327:2; M"B 327:12; Rambam 11:6
[79] See previous Q&A and footnotes there! However see Piskeiy Teshuvos 327:4 that onl;y prohibits doing so to new leather.
[80] Piskeiy Teshuvos 327:4

May one soften a new baseball glove on Shabbos?
No.

May one enter shoetrees into his shoes on Shabbos to upkeep the shoes?[81]
One may do so if his intent is to simply **prevent** the leather from shrinking, such as by wet shoes, [and only if within the process of inserting the shoe tree he does not stretch out the shoe[82]][83]. However one may not do so if his intent is to stretch the leather of the shoe, or to undo its folds, as this action contains the tanning prohibition.[84]

[81] SSH"K 15:48; Piskeiy Teshuvah 308:15
[82] Piskeiy Teshuvah ibid
[83] Michzeh Eliyahu 42 [Rav Pesach Eliyahu Faulk Sheyichyeh, Rav in Gateshead]; Toras Shabbos 302:13; SSH"K ibid
[84] So rules Minchas Yitzchak 9:58; SSH"K; Piskeiy Teshuvos, based on Admur 308:42 which rules: "A shoe, whether new or old, which is fastened onto a shoe-tree is permitted to be removed from it, whether by removing the shoe tree from the shoe or whether by removing the shoe from the shoe-tree, as there is no prohibition involved in moving the shoe-tree, as the shoe-tree has the status of a vessel, and it is just that it is designated for a prohibited use [being that it removes the folds and stretches the leather-Minchas Yitzchak ibid], [of which the law is] that it is permitted to move it in order to use its space, which in this case refers to the inner space of the shoe in which the shoe-tree is inside of."

THE LAWS OF TAKING MEDICINE, TREATING THE SICK, AND APPLYING FIRST AID ON SHABBOS

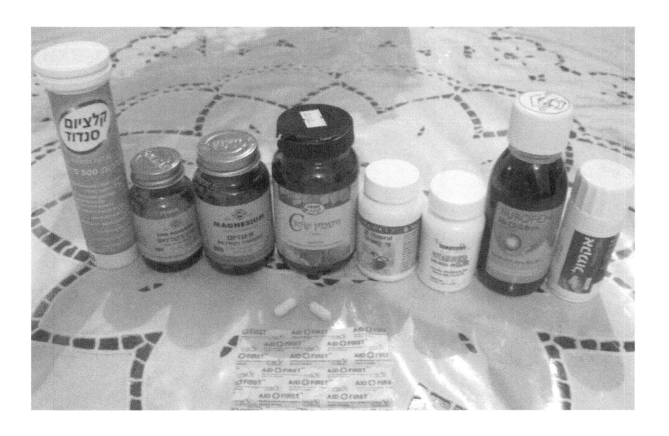

Based on Shulchan Aruch Chapter 328

Translation
Shulchan Aruch
Chapters 328-329

TRANSLATION CHAPTER 328
The laws of a sick person on Shabbos
Contains 55 Halachos

Introduction:

The following chapter will discuss the laws of treating illnesses on Shabbos. Healing on Shabbos is in it of itself a Rabbinical prohibition even when done without any other Shabbos transgressions. At times healing is allowed even when it involves transgressing other Shabbos prohibitions in the process, and at times is forbidden even when no other prohibitions are transgressed.

Healing on Shabbos

Halacha 1
One who is not in danger and can walk:

One who has a mere ache in which there is no concern of danger at all and he has strength, and walks like a healthy person, then it is forbidden to do any form of healing for him on Shabbos even through a gentile, with exception to the ways that will be explained.

Furthermore, even to do something which contains no resemblance even of the slightest to any form of even Rabbinically forbidden labor and there is thus no prohibition at all for a healthy person to do so, nevertheless since [the ill person] is doing so for healing and it is recognizable that he is doing so for healing [therefore] it is forbidden to be done.

The reason for this is: due to a decree that he may come to grind herbs for healing if it were to be allowed to deal with medical issues on Shabbos and he will thus be liable for grinding.

Halacha 2
A life threatening illness:

One who has a life-threatening illness it is a Mitzvah to transgress Shabbos on his behalf [to help heal him] and those which act with alacrity [and do so first] are praised. One who seeks [Halachic advice to verify if he is allowed to save him] is spilling blood [through this delay] and the one who is asked [such a question] is to be ashamed because he should have made a public speech mentioning that it is allowed.

Even a questionable life-threatening situation pushes off [the prohibitions of] Shabbos.

The reason for this because: it says [in the verse] "That one should do and <u>live</u> by them" and what is "and live by them" trying to teach us? It is saying that one should see to it that one will for certain live through doing the Mitzvah and should not [do so if] he will come through this [Mitzvahs] to a case of a possible life-threatening danger.

Must use a known treatment or one prescribed by a medical expert: Nevertheless, even if there is a definite danger one may only transgress Shabbos for medical treatment that is known to all or is done by a professional [doctor]. When it is a known form of healing then even if one does not know if he will be cured through it or not, one transgresses Shabbos out of doubt [that perhaps it will heal].

Halacha 3
A wound in an inner limb:

The definition of an inner limb: Any internal wound, which includes all wounds in limbs that are located from one's teeth and inward, including the teeth [and one's gums[1]], one is to desecrate Shabbos on behalf of [healing them].

The definition of a wound: However, this only refers to [a type of wound that has] impaired one's teeth or any one of the other inner limbs due to a wound, or that has a blister and the like. However mere aches and pains alone [which one knows is not associated with a wound or blister[2]] are not considered a wound and one may not transgress Shabbos for them even if it involves tremendous pain. [However, if one feels great pain and is unaware of whether or not it is a result of a wound or of a blister, then he may desecrate

---

[1] Ketzos Hashulchan 126 Halacha 3
[2] Ketzos Hashulchan 126 footnote 6, and so rules Mishneh Berurah

Shabbos to treat it.[3]]

One who is in so much pain that his entire body feels week: [However] if one is in such pain that his entire body feels [week and] sick then it is allowed to desecrate Shabbos through a gentile even by [having him do] a Biblical prohibition.

One who is not in such pain: (If he is not in so much pain then he is [nevertheless] allowed to have done through a gentile any [form of treatment] which is [only] Rabbinically prohibited) as will be explained [in Halacha 20].

A toothache which has made one weak: Therefore, one who has such a tooth ache that he is in such pain that his entire body feels sick (is allowed to transgress Shabbos through a gentile) [and] may tell the gentile to remove [the tooth].

The reason it is allowed despite ones assistance that he is giving to the dentist: Now, although the Jew is helps him locate the tooth and slightly assists him to take it out, [nevertheless] this does not pose a problem because his help is not meaningful as even if the Jew were to not help him in this assistance [that he is giving] but would also not stop [the gentile from doing his job] the gentile would be able to do it himself.

A toothache which has not made one weak: (And according to those opinions which say that any action which is not done for its own use is only Rabbinically forbidden then it is permitted to remove [the tooth] through a gentile even if the entire person's body has not become sick [so long as it is more than a mere ache] as will be explained [in Halacha 20])

Halacha 4
An inner wound is assumed to be deadly unless known otherwise:
A wound in an inner limb does not need to be evaluated [by a professional] and rather even by a standard wound in which there is no [available] professional to recognize [the danger in such a wound], that it needs an immediate cure [on Shabbos], as well as [even] if the patient himself does not mention anything, one may do for [this patient] anything which is regularly done for [a sick person] during the week.

The allowance to do everything that is normally done on a weekday: [One may make for him] foods and remedies which are good for a sick person, even if there is no danger at all involved in refraining from doing [these actions], as nevertheless there is danger involved in his illness.

If the inner wound is known to not be of danger: However, when one knows and recognizes that this illness [can be] delayed [from being treated now] and thus does not need to have Shabbos transgressed for it, then one is not allowed to transgress Shabbos to treat it even though it is a wound in an inner limb. Certainly, this applies if the patient or a medical professional says that it does not need immediate attention.

Other Opinions regarding doing actions which are not a necessity: [However] there are opinions which say that even in a scenario that one needs to desecrate Shabbos a Jew is only allowed to do those forbidden actions which there is possibility that a lack of doing them can put him in danger. However, any action that if refrained from doing will not cause danger, then even though the patient requires it and it is accustomed to do so for him during the week one may only do so on Shabbos through gentiles as is the law by the needs of any sick person which is not in danger.

The Final Ruling: (One is to follow the latter opinion in these provinces which are likewise accustomed to be strict even regarding an action in which there is danger if refrained from doing, to not do so through a Jew so long as it could be done through a gentile without any wait and delay at all as will be explained [in Halacha 13], thus by an action in which refraining from doing involves no danger at all one is to do it through a gentile even if there is suspicion that he may take his time doing it. However, if there is no gentile available at all then one may rely on the first opinion, although nevertheless every meticulous person should worry for himself regarding [transgressing] a Biblical prohibition).

---

[3] see previous note

Halacha 5
A wound on in outer limb:
[Regarding] a wound which is not in an inner limb one is to council with a medical professional and the patient. If one of them say that it requires desecration of Shabbos or says that if one does not desecrate Shabbos it is possible that the sickness will get worse, and it is a scenario that is possible that if the sickness were to worsen that it may become lethal, then one transgresses [for the wound].

However, if [the illness will] not [eventually become lethal if left untreated] then we do not transgress Shabbos.

Halacha 6
A wound on the palms, swallowing a leech, and getting bit by a poisonous creature:
A wound which is on the back of the hand or back of the foot [not including the back of one's fingers[4]], even if it occurred on its own without getting hit by iron, as well as one who has swallowed a leech, which is a small worm that is found in water and when it comes in contact with the skin of a person it sucks out the blood until it inflames to [the size of a] small barrel, and when a person swallows it in water it sucks moisture out from his stomach and causes his stomach to become swollen, as well as one who was bitten by a rabid dog or one of the deadly creeping creatures, even if it is questionable whether they kill or not, they are considered like an internal wound [of which one is to desecrate Shabbos for].

Halacha 7
A wound from iron, blisters, and fever:
As well Shabbos is to be desecrated for any wound that resulted from iron, even if the wound is on the exterior of one's skin and is not on the back of one's hand and feet.

As well one is to desecrate Shabbos for boils which sprang up by the rectum and on furuncle[5] (which is called flunkero in the vernacular) and for one who has a very heavy fever or even if it is not such high fever, but the fever is accompanied with shivering, meaning with [feeling] cold (called shvidrin in the Yiddish) in a case that the fever and shivering came simultaneously. However, the common fever which is at first hot and then cold involves no danger.

Halacha 8
Treating blood accumulation:
One who has blood build up (in a scenario that could be life threatening) is to have his blood let even if he is able to walk on his feet, and even if it is the first day that he has had the blood build up.

(And if there is no danger involved then he is allowed to cool himself down in water being that doing so appears like he is cooling himself off and not that he is intending to do so for healing)

Halacha 9
Eye Pain
One has not yet begun to heal: One who has a pain in his eyes or in one of his eyes and there is fluid in it or there are tears pouring out of it as a result of the pain, or there is blood pouring out of it or it has pus which continuously congeals, or the pain [feels] like the prickling of a needle or it is burning and feverish, then one is to transgress Shabbos on the outset of all these sicknesses.

The reason for this is: as there is danger at that time because if the eyeball will become removed, he will die because eyesight is dependent on the heart.

One has begun to heal: However towards the end of all these sicknesses, which is defined as when he is already on his way to being healed and there only remains a small amount of the sickness, [such as that] it [only] slightly burns, then one may not transgress Shabbos even through a gentile with exception to a

---

[4] Ketzos Hashulchan 126 Footnote 1
[5] A skin inflammation

Rabbinical prohibition, such as to apply [to the eye a remedy of] herbs which had been grinded the day before [meaning before Shabbos] as will be explained [in Halacha 21].

Halacha 10
What to do in case of split opinion, and is the opinion of an amateur taken into account?

All Doctors agree that is dangerous: Any illness of which doctors say is life threatening, even if it is located on the outside of the skin, one is to transgress Shabbos to treat it.

A split of opinion amongst two doctors: If one doctor says that [it is life threatening and thus] Shabbos must be transgressed, while a second doctor says that [it is not life threatening and thus] one does not need to desecrate Shabbos for it, then one is to desecrate Shabbos for it because in case of doubt that a life is in danger we rule leniently [against the prohibition and force Shabbos to be transgressed]. [However, see chapter 618 Halacha 4 regarding if the patient himself agrees with the doctor claiming it is not lethal, as well see there for other cases.]

An amateur says that the illness may be life threatening: [Furthermore] even if there is no professional doctor [giving an opinion] but there is one person which says that he recognizes the sickness and its appears to him that Shabbos needs to be desecrated, then one is to desecrate Shabbos based on his word because every person is considered to be slightly expertise [in the lethalness of illnesses] and in case of doubt that a life is danger we rule leniently.

([Furthermore] even if [the amateur] says that it is questionable whether one needs to desecrate Shabbos, one is to desecrate it if he says he recognizes this illness).

A split of opinion amongst an amateur and medical professional: Nevertheless, [the opinion of the amateur] does not override the opinion of a professional doctor which says that [the illness] does not require Shabbos to be transgressed even if [the amateur] says that it definitely [is life threatening and] needs Shabbos to be transgressed.

The invalidity of the opinion of an amateur gentile: All the above [leniency to take into account the sole opinion of an amateurs] with regards to a Jewish [amateur], however a typical non- medical professional gentile is not considered like a professional to allow one to desecrate Shabbos based on their opinion when there is no Jew around that recognizes this illness.

Halacha 11
One who refuses to accept treatment:

If [the sick person] refuses to accept the treatment because he does not want Shabbos to be desecrated on his behalf, then he is to be forced [into taking it] as this is a ludicrous form of [supposed] piety.

Halacha 12
A split opinion between the doctor and patient:

If the patient says that he needs a certain treatment [for his illness to be done on Shabbos as he feels that his illness is life threatening] and the doctor says that he does not require [any immediate medication] then we listen to the patient because [only ones own] heart [truly] knows the [severity of the] pain of his soul.

If the doctor claims the treatment requested is damaging: [However] if the doctor says that the requested treatment will damage him [even further], one is to listen to the doctor.[6]

---

[6] However regarding Yom Kippur, the following is Admur's ruling in chapter 618 "Any person which is sick and knows that the day is Yom Kippur and nevertheless says that he needs to eat is to be fed even if a hundred doctors say that he does not need to eat, even if they say that the eating will make things worse. The reason for this is because we do not assume that the person is a sinner that will eat on Yom Kippur, thus if he is saying that he needs to eat despite the doctors he must really feel he needs to eat, which is something that only he can feel and not the doctors." Vetzaruch Iyun!

Halacha 13
Who is allowed to desecrate the Shabbos for the ill person and may one delay doing so until after Shabbos?

May a treatment be started on Shabbos if the doctors say that he will regardless be able to live until after Shabbos? A deathly ill person which was diagnosed on the day of Shabbos that he requires a known treatment which contains Shabbos prohibited labor [and the treatment must be] done for the next eight days, then we do not say "let us wait until night [to begin the treatment] in order so we only transgress one Shabbos". Rather we desecrate Shabbos immediately even though that through doing so one will desecrate two Shabbosim.

The reason: Now, although we know for certain that [the patient] will not die today being that he was evaluated to live through the eight days [of the required treatment], nevertheless we are worried that perhaps he may die after the eight days, if the treatment were not to be started immediately.

Must a treatment that does not involve Shabbos desecration be given over one that does? However in a scenario that one can begin [preparing] the treatment immediately [in a form] that does not contain desecrating Shabbos but [because of this it] will be delayed a slight amount of time [until it is ready to be applied to the patient], then one may not desecrate Shabbos just in order to prepare the treatment in the shortest amount of time possible without any delay, if the situation is that there is no danger at all involved in this short delay [in the application of the treatment].

The reason for this restriction is: because [the prohibitions of] Shabbos are [simply] overruled in a life-threatening situation and are not completely revoked [from being in affect], [thus] in any scenario that something can be done to save a person without desecrating Shabbos, Shabbos is not overruled for him.

Must desecration of Shabbos be done by an available gentile or child rather than an adult Jew? Nevertheless, even [in a scenario that] we have in front of us gentiles and children under the age of Mitzvahs we do not say that [since] one is able to [give the treatment] through these people and avoid desecrating Shabbos through a Jew who is above the age of Mitzvahs [therefore it should be forbidden for a Jew above the age of Mitzvahs to do so. Rather we say that an adult Jew is to do it].

The reason for this allowance is: because since the only option in saving him is through doing an action which is forbidden on Shabbos, therefore Shabbos is overruled on his behalf for [all] Jews which are obligated to save him and there is no transgression of Shabbos here at all.

The Rabbinical prohibition in giving over the job to a gentile or child: Furthermore, even if a Jew wishes to be strict upon himself [to not transgress Shabbos and thus wishes] to do the required labor through a gentile or child, or [he wishes to have them do it] because he does not desire to trouble himself [to do so], there is a Rabbinical prohibition in [him refraining from doing it himself].

The Reason: as perhaps the bystanders will now say that with utter difficulty was [transgressing Shabbos] permitted [to be done] for a life-threatening situation and [they will think that] initially it is not permitted to transgress Shabbos through a Jew that is above the age of Mitzvahs, and this may then lead to that where a gentile or child cannot be found they will not wish to desecrate Shabbos through an esteemed religious leader.

May women be entrusted the responsibility of saving lives? [Furthermore] even by women which are obligated in Mitzvahs [of Shabbos] and there thus exist no such worry [that if given to them to desecrate Shabbos one may think that doing so is not so suitable] nevertheless we do not place upon them alone the responsibility and duty in dealing [with life threatening situations], that [the treatments] should be done through their hands [alone], as perhaps they will be lazy [in doing so with alacrity] or negligent in it.

Having women take part in the treatment: However, women may be joined together with Jewish men, if the man will receive the overall responsibility [of the treatment] and the woman will be directed by the Jewish man, as since the Jewish man is dealing with the treatment, she too will do so with alacrity due to his [presence].

Doing all the treatments through Torah Scholars: Nevertheless, the greatest form of fulfilling this Mitzvah is to try to have all the [necessary Shabbos desecrations] done through Jews which are great [Torah] scholars and not through the simple folk and women.

The reason for why the treatment should not be done by the simple folk and woman is: in order so that

Shabbos not be considered frivolous in their eyes and thus have them come to be lenient even in situations that are not life threatening. As well [another reason that great scholars should do so is] in order to publicly rule through a practical case [that Shabbos is allowed to be desecrated in these situations].

Other Opinions:[7]
Do the labor with an irregularity: [However] there are opinions which say that since [in life threatening cases the] Shabbos [prohibitions] are [merely] being overruled and the [holiness of Shabbos has not been] revoked at all, [therefore] whatever [treatment] is possible to be done without Biblically transgressing [Shabbos] is required to be done through not transgressing a Biblically forbidden action and therefore if one is able to do [a transgression] without suspension and delay through an irregular form [of action used for that transgression], then one is to do it with an irregularity, as through doing so there is no Biblical transgression.
Have an available gentile do it: As well [they say that], if one is able to do [the transgression] through a gentile without any delay at all, then one is Biblically required to do so through a gentile, [as according to this opinion] it was only [Rabbinically] forbidden to do so through a gentile in a scenario that there is worry that he may do so lazily and thus come to delay and suspend [the treatment], however [they did not prohibit asking a gentile] if a Jew is actively supervising him and hastening him in a way that there is no worry at all [of possible delay].

The Final Ruling:
The main Halachic opinion is like the first opinion[8], although the custom in these countries is like the latter opinion. Nevertheless, it is best not to follow this custom[9] because there is worry that perhaps since people will now see that the treatments are only done through a gentile, they will come to think that it is always forbidden to do so through a Jew, and occasionally there will not be a gentile available and the ill person will be endangered as a result of their delay in waiting for the arrival of a gentile.
[However, regarding the dispute in doing the actions with an irregularity the Alter Rebbe here does not give a final ruling, and one thus is to be stringent when there is no delay involved in doing so[10]].
Those who follow the custom must announce to all: At the very least one who wants [to follow the custom and] do so through a gentile is to make it publicly known at that time that it is permitted for a Jew himself to transgress Shabbos [and it is only not being done through a Jew] because a gentile is readily available. [As well when one does the action with an irregularity, he is to announce that in truth it is permitted to do even without an irregularity[11].]

Halacha 14
Being swift to transgress Shabbos when necessary:
Whomever is swift to transgress Shabbos for a life-threatening situation is praised [for doing so] even if [in the process of doing so hastily] he has done with it an additional [unnecessary] transgression[12], such as for example one spread out a net to remove a child that fell in a river and consequently caught with fish with it, as well as any case of the like.

Halacha 15
A baby which has gotten locked in a room:
If a child has gotten locked in a room one may break down the door and take him out, because there is

---

[7] Rama, in the name of the Ramban and Oar Zarua. The first opinion is the view of the Michaber [12] in the name of the Rambam.
[8] So rules Taz.
[9] So rules also Taz and Mishneh Berurah 37, albeit for the reason that the gentile will do so at a slower pace. However according to Admur, even when we know for certain that a gentile will not do so at a slower pace, nevertheless one is to do so himself.
[10] Ketzos Hashulchan 135 footnote 10. See there for reasoning.
[11] Ketzos Hashulchan 135 footnote 10.
[12] Lit. has fixed another matter

chance that the baby will get frightened and die.

Halacha 16
May a kosher animal be slaughtered if there is non-kosher meat readily available?
If there is a deathly ill person [above the age of Mitzvahs[13]] which needs meat and there is no kosher meat available, then] one slaughters [a Kosher animal or bird] for him.

The reason that: we do not say that he should be fed non-kosher food which contains only a prohibition of a negative command [without the capital punishment] rather than transgress Shabbos which is a prohibition [which contains the penalty] of stoning, [is] because Shabbos has already been overruled with regards to lighting the fire and cooking [the meat].

Another reason: As well, in [eating] non-kosher meat one transgresses on every single *kezayis* [of meat eaten] and even if one were to [verify that the ill person only] eat less than a *kezayis* [within the time of Pras], [nevertheless] there is [still] a Biblical prohibition [being transgressed] with every single bite [of the meat]. On the other hand, by slaughtering, one is only transgressing a single prohibition although that it is [more] severe.

Another reason: Furthermore, perhaps the sick person will be disgusted in eating non-Kosher food and will refrain [from eating it] and will thus be endangered.[14]

If one needs to eat meat immediately: Nevertheless, if the sick person needs to eat right away and the non-kosher meat is readily available and the slaughtered meat will be delayed [in arriving to him], then he is to be fed the non-kosher meat.

If one needs boiled wine for a deathly ill person: However[15] if [the ill person] needs wine to be heated up for him, then a Jew should fill up [the pot with the wine so that the wine not become Yayin Nesech] and based on the custom explained above [in Halacha 13] the gentile should heat it up supervised [by the Jew] (see Yorah Deah chapter 153 and 155) that he [the gentile] not touch [the wine] prior to it reaching a boil[16], and even if he touches it there is no problem involved, as even so there will only be a Rabbinical prohibition [involved in drinking it]. This is opposed to if the Jew heats it up in which case, he will be doing a Biblical transgression [and thus according to the custom explained above it is better to have a gentile cook it and take the chance of him touching it. However, based on the above ruling that one should not follow this custom and rather do the transgression himself, the same applies in this case].

There is no need to worry that [if the gentile were to touch it] perhaps the sick person will be disgusted in drinking it being that its prohibition is not so severe.

Halacha 17
If many dates were picked when only one was needed:
[If] the doctors evaluated that [the patient] needs one fig and ten people ran and each one brought back one fig, they are all exempt of liability and they all receive reward from G-d even if [the patient] became better from the first fig.

Halacha 18
Three figs on one stem verses two on individual stems:
If [the patient] was evaluated to require two figs and they only found two figs which were attached [to the tree] each one to a separate stem or on their own, as well as [they found] three figs which were all three attached to the same stem, then one is to cut the stem which has the three on it [rather then cut two

---

[13] See end of next note

[14] Each one of these three reason is itself enough of a reason to slaughter the animal rather than feed non-kosher food to the patient. [Ketzos Hashulchan 135 footnote 6]. The Ketzos Hashulchan [135 footnote 6] adds another two reasons 1) The Mordechaiy says because eating non-kosher food is looked down upon [even in such a scenario]. 2) The Nitziv writes that non-kosher food creates evil tendencies in one's nature. Regarding a child, the Ketzos Hashulchan [there footnote 8] based on Mishneh Berurah rules that one is to rather feed him non-kosher then to slaughter for him on Shabbos.

[15] Meaning that in the following case it is better for the Jew to eat non-kosher rather than have a Jew transgress a Shabbos prohibition.

[16] However once the wine has reached a boil it is no longer prohibited by the touch of a gentile.

individual figs] as although that by doing so one is increasing in the amount of figs [that are being detached] nevertheless he is lessening the amount of detaching [that he must do] which is the main aspect of the prohibition [in detaching fruits].

Two on one stem verses three on one stem: However if there were two on one stem and three on another single stem then one may only cut the stem that has two on it because it is forbidden to increase onto the amount [needed for] the forbidden action to be done, even though that [that in this case cutting the stem with three] is not increasing the amount of effort needed for the action being that [all three figs will be cut] simultaneously.

If the matter is urgent: Nevertheless, if the matter is urgent then we are not particular about this so one not come to push it off and delay it.

Halacha 19
A person which is bedridden or feels weak in his entire body:

Having a gentile do forbidden work: A sick person that is bedridden due to his illness and is not in danger or [a person] that has an ache that pains him to the point that his entire body is weakened due to it, in which case even though he is able to walk he is considered like one who is bedridden, then all of his needs may be done through a gentile, even complete Biblical prohibitions such as to bake for him or to cook for him if he needs this done.

The reason that Bishul Akum has been allowed: Now, although all forbidden foods, even those [forbidden only] Rabbinically, were not permitted for a sick person that is not in danger [to eat from them], nevertheless [the Sages] permitted [this sick person] on Shabbos in which there is no other available option [to eat food cooked by a gentile which contains the prohibition of] Bishul Akum due to that the food is permitted in it of itself and it is only that an action of the gentile is causing its prohibition.

The prohibition for a Jew to Biblically transgress even when there is a limb in danger: However a Jew may not transgress Shabbos in doing a Biblical prohibition even if there is danger of [losing] a limb, so long as there is no danger of life.

The allowance for a Jew to Rabbinically transgress when there is danger of a limb: [However] for a Jew to transgress Shabbos by doing a Rabbinical prohibition [directly] with his hands, such as for example to administer to him any treatment [of healing] which is prohibited due to the decree of [that he may come] to crush herbs[17], even though doing so in it of itself involves no remote prohibition even Rabbinically, or even if it itself does involve doing a Rabbinical prohibition in its process, then it is allowed to be done without any irregularities from the way it is typically done during the week if there is a danger of a limb involved even though he is not bedridden and his entire body does not feel sick.

The allowance for a Jew to Rabbinically transgress with an irregularity when one is bedridden: However if there is no danger of a limb although he is bedridden or is in so much pain that his entire body feels week, then we do not allow a Jew to do something for him which is Rabbinically forbidden unless done in an irregular fashion then the normal way that it is done during the week.[18]

Doing even Biblical prohibitions with an irregularity: [Furthermore] when doing an irregularity it is allowed to even do a Biblical prohibition [if it cannot be done through a gentile[19]], such as for example one who is moaning [in pain from the heart] (of which it is permitted for him to suckle the milk of an animal) with his mouth as will be explained [in Halacha 40], as since he is changing from the regular way in which it is done it is only Rabbinically prohibited.

Medicine for one who is bedridden: However if one needs to eat foods which are recognizable that they are administered for healing, then although doing so is a Rabbinical prohibition due to [a decree] that one may come to grind up herbs as will be explained [in Halacha 43], nevertheless since (this is something

---

[17] But the treatment itself does not involve crushing herbs or any other biblical prohibition.

[18] Now, although earlier we stated that one may ask a gentile to do even a Biblical prohibition, which itself is a Rabbinical prohibition, nevertheless there this is because the Jew is merely commanding the gentile to do so and is not doing any action and thus the Sages were not as strict to require the gentile too to do a Biblical action with an irregularity. [Ketzos Hashulchan 134 footnote 5]

[19] Ketzos Hashulchan 134 Halacha 4

which is impossible to do through a gentile[20] and he is) sick throughout his entire body, [therefore] [the Sages] permitted for him to do so.

Other Opinions: [However] there are opinions which prohibit [the ill person from taking medicine].

The Final Ruling: Regarding the final ruling, in a [dispute over a] Rabbinical prohibition one may follow the lenient opinion.

Halacha 20
One who is in tremendous pain but is not bedridden and does not feel weak throughout his entire body:
Doing a Rabbinical prohibition with an irregularity: If one has not become bedridden [due to his illness] and as well is not suffering so much to the point that his entire body feels weak (but nevertheless is in tremendous pain) then it is allowed to do for him through a Jew any Rabbinical prohibition which will be done with an irregularity even if it is a forbidden action[21].

Doing a Rabbinical prohibition without an irregularity/Taking medicine: However, it is forbidden for him to eat foods which are recognizable that they are being administered for medication, and certainly [to do] other Rabbinical prohibitions without an irregularity [is forbidden] even if they do not contain any resemblance of a Biblically forbidden action. As well [one may not] do a Biblical prohibition through a gentile being that doing so is a complete Rabbinical prohibition which is being done without any irregularity. [However, to have a gentile do a Rabbinical prohibition is allowed.]

One who is only slightly ill:
Having a gentile do a Rabbinical prohibition: If one is not in tremendous pain and does not have a sickness which incorporates his entire body[22] but rather [only] a minor illness, then it is permitted for him to do all Rabbinical prohibitions through a gentile even without [having the gentile do so with] an irregularity as was explained in chapter 307 [Halacha 12].

Having a Jew do a forbidden action: However [one may] not [do any forbidden action, even Rabbinical] through a Jew even when done with an irregularity.

Medication: Therefore [on the one hand] it is permitted to have applied an external medical treatment through a gentile which places [the medicine] on him, since he [the Jew] is not doing any action in having this done. As although he does slightly assist [the gentile] [in applying the treatment] [nevertheless] it is meaningless and does not pose a problem as explained above [in Halacha 3] [and thus is allowed due to it being a Rabbinical prohibition done by a gentile].

(However [on the other hand] it is forbidden for [the sick person] to eat foods that are recognizable that they are eaten as medication as will be explained).

One who has a mere ache:
However, if one is not even slightly sick but simply has a mere ache it is forbidden to do for him even through a gentile any action which is recognizable that it is being done for healing as was explained above [in Halacha 1].

Halacha 21
Giving assistance to a gentile which is giving the medical treatment:
Having the sick person himself assist in his treatment: Anything which is if forbidden to be done [for the ill person] through a Jew is also forbidden to be done by the sick person himself, however if a gentile does it is permitted for the sick person to slightly assist him, such as for example a gentile which is applying ointment to the eye of a Jew towards the conclusion of his sickness in which his [eyes] slightly burn, then it is permitted for him to open and close his eyes in order so that the ointment enter into it well, being that assisting [the gentile] is [considered] meaningless so long as the gentile is capable of doing [the

---

[20] Meaning that here the prohibition is in the actual eating the medication which is something that only the patient can do, and thus should ideally be prohibited due to that it cannot be done with an irregularity, nevertheless this itself is the reason to permit it as there is no other way to administer the medication.

[21] Meaning that even a Rabbinical prohibition which is rooted in a Biblical prohibition is permitted to be done with an irregularity.

[22] Meaning that his entire body does not feel sick due to the illness.

treatment] himself without the help of the Jew and just having the Jew not refrain him from doing it as explained above [in Halacha 3].

[Furthermore] even if the gentile is doing for him a Biblically forbidden action in a scenario where it is permitted [for a Jew to have him do so then] the sick person is allowed to assist him in the way explained [two lines above that the gentile would anyways be able to do it].

The Reason: (Now, although one who assists in doing a Biblical prohibition is [transgressing a] fully fledged Rabbinical prohibition as will be explained in chapter 346[23] and [thus] even upon assisting in doing a Rabbinical prohibition he [transgresses] at the very least a Rabbinical decree upon a Rabbinical decree [which is also forbidden], nevertheless here since [the Sages] rescinded the Rabbinical prohibition of asking a gentile [to do a forbidden act] for the need of a sick person, so too we rescind the Rabbinical prohibition of assisting him being that this too is for the need of the sick person. As through the assistance the treatment is done much better from how it were to be done through the gentile alone, such as for example [having the patient] close his eyes so that the ointment get absorbed in well and so too to open the eyes for the ointment to be entered into, or to open ones mouth for ones tooth to be removed [in which in all of these cases] although the gentile could have done [these actions] himself nevertheless the Sages did not require this, to place this responsibility on the gentile, and not allow the patient, for whom the treatment must be done to, to comply.)

Having another Jew assist the gentile: (However when the gentile does other matters that are forbidden even Rabbinically then a Jew (other than the patient) may not assist him with the treatment since there is no need at all for his assistance being that the gentile is capable of doing it all himself.

However, if there is a need for his assistance that through assisting the treatment will work better than if it were to be done by the gentile alone, then it is permitted for even another Jew to slightly assist him.)

If the assistance is critical for the treatment: [However] if it is impossible to do [the treatment] without the assistance of a Jew then it is forbidden even for the sick person himself to assist.

Halacha 22
The status of a child with regards to desecrating Shabbos on their behalf:
It is permitted to ask a gentile to cook a food for a child which does not have anything else to eat, as the typical needs of a child has the Halachic status of the needs of a sick person that is not in danger [which was explained in Halacha 19 above regarding what may be done for him].

It is permitted to feed a child Muktzah [food[24]] even with one's hands if it is impossible to do so in a different way [meaning that no gentile is available[25]].

Halacha 23
May one ask a gentile to do an action which will only be needed after Shabbos?
[The Sages] only permitted asking a gentile to do something for a sick person if it is needed on Shabbos, however not if it is only needed for after Shabbos.

Halacha 24
Lighting a bonfire for a lethally ill person:
One who let blood: One who has had his blood let and became cold is considered to be in [lethal] danger and one is to make for him a bonfire on Shabbos even in the season of *Tammuz* [the hottest summer month].

Other ill people: However, for other sick people even though they are lethally sick, nevertheless [since] the coldness is not a danger for them as it is possible to warm them up with clothing, therefore one may only make a bonfire for them through a gentile, unless there are no [available] clothes to warm them up with.

---

[23] Perhaps this refers in truth to 347 Halacha 1 and 3.
[24] Such as fruits that fell off the tree on Shabbos and the like
[25] Ketzos Hashulchan 134 footnote 18

Other Opinions: [However] according to those opinions which say any deathly ill person may have done for him through a Jew anything that is normally done during the week [for ill people], even if refraining from doing a particular matter will not cause him danger, (then nevertheless) [here too] one is also allowed to make a bonfire for the patient through a Jew as is done during the week.

The Final Ruling: (It was already explained [above Halacha 4] how one should follow in these countries).

Halacha 25
Placing wine in the eye:
One may not place wine into an eye because it is recognizable that one is doing so for healing purposes, although it is permitted to place it on top of the eye[26] because [doing so] only appears like one is rinsing [his eyelid] and not like he is intending to do so for healing purposes.

Closing and opening the eye: [However] this is only [permitted] so long as that one does not open and close his eyes, however if he does open and close [his eyes] so the wine penetrates into it, then it is recognizable that he is intending to do so for healing purposes and it is thus forbidden.

The law today: Today that it is no longer accustomed to rinse [one's eye] with wine it is forbidden [to rinse one's eye with it] under all circumstances [even if he does not open and close his eyes] if his intention in doing so is for healing.

Halacha 26
Placing tasteless saliva on one's eyes:
Tasteless saliva, which is defined as all the saliva that one has after awaking from his sleep [at night] prior to having tasted anything, is potent and has healing powers, and is forbidden to be placed even on the eyelids being that doing so does not appear as if he is rinsing them as it is not common to rinse with saliva due to its repulsiveness.

Saliva mixed with water: However, if one washes his mouth with water and then passes it on his eyes, then although that tasteless saliva is mixed into that water it is [nevertheless] permitted being that it is not repulsive to rinse [one's eyes] with such water [and thus does not appear that one is doing so for healing purposes].

One who is unable to open his eyes: One who is unable to open his eyes is allowed to damp them even with pure tasteless saliva, being that [the Sages] only prohibited doing so when done with intent of healing and this [purpose to help one's eyes open] is not considered healing.

Halacha 27
Applying collyrium to one's eyes on Shabbos:
Soaking it before Shabbos: One may soak liquidly and clear collyrium[27] before Shabbos and place it over his eyelids on Shabbos for healing.

The Reason: There is no decree here that one may come to grind herbs as since one was required to soak it before Shabbos this thus serves for him as a reminder that he may not make medicines on Shabbos[28]. There is no need to worry that the above gives onlookers a bad impression [and may lead them to think that medication is allowed to be taken on Shabbos] as [rinsing one's eyes with it] simply appears like one is washing them as since [the collyrium] is liquidly and clear it appears to the onlooker as if it is wine.[29]

Opening and closing the eyes: Nonetheless, one may not open and close his eyes [upon placing it on them] as when done so it is evident that that his intentions [in placing it there] [are for healing purposes.

Thick collyrium: However thick collyrium is forbidden to place on one's eyelids on Shabbos because it is

---

[26] Seemingly this refers to placing it on the eye lid when closed. See Rashi on Shabbos 108b

[27] In eye care, a collyrium is a lotion or liquid wash used as a cleanser for the eyes, particularly in diseases of the eye. Pre-modern medicine distinguished two kinds of collyriums: the one liquid, the other dry. Liquid collyriums were composed of ophthalmic powders, or waters, such as rose-water, plantain-water, that of fennel, eyebright, etc, in which was dissolved tutty, white vitriol, or some other proper powder. The dry collyriums were troches of rhasis, sugar-candy, iris, tutty prepared and blown into the eye with a little pipe.

[28] Lit. Deal with healing on Shabbos

[29] However today that no one washes with wine doesn't even this appear like healing to the onlooker?

evident that it is done for healing purposes. Although if one placed it [on his eyelids] from before Shabbos then it is permitted [to be left there over Shabbos] as explained in chapter 252 Halacha 14].

Halacha 28
Removing scabs and applying ointments to it:

Smearing the wound with oil: One may remove the scab of a wound [with one's hands[30]] and may smear the wound with oil in places that it is common to smear oil also when there is no healing intended [i.e. for pleasure] as explained in chapter 327 [Halacha 1].

Smearing it with fat: However, one may not smear it with fat because it [causes it to] melt and is forbidden for the reason explained in chapter 326 [Halacha 10]

Final stage of the wound: Even in the final stage of the wound, which is defined as when it has already healed and one feels no pain from it, it is permitted to remove the scab and to smear it with oil for mere pleasure [even in places that oil is never smeared for mere pleasure[31]].

Applying an oil and water mixture: However, one may not apply a mixture of oil and hot water over a wound, and not over a bandage which is to be placed over the wound being that doing so is evident that it is being done for healing purposes. However, one may place it on his skin that is on the side of the wound and have it flow and drip onto the wound as when done so it is not recognizable that one's intention is for healing. Although it is permitted to place on it plain oil in places that it is common to smear oil even [for pleasure,] when there is no intention for healing. As well it is permitted to place on it plain hot water that was heated from before Shabbos.

Applying oil or water to a bandage:

(As well it is permitted to place plain oil) over a pad which will be placed on [the wound]. (However hot water even plain, may not be placed (if the pad is not designated for this purpose) due to a decree that one may come to squeeze it [and be liable for the laundering prohibition], although by oil there is no decree made that one may come to squeeze it as was explained in chapter 320 [Halacha 21].

Halacha 29
Placing pads and bandages on a wound on Shabbos:

New: It is permitted to place on a wound a sponge and pieces of dry clothing if they are new being that doing do is not done for healing but rather to prevent one's clothing from irritating the wound.

Old: However, one may not place old pieces of clothing on it [being] that they contain healing powers. However, this only applies if [the old pieces] were never yet placed on a wound, though if they had already been placed on a wound then they no longer have healing powers despite the fact that they are old, and it is thus permitted to place them on a wound on Shabbos.

Halacha 30
Placing leaves on a wound on Shabbos:

One may place a [non-Muktzah] leaf over a wound on Shabbos, as it is only placed as a safeguard [from irritation], with exception to grape leaves being that they are used for healing. The same applies for all leaves which heal [that they may not be placed on wounds].

If one placed them [on the wound] from before Shabbos and removed them from it after dark [i.e. after Shabbos already began] even purposely then it is permitted to replace them.

The reason for this is: As [the Sages] only forbade all healing treatments [from being done] due to a decree that one may come to grind herbs, when [the treatment] is being given on Shabbos for its first time, however not when one already began the treatment from before Shabbos and is only returning it on Shabbos.

---

[30] However, with a vessel is forbidden [Ketzos Hashulchan 136 footnote 22
[31] M"B, brought in Ketzos Hashulchan 136 footnote 20

Replacing a dressing which contains ointment on a wound on Shabbos:

Removed purposely: However, a poultice[32] which one removed from his wound purposely, even while still being held in his hand, is forbidden to be replaced due to a decree that one may come to smear and smoothen the bumps that are in it and will come to be liable for the smoothening prohibition as was explained in chapter 314 [Halacha 21].

Fell off wound but did not hit ground: However, if it slipped off the wound on its own after dark [but still remained attached to one's skin] then the Sages did not make a decree in such a case and it is permitted for him to return it. [Furthermore] even if it fell off of him completely it has the same status as if it had slipped away [from only the wound and has remained on his skin].

If fell onto the ground: However, this only applies if it fell onto a vessel. However, if it fell onto the floor then if he wishes to return it [to the wound] it is as if he is placing it on Shabbos for its first time and is forbidden due to a decree that he may come to smoothen it and due to the decree that he may come to grind herbs.

Replacing it through a gentile: Although through a gentile it is permitted to place it on the wound even initially if it is causing him pain and slight illness as was explained above [in Halacha 20]. However, it is forbidden to tell the gentile to initially make the dressing on Shabbos [by smearing ointment on the bandage], as smearing onto the bandage is a Biblical prohibition and doing so through a gentile is a complete Rabbinical prohibition which was only permitted [to be done] if one's entire body has fallen ill or if a limb is in danger [of being destroyed] as was explained above [in Halacha 19].

Removing the poultice to clean the wound: One may open part of the poultice and clean the mouth of the wound and then return it, and then go and open its other side and clean the mouth of the wound and then return it as since he does not remove the entire poultice [in the process] therefore he may return it. However, he may not clean the bandage [of the ointment] being that doing so [transgresses the] smearing [prohibition].

Halacha 31
Applying a poultice on Shabbos to a healed wound:
A wound which has healed one is allowed to place on it a poultice initially on Shabbos being that it merely protects it from getting irritated by his clothes.

The Reason: [The Sages] were not worried that one may come to smear it or [come to] grind herbs as since it has already healed the person is not so nervous regarding it that he will come to smear and grind herbs [to cure it more].

Halacha 32
Puncturing a pimple/boil on Shabbos:
Punctures it to let in air to heal it: One who breaks [open] a boil on Shabbos, if he does so in order to make for it an opening for air to enter through it to heal it, then he is liable for [the prohibition of] "Makeh Bepatish".

The reason for this is: being that he has fixed for it an opening and anyone which fixes an opening in any item detached [from the ground] is liable for fixing a vessel, which is an offshoot of the "Makeh Bepatish" prohibition as explained in chapter 314 [Halacha 2]. And what difference does it make if one has fixed a vessel or fixed a wound, and thus also in the fixing of a hole in the wound contains the prohibition of "Makeh Bepatish".

Now, although one is only liable on a hole made to enter and remove [something] thorough it as was explained there, [nevertheless here too one is liable] as this opening too is made to enter through it air and to constantly remove puss through it.

Punctures it to release the puss that is causing him pain: [However] if one breaks it open only in order to remove its puss which is causing him pain and not in order to enter air into it for purposes of healing, then

---

[32] This refers to a dressing or pad which has ointment smeared over it which is then placed on the wound

it is permitted.

The reason: Now, although that one consequently creates a hole which is fit to [have something] entered and removed through it, nevertheless since he does not have a need for it this is considered an action done not for its own use [which is not Biblically forbidden]. [Furthermore] even according to those opinions which say that an action which one does not do for its own use one is [also] liable on nevertheless here since the liability is due to fixing the wound thus if he does not care for this "fixing" and does not intend for it, then even though it consequently occurs [through him breaking open the boil], [nevertheless] this is not considered fixing at all and is as if he has done nothing. Albeit there does remain reason to decree against doing so due to that he may come to intend to make the hole [for healing, nevertheless] in a case of pain [the Sages] did not make such a decree.

Other Opinion: [However] there is an opinion which says that [the Sages] only permitted [breaking the boil] if one cares in doing so to merely remove its current puss and does not care if the boil will close back up. However, if he desires that it remain open in this form in order for it to constantly remove its puss, then although he does not intend for air to enter through it [for healing] [nevertheless] it is forbidden.

The Final Ruling: It is proper to suspect for this latter opinion and to puncture the boil/pimple through a gentile [when done with intent to remain constantly open].

Halacha 33
Scratching a pimple/boil on Shabbos
However, it is forbidden to scratch a boil [on Shabbos] as doing so removes blood and contains the prohibition of inflicting a wound.

The difference between scratching and puncturing: This is not similar to [puncturing it to remove puss] being that puss is not attached and absorbed within the skin and is rather as if it is deposited there within a vessel and upon opening the boil to remove [the puss] it is merely like one is opening a vessel to remove its content. This is opposed to blood which is attached and absorbed within the skin.

Halacha 34
Widening the hole of a wound on Shabbos and the laws of an Apturah:
A hole that is in a wound which was already opened [from before Shabbos] and one wishes to broaden it on Shabbos even only slightly it is forbidden [to be done].

Unplugging it: However, if it had closed up then it remains questionable whether one is allowed to go ahead and reopen it on Shabbos as it was originally just as it is permitted to reopen a hole of a vessel that got plugged as explained in chapter 314 [Halacha 6].

The hole of an Apturah: As well those that have a hole in their arm that is called (*aptora*) and this hole got slightly stuffed up then there is doubt as to whether or not one is allowed to place legumes inside of it in order to open it.

Placing a poultice on the Apturah: [However] a poultice is allowed to be placed on the (Apturah) being that it is like a wound which has healed which is permissible to place on it a poultice on it (as was explained in this chapter [Halacha 31])

Other Opinion: [However] there is an opinion which prohibits placing [a poultice) on an (*Apturah*).

The Final Ruling: (One is to suspect for their opinion [and thus be stringent]).

Cleaning the Apturah: If one is certain that cleaning [the Apturah] will extract blood then he may not clean it on Shabbos as [although one has no intention to extract blood, nevertheless] it is inevitable.

Switching the bandage of a wound:
By an Apturah: However, it is permitted to switch the current [garment which is covering the Apturah with] a different garment, as if one will not do so then it will smell, and [thus we allow it to be done as we take great precaution] to insure the dignity of people as well as that there is pain from it.

By a wound without a hole: However the above [allowance] only refers to this type of wound [called Apturah] being that it has a hole, however a wound which does not have a hole it is forbidden to change the garment or paper [for another] (because) one draws out puss from the wound (through removing [the cloth] from on it) and it is forbidden due to the "detaching" prohibition, as will be explained [in Halacha 54].

Placing sugar on a wound: Certainly, one may not place [sugar] (*tzuker zlab*) on a wound which does not have a hole.

Halacha 35
Applying wine and vinegar to suppress a wound:

Wine for the un-pampered: One who hurt his hand or leg not as a result of iron may constrict it with wine in order to suppress the blood [flow].

Vinegar: However [he may] not [suppress it] with vinegar because it is potent and thus contains the healing prohibition.

Wine for the pampered: If one is pampered then even wine helps [cure the wound] as does vinegar and it is forbidden [to be placed] when the wound is not on the back of his hand or the back of his foot, as if it is then it is permitted to desecrate Shabbos for it by even doing a Biblical prohibition. Similarly, if [the wound] resulted from a blow from iron [then it too may have Shabbos desecrated for it] as mentioned above [in Halacha 7].

Halacha 36
Dislocated arm or leg on Shabbos:

One who dislocated his arm or foot, which is defined as if the bone came out of its socket, may not rub it with a lot of cold water being that this heals it. Rather he is to wash it regularly [as he washes it during the week] and if it gets healed [in the process] then so be it[33].

Halacha 37
Removing a nail or pieces of skin from ones nail on Shabbos:

If majority of it has begun peeled off: A nail which is in the process of peeling off and cuticles, which are thin strings [of skin] which have [begun] separating off of the skin of the finger that surrounds the nail, if majority of it has peeled off then since they are close to becoming [completely] disconnected [therefore] there is no Biblical shearing prohibition applicable to it even when cut off with a vessel, although it is Rabbinically forbidden [to do so with a vessel].

Removing it with one's hands: However, to remove it with one's hand, [being that it] is not the common way of shearing is permitted to do even initially if they are irritating him, so long as they have peeled off towards the top, meaning that it had begun to peel off on the side of the nail [as opposed to under the nail].

Other Opinions:[34] [However] there are opinions which say that towards the top means towards the body and not towards the nail.

The Final Ruling: One needs to suspect for both explanations [and thus it is never permitted to peel the skin or nail off even when majority of it has begun to peel off[35]].

If only minority of the nail or skin has peeled off: If majority of [the skin or nail] did not peel off and one took it off with his hand then he is exempt [from Biblical liability] although has done a [Rabbinical] prohibition. [However] if one cut it with a vessel then he is liable for shearing. [Furthermore] even according to those opinions that say that an action which is not done for its own use one is not liable on, [nevertheless] there are opinions which say that by shearing one is liable according to everyone for the reason to be explained in chapter 340 [Halacha 2].

---

[33] Lit. "it heals"
[34] Rabeinu Tam. The former opinion is that of Rashi.
[35] Mishneh Berurah 99

Halacha 38
A Toothache:

A minor ache: One who has a toothache may not gargle vinegar and then spit it out being that it is recognizable that he is doing it for healing. However, he may gargle and swallow it or dip a piece of bread into it and eat it as is normally done during the week.

Even through a gentile it is forbidden to do any [treatment] for him even if there is no resemblance of a forbidden action even Rabbinical, if it is recognizable that [the treatment] is being done for healing.

A major ache: However this only applies by a mere [tooth] ache, however he is in so much pain that his entire body is weakened because of it, then he is permitted to do through a gentile [even Biblical prohibitions, and if his entire body is not in weakened but he nevertheless feels pain to the point that he is slightly sick then a gentile may nevertheless do for him[36]] anything which is only Rabbinically prohibited, as was explained above [in Halacha 19].

Halacha 39
A sore throat:

Gargling oil: One who has a sore throat may not gargle oil, which means to retain oil in his mouth [for a period of time] prior to swallowing it as doing so is evident that one's intentions are for healing.

Swallowing oil: However, he may swallow the oil and if he gets healed in the process, so be it[37].

Other Opinions: [However] there are opinions which prohibit to even swallow the oil because [plain] oil damages the body and it is only common to drink it for healing purposes.

The Final Ruling: It all depends on the place and time that one is [living] in, that if it is not common for healthy people to drink it then it is forbidden [to be done].

Drinking the oil down in a drink: However, it is permitted to place a lot of oil in beet juice (*Inigrone*) and then swallow it as in such a case it does not damage the body and it is not apparent that it is being done for healing but rather simply for drinking. Nonetheless one must swallow it immediately and not retain it in his mouth, and it goes without saying that he may not spit it out a then it is recognizable that he is doing so for healing.

Halacha 40
Sucking the milk from an animal:

As a cure for heart pain: One who is moaning from heart pain of which his treatment is to suckle with his mouth from an animal, is permitted to suckle on Shabbos.

The Reason: As doing so is [merely] detaching in an irregular manner as it is not common to suckle milk [from the animal breast] with one's mouth but rather to milk it into a vessel and drink from it, therefore there is no Biblical prohibition involved in this nursing but rather merely Rabbinical and in a case of pain [the Sages] did not make their decree.

Due to hunger: However, this allowance only applies to one with heart pain however one who is merely hungry it is forbidden for him to nurse from an animal on Shabbos.

However, on Yom Tov it is permitted to nurse [from it] (if it is impossible to milk it through a gentile and also if he does not have food into which he can milk into).

Halacha 41
Pumping milk from a woman's breast on Shabbos:

Into a cup and the like: A woman may not squeeze milk from her breasts into a cup or into a pot in order to nurse [the milk] to her child.

The reason for this is: because one who milks into a vessel is completely detaching and is liable for the threshing prohibition, and it was only permitted to do a Biblical prohibition in a case of life-threatening danger.

---

[36] This insert is placed by the Ketzos Hashulchan (chapter 128 footnote 9). Without it the statement contradicts what was explained above in Halacha 19. So rules also Mishneh Berurah 100.

[37] Lit. "then he gets healed"

Trickling milk in order to stimulate her child to nurse: However, it is permitted for a woman to squeeze out some milk [and have it trickle down her skin and the like[38]] in order to stimulate her child to take hold of her breast and nurse. [However, she may not squeeze the milk into his mouth in order to stimulate him.[39]]

The reason for this is because: as since this milk [that is squeezed] is going to waste it does not contain a Biblical "detaching" prohibition, but rather a Rabbinical prohibition as explained in chapter 320 [Halacha 21] and for the need of a child [the Sages] did not apply their decree.[40]

Squirting milk onto one who is spellbound: However, it is forbidden to squirt from her milk onto one who has been overtaken by an evil spell, as he is not in any danger and is not in great pain for us to rescind for him a Rabbinical prohibition to be done through a Jew, as [opposed to] what was permitted by one who has heart ache and the like. See chapter 330 [Halacha 9].

Halacha 42
Chewing gum and applying [liquid] toothpaste to one's teeth:

For medical purposes: One may not chew a species of resin called Mastichi[41] and may not rub a drug on one's teeth when one's intention in doing so is for healing purposes.

To remove bad odor: However, if he is only doing so to [remove bad] odor from his mouth, then it is allowed [to rub an herb or chew the gum].[42]

Halacha 43
Taking medications and foods which are eaten for medication.

Eating foods and drinks that are common day foods for medication: All foods and drinks which are foods [eaten] by healthy people is allowed to be eaten and drank for healing even though they have bad side effects for certain things, and it is thus slightly recognizable that one's intention is for healing.

Example: For example [to eat the] spleen [of an animal] which is bad for ones stomach but helps and is good for teeth, or a vetch[43] that is bad for ones teeth but is good to heal the stomach, nevertheless since it is common at times for healthy people to eat it as well when not intending for healing, it is therefore permitted to eat it even when eaten for healing.[44]

Foods which are eaten only for medication: All foods and drinks which are not foods eaten by a healthy person are forbidden to be eaten or drunk for healing due to a decree that one might come to grind spices. However, this [restriction] is only if one has a mere ache and strengthens himself and walks like a healthy person even if it hurts him tremendously, however if his entire body feels sick as a result [of the pain] then even though he strengthens himself and walks, and it goes without saying if he has become bedridden, then it has already explained above [Halacha 19] that there are opinions that permit [him to take medicine].

One who does not intend to eat them for healing: However, if one does not have a any ache at all and does not intend at all [to eat an item] for healing but rather for a different usage, such as for example, one who eats sweet resin and swallows a raw egg in order to sweeten his voice, then it is permitted. However, when he does so intending for healing then it is forbidden even if he is completely healthy and does not

---

[38] See reason and footnote below.

[39] Ketzos Hashulchan 138 footnote 30. See next note.

[40] Thus, one may not squirt the milk into the mouth of the baby as in such a case it is not going to waste. This is unlike the understanding of the Mishneh Berurah [328:112] based on the Shevulay Haleket that one may squirt into the baby's mouth. In the Sharreiy Tziyon the Mishneh Berurah queries how come this is allowed. According to the Alter Rebbe the query does not apply as in truth it is not allowed.

[41] This is a type of resin with a pleasant smell which comes out of a tree. [Mishneh Berurah 114]

[42] See next Halacha note 31

[43] A leguminous plant with small flowers. Use: silage, fodder.

[44] This only applies to actions which are also done for pleasure and satiation and thus are not evident that one is currently doing so for healing, although if the action is done for a type of healing which is not Halachically defined as healing, such as to swallow a raw egg to sweeten ones voice or place mouthwash in ones mouth to remove a bad smell, then when done for healing it is nevertheless forbidden even though it is no recognizable for others. [See Ketzos Hashulchan 134 footnote 16]

have any ache.[45]

Halacha 44
Inducing vomiting:

For no medical purpose: It is forbidden to induce oneself to vomit for a non-healing purpose even during the week because doing so wastes the food that was in his stomach, as by doing so he becomes hungry and goes back and eats again.

To relieve a stomachache during the week: [However] if one is in pain during the week from having eaten too much then it is permitted [to induce vomit] even using a medication.

On Shabbos: [However] on Shabbos it is forbidden to use medication [to induce vomiting] being that this is similar to healing. Although it is permitted to enter one's finger into his mouth until he vomits.

[It is forbidden to induce vomiting on Yom Kippur even if one has a stomachache. See chapter 608]

Halacha 45

Placing a hot empty cup over an aching stomach: One who feels pain in his stomach is permitted to place on it a cup from which hot water had been poured even though [the cup] still contains steam [from the hot water].

Elevating one's ear tendons: As well it is permitted to elevate ones ears, meaning the cartilage of one's ear which at times droop downwards and cause the cheek[46] [bones] to break up[47]. They may be elevated whether by hand or by using a utensil.

Elevating the cartilage opposite one's heart: Similarly one may elevate the cartilage that is opposite the heart which has drooped inwards towards the heart [and thus interferes with breathing[48]].

The Reason that the above is allowed to be done is: because each one of these issues are never healed using medications and thus there is no worry that one may come to grind [herbs], [and hence we allow it to be treated] because one has pain from the above[49].

Halacha 46
Sobering up on Shabbos using different tactics:

Using an oil and salt mixture: Similarly, one who is drunk of which his cure [to make him sober] is to smear [a mixture of[50]] oil and salt on the palms of his hands and feet, it is permitted to smear [the oil] on them on Shabbos for the above-mentioned reason [that normally there is no medication administered for this ailment].

Sniffing ash: One may not learn from this the allowance that some places have accustomed themselves to, to sniff ash of a grinded herb into one's nostrils in order to sober up from ones drunken state, because this ash has similar affects to medication regarding other matters as well, and it is thus relevant to decree upon it that one may come to grind herbs.

Halacha 47
Massages and exercise on Shabbos:

It is forbidden to massage one's body with force even for mere pleasure as was explained in chapter 327 [Halacha 2]. It goes without saying [that this is forbidden to be done] in order to exercise and sweat. Similarly, it is forbidden to exercise in other forms in order so one sweats for healing purposes due to a

---

[45] see previous note for the reason why here it is forbidden when done for healing.

[46] Based on Rashi in Avodah Zara 22b. Vetzaruch Iyun Gadol on the Mishneh Berurah [134] who quotes Rashi to say that it causes the ears to break up, while in Rashi there the version is "the cheeks".

[47] Rashi there "thus putting one in danger" However from the reason mentioned below this does not seem to be the case according to the Shulchan Aruch

[48] Mishneh Berurah 135

[49] Seemingly if there were no pain involved, we would still prohibit it due to that others may come to think that all forms of healing are allowed just like this one is.

[50] Mishneh Berurah 128

decree that one may come to grind and drink herbs which cause one to sweat.

Dealing with constipation:
It is forbidden to press upon the stomach of a [constipated] baby in order to help the feces come out as one may come to give [the baby] to drink medications which causes diarrhea. [However, if the child is in pain and cannot release the bowel movement on his own, then certainly one may even give him medicine, as the needs of a child are like the needs of one who is bedridden.[51]]

Halacha 48
Bathing for healing purposes:
Waters that are commonly bathed in [on Shabbos]: One may bathe for healing purposes in waters of Gerar and waters of Chamson and waters of Tiberius and in the pure waters of the Mediterranean Sea even though that they are salty [and thus have a greater healing affect[52]].[53]

The reason for this allowance is: because it is common to bath in them even not for healing purposes and it is thus not evident that [one is bathing in them] with intent for healing.

Waters that are not commonly bathed in: However [one may not bathe for healing purposes] in foul water of the Mediterranean Sea, and not in flax water[54] being that they are repugnant, and it is [thus] uncommon to bathe in them for non-medical purposes.

To dip and leave: However, this restriction only applies if one remains in the water [for some time], however if one does not remain in them [and rather dips and leaves] then it is permitted [even in the foul waters] being that it simply appears as if he is cooling himself off [in them].

Tiberius hot springs: In places that it is common to only bathe in Tiberius hot springs for healing purposes, then it is forbidden to bathe in them on Shabbos for healing even if he does not remain in the waters [a long time].

Halacha 49
Inducing diarrhea on Shabbos:
Through bathing: One may not bathe in waters that have a laxative effect [causing diarrhea], and not in quicksand.

Through drinking: And one may not drink liquids which cause diarrhea even if they are foods eaten by healthy people [and thus are not forbidden due to the decree of coming to grind spices] and one is not drinking it for healing purposes at all.

The reason for this is because: all the above actions cause pain while Shabbos is called a day of pleasure.

Halacha 50
Charming snakes
One may charm[55] snakes and scorpions on Shabbos so they do not cause injury even if they are not pursuing oneself, and doing so does not contain the trapping prohibition even according to those opinions which hold liable one who does an action that is not needed for itself.[56]

Halacha 51
Eye Care on Shabbos:
One may place a vessel over an eye in order to cool [the eye] down as long as the vessel is permitted to be

---

[51] Ketzos Hashulchan 128 footnote 20

[52] Mishneh Berurah 138

[53] Seemingly although the custom is not to bathe even in cold water on Shabbos, nevertheless for healing it is allowed. Vetzaruch Iyun.

[54] Lit. Water that had material soaking in it

[55] Snake charming is the practice of apparently hypnotizing a snake by simply playing an instrument. A typical performance may also include handling the snakes or performing other seemingly dangerous acts, as well as other street performance staples, like juggling and sleight of hand. The practice is most common in India, though other Asian nations such as Pakistan, Bangladesh, Sri Lanka, Thailand, and Malaysia are also home to performers, as are the North African countries of Egypt, Morocco and Tunisia. Seemingly playing an instrument is allowed on Shabbos in order to restrain a dangerous snake, just like it is allowed to trap them, which is also a Rabbinical prohibition.

[56] As explained in chapter 316 Halacha 17

moved [not-Muktzah].

Similarly, what is done to a person which feels eye pain in which they surround [his eye] with a ring in order to restrain the inflammation [of the eye is likewise allowed to be done on Shabbos].

Halacha 52
Fixing a dislocation or break on Shabbos:

Dislocation: A bone which has become dislocated is forbidden to be returned to its socket [on Shabbos] being that doing so is similar to building (in addition to the fact that all healing treatments are forbidden [on Shabbos when no danger is involved]).[57] Even to rub it a lot with cold water is forbidden as explained above [in Halacha 36].

A Break: However, a bone which has broken may be returned to its place [by a gentile[58]] as if one does not return it there on Shabbos the limb will be in danger and in scenarios of danger for a limb [the Sages] did not make their decree.

Halacha 53
Treating a bleeding wound on Shabbos:

It is forbidden to place a garment cloth on a wound that is bleeding.

The Reason is: because the blood will dye it. Now, although one is ruining [the cloth in this dying, as he is simply staining it] nevertheless it is Rabbinically forbidden [to be done].

A red cloth: It is certainly [prohibited to place on the bleeding wound] a red garment, being that one is fixing it [by dying it with its natural red color].

Squeeze out the blood: It is not allowed for one to squeeze out the blood from the wound prior [to placing the cloth on it] as doing so consists the wounding prohibition as explained above [in Halacha 33].

Wrapping spider webs around it: Thus, how is one to treat a bleeding wound? One is to wrap around it spiders web and cover with it all the blood and the entire wound and afterwards wrap a rag around it.

Other Opinions: There are opinions which question [whether it is allowed] and prohibit wrapping [the wound in] spider webs being that they have healing powers.

Rinsing off the blood: Rather [according to this latter opinion] one is to rinse [off the wound] in water or wine [prior to applying bandage to it] in order to remove the blood which is on the wound and afterwards [one may] wrap a rag on it.

The Final Ruling: It is proper[59] to suspect for this latter opinion, although the main Halachic ruling follows the first opinion.

Kutras Achron in chapter 302:

Cloths that are designated specifically for wiping on: May be used for wiping blood and is not a problem of dying, as we only say a problem of dying when it is not in a way of wiping, or it is but is done to a random cloth.[60]

Halacha 54
Sucking out blood from a wound:

It is forbidden to suck blood with one's mouth from the wound due to the wounding prohibition.

Doing Metzitzah by a Bris: By a circumcision [sucking the blood of the circumcised area] was only permitted because [lack of doing so] poses danger.

Sucking the blood in one's gums: Therefore, it is forbidden to suck blood which is between the teeth [in ones gums].

---

[57] This follows the ruling of the Magen Avraham. However, the Michaber [47] argues and hold that even a dislocation is permitted to be returned on Shabbos. According to all if the doctor says that there is danger of a limb involved then a Jew may replace it. [Mishneh Berurah 145] As well if one is in extreme pain then he may tell a gentile to do it, as explained in Halacha 20.

[58] Or by a Jew with an irregularity as explained above in Halacha 19

[59] Lit. good

[60] Kuntrus Achron in 302

The reason: Now, although that doing so is separating [the blood] in an irregular way, nevertheless it is Rabbinically forbidden.

Placing a substance on a wound which draws out puss and blood: Likewise, it is forbidden to place on a wound a substance which draws out the blood and the puss due to the detaching prohibition, as although the substance is drawing out [the blood and puss] on its own nevertheless since it is being placed there in order to draw it out, it is as if one is wounding and detaching with one's hands.

Halacha 55
Treating constipation with a rectum insert

It is forbidden to place a string[61] into one's rectum as is commonly done for one suffering from constipation, unless one places it with an irregularity, [which is] by grasping it with two fingers and placing it in delicately.

The Reason: [This is needed to be done in order to prevent] tearing membranes [of the rectum] as explained in chapter 312 [Halacha 12].

Inserting an enema: Although it is forbidden to insert an enema[62] even through an irregularity, even if one had prepared it from the day before [before Shabbos] (because of the decree that one may come to grind spices) unless one is sick.

As well even by a sick person one needs to be careful not to come to do a Biblical prohibition (as well) as that if it is possible to do it through a gentile then it is to be done through a gentile.

---

[61] Any cylindrical body such as made of wax or fat or paper or other materials [Mishneh Berura 151]
[62] The insertion of a liquid into the bowels via the rectum as a treatment, especially for constipation.

TRANSLATION CHAPTER 329
For whom may one transgress Shabbos
Contains 10 Halachos

Halacha 1
Extinguishing a lethal fire:
Any life-threatening situation overrides [the] Shabbos [prohibitions], and whoever is quick [to transgress in order to save a life] is praised.

Children or sick people are endangered: Even if a fire ignited in a different courtyard and one is worried that it may spread into one's own courtyard and it will pose danger, such as for example if there is a sick person or children [in his courtyard] and there is no time [for them] to run away before it will reach [them], then one is to extinguish [the fire] to prevent it from spreading.

It is possible to carry them out: Even if it is possible to escape [by carrying the children and ill person] through a Biblically considered public domain, then it is [still] better to extinguish [the fire, rather than escape].

The reason for this is: because extinguishing [a fire] is an action which is not done for its own use [and is thus only Rabbinically forbidden] as mentioned in chapter 278 [Halacha 1], while carrying out a sick person or children which are not able to walk is a Biblical prohibition as explained in chapter 308 [Halacha 81].

Halacha 2
Removing an unknown person from danger on Shabbos:
We do not follow after the majority [of a population's ethnic group] by a life-threatening situation [as will be explained].

A mound fell in an area that a Jew was definitely around: It goes without saying that if there nine gentiles and one Jew standing in a courtyard and a building fell on one of them in that courtyard, and it is not known if it was a Jew [upon whom it fell] or a gentile, that one may undo the mound.

The reason for this is: being that the Jew and the gentiles were set in that courtyard and anything which is set is considered [a ratio of] half and half [even though in truth there is less than half of it] and in a case of doubt regarding if there is a life-threatening situation [to a Jew] we rule leniently.

If one person separated from the group: [Furthermore] even if one person left to a different courtyard and [in that courtyard] a building fell on him in which case it is appropriate to follow the majority [of people, and thus not allow to remove the mound on Shabbos], even so we clear [the rubble] from on top of him.

The Reason: As since the original establishment [of 50:50] has remained in its state (at the time [that the person] left the [50:50] establishment) we therefore consider [this person who separated] as if he were still established with them to be lenient in a life-threatening situation.

If the entire group left one after the other: However, if the [entire] group uprooted from [their original place of establishment] one after the other, and at the time of the uprooting one of the group members left to a different courtyard and there a building fell on him, then one may not uncover it for him.

The reason for this restriction is: as since the original [50/50] establishment has already moved from its place (when this person separated from them) it is thus impossible to be lenient in it due to the concept of a [50/50] establishment and we [thus] go after the majority of which were gentiles.

If the entire group left together: However if the entire group left together, then they are still considered established together and when one person separates from them, he has separated from a [50/50] establishment and one is to undo the mound from on top of him.

An abandon baby in a city of majority gentile population: Likewise, an [abandoned] baby which was found in a city that is majority gentile, there are opinions which say that one may not desecrate Shabbos for him, as since every day everyone separates from their established area we therefore go after the majority (as is explained in Even Haezer Chapter 4 [Halacha 34[63]], [although] see there for opinions which argue[64]).

Halacha 3
If there are many doubts involved in the case:

One which fell upon him a mound and there is doubt as to whether he is still alive or already dead, [and] a doubt if he is under there or he is not under there, and even if one were to say that he is under there is doubt as to whether he is a Jew or a gentile, one is to undo the mound from upon him even though there are many doubts involved.

The reason for this is: because the Torah says "you should live by them" that it cannot be made to lead under any circumstances towards the death of a Jew through keeping the Mitzvahs.

Saving a life even only momentarily:

Even if [the victim] was found to be crushed and is thus is only able to live momentarily, [nevertheless] one is to undo the mound up to his nose and check him [for if he still has life] and if he is still alive then one is to undo the mound and take him out for him to live whatever amount longer [that doing so will allow him to live]. [However] if one did not feel life in his nose, then he has certainly already dead even if he was not crushed.

Checking if the person is already dead:

Whether [the victim] got hit first on his head or first on his feet and one sees that there is no life in his heart, even so one is to check up to his nose, as the main evidence of whether there is life is in the nose, as it says [in the verse] "all that have a soul of life in their nose".

Halacha 4
If the upper part of the mound had dead people found in it:

If one found the upper [bodies in the mound] to be dead one does not assume that the lower ones have already also died and rather is to undo the mound from on top of them as perhaps they are still alive.

There was an incident [which proves this point as a mound fell and the searchers found] the top ones to be dead and the bottom ones were found alive.

Halacha 5
Saving a robber from death on Shabbos:

One who comes through a tunnel [to rob a house] in a scenario that [the robber] has given up his blood and it is permitted [for the homeowner] to kill him [in self-defense], and a mound fell on him there [in the tunnel] one may not undo it for him (as one is not commanded to help him live).

Halacha 6
Fighting battle against gentiles on Shabbos:

For monetary purposes: Gentiles which have sieged a city of Jews, if they have come to for monetary purposes [to loot the town] then one may not desecrate Shabbos.

To defend lives: However, if they have come to kill the inhabitants, even if they have come as they do typically but there is worry that perhaps they have come to kill, and even if they have still not yet come but they are preparing to come, then the town may go out to greet them with weapons and they may desecrate Shabbos on their behalf [to defend themselves].

A border town: A city that rests near the border, then even if the gentiles only want to come for purposes of [taking] hay and straw, one is to desecrate Shabbos as [otherwise] perhaps the city will be conquered [by the gentiles] and from there it will be easy to conquer the remainder of the land.

---

[63] The Michaber there rules like the Rambam, that if majority of the town are gentiles then one may not remove a mound from an Asufi on Shabbos.

[64] The Rama there rules that even if the majority of the population are gentiles one may still desecrate Shabbos to save the Asufis life, as we view the Jews in the city as Kavua and thus is 50:50.

Halacha 7

Other Opinions: There are opinions which say that in these days that we live between non-Jews which loot and kill, then even if they have only come [to steal] money, [nevertheless] one is to desecrate Shabbos due to them.

The reason for this is: because if the Jew will not allow the robbers to steal and loot then they will kill the Jew, and it is presumable that a person does not stand by and allow his money to be taken and there is thus worry that perhaps one person will stand up against the robbers and they will kill him, and this is thus a situation of life and death.

The Final Ruling: Nevertheless, it all depends on the situation.

However, robbers came upon a single person to rob his money, then he is to let them take everything he has and may not desecrate Shabbos even to do a Rabbinical prohibition, with exception to ways explained in chapter 301 [Halacha 38].

Halacha 8

Helping save another Jew:

When there is no danger involved for the rescuer: One who sees a ship, which contains Jews, drowning in the sea, as well as [one who sees] a river that is drowning [another person], as well as [one who sees] a Jew being chased by a gentile then it is a commandment upon every individual to desecrate Shabbos in order to save them, even if there is doubt as to whether they will be saved.

When there is danger involved for the rescuer: Nevertheless, if there is danger [involved in trying to save the Jew] one may not endanger himself in order to save his friend because [in the meantime] he is not within the range of danger. [This applies] even if one is witnessing the death of his friend and even if his danger [in trying to save him] is doubtful while his friend's is certain, nevertheless [he is not to put himself in danger to save him]. [However, see supplement that this is only in accordance to one opinion].

The reason for this is: as the verse states, "You shall live by them" and not that one should come into doubt of death through fulfilling the Mitzvah of "Do not stand by the blood of your friend".

Supplement from Choshen Mishpat Hilchos Nizkeiy Haguf Vehanefesh Halacha 7:

One who sees a friend drowning in the sea or that murderers are coming upon him and he is able to personally save him or to hire someone to help save him, then he is obligated to trouble himself to hire others to save him, and he then returns and collects the money from the victim if the victim has the money, and if not then he may not refrain from [paying to help save him], and if he does refrain from doing so then he transgresses the command of "do not idle while your friends blood is being spilled".

When there is danger involved for the rescuer: Even to enter oneself into a questionable case of danger one must do in order to help save his friend from definite death. (However, there are opinions which argue on this, and Safek Nefashos Lehakel).

Halacha 9

Returning home with the weapons:

Whoever is going out to save may return with their weapons to their towns if they fear from the gentiles to remain in the area of conquest as is explain in chapter 407 [Halacha 3].

Halacha 10

Saving a Jew from forcibly giving up his religion:

One who gentiles are trying to force to give up his religion regarding whether one may desecrate Shabbos to save him was explained in the end of chapter 306 [the last Halacha].

TRANSLATION CHAPTER 330
The Laws of a Yoledes on Shabbos
11 Halachas

Halacha 1

Like a dangerously ill person: A Yoledes [woman in labor] is [considered] like a dangerously ill person and one [thus] is to desecrate Shabbos on her behalf for all of her needs. [Thus, the following may be done:]

Calling a midwife: One may call a midwife for her from one place to another.

Helping her give birth: One may help her give birth.

Turning on the light: At night one may light a candle for her. [Furthermore] even if she is blind and even if the other women which are assisting her do not require this candle, as they are able to fully assist her without a candle, [nevertheless] one lights a candle for her.

The reason: as although she [the patient] cannot see she becomes calmer upon knowing that there is light here, as she tells herself that if there is anything that she needs my friends can see and can do so for me. However, if she were to know that there is no candle here then there is worry that she will become endangered due to fear in her heart, as she will fear that perhaps the assistors are not doing properly what she needs done.

The requirement to use an irregularity upon desecration: Nevertheless [despite the fact that she is considered like a dangerously ill patient], since the pain of a Yoledes is natural and not [even] 1 of 1000 die from childbirth, therefore the Sages were stringent to require one to change [from his way of normally doing the action needed of desecrating Shabbos] in whatever he is able to change in it.

For example: If one needs to bring the woman a vessel through a public area then her assistant should bring it through tying it to her hair which is carrying in an irregular way and does not contain a Biblical prohibition. The same applies for all cases of the like.

If she [the Yoledes] needs oil then her friend should not smear oil on her hair and then come to her [the Yoledes] and squeeze the oil out, rather she should bring it in a vessel which is hanging on her hair, as it is better to carry [the oil] with a vessel in an irregular way, without any other prohibition, then to add in doing the squeezing prohibition, even though that squeezing hair is only Rabbinically forbidden as was explained in chapter 326 [Halacha 5].

Halacha 2

Being a midwife for a gentile woman: One may not assist a gentile to give birth even if the needed assistance does not involve desecrating Shabbos, such as [in a case that] the baby has already detached [from the womb and begun] to exit, in which case removing it does not involve [the prohibition of] uprooting an item from its area of growth. Furthermore, [even] if the Jewish woman is a known midwife and she receives payment [for assisting in birth], in which case it is permitted for her during weekdays to assist gentile women in giving birth due to [that refusing to do so will cause] enmity, nevertheless on Shabbos [since] there is no enmity [involved in refusing to assist, and thus it remains forbidden to help a gentile woman give birth].

The reason that there is no enmity on Shabbos is because: the Jewish midwife is able to excuse herself [from assisting without causing hatred] by saying "Our women which keep Shabbos are permitted to be assisted in giving birth on Shabbos, however your women which do not keep Shabbos it is forbidden for us to assist them in giving birth".

The Law by an Arab woman: [Furthermore] even an Arab woman, which is not an idolater, (and there is thus no prohibition to assist them in giving birth during the week as there is by idolatress gentiles in which it was forbidden due to that she is assisting a idolatress child to be born, nevertheless on Shabbos) it is forbidden [to assist her] due to it being an unnecessary act, as will be explained in Chapter 332 [Halacha 1], (being that it is possible to excuse oneself from giving assistance without causing hatred).

The law by Karite women: However, the Karaim since they keep Shabbos it is permitted to assist them in giving birth (in exchange for reward [and only] in matters that do not contain desecration of Shabbos. [This may be done] due to enmity)

If one is not able to excuse himself without causing enmity: Even by idolatress gentile women if it is impossible to excuse oneself [from assisting] without causing enmity, it is permitted [to assist] in matters that do not contain desecration of Shabbos.

Halacha 3
The definition of a Yoledes: From when is a [woman] defined as a Yoledes [in the process of giving birth] to be allowed to desecrate Shabbos [on her behalf]? From when she sits on the birthing stool[65], or from the time that the blood is drooling out, or from the time that her friends [have to] carry her by her arms due to her not having strength to walk.

Once any of the above has begun to occur one is [allowed] to desecrate Shabbos on her behalf for all her needs which are able to be done now without delay[66].

Calling a midwife: However, to call a midwife from place to place which is a matter which takes time and delay is permitted to be done prior to this [i.e. to her reaching the above mentioned state] from the time that she feels a little [need to give birth], even if she is in doubt.

Preparing matters from before Shabbos: It is proper to beware that when the 9th month arrives one prepares all [the matters that would require desecration in the event she was to give birth on Shabbos] from before Shabbos in order so they will not be required to desecrate Shabbos.

Halacha 4:
Desecrating Shabbos for a woman which is after birth:
First three days after birth: Throughout the entire first three days after birth the Yoledes is considered like a definite dangerously ill person.

The reason for this is because: her limbs are loose, and she is physically crushed.

The allowance to desecrate Shabbos without the orders of an expert: Therefore, one is to desecrate Shabbos on her behalf even if she claims that it is unnecessary, but her comrades claim that she needs it. Even if there is no midwife or doctor amongst them one is to do for her all her needs, as the matters that are done for a Yoledes during the week are well known to all. Even if she eats the foods of other [healthy] people [and thus it appears that she is healthy] we say that [this is because] she temporarily does not feel [her ill state], but [in truth] if she were to eat cold foods or other foods that a dangerously ill person refrains from eating, she would fall in danger.

Not to desecrate Shabbos if medical experts say it's unnecessary: However, if a midwife or a doctor say that there is no need to desecrate Shabbos, [the comrades] are to listen to them.

The reason for this is: because there are many Yoldos which do not have hot food made for them daily, and so is the custom today in some places that they eat on Shabbos the foods heated from the day before.

Halacha 5:
After 3 days but before 7 days after birth:
From [after] three [days after birth] until the end of the seventh [day], if she says "I do not need [Shabbos desecrated] "then it is not to be desecrated even if her comrades claim that she does need [it done].

The reason for this is: because she is no longer considered endangered with regards to those matters which her comrades commonly do for her during the week, and it is [thus] possible for her to wait until the night [after Shabbos to have those things done].

---

[65] A birthing stool is a stool which has been specifically designed for use during childbirth. It allows a woman to sit or squat while giving birth with support to help her if she begins to feel fatigued.
[66] Meaning that those matters which do not take time to do may only be done from when she reaches this state.

If a midwife or doctor say she needs an action done: The above is with exception to if a midwife or doctor say that she needs [Shabbos desecrated for her], in which case Shabbos is likewise desecrated for other ill patients, as was written in chapter 328 [Halacha 10].

If the Yoledes does not voice an opinion: All the above is when she claims that she does not need Shabbos desecrated, however ordinarily when she does not voice an opinion and her comrades do not know [if she needs it done or not], then Shabbos is desecrated [for her]. However, if her comrades say that she does not need [Shabbos desecrated], then it is not to be desecrated.

If the Yoledes claims she needs Shabbos desecrated: However, the above is with exception to if she says "I do need [Shabbos desecrated] ", in which case even if 100 doctors say she does not need Shabbos desecrated, [nevertheless] it is to be desecrated.

The reason for why she is believed over the doctors is: because one's own heart knows the bitterness of his soul, and as will be explained in chapter 618 [Halacha 1] regarding other ill patients.

From after seven days:
From the end of seven days and onwards, even if she says she needs [Shabbos desecrated], it is not to be desecrated for her behalf. Rather she is considered until thirty days like a non-dangerously ill person, of which all their needs may be done by a gentile, with exception to the matter of a heater of which if she needs it, it is to be done by a Jew being that feeling cold is a danger for her for the entire duration of the thirty days, and even in the time of Tamuz.

Regarding if others are allowed to warm up opposite this bonfire [which was heated for her] was explained in Chapter 276 [Halacha 13].

Halacha 6:
How to calculate the 7 days:
These [above mentioned] days are not counted through 24 hours [per day], but rather if she gave birth on Wednesday close to night, then when the entrance of night of Shabbos arrives, it is already the fourth day from her birth, even though she had not completed three 24-hour days until close to the night of Shabbos. The same applies for [calculating] the seven days and thirty days.

Halacha 7:
The law if a woman died r"l during childbirth:
A woman which sat on the birthing stool and died, one is to bring a knife on Shabbos even through a public property, and tear her stomach and take out the baby as perhaps [the baby] will be found alive.

The reason for why we suspect that he is alive: Now, although majority of times the infant dies prior to the mother, nevertheless by the danger of a life we do not follow the majority, and at times it is able to live after its mother's death. Now, although this infant never had a living status, Shabbos is to be desecrated due to doubt just as one who did have a living status.

The reason for why today we are no longer accustomed to tear the mothers stomach: The reason that [cutting the mother's stomach] is not in practice today even during the week is because we are no longer expert in the mother's death to such close proximity that the child still can live, as [we suspect that] perhaps she fainted and if her stomach were to be torn she will die, and thus one needs to wait [to verify whether she has died or merely fainted] and until then the child has certainly died.

Halacha 8:
What may be done for the newborn on Shabbos?
The child which is born on Shabbos may have all of his needs done for him.
One may:
1. Bathe him,
2. Salt him in order so his flesh harden,

3. Bury the placenta in order to warm the infant[67],
4. Cut the umbilical cord,
As all these matters the infant has pain from them if they are not done for him, and since they do not contain any Biblical work the Sages allowed it [to be done].

If the child was born prematurely:

Certainly, born in 7th or 9th: The above allowance applies by a livable baby, which is defined as a baby which was for certain born in the ninth or seventh [month] (such as if the husband separated from her after [the original] marital relations [which got her pregnant]).

Questionably or Certainly born in 8th: However if the child was born in the eighth month, or if it is questionable whether it was born after seventh or eighth, then one does not desecrate Shabbos for him whether for the above matters, whether for matters which lack of performing can endanger him, such as to undo a mound that is over him, unless his hair and nails have completed growing, in which case he certainly was fully developed by the seventh months and it just delayed leaving his mother's womb after having been fully developed. Therefore, even if he is for certain born in the eighth, such as if her husband separated from her after having marital relations, his status is like one who was born in the seventh month for all matters and he is [thus] to be circumcised on Shabbos.

However, if his hair was smitten and his nails are not complete when born, then even if he is questionably a child of the eighth month, his ruling is like one who is for certain of the eighth month for all matters. Furthermore even regarding life threatening matters in which one [is ordinarily allowed to] desecrate [even] when there is a doubt, even by a fetus which never had a living status due that we suspect that perhaps he has developed enough months and his hair and nails are complete, nevertheless here where we see that [his nails and hair] are not complete it is close to certain that he was born in the eighth [month], [and he] would not have been complete until the ninth month, and he hurried to be born prior to the time and he is a stillborn.

Moving the eighth month baby who did not complete his nails/hair: Even to move such a baby is forbidden the same way it is forbidden to move a stone. Therefore, one does not circumcise this child on Shabbos.

The reason he is not allowed to be circumcised on Shabbos: We do not say let us circumcise the child in any event as if the child is a seventh month old then his circumcision overrules Shabbos and if he is an eighth month child then there is no Shabbos desecration here in the circumcision, as it is like merely cutting meat. [The reason for this is] as since it is close to certain that it is an eighth month child the Sages did not want to allow moving him on behalf of his circumcision in a scenario where it is close to certain that his circumcision is meaningless.

Other Opinions: There are those which argue on this and say that since it is possible that he is a seventh month child and all seventh month children are not stillborns despite that their hair and nails have not fully developed, therefore there is no prohibition at all to carry him on Shabbos, and so too he is to be circumcised on Shabbos in any event.

According to all cannot desecrate Shabbos for this child: However, one may not desecrate Shabbos for him according to all whether for matters in which there is danger [for the child] if they are not done, whether for matters that [the Sages] permitted to do for the child on the day that he was born due to his pain even though that [doing these actions] do not contain a Biblical prohibition.

The custom today-To circumcise and move babies born in eighth: Based on this [latter] opinion today we circumcise all children even if he was born in the eighth month as we are not expert in the months of pregnancy as at times a woman conceives near her immersion and at times she does not conceive until later and it is possible that the child is a seventh month child, and even though that his hair and nails have not fully developed he is to be circumcised, and so too it is permitted to move him on Shabbos.

---

[67] This had a supernatural effect in warming the child [M"B]

The Final Ruling: (Regarding the final ruling in a Rabbinical matter one follows the lenient opinion and therefore one who is lenient to move the child like the latter opinion does not lose [following religious law], however with regards to circumcision on Shabbos it is better to sit and do nothing, as it is proper to suspect for the words of the forbidding opinions, [as] although there is no prohibition in moving the child there is a prohibition in circumcising the child on Shabbos for no need as similarly there is a prohibition in cutting the umbilical cord on Shabbos even according to the latter opinion as was explained [above].)

Halacha 9:
Is it permitted for a woman to squeeze out milk from her breast:
Even a child which is for certain an eighth month [child], which is [therefore] forbidden to move according to all, his mother may bend over him and nurse him due to the pain of the milk which pains her. Similarly, she herself may remove with her hands the milk which is causing her pain.

The reason for this allowance is: as since this milk is going to waste it does not contain the [Biblical] detaching prohibition but rather [only] the Rabbinical, and due to her pain they did not decree [against removing it].

Halacha 10:
Straightening the child's limbs:
One may straighten the limbs of a livable child which have dislocated due to the pain of the birth. However, this is only allowed to be done on the day of the birth, however afterwards it is forbidden.
The reason for this is: because it appears like building.

To wrap him in his clothing: However, to wrap him in his clothing in order to straighten his limbs is always permitted as this is the ordinary way of doing things during the week and it does not appear like building on Shabbos. However, an infant which is not wrapped during the week and his limbs have bent on Shabbos, it is forbidden to wrap him in order to straighten them.

Halacha 11
Lifting up the foreskin of the throat:
If the foreskin of the throat of the infant fell it is permitted to place a finger into his mouth and remove the foreskin to its place even though that at times this will cause him to vomit.

Compilation of Halachas Summaries and Q&A

Introduction:
The following chapter will discuss the laws of treating illnesses on Shabbos. Healing on Shabbos is in it of itself a Rabbinical prohibition even when done without any other Shabbos transgressions. At times healing is allowed even when it involves transgressing other Shabbos prohibitions in the process, and at times is forbidden even when no other prohibitions are transgressed.

CHAPTER 1: THE LAWS OF ONE WHOSE LIFE IS IN DANGER

1. The obligation to help save someone's life even if it involves desecrating Shabbos:
A. The Mitzvah and its reason:[1]
One who has a life-threatening illness it is a Mitzvah [and obligation[2]] to transgress Shabbos on his behalf [to help heal him] and those which act with alacrity [and do so first] are praised.

Asking a Rav: One who seeks [Halachic advice to verify if he is allowed to save a person who he knows is in danger[3]] is spilling blood[4] [through this delay] and the one who is asked [such a question] is to be ashamed[5] because he should have made a public speech mentioning that it is allowed.[6] [It is obligatory upon every Rav to be well versed in these laws in order so he does not have to delay a treatment until he verifies the matter in Sefarim.[7]]

If there is doubt whether the situation is life threatening:[8] Even a questionable life-threatening situation pushes off [the prohibitions of] Shabbos.

If there is doubt if the person is alive or dead, Jew or gentile:[9] One which a mound fell upon him and there is doubt as to whether he is still alive or already dead, [and] a doubt if he is under there or he is not under there, and even if one were to say that he is under there is doubt as to whether he is a Jew or a gentile, one is to undo the mound from upon him even though many doubts are involved.

The reason for all the above is because:[10] It says [in the verse] "That one should do and <u>live</u> by them" and what is "and live by them" trying to teach us? It is saying that one should see to it that one will for certain live through doing the Mitzvah and should not [do so if] he will come through this [Mitzvos] to a case of a possible life-threatening danger.

Q&A
If one is not knowledgeable of whether the injury or illness can be life-threatening, is he to ask a doctor/Rav or is he to desecrate Shabbos due to doubt?
Yes, he must ask a doctor/Rav in such a case.

---

[1] Admur 328:2; Michaber 328:2; Mishneh Yuma 83a

[2] As the Torah states "Lo Saamod Al Dam Reiacha" [M"B 328:6; See also Admur 329:8 and Hilchos Shemiras Haguf Vehanefesh 7]

[3] See M"B 328; This means that in the event that

[4] Admur ibid; Michaber ibid; Yerushalmi Yuma 8:5
The reason: As through doing so the treatment is being delayed and he may eventually die due to this delay. [M"B 328:6]

[5] Admur ibid; Yerushalmi ibid; M"A 328:1; M"B 328:4

[6] Admur ibid; M"A 328:1; Terumos Hadeshen 1:58; 2:156; M"B 328:4

[7] Kaf Hachaim 328:10; Mateh Efraim 618:16; M"B 618:24

[8] Admur ibid; Michaber 329:3; Mishneh Yuma ibid

[9] Admur 329:3; Michaber 328:3; Mishneh Yuma ibid

[10] Admur 328:2 and 329:3; Shmuel Yuma 85b; M"B 328:4; Biur Halacha 329:3 "Ela"
Other reasons in Admur-Opinion of Rebbe Shimon Ben Minasya: Rebbe Shimon Ben Minasya in Yuma 85b says the reason one is allowed to desecrate Shabbos is because "Let one desecrate one Shabbos so he can fulfill many Shabbosos". [brought in Admur 306:29 as the reason for why one may desecrate Shabbos; Brought in Tanya chapter 24 as the only reason] According to this reason if one will not come to fulfill many Shabbosos [such as if he will die momentarily regardless, or is a Shoteh or Katan] then he may not desecrate Shabbos. [See Biur Halacha 329:3 "Ela"; Minchas Elazar 1:9]

If the danger is not immediate, and there is time to take advice with a Rav in terms of the proper action, may one do so?[11]

Yes, and so is the custom. The above disparaging of asking a Rav is only when it is an emergency that requires immediate attention.

B. Helping to save a life even he will further live only momentarily:[12]

Even if [the victim] was found to be crushed and is thus only able to live momentarily, [nevertheless] one is to undo the mound up to his nose and check him [for if he still has life] and if he is still alive then one is to undo the mound and take him out for him to live whatever amount longer [that doing so will allow him to live]. [This applies even if the person has no chance of living enough to fulfill another Mitzvah, or guard Shabbos, or to ever regain consciousness, nevertheless for those few moments one is to desecrate Shabbos.[13]] [However] if one did not feel life in his nose, then he has certainly already died, even if he was not crushed.

C. One who refuses to accept treatment:[14]

If [the sick person] refuses to accept the treatment because he does not want Shabbos to be desecrated on his behalf, then he is to be forced [into taking it] as this is a ludicrous form of [supposed] piety.[15] [This certainly applies during the week, that we force him to take a medicine or listen to doctors' orders even to cut off a limb, even if he does not want to do it due to the pain and ridicule he will have to live with.[16]]

---

[11] Aruch Hashulchan 328:2 based on Or Zarua 108 and Gemara Menachos 64a; Shevet Halevi 3:36

[12] Admur 329:3; Michaber 329:4; Yuma 85a

Opinion of Or Hachaim Hakadosh: Some write that one may not desecrate Shabbos for the mere extending of a moment of life unless he will live until the next Shabbos. [Or Hachaim Hakadosh Ki Sisa 31:16] This is seemingly based on the opinion of Rebbe Shimon Ben Minasya in Yuma 85b that the reason one is allowed to desecrate Shabbos is because "Let one desecrate one Shabbos so he can fulfill many Shabbosos", and hence here since he will not come to fulfill many Shabbosos therefore one may not desecrate Shabbos. [Biur Halacha 329:3 "Ela"; Minchas Elazar 1:9] However in truth one cannot say he is based on their opinion as even Rebbe Shimon agrees with the above ruling of the Gemara which is not brought with any differentiation, as even one more moment of fulfilling Shabbos is worthy of desecrating Shabbos, even according to this opinion, while the Or Hachaim requires him to live until the next Shabbos. Furthermore, we do not rule like Rebbe Shimon Ben Minasya! Rather one must say the Or Hachaim is simply giving a commentary according to Derush and not according to the final Halacha. [Minchas Elazar ibid] Other answers on the Or Hachaim are suggested amongst the Poskim and Mefarshim. [See Minchas Elazar ibid in name of many Poskim; Daas Torah; Orchos Chaim; Oheiv Yisrael; Sefas Emes; Minchas Chinuch Moseich Shabbos]

Opinion of Rebbe Shimon Ben Minasya: See above that according to the reason Rebbe Shimon Ben Minasay in Yuma ibid one would not be allowed to desecrate Shabbos if the person cannot live to fulfill another Shabbos, or more Mitzvos on that same Shabbos. [Biur Halacha 329:3 "Ela"; Minchas Elazar 1:9]

Case of Goses, or terminal illness: See Q&A below and Rama Y.D. 339:1; Piskeiy Teshuvos 329:30

[13] Biur Halacha 329:3 "Ela"; Minchas Elazar 1:9

The reason: As in those few moments he can think thoughts of Teshuvah. [Meiri, brought in Biur Halacha ibid; Chasam Sofer Haazinu] Furthermore, even if he cannot think words of Teshuvah, every moment of Jewish life in this world is precious. [Biur Halacha ibid] As every person is given an exact amount of time to live in this world and perhaps, he needs those extra seconds to fulfill his mission and not come back down in a Gilgul a second time. [Halachos Ketanos 2:38; Tzitzis Eliezer 8:15-3; See Piskeiy Teshuvos 329:6]

[14] Admur 328:11; M"A 328:6; Radbaz 4:67; Kneses Hagedola; Mor Uketzia 328; M"B 328:6; See also Admur 618:1 regarding eating on Yom Kippur

Custom of some Tzaddikim: Some Tazaddikim were accustomed to give up their lives rather than be Michalel Shabbos, as they held one may trust in Hashem rather than listen to the doctors. [See Avnei Nezer 7:193 in name of Ramban and Even Haezra] It is likewise recorded that the Riva refused to eat on Yom Kippur despite the doctors' orders and he dies as a result. [Radbaz 1:444] Some Poskim defend this practice. [Avnei Nezer ibid] Other Poskim negate it. [See Radbaz ibid] According to all this may be done only for people that are on a very high level of trust in Hashem. [Sheveit Halevi 8:251] However other people may not rely on a miracle. [Rashba 1:413; Chovos Halevavos Bitachion 4]

[15] The reason: Although in Yoreh Deah 157:1 the Michaber rules like the Rishonim [Rabbeinu Yerucham] that say by all Mitzvos one may choose to die rather than transgress, nevertheless this is only in a case that the gentile wants him to transgress for the sake of transgressing his religion, in which case there is a Kiddush Hashem if he is killed. However, in this case there is no Kiddush hashem involved, and hence one may not be stringent upon himself. [Radbaz ibid]

[16] Mor Uketzia 328

D. No need for atonement:[17]
Anyone which extinguished a fire which posed a possible danger does not need atonement and is not allowed to be stringent on himself and do acts of repentance on it even if he so wishes.[18] [One is not to have any worry or sadness over the fact he had to desecrate Shabbos.[19]]

E. Being swift to transgress Shabbos to save a life even if doing so swiftly involves additional transgressions:[20]
Whomever is swift to transgress Shabbos for a life-threatening situation is praised [for doing so] even if [in the process of doing so hastily] he has done with it an additional [unnecessary] transgression[21], such as for example one spread out a net to remove a child that fell in a river and consequently caught fish with it, as well as any case of the like. [However, if the matter is not so urgent then when possible to lessen the amount of prohibition done, then one must do so as will be explained in Halacha 3B.[22]]

F. If many figs were picked when only one was needed:[23]
[If] the doctors evaluated that [the patient] needs one fig and ten people ran and each one brought back one fig, they are all exempt of liability and they all receive reward from G-d even if [the patient] became better from the first fig.

G. May a treatment be started on Shabbos if the doctors say that he will regardless live until after Shabbos?[24]
A deathly ill person which was diagnosed on the day of Shabbos that he requires a known treatment which contains Shabbos prohibited labor [and the treatment must be] done for the next eight days, then we do not say "let us wait until night [to begin the treatment] in order so we only transgress one Shabbos". Rather we desecrate Shabbos immediately even though that through doing so one will desecrate two Shabbosim. [If, however, one knows that there will be no danger at all involved in delaying the treatment then one must do so.[25]]

The reason: Now, although we know for certain that [the patient] will not die today being that he was evaluated to live through the eight days [of the required treatment], nevertheless we are worried that perhaps he may die after the eight days, if the treatment were not to be started immediately.

Summary of the obligation to help save someone's life even if it involves doing Shabbos transgressions:

It is a Mitzvah to do everything possible to help save a Jews life, even if it involves transgressing Biblical prohibitions, and one who delays doing so even in order to receive Halachic permission is considered to have spilled blood. Even in a case of doubt as to whether the person is in life threatening danger one is to do all that is possible to save him.[26] Even if one will only be able to help

---

[17] Admur 334:28; Darkei Moshe 334:7; Or Zarua 2:38; Chavos Yair 236; Shaareiy Teshuvah 334:2; M"B 334:78 in name of Nezer Yisrael in name of Zechor Leavraham;

Other opinions: Some Poskim rule that an individual may choose to fast for atonement if he desecrated Shabbos Biblically being that Shabbos is Dchuya by Pikuach Nefesh and not Hutar, although we do not rule this way to anyone who asks. [Chavos Yair ibid; see Piskeiy Teshuvos 3287 footnote 61]

[18] The reason: As this can cause himself [or others] to be lax in extinguishing a fire the next time it occurs. [ibid]

[19] Tashbatz 1:54; Shulchan Shlomo 334:4; Chasam Sofer 85 "Just as one is not to be pained for doing Mila on Shabbos, so too regarding Pikuach Nefesh"

[20] Admur 328:14; Michaber 328:13; Braisa Yuma 84b

[21] Lit. has fixed another matter

[22] Based on 328:13 and 18; Biur Halacha 328:15 "Viyeish Lahem Sechar Tov"

[23] Admur 328:17; Michaber 328:15; Menachos 64a

[24] Admur 328:13; Michaber 328:11; Yuma 84b

[25] M"B 328:32

[26] Admur 328:2

him live for a very short amount of time, he is to save him.[27] One who is swift to transgress Shabbos to save a life even on account of doing additional prohibitions is praised.[28] However if the matter is not so urgent then if it is possible to lessen the amount of prohibition done, one must do so.[29] If the patient refuses to accept treatment then he is to be forced into it.[30]

Even if the treatment can be pushed off until after Shabbos one is not to do so, due to worry that perhaps by then he may not be able to be cured anymore by that time.[31]

Q&A

Is one to Daven to Hashem that he does not have to desecrate Shabbos do to Pikuach Nefesh, such as that his wife not give birth on Shabbos?[32]

Yes, one is to Daven for this.[33]

May one study medicine on Shabbos?

One may read books of medicine.[34] However one may not transgress any Biblical or Rabbinical command for the sake of learning medicine and a cure for illness, being there is not any immediate danger in the vicinity.[35]

---

2. On behalf of whom may one transgress Shabbos?

A. Saving a child:[36]

One is to desecrate Shabbos in order to save the life of a child, even though they are not obligated in Mitzvos.[37]

B. Saving a gentile:[38]

One may not desecrate Shabbos to save a gentile.[39] This applies even if the gentile is not an idol worshiper, such as a Yishmaeili, that although one may save his life during the week, one may not do so on Shabbos if it involves Chilul Shabbos.[40] However an idol worshiper, even during the week it is forbidden to save their lives.[41]

---

[27] Admur 329:3

[28] Admur 328:14

[29] Admur 328:18

[30] Admur 328:11

[31] Admur 328:13

[32] Sefer Chassidim 753

[33] The reason: As Shabbos Is Dchuya by Pikuach Nefesh and not Hutra.

[34] Admur 307

[35] Noda Beyehuda Tinyana Y.D. 210; Chasam Sofer Y.D. 337; Chazon Ish 208:7; Piskeiy Teshuvos 328:4

[36] Admur 306:29 in parentheses; see Admur 392:2; M"A 329:2; Even Haezer 4:34 from which it is understood as a simple fact that one is Michaleil Shabbos for a Jewish child

[37] The reason: One may desecrate Shabbos to save a child in order so he fulfill many Shabbasos when he is older. [Admur ibid] However Tzaruch Iyun, as in 328:2 Admur rules that we desecrate Shabbos because of the verse of Vechaiy Bahem. See Biur Halacha 329:4 "Ela" that it is because of Vechaiy Bahem that one may save a child.

[38] See Admur 329:2 and 330:2; Michaber 329:2; Yuma 84b; Avoda Zara 26

[39] See Likkutei Sichos 27 p. 33 that the entire reason one may desecrate Shabbos to save a life is because Shabbos is a sign between us and Hashem, and is not relevant to gentiles.

[40] Admur 330:2

Ger Toshav: Vetzaruch Iyun regarding if one is to desecrate Shabbos for a Ger Toshev, as one is commanded to help him live [see Admur 329:5] Likewise Tzrauch Iyun why no mention is made in Poskim regarding Tzaar Baalei Chaim of the gentile, as is said regarding an animal, and according to some opinions Rabbinical Melacha may be performed for the animal, would not the same apply to a gentile [that is not an idolator] and even more so?

[41] See Admur ibid; Michaber Choshen Mishpat 425:5

Q&A

Practically, today may one give medical treatment to a gentile on Shabbos, and may he desecrate Shabbos on his behalf?[42]

> ➤ *Example: May a paramedic who was called to an area transgress Shabbos to assist a gentile in medical need? May a Dr. that is on call transgress Shabbos on behalf of a gentile patient? May a Jewish bystander call an ambulance if he sees a gentile in need?*

Yes.[43] This is due to fear of spreading anti-Semitism if one were to refrain from assisting a gentile in a time that he requires medical assistance.[44] It is thus allowed to perform even Biblical transgressions.[45]

<u>What to have in mind</u>: Some Poskim[46] rule that while one is desecrating Shabbos on behalf of the gentile, he is to constantly think that he is doing so simply to save himself or other Jews from danger, and then it is considered like a Melacha Sheiyna Tzarich Legufa which many Poskim allow to be done to help save a gentile.

<u>In a situation that no one will know that the Jew did not give assistance</u>: In the event that one knows for certain that no one will discover him ignoring the giving of assistance to the gentile, then he may not desecrate Shabbos on his behalf. Thus, if one sees a gentile in need from his stained windows and it will be unnoticed to anyone that he did not give assistance, then he may not do so if it involves transgressing Shabbos. However, some Poskim[47] rule that in all cases one is to desecrate Shabbos being that it is possible that unknowingly to oneself one may come to refrain from assistance in a case that it will bring enmity.

May one desecrate Shabbos to save a Jew which does not keep Shabbos, or a heretic?[48]

<u>Letter of the law</u>: One may not desecrate Shabbos for a Jew that is Halachically defined as a heretic[49] [Min and Apikores], or one who transgresses even one Mitzvah Lehachis, for the sole purpose of rebelling against the Torah.[50] One may however desecrate Shabbos for a Jew that desecrates the Mitzvos "Leteiavon", for his own person lusts.[51] Some Poskim[52] however rule that one may not desecrate Shabbos for a Jew that desecrates Shabbos in public even if he does so only for pleasure. One may however desecrate Shabbos to save a Jew that is a Tinok Shenishbah, which is defined as one who was brought up with a secular upbringing, even if he does not believe in any of the Torah or Mitzvos and transgresses Shabbos openly.[53] Furthermore, in any case that not assisting the Jew can cause enmity, one is to desecrate Shabbos to help him even if he is defined as Min and Apikores, as

---

[42] Piskeiy Teshuvos 330:3 [new]

[43] See Chasam Sofer Yoreh Deah 131; Coshen Mishpat 194, brought in Pischeiy Teshuvah Yoreh Deah 154:2; Divrei Chayim 2:25; Yad Shalom 57; Kaf Hachaim 330:14; Igros Moshe 4:49; Chelkas Yaakov 2:54, 141; Minchas Yitzchak 1:53, 3:20; Divrei Yatziv 1:53; Tzitz Eliezer 8:15-6; Yabia Omer 8:38; Beir Moshe 5:164; See Piskeiy Teshuvos 329:3 footnote 11

<u>Opinion of Mishneh Berurah</u>: The Mishneh Berurah 330:8 rules it is forbidden to transgress Biblical prohibitions even in a case that it can lead to enmity. Furthermore, possibly even Rabbinical prohibitions are forbidden to transgress. Nevertheless, the Poskim argue on his ruling. [All Poskim ibid; See Igros Moshe and Divrei Yatziv ibid]

[44] Due to the advanced communication and the constant anticipation of reasons to use to hate and attack Jews the matter can lead to actual danger for other Jews if one were to refuse to treat them.

[45] Poskim ibid

[46] Shearim Hametzuyanim Behalacha 92:1; Tzitz Eliezer 8:15-6

[47] Igros Moshe ibid that so was the Takana of the Daled Aratzos

[48] Piskeiy Teshuvos 329:2

[49] See Michaber Yoreh Deah 158:2 and Choshen Mishpat 425:5

[50] Michaber Choshen Mishpat 425:5; P"M 328 M"Z 6; M"B 329:9

[51] M"B ibid; Rama Yoreh Deah 251:2

[52] P"M ibid; Kaf Hachaim 328:8 in name of Kol Yehuda 7; Orchos Chaim 328:4; See Piskeiy Teshuvos 329:5 footnote 20

[53] Rav Akiva Eiger, brought in Beis Meir 330, regarding bneing a midwife to a Mumar woman; Chazon Ish Yoreh Deah 2:28; See Rambam Mamarim 3:3; Piskeiy Teshuvos 329:5 footnote 21

<u>Other opinions</u>: See Beis Meir ibid that one may not desecrate Shabbos for a Tinok Shenishba being that he will not fulfill future Shabbosos; Practically, we do not rule like the Beis Meir, as explains the Biur Halacha 329:4 "Ela".

explained above regarding a gentile.

<u>Ruling today:</u>[54] All non-religious Jews today are defined as a Tinok Shenishbah[55] and one is hence obligated to transgress Shabbos on their behalf of saving them just as with any other Jew. This applies even if the Jew was brought up in a religious home and later left being observant.[56] This is in addition to the fact that refraining from doing so will cause enmity and is thus allowed just like by a gentile[57], as well as that perhaps the Jew has repented due to their illness.[58]

B. Transgressing Shabbos to help save a person which is questionably Jewish:[59]

We do not follow after the majority [of a population's ethnic group] by a life-threatening situation [as will be explained].

A mound fell in an area that a Jew was definitely around:[60] It goes without saying that if there nine gentiles and one Jew standing in a courtyard and a building fell on one of them in that courtyard, and it is not known if it was a Jew [upon whom it fell] or a gentile, that one may undo the mound.

The reason for this is:[61] being that the Jew and the gentiles were set in that courtyard and anything which is set is considered [a ratio of] half and half [even though in truth there is less than half of it] and in a case of doubt regarding if there is a life-threatening situation [to a Jew] we rule leniently.

If one person separated from the group:[62] [Furthermore] even if one person left to a different courtyard and [in that courtyard] a building fell on him in which case it is appropriate to follow the majority [of people, and thus not allow to remove the mound on Shabbos], even so we clear [the rubble] from on top of him.

The Reason:[63] As since the original establishment [of 50:50] has remained in its state (at the time [that the person] left the [50:50] establishment[64]) we therefore consider [this person who separated] as if he were still established with them to be lenient in a life-threatening situation. [Meaning that the novelty of the leniency by Pikuach Nefesh is that even though in general we apply the rule of that whenever the item separates, we follow majority, by Pikuach Nefesh we still extend the status of Kavua, even when one separated.[65]]

If the entire group left one after the other:[66] However if the [entire] group uprooted from [their original place of establishment] one after the other[67], and at the time of the uprooting one of the group members left to a different courtyard and there a building fell on him, then one may not uncover it for him.

The reason for this restriction is:[68] as since the original [50/50] establishment has already moved from its

[54] Chazon Ish Yoreh Deah 2:16 and 28; See Yaavetz 1:30; Chasam Sofer Y.D. 341; Maharhm Shick 140; Beis Yitzchak Y.D. Treifos 29; Hisorerus Teshuvah 1:169; Chelkas Yaakov 1:45 and 154; Minchas Yitzchak 1:53; 3:20; 10:31 letter 14; 10:151; Igros Moshe E.H. 2:59; Sheivet Halevy 3:36; 5:48; 10:65; Mishneh Halachos 5:55; Tzitz Eliezer 8:15; 9:17; Yabia Omer 8:38; Piskeiy Teshuvos 329:5 and footnote 23

[55] This applies even though they are fully aware of the Jewish religion, and know full well that they are Jewish, nevertheless they are considered Anuss/Tinok Shenishba being that they grew up with a secular upbringing, and according to all opinions are not considered to be in the category of Moridin/heretic. [Admur Ribis 79; Darkei Moshe 159; Rambam Mamarim 3:3; Chazon Ish Yoreh Deah 2:16; Zekan Ahron 12; Binyan Tziyon 23; Milameid Lehoil 29;]

<u>Other opinions:</u> Some Poskim rule that those Tinokos Shenishbu which discovered that they are Jewish and are aware of the Jewish religion and nonetheless continue their secular lifestyle are not considered Tinokos Shenishbu. [Ramban and Nimmukei Yosef brought in Darkei Moshe ibid and Beis Yosef Y.D. 159; See also Teshuvos Vehanhagos 5:95; 6:90; Bina Vedaas Miluim in anme of Rav SZ"A; Betzeil Hachochma 2:76; Shevet Halevi 9:198; Yissa Yosef 3:97; See Piskeiy Teshuvos ibid footnote 22] Nevertheless, even according to this approach it is still permitted/obligated to desecrate Shabbos on their behalf due to enmity, as we rule by gentiles.

[56] Chazon Ish Yoreh Deah 2:16; See Minchas Asher 1:10; Piskeiy Teshuvos 329:5 and footnote 24

[57] Minchas Yitzchak ibid

[58] Chasam Sofer Y.D. 341; Mahrahm Shick 140; Yisa Yosef ibid

[59] Admur 329:2; Michaber 329:2; Yuma Mishneh 83a and Gemara 84b

[60] Admur ibid; M"B 329:3; Yuma ibid

[61] Admur ibid; Yuma ibid

[62] Admur ibid; Michaber ibid; Yuma ibid

[63] Admur ibid; Michaber ibid; Rashi ibid

[64] Admur ibid based on Gemara ibid; Rosh and Michaber ibid

[65] M"A 329:2; M"B 329:5 in name of Bahag and Tosafus Yuma; See Shaar Hatziyon 329:6

[66] Admur ibid; Michaber ibid; Yuma ibid

[67] Admur ibid; M"A 329:2 in name of Issur Viheter 59:38; M"B 327:7

[68] Admur ibid; Michaber ibid; Yuma ibid

place (when this person separated from them) it is thus impossible to be lenient in it due to the concept of a [50/50] establishment and we [thus] go after the majority of which were gentiles. [From here we learn that not in all cases do we desecrate Shabbos in a case of doubt, and only when the doubt is considered a Halachic doubt may one desecrate Shabbos. We find a similar ruling regarding if two doctors say the illness is not dangerous and one doctor says it is in which case, we follow the majority.[69]]

If the entire group left together:[70] However if the entire group left together, then they are still considered established together and when one person separates from them, he has separated from a [50/50] establishment and one is to undo the mound from on top of him.

An abandoned baby in a city of majority gentile population:[71] Likewise an [abandoned] baby which was found in a city that is majority gentile, there are opinions[72] which say that one may not desecrate Shabbos for him, as since every day everyone separates from their established area we therefore go after the majority (as is explained in Even Haezer Chapter 4 [Halacha 34], [although] see there for opinions[73] which argue). [If, however, the city contains majority Jews, or even 50% Jews, then one desecrates Shabbos on his behalf according to all opinions.[74] Practically, we rule like the lenient opinion that one may desecrate Shabbos for a Jew.[75]]

Summary:
May one desecrate Shabbos to help save a person if one does not know if he is Jewish?[76] Whenever there is a gathering of people of which there is at least one Jew within the gathering then one may save any person that is in danger within that gathering if it is unknown if he is that Jew or not, whether the danger occurred in the area of the gathering or after he personally left the gathering. However, if every individual separated [in different directions or] one after the other, then one may not desecrate Shabbos for an unknown person unless the majority of the group was Jewish.
An abandon baby found on Shabbos: May not have Shabbos desecrated on its behalf unless the majority of the city is Jewish. Although there are those which argue. Practically we are lenient.
As explained in A, in all cases where not transgressing Shabbos can lead to enmity and anti-Semitism, then one is to transgress Shabbos to save a life even if one knows for certain the person is a gentile, and certainly if there is doubt, even though from the letter of the law we do not allow to desecrate Shabbos in this case of doubt.

---

[69] See Piskeiy Teshuvos 329 footnote 4; Aruch Hashulchan 329:5; Beis Yitzchak 53; Shaareiy Yosher 4; Shevet Halevi 1:60; Chayeh Adam 95

[70] Admur ibid; M"A 329:2 in name of Issur Viheter; M"B 327:7

[71] Admur ibid; M"A 329:2; Even Haezer 4:34; M"B 329:6; Yuma ibid; Mishneh Machshirin 2

[72] First opinion in Admur ibid and M"B ibid; ruling of M"A 329:2; ruling of Michaber Even Haezer 4:34 which rules like the Rambam, that if majority of the town are gentiles then one may not remove a mound from an Asufi on Shabbos, and he is considered like a gentile for all matters

[73] Second opinion in Admur ibid and M"B ibid; ruling of Rama Even Haezer 4:34 which rules like the Tur, Ramban and Rashba that even if the majority of the population is gentiles one may still desecrate Shabbos to save the Asufis life. This opinion is omitted by the M"A ibid, although is brought by Admur and M"B ibid and P"M 329 A"A 2
The reason: As we view the Jews in the city as Kavua and thus is 50:50. [Beis Shmuel 4:58; M"B ibid] Some however explain the reason is because the Rama rules like Shmuel in Yuma ibid that we do not follow the majority in Hilchos Shabbos, while the Michaber does not rule like Shmuel.

[74] Michaber ibid

[75] M"B ibid in name of Gr"a; Kaf Hachaim 328:8 in name of Tosefes Shabbos that by Pikuach Nefesh we follow the lenient opinion; See Piskeiy Teshuvos 329 footnote b6

[76] Admur 329:2

Q&A

If a child was found on the road [between cities[77]], may one desecrate Shabbos on his behalf?[78]

If the travelers of this road are majority gentile, then one may not desecrate Shabbos on behalf of the child. This applies according to all opinions.[79] If, however, majority or even half of the passersby are Jewish, one is to desecrate Shabbos on their behalf.

May one desecrate Shabbos on behalf of a person who one does not know if he is Jewish or not, such as a randomly injured bystander within the city?

Yes. This follows the same law as an abandon child, in which case we are lenient.

What is one to do if he witnessed a car accident between two cars or a pedestrian and does not know if the person is Jewish?[80]

If the accident occurred in the city, then one is to desecrate Shabbos on their behalf even if the majority population is gentile. If, however, the accident occurred on a road between the cities one is not allowed to desecrate Shabbos if the majority of the travelers are gentile, unless this can bring towards enmity, in which case one is to do so.

C. Transgressing Shabbos to save the life of an animal:[81]

It is forbidden to transgress Shabbos on behalf of an animal, even if it is in a state of lethal danger. It is forbidden to transgress even Rabbinical prohibitions, including the prohibition of Muktzah, even if the animal will die as a result.[82] Nonetheless, in certain cases the Sages were lenient to permit certain light Rabbinical prohibitions for the sake of saving an animal, as will be explained.[83]

Moving an animal out of danger: It is forbidden to even move an animal for the sake of saving its life due to the Muktzah prohibition. Thus, if an animal is drowning one may not lift the animal out of the water.

Case of great loss: In a case that [one owns the animal and] not saving its life can lead to great loss, one may be lenient to move the animal in order to save its life.

May the limb of an animal?[84] Although it is forbidden to shake an item that is Muktzah, even if one will not actually move it, nevertheless in a case of pain it is permitted to hold the limbs of an animal, [such as in order to apply treatment] so long as one does not lift both of its legs or its body.

Amira Lenachri:[85] One may ask a gentile to perform even Biblical transgressions for the sake of saving an animal.[86] [This applies even if one owns the animal, and certainly if one does not own the animal.]

---

[77] So is implied from Poskim ibid, and so learns Piskeiy Teshuvos 329:2

[78] P"M 329 A"A 2; M"B 329:6; Kaf Hachaim 329:9

[79] The reason: As on the road there is no Kevius, and hence we follow the majority. [ibid]

[80] Piskeiy Teshuvos 329:2

[81] Admur 305:26; M"A 305:11; Taz 305:11; M"B 305:70 and 332:6; Rambam 25:26

[82] Admur ibid; M"A ibid; Taz ibid; M"B ibid; Rambam ibid

Why it is not permitted to transgress due to Tzaar Baalei Chaim: Although preventing Tzaar Baalei Chaim is a Biblical command, and one is hence Biblically obligated to help save an animal from pain [and certainly from death] [Admur ibid; Hilchos Ovrei Derachim 3-4; M"B 305:69] nevertheless the Sages did not permit to perform [even Rabbinical transgressions such as] Muktzah for the sake of saving the life of an animal. The Sages have the power to usurp a Biblical command in a way of Sheiv Veal Taaseh. [Admur ibid; See Yevamos 90a]

Other opinions in Admur and other Poskim: Some Poskim rule it is permitted to move an animal away from danger [or perform any Rabbinical transgression on his behalf] due to [the Biblical command to prevent] Tzaar Balaei Chaim [2nd opinion in Admur ibid, brought in parentheses; Shiltei Giborim Shabbos 128b in name of Riaz, in name of Tosafus Rid, brought in Bach 308; Elya Raba 305:18] Practically, Admur ibid concludes in parentheses that one is to be stringent unless it is case of case of great loss. Other Poskim however rule that one in a case of pain to the animal [and certainly in a case of eventual death], the Muktzah prohibitions do not apply, even if the case does not involve great loss. [Elya Raba brought in M"B 305:70; Chazon Ish 52:16]

[83] Such as placing vessels under it [305:26] or moving a limb of an animal [308:79] or helping it give birth in a case of danger to the animal [Biur Halacha "Ein Meyaldin"; Kaf Hachayim 332:1]

[84] Admur 308:79; ; Michaber 308:40; Shabbos 128

[85] Admur 332:3 and Michaber 332:4 regarding bloodletting, and 305:26 regarding Muktzah; M"B 332:6 in name of Chayeh Adam in all cases that the animal is sick

D. Saving a Jewish robber from death on Shabbos:[87]

One who comes through a tunnel [to rob a house] in a scenario that [the robber] has given up his blood[88] and it is permitted [for the homeowner] to kill him [in self-defense][89], and a mound fell on him there [in the tunnel] one may not undo it for him (as one is not commanded to help him live[90]).

Q&A

May one desecrate Shabbos to help save one who is committing suicide?[91]

Some Poskim[92] rule it is permitted/obligation to desecrate Shabbos to help save a person who is in danger due to trying to commit suicide.[93] Other Poskim[94] rule that one may not desecrate Shabbos for such a person.[95] Practically, the Poskim[96] conclude that one is permitted and obligated to desecrate Shabbos on his behalf. It is permitted and an obligation to desecrate Shabbos to prevent one from committing suicide, if he is threatening to do so and there is considerable worry that he is serious of his intents.[97]

May one desecrate Shabbos on behalf of a Jew that is liable for death under Beis Din?

Some Poskim[98] rule it is forbidden to do so.[99] However other Poskim[100] rule it is permitted.[101]

---

[86] The reason: As the Sages felt if they were not to allow the Jew to ask a gentile to help save the animal, the Jew out of panic may come to do so himself. [ibid]

[87] Admur 329:5; M"A 329:4; M"B 329:9; Sanhedrin 72b

[88] See Rama Choshen Mishpat 425:1 and Smeh 425:6

[89] The law today: See Mishnas Yosef 1:25and Piskeiy Teshuvos 329:4 that this only applies today in cases that one may legally kill the intruder. However, in those places that one may not kill the intruder then one is to desecrate Shabbos on his behalf. The reason is because the intruder has not given up his life in those states in which he may not be killed. However, from Admur ibid it is implied that even in such a case one may not desecrate Shabbos, as according to Halacha one is allowed to kill him, and one is thus not commanded to help him live, which consequently prohibits transgressing Shabbos on his behalf.

[90] Admur ibid in parentheses; See Beis Shmuel Even Haezer 4:59 that anyone who one is not obligated to help live one may not desecrate Shabbos on their behalf.

Reason of M"A: The M"A and M"B ibid write the reason one may not desecrate Shabbos on his behalf is because he is "Bar Katila", deserving of death. Admur ibid changes the wording from the M"A possibly because one can argue that perhaps although he is deserving of death he is not obligated to be killed, and hence perhaps it is permitted to desecrate Shabbos on his behalf if one so chooses. Thus, Admur emphasizes that one may not desecrate Shabbos being that one is not obligated to help him live, and only those which one is commanded to help live may one desecrate Shabbos on their behalf. [See Koveitz Ohalei Sheim 2:138]

Why one may not desecrate Shabbos if the danger has been eliminated? See Minchas Shlomo 1:7; Chelkas Yaakov 155; Mishnas Yosef ibid; Piskeiy Teshuvos 329:4 footnote 16

[91] See Piskeiy Teshuvos 329:1

[92] Maharam Merothenberg 59; Birkeiy Yosef 301:6; Rav Poalim 3:29; Cheker Halacha 2:6, brought in Kaf Hachaim 328:124; Maharil Diskin 5:34; Chelkas Yoeiv 2:88

[93] The reason: As one is obligated to help him live.

[94] Chachmas Shlomo 329; Iyun Yaakov Yuma 35; Minchas Chinuch Komeitz Lemincha 237; Maharam Yafa 13

[95] The reason: As one is not commanded to help save such a person even during the week. [Minchas Chinuch ibid] Alternatively because one may not push of an Aseh dur to Peshia. [Chochmas Shlomo]

[96] Igros Moshe 1:127; Y.D. 2:174; Chelkas Yaakov 155; Minchas Yitzchak 5:8; Kinyan Torah 1:100; Bitzeil Hachachma 1:67; Tzitz Eliezer 8:15; 9:17; Lehoros Nasan 5:28; Mishneh Halacha 8:15; Yabia Omer 8:37; Divrei Yatziv 1:167

[97] Nishmas Avraham Tinyana 306:6

[98] Biur Halacha 329:4 "Ela"; Tehila Ledavid 329:5; Yeshuos Malko on Rmabam 2:1; Doveiv Meisharim 4:52; See Piskeiy Teshuvos 329:4 footnote 18

The reason: As he has given up his life, similar to a robber and the like. [ibid]

[99] The reason: As he has given up his life, similar to a robber and the like. [ibid]

[100] P"M 329 A"A 4; See Shevet Halevi 5:48

[101] The reason: As it is forbidden for Beis Din to kill him on Shabbos and one is to desecrate Shabbos even to extend momentary life. [ibid]

E. Checking if the person is already dead:[102]

If one does not feel life in his nose, then he has certainly already dead[103] even if he was not crushed. Whether one discovered his headfirst or one discovered his feet first[104] and one sees that there is no life in his heart, even so one is to check up to his nose, as the main evidence of whether there is life is in the nose, as it says [in the verse] "all that have a soul of life in their nose".[105]

Q&A

May one turn on a resuscitation machine to help revive one who is not breathing?[106]
Yes.

May one desecrate Shabbos for one who is in a coma, is insane, is a Cheresh or a Katan?
Yes.[107] However some Poskim[108] have left this matter in question.

May one desecrate Shabbos for one who is a Goses?
Some Poskim[109] rule one is not to desecrate Shabbos on his behalf, to help him live. Other Poskim[110] however rule one may desecrate Shabbos on his behalf, to help lengthen his life. Some Poskim[111] rule that while one may desecrate Shabbos to save the life of a Goses, one is not obligated to do so if there is no chance of recovery. Other Poskim[112] rule that if there is no chance of recovery and the person is living with excruciating pain, then even during the week it is forbidden to do actions that lengthen his life and pain in this world. A Rav who is expert in the medical field is to be contacted in all circumstances.

Is one who is brain dead and attached to a respirator considered dead?[113]
Some Poskim[114] rule that one who is 100% brain dead is considered dead, as it is impossible for him to breathe on his own and accordingly one would not be allowed to desecrate Shabbos on his behalf.[115] Other Poskim[116] however rule that he is considered alive and one may hence desecrate Shabbos on his behalf.[117] Practically, a Rav who is expert in the medical field is to be contacted.

---

[102] Admur 329:3; Michaber 329:4; Yuma Mishneh 83a; Gemara 84a

[103] Admur ibid; Michaber ibid; first opinion in Yuma ibid
Other opinions in Gemara: Other opinions in the Gemara hold that one is to check the heart for life.

[104] Admur ibid; Michaber ibid; See Rav Papa in Gemara ibid

[105] Admur ibid; M"B ibid; Rav Papa ibid

[106] Nishmas Avraham 329:5; Teshuvos Vehanhagos 6:221-222Piskeiy Teshuvos 329:3

[107] Biur Halacha 329:4 "Ela"; Teshuvos Vehanhagos 1:861; Piskeiy Teshuvos 329:6

[108] Halachos Ketanos 2:38

[109] Beis Yaakov 59, brought in Gilyon Maharsha Y.D. 339, based on Shach 339:1 who quotes Ran, and no mention is made that one can desecrate Shabbos on his behalf.

[110] Shvus Yaakov 3:13, brought in Gilyon Maharsha Y.D. 339; Tosafus Nida 44b; Chasam Sofer 338; Minchas Chinuch 32 Mileches Hotza; Biur Halacha 329:4 "Ela"; Teshuvos Vehanhagos 1:861; Piskeiy Teshuvos 329:6; Poskim in Nitei Gavriel 2:4 footnote 5

[111] Teshuvos Vehanhagos ibid; Minchas Shlomo 1:91-24; Shevet Halevi 8:86; Divrei Moshe 1:95; See Piskeiy Teshuvos ibid footnote 30

[112] See Igros Moshe Y.D. 3:132; Tzitz Eliezer 13:89

[113] For the most updated and thorough research on this subject, including the different approaches, supports in the Poskim, and practical rulings of the leading Rabbanim of today as interviewed by the writers-see the journal of the RCA [110 pages long] on this issue titled *"Halachic Issues in the Determination of Death and in Organ Transplantation"*

[114] Igros Moshe Y.D. 3:132; 8:54; For an in depth analysis as to the true opinion of the Igros Moshe-see the above journal; The Rabbanut Hareishit in 1986, under the council of Rav Mordechai Eliyahu, Rav Shapiro, Rav Zalman Nechemia Goldberg and leading physicians in the Machon Shlezinger institute of Shaareiy Tzedek, have accepted this approach. See the above journal for further discussions they had with the above Rabbanim and if any retracted their rulings.

[115] The reason: As we rule that we follow the breath and not the heart, and hence if he can no longer breathe on his own he is considered dead even if his heart still beats. [ibid] See also Chasam Sofer Y.D. 338 for a Teshuvah that supports this stance.

[116] Tzitz Eliezer 10:25; 13:89 based on Chasam Sofer and Chacham Tzvi and Rashi in Yuma ibid; Minchas Yitzchak 5:7; Rav Elyashiv; Rav SZ"A as detailed in the above journal

[117] The reason: As in actuality he is still breathing, and his heart works. It is thus not similar to the case of the Gemara in which case his breathing has stopped and cannot be returned. Alternatively, even the beating of the heart is a sign of life, as implied from Rashi ibid and Chasam Sofer. Alternatively, it is not possible to determine 100% brain death.

F. Must one help save another Jew if there is danger involved for himself?[118]

Although it is a commandment upon every individual to desecrate Shabbos in order to save them, even if there is doubt as to whether they will be saved, nevertheless if there is danger [involved in trying to save the Jew] one may not endanger himself in order to save his friend because [in the meantime] he is not within the range of danger. [This applies] even if one is witnessing the death of his friend and even if his danger [in trying to save him] is doubtful while his friend's is certain, nevertheless [he is not to put himself in danger to save him]. [However, see supplement that this is only in accordance to one opinion].

The reason for this is: as the verse states, "You shall live by them" and not that one should come into doubt of death through fulfilling the Mitzvah of "Do not stand by the blood of your friend".

Supplement from Choshen Mishpat Hilchos Nizkeiy Haguf Vehanefesh Halacha 7:

One who sees a friend drowning in the sea or that murderers are coming upon him and he is able to personally save him or to hire someone to help save him, then he is obligated to trouble himself to hire others to save him, and he then returns and collects the money from the victim if the victim has the money, and if not then he may not refrain from [paying to help save him], and if he does refrain from doing so then he transgresses the command of "do not idle while your friends blood is being spilled".

When there is danger involved for the rescuer: Even to enter oneself into a questionable case of danger there are opinions[119] who say that one must do in order to help save his friend from definite death. (However, there are opinions[120] who argue on this, and Safek Nefashos Lehakel).

Conclusion:

In Hilchos Shabbos Admur rules that one may not enter himself into the Sakana. In Nizkei Haguf he brings a dispute and concludes that Safek Nefashos Lihakel, that he may be lenient not to save his life.[121] Perhaps regarding Shabbos, since the verse of Vechai Bahem does not apply, one may not desecrate Shabbos to save him. However, regarding the weekday, one can choose to do so. In all cases one must heavily measure this matter to determine if in truth he is in questionable danger if he tries to save him.[122]

Q. Saving a Jew from forcibly giving up his religion:[123]

One who gentiles are trying to force him to give up his religion, then regarding whether one may desecrate Shabbos to save him is explained in the end of chapter 306 [the last Halacha].

Chapter 306/29:

Desecrating Shabbos in order to help save a Jew from leaving Judaism: [124]

One who discovered on Shabbos that gentiles have kidnapped his daughter from his home for the purposes of removing her from the Jewish people [and make her live like a gentile], it is a Mitzvah for him to travel and place effort to save her.

Transgressing Biblical prohibitions: He may travel even past the distance of 12 Mil[125] [which is the Biblical Techum Shabbos according to some Poskim[126]], and he may even perform complete Biblical

---

[118] Admur 329:8; Issur Viheter 59:38; Elya Zuta 329:4; Smeh 426:2 based on omission of all Rishonim and Poskim; M"B 329:19

[119] Hagahos Maimanos Rotzeiach 1:14 in name of Yerushalmi; Radbaz Leshonos Harambam 1582

[120] Smeh 426:2 based on omission of all Rishonim and Poskim

[121] This difference of ruling s well as the parentheses given by Admur in Nizkei Haguf is discussed by the Rebbe in Likkutei Sichos 28 p. 153 footnote 19. The Rebbe does not give any concluding stance on this subject.

[122] Choshen Mishpat 426:2; M"B 328:19; Shevet Halevi 8:87; See Piskeiy Teshuvos 329:9

[123] Admur 329:10; Rama 329:8

[124] Admur ibid; Michaber 30614; Tosafus Shabbos 4a; Eiruvin 32:b; Gittin 41:b

[125] Admur ibid; Michaber ibid; Tosafus ibid

[126] M"B 306:57

prohibitions if, necessary, to save her.[127]

Doubt if will be successful:[128] This may be done even if it is only a doubt as to whether he will be successful in saving her.[129]

Child:[130] This may be done even if the daughter is a child and is not yet obligated in Mitzvos, one is nevertheless to desecrate Shabbos in order to save her.[131]

Forcing the father:[132] If the father does not desire to help save her, he is to be forced to do so.

Another person's child:[133] This law applies even to another person's child, another person's son or daughter which is not one's relative, nevertheless if he has ability to try to fulfill this Mitzvah and save the child, then he must do so and he is to be forced[134] into helping in any way he can. This applies even if it is a mere doubt in whether he will be successful, and even if he will have to transgress Biblical prohibitions in order to do so.

What is the law if the child ran away on his own accord?
Some Poskim[135] rule it is forbidden to desecrate Shabbos to help save him. Other Poskim[136] rule it is permitted even if the child did so purposely.

May one invite a non-religious guest for Shabbos if he will desecrate Shabbos in order to come to you?[137]
Some Poskim[138] rule it is forbidden to invite guests to one's home for the Shabbos meal if this will cause him to desecrate Shabbos, such as to drive, in order to arrive there.[139] If, however, the home is close by and it is possible that the guest will choose to walk over rather than drive, it is permitted to invite him even though one does not know for certain whether he will arrive by foot or will drive.[140] Other Poskim[141] however rule it is permitted to invite the guest even if one knows that he will drive.[142] Nevertheless, those that are lenient are to abide by the following four conditions:

---

[127] Admur ibid; Darkei Moshe; Beis Yosef; M"B 306:57

[128] Admur ibid; Kuntrus Achron 306:1; Levush

[129] The reason: As this matter is treated like Pikuach Nefesh in which case one desecrates Shabbos even for a questionable saving of life. There is no greater Pikuach Nefesh than this in which case she will leave the Jewish people and desecrate Shabbos her entire life. [Admur ibid; M"A 306:29; Taz 306:5; M"B 306:57] It is better that we desecrate one Shabbos on her behalf than have her desecrate many Shabbasos, as it is due to this reason that we desecrate Shabbos for Pikuach Nefesh, as the Torah stated "desecrate one Shabbos in order so he guard many Shabbasos". [Admur ibid; first opinion in Yuma 85b; See Admur 328:2 that rules like Shmuel]

[130] Admur ibid in parentheses; Elya Raba 306:33; M"B 306:57
Other opinions: Some Poskim leave this matter in question. [M"A 306:29, brought in M"B ibid]

[131] The reason: One may desecrate Shabbos to save her in order so she fulfill many Shabbasos when she is older. It is also for this reason that one may desecrate Shabbos for the Pikuach Nefesh of a Katan. [Admur ibid in parentheses] However Tzaruch Iyun, as in 328:2 Admur rules that we desecrate Shabbos because of the verse of Vechaiy Bahem. See Biur Halacha 329:4 "Ela" that it is because of Vechaiy Bahem that one may save a child.

[132] Admur ibid; Michaber ibid

[133] Admur ibid; Malbushei Yom Tov; Olas Shabbos 306 end; Elya Zuta 306:12; M"B 56

[134] Admur ibid; See however Shaar Hatziyon 306 footnote 44

[135] Shvus Yaakov 1:16; M"B 306:56

[136] Nachals Shiva 83

[137] See Ratz Katzevi 8:28 for a through discussion on this matter; See Hearos Ubiurim 1037:137 and 1039 p. 81; See Hiskashrus 929:15 that when the Rebbe was addressed this question by Shluchim he forwarded the person to Rav Dworkin

[138] Igros Moshe 1:99 regarding prohibition to invite to Shul; Mishneh Halachos 16:31 regarding inviting to house; Shevet Halevi 8:165-6; 8:256-2 [regarding inviting to Simcha]; Chishukei Chemed of Rav Zilbirshtram, in name of Rav Elyashiv; Rav A.L. Cohen, Rav of Beitar, in response to the authors question

[139] The reason: This is forbidden due to Lifnei Iver, or due to the prohibition of helping another do a sin [Misayeia], or due to the prohibition of Meisis. [Igros Moshe ibid; Shevet Halevi ibid; See Ratz Katzevi 28 chapter 1-2] Or due to it being a Chilul Hashem. [Shevet Halevi ibid]

[140] See Admur 347:4; M"A 347:4; Igros Moshe ibid

[141] Rav SZ"A in Minchas Shlomo 2:4-10; Teshuvos Vehanhagos 1:358; Rav Weiss in Ratz Katzevi ibid; See response of Rav Dworkin, brought ion Hiskashrus ibid

[142] The reason:
a) As Lifnei Iver only applies when the person would not be able to transgress without the help of the other person, and thus here, since the Jew would drive his car even without the invitation, it is therefore not forbidden due to Lifnei Iver. [Rav Asher Weiss based on Avoda Zara 6b; See Ratz Katzevi 28 chapter 1; See Admur 347:2-3]
b) It likewise does not involve the Rabbinical prohibition of helping others due a sin, as this prohibition does not apply to a Mumar [See Shach 151:6; Rav Weiss in Ratz Katzevi 28:3] or because it only applies when one gives assistance to the actual prohibition. [Maharsham; See Rav

1. Invite him for the entire Shabbos, beginning with Mincha of Erev Shabbos so a) He can arrive before Shabbos and b) He can stay until after Shabbos.[143] A good advice is to make the mealtime earlier, before Shabbos, so he can arrive beforehand.[144] [One does not have to wait for the guest to verify this invitation, but simply must let him know. He is certainly not to tell the guest that he may drive if he chooses, and is not to affirm such a question.]
2. Let the person know that it is forbidden to drive on Shabbos.[145]
3. Some Poskim[146] due not require the above, although rule that one must ask them not to park near your house if they do decide to come by car.

Summary of whose life one is obligated to save:

<u>Danger is involved for the rescuer:</u>[147] Then even if the danger is only a doubt while the danger of the victim is certain, nevertheless one is not allowed to enter himself into danger in order to try to save him.

<u>Saving a robber from death on Shabbos:</u>[148] One who is in the process of robbing a home and falls in danger may not have Shabbos desecrated for him.

<u>May one desecrate Shabbos to help save a person if one does not know if he is Jewish?</u>[149] Whenever there is a gathering of people of which there is at least one Jew within the gathering then one may save any person that is in danger within that gathering if it is unknown if he is that Jew or not, whether the danger occurred in the area of the gathering or after he personally left the gathering. However, if every individual separated [in different directions or] one after the other, then one may not desecrate Shabbos for an unknown person unless the majority of the group was Jewish.

<u>An abandon baby found on Shabbos:</u> May not have Shabbos desecrated on its behalf unless the majority of the city is Jewish. Although there are those which argue.

<u>May one desecrate Shabbos if it is unknown if the person is still alive?</u>[150] Yes. In any case of doubt, even if it involves many doubts such as he may not even be Jewish, and he may not even be alive, nevertheless one is commanded to desecrate Shabbos for him.

<u>When is one considered dead that Shabbos may no longer be desecrated for him?</u>[151] When there is no longer sign of life from his nose, even if there is no sign of life from his heart.

SZ"A in Minchas Shlomo 2:90 for a similar ruling regarding renting houses to Michalilei Shabbos] or because it does not apply when done to save the person from a prohibition. [Rav Akiva Eiger Y.D. 181:6] In other words, when done for Kiruv purposes, he is not helping him do an Aveira but rather a Mitzvah. [Minchas Shlomo 1:35 regarding giving food to a non-religious person even though he may not wash or say a blessing; Teshuvos Vehanhagos ibid; Ratz Katzevi 28:4-5]

c) It is permitted to desecrate Shabbos for the sake of saving a Jew from heresy. [See Admur 306:29; See Ratz Katzevi 28 chapter 4; See Shevet Halevi 6:36 that in certain cases we say "sin in order to benefit your friend"; This response was given regarding a person traveling for Shabbos for Kiruv purposes to a Yishuv that may not have a Minyan, and hence the questioner asked whether he should miss a Minyan for Kiruv purposes, and on this the Shevet Halevi answered that we learn from 306 That one may desecrate Shabbos to help save a soul from Shemad. Thus, perhaps here too, although here one is causing his friend to stumble and transgress Shabbos, which transgresses Lifnei Iver, nevertheless this is all being done for the sake of being Mikaeiv him. However, see Shevet Halevi 8:165-6; 8:256-2 who in conclusion rules stringently regarding this question.]

[143] Rav SZ"A, brought in Rat Katzevi 28:5 in length; Directive of Rav Dworkin, brought in Hiskashrus 929:15

[144] Rav Zalman Nechmia Goldberg in letter printed in Ratz Katzevi p. 516

[145] See Igros Kodesh 14 p. 98 regarding inviting people to Hakafos if they will drive on Shabbos/Yom Tov.

[146] Teshuvos Vehanhagos ibid

[147] Admur 329:8

[148] Admur 328:5

[149] Admur 329:2

[150] Admur 329:3

[151] Admur 329:3

3. Who should do the desecration of Shabbos for the ill person-Jew, Gentile, Man, Woman, Child?[152]
A. First Opinion:[153]

Must desecration of Shabbos be done by an available gentile or child rather than an adult Jew? [Despite the ruling that when the treatment is not urgent, and there is thus no danger involved in taking more time to prepare the treatment in a way that will lessen the amount of transgressions to be done, then one must do so, nevertheless] even [in a scenario that] we have in front of us gentiles and children under the age of Mitzvos we do not say that [since] one is able to [give the treatment] through these people and avoid desecrating Shabbos through a Jew who is above the age of Mitzvos [therefore it should be forbidden for a Jew above the age of Mitzvos to do so. Rather we say that an adult Jew is to do it].

The reason for this allowance is: because since the only option in saving him is through doing an action which is forbidden on Shabbos, therefore Shabbos is overruled on his behalf for [all] Jews which are obligated to save him and there is no transgression of Shabbos here at all.

The Rabbinical prohibition in giving over the job to a gentile or child: Furthermore, even if a Jew wishes to be strict upon himself [to not transgress Shabbos and thus wishes] to do the required labor through a gentile or child, or [he wishes to have them do it] because he does not desire to trouble himself [to do so], there is a Rabbinical prohibition in [him refraining from doing it himself].

The Reason: as perhaps the bystanders will now say that with utter difficulty was [transgressing Shabbos] permitted [to be done] for a life-threatening situation and [they will think that] initially it is not permitted to transgress Shabbos through a Jew that is above the age of Mitzvos, and this may then lead to that where a gentile or child cannot be found then they will not wish to desecrate Shabbos through an esteemed religious leader.

May women be entrusted the responsibility of saving lives? [Furthermore] even by women which are obligated in Mitzvos [of Shabbos] and there thus exist no such worry [that if given to them to desecrate Shabbos one may think that doing so is not so suitable] nevertheless we do not place upon them alone the responsibility and duty in dealing [with life threatening situations], that [the treatments] should be done through their hands [alone], as perhaps they will be lazy [in doing so with lack of alacrity] or negligent in it.

Having women take part in the treatment: However, women may be joined together with Jewish men, if the man will receive the overall responsibility [of the treatment] and the woman will be directed by the Jewish man, as since the Jewish man is dealing with the treatment, she too will do so with alacrity due to his [presence].

Doing all the treatments through Torah Scholars: Nevertheless, the greatest form of fulfilling this Mitzvah is to try to have all the [necessary Shabbos desecrations] done through Jews which are great [Torah] scholars and not through the simple folk and women. [Obviously however this should only be done if it will cause no delay in the treatment. Thus, one should not search for a Torah Scholar but rather if a Torah scholar is at the scene then he should be the one to do the prohibited actions.]

The reason for why the treatment should not be done by the simple folk and woman is: in order so that Shabbos not be considered frivolous in their eyes and thus have them come to be lenient even in situations that are not life threatening. As well [another reason that great scholars should do so is] in order to publicly rule through a practical case [that Shabbos is allowed to be desecrated in these situations].

B. Other Opinions:[154]

[However] there are opinions which say that since [in life threatening cases the] Shabbos [prohibitions] are [merely] being overruled and the [holiness of Shabbos has not been] revoked at all, [therefore] whatever [treatment] is possible to be done without Biblically transgressing [Shabbos] is required to be done through not transgressing a Biblically forbidden action and therefore if one is able ...., as well as if one is able to do [the transgression] through a gentile without any delay at all, then one is Biblically

---

[152] Admur 328:13
[153] The first opinion is the view of the Michaber 328:12 in the name of the Rambam
[154] Rama, in the name of the Ramban and Oar Zarua.

required to do so through a gentile.

The reason that a gentile is trusted to do the treatment: [as according to this opinion] it was only [Rabbinically] forbidden to do so [i.e. the treatment] through a gentile in a scenario that there is worry that he may do so lazily and thus come to delay and suspend [the treatment], however [they did not prohibit asking a gentile] if a Jew is actively supervising him and hastening him in a way that there is no worry at all [of possible delay].

C. The Final Ruling:

Halacha like 1st, Custom like 2nd, best to do like 1st: The main Halachic opinion is like the first opinion[155], although the custom in these countries is like the latter opinion. Nevertheless, it is best not to follow this custom[156] because there is worry that perhaps since people will now see that the treatments are only done through a gentile, they will come to think that it is always forbidden to do so through a Jew, and occasionally there will not be a gentile available and the ill person will be endangered as a result of their delay in waiting for the arrival of a gentile.

Those who follow the custom of the second opinion must announce to all: At the very least one who wants [to follow the custom and] do so through a gentile is to make publicly known at that time that it is permitted for a Jew himself to do so [and it is only not being done through a Jew] because a gentile is readily available

---

Summary-Who should do the desecration of Shabbos for the ill person?[157]

[If there are a number of people to choose from without delay to help save the person's life then] it should not be administered to women, children, gentiles, or ignoramuses but rather should be done completely by the Torah scholars and leaders. However, it is permitted from the letter of the law to allow women to help in the treatment, having a Jewish man supervise. However, there is a Rabbinical prohibition to appoint a gentile or child to administer the treatment in place of a Jew [even if there is a Jew supervising[158]].

Those people of communities which hold of the opinion that argues on the above, and holds that the treatment __must__ even initially be done through a gentile/child under Jewish adult supervision when there is no delay in administering it to them, should not follow this custom, and those who do follow the custom must announce the reason that they themselves are not administering the treatment is because there is no delay involved in having the gentile do it.

[Whenever there is delay involved in administering the responsibility for the treatment to someone else, according to all, it is to be done by whoever has the ability to help immediately.]

Q&A
Should a gentile doctor be given over the treatment of a Jewish patient instead of a Jewish doctor?

No, specifically the Jewish doctor[159] should be chosen as ruled above.

---

[155] So rules Taz.

[156] So rules also Taz and Mishneh Berurah 37, albeit for the reason that the gentile will do so at a slower pace. However according to Admur, even when we know for certain that a gentile will not do so at a slower pace, nevertheless one is to do so himself.

[157] Admur 328:13

[158] So is implied from the fact that Admur only mentions supervision regarding a woman, as well as from the second opinion which only allows it to be done with Jewish supervision thus implying that according to the first opinion, of which we rule in accordance of, this too is not allowed.

[159] This applies even [and maybe even more so] if the doctor is not religious, as is evident from the reason mention for why a Jew is to be chosen over a gentile.

Should a religious doctor be given to take care of the treatment over a non-religious Jewish doctor?[160]
If they are both equally expertise, then the religious doctor must be given the care for the treatment according to all opinions [even according to the second opinion which prefers a gentile over a Jew] being that he will diminish in the Shabbos transgressions when possible. If, however, the other doctor is more expertise then obviously he should be chosen over the religious doctor.

May a female nurse be initially entrusted with care for the patient or is one to request specifically a man?[161]
There is no suspicion that these women will do their job lazily and they thus may be entrusted. Nevertheless, a man should try to only have a male give him treatment as to avoid the prohibitions involved in touching women.

4. Which treatments may be done?

A. Must use a known treatment or one prescribed by a medical expert:[162]
Even if there is a definite danger one may only transgress Shabbos for medical treatment that is known to all or is done by a professional [doctor]. When it is a known form of healing then even if one does not know if he will be cured through it or not, one transgresses Shabbos out of doubt [that perhaps it will heal]. *[See Q&A regarding a Kemiah and Homeopathic treatments]*

Summary of which treatments may be used?
One may only do a treatment that is either being administered by an expert, or is known to be able to cure the person.[163]

Q&A

May one do forms of treatment that work in accordance to Segula and are not recognized by science?[164]
Some Poskim[165] rule that any treatment that is based on Segula [supernatural healing] and not due to scientific understanding, is forbidden to performed on Shabbos if they involve Shabbos desecration. This applies even to those treatments mentioned in Chazal that work based on Segula.[166] Other Poskim[167] however rule that even treatments that work based on Segula may be used on Shabbos so long as they have been proven to work or have been written by Chazal. Practically, one may be lenient so long as it has been verified to have healing abilities, even if it works as a way of Segula.[168] If this is not the case then it may only be given if the patient is asking for it and doing so will calm him down.

May one write a Kemiah [Kabalistic charm] for the patient?[169]
Patient is asking for it: If the patient is asking for this and it will calm him down and help him live then this may be done.

---

[160] Piskeiy Teshuvos 328:9
[161] Ketzos Hashulchan 135 footnote 9
[162] Admur 328:2
[163] Admur 328:2
[164] Piskeiy Teshuvos 328:4 [old] 328:5 [new]
[165] Radbaz 1436; 1526 [2:153] based on Rambam Pirush Hamishnayos Yuma 8:4
[166] The reason: As the treatments that are based on Segula are mild and don't work well. [Radbaz 1436] Alternatively, the Rambam holds that these treatments don't really help and are not a Refua at all. [Radbaz 1526]
[167] Rashba 1:413; 167; 865; 4:245; Tzemach Tzedek 38; Many Poskim in Piskeiy Teshuvos ibid
[168] So rules Tzemach Tzedek ibid and majority of Achronim
[169] Piskeiy Teshuvos 328:4

Patient is not asking for it: If the patient is not asking for the Kemia and one simply desires to use it to try to heal the patient then it follows the same dispute as mentioned above: Some Poskim[170] rule that it is forbidden to be written in all cases. Other Poskim[171] rule that it may be written if it has been proven to work three times and the person writing it has written at least three working charms. Practically, one may be lenient in this matter.[172]

May one do homeopathic treatments and other forms of natual treatment which are not recognized by conventional medicine?[173]
If the treatment has become accepted by medical experts and has been experienced with for a while and is verified to have healing abilities then it is allowed to be done without limitation, even if it works as a way of Segula.[174] If this is not the case then it may only be given if the patient is asking for it and doing so will calm him down.

B. Must a treatment that does not involve Shabbos desecration be given over one that does?[175]
If there is no danger involved for the patient in doing the permitted method: In a scenario that one can begin [preparing] the treatment immediately [in a form] that does not contain desecrating Shabbos but [because of this it] will be delayed a slight amount of time [until it is ready to be applied to the patient], then one may not desecrate Shabbos just in order to prepare the treatment in the shortest amount of time possible without any delay, **if the situation is that there is no danger at all involved in this short delay** [in the application of the treatment].
The reason for this restriction is: because [the prohibitions of] Shabbos are [simply] overruled in a life-threatening situation and are not completely revoked [from being in affect], [thus] in any scenario that something can be done to save a person without desecrating Shabbos, Shabbos is not overruled for him.
An example of the above Halacha:[176] If [the patient] was evaluated to require two figs and they only found two figs which were attached [to the tree] each one to a separate stem or on their own, as well as [they found] three figs which were all three attached to the same stem, then one is to cut the stem which has the three on it [rather then cut two individual figs] as although that by doing so one is increasing in the amount of figs [that are being detached] nevertheless he is lessening the amount of detaching [that he must do] which is the main aspect of the prohibition [in detaching fruits].
However if [the patient] was evaluated to require two figs and there were two on one stem and three on another single stem then one may only cut the stem that has two on it because it is forbidden to increase onto the amount [needed for] the forbidden action to be done, even though that [that in this case cutting the stem with three] is not increasing the amount of effort needed for the action being that [all three figs will be cut] simultaneously.
If the matter is urgent:[177] Nevertheless if the matter is urgent then we are not particular about this so one not come to push it off and delay it.

---

[170] Radbaz 1436; 1526 based on Rambam Pirush Hamishnayos Yuma 8:4; Uvacharta Bachaim [Rav Shlomo Kluger 87]; Shevet Halevi 5:55; Tzitz Eliezer; See Nishmas Avraham 301 p. 285
[171] So rules Tzemach Tzedek 38
[172] So rules Tzemach Tzedek ibid and majority of Achronim
[173] Shevet Halevi 5:55; Piskeiy Teshuvos 328:4 [old] 328:5 [new]
[174] Vetzaruch Iyun why not just say like Admur that it may be done if "is either being administered by an expert, or is known to be able to cure the person."
[175] Admur 328:13
[176] Admur 328:18
[177] Admur 328:18

Summary of must a treatment that does not involve Shabbos desecration be given over one that does:

If one can do a treatment without transgression that will take a little more time than doing a treatment with transgression, then if there is no danger in this short delay, one must do the former.[178] Certainly then if one can do a permitted or forbidden treatment and neither take more time than the other, one must do the permitted treatment. Nevertheless, if the matter is urgent then we are not particular about this so one not come to push it off and delay it.[179]

Q&A

What's Halachically better, to drive to the hospital oneself or to call an ambulance?[180]

Emergency: In all cases of emergency that medical assistance is immediately required even prior to reaching the hospital then obviously an ambulance is to be taken.

Non-Emergency: If the matter is not this urgent then it is better for a religious Jew to drive the patient to the hospital rather than call an ambulance.[181] [**However see footnote with regards if one knows that the driver is a gentile**[182]]. However, if no religious Jew is available to drive then it is better to call an ambulance then have a non-religious Jew do the driving.[183]

If a light needs to be turned on and one has different options of which light to use is there preference of one type of light over another?[184]

Yes. It is better to turn on a fluorescent light then to turn on a regular light bulb. As well it is better to turn on a smaller light bulb then a larger light bulb.

Q&A with regards to getting help from neighbor in order to prevent desecration of Shabbos

Should one ask a neighbor to drive the patient to the hospital rather than call an ambulance?[185]

One is not obligated to ask his neighbor to drive the patient to the hospital if his neighbor is currently sleeping or if by doing so his neighbor will end up being stuck away from his family for Shabbos.

Must one drive his sick neighbor to the hospital in order to prevent an ambulance from being called?[186]

One is not obligated to drive the patient to the hospital if by doing so he will end up being stuck away from his family for Shabbos. Nevertheless, as a meticulous act of kindness and sanctification of G-d's name it is best for one to help diminish as much desecration as possible.

---

[178] Admur 38:13

[179] Admur 328:18

[180] Piskeiy Teshuvos 328:13

[181] As by doing so one diminishes in the transgression of making the phone call, as well as the ambulance drivers usually are not careful in matters of desecration of Shabbos which are not needed, such as driving back to the station, while a religious driver will be. [Now, although the Ketzos Hashulchan 140: footnote 3 rules the opposite that it is better to take an ambulance then to have one drive, this was only because back then the cars would drive back home, which was forbidden, while the ambulances would drive back to their station which was permitted due to that they need to be on call. However today even the Ketzos Hashulchan would agree that it is better for a religious Jew to drive as the religious driver will not drive back home. Thus, there is desecration of Shabbos being saved.]

[182] Tzaruch Iyun if according to Admur which rules that a Jew is to do the desecration over a gentile, if this applies even in this case [that a Jew should do the driving rather than call a gentile ambulance] being that here people will simply think that the gentile ambulance was contacted not because that a Jew cannot do the driving but rather because it is an emergency, and there is thus no longer a worry that people may come to think that the Jew cannot drive. Furthermore, it is evident to all that the Jew had to call the gentile ambulance and it is thus evident to all that a Jew may desecrate Shabbos to save a life. Thus, it seems clear that in a case that a gentile ambulance driver is available he should be contacted rather than have a religious Jew drive to the hospital, being that although one adds in the phone call he nevertheless diminishes the entire transgression of driving. To note that so rules Piskeiy Teshuvos 328:13

[183] As he will do extra Shabbos transgressions unnecessarily.

[184] Piskeiy Teshuvos 328:14

[185] Piskeiy Teshuvos 328:13; SSH"K 40:72

[186] Piskeiy Teshuvos 328:13; SSH"K 40:72

> **Must one provide his Shabbos food for his sick neighbor in order to prevent them from needing to cook food on Shabbos?**[187]
>
> One is not obligated to provide his neighbor with hot food or his candles and the like in order to prevent the neighbor from needing to desecrate Shabbos. Nevertheless, as a meticulous act of kindness and sanctification of G-d's name it is best for one to help diminish as much desecration as possible.

C. Must one do the Biblical prohibitions involved in the treatment with an irregularity?[188]

Note: The dispute brought below is brought by Admur in conjunction with the two opinions mentioned in Halacha 2. The 1st opinion here is in accordance to the First opinion there and the second opinion here is the same opinion as the second opinion there!

First Opinion-No need for irregularity:[189] [One need not do the forbidden actions using an irregularity[190].]

The reason for this allowance is: because since the only option in saving him is through doing an action which is forbidden on Shabbos, therefore Shabbos is overruled on his behalf for [all] Jews which are obligated to save him and there is thus no transgression of Shabbos here at all.

Other Opinions[191]*- Do the labor with an irregularity*: [However] there are opinions which say that since [in life threatening cases the] Shabbos [prohibitions] are [merely] being overruled and the [holiness of Shabbos has not been] revoked at all, [therefore] whatever [treatment] is possible to be done without Biblically transgressing [Shabbos] is required to be done through not transgressing a Biblically forbidden action and therefore if one is able to do [a transgression] without suspension and delay through an irregular form [of action used for that transgression], then one is to do it with an irregularity, as when done so there is no Biblical transgression.

The Final Ruling: The main Halachic opinion is like the first opinion[192], although the custom in these countries is like the latter opinion. Nevertheless, it is best not to follow this custom[193] because there is worry that perhaps since people will now see that the treatments are only done through a gentile, they will come to think that it is always forbidden to do so through a Jew, and occasionally there will not be a gentile available and the ill person will be endangered as a result of their delay in waiting for the arrival of a gentile. [However, regarding the dispute in doing the actions with an irregularity the Alter Rebbe here does not give a final ruling, and one thus is to be stringent when there is no delay involved in doing so.[194]]

Those who follow the custom must announce to all: At the very least one who wants [to follow the custom, when one does the action with an irregularity, he is to announce that in truth it is permitted to do even without an irregularity[195].]

---

[187] Piskeiy Teshuvos 328:13; SSH"K 32:74

[188] Admur 328:13

[189] The first opinion is the view of the Michaber [12] in the name of the Rambam.

[190] Although Admur does not mention this explicitly in the 1st opinion, nevertheless, so is implied from Admur in a) the reasoning of the first opinion with regards to having a Jew do it over a gentile implies this to be the case as well regarding an irregularity. B) In the second opinion there Admur states that their ruling of having a gentile to so over a Jew is a result of them holding that an irregularity must be done, thus implying that the 1st opinion does not hold that an irregularity must be done. C) So learns Ketzos Hashulchan mentioned below.

[191] Rama, in the name of the Ramban and Or Zarua. The first opinion is the view of the Michaber [12] in the name of the Rambam.

[192] So rules Tzemach Tzedek O"H 38; Minchas Yitzchak 10:31-16

[193] So rules also Taz and Mishneh Berurah 37, albeit for the reason that the gentile will do so at a slower pace. However according to Admur, even when we know for certain that a gentile will not do so at a slower pace, nevertheless one is to do so himself.

[194] Ketzos Hashulchan 135 footnote 10. See there for reasoning.

[195] Ketzos Hashulchan 135 footnote 10.

Summary-Must one do the Biblical prohibitions involved in the treatment with an irregularity?[196]

If doing so will delay the treatment, then one is to do so regularly. If not, then it is disputed whether it must be done with an irregularity [and one should be stringent regarding a Biblical prohibition[197]].

Q&A

In cases that an action may only be done with an irregularity, what is defined to be an irregularity?

One is to ask a Rav what is considered an irregularity for each particular forbidden action that he must do.[198]

Is doing an action with two people if it is normally done alone considered an irregularity?[199]

Some Poskim[200] rule it is considered an irregularity and therefore all forbidden acts that need to be done should, if possible, be done jointly with two people. Such as they lift the telephone off the hook together. Others[201] however argue that this does not constitute an irregularity as one is in any case still Biblically liable by a prohibition done jointly, as well as the exemption does not apply to simple acts such as lifting the telephone[202].

How may one dial the telephone with an irregularity?[203]

Some Poskim[204] say one is to have two people lift it together. Others say[205] that it should be lifted using one's elbows and the like.

D. May non-urgent actions be done?[206]

The allowance to do everything that is normally done on a weekday: [One may make for him] foods and remedies which are good for a sick person, even if there is no danger at all involved in refraining from doing [these actions], as nevertheless there is danger involved in his illness.

Other Opinions regarding doing actions which are not a necessity: [However] there are opinions which say that even in a scenario that one needs to desecrate Shabbos a Jew is only allowed to do those forbidden actions which there is possibility that a lack of doing them can put him in danger. However, any action that if refrained from doing will not cause danger, then even though the patient requires it and it is accustomed to do so for him during the week one may only do so on Shabbos through gentiles as is the law by the needs of any sick person which is not in danger.

The Final Ruling: (One is to follow the latter opinion in these provinces which are likewise accustomed to be strict even regarding an action in which there is danger if refrained from doing, to not do so through a Jew so long as it could be done through a gentile without any wait and delay at all as will be explained [in 328/13], thus by an action in which refraining from doing involves no danger at all one is to do it through a gentile even if there is suspicion that he may take his time doing it. However, if there is no gentile available at all then one may rely on the first opinion, although nevertheless every meticulous person should worry for himself regarding [transgressing] a Biblical prohibition).

---

[196] Admur 328:13
[197] Ketzos Hashulchan 135 footnote 10. See there for reasoning.
[198] Ketzos Hashulchan chapter 134 Halacha 4
[199] Piskeiy Teshuvos 328:8
[200] SSH"K 32:28
[201] Minchas Yitzchak 10:31; Bear Yitzchak 14
[202] Being that the prohibition is not an elongated process, as would be the case by crushing herbs and the like, but is rather a single movement of lifting the telephone, and in such cases, we do not apply the exemption of two people doing it together. [Minchas Yitzchak ibid]
[203] Piskeiy Teshuvos 328:8
[204] SSH"K 32:28
[205] Piskeiy Teshuvos ibid
[206] Admur 328:4

E. An example of the above dispute in D-Lighting a bonfire for a lethally ill person over warming him with clothes:[207]

One who let blood: One who has had his blood let and became cold is considered to be in [lethal] danger and one is to make him a bonfire on Shabbos even in the season of *Tammuz* [the hottest summer month].

Other ill people: However, for other sick people even though they are lethally sick, nevertheless [since] the coldness is not a danger for them as it is possible to warm them up with clothing, therefore one may only make a bonfire for them through a gentile, unless there are no [available] clothes to warm them up with.

Other Opinions: [However] according to those opinions which say any deathly ill person may have done for him through a Jew anything that is normally done during the week [for ill people], even if refraining from doing a particular matter will not cause him danger, (then nevertheless) [here too] one is also allowed to make a bonfire for the patient through a Jew as is done during the week.

The Final Ruling: (It was already explained [above Halacha D] how one should follow in these countries).

Summary of D/E-May non-urgent actions be done?

All actions that are normally done during the week for this type of patient, which are insignificant for his survival, and thus he will live even without these actions being done, one is to only do them through a gentile. If no gentile is available then he may do so himself, although a meticulous person should worry of a possible Biblical prohibition in doing so.[208] Thus if the patient can be warmed up with clothing, then it is forbidden [based on the custom in these countries] to light a fire for him through a Jew but rather only through a gentile.[209]

Q&A

May one travel to a hospital of their choice or must they go the closest available hospital?[210]

One may travel to whichever hospital he/she feels that they will receive the best medical treatment or care. However, one may not travel to a further hospital simply to save money.

May the relatives of a deathly ill patient be alerted to come visit him?[211]

They may be alerted through a gentile and may come to visit the patient through being driven by a gentile, although must make sure to not transgress any Shabbos transgressions in the process, such as carrying, lights of car etc.] If the medical doctor however says that their visit is a matter of life and death for the patient [meaning that if they do not visit him his illness may become more severe] then the relatives may do whatever is needed to get there even if it involves Biblical prohibitions.

May a relative or friend accompany the patient to the hospital?[212]

Any relative or friend who will help the patient keep calm may travel with them. This applies even if there are other people in the car, such as a medic or EMT, and even if the patient says that he/she does not need the escort of the relative or friend.[213] [However care must be taken to avoid Chilul Shabbos in the process, such as not to carry items with him/her if there is no Eiruv.] However, there are Poskim[214] which are less lenient and only allow an escort in a case that the patient is asking for

---

[207] Admur 328:24
[208] Admur 328:4
[209] Admur 328:24
Vetzaruch Iyun if in this case that clothing are available, but no gentile is available, if he himself may light the fire and follow the Michaber? How would the Alter Rebbe rule in this case that in any event?
[210] Piskeiy Teshuvos 330:3
[211] Piskeiy Teshuvos 328:4
[212] Piskeiy Teshuvos 330:3
[213] So rules Chazon Ish and Az Nidbaru 1:29
[214] So is implied from Igros Moshe 1:132; Teshuvos Vehanhagos 2:177-Although there he says that by a woman giving birth for her 1st few times one may be lenient even if she says that she does not need him.

one, or is evident that she needs it.

May a Tzaddik or Torah Scholar be alerted to pray for the patient if doing so involves prohibitions?[215]
Such as sending a gentile to give a written note to the Tzaddik and the like.
If doing so will calm the patient down, then the prohibitions involved may be done through a gentile.
If the patient however asks for this to be done and the medical doctor says that it is a matter of life and death for the patient [meaning that if they do not visit him his illness may become more severe] then they may do whatever is needed to reach the Tzaddik, even if it involves Biblical prohibitions.

May a doctor/EMT which drove a patient to the hospital return home on Shabbos?[216]
See Halacha 6 Q&A there!

May one who was released from a hospital on Shabbos return home on Shabbos?[217]
It is forbidden for one to drive back home. Although if there is no comfortable area where one can wait until after Shabbos[218] there is room to allow him/her to have a gentile drive her home, so long as her house is within Techum Shabbos.[219]

F. May a kosher animal be slaughtered if there is non-kosher meat readily available?[220]
If there is a deathly ill person [above the age of Mitzvos[221]] which needs meat and there is no kosher meat available, then] one slaughters [a Kosher animal or bird] for him.
The reason that: we do not say that he should be fed non-kosher food which contains only a prohibition of a negative command [without the capital punishment] rather than transgress Shabbos which is a prohibition [which contains the penalty] of stoning, [is] because Shabbos has already been overruled with regards to lighting the fire and cooking [the meat].
Another reason: As well, in [eating] non-kosher meat one transgresses on every single *kezayis* [of meat eaten] and even if one were to [verify that the ill person only] eat less than a *kezayis* [within the time of Pras], [nevertheless] there is [still] a Biblical prohibition [being transgressed] with every single bite [of the meat]. On the other hand, by slaughtering, one is only transgressing a single prohibition although that it is [more] severe.
Another reason: Furthermore, perhaps the sick person will be disgusted in eating non-Kosher food and will refrain [from eating it] and will thus be endangered.[222]
If one needs to eat meat immediately: Nevertheless, if the sick person needs to eat right away and the non-kosher meat is readily available and the slaughtered meat will be delayed [in arriving to him], then he is to be fed the non-kosher meat.
If one needs boiled wine for a deathly ill person: However[223] if [the ill person] needs wine to be heated up for him, then a Jew should fill up [the pot with the wine so that the wine not become Yayin Nesech] and

---

[215] Piskeiy Teshuvos 328:4
[216] Piskeiy Teshuvos 329:5
[217] Piskeiy Teshuvos 330:1
[218] This includes if one will not be able to pray with a Minyan or eat the Shabbos meals. [Teshuvos Vehanhagos ibid]
[219] SSH"K 36:10; Teshuvos Vehanhagos 2:174-However there the allowance is only if the gentile is any ways traveling to their area, or one hints to a gentile ambulance driver to do so. However, to ask a regular gentile to drive them back he does not allow.
[220] Admur 328:16
[221] See end of next note
[222] Each one of these three reason is itself enough of a reason to slaughter the animal rather than feed non-kosher food to the patient. [Ketzos Hashulchan 135 footnote 6]. The Ketzos Hashulchan [135 footnote 6] adds another two reasons 1) The Mordechay says because eating non-kosher food is looked down upon [even in such a scenario]. 2) The Nitziv writes that non-kosher food creates evil tendencies in one's nature. Regarding a child, the Ketzos Hashulchan [there footnote 8] based on Mishneh Berurah rules that one is to rather feed him non-kosher then to slaughter for him on Shabbos.
[223] Meaning that in the following case it is better for the Jew to eat non-kosher rather than have a Jew transgress a Shabbos prohibition.

based on the custom explained above [in Halacha 13] the gentile should heat it up supervised [by the Jew] (see Yorah Deah chapter 153 and 155) that he [the gentile] not touch [the wine] prior to it reaching a boil[224], and even if he touches it there is no problem involved, as even so there will only be a Rabbinical prohibition [involved in drinking it]. This is opposed to if the Jew heats it up in which case, he will be doing a Biblical transgression [and thus according to the custom explained above it is better to have a gentile cook it and take the chance of him touching it. However, based on the above ruling that one should not follow this custom and rather do the transgression himself, the same applies in this case].

There is no need to worry that [if the gentile were to touch it] perhaps the sick person will be disgusted in drinking it being that its prohibition is not so severe.

Summary of Kosher verses non-Kosher food:
If the patient does not need to eat urgently, then one is to provide him with Kosher food despite non-kosher food being readily available, even if proving the kosher food involves a Shabbos prohibition.[225]

Q&A

May one salt the meat to remove its blood?[226]
Some Poskim[227] permit this to be done. Others[228] only permit this to be done through a gentile as the prohibition of eating cooked blood is only Rabbinical.

Is there a Halachic difference between slaughtering a cow and a chicken if both are available?[229]
No, as the transgression of killing an animal is equal to both. Nevertheless, there are those[230] which are stringent.

---

5. Cases that are defined as life threatening situations:
A. A wound in an inner limb is assumed to be deadly unless known otherwise:

The definition of an inner limb:[231] Any internal wound, which includes all wounds in limbs that are located from one's teeth and inward, including the teeth [and one's gums[232]], one is to desecrate Shabbos on behalf of [healing them].

The definition of a wound[233]: However, this only refers to [a type of wound that has either] impaired one's teeth or any one of the other inner limbs due to a wound, or that has a blister and the like. However mere aches and pains alone [which one knows is not associated with a wound or blister[234]] are not considered a wound and one may not transgress Shabbos for them even if it involves tremendous pain. [However, if one feels great pain and is unaware of whether or not it is a result of a wound or of a blister, then he may desecrate Shabbos for it.[235]] [As well], if one is in such pain that his entire body feels [weak and] sick then it is allowed to desecrate Shabbos through a gentile even by [having him do] a Biblical prohibition. (If he is not in so much pain then he is [nevertheless] allowed to have done through a gentile any [form of treatment] which is [only] Rabbinically prohibited) as will be explained [in chapter 2 Halacha 2-4].

An inner wound is assumed to be life threatening and does not require medical evaluation to determine

---

[224] However once the wine has reached a boil it is no longer prohibited by the touch of a gentile.
[225] Admur 328:16
[226] Piskeiy Teshuvos 328:12
[227] Daas Torah 14; Maharam Shik 138
[228] Beis Shearim 111
[229] Piskeiy Teshuvos 328:12
[230] Kaf Hachaim 328:87
[231] Admur 328:3
[232] Ketzos Hashulchan 126 Halacha 3
[233] Admur 328:3
[234] Ketzos Hashulchan 126 footnote 6, and so rules Mishneh Berurah
[235] see previous note

this:[236] A wound in an inner limb does not need to be evaluated [by a professional] and rather even by a standard wound in which there is no [available] professional to recognize [the danger in such a wound], that it needs an immediate cure [on Shabbos], as well as [even] if the patient himself does not mention anything, one may do for [this patient] anything which is regularly done for [a sick person] during the week.

If the inner wound is known to not be of danger: [237] However when one knows and recognizes that this illness [can be] delayed [from being treated now] and thus does not need to have Shabbos transgressed for it, then one is not allowed to transgress Shabbos to treat it even though it is a wound in an inner limb. Certainly, this applies if the patient or a medical professional says that it does not need immediate attention.

B. A wound on an outer limb-Some require evaluation:

A general outer wound requires evaluation of a doctor or patient to determine if lethal [other than those to be mentioned below]:[238] By a wound which is not in an inner limb, one [needs to] council with a medical professional and the patient [to determine if it's lethal]. If one of them say that it requires desecration of Shabbos or says that if one does not desecrate Shabbos then it is possible that the sickness will get worse, and it is a scenario that is possible that if the sickness were to worsen that it may become lethal, then one transgresses [for the wound]. However, if [the illness will] not [eventually become lethal if left untreated] then we do not transgress Shabbos.

C. A wound on the back of the hand or foot:[239]

A wound which is on the back of the hand or back of the foot [not including the fingers[240]], even if it occurred on its own without getting hit by iron, they are considered like an internal wound [of which one is to desecrate Shabbos for].

D. A wound from iron:[241]

As well Shabbos is to be desecrated for any wound that resulted from iron, even if the wound is on the exterior of one's skin and is not on the back of one's hand and feet. *[See Q&A if this applies even if one got a simple cut with a knife and cases of the like]*

E. Blisters by the rectum:[242]

As well one is to desecrate Shabbos for boils which sprang up by the rectum.

F. Furuncle [by the rectum[243]]: [244]

As well one is to desecrate Shabbos for furuncle[245] (which is called flunkero in the vernacular).

G. Fever accompanied with shivering: [246]

As well one is to desecrate Shabbos for one who has a very heavy fever or even if it is not such high fever but the fever is accompanied with shivering, meaning with [feeling] cold (called shvidrin in the Yiddish) in a case that the fever and shivering came simultaneously. However, the common fever which is at first hot and then cold involves no danger.

---

[236] Admur 328:4
[237] Admur 328:4
[238] Admur 328:5
[239] Admur 328:6
[240] Ketzos Hashulchan 126 Footnote 1
[241] Admur 328:7
[242] Admur 328:7
[243] So is implied from Admur, however see Q&A that also on the lips is dangerous.
[244] Admur 328:7
[245] A skin inflammation
[246] Admur 328:7

[See Q&A regarding high fever not accompanied by common cold. For fever due to common cold or virus- see end of Chapter 3]

H. Swallowed a leech:[247]
One who has swallowed a leech, which is a small worm that is found in water and when it comes in contact with the skin of a person it sucks out the blood until it inflames to [the size of a] small barrel, and when a person swallows it in water it sucks moisture out from his stomach and causes his stomach to become swollen, is to be considered like an internal wound [of which one is to desecrate Shabbos for].

I. Bitten by rabid dog or another deadly creature:[248]
One who was bitten by a rabid dog or one of the deadly creeping creatures [such as a scorpion or lethal snake[249]], even if it is questionable whether they kill or not, they are considered like an internal wound [of which one is to desecrate Shabbos for]. *[See Q&A regarding wasps and bees]*
Charming snakes and other deadly creatures to prevent injury:[250] One may charm[251] snakes and scorpions on Shabbos so they do not cause injury even if they are not pursuing oneself, and doing so does not contain the trapping prohibition even according to those opinions which hold liable one who does an action that is not needed for itself.[252]

J. Treating blood accumulation:[253]
One who has blood build up (in a scenario that could be life threatening) is to have his blood let even if he is able to walk on his feet, and even if it is the first day that he has had the blood build up. (And if there is no danger involved then he is allowed to cool himself down in water being that doing so appears like he is cooling himself off and not that he is intending to do so for healing)

K. Eye Pain:[254]
One has not yet begun to heal: One who has a pain in his eyes or in one of his eyes and there is fluid in it or there are tears pouring out of it as a result of the pain, or there is blood pouring out of it or it has pus which continuously congeals, or the pain [feels] like the prickling of a needle or it is burning and feverish, then one is to transgress Shabbos on the outset of all these sicknesses.
The reason for this is: as there is danger at that time because if the eyeball will become removed, he will die because eyesight is dependent on the heart.
One has begun to heal: However towards the end of all these sicknesses, which is defined as when he is already on his way to being healed and there only remains a small amount of the sickness, [such as that] it [only] slightly burns, then one may not transgress Shabbos even through a gentile with exception to a Rabbinical prohibition, such as to apply [to the eye a remedy of] herbs which had been ground the day before [meaning before Shabbos] as will be explained.

---

[247] Admur 328:6
[248] Admur 328:6
[249] Ketzos Hashulchan
[250] Admur 328:50
[251] Snake charming is the practice of apparently hypnotizing a snake by simply playing an instrument. A typical performance may also include handling the snakes or performing other seemingly dangerous acts, as well as other street performance staples, like juggling and sleight of hand. The practice is most common in India, though other Asian nations such as Pakistan, Bangladesh, Sri Lanka, Thailand, and Malaysia are also home to performers, as are the North African countries of Egypt, Morocco and Tunisia. Seemingly playing an instrument is allowed on Shabbos in order to restrain a dangerous snake, just like it is allowed to trap them, which is also a Rabbinical prohibition.
[252] As explained in chapter 316 Halacha 17
[253] Admur 328:8
[254] Admur 328:9

L. A baby which has gotten locked in a room:[255]

If a baby has gotten locked in a room one may break down the door and take him out, because there is chance that the baby will get frightened and die. *[See Q&A regarding a lost child]*

M. A sinking ship; drowning person; a Jew being chased by a gentile:[256]

One who sees a ship, which contains Jews, drowning in the sea, as well as [one who sees] a river that is drowning [another person], as well as [one who sees] a Jew being chased by a gentile then it is a commandment upon every individual to desecrate Shabbos in order to save them, even if there is doubt as to whether they will be saved.

N. Extinguishing a lethal fire:[257]

Any life-threatening situation overrides [the] Shabbos [prohibitions] and whoever is quick [to transgress in order to save a life] is praised. Thus...

Children or sick people are endangered: Even if a fire ignited in a different courtyard and one is worried that it may spread into one's own courtyard and it will pose danger, such as for example if there is a sick person or children [in his courtyard] and there is no time [for them] to run away before it will reach [them], then one is to extinguish [the fire] to prevent it from spreading.

It is possible to carry them out: Even if it is possible to escape [by carrying the children and ill person] through a Biblically considered public domain, then it is [still] better to extinguish [the fire, rather than escape].

The reason for this is: because extinguishing [a fire] is an action which is not done for its own use [and is thus only Rabbinically forbidden] as mentioned in chapter 278 [Halacha 1], while carrying out a sick person or children which are not able to walk is a Biblical prohibition as explained in chapter 308 [Halacha 81].

O. Fighting Robbers/Enemy Soldiers:[258]

Robbers which attack a town:[259] Gentiles which have placed in siege a city of Jews, if they have come for monetary purposes [to loot the town] then one may not desecrate Shabbos.

Other Opinions[260]: There are opinions which say that in these days that we live between non-Jews which loot and kill, then even if they have only come [to steal] money, [nevertheless] one is to desecrate Shabbos due to them.

The reason for this is[261]: because if the Jew will not allow the robbers to steal and loot then they will kill the Jew, and it is presumable that a person does not stand by and allow his money to be taken and there is thus worry that perhaps one person will stand up against the robbers and they will kill him, and this is thus a situation of life and death.

The Final Ruling:[262] Nevertheless, it all depends on the situation.

Robbers which attack an individual:[263] However robbers which came upon a single person to rob his money, then he is to let them take everything he has and may not desecrate Shabbos even to do a Rabbinical prohibition, with exception to ways explained in chapter 301 [Halacha 38]. *[See Q&A regarding a robber robbing a bank, one's friend's house, and fighting back the robber]*

Robbers which attack a border town:[264] A city that rests near the border, then even if the gentiles only want to come for purposes of [taking] hay and straw, one is to desecrate Shabbos as [otherwise] perhaps

---

[255] Admur 328:15
[256] Admur 329:8
[257] Admur 329:1
[258] Admur 329:6-7
[259] Admur 329:6
[260] Admur 329:7
[261] Admur 329:7
[262] Admur 329:7
[263] Admur 329:7
[264] Admur 329:6

the city will be conquered [by the gentiles] and from there it will be easy to conquer the remainder of the land.

Returning home with the weapons:[265] Whoever is going out to save [others] may return with their weapons to their towns if they fear from the gentiles to remain in the area of conquest as is explain in chapter 407 [Halacha 3].

Saving one's belongings from robbers: [266]

If robbers are coming to search and rob from one's home, it is permitted for one to move valuable Muktzah items[267], in order to save them from the robbers. It is forbidden according to all to move Muktzah items which are not of much value.[268]

May one carry the items outside if there is no Eiruv? It is forbidden for one to carry the items into a Karmalis.[269] Hence, one may only save the items into an area that has an Eiruv.

P. Murderers:[270]

If gentiles have come to kill the inhabitants, even if they have come as they do typically but there is worry that perhaps they have come to kill, and even if they have still not yet come but they are preparing to come, then the town may go out to greet them with weapons and they may desecrate Shabbos on their behalf [to defend themselves].

Returning home with the weapons:[271] Whoever is going out to save [others] may return with their weapons to their towns if they fear from the gentiles to remain in the area of conquest as is explain in chapter 407 [Halacha 3].

Q. Saving people within a collapsed building:[272]

One which fell upon him a mound and there is doubt as to whether he is still alive or already dead, [and] a doubt if he is under there or he is not under there, and even if one were to say that he is under there is doubt as to whether he is a Jew or a gentile, one is to undo the mound from upon him even though that there involves here a lot of doubts.

The reason for this is: because the Torah says "you should live by them" that it cannot be made to lead under any circumstances towards the death of a Jew through keeping the Mitzvos.

Saving a life even only momentarily: Even if [the victim] was found to be crushed and is thus only able to live momentarily, [nevertheless] one is to undo the mound up to his nose and check him [for if he still has life] and if he is still alive then one is to undo the mound and take him out for him to live whatever amount longer [that doing so will allow him to live]. [However] if one did not feel life in his nose, then he has certainly already dead even if he was not crushed.

Checking if the person is already dead: [273] Whether [the victim] got hit first on his head or first on his feet and one sees that there is no life in his heart, even so one is to check up to his nose, as the main evidence of whether there is life is in the nose, as it says [in the verse] "all that have a soul of life in their nose".

If the upper part of the mound had dead people found in it: [274] If one found the upper [bodies in the

---

[265] Admur 329:9

[266] Admur 334:2; 301:40

[267] As there are opinions which rule one may move Muktzah in a case of great loss. Furthermore, even according to those which rule Muktzah is forbidden to be moved even in a case of great loss, there are opinions which say in such a case moving Muktzah is allowed, as if it were to be forbidden, out of panic, one may come to transgress an even more severe sin, such as extinguishing the fire. Practically with the joint of these two opinions one may be lenient to move out his Muktzah items from the fire. [ibid]

[268] As in such a case there is no great loss, and one is not panicky about it.

[269] There are opinions which rule that it is even permitted to carry into a Karmalis the items which one desires to save, as if we were to forbid this, they may come, due to panic, to transgress a more sever sin such as burying the money. Nevertheless, many Poskim argue on this opinion and practically one may not be lenient, and it is only by Muktzah that some Poskim also rule that Muktzah is permitted to be moved in a case of great loss, that we combine the opinions and allow one to be lenient. [ibid]

[270] Admur 329:7

[271] Admur 329:9

[272] Admur 329:3

[273] Admur 329:3

[274] Admur 329:4

mound] to be dead one does not assume that the lower ones have already also died and rather is to undo the mound from on top of them as perhaps they are still alive.

There was an incident [which proves this point as a mound fell and the searchers found] the top ones to be dead and the bottom ones were found alive.

R. Extinguishing a candle for the ill which need sleep:[275]

It is permitted to extinguish a candle for an ill person to sleep, if he is sick in a way that there is worry of danger if he does not sleep.

The reason for this is because: Danger of life pushes away [the] Shabbos [prohibitions] even by a worry of questionable danger.

R. Extinguishing candles due to fear of bandits:[276]

Similarly, one who fears that bandits may come to kill him is permitted to extinguish a candle to prevent them from seeing him.

The reason for this is because: Danger of life pushes away [the] Shabbos [prohibitions] even by a worry of questionable danger.

Prohibition to extinguish to prevent theft or for the non-lethally ill: However, if there is no worry of danger of life but rather danger of one's money, as well as for an ill person which is not in danger, it is Rabbinically forbidden to extinguish the candle [although] if he [transgressed and] extinguished it he is exempt [from Biblical liability].

Practical definition of life-threatening wounds, illnesses and situations which are included in the above Mitzvah to desecrate Shabbos:

A wound in an inner limb: A wound in an inner limb is defined as all wounds to limbs that are inwards from ones teeth, including ones teeth, which have impaired the use of the limb, or if the limb has grown a blister and the like.[277] Such wounds are considered deadly and do not require any medical evaluation to determine this, although if one knows that the wound is not deadly, then one may not desecrate Shabbos for it.[278]

Mere aches and pains in the inner limbs which are for certain not a result of a wound or blister are not considered a lethal wound and thus do not have the laws of ones whose life is in danger.[279]

A wound in an outer limb: Is only considered lethal if evaluated by a professional which confirms this to be the case or that this will be lethal if left untreated, or if the patient himself says so.[280] This is with exception to a wound on the back of his feet or hands which are always considered lethal just like an inner wound.[281] As well any wound which resulted from iron is considered lethal, even if it is only an exterior wound.[282]

Swallowed a leech:[283] Is considered lethal.

Bitten by a rabid dog:[284] Is considered lethal.

A boil on the rectum:[285] Is considered lethal.

Fever:[286] If the fever is very high, or even if not very high but was simultaneously accompanied with

---

[275] Admur 278:1
[276] Admur 278:1
[277] Admur 328:3
[278] Admur 328:4
[279] Admur 328:3
[280] Admur 328:5
[281] Admur 328: 6
[282] Admur 328:7
[283] Admur 328:6
[284] Admur 328:6
[285] Admur 328:7
[286] Admur 328:7

shivering is considered lethal. However, a typical fever is not considered lethal.

Blood accumulation: Is at times lethal[287], and one is to thus light a bon fire for him even in the summer, even if he has warm clothing.[288]

Eye Pain:[289] One has pain in his eye and there is fluid in it or there are tears pouring out of it as a result of the pain, or there is blood pouring out of it or it has pus which continuously congeals, or the pain [feels] like the prickling of a needle or it is burning and feverish, then it is lethal and one is to transgress Shabbos on the outset of all these sicknesses. However if it has already begun to heal then it is no longer lethal.

A baby locked in a room[290]: Can be life threatening if the child is scared and thus the door may be broken down.

A scorpion sting:[291] Is dangerous and one may desecrate Shabbos for it. A known cure is to capture the scorpion, kill it and fry it and then place it on the wound. This thus may be done even on Shabbos.

A poisonous snake:[292] Is lethal and one may desecrate Shabbos for it.

A lethal fire:[293]Any fire which is threatening the lives of people which do not have the ability to escape, such as old and sick people as well as children, then one is to extinguish the fire on Shabbos. If the old, sick or children are unable to walk out but are able to be carried out, then if one will carry them to a public domain, he is to extinguish the fire rather than carry them.[294]

Fighting off a robber on Shabbos:[295] If [one knows for certain that] they came to rob his money and not to take his life then one is to let them take all of his possessions and may not desecrate Shabbos even with a Rabbinical prohibition. [If, however, there is any worry that the robber will attempt a physical attack then one may desecrate Shabbos and call the police.[296]]

Fighting battle against gentiles on Shabbos:[297]

By a border town even if gentiles come to steal hay and straw they are to be battled on Shabbos.

By a non-border town, if they are coming for monetary purposes then one may not desecrate Shabbos to fight them unless one fears that it may lead to a dangerous situation where lives may be threatened in which case he is to desecrate Shabbos.

In all cases that battling on Shabbos is permitted the people may return with their weapons if they fear remaining where they currently are.[298]

A dangerously ill person which needs sleep: May have the light turned off for him if there is danger involved in not doing so.

Q&A

May one desecrate Shabbos for the above-mentioned symptoms defined as life threatening even today when modern medicine has diminished the severity of these symptoms?[299]

All the above-mentioned illnesses are considered life threatening even if the doctor and patient both say that it is not, as this was the tradition of the Sages.[300] However, some have written[301] that those symptoms which all doctors today have agreed that they are not life threatening lose their life-

---

[287] Admur 328:8

[288] Admur 328:24

[289] Admur 328:9

[290] Admur 328:15

[291] Admur 328:6, Ketzos Hashulchan 137 footnote 1. See also chapter 316

[292] Admur 328:6, and chapter 316

[293] Admur 329:1

[294] However, in a Karmalis, seemingly if they have the ability to be carried out, one must do so rather than extinguish the fire. [so is implied from Admur]

[295] Admur 328:7

[296] SSH"K 41:25 Upashut.

[297] 328:6-7

[298] Admur 328:8

[299] Piskeiy Teshuvos 328:3

[300] M"B 328:8; Minchas Shabbos 92:132; Sdei Chemed 9:5

[301] See in Piskeiy Teshuvos ibid

threatening status.

May one desecrate Shabbos for even a mere cut due to a metal knife?[302]
A previously used knife: One may desecrate Shabbos in all cases by a cut from a used knife due to suspicion that they may have rust on them which could enter into one blood stream and be lethal.
A new knife: However, by a new knife [as well as a freshly sharpened knife] in which the rust suspicion does not apply, then if it one got a shallow cut one may not desecrate Shabbos for it[303]. However, by a deep cut[304] one may desecrate Shabbos unless there is a doctor present which states otherwise.[305]

May one desecrate Shabbos if he was hit by a metal or wooden[306] item and no blood came out but a bruise was formed?[307]
If a doctor is readily available, then he is to be spoken with and one is to do in accordance to his diagnosis.
If no doctor is available then one may desecrate Shabbos due to the doubt, however one must try to diminish as much as possible in the desecration being done.
If a red streak has formed from the area of the wound, then one may desecrate Shabbos due to fear of blood poisoning.[308]
Regarding placing a bandage soaked with medical ointment over the wound: One must be careful to avoid the laundering prohibition. Thus, one is to only dip a very white and clean cloth into water which had wine or other colored liquid poured into it before Shabbos [or on Shabbos if one did not do so before hand]. As well if one needs to squeeze the liquid out from the cloth then one may only do so if the liquid goes to waste.[309]

May one desecrate Shabbos to search for a lost child?[310]
If there is worry for the safety of the child, then one may do all Shabbos prohibitions in order to find him.

May one contact the police or the relatives in a case of a lost child which one has found?[311]
If the child is hysterical to be with his relatives then this may be done.

Q&A on robbers
If the robber is simply coming for the money, must the owner comply with his commands, such as giving him the key to the safe if he is asked for it, or may he fight back and desecrate Shabbos?[312]
If there is suspicion that this robber may come to physically hurt him [such as a typical unknown robber] then one may desecrate Shabbos as whenever the unknown robber gives commands to the owner, he receives the status of a Rodef and may even be killed by the owner, let alone have Shabbos desecrated on his behalf.

---

[302] Ketzos Hashulchan 136 footnote 2, so rules Piskeiy Teshuvos 328:5
[303] As is implied from the Issur Viheter 53:22 which only allows a gentile to give care to the cut.
[304] Piskeiy Teshuvos ibid writes that this refers to a cut by one's veins or arteries, however from Ketzos Hashulchan ibid it is evident that it refers to any deep cut.
[305] As the Tevuas Shur 44 rules that even a mere cut with a knife is dangerous, and thus certainly by a deep cut one is to be stringent.
[306] So writes Ketzos Hashulchan 136 footnote 2
[307] Ketzos Hashulchan 136 footnote 2, so rules Piskeiy Teshuvos 328:5
[308] Piskeiy Teshuvos 328:5
[309] Based on Ketzos Hashulchan 136 footnote 2
[310] SSH"K 41:28; Piskeiy Teshuvos 328:11
[311] SSH"K 41:28; Piskeiy Teshuvos 328:11
[312] SSH"K 41:25 footnote 70; Piskeiy Teshuvos 329:4

May one fight off the robber to prevent his money from getting stolen if he knows the robber does not intend to harm him?
Being that this can lead one to need to desecrate Shabbos, as the robber will certainly fight back and will then have the status of a Rodef, it is questionable whether it is allowed.[313] However see above that if the robber is giving him commands then the robber has the status of a rodef and one may desecrate Shabbos.

May one call the police if he sees a robber entering another person's house?[314]
If the house is empty of people and there is no suspicion that the robber will enter into a house in which someone is at home, then one may not call the police or desecrate Shabbos in any way. If, however, there are people in the home or there is suspicion that he will try to enter into a nearby home with people inside, then if one suspects that this may lead to a confrontation between the robber and the owner, he may call the police.

May one call police if he has discovered his house was burglarized?
If one entered his home and discovered, it was burglarized it is forbidden to call police until after Shabbos.

May one call the police if he sees robbers entering into a bank or the like?[315]
If the bank is empty then no, as there is no physical danger involved for anyone.

A list of different symptoms which are to be considered life threatening:[316]
Burn: A strong burn which has spread to a large portion of one's body.
Poison: The consumption of any poison or a large amount of medicine which is determined as poison.
Swallowing a needle
Bees/wasps: A bee or wasp sting to one who is allergic to them or is currently having an allergic reaction.
Cat's: The scratch of a cat.
Cut under one's nail: A shard or splinter which has entered under one's nail.
Furnucle: If large then anywhere on the body is lethal. On the lips even if small.
A fever that is not the result of the common cold or virus:[317] If the fever is above 39C [102.2 F] then it may be lethal as it may be a result of some inner illness and one may thus desecrate Shabbos for it.
A Fever above 40 C [104 F]:[318] Is considered life threatening which one may desecrate Shabbos for.
Cut in a vein or artery: Is life threatening.[319]

May one call the electric company if wires have fallen in a public area?[320]
Yes.[321]

May one call police if he sees a suspicious object due to fear it may contain a bomb?[322]
Yes.

---

[313] SSH"K 41 footnote 70 in name of Rav SZ"A
[314] SSH"K 41:25; Piskeiy Teshuvos 329:4
[315] SSH"K 41:25; Piskeiy Teshuvos 329:4
[316] SSH"K 32:11; Piskeiy Teshuvos 328:5
[317] Piskeiy Teshuvos 328:6
[318] Piskeiy Teshuvos 328:6
[319] SSH"K 32:11
[320] SSH"K 41:22
[321] It can be fatal for one to touch a downed electric wire, and being it is difficult to secure that no one will come near the wires, one is to contact help immediately.
[322] SSH"K 41:38

May one call police to capture a wild dog?[323]
If one suspects the dog may contain rabies, it is permitted to do so.

May one call police in case of a fight between two people?[324]
If there is possibility that the fight can lead to danger of life, one is to do so.

Mental illness, Manic episode:
See Piskeiy Teshuvos 328:31

---

6. Illnesses which require a Doctors evaluation:[325]

Introduction: All ailments which are not listed above [Halacha 4] as being life threatening require evaluation to determine their lethalness. The laws dealing with this evaluation and conflicting opinions will be discussed below.

A. All Doctors which did the evaluation agree that is dangerous:

Any illness of which doctors say is life threatening, even if it is located on the outside of the skin, one is to transgress Shabbos to treat it.

B. What to do in a case of split of opinion amongst two doctors:

If one doctor says that [it is life threatening and thus] Shabbos must be transgressed, while a second doctor says that [it is not life threatening and thus] one does not need to desecrate Shabbos for it, then one is to desecrate Shabbos for it because in a case of doubt that a life is danger we rule leniently [against the prohibition and force Shabbos to be transgressed]. [However see chapter 618 Halacha 4 regarding if the patient himself agrees with the doctor claiming it's not lethal, as well see there for other cases.]

C. A split opinion between the doctor and patient:[326]

If the patient says that he needs a certain treatment [for his illness to be done on Shabbos as he feels that his illness is life threatening] and the doctor says that he does not require [any immediate medication] then we listen to the patient because [only ones own] heart [truly] knows the [severity of the] pain of his soul. *[See Q&A regarding if the patient says that it is not lethal!]*
If the doctor claims the treatment requested is damaging: [However] if the doctor says that the requested treatment will damage him [even further], then one is to listen to the doctor.[327]

D. The opinion of a Non-Medical professional:

An amateur says that the illness may be life threatening: [Furthermore] even if there is no professional doctor [giving an opinion] but there is one person which says that he recognizes the sickness and it appears to him that Shabbos needs to be desecrated, then one is to desecrate Shabbos based on his word because every person is considered to be slightly expertise [in the lethalness of illnesses] and in case of doubt that a life is danger we rule leniently.
([Furthermore] even if [the amateur] says that it is questionable whether one needs to desecrate Shabbos, one is to desecrate it if he says he recognizes this illness).

---

[323] Based on SSH"K 41:23
[324] SSH"K 41:26
[325] Admur 328:10
[326] Admur 328:12
[327] *However regarding Yom Kippur the following is Admur's ruling in chapter 618:*"Any person which is sick and knows that the day is Yom Kippur and nevertheless says that he needs to eat is to be fed even if a hundred doctors say that he does not need to eat, even if they say that the eating will make things worse. The reason for this is because we do not assume that the person is a sinner that will eat on Yom Kippur, thus if he is saying that he needs to eat despite the doctors he must really feel he needs to eat, which is something that only he can feel and not the doctors." Vetzaruch Iyun!

A split of opinion amongst an amateur and medical professional: Nevertheless, [the opinion of the amateur] does not override the opinion of a professional doctor which says that [the illness] does not require Shabbos to be transgressed even if [the amateur] says that it definitely [is life threatening and] needs Shabbos to be transgressed.

The invalidity of the opinion of an amateur gentile: All the above [leniency to take into account the sole opinion of an amateurs] with regards to a Jewish [amateur], however a typical non- medical professional gentile is not considered like a professional to allow one to desecrate Shabbos based on their opinion when there is no Jew around that recognizes this illness.

E. The opinion of a woman or gentile doctor:[328]

If the doctor is a woman or gentile, they have the same status as a Kosher Jew regarding this matter [of determining if the symptom is life threatening or not] whether to be stringent or to be lenient. They are [therefore] believed to even contradict a Jewish religious Doctor [which says that it is not life threatening].

Summary of illnesses which require evaluation:

A condition which a doctor or person says it is life threatening [and the patient gives no opinion[329]]: Any condition which all doctors say is lethal, or if even one Jewish person which recognizes the illness says that it is lethal, or that it may be lethal [having no doctor dissenting his view] one is to desecrate Shabbos for even a wound on the outside of the skin. Furthermore, even if there is a split of opinion amongst two doctors one is to desecrate Shabbos. However, if an amateur says it's lethal while a doctor says it's not then we listen to the view of the doctor. As well the opinion of an amateur gentile is never taken into account.[330] [If more than one doctor says that it is not lethal, and there is only one doctor who says that it is lethal, one may not desecrate Shabbos unless the dissenting doctor is a greater medical expert then the opposing doctors. However whenever two doctors claim that it is lethal, they override even a hundred doctors which are greater experts which claim that it is not.[331]] For more detailed cases refer to Hilchos Yom Kippur chapter 618.

If the patient says it is lethal:[332] Then even if the doctor[s] contradicts him one listens to the patient unless the doctor says that the treatment is further damaging to the patient.

Q&A

May one desecrate Shabbos if he does not know whether the matter is life threatening and there is no Doctor available?

Seemingly, if one suspects that the matter may be life threatening then one may do so.

What is the law if the patient says that the ailment is not lethal?[333]

Then if there is no doctor around which contradicts his statement then one must listen to the patient.

---

7. The law of Techum Shabbos by one who helped save another Jew:[334]

All that have gone to help save Jewish souls from gentiles or from [drowning in] a river or from [dying] in a collapsed building, then they have 2000 cubits [.60 mile] radius from every direction from the area that they came to save the person.

---

[328] Admur 618:6 Regarding eating on Yom Kippur. However, see Piskeiy Teshuvos 328:7 regarding other opinions.
[329] Regarding if the patient gives an opinion, see next case regarding if he says it is lethal, and chapter 618 regarding if he says it is not lethal.
[330] Admur 328:10
[331] Chapter 618 Halacha 4-5
[332] Admur 328:12
[333] Ketzos Hashulchan 136
[334] Admur 407:3

If one fears danger in remaining in the area: However, if the gentiles are powerful and the saviors fear remaining in the area where they accomplished saving the Jew, then they may return on Shabbos to their areas and carry their weapons with them.

A midwife:[335] One who left the Techum due to Pikuach Nefesh, such as a midwife which left to help a woman give birth and cases of the like, he has 2000 cubits radius from every direction from the destination. This [radius distance of walking] is allowed in order not to cause one to stumble in the future, as if one were limited to the 4 cubits of his destination, he may refrain from going [to help someone on] the next opportunity. In a case that one arrived to a city, then he has the same Techum as do the inhabitants of the city and [may hence walk up to] 2000 cubits from outside the city parameters.

Summary:

One who traveled outside of Techum Shabbos to help save another Jew may walk within 2000 cubits from his destination. If he arrived in a city, he has the same Techum as do the city inhabitants.

Q&A

May a doctor/EMT which drove a patient to the hospital return home on Shabbos?[336]

If one estimates that he will be needed to assist more urgent cases in his hometown then he may ask a gentile to drive him home, and if need be even drive home himself.

If, however, he does not estimate this to be the case, then he may nevertheless ask a gentile to drive him back home[337], however he may not drive back home himself in his own car. If, however, there is no gentile available and there is worry that prohibiting the doctor from driving back will cause him to delay or neglect helping in emergency another time, then there is room to be lenient.[338]

---

[335] Admur 407:1

[336] Piskeiy Teshuvos 329:5

[337] As if we were to not allow him to be lenient by Rabbinical matters there is suspicion that he may delay going next time. This is similar to the allowance for the soldiers to carry back their weapons.

[338] So rules Igros Moshe 4:80

CHAPTER 2: PROVIDING TREATMENT TO ILLNESSES AND AILMENTS WHICH ARE NOT DEADLY

Introduction:
The following chapter will discuss the various levels of illness that a person may have, and which level of prohibitions may be done in order to help treat them.

Medication in general, even if it involves no Shabbos prohibition in its form of treatment, such as swallowing a pill, is Rabbinically forbidden to be taken on Shabbos unless the form sickness is severe enough to allow it to be taken, as will be explained below within each category of illness. There are however certain forms of medical treatment which are allowed in all cases due to them not being recognized to the bystander as being medication. This matter will be discussed in Halacha 7.

This chapter will discuss the general levels of illness and their respective laws. Chapter 3 will list particular medical symptoms and their respective laws regarding giving treatment on Shabbos!

1. The law of one who has a limb that is in danger but is not in a life-threatening situation:[339]

Having a gentile do forbidden work: All of one's needs may be done through a gentile, even complete Biblical prohibitions, such as to bake for him or to cook for him if he needs this done.

The prohibition for a Jew to Biblically transgress even when there is a limb in danger: However, a Jew may not transgress Shabbos in doing a Biblical prohibition even if there is danger of [losing] a limb, so long as there is no
danger of life.

The allowance for a Jew to Rabbinically transgress when there is danger of a limb: [However] for a Jew to transgress Shabbos by doing a Rabbinical prohibition [directly] with his hands, such as for example to administer to him any treatment [of healing] which is prohibited due to the decree of [that he may come] to crush herbs[340], even though that doing so in it of itself involves no remote prohibition even Rabbinically, or even if it itself does involve doing a Rabbinical prohibition in its process, then it is allowed to be done without any irregularities from the way it is typically done during the week if there is a danger of a limb involved even though he is not bedridden and his entire body does not feel sick.

Doing even Biblical prohibitions with an irregularity: [Furthermore] when doing an [action using an] irregularity it is allowed to even do a Biblical prohibition [if it cannot be done through a gentile[341]].

The law of one who has a limb that is in danger but is not life threatening:[342]

Having a gentile do the treatment: All prohibitions needed to be done in order to treat him may be done through a gentile, including even cooking and baking, which presents aside for a Shabbos prohibition, also a Kashrus prohibition.

Having a Jew do the treatment: It is permitted for a Jew to do a Biblical prohibition with an irregularity, although without an irregularity it is forbidden. However, a Rabbinical prohibition may be done even regularly.

Medicine: May be taken according to all.

---

[339] Admur 328:19

[340] But the treatment itself does not involve crushing herbs or any other biblical prohibition.

[341] Ketzos Hashulchan 134 Halacha 4 with regards to one who is bedridden. Seemingly this would apply in this case as well. So also learns Piskeiy Teshuvos 328:15

[342] Admur 328:19

Q&A

What is the definition of the danger of a limb?[343]

If there is danger that the limb will no longer function normally if it is not immediately treated, then it is defined as that the limb is in danger even though it will still somewhat function.

In cases that an action may only be done with an irregularity, what is defined to be an irregularity?[344]

One is to ask a Rav what is considered an irregularity for each particular forbidden action that he must do.

Is a Biblical action not done for its own use considered a Rabbinical action and allowed to be done by a Jew in cases that only a Rabbinical action is allowed to be done?[345]

No. It is considered like a Biblical action being that it appears like one is doing an actual Biblical prohibition. [However, to ask a gentile to do so in cases that only Rabbinical action may be done by a gentile is allowed according to those which hold that it is only considered a Rabbinical action.[346]]

---

2. The law of one which is bedridden or feels weak in his entire body but is not in danger:[347]

Having a gentile do forbidden work: A sick person that is bedridden due to his illness and is not in danger or [a person] that has an ache that pains him to the point that his entire body is weakened due to it, in which case even though he is able to walk he is considered like one who is bedridden, then all of his needs may be done through a gentile, even complete Biblical prohibitions such as to bake for him or to cook for him if he needs this done.

[Regarding giving assistance to a gentile which is giving the medical treatment-See Halacha 8]

The reason that Bishul Akum has been allowed: Now, although all forbidden foods, even those [forbidden only] Rabbinically, were not permitted for a sick person that is not in danger [to eat from them], nevertheless [the Sages] permitted [this sick person] on Shabbos in which there is no other available option [to eat food cooked by a gentile which contains the prohibition of] Bishul Akum due to that the food is permitted in it of itself and it is only that an action of the gentile is causing its prohibition.

The prohibition for a Jew to Biblically transgress: However, a Jew may not transgress Shabbos in doing a Biblical prohibition even if there is danger of [losing] a limb [and certainly if he is merely bedridden or weak], so long as there is no danger of life.

The allowance for a Jew to Rabinically transgress with an irregularity when one is bedridden: [Although when there is danger of a limb a Jew is allowed to transgress Rabbinical prohibitions in their regular fashions, nevertheless] if there is no danger of a limb, then although he is bedridden or is in so much pain that his entire body feels weak, we do not allow a Jew to do something for him which is Rabbinically forbidden unless done in an irregular fashion then the normal way that it is done during the week.[348]

Doing even Biblical prohibitions with an irregularity: [Furthermore] when doing an irregularity it is allowed to even do a Biblical prohibition [**see footnote for other opinions[349]**] [if it cannot be done

---

[343] Ketzos Hashulchan 138 footnote 18

[344] Ketzos Hashulchan chapter 134 Halacha 4

[345] Ketzos Hashulchan chapter 138 footnote 5

[346] As rules Admur in Halacha 3

[347] Admur 328:19

[348] Now, although earlier we stated that one may ask a gentile to do even a Biblical prohibition, which itself is a Rabbinical prohibition, nevertheless there this is because the Jew is merely commanding the gentile to do so and is not doing any action and thus the Sages were not as strict to require the gentile too to do a Biblical action with an irregularity. [Ketzos Hashulchan 134 footnote 5]

[349] As rules Admur so rules Igleiy Tal Tochen 18; Tehila Ledavid 22.

However the M"B [57] rules that only Rabbinical transgressions may be done with an irregularity and not Biblical transgressions.

Regarding the reason for why according to Admur a Rabbinical transgression may only be done with an irregularity while a Biblical transgression done with an irregularity [which is considered a typical Rabbinical transgression] is allowed-see Ketzos Hashulchan 134 footnote 6.

through a gentile[350]], such as for example one who is moaning [in pain from the heart] (of which it is permitted for him to suckle the milk of an animal) with his mouth as will be explained, as since he is changing from the regular way in which it is done it is only Rabbinically prohibited.

Medicine for one who is bedridden: However if one needs to eat foods which are recognizable that they are administered for healing, then although doing so is a Rabbinical prohibition due to [a decree] that one may come to grind up herbs as will be explained [in Halacha 43], nevertheless since (this is something which is impossible to do through a gentile[351] and he is) sick throughout his entire body, [therefore] [the Sages] permitted for him to do so.

Other Opinions: [However] there are opinions which prohibit [the ill person from taking medicine].

The Final Ruling: Regarding the final ruling, in a [dispute over a] Rabbinical prohibition one may follow the lenient opinion.

Making medicines:[352] If one needs to prepare the medicine, such as to mix a medicinal ointment together, then it may only be done using an irregularity. Thus, if one needs to make an oil/wine mixture it may not be mixed on Shabbos and rather one is to place each liquid separately on the required area. The reason for this is because it is forbidden to do any prohibition, even Rabbinical, without an irregularity if the patient is not deathly ill.

Summary-A person which is bedridden or feels weak in his entire body:

Having a gentile do the treatment: All prohibitions needed to be done in order to treat him may be done through a gentile, including even cooking and baking, which presents aside for a Shabbos prohibition, also a Kashrus prohibition.

Having a Jew do the treatment: It is permitted for a Jew to do any prohibition, even Biblical, when it is done with an irregularity [although a Biblical prohibition may only be done with an irregularity if it cannot be done through a gentile[353]]. A Rabbinical prohibition too may only be done with an irregularity.

Taking medicine: One may be lenient to allow medicine to be taken, even though doing so is a Rabbinical prohibition done without an irregularity.

Making medicines:[354] If one needs to prepare the medicine, such as to mix a medicinal ointment together, then it may only be done using an irregularity.

Q&A

In cases that an action may only be done with an irregularity, what is defined to be an irregularity? [355]

One is to ask a Rav what is considered an irregularity for each particular forbidden action that he must do.

Is a Biblical action not done for its own use considered a Rabbinical action and allowed to be done by a Jew in cases that only a Rabbinical action is allowed to be done?[356]

No. It is considered like a Biblical action being that it appears like one is doing an actual Biblical prohibition. [However, to ask a gentile to do so in cases that only Rabbinical action may be done by a gentile is allowed according to those which hold that it is only considered a Rabbinical action.[357]]

---

[350] Ketzos Hashulchan 134 Halacha 4

[351] Meaning that here the prohibition is in the actual eating the medication, which is something that only the patient can do, and thus should ideally be prohibited due to that it cannot be done with an irregularity, nevertheless this itself is the reason to permit it as there is no other way to administer the medication.

[352] Admur 331:1

[353] Ketzos Hashulchan 134 Halacha 4

[354] Admur 331:1

[355] Ketzos Hashulchan chapter 134 Halacha 4

[356] Ketzos Hashulchan chapter 138 footnote 5

[357] As rules Admur in Halacha 3

May one who is bedridden or weak in his entire body take medicine for a mere ache?[358]

No. Medicine may only be taken for those symptoms that cause him to be bed ridden or weak in his entire body.

Do the leniencies of a bedridden person apply even if he caused himself to reach this state, such as a failed suicide attempt?[359]

Some write[360] that in such a case he may not be lenient in any of the Shabbos prohibitions.

May one take medication if he suspects that lack of doing so can lead to being bedridden or weak in his entire body?[361]

Yes.

May one ask a child to do Melacha for a non-dangerously ill person who is bedridden?

A Biblical prohibition: No. A child has the same status as an adult in these regards.[362] Hence just as an adult may only do a Biblical prohibition with an irregularity, and only if a gentile is unavailable, so too a child may only ask to do so in these circumstances. This applies even if it is the child himself which is ill and is being asked to do Melacha for his own treatment.[363]

A Rabbinical prohibition: If no gentile is available [and one cannot do so with an irregularity[364]] seemingly one may be lenient to have a child do so, on his own behalf, such as if the child is sick.[365] However on behalf of another that is sick it requires further analysis if the child may do so.[366] In all cases if one can do so on his own with an irregularity then one should not ask a child to do so without an irregularity.

May a child be asked to plug in or turn on a nebulizer for one who needs it?

No[367], unless it is a matter of danger or can lead to it, in which case even an adult may do so, and it is even better that an adult do so. This includes even if the child needs it for himself.

Doing so with an irregularity: It is however permitted to be done with an irregularity, even by an adult, for one who is bedridden, if no gentile is available. It requires clarification as to what would be considered an irregularity in this case.

---

[358] Igros Moshe 5:51

[359] Piskeiy Teshuvos 329:1

[360] Tzitz Eliezer 10:25

[361] SSH"K 34:16; Piskeiy Teshuvos 328:2

[362] As it is a Biblical prohibition to ask a child to transgress Shabbos or do any sin. [265:10; 343:5] Hence asking a child to do a Biblical prohibition which is forbidden for an adult does not make it any more lenient, and hence is not allowed.
Background of above ruling:
In 343:5 Admur rules it is Biblically forbidden to feed a child any Issur, although it is unclear from there if other Issurim are as well Biblical. However, in 265:10 Admur states explicitly that asking a child is Biblically forbidden.
VeTzaruch Iyun based on this from 328:134 that implies that asking a child to transgress Shabbos in a case of danger is better than having an adult do it, hence implying there is no Biblical prohibition involved in asking him!!
A. Perhaps one can say that the Issur in asking a child is not in having him do the transgression but in asking him to do something which he is not allowed to do. However, in a case of danger since even a Jew may do so, asking the child is not forbidden at all, and hence there is no prohibition at all taking place, as the child is not commanded in Mitzvos and the adult was allowed to ask him. If however an adult transgresses, then although it is allowed and a Mitzvah, it is merely Dechuyah and is similar to an amputation which is done to save one's life.
Hence the advantage of asking a child is that it goes from dechuyah or Hutrah

[363] Admur 343:5

[364] As otherwise it is better for one to do so with an irregularity which is permitted according to all by a Rabbinical prohibition in case of a bedridden person, and not enter oneself in a dispute regarding having a child do a Rabbinical prohibition for his own sake.

[365] Admur 343:6

[366] As the allowance in 343:6 is only for the sake of a Mitzvah. Vetzaruch Iyun if a bedridden person can be equated to the sake of a Mitzvah to be lenient.

[367] As electricity is viewed as a Biblical transgression, and asking a child is Biblically forbidden as explained above.

3. One who is in tremendous pain but is not bedridden and does not feel weak throughout his entire body: [368]

Doing a Rabbinical prohibition with an irregularity: If one has not become bedridden [due to his illness] and as well is not suffering so much to the point that his entire body feels weak (but nevertheless is in tremendous pain) then it is allowed to do for him through a Jew any Rabbinical prohibition which will be done with an irregularity even if it is a forbidden action.[369]

Doing a Rabbinical prohibition without an irregularity/Taking medicine: However, it is forbidden for him to eat foods which are recognizable that they are being administered for medication, and certainly [to do] other Rabbinical prohibitions without an irregularity [is forbidden] even if they do not contain any resemblance of a Biblically forbidden action. As well [one may not] do a Biblical prohibition through a gentile being that doing so is a complete Rabbinical prohibition which is being done without any irregularity.

Having a gentile do a Rabbinical prohibition: It is permitted for one to do all Rabbinical prohibitions through a gentile even without [having the gentile do so with] an irregularity as was explained in chapter 307 [Halacha 12].

[Regarding giving assistance to a gentile which is giving the medical treatment-See Halacha 8]

Medication: Therefore [on the one hand] it is permitted to apply an external medical treatment through a gentile which places [the medicine] on him, since he [the Jew] is not doing any action in having this done. (However [on the other hand] it is forbidden for [the sick person] to eat foods that are recognizable that they are eaten as medication as will be explained). [As well any and all forms of recognizable medical treatment are forbidden to be applied by a Jew, as will be explained in Halacha 7 **[See there],** unless done using an irregularity.]

One who is in tremendous pain but is not bedridden and does not feel weak throughout his entire body:[370]

Having a gentile do the treatment: Only a Rabbinical prohibition may be done. He may do so even regularly.

Having a Jew do the treatment: Only a Rabbinical prohibition done with an irregularity may be done.

Taking medicine: Is forbidden.

Q&A

In cases that an action may only be done with an irregularity, what is defined to be an irregularity?[371]

One is to ask a Rav what is considered an irregularity for each particular forbidden action that he must do.

Is a Biblical action not done for its own use considered a Rabbinical action and allowed to be done by a Jew in cases that only a Rabbinical action is allowed to be done?[372]
No. It is considered like a Biblical action being that it appears like one is doing an actual Biblical prohibition. [However, to ask a gentile to do so in cases that only Rabbinical action may be done by a gentile is allowed according to those which hold that it is only considered a Rabbinical action.[373]]

4. One who is only slightly ill:[374]
Having a gentile do a Rabbinical prohibition: If one is not in tremendous pain and does not have a sickness which incorporates his entire body[375] but rather [only] a minor illness, then it is permitted for him to do all Rabbinical prohibitions through a gentile even without [having the gentile do so with] an irregularity as was explained in chapter 307 [Halacha 12]. *[Regarding giving assistance to a gentile which is giving the medical treatment-See Halacha 8]*
Having a Jew do a forbidden action: However [one may] not [do any forbidden action, even Rabbinical] through a Jew even when done with an irregularity.
Medication: Based on the above [on the one hand] it is permitted to apply an external medical treatment through a gentile which places [the medicine] on him, since he [the Jew] is not doing any action in having this done. (However [on the other hand] it is forbidden for [the sick person] to eat foods that are recognizable that they are eaten as medication as will be explained). [As well any and all forms of recognizable medical treatment are forbidden to be applied by a Jew, as will be explained in Halacha 7 **See There!**]

Summary-One who is only slightly ill:[376]
Having a gentile do the treatment: All Rabbinical prohibitions may be done. The gentile may do so regularly.
Having a Jew do the treatment: A Jew may not do any prohibition, even Rabbinical and even with an irregularity. Thus, even an action which involves no prohibition but is recognizable that it is being done for healing may not be done.
Taking medicine: Is forbidden.

5. One who has a mere ache:[377]
One who [is not even slightly sick but simply[378]] has a mere ache [in which there is no concern of danger at all and he has strength, and walks like a healthy person[379]], it is forbidden to do any [action which is recognizable that it is being done as a[380]] form of medical treatment for him on Shabbos even through a gentile, with exception to the ways that will be explained in Halacha 7 **See there!**

---

[372] Ketzos Hashulchan chapter 138 footnote 5
[373] As rules Admur in Halacha 3
[374] Admur 328:20
[375] Meaning that his entire body does not feel sick due to the illness.
[376] Admur 328:20
[377] Admur 328:1 and 20
[378] Admur 328:20
[379] Admur 328:1
[380] Admur 328:20

Summary- One who has a mere ache:[381]
It is forbidden for one to do any prohibition, even through a gentile. Thus, even an action which involves no prohibition but is recognizable that it is being done for healing may not be done. Actions that are not recognizably done for healing may be done as will be explained.
Taking medicine: Is forbidden.

Illness Chart and their relative laws

Level of illness	Jew-Biblical	Jew Rabbinical	Gentile-Biblical	Gentile-Rabbinical	Medicine
Danger of limb	*Permitted [shinui]*[382]	*Permitted*	*Permitted*	*Permitted*	*Permitted*
Bedridden or weak in entire body	*Permitted [shinui]*[383]	*Permitted [Shinui]*	*Permitted*	*Permitted*	*Permitted*
Tremendous pain	*Forbidden*	*Permitted [Shinui]*	*Forbidden*	*Permitted*	*Forbidden*
Slight illness	*Forbidden*	*Forbidden*	*Forbidden*	*Permitted*	*Forbidden*
Slight ache	*Forbidden*	*Forbidden*	*Forbidden*	*Forbidden*	*Forbidden*

6. The status of a child with regards to desecrating Shabbos on their behalf and giving them medicine:[384]

Having a gentile cook food for him: It is permitted to ask a gentile *[See Q&A regarding a Jew]* to cook a food for a child *[See Q&A regarding the definition of a child]* which does not have anything else to eat, as the typical needs of a child has the Halachic status of the needs of a sick person that is not in danger [which was explained above regarding what may be done for him]. *[See Q&A regarding if non-food related transgressions may also be done for the child]*
Moving Muktzah for a child: It is permitted to feed a child Muktzah [items[385] such as food[386]] even with ones hands if it is impossible to do so in a different way [meaning that no gentile is available[387]].

Summary-The status of a child with regards to desecrating Shabbos on their behalf:
The typical need of a child [which still needs its mother in order to be fed baby foods[388]] has the Halachic status of the needs of a sick person that is not in danger. Thus, it is permitted to ask a gentile

---

[381] Admur 328:20 and Halacha 1
[382] If no gentile is available.
[383] If no gentile is available.
[384] Admur 328:22
[385] SSH"K 15:18 writes that all Muktzah items may be moved for a child's need if no other is available.
[386] Such as fruits that fell off the tree on Shabbos and the like
[387] Ketzos Hashulchan 134 footnote 18
[388] Ketzos Hashulchan 134 footnote 18

to cook a food for a child which does not have anything else to eat.

As well it is permitted to feed a child Muktzah food even with one's hands if it is impossible to do so in a different way.

Q&A

Until what age are the typical needs of a child considered to be like the needs for one who is bedridden?[389]

This matter is disputed in the Poskim:

Some Poskim[390] say that it is dependent on if he still needs to be fed foods by his mother. Thus, once the child begins eating like an adult [on his own] then he is no longer considered like one who is ill. Other Poskim[391] brings that until the age of 9 a child is considered like one who is ill. Other Poskim[392] rule that the child is only considered like an ill person until the age of 2-3. Other Poskim[393] rule that the child is only considered like an ill person until the age of 6.

What needs of a child may be done as if he were bedridden?

Some Poskim[394] rule that only with regards to making food for the child is the child considered like a bedridden patient to which a gentile may do all of his needs. However, with regards to other matters one may not be lenient any more than any other person. Other Poskim[395] however view that the child has the same status as a bedridden patient with regards to all matters [and so seems to be the opinion of Rama/Admur[396]].

May a child which is sick be given medicine even if he is not bedridden etc?

Seemingly one may give medicine to any child under Bar or Bas Mitzvah, even if the child is not bedridden, and is above the age mentioned above which considers a childlike one who is bedridden.[397]

If a child needs food made for him to eat which involves a Shabbos transgression may it be done through a Jew?

If there is no gentile available, then it may be done by a Jew with an irregularity being that the child has

---

[389] See Shabbos Kehalacha Vol. 1 p. 214

[390] Ketzos Hashulchan 134 footnote 18; Aruch Hashulchan 328:20

[391] Minchas Yitzchak 1:78; SSH"K

[392] Sheivit Halevy, Chazon Ish, Rav SZ"A

[393] Tzitz Eliezer 8:15-12

[394] Tehila Ledavid 308:47 and 328:24

[395] Minchas Yitzchak 1:78

[396] This opinion seems to be supported by the Halacha above which states that "the general needs of a child are viewed as the needs of a sick person".

[397] If the child is young enough to be considered even when healthy like a bedridden person, then definitely it is allowed. However perhaps one can argue that even if the child is above this age he may be given medicine under any scenario so long as he is under the age of Mitzvos based on a ruling in chapter 343 that one may be lenient to feed a Rabbinical prohibited food to a slightly sick child if there is no gentile available to do so and thus so too here since medicine is only a Rabbinical prohibition one may be lenient.

Furthermore, one can say that even according to the stringent opinion there [in chapter 343] here they would agree to this leniency because they only hold of a prohibition in cases that the food is in it of itself Rabbinically not kosher. However, if it is Kosher in it of itself and just cannot be eaten due to a separate Rabbinical prohibition, such as the prohibition to eat prior to Kiddush, then they too agree that the child may be given food. Thus, here too being that the medicine is kosher in it of itself and it's just a side prohibition that prohibits it, therefore according to all it is allowed to be given to a slightly ill child.

a status of a bedridden person.[398] Furthermore if there is worry that delay of the feeding can lead to illness then all transgressions may be done as for a lethally ill patient.[399]

May one smear a cream onto a child's skin one's skin[400]?[401]
This may only be done to a child not older than the age mentioned above, **and** only if it is a type of cream which needs to be rubbed completely into the skin and it is not common to leave any of visible cream on the skin[402]. If the cream is common to be left visibly on the skin, then it is forbidden to be placed. [However according to Ketzos Hashulchan[403] which argues that there is no smoothening prohibition by soap, seemingly here too it would be allowed even if the cream is visible.]

May one smear oil on a baby for healing purposes [such as he has a rash and the like]?[404]
Yes, as a child is always viewed as a non-lethally ill patient of which it is permitted for one to give them medication on Shabbos.

---

7. Taking Medicine and other medical treatments which involve no Shabbos prohibition:

A. The General Rule:[405]
[In all cases mentioned above where medication is forbidden to be given {cases 4-5, and 3 unless done with an irregularity}] then even to do something which contains no resemblance even of the slightest to any form of even Rabbinically forbidden labor and there is thus no prohibition at all for a healthy person to do so, nevertheless since [the ill person] is doing so for healing and it is recognizable that he is doing so for healing [therefore] it is forbidden to be done.
The reason for this is: due to a decree that he may come to grind herbs for healing if it were to be allowed to deal with medical issues on Shabbos and he will thus be liable for grinding.

B. Taking medications and eating foods for the purpose of medication:[406]
Eating common foods and drinks that are used for medication: All foods and drinks which are foods [eaten] by healthy people are allowed to be eaten and drank for healing even though they have bad side effects for certain things and it is thus slightly recognizable that one's intention is for healing.
Example: For example [to eat the] spleen [of an animal] which is bad for ones stomach but helps and is good for teeth, or a vetch[407] that is bad for ones teeth but is good to heal the stomach, nevertheless since it is common at times for healthy people to eat it as well when not intending for healing, it is therefore permitted to eat it even when eaten for healing.[408] **[See Q&A regarding Aspirin]**
Foods which are eaten only for medication: All foods and drinks which are not foods eaten by a healthy person are forbidden to be eaten or drunk for healing due to a decree that one might come to grind spices. However, this [restriction] is only if one has a mere ache and strengthens himself and walks like a healthy

---

[398] So is evident from Admur. However those which rule like M"B would forbid a Jew from doing Biblical transgressions.
[399] Chazon Ish 59:4 brought in Piskeiy Teshuvos 328:16
[400] Doing so may involve a smearing prohibition, as well as a taking medicine prohibition.
Due to the medicine prohibition, it may never be done to one who is not defined as bed ridden or weak in his entire body.
[401] Minchas Yitzchak 7:20; Piskeiy Teshuvos 328:18 Vetzaruch Iyun from Piskeiy Teshuvos 327:1 which contradicts this ruling here and rules that it is always forbidden.
[402] As in such a case there is no smoothening prohibition, as is proven from the fact that no smoothening prohibition was mentioned regarding soap. [Daas Torah brought in Minchas Yitzchak ibid].
[403] 146:32.
[404] Beir Moshe 1:36, brought in Piskeiy Teshuvos 327:1
[405] Admur 328:1
[406] Admur 328:43
[407] a leguminous plant with small flowers. Use: silage, fodder.
[408] This only applies to actions which are also done for pleasure and satiation and thus are not evident that one is currently doing so for healing, although if the action is done for a type of healing which is not Halachically defined as healing, such as to swallow a raw egg to sweeten ones voice or place mouthwash in ones mouth to remove a bad smell, then when done for healing it is nevertheless forbidden even though it is no recognizable for others. [See Ketzos Hashulchan 134 footnote 16]

person even if it hurts him tremendously, however if his entire body feels sick as a result [of the pain] then even though he strengthens himself and walks, and it goes without saying if he has become bedridden, then it has already explained above [Halacha 19] that there are opinions that permit [him to take medicine].

One who does not intend to eat them for healing: However, if one does not have any ache at all and does not intend at all [to eat an item] for healing but rather for a different usage, such as for example, one who eats sweet resin and swallows a raw egg in order to sweeten his voice, then it is permitted.

A healthy person which intends on eating something for healing: However, when he does [drink the egg or chew the resin] intending for healing then it is forbidden even if he is completely healthy and does not have any ache [and is merely taking the medication in order to gain more strength[409]]. [**See Q&A regarding Vitamins**].[410]

C. Giving medical treatment for symptoms which are never treated through medicine:[411]

Introduction: The above prohibition of giving recognizable medical treatment only applies when the illness is at times treated for using medicine, as in such a case there is suspicion that one may come to grind herbs make the medication. However…]

Placing a hot empty cup over an aching stomach: One who feels pain in his stomach is permitted to place on it a cup from which hot water had been poured even though [the cup] still contains steam [from the hot water].

Elevating ones ear tendons: It is permitted to elevate ones ears, meaning the cartilage of one's ear which at times droop downwards and cause the cheek[412] [bones] to break up[413]. They may be elevated whether by hand or by using a utensil.

Elevating the cartilage opposite ones heart: Similarly one may elevate the cartilage that is opposite the heart which has drooped inwards towards the heart [and thus interferes with breathing[414]].

The Reason that the above is allowed to be done is: because each one of these issues are never healed using medications and thus there is no worry that one may come to grind [herbs], and [thus we allow it to be treated] because] one has pain from the above[415]. [However, if there is no pain involved then it would be prohibited due to it being a mundane act.[416]] [**See Q&A regarding wearing braces**]

D. Making medicines:[417]

If one needs to prepare medicine for one who is bedridden or weak in his entire body[418], such as to mix a medicinal ointment together, then it may only be done using an irregularity. Thus, if one needs to make an oil/wine mixture it may not be mixed on Shabbos and rather one is to place each liquid separately on the required area. The reason for this is because it is forbidden to do any prohibition, even Rabbinical,

---

[409] M"B

Some learn that the above prohibition for "even if he is completely healthy and does not have any ache" only applies by one who has a weak nature and although is healthy desires to strengthen his strength. However one who is completely healthy and just takes it as preventive medication, then it is allowed.

[410] see previous note for the reason why here it is forbidden when done for healing.

[411] Admur 328:45

[412] Based on Rashi in Avodah Zara 22b. Vetzaruch Iyun Gadol on the Mishneh Berurah [134] who quotes Rashi to say that it causes the ears to break up, while in Rashi there the version is "the cheeks".

[413] Rashi there "thus putting one in danger" However from the reason mentioned below this does not seem to be the case according to the Shulchan Aruch

[414] Mishneh Berurah 135

[415] So rules also Michaber.

This however only applies in cases that there is no other way to heal the ailment. If however there is another way available to heal the ailment which is not noticeable to others as a form of healing, then it is therefore forbidden to do treat it in a way that is noticeably done for healing. [Ketzos Hashulchan 138 footnote 18 based on the ruling of Admur by rubbing water on a dislocated limb, brought below in Chapter 3 Halacha 6A]

[416] So rules M"B [136] in name of Magen Avraham .

[417] Admur 331:1

[418] The case in 331:1 refers to a child which has the status of a bedridden person, or any person which is bedridden. It is however to prepare medicine even with an irregularity for one who is not bedridden or weak in his entire body, even if he is in tremendous pain.

without an irregularity if the patient is not deathly ill.[419]

Summary-Taking medicine and doing other treatments which do not contain any other Shabbos prohibitions:

The rule:[420] **a)** Any action done for healing which is **a)** evident that it is being done for healing **and b)** of which the symptom that is being treated is at times treated through medication[421], is Rabbinically forbidden to be done in all cases explained above that a regular Rabbinical prohibition may not be done, even if the treatment does not involve any other prohibition. However, if the action is **a)** not being done for healing [**and** the person is not currently sick[422]], **or b)** is being done for healing but is not evident to others that it is being done for healing[423], [or **c)** it is done for healing but is never anyways cured through medication, and the person is in pain[424]], then it may be done on Shabbos so long as it involves no other prohibitions.

Eating foods for medication:[425] Is permitted by all foods that are at times commonly eaten by healthy people. However, if only eaten for healing then it's forbidden unless ones intentions in eating it are not for healing purposes, and he does not have any ache.

Thus, all medical pills are forbidden to be taken on Shabbos unless one falls into category 1-2 of the severity of illnesses mentioned above.

In short: One may only take medication on Shabbos if either:
1. One is bedridden.
2. One is weak in his entire body
3. One is healthy and strong, and thus is not taking it as medicine.
4. It is normally eaten as food and is thus not recognizable to others that it is medicine.
5. The ailment is never treated through medicine, and one is in pain and there is no other way to treat it then one may do a recognizable medical treatment [but may not administer medication[426]].

A list of medical symptoms and their laws regarding if treatment may or may not be done for them will be brought in Chapter 3 See There!

Q&A

If one commonly takes a certain pill for non-medicinal purposes, may he take it to relieve pain?
No.[427] Furthermore, one may not even take it for non-medicinal purposes if in truth he is in pain and the pill will relieve this pain.[428]

---

[419] Vetzaruch Iyun: A) Does this Halacha in 331:1 apply to all medicines that it is forbidden to make them without a Shinuiy? B) Why can't one mix it regularly and then pour it on with a Shinuiy? So long as it is administered with a Shinuiy should it not be valid?

[420] Admur 328:43

[421] Admur 328:45-46

[422] So is implied from 328:43 that even when taken for other intentions it may not be taken if one has an ache which is healed in the process. As Admur states: "*However if one does not have a any ache at all and does not intend at all [to eat an item] for healing but rather for a different usage, such as for example, one who eats sweet resin and swallows a raw egg in order to sweeten his voice, then it is permitted.*"
However, this only applies in cases that the food is not normally eaten for eating purposes, if however it is normally eaten then it may be taken even intentionally for heating being that it is not recognizable, as will be explained in B.

[423] This only applies to actions which are also done for pleasure and satiation and thus are not evident that one is currently doing so for healing, although if the action is done for a type of healing which is not defined as healing, such as to swallow a raw egg to sweeten one's voice or place mouthwash in ones mouth to remove a bad smell, then when done for healing it is nevertheless forbidden even though it is no recognizable for others. [See Ketzos Hashulchan 134 footnote 16]

[424] Halacha 45-46

[425] Halacha 43

[426] As if one administers medicine it once again becomes relevant to decree against it that one may come to grind the herbs and make the medicine.

[427] Based on Ketzos Hashulchan 134 footnote 16 brought in previous footnotes.

[428] As explained in summary above, see footnote there.

May medicine be taken through an irregularity?[429]

Some Poskim[430] allow this to be done. Others[431] forbid it, and others which limit this allowance.[432]

The following are the cases which there are Poskim which are lenient to allow.

Dissolving the medicine in liquid from before Shabbos: One may before Shabbos dissolve medicine within a liquid and then drink it on Shabbos so long as it is not noticeable to the on looker that he is taking a medicinal drink.[433] Some[434] even allow the medicine to be dissolved in the liquid on Shabbos in an irregular fashion, if one forgot to do so before Shabbos. However other Poskim[435] argue that it may not be done on Shabbos at all.

Crushing the medicine into powder and mixing it with sugar before Shabbos: If done before Shabbos may be taken on Shabbos.[436]

Wrapping the pill in a piece of tissue and swallowing it: Some Poskim[437] allow one to do so.

May one take aspirin and other pain reliever drugs on Shabbos?[438]

If one is bedridden or is in so much pain that his entire body feels weak then any pain reliever may be taken.[439]

If one does not have the above-mentioned level of pain then: All pain relievers which are not commonly taken unless one feels sick or is in pain according to all may not be taken on Shabbos. If they are regularly taken by even healthy people as preventive measures, then some allow one to take it even for when one is in pain. Thus, regarding Aspirin and the like: Some Poskim[440] have ruled that Aspirin [and pain killers of the like] may be taken in any circumstance being that it has become a common drug even for the healthy people in order to prevent heart disease. Other Poskim[441] however have questioned this allowance being that it has been discovered that aspirin has negative side effects and thus many people avoid taking it unless they need too. Other Poskim[442] have explicitly forbidden it. *Regarding opinion of Admur see footnote below.*[443]

---

[429] Piskeiy Teshuvos 328:17

[430] For which Poskim: See the lenient cases below and the Poskim which rule this way.

[431] Halachos Mahrsham on Orchos Chayim 328:27

[432] See Igros Moshe in footnote below which only allows dissolving the medicine before Shabbos in liquid, if this is the normal way of taking the medicine. Otherwise, it is forbidden.

[433] Ketzos Hashulchan 138 footnote 31 regarding making soda to relieve stomach pain. Thus, it is possible to learn into him as learns the Igros Moshe that this allowance is limited to only those cases where the medicine is usually taken in a drink. However, see Minchas Yitzchak 6:28 which clearly learns the allowance of the Ketzos Hashulchan to be in all cases; Beir Moshe 1:33 permits it in all cases; Minchas Yitzchak 6:28 allows to rely on Ketzos Hashulchan in a case of great pain; Igros Moshe 2:86 allows only in cases that this is the normal way of taking the medicine is normally taken in a drink; Sheivet Halevy 3:36; Shearim Hametzuyanim Behalacha 91:2

[434] Ketzos Hashulchan ibid. Vetzaruch Iyun why this was omitted by the Piskeiy Teshuvos.

[435] Beir Moshe ibid; Daas Torah 37; Sheivet Halevy ibid

[436] Beir Moshe 4:31-32

[437] SSH"K 34 footnote 6 in name of Orchos Chayim 532:102

[438] See Piskeiy Teshuvos 328:2

[439] See chapter 2 Halacha 2

[440] Brought in Beir Moshe 2:32

[441] Beir Moshe 1:33 which forbade this completely. Beir Moshe 2:32 which after hearing testimony that Gedolei Haposkim have allowed it, nullifies his opinion to the allowance, although questions if it is still relevant today being that people do not use it when healthy due to negative side effects.

[442] SSH"K 34:3 and 6 forbids all medicines in all cases of pain unless one is bed ridden or his entire body is weak, as is the simple ruling of SHU"A.

Minchas Yitzchak 3:35 rules that despite that aspirin is taken by healthy people nevertheless since its main intent is for medication, therefore it may not be taken for a mere ache. However, if one is in great pain, he leans to allow it.

Ketzos Hashulchan 138:31 regarding headaches rules that "it is difficult to allow medicine to be taken even by a strong headache unless one feels week in his entire body". Thus, implying that he too does not hold of the aspirin allowance [which had already been around for about 30 years before him writing this ruling].

[443] Opinion of Admur: Seemingly according to Admur taking pain killers to relieve pain is forbidden even if the fact were that healthy people always take it. This is learned from Admur in 328:34 which rules: "However when he does eat raw egg or resin [foods that are taken even by the healthy] intending for healing then it is forbidden even if he is completely healthy and does not have any ache [and is merely taking the medication in order to gain more strength]", and as infers the Ketzos Hashulchan from here that those foods eaten for a type of healing which is not defined as healing [such as egg to sweeten ones voice and likewise pills to prevent illness], then when done for actual healing then it is nevertheless forbidden even though it is no recognizable for others.

Dissolving the medicine from before Shabbos: According to all one may dissolve aspirin and other pain killers in water before Shabbos and then drink it on Shabbos upon need.[444]

May one take Vitamins?[445]

This matter is disputed in the Poskim:

Some Poskim-Always allowed: Some Poskim[446] rule that it is always permitted being that today it has become like food of a healthy person, which is permitted to be taken even if one is sick.[447] [**For Opinion of Admur- See footnote[448]]**

Other Poskim-Depends on vitamin: Other Poskim[449] rule that those vitamins which are meant for one who is weak natured, in order to give him strength, may not be taken [for strength purposes] unless he is bedridden or weak in his entire body.[450] However those vitamins which are meant for one whom is also perfectly strong and healthy, and are meant to be taken simply to prevent illness and not to strengthen ones weakness, may be taken on Shabbos being that this is not considered to be a healing.[451]

Other Poskim-Always Forbidden: Other Poskim[452] however rule that all vitamins are forbidden.[453]

As a supplement for foods:[454] Some write that if one takes vitamins as a supplement for a food then it is allowed as it is no different than him eating food to gain strength.

Pregnant/nursing/Children: May take vitamins, although is best if possible, to push this off to before or after Shabbos.[455]

May one insert a rectal suppository for medication?[456]

Being that this contains medicine it may only be done through a large irregularity, such as placing it in from the wide side. However, to place it in with two fingers is not considered enough of an irregularity. There is no prohibition in cutting the suppository in half.[457]

Thus according to Admur since aspirin is taken by healthy people for a [non-Halachic] health purpose, it may not be taken for a Halachic health purpose such as to relieve pain even though it is not recognizable that one is taking it for this purpose.

[444] Beir Moshe 1:33

[445] Piskeiy Teshuvos 328:30

[446] Beir Moshe 1:33-1. Vetzaruch Iyun Gadol from Piskeiy Teshuvos which does not mention that the Beir Moshe allows taking vitamins in all situations.

[447] Thus, he certainly does not learn like the ruling of Ketzos Hashulchan in Admur that something which is only taken for a health reason that is not Halachically defined as health, may not be taken when done for actual health.

[448] Seemingly according to Admur vitamins would be forbidden for one who is taking them to gain strength, as we explained in opinion of Admur regarding aspirin. Thus Admur does not hold of the 1st opinion that permits it without limitation. Regarding the other opinions there is room in Admur to rule like the 2nd or third opinion. Vetzaruch Iyun.

[449] Igros Moshe 3:54

[450] As writes Rama/Admur: "However when he eats [foods normally eaten for health reasons] intending for healing then it is forbidden **even if he is completely healthy and does not have any ache.**"

[451] They learn that the above ruling "even if he is completely healthy and does not have any ache" only applies by one who has a weak nature and although is healthy desires to strengthen his strength. However, one who is completely healthy and just takes it as preventive medication, then it is allowed. It is possible to read this opinion into Admur as well.

[452] Mishneh Halachos 4:51, and so seems to learn Rav SZ"A as brought in SSH"K that it may only be taken as a food supplement and not to gain strength.

[453] As he views all vitamins as to be defined as strengthening ones system and it is thus considered like medicine and not like the food of the healthy.

[454] SSH"K 34 footnote 84 in name of Rav SZ"A

[455] Piskeiy Teshuvos 328:30 in name of Az Nidbaru

[456] Piskeiy Teshuvos 328:39; Ketzos Hashulchan 138 footnote 31 regarding treating hemorrhoids.

[457] SSH"K 33 footnote 30 in name of Rav SZ"A being that this is similar to food which does not contain a cutting prohibition.

May one cut a medicine in half [for one who may take medicine on Shabbos], such as to achieve a smaller dose for a child and the like?[458]
Yes. The prohibition of Tikkun Keli does not apply by medicine just as it does not apply towards food, and hence one may cut it to a small size for Shabbos use.[459]
Suppository: There is no prohibition in cutting a suppository in half on Shabbos.[460]

May one take medication if he suspects that lack of doing so can lead to being bedridden or weak in his entire body?[461]
Yes.

If one started a medication before Shabbos may he continue taking it into Shabbos?[462]
If not taking the medication on Shabbos can cause one to get sick to the point that he is bedridden or his entire body feels weak, then it may be taken on Shabbos.[463] This applies even if the person at the moment feels healthy.[464]
If not taking the medication on Shabbos will not cause one to become sick to the extent mentioned above, then some Poskim[465] rule that it may not be taken, [seemingly even if due to this the medicine will be of no effect[466]]. Other Poskim[467] however allow it to be taken being that he began taking it from before Shabbos.

Are medicines Muktzah?[468]
Yes, they are considered Muktzah Machmas Gufo and thus may not be moved with exception to when they are allowed to be taken.[469]

May one open the closed covering of pills?[470]
Yes, so long as he does not tear letters in the process. It is thus best to try to open it from the plastic side in contrast to the tinfoil side which has letters written on it.

In a situation that one is allowed to take medicine[471] may one mix a medicinal drink on Shabbos?[472]
It may only be done using an irregularity. Thus, if one needs to mix two different liquids it may not be done on Shabbos [as there is no way to do so in an irregular form].

---

[458] SSH"K 33 footnote 36 in name of Rav SZ"A; Piskeiy Teshuvos 328:39; 322 footnote 20 [New]
[459] See Michaber 322:4 "Animal food does not contain within it [the prohibition of] fixing a vessel."; Admur 314:11 " As animal fodder is soft and does not last, as will be explained in chapter 322 [Halacha 4], in a case that one modifies the food to become an independent vessel, **being that it is not at all common to initially make a vessel out of food**, due to the fact that it does not last long."
[460] The reason: Being that this is similar to food which does not contain a cutting prohibition. [SSH"K ibid]
[461] SSH"K 34:16; Piskeiy Teshuvos 328:2
[462] Piskeiy Teshuvos 328:28
[463] Igros Moshe Orach Chayim 5:53; SSH"K 34:17
[464] SSH"K ibid
[465] Igros Moshe ibid
[466] So is implied from Igros Moshe, and so explains Piskeiy Teshuvos ibid
[467] Minchas Shabbos 91:9; SSH"K 34:17
[468] Piskeiy Teshuvos 328:27
[469] Minchas Shabbos 88:16 See there regarding if one was sick before Shabbos and thus knew that medicine would be needed on Shabbos if even healthy people may move it for themselves.
[470] Piskeiy Teshuvos 314:3
[471] Cases 1 and 2 mentioned above
[472] Admur 331:1 regarding mixing wine with oil in which Admur rules that it may not be done unless one is deathly ill, being that it is forbidden to make medicine on Shabbos without an irregularity. This implies that two liquids cannot physically be mixed in a way that is defined as irregular.

Q&A on different forms of medications:

May a person who is in pain bathe in hot water heated before Shabbos?[473]

Yes, even if his entire body does not feel sick.[474]

May one place a wet cloth over his head to treat a fever or a headache?[475]

Yes[476] as there is no external herbal medication that is given for these matters and it thus does not contain a healing prohibition.[477] However, one must be careful to avoid the laundering prohibition. Thus, one is to only dip a very white and clean cloth into water which had wine or other colored liquid poured into it before Shabbos [or on Shabbos if one did not do so before hand]. As well one may not squeeze the water out of the cloth.[478]

May one wear detachable braces on Shabbos?[479]

Some Poskim rule that it is allowed as there is no medication that is given for these matters and it thus does not contain a healing prohibition. As well one is allowed to go into public property while wearing them. [This ruling however requires further analysis as what pain is involved in not wearing braces, as Admur here seemingly rules that the allowance only applies in a case of pain.]

May one wear a back brace and items of the sort?[480]

Yes, as there is no medication that is given for these matters and it thus does not contain a healing prohibition. As well one is allowed to go into public property while wearing them.

May one take Sleeping pills:[481]

Some Poskim[482] rule that it may be taken on Shabbos being that this is not considered to be a medical treatment.

Other Poskim[483] however rule that it is forbidden being that although this is not defined as an illness, nevertheless the pill is made through grinding and thus has the medicine decree apply to it as well.

Some[484] mediate between these two opinions and rule that it may be taken if one is in extreme pain due to inability to fall asleep.

May one take "stay awake pills"?

This is subject to the same debate as sleeping pills-See above.

May one use nose drops?[485]

No[486], unless one is bedridden or feels weak in his entire body.[487] However there are Poskim[488] who

---

[473] Rav Akivah Eiger brought in Biur Halacha and Ketzos Hashulchan 133 footnote 1

[474] So rules Rav Akivah Eiger based on 307:5 in which the Michaber writes that one may a ask a gentile to carry hot water for oneself if he is pain so he can bathe in it. Thus, we see that it is permitted to wash in hot water to remove pain. So, rules also Admur in 307:12. Thus it seems that Admur also rules that this is allowed. Now, regarding why here in the above Halacha no mention is made of water heated from before Shabbos, simply the reason for this is because this Halacha is addressing the issue of healing on Shabbos, which is only problematic by springs and other bodies of water as opposed to hot water found within a vessel. Thus, regarding the bathing prohibition, in truth it does not apply at all when a person is in pain, and one may bathe in water heated before Shabbos to release pain.

[475] Piskeiy Teshuvos 328:35 in name of Az Nidbaru

[476] The Ketzos Hashulchan allows this to reduce fever. The Az Nidbaru extends this allowance to even a head ache.

[477] Therefore it is permitted even for a head ache which in general one may not take medicine for. However, by fever one may even take medicine and thus this reasoning is not needed.

[478] Based on Ketzos Hashulchan 136 footnote 2 and 138 footnote 31

[479] Piskeiy Teshuvos 328:35; SSH"K 34:29

[480] Piskeiy Teshuvos 328:35; SSH"K 34:29

[481] Piskeiy Teshuvos 328:31

[482] Ketzos Hashulchan chapter 138 footnote 31; Beir Moshe 1:33-19 regarding "stay awake pills".

[483] Minchas Yitzchak 3:21 regarding stay awake pills. The same applies for sleeping pills; Az Nidbaru 14:10

[484] SSH"K 33:16

[485] Piskeiy Teshuvos 328:33

[486] Being that they are used only for healing.

[487] Minchas Yitzchak 8:5. Ketzos Hashulchan 138 footnote 31 towards end. This is not similar to sniffing tobacco which is done for pleasure.

rule that if not taking the drops will cause mucus droppings which will be embarrassing then one may be lenient and it thus may be taken.

May one take anti-depressants and other medications meant for mental health on Shabbos?
Seemingly this is allowed.[489]

May one sniff or smell a substance that will clear his nasal passages?
If the substance is snuffed or smelled even for pleasure, such as is the case by tobacco, then it may be used even if it will clear the passageway, as it is not recognizable that it is being done for healing.[490]
If the substance is only used for the purpose of clearing nose passage, then: Some Poskim[491] rule that this is forbidden as by doing so one temporarily heals the extra mucus flow which derives. Other Poskim[492] rule that it is allowed as it does not actually heal the mucus flow but temporarily stops it.

Medications which relate to marital relations
May one take fertility pills to help for conception?[493]
Yes, as there is no apparent illness.[494] However, some Poskim[495] write that it is best to dissolve the pill in water before Shabbos and then drink it.[496]

May a man take Viagra on Shabbos if necessary, for him to have intimacy?[497]
Yes.[498]

May one take contraceptive pills?[499]
One who has consulted with a Rav and received permission to be on a contraceptive may take the pills on Shabbos, as there is no apparent illness.

May one take heart medication[500] for use prior to and after marital relations?[501]
One is to dissolve the pill in water <u>before Shabbos</u> and may then drink it on Shabbos, as in such a way it is not noticeable that one is taking medication.[502]
If this was not done then it is forbidden to take the pills on Shabbos, even through dissolving them in liquid[503], unless it is one's wife's night of Mikveh.[504]

---

[488] Rav SZ"A in SSH"K 134 footnote 52

[489] As A) Tzaruch Iyun if things taken for mood issues are considered medicine. If so, then maybe coffee should be considered medicine? [see above by stay awake pills], as well these medicines are usually taken every day, and thus have a further leniency mentioned in some Poskim that a medicine started from before Shabbos may be taken on Shabbos. As well if one were to consider depression as a medical illness, and thus its medication is considered a medicine then it should be permitted for this reason itself, as when one is depressed, he does not feel like moving from his bed and is thus similar to being bedridden, for which taking medicine is allowed.

[490] Mishneh Berurah 328:127; Ketzos Hashulchan 138 footnote 31 towards end

[491] Ketzos Hashulchan ibid

[492] Beir Moshe 1:33

[493] Piskeiy Teshuvos 328:1

[494] Beir Moshe 1:33

[495] See Piskeiy Teshuvos 328:1

[496] See Piskeiy Teshuvos 328:1

[497] Encyclopedia Hilchatit Refuit [Shteinberg] 7 p. 475 in name of Koveitz Assia 73-74 p. 27; Mayan Omer 2:249; See also Poskim in previous and coming Q&A

[498] The reason: As there is no real illness, and medicine is permitted to be taken by one who is healthy for non-medicinal purposes, as rules Admur 328:43 regarding swallowing eggs to better one's voice. Furthermore, it is being done for the sake of a Mitzvah. Furthermore, even if it were to be defined as an illness, it should be defined as Sakanas Eiver for which medicine taking is permitted. [See Poskim ibid]

[499] Beir Moshe 1:33; So rules Piskeiy Teshuvos 280:2

[500] People that suffer from high blood pressure may need to take medication prior to having marital relations so their blood pressure not sore too high.

[501] Piskeiy Teshuvos 280:2

[502] Beir Moshe 1:33-9

[503] So rules Beir Moshe ibid and so is implied from Minchas Yitzchak 1:108 which only writes with regards to Leil Tevilah.

[504] Beir Moshe ibid, Minchas Yitzchak ibid

May one smear a cream onto one's skin[505]?[506]
This may only be done to a child [not older than age 9[507]] or to one who is bedridden or ill, **and** only if it is a type of cream which needs to be rubbed completely into the skin and it is not common to leave any of visible cream on the skin[508]. If the cream is common to be left visibly on the skin then it is forbidden to be placed. [However according to Ketzos Hashulchan which argues that there is no smoothening prohibition by soap, seemingly here too it would be allowed even if the cream is visible.]

Regarding taking a laxative, alka seltzer and other medicines for specific medical conditions-see next chapter under their relevant topic.

8. Giving assistance to a gentile which is giving the medical treatment:[509]
Having the sick person himself assist in his treatment: Anything which is if forbidden to be done [for the ill person] through a Jew is also forbidden to be done by the sick person himself, however if a gentile does it, it is permitted for the sick person to slightly assist him, such as for example a gentile which is applying ointment to the eye of a Jew towards the conclusion of his sickness in which his [eyes] slightly burn, then it is permitted for him to open and close his eyes in order so that the ointment enter into it well, being that assisting [the gentile] is [considered] meaningless so long as the gentile is capable of doing [the treatment] himself without the help of the Jew and just having the Jew not refrain him from doing it as explained above.
[Furthermore] even if the gentile is doing for him a Biblically forbidden action in a scenario where it is permitted [for a Jew to have him do so then] the sick person is allowed to assist him in the way explained [two lines above that the gentile would anyways be able to do it].
The Reason: (Now, although one who assists in doing a Biblical prohibition is [transgressing a] fully fledged Rabbinical prohibition as will be explained in chapter 346[510] and [thus] even upon assisting in doing a Rabbinical prohibition he [transgresses] at the very least a Rabbinical decree upon a Rabbinical decree [which is also forbidden], nevertheless here since [the Sages] rescinded the Rabbinical prohibition of asking a gentile [to do a forbidden act] for the need of a sick person, so too we rescind the Rabbinical prohibition of assisting him being that this too is for the need of the sick person. As through the assistance the treatment is done much better from how it were to be done through the gentile alone, such as for example [having the patient] close his eyes so that the ointment get absorbed in well and so too to open the eyes for the ointment to be entered into, or to open ones mouth for ones tooth to be removed [in which in all of these cases] although the gentile could have done [these actions] himself nevertheless the Sages did not require this, to place this responsibility on the gentile, and not allow the patient, for whom the treatment must be done to, to comply.)
{Thus, although one does slightly assist [the gentile] [in applying the treatment] [nevertheless] it is meaningless and does not pose a problem[511], as even if the Jew were to not help him in this assistance [that he is giving] but would also not stop [the gentile from doing his job] then the gentile would be able to do it himself.[512]}

---

[505] Doing so may involve a smearing prohibition, as well as a taking medicine prohibition.
Due to the medicine prohibition it may never be done to one who is not defined as bed ridden or weak in his entire body.
[506] Minchas Yitzchak 7:20; Piskeiy Teshuvos 328:18 Vetzaruch Iyun from Piskeiy Teshuvos 327:1 which contradicts this ruling here and rules that it is always forbidden.
[507] Regarding all the opinions in the age of the child-See "The Laws of taking Medicine" Chapter 2 Halacha 6
[508] As in such a case there is no smoothening prohibition, as is proven from the fact that no smoothening prohibition was mentioned regarding soap. [Daas Torah brought in Minchas Yitzchak ibid].
[509] Admur 328:21
[510] Perhaps this refers in truth to 347 Halacha 1 and 3.
[511] Admur 328:3 and 20
[512] Admur 328:3

Having another Jew assist the gentile: (However when the gentile does other matters that are forbidden even Rabbinically then a Jew (other than the patient) may not assist him with the treatment since there is no need at all for his assistance being that the gentile is capable of doing it all himself.

However, if there is a need for his assistance that through assisting the treatment will work better than if it were to be done by the gentile alone, then it is permitted for even another Jew to slightly assist him.)

If the assistance is critical for the treatment: [However] if it is impossible to do [the treatment] without the assistance of a Jew then it is forbidden even for the sick person himself to assist.

Having the patient or other Jews give assistance to a gentile which is giving the medical treatment:[513]

In all the above cases {cases 2, 3, 4} that a gentile may administer treatment but a Jew may not do even a Rabbinical prohibition [without an irregularity], assistance may be given, to the gentile which is doing the treatment, by any Jew if **a)** it does not involve any other prohibition[514] **and b)** The gentile is able to administer the treatment himself even without this assistance, **and c)** The treatment will work better with this assistance.

If the treatment does involve a Biblical or Rabbinical prohibition, then only the patient himself may assist the gentile [in matters that his assistance have no prohibition involved].

---

9. May one ask a gentile to do an action which will only be needed after Shabbos?[515]

[The Sages] only permitted asking a gentile to do something for a sick person if it is needed on Shabbos, however not if it is only needed for after Shabbos.

Summary:

In all the above cases the Sages only permitted asking a gentile to do something for a sick person if it is needed on Shabbos, however not if it is only needed for after Shabbos.

Compilation-May one who has a localized pain, such as a headache, foot pain, back pain, and the like, take a pain killer on Shabbos?

*Important note: This Halacha is dealing with the very specific case of taking pain killers for a non-lethal localized pain. It does not refer to illnesses, such as fever, or other medical conditions, or people who do not have any pain, illness or medical condition, which contains its own article.

A. Background:

The Sages prohibited taking medicine on Shabbos due to a decree that this can lead one to grind medicinal herbs which is Biblically forbidden due to the grinding prohibition.[516] This prohibition applies even today.[517] This prohibition applies even if one is slightly ill, and even if one is in great pain.[518] However this restriction only applies if one has a mere ache and is able to strengthen himself and walk like a healthy person, even if it hurts him tremendously.[519] However, if his entire body feels weak or sick as a result [of the pain] then even though he strengthens himself and walks, and it goes without saying if

---

[513] Halacha 21

[514] As ideally the mere giving of treatment is itself a prohibition, thus the case here is discussing that no other prohibitions are involved in the assistance given.

[515] Admur 328:23

[516] Admur 328:1, 19-20, 43; Michaber 328:1; Mishneh Shabbos 109b, 111a and Gemara 53b

[517] See Ketzos Hashulchan 134 footnote 7; Piskeiy Teshuvos 328:2

[518] Admur 328:20 in parentheses; 328:43; Michaber 328:37; Mishneh Shabbos 109b

[519] Admur 328:43; Michaber ibid

he has become bedridden, then some Poskim[520] rule that he may take medicine, and so is the final ruling.[521]

B. The ruling:[522]

Very painful to point of weakness: If one is experiencing pain to the point that it drains one's energy and makes one's entire body feel weak, then any pain reliever may be taken on Shabbos to relieve the pain.

Painful, but able to function-Pain relievers that are not regularly taken unless sick [i.e. prescription drugs, Tylenol, ibuprofen]: All pain relievers which are not commonly taken by people unless they feel sick, or are in pain, may not be taken on Shabbos, even if one is in pain, so long as he can still walk and function like a normal person. [Thus, all prescription drugs, and all OTC [i.e. Over-The-Counter] pain relievers which healthy people do not take daily as preventive medicine, may not be taken. An example of such pain relievers are all forms of opioids, Tylenol, ibuprofen, and most over the counter pain killers.]

Painful, but able to function-Pain relievers that are taken regularly even by healthy people [i.e. Aspirin]: Pain relievers which are regularly taken even by healthy people as preventive medicine, such as aspirin to lower the risk of heart disease, are debated in whether they are defined as medicine, and as to whether it may be taken by one who is in pain. Some Poskim[523] rule that Aspirin may be taken in any circumstance being that it has become a common drug used by even healthy people in order to prevent heart disease. However, the majority of Poskim[524] rule that even such medicines are forbidden to be taken for medicinal purposes, just like all other medicine, and so is the implied ruling of Admur in his Shulchan Aruch.[525] This is especially in light of the fact that it has been discovered that aspirin has negative side effects and thus many people avoid taking it unless they need to, thus eroding the entire basis of the lenient approach. Practically, it is forbidden to be taken unless one is in great pain, which has weakened his body, as explained above.

---

[520] 1st and Stam opinion in Admur 328:19 *"A sick person that is bedridden due to his illness and is not in danger or [a person] that has an ache that pains him to the point that his entire body is weakened due to it, in which case even though he is able to walk he is considered like one who is bedridden, then.....if one needs to eat foods which are recognizable that they are administered for healing, then although doing so is a Rabbinical prohibition due to [a decree] that one may come to grind up herbs as will be explained [in Halacha 43], nevertheless since (this is something which is impossible to do through a gentile and he is) sick throughout his entire body, [therefore] [the Sages] permitted for him to do so."*; Rama 328:37; Beis Yosef 328; M"A 328:44; Implication of Maggid Mishneh 21:20 and Ran 14; See Biur Halacha 328:37 "Vechein"

Other opinions: Some Poskim rule it is forbidden to take medicine on Shabbos even if one is bedridden due to the pain or illness. [2nd opinion in Admur ibid; Taz 328:25; Bach 328; Olas Shabbos 328:42]

[521] Admur 328:19 *"Regarding the final ruling, in a [dispute over a] Rabbinical prohibition one may follow the lenient opinion."*; 328:43 *"It has already explained above [Halacha 19] that there are opinions that permit [him to take medicine]."* See Biur Halacha 328:37 "Vechein" who leans to be stringent; See See Ketzos Hashulchan 134 footnote 7; Piskeiy Teshuvos 328:2

[522] See Ketzos Hashulchan 138:31 *"It is difficult to allow medicine to be taken even by a strong head ache unless one feels week in his entire body"*; SSH"K 34:3 and 6; Piskeiy Teshuvos 328:2 [old]

[523] Opinion of Rav Shteif, recorded in Beir Moshe 2:32

[524] SSH"K 34:3 and 6 forbids all medicines in all cases of pain, unless one is bed ridden or his entire body is weak, as is the simple ruling of SHU"A; Piskeiy Teshuvos [new] 328 footnote 499 that majority of Poskim argue on the above leniency; Minchas Yitzchak 3:35 rules that although aspirin is taken by healthy people, nevertheless, since its main intent is for medication, therefore it may not be taken for a mere ache. However, if one is in great pain, he leans to allow it.; Ketzos Hashulchan 138:31 writes regarding headaches rules that *"it is difficult to allow medicine to be taken even by a strong head ache unless one feels week in his entire body"*. Thus, implying that he too does not hold of the aspirin allowance [which had already been around for about 30 years before him writing this ruling]. This is furthermore understood from his ruling in Ketzos Hashulchan 134 footnote 16, brought in next footnote. The Beir Moshe in 1:33 forbids this completely, although in Beir Moshe 2:32 he writes that after hearing testimony that some Gedolei Haposkim have allowed it, nullifies his opinion to the allowance, although questions if it is still relevant today being that people do not use it when healthy due to negative side effects; See Beir Sarim 3:43; Minchas Asher 2:38

[525] Opinion of Admur: Seemingly according to Admur taking pain killers to relieve pain is forbidden even if the fact were that healthy people always take it. This is learned from Admur in 328:34 in which he writes: *"However when he does eat raw egg or resin [foods that are taken even by the healthy] intending for healing then it is forbidden even if he is completely healthy and does not have any ache [and is merely taking the medication in order to gain more strength]"*, and as infers the Ketzos Hashulchan 134 footnote 16 from here that those foods eaten for a type of healing which is not defined as healing [such as egg to sweeten ones voice and likewise pills to prevent illness], then when done for actual healing it is nevertheless forbidden even though it is no recognizable for others. Thus, according to Admur since aspirin is taken by healthy people for a [non-Halachic] health purpose, it may not be taken for a Halachic health purpose such as to relieve pain even though it is not recognizable that one is taking it for this purpose.

Summary:

It is forbidden for one who has localized pain to take pain killers on Shabbos unless he is in pain to the point that it depletes his energy and makes him feel weak in his entire body, in which case any pain killer may be taken regularly.

Q&A

If one is unsure as to whether he is weak in his entire body due to the pain, may he take the medicine?

Some Poskim[526] rule it is permitted to do so.

Word of Advice-Dissolving the medicine from before Shabbos:[527]

One who feels that he may need to take pain killers on Shabbos, but will not reach the state of being weak in his entire body due to the pain, may dissolve the pain killer in water before Shabbos and then drink the solution on Shabbos upon need.[528] [One is to dissolve the pill in juice or colored soda water, in a way that the solution will not be recognizable that it contains medicine.]

---

[526] Shut Rav Akiva Shlezinger 1:122; Piskeiy Teshuvos 328:2

[527] Beir Moshe 1:33; See Ketzos Hashulchan 138: footnote 31; Minchas Yitzchak 6:28; Igros Moshe 2:86 allows only in cases that this is the normal way of taking the medicine, that it is normally taken in a drink; Sheivet Halevy 3:36; Shearim Hametzuyanim Behalacha 91:2

[528] The reason: As any action which is being done for healing but is not evident to others that it is being done for healing may be done on Shabbos. [See Admur 328:43; Ketzos Hashulchan 134 footnote 16]

CHAPTER 3: LIST OF MEDICAL SYMPTOMS AND THEIR RESPECTIVE LAWS REGARDING THEIR TREATMENT ON SHABBOS

Important Note:

The laws here on the most part relate to classical symptoms which are a mere ache, and what treatments are defined as recognized medical treatments and thus may not be done. This however does not negate any of the laws explained in the previous chapter of the different levels of illnesses and their respective laws. Thus, if in any of the below mentioned cases one has reached a severity of illness as those mentioned above which allow desecration of Shabbos to a certain extent, then all those laws apply.

---

1. Eye care:
A. Placing ointment in one's eye:
❖ ***Placing tasteless saliva on one's eyes:[1]***

Tasteless saliva, which is defined as all the saliva that one has after awaking from his sleep [at night] prior to having tasted anything, is potent and has healing powers, and is forbidden to be placed even on the eyelids being that doing so does not appear as if he is rinsing them as it is not common to rinse with saliva due to its repulsiveness.

Saliva mixed with water: However, if one washes his mouth with water and then passes it on his eyes, then although that tasteless saliva is mixed into that water it is [nevertheless] permitted being that it is not repulsive to rinse [one's eyes] with such water [and thus does not appear that one is doing so for healing purposes].

❖ ***Applying collyrium to one's eyes:[2]***

Soaking it before Shabbos: One may soak liquidly and clear collyrium[3] before Shabbos and place it over his eyelids on Shabbos for healing.

The Reason: There is no decree here that one may come to grind herbs as since one was required to soak it before Shabbos this thus serves for him as a reminder that he may not make medicines on Shabbos[4]. There is no need to worry that the above gives onlookers a bad impression [and may lead them to think that medication is allowed to be taken on Shabbos] as [rinsing one's eyes with it] simply appears like one is washing them as since [the collyrium] is liquidly and clear it appears to the onlooker as if it is wine.[5]

Opening and closing the eyes: Nonetheless, one may not open and close his eyes [upon placing it on them] as when done so it is evident that that his intentions [in placing it there] are for healing purposes.

Thick collyrium: However thick collyrium is forbidden to place on one's eyelids on Shabbos because it is evident that it is done for healing purposes. Although if one placed it [on his eyelids] from before Shabbos then it is permitted [to be left there over Shabbos] as explained in chapter 252 Halacha 14].

❖ ***Placing wine in the eye:[6]***

One may not place wine into an eye because it is recognizable that one is doing so for healing purposes,

---

[1] Admur 328:26
[2] Admur 328:27
[3] In eye care, a collyrium is a lotion or liquid wash used as a cleanser for the eyes, particularly in diseases of the eye. Pre-modern medicine distinguished two kinds of collyriums: the one liquid, the other dry. Liquid collyriums were composed of ophthalmic powders, or waters, such as rose-water, plantain-water, that of fennel, eyebright, etc, in which was dissolved tutty, white vitriol, or some other proper powder. The dry collyriums were troches of rhasis, sugar-candy, iris, tutty prepared and blown into the eye with a little pipe.
[4] Lit. Deal with healing on Shabbos
[5] However today that no one washes with wine shouldn't we say that it does appear like healing to the onlooker?
[6] Admur 328:25

although it is permitted to place it on top of the eye[7] because [doing so] only appears like one is rinsing [his eyelid] and not like he is intending to do so for healing purposes.

Closing and opening the eye: [However] this is only [permitted] so long as that one does not open and close his eyes, however if he does open and close [his eyes] so the wine penetrates into it, then it is recognizable that he is intending to do so for healing purposes and it is thus forbidden.

The law today: Today that it is no longer accustomed to rinse [one's eye] with wine it is forbidden [to rinse one's eye with it] under all circumstances [even if he does not open and close his eyes] if his intention in doing so is for healing.

Summary-Placing ointment in one's eyes for healing[8]:
May only be done if it is not evident that one is doing so for healing purposes.

B. Treatment for one who is unable to open his eyes:[9]
One who is unable to open his eyes is allowed to damp them even with pure tasteless saliva, being that [the Sages] only prohibited doing so when done with intent of healing and this [purpose to help one's eyes open] is not considered healing.

Summary- One who is unable to open his eyes[10]:
May wet them with even medical ointment as doing so is not considered a treatment.

C. Treating eye irritation:[11]
One may place a vessel over an eye in order to cool [the eye] down as long as the vessel is permitted to be moved [not-Muktzah].

Similarly, what is done to a person which feels eye pain in which they surround [his eye] with a ring in order to restrain the inflammation [of the eye is likewise allowed to be done on Shabbos].

Question:
May my son use eyedrops on Shabbos to prevent his lens number from going up?

Answer:
Yes, if he is under 9 years old, or if lack of doing so can cause a significant loss of eyesight later on.

Background: Ideally, eyedrops are forbidden on Shabbos for medicinal purposes unless it is done for a specific active condition such as an eye infection [as opposed to mere dryness of the eye, or slight pain]. It is questionable as to how to judge the purpose for which the eyedrops are intended for, and if it is to be viewed similar to dryness, which is forbidden, or like a Sakanas Eiver which is permitted. Practically, if your son is under 9 years old you may do so for any medicinal purpose including the one you mentioned. If he is above age 9, then seemingly this matter would depend on how bad the eyesight can be damaged if the eyedrops are not given during the 24 hours period of Shabbos, and whether one can rely on those Poskim who rule that if one started a treatment before Shabbos than one may continue

---

[7] Seemingly this refers to placing it on the eye lid when closed. See Rashi on Shabbos 108b
[8] Admur 328:27
[9] Admur 328:26
[10] Admur 328:26
[11] Admur 328:51

on Shabbos. However, my leaning stance would be that if it can damage the eyesight to the point that one will have abnormal difficulty seeing, or higher than average eye prescriptions even later on in life, then one may do so.

Sources: See Admur 328: 9,22, 26-27; 51; Michaber 328:9; Minchas Yitzchak 1:78; See Piskeiy Teshuvos 328:22; Choveret Asia 48:79

2. Mouth and Teeth ailments:
A. Removing an aching tooth:[12]
A toothache which has made one weak: Based on the laws of the different levels of severity of illnesses listed in Chapter 2, one who has a tooth ache which causes him such pain that his entire body feels sick (is allowed to transgress Shabbos through a gentile) [and] may tell the gentile to remove [the tooth].
The reason it is allowed despite ones assistance that he is giving to the dentist: Now, although the Jew helps him locate the tooth and slightly assists him to take it out, [nevertheless] this does not pose a problem because his help is not meaningful as even if the Jew were to not help him in this assistance [that he is giving] but would also not stop [the gentile from doing his job] then the gentile would be able to do it himself.
A toothache which has not made one weak:[13] (And according to those opinions which say that any action which is not done for its own use is only Rabbinically forbidden then it is permitted to remove [the tooth] through a gentile even if the entire person's body has not become sick [so long as it is more than a mere ache] as was explained [in Halacha 328/20]) [**See Q&A regarding tooth which its majority has begun coming out**]

B. Taking medicine:[14]
A minor ache: One who has a toothache may not gargle vinegar and then spit it out being that it is recognizable that he is doing it for healing. [The same applies to taking any medicine, that doing so is forbidden, unless the ache is so strong that he is bedridden due to it as will be explained next.] However, he may gargle and swallow it or dip a piece of bread into it and eat it as is normally done during the week. Even through a gentile it is forbidden to do any [treatment] for him even if there is no resemblance of a forbidden action even Rabbinical, if it is recognizable that [the treatment] is being done for healing.
A major ache: However this only applies by a minor [tooth] ache, however if he is in so much pain that his entire body is weakened because of it, then he is permitted [take medicine[15] and may] do through a gentile [even Biblical prohibitions, and if his entire body is not weakened but he nevertheless feels pain to the point that he is slightly sick then a gentile may nevertheless do for him[16]] anything which is only Rabbinically prohibited, as was explained above.

Summary:
Removing the tooth: If it hurts to the point that one's entire body feels weak, then he may ask a gentile to pull it out. According to some even if one's entire body is not weak from the pain, but is more than a mere ache, then one may ask a gentile to remove it.[17]

---

[12] Admur 328:3
[13] Admur ibid; Mamar Mordechai, brought in M"B 316:30
Other opinions: Some Poskim rule that removing a tooth for medical purposes [or doing any bruise for medical purposes] is considered a Melacha Shetzricha Legufa. [M"A 316:15; 328:3; M"B 316:30]
[14] Admur 328:38
[15] As explained in Chapter 2 Halacha 2
[16] This insert is placed by the Ketzos Hashulchan [Chapter 128 footnote 9]. Without it the statement contradicts what was explained above in Halacha 19. So rules also Mishneh Berurah 328:100.
[17] Admur 328:3

Gargling vinegar: If it is a mere ache then one may not even gargle vinegar and the like and then spit it out. Although he may gargle it and swallow it or dip his bread in it and eat it, as then it is not noticeable that he is eating it as medicine.[18] If, however, the pain is so strong that one feels weak in his entire body then all medicine may be taken.

Medicine: Is forbidden unless one is bedridden or weak throughout his entire body.

Q&A

May one pull out a loose tooth?[19]

If majority of the tooth has already detached and pulling it out will not release blood, then it is allowed to be pulled out if it is causing one pain.[20]

May one wear detachable braces on Shabbos?[21]

See Chapter 2 Halacha 7 Q&A there!

Question:

I suffer from dull tooth pain. May I bite on a clove on Shabbos for the sake of relieving it?

Answer:

You should only do so in the process of eating such as to add cloves to a salad or other food and eat it within that food, however you should not need it plain. If, however, the pain is so strong that you feel weak in your entire body, then you may chew the clove regularly and even take medicine, as is the law of allowance by anyone who is sick.

Explanation: It is forbidden to take medicine on Shabbos even if one is in pain unless one is sick, which is defined as feeling weakness throughout the entire body. This restriction applies even against eating foods for medicinal purposes if it is being done in a way that is evident to all that its purpose is for medicine. However, the restriction does not apply if one consumes the food in the regular way of eating even if its true intent is for medicinal purposes, being that this intent is not apparent to others. Accordingly, we concluded above that while certainly one may eat the clove as part of an ingredient of his food or salad, even if his intent is for medicinal purposes being that there are plenty of healthy people who do so, and it is hence not apparent to others that is being done for medicinal purposes, nonetheless, he should not chew it plain being that, as far as I'm aware, this is not normally done by even a minority of healthy people for eating purposes and will hence be viewed by others as being done for medicinal purposes.

Sources: Admur 328:1 [regarding general medicine prohibition]; Admur 328:38 [regarding the permitted and forbidden ways of treating toothache based on the intensity of the ache and on whether the treatment appears like medicine to others]; Admur 328:43 and Ketzos Hashulchan 134 footnote 16 [regarding if the general prohibition of medicine applies to foods]; See Piskeiy Teshuvos 328:61 footnote 485 that while it is permitted to eat garlic in salad for medicinal purposes, it is not permitted to eat garlic plain for medicinal purposes being that not even a minority of people do so.

---

[18] Admur 328:38

[19] Sheivet Halevy 5:39, brought in Piskeiy Teshuvos 328:24

[20] As this is similar to a nail which has peeled off its majority which ideally may be removed. [Although practically may not due to what will be explained in the Halacha dealing with it.]

[21] Piskeiy Teshuvos 328:35; SSH"K 34:29

C. Chewing medicinal gum and applying toothpaste to one's teeth:[22]

For medical purposes: One may not chew a species of resin called Mastichi[23] and may not rub a drug on ones teeth when ones intention in doing so is for healing purposes.

To remove bad odor: However, if he is only doing so to [remove bad] odor from his mouth, then it is allowed [to rub an herb or chew the gum].[24]

Summary-Chewing medicinal gum and applying toothpaste to one's teeth:[25]
One may not do so for medical purposes. However, one may do so in order to remove bad odor from one's mouth.

Q&A

May one brush his teeth on Shabbos?
One may place thin creamy toothpaste on his hand and then smear it on his teeth.[26] It is forbidden to place it directly on a toothbrush and then smear it as doing so is a mundane act.[27] Practically the custom is to avoid brushing one's teeth at all on Shabbos. [See Piskeiy Teshuvos 326/3 for all details]

May one use mouthwash to remove bad odor?[28]
Yes, this is permitted.

May one floss his teeth on Shabbos?
One may floss his teeth so long as he beware not to cause bleeding. Likewise, it is forbidden to cut the piece of floss off on Shabbos due to the prohibition of Tikkun Keli.

---

3. A sore throat:[29]

Gargling oil: One who has a sore throat may not gargle oil, which means to retain oil in his mouth [for a period of time] prior to swallowing it as doing so is evident that one's intentions are for healing.

Swallowing oil: However, he may swallow the oil and if he gets healed in the process, so be it[30].

Other Opinions: [However] there are opinions which prohibit to even swallowing the oil because [plain] oil damages the body and it is only common to drink it for healing purposes.

The Final Ruling: It all depends on the place and time that one is [living] in, that if it is not common for healthy people to drink it then it is forbidden [to be done].

Drinking the oil down in a drink: However, it is permitted to place a lot of oil in beet juice (*Inigrone*) and then swallow it as in such a case it does not damage the body and it is not apparent that it is being done for healing but rather simply for drinking. Nonetheless one must swallow it immediately and not retain it in his mouth, and it goes without saying that he may not spit it out, as then it is recognizable that he is doing so for healing.

---

[22] Admur 318:42
[23] This is a type of resin with a pleasant smell which comes out of a tree. [Mishneh Berurah 328:114]
[24] See next Halacha note 31
[25] Admur 318:42
[26] Doing so is not a problem of smearing being that the prohibition only applies if one smoothens out the bumps of which there is no concern regarding one's teeth. However, a thick toothpaste is forbidden due to Nolad as it becomes liquidly when placed in the mouth.
[27] Ketzos Hashulchan 138 footnote 31
[28] Piskeiy Teshuvos 328:26 based on 328:42
[29] Admur 328:39
[30] Lit. "then he gets healed"

Summary-A sore throat:

Gargling oil: One who has a sore throat may not gargle oil, even if he intends to swallow it. However, he may swallow the oil in an area where it is common to drink oil, and if he gets healed in the process, so be it. However, in places where this is not common then it is forbidden. However, it is permitted to place a lot of oil in beet juice and then swallow it, although one must swallow it immediately and may not retain it in his mouth, or spit it out.

Medicine: Is forbidden unless one is bedridden or weak throughout his entire body.

Q&A

May one drink a hot tea to sooth a sore throat?

Yes, as it is not recognizable that one is doing so for healing purposes.

May one gargle salt water for a salt throat?

No, as it is recognizable one is doing so for medical purposes. If, however, one is bedridden or weak in his entire body, then this is allowed.

4. Stomach care:

A. Inducing vomiting:[31]

For no medical purpose: It is forbidden to induce oneself to vomit for a non-healing purpose even during the week because doing so wastes the food that was in his stomach, as by doing so he becomes hungry and goes back and eats again.

To relieve a stomachache during the week: [However] if one is in pain during the week from having eaten too much then it is permitted [to induce vomit] even using a medication.

On Shabbos: [However] on Shabbos it is forbidden to use medication [to induce vomiting] being that this is similar to healing. Although it is permitted to enter one's finger into his mouth until he vomits.

[It is forbidden to induce vomiting on Yom Kippur even if one has a stomachache. See chapter 608]

Summary-Inducing vomiting:[32]

Is forbidden for a non-healing purpose even during the week because doing so wastes the food that was in his stomach. However, if one is in pain from having eaten too much then during the week it is permitted to induce vomit even using a medication. However, on Shabbos it is forbidden to use medication [to induce vomiting] being that this is similar to healing. Although it is permitted to enter one's finger into his mouth until he vomits.

B. Treating stomach pains with a vessel of hot water:[33]

A large amount of water: One who has stomach pains is forbidden to place on his stomach a vessel that has hot water.

The reason for this is: because he may come to spill it on majority of his body, and it will thus be considered as if he has washed majority of his body in hot water.

A small amount: [Furthermore] even if there is only a small amount of hot water [in the vessel] which is not enough to wash majority of one's body [if it were to spill], then nevertheless if it were heated on Shabbos even a little, [even if this were] to the point that it is not [yet] Yad Soledes, it is forbidden [to place in a vessel on one's body for the reason] explained [in the Laws of Bathing Halacha 1, that one may not bathe even minority of one's body in water heated on Shabbos].

---

[31] Admur 328:44
[32] Admur 328:44
[33] Admur 326:5

On a weekday: [Furthermore] even on a weekday this is not allowed to be done because of the possible danger [that it involves] as at times the water is very hot [and may come to spill on one's body and give him a serious burn].

Placing hot clothing on it: However, it is permitted to heat up clothing and place them on ones stomach even on Shabbos. [**See Q&A regarding am electric heating blanket**]

Placing a hot empty cup over an aching stomach:[34] One who feels pain in his stomach is permitted to place on it a cup from which hot water had been poured even though [the cup] still contains steam [from the hot water].

The Reason that the above is allowed to be done is:[35] because each one of these issues are never healed using medications and thus there is no worry that one may come to grind [herbs], and [thus we allow it to be treated] because] one has pain from the above.[36] [However, if there is no pain involved then it would be prohibited due to it being a mundane act.[37]]

Summary-Placing hot items over an aching stomach:

Is allowed if there is no hot water in it, even if it still contains steam.[38] However if it has hot water in it then it is forbidden even during the week due to worry that one may receive a burn if it were to spill.[39] On Shabbos this is forbidden also due to the bathing prohibition, unless it were heated before Shabbos and does not contain enough water to wet majority of one's body if it were to spill. [However, nevertheless it would remain forbidden due to danger.]

Q&A

If the water is placed in a closed bottle may one place it on his stomach?

Yes, as there is now no suspicion that it will spill.[40] [As well there is no medication prohibition involved here as is seen from the fact that Admur makes no mention of it.]

May one place an electric heating blanket [which was left on from before Shabbos] over an aching stomach?[41]

Yes.[42]

C. Dealing with constipation-Inducing Diarrhea:

Pressing down on the stomach[43]: It is forbidden to press upon the stomach of a [constipated] baby in order to help the feces come out as one may come to give [the baby] to drink medications which causes diarrhea. [However, if the child is in pain and cannot release the bowel movement on his own, then certainly one may even give him medicine, as the needs of a child are like the needs of one who is bedridden.[44]]

❖ *Inducing diarrhea on Shabbos:[45]*

Through bathing: One may not bathe in waters that have a laxative effect [causing diarrhea], and not in quicksand.

---

[34] Admur 328:45
[35] Admur 328:45
[36] So rules also Michaber.
[37] So rules M"B [328:136] in name of Magen Avraham .
[38] Admur 328:45 and chapter 326 Halacha 5
[39] Chapter 326 Halacha 5
[40] Beir Moshe 1:33-15
[41] Piskeiy Teshuvos 328:32
[42] Igros Moshe 3:50
[43] Admur 328:47
[44] Ketzos Hashulchan 128 footnote 20
[45] Admur 328:49

Through drinking: And one may not drink liquids which cause diarrhea even if they are foods eaten by healthy people [and thus are not forbidden due to the decree of coming to grind spices] and one is not drinking it for healing purposes at all.

The reason for this is because: all the above actions cause pain while Shabbos is called a day of pleasure.

❖ *Treating constipation with a rectum insert:*[46]

It is forbidden to place a string[47] into one's rectum as is commonly done for one suffering from constipation, unless one places it with an irregularity, [which is] by grasping it with two fingers and placing it in delicately.[48]

The Reason: [This is needed to be done in order to prevent] tearing membranes [of the rectum] as explained in chapter 312 [Halacha 12].

Inserting an enema: Although it is forbidden to insert an enema[49] even through an irregularity, even if one had prepared it from the day before [before Shabbos] (because of the decree that one may come to grind spices) unless one is sick. As well even by a sick person one needs to be careful not to come to do a Biblical prohibition (as well) as that if it is possible to do it through a gentile then it is to be done through a gentile.

Summary- Dealing with constipation:

It is forbidden to press down on the stomach[50] or do anything or eat anything which will have a laxative effect on one's stomach and cause one to have diarrhea even if it does not appear that one is doing so for this purpose.[51] One may however place an insert into his rectum to help with the constipation as long as one inserts it with an irregularity which is defined as using two of one's fingers as opposed to one's hand. However, it is forbidden to insert an enema.[52]

Q&A

May one take a laxative drug to help with constipation?[53]

No[54], unless the constipation is causing one pain to the point that his entire body feels weak.

May one insert a rectal suppository to treat constipation?[55]

Being that this contains medicine it may only be done through a large irregularity, such as placing it in from the wide side. However, to place it in with two fingers is not considered enough of an irregularity. There is no prohibition in cutting the suppository in half.[56]

May one who has hemorrhoids apply ointment to the area?

See Tzitz Eliezer 11/37

May one who has hemorrhoids soak his bottom in hot water?

Yes[57]. However, some Poskim[58] question whether this is allowed in case that one is not bedridden or

---

[46] Admur 328:55

[47] Any cylindrical body such as made of wax or fat or paper or other materials [Mishneh Berura 151]

[48] Vetzaruch Iyun why is this not forbidden due to the medicine prohibition? How does doing it with a Shinui help in this regard? Why is only an enema forbidden and not this?

[49] The insertion of a liquid into the bowels via the rectum as a treatment, especially for constipation.

[50] Admur 328:47

[51] Admur 328:49

[52] Admur 328:55

[53] Piskeiy Teshuvos 328:29; SSH"K 34:11

[54] As is evident from the ruling above

[55] Piskeiy Teshuvos 328:39; Ketzos Hashulchan 138 footnote 31

[56] SSH"K 33 footnote 30 in name of Rav SZ"A being that this is similar to food which does not contain a cutting prohibition.

[57] So rules Tzitz Eliezer 12:44 and Beir Moshe 1:33, and so is implied from fact that one may bathe in hot water to relive pain. [See Ketzos Hashulchan 133 footnote 1, mentioned above in Chapter 2 Halacha 7 Q&A there.]

[58] Nishmas Avraham 22

feeling weak due to the pain.[59]

5. Dislocated or broken arm or leg:[60]

Note: In all cases that doctors say that the dislocation or break is lethally dangerous one may obviously desecrate Shabbos to heal it immediately as explained in Chapter 1.

A. Dislocation:

Rubbing it with water:[61] One who dislocated his arm or foot, which is defined as that the bone came out of its socket, he may not rub it a lot with cold water being that this heals it[62]. Rather he is to wash it regularly [as he washes it during the week] and if it gets healed [in the process] then so be it[63].

Returning it to its socket:[64] A bone which has become dislocated is forbidden to be returned to its socket [on Shabbos] being that doing so is similar to building (in addition to the fact that all healing treatments are forbidden [on Shabbos when no danger is involved]). [**See footnote for opinion of Michaber**[65]] Even to rub it a lot with cold water is forbidden as explained above. [**See Q&A regarding if there is fear for the limb or if one is in extreme pain**]

B. Returning a broken bone to its proper positioning:

However, a bone which has broken may be returned to its place as if one does not return it there on Shabbos the limb will be in danger and in scenarios of danger for a limb [the Sages] did not make their decree. [**See Q&A regarding making a cast and x-ray**]

Summary- Dislocated arm or leg on Shabbos:

Dislocated bones may **not** be returned to its socket on Shabbos due to a building prohibition [unless one is in bedridden in which case a gentile may do so].[66] As well one may not rub the area with a lot of cold water, although may wash it regularly.[67] However if the dislocation is due to a break in the bone then one may return it on Shabbos as the limb is considered to be in danger.[68]

Q&A

If one is in great pain and there is fear that the limb will not be able to function properly any more if it is not returned to its socket may one be lenient to return it?[69]

Yes[70], it may be done regularly by a Jew as this is considered that the limb is in danger.[71]

If one is in extreme pain but there is no fear of damaging the limb what is he to do?

If one is in extreme pain then he may tell a gentile to return the limb to its socket, as explained in Chapter 2 Halacha 3.

---

[59] Seemingly due to that they hold this is recognizable that it is done for healing.

[60] Admur 328:36

[61] Admur 328:36

[62] Now although as explained in Chapter 2 Halacha 7 that the medicine prohibition only applies in cases that the healing is done thru medicine, while here it is not done through medicine, nevertheless since it is possible to heal it through washing it regularly it is therefore forbidden to do it in a way that is noticeable. [Ketzos Hashulchan 138 footnote 18]

[63] Lit. "it heals"

[64] Admur 328:52

[65] This follows the ruling of the Magen Avraham. However, the Michaber [47] argues and hold that even a dislocation is permitted to be returned on Shabbos.

[66] Admur 328:36

[67] Admur 328:52

[68] Admur 328:52

[69] Ketzos Hashulchan 138 footnote 18; Piskeiy Teshuvos 328:38

[70] The M"B writes that according to all if the doctor says that there is danger of a limb involved then a Jew may replace it. [Mishneh Berurah 145] This applies as well if one knows the danger of the dislocation even if there is no doctor. [Ketzos Hashulchan ibid]

[71] Why is an irregularity not required is this not a biblical prohibition?

May a cast be made for a broken limb?[72]

No as doing so involves Biblical prohibitions. The limb is rather to be placed in a sling until after Shabbos.

May an x-ray be taken?[73]

Doing so involves a Biblical prohibition.[74]

6. Skin care:

A. Puncturing a pimple/boil on Shabbos:[75]

Punctures it to let in air to heal it: One who breaks [open] a boil on Shabbos, if he does so in order to make for it an opening for air to enter through it to heal it, then he is liable for [the prohibition of] "Makeh Bepatish".

The reason for this is: because he has fixed for it an opening, and anyone which fixes an opening in any item detached [from the ground] is liable for fixing a vessel, which is an offshoot of the "Makeh Bepatish" prohibition as explained in chapter 314 [Halacha 2]. And what difference does it make if one has fixed vessel or fixed a wound, and thus also in the fixing of a hole in the wound contains the prohibition of "Makeh Bepatish."

Now, although one is only liable on a hole made to enter and remove [something] thorough it as was explained there, [nevertheless here too one is liable] as this opening too is made to enter through it air and to constantly remove puss through it.

Punctures it to release the puss that is causing him pain: [However] if one breaks it open only in order to remove its puss which is causing him pain and not in order to enter air into it for purposes of healing, then it is permitted.

The reason: Now, although that one consequently creates a hole which is fit to [have something] entered and removed through it, nevertheless since he does not have a need for this, it is considered an action done not for its own use [which is not Biblically forbidden]. [Furthermore] even according to those opinions which say that an action which one does not do for its own use one is [also] liable on nevertheless here since the liability is due to fixing the wound thus if he does not care for this "fixing" and does not intend for it, then even though it consequently occurs [through him breaking open the boil], [nevertheless] this is not considered fixing at all and is as if he has done nothing. Albeit there does remain reason to decree against doing so due to that he may come to intend to make the hole [for healing, nevertheless] in a case of pain [the Sages] did not make such a decree.

Other Opinion: [However] there is an opinion which says that [the Sages] only permitted [breaking the boil] if one cares in doing so to merely remove its current puss and does not care if the boil will close back up. However, if he desires that it remain open in this form in order for it to constantly remove its puss, then although he does not intend for air to enter through it [for healing] [nevertheless] it is forbidden.

The Final Ruling: It is proper to suspect for this latter opinion and to puncture the boil/pimple through a gentile [when done with intent to remain constantly open].

---

[72] Sheivet Halevy 6:25; Piskeiy Teshuvos 328:38

[73] Piskeiy Teshuvos 328:38

[74] However, the Beir Moshe [7:50] rules that x-rays involve only a Rabbinical writing prohibition being that the x-ray is only understandable by experts.

[75] 328:32

B. Scratching a pimple/boil on Shabbos:[76]
However, it is forbidden to scratch a boil [on Shabbos] as doing so removes blood and contains the prohibition of inflicting a wound.
The difference between scratching and puncturing: This is not similar to [puncturing it to remove puss] being that puss is not attached and absorbed within the skin and is rather as if it is deposited there within a vessel and upon opening the boil to remove [the puss] it is merely like one is opening a vessel to remove its content. This is opposed to blood which is attached and absorbed within the skin.

Summary:
It may only be done if the following two conditions are fulfilled:
1. Condition 1: When in pain it is permitted to be done in order to temporarily remove its puss and relieve the pain. However, for it to permanently remain open and ooze puss is proper to only be done through a gentile. However, to puncture it so it heals through having air enter into it is Biblically forbidden.[77]
2. Condition B: As well it is only permitted to be done if through doing one will not make a new wound that releases blood. However, blood that is mixed with the puss does not pose a problem.[78]

C. Cutting off a blister:[79]
It is forbidden to cut a blister from one's body whether with one's hand [or teeth[80]] whether with a vessel, whether for himself, whether for others, whether it is [filled with] puss [blister], whether it is dry. And if one cut a puss [filled] blister with a vessel he is liable for shearing according to those which hold one liable for shearing even if he does not require that which is being sheared.

Summary
It is a Biblical prohibition according to some to cut it off with a vessel, whether it is a dry or mucus filled blister. It is Rabbinically forbidden to remove it with one's hands [or teeth].

D. Removing a nail or pieces of skin from one's nail on Shabbos:[81]
If majority of it has begun peeling off: A nail which is in the process of peeling off and cuticles, which are thin strings [of skin] which have [begun] separating off of the skin of the finger that surrounds the nail, if majority of it has peeled off then since they are close to becoming [completely] disconnected [therefore] there is no Biblical shearing prohibition applicable to it even when cut off with a vessel, although it is Rabbinically forbidden [to do so with a vessel].
Removing it with one's hands: However, to remove it with one's hand, [being that it] is not the common way of shearing is permitted to do even initially if they are irritating him, so long as they have peeled off towards the top, meaning that it had begun to peel off on the side of the nail [as opposed to under the nail].
Other Opinions[82]: [However] there are opinions which say that towards the top means towards the body and not towards the nail.
The Final Ruling: One needs to suspect for both explanations [and thus it is never permitted to peel the

---

[76] Admur 328:33
[77] Admur 328:32
[78] Admur 328:33
[79] Admur 340:3
[80] Ketzos Hashulchan 143 in name of Mishneh Berurah.
[81] Admur 328:37
[82] Rabeinu Tam. The former opinion is that of Rashi.

skin off even when majority of it has begun to peel off[83]] [**Regarding the nail-See Q&A**].

If only minority of the nail or skin has peeled off: If majority of [the skin or nail] did not peel off and one took it off with his hand then he is exempt [from Biblical liability] although has done a [Rabbinical] prohibition. [However] if one cut it with a vessel then he is liable for shearing. [Furthermore] even according to those opinions that say that an action which is not done for its own use one is not liable on, [nevertheless] there are opinions which say that by shearing one is liable according to everyone for the reason to be explained in chapter 340 [Halacha 2].

Summary-Removing a nail or pieces of skin from one's nail on Shabbos:[84]

If they are not irritating him: Then it is forbidden in all cases to peel off a nail or skin.

If they are irritating him: Then regarding-

- Pieces of skin: Is forbidden to be removed whether with one's hands or with a vessel, even if it is irritating him and majority of it has peeled off. When done with a vessel and majority has not yet peeled off then it is Biblically forbidden due to shearing.

- A Nail: When done with a vessel and majority has not yet peeled off then it is Biblically forbidden due to shearing. If majority has peeled off, then it is Rabbinically forbidden to remove it with a vessel. Regarding removing it by hand-see Q&A.

Q&A

May one remove a nail which has peeled off in its majority?[85]

Some Poskim[86] rule that it is allowed to be removed by hand [or teeth] if they are irritating him, as the dispute with regards to what is considered going upwards and downwards was only with regards to pieces of skin and not with regards to the nail. Whatever the case one must beware that no blood is extracted in the process.[87]

May one apply Vaseline to dry lips on Shabbos?

Vaseline may not be applied onto dry lips even if one will merely dab it on as opposed to smearing it, due to the healing prohibition. However, it may be dabbed on fresh skin or lips for mere pleasure.[88] It may not be smeared due to a possible smearing prohibition.[89]

May one apply powder or a spray to feet with bad odor?[90]

Some Poskim[91] rule that one may not do so on Shabbos due to the healing prohibition, although one may mix it in water before Shabbos and then use it to wash one's feet in a way that appears that one is simply washing the feet. However other Poskim[92] rule that powder or spray may be placed in order to remove bad smell even if it now gives a good smell.[93]

If the powder has healing powers, then it is forbidden [to be placed on feet which require healing according to all] due to the healing prohibition.

---

[83] Ketzos Hashulchan 143:1; Mishneh Berurah 99
[84] Halacha 37
[85] Piskeiy Teshuvos 328:25
[86] Ketzos Hashulchan 143:1 and footnote 3; Az Nidbaru
[87] So rules Peri Megadim M"Z 328:23, brought in Taharah Kihalacha 19:79-2, Upashut!
[88] Beir Moshe 1:36-4; 2:29-3
[89] See Beir Moshe [1:36-4] where he discusses the reasons for why it may even be smeared being that it is too soft of an item to contain the smearing prohibition as well as that its main intent is to be absorbed within the skin. However, in his conclusion he rules not to be lenient to smear it and rather may only dab it. See also Beir Moshe 2:29-3.
Vetzaruch Iyun from Ketzos Hashulchan regarding if this really contains smearing. [See Misc laws of Shabbos" The laws of smearing]
[90] Ketzos Hashulchan chapter 138 footnote 31; Piskeiy Teshuvos 328:26
[91] Ketzos Hashulchan chapter 138 footnote 31; Kinyan Torah ; See also Beir Moshe 1:34
[92] See Piskeiy Teshuvos 328:26
[93] Beir Moshe 1:34; Piskeiy Teshuvos 328:26

7. Treating wounds:

Note: Wounds which come from result of getting cut or hit with metal are considered lethal and its laws were explained above in Chapter 1. See there!

A. Cleaning the blood of a wound:[94]

Placing a [non-designated] cloth on a wound: It is forbidden to place a garment cloth on a wound that is bleeding.

The Reason is: because the blood will dye it. Now, although one is ruining [the cloth in this dying, as he is simply staining it] nevertheless it is Rabbinically forbidden [to be done].[95]

A red cloth: It is certainly [prohibited to place on the bleeding wound] a red garment, being that one is fixing it [by dying it with its natural red color].

Squeeze out the blood:[96] It is not allowed for one to squeeze out the blood from the wound prior [to placing the cloth on it] as doing so contains the wounding prohibition as explained.

Wrapping spider webs around it: Thus how is one to treat a bleeding wound? One is to wrap around it spiders web and cover with it all the blood and the entire wound and afterwards wrap a rag around it.

Other Opinions: There are opinions which question [whether it is allowed] and prohibit wrapping [the wound in] spider webs being that they have healing powers.

Rinsing off the blood and then applying the bandage: Rather [according to this latter opinion] one is to rinse [off the wound] in water or wine [prior to applying the bandage to it] in order to remove the blood which is on the wound and afterwards [one may] wrap a rag on it. [**See Q&A regarding if this may be done if one knows that it will still continue to bleed after bandaging it**].

The Final Ruling: It is proper[97] to suspect for this latter opinion [to rinse off the blood rather than use a spiders web], although the main Halachic ruling follows the first opinion.

Cloths that are designated specifically for wiping on:[98] May be used for wiping blood and is not a problem of dying, as we only say a problem of dying when it is not in a way of wiping, or it is but is done to a random cloth.

Cleaning the blood of a wound:[99]

Is forbidden to be done with any cloth, irrelevant of color, which is not designated for that purpose due to the dying prohibition. If thus there are no pre-designated cloths available, one is to rinse it off with water and then place the cloth on it prior to it beginning to bleed.

Q&A

May a bandage be placed over a bleeding wound?

Yes, as bandages are designated for this purpose.

May one wrap a towel over a bleeding wound?

Seemingly no as towels are not meant to be used to dry colored liquids but rather to dry water. Vetzaruch Iyun

---

[94] Admur 328:53 and Kuntrus Achron 301

[95] Vetzaruch Iyun why here Admur only brings the stringent opinion brought in Halacha 3 regarding wiping-stained hands on a cloth, while there in Halacha 3 he also brings a lenient opinion. In any event the final ruling remains as explained there in Halacha 3, like the stringent opinion.

[96] 1st opinion in Admur 328:53; 1st opinion in Michaber 328:48; Rokeaich 70; Kol Bo 31

The law of Muktzah regarding the spider web: The above ruling implies that spiders' webs are not Muktzah. See also Leket Yosher *"One time a spiders web was made on the faucet and he [the Terumas Hadeshen] said that it is permitted to break it on Shabbos."* See, however, Tehila Ledavid 328:79 that for the sake of relieving pain, the Sages permitted the moving of Muktzah. However, from Leket Yosher ibid, it is implied that it is permitted even not for the sake of relieving pain, as well as that no such allowance is recorded in Admur regarding Muktzah, and on the contrary, he explicitly mentions the Muktzah prohibition even in a case of pain. [See Admur 308:56 regarding placing raw cloth materials on a wound and 328:51 regarding eye pain] Thus, one must conclude that according to the Poskim ibid, cobwebs are not Muktzah on Shabbos. On the other hand, perhaps one can establish the case to be referring to cobwebs that were already prepared before Shabbos. Vetzaruch Iyun.

[97] Lit. good

[98] Kuntrus Achron 302

[99] Admur 328:53 and Kuntrus Achron 301

May one place a tissue or disposable napkin on the wound?[100]
Yes.[101]

One who has cleaned a wound from blood, may he place on it a bandage even though he knows that it will eventually continue to bleed?[102]
The Machatzis Hashekel requires that it be cleaned until the blood stops secreting.
However, the Avneiy Nezer rules that once the wound is clean one may put it on being that even if it later bleeds this is only Grama and is allowed, and so seems to be the opinion of the Poskim.

B. Squeezing out the blood:[103]

It is not allowed for one to squeeze out the blood from the wound prior [to placing the cloth on it] as doing so consists of the wounding prohibition as explained above.

❖ Sucking out blood from a wound:[104]

It is forbidden to suck blood with one's mouth from the wound due to the wounding prohibition.
Doing Metzitzah by a Bris: By a circumcision [sucking the blood of the circumcised area] was only permitted because [lack of doing so] poses danger.
Sucking the blood in ones gums: Therefore it is forbidden to suck blood which is between the teeth [in ones gums].
The reason: Now, although that doing so is separating [the blood] in an irregular way, nevertheless it is Rabbinically forbidden.

Squeezing blood out of a wound:
Is forbidden.[105] Likewise it is forbidden to suck out blood from a wound, including from ones gums due to the wound prohibition. However, by a Bris, Metzitza it is permitted.

C. Applying ointments to a wound:[106]

Smearing the wound with oil: One may remove the scab of a wound [with one's hands[107]] and may smear the wound with oil in places that it is common to smear oil also when there is no healing intended [i.e. for pleasure] as explained in chapter 327 [Halacha 1].
Smearing it with fat: However, one may not smear it with fat because it [causes it to] melt[108] and is forbidden for the reason explained in chapter 326 [Halacha 10]
Final stage of the wound: Even in the final stage of the wound, which is defined as when it has already healed and one feels no pain from it, it is permitted to remove the scab and to smear it with oil for mere pleasure [even in places that oil is never smeared for mere pleasure[109]].

---

[100] SSH"K 14:19; Piskeiy Teshuvos 320:11 based on Admur Kuntrus Achron 302
This is unlike the ruling of Rav Farkash in Tahara Kehalacha 10:28 which rules that tissues should not be used as they are not specifically designated for this purpose. Vetzaruch Iyun Gadol from where he understood that they must be designated for a specific form of wiping, as opposed to general wiping.
[101] As they are designated for wiping on, and thus do not contain a dyeing prohibition.
[102] Ketzos Hashulchan chapter 136 footnote 11
[103] Admur 328:53
[104] Admur 328:54
[105] Halacha 53
[106] Admur 328:28
[107] However, with a vessel is forbidden [Ketzos Hashulchan 136 footnote 22
[108] As for why it is not forbidden due to the smoothening prohibition-See "The Laws of melting..." where the Ketzos Hashulchan explains why there is no Mimacheik prohibition by soap.
[109] M"B, brought in Ketzos Hashulchan 136 footnote 20

Applying an oil and water mixture: However, one may not apply a mixture of oil and hot water over a wound, and not over a bandage which is to be placed over the wound, being that doing so is evident that it is being done for healing purposes. However, one may place it on his skin that is on the side of the wound and have it flow and drip onto the wound as when done so it is not recognizable that one's intention is for healing. Although it is permitted to place on it plain oil in places that it is common to smear oil even when there is no intention for healing. As well it is permitted to place on it plain hot water that was heated from before Shabbos.

❖ **Applying ointment/liquids to suppress the bleeding of a wound:**[110]
Wine for the un-pampered: One who hurt his hand or leg not as a result of iron may constrict it with wine in order to suppress the blood [flow].
Vinegar: However [he may] not [suppress it] with vinegar because it is potent and thus contains the healing prohibition.
Wine for the pampered: If one is pampered then even wine helps [cure the wound] as does vinegar and it is forbidden [to be placed] when the wound is not on the back of his hand or the back of his foot, as if it is then it is permitted to desecrate Shabbos for it by even doing a Biblical prohibition. Similarly, if [the wound] resulted from a blow from iron [then it too may have Shabbos desecrated for it] as mentioned above [in Halacha 7].

Summary-Applying ointments to a wound:[111]
Is permitted so long as it is common to apply that ointment there even for pleasure purposes, and it is a liquidly substance, [as opposed to creamy, **Regarding creams see Q&A below**]. Thus, water may be applied, as well as oil in those places which smear oil also for pleasure. However, all medical ointments are forbidden being that they are only used for medication. However, one may place it on his skin that is on the side of the wound and have it flow and drip onto the wound as when done so it is not recognizable that one's intention is for healing.
Liquids that suppress bleeding: All non-healing substances may be used to suppress blood flow thus one may apply wine to it if he is not pampered. However, it is forbidden to apply a healing substance to suppress the blood flow. Thus vinegar, and wine for the pampered may not be used.

Q&A
May one place Dermatol/Hydrogen Peroxide or other disinfecting liquids on a wound?
Some Poskim[112] rule that it is forbidden to do so due to the healing prohibition. [Thus, in all cases that healing is allowed, such as there is danger involved, or one is bed ridden or weak in his entire body, or for a child, or if having a gentile apply it if one is in pain then it may be placed.] Other Poskim[113] rule that if the liquid is simply disinfecting the wound and does not have other healing powers then it is allowed, as disinfection is not defined as healing. However, there are Poskim[114] which rule that it is allowed [even if it has the ability to heal] being that one's main intent is to suppress the bleeding and not to heal the wound.[115]

---

[110] Admur 328:35
[111] Halacha 28
[112] So rules Az Nidbaru and so is the simple understanding from the Halacha mentioned above.
[113] Beir Moshe 6:38
[114] SSH"K 35:12 footnote 17 in name of Rav SZ"A; Beir Moshe 6:38
[115] So explains Rav SZ"A there. Vetzaruch Iyun Gadol on this reasoning from the ruling here in Admur and Tur/SH"A 29 regarding wine and vinegar which implies that it may not be placed to suppress the blood flow if it can heal. However according to the reason given by the Beir Moshe the allowance would still apply despite the above ruling of Admur.

May one smear a cream onto the wound[116]?[117]
This may only be done to a child [not older than age 9[118]] or to one who is bedridden or ill[119], **and** only if it is a type of cream which needs to be rubbed completely into the skin and it is not meant to leave any of visible cream on the skin[120]. If the cream is common to be left visibly on the skin, then it is forbidden to be placed.

D. Placing a substance on a wound which draws out puss and blood:[121]
It is forbidden to place on a wound a substance which draws out the blood and the puss due to the detaching prohibition, as although the substance is drawing out [the blood and puss] on its own nevertheless since it is being placed there in order to draw it out, it is as if one is wounding and detaching with one's hands.

Summary:
One may not apply any substance to one's skin which draws out blood or puss due to the detaching prohibition.[122]

E. Placing sugar on a wound:
Certainly, one may not place [sugar] (*tzuker zlab*) on a wound which does not have a hole.

Placing sugar on a wound:[123]
Is forbidden.

F. Widening the hole of a wound on Shabbos and the laws of an Apturah:[124]
A hole that is in a wound which was already opened [from before Shabbos] and one wishes to broaden it on Shabbos even only slightly it is forbidden [to be done].
Unplugging it: However, if it had closed up then it remains questionable whether one is allowed to go ahead and reopen it on Shabbos as it was originally just as it is permitted to reopen a hole of a vessel that got plugged as explained in chapter 314 [Halacha 6].
The hole of an Apturah: As well those that have a hole in their arm that is called (*aptora*) and this hole got slightly stuffed up then there is doubt as to whether or not one is allowed to place legumes inside of it in order to open it.

---

[116] Doing so may involve a smearing prohibition, as well as a taking medicine prohibition.
Due to the medicine prohibition, it may never be done to one who is not defined as bed ridden or weak in his entire body.
[117] Minchas Yitzchak 7:20; Piskeiy Teshuvos 328:18 Vetzaruch Iyun from Piskeiy Teshuvos 327:1 which contradicts this ruling here and rules that it is always forbidden.
[118] Regarding all the opinions in the age of the child-See "The Laws of taking Medicine" Chapter 2 Halacha 6
[119] This applies even if the cream is not a medical lotion and thus does not contain any healing prohibition when placed, as there are opinions which hold that the smoothening prohibition applies even in a case that the cream is completely absorbed, and it is only in a case of an ill person that the Daas Torah said one may be lenient like the Magen Avraham [see Minchas Yitzchak 7:20]. [Seemingly however according to the Magen Avraham and those Poskim which rule likewise, such as the Mishneh Berurah, one may absorb non medical cream onto a healthy person.]
[120] As in such a case there is no smoothening prohibition, as is proven from the fact that no smoothening prohibition was mentioned regarding soap. [Daas Torah brought in Minchas Yitzchak ibid]. However, see above that some Poskim hold that there is no smoothening prohibition at all by soap and that is the reason that no prohibition was mentioned.
[121] Admur 328:54
[122] Admur 328:54
[123] Admur 328:34
[124] Admur 328:34

Placing a poultice on the Apturah: [However] a poultice is allowed to be placed on the (Apturah) being that it is like a wound which has healed which is permissible to place on it a poultice on it (as was explained in this chapter [Halacha 31])
Other Opinion: [However] there is an opinion which prohibits placing [a poultice] on an *(aptora)*.
The Final Ruling: (One is to suspect for their opinion [and thus be stringent]).

Summary-Widening the hole of a wound:
Is forbidden due to the building prohibition.

G. If cleaning a wound will cause blood to come out:[125]
If one is certain that cleaning [a wound] will extract blood then he may not clean it on Shabbos as [although one has no intention to extract blood, nevertheless] it is inevitable.

H. Placing pads and bandages on a wound on Shabbos:[126]
New: It is permitted to place on a wound a sponge and pieces of dry clothing if they are new being that doing do is not done for healing but rather to prevent one's clothing from irritating the wound.
Old: However, one may not place old pieces of clothing on it [being] that they contain healing powers. However, this only applies if [the old pieces] were never yet placed on a wound, though if they had already been placed on a wound then they no longer have healing powers despite the fact that they are old, and it is thus permitted to place them on a wound on Shabbos.
Regarding bandages which contain ointments on them-see next two Halachas!

Placing a dry bandage on a clean wound:[127]
All pads and bandages may be placed on a wound. Used clothing which have never before been placed on a wound may not be used for its first time on Shabbos. [Regarding using cloths and the like which do not have the status of a vessel, see chapter 308 Halacha 56 for the Muktzah laws that relate to this.]

Q&A
May one cut or tear a bandage to make it a better fit?[128]
Doing so is forbidden due to the "Make Bepatish" prohibition.

May one use a piece of tape to tape the bandage onto one's skin?[129]
One may not do so due to the sewing prohibition.[130]
However, if there is no other option of attaching the bandage to the wound then there is an opinion[131] which allows one to tape the bandage to one's skin if both ends of the tape are on one's skin. [Meaning the bandage is in the middle of the tape.] [However, the tape must be cut before Shabbos as

---

[125] Admur 328:34
[126] Admur 328:29; 308:56: *"There is no transgression involved in placing designated combed flax and spun wool on top of a wound on Shabbos, regarding [the prohibition of] healing [on Shabbos] which was decreed against due to that one may come to grind herbs, as will be explained in chapter 328 [Halacha 1], as these [materials] do not heal, and they are only placed on [wounds] in order to prevent ones clothing from irritating the wound."*
[127] Halacha 29
[128] Piskeiy Teshuvos 328:21; Tzitz Eliezer 8:15-14-6
[129] Piskeiy Teshuvos 328:21
[130] As one is sewing the tape onto the bandage. Tzitz Eliezer 8:15-14-6-unless is a time of need, as will be explained; SSH"K 34:25 in all cases even in a time of need.
[131] Tzitz Eliezer 8:15-14-6

will be explained in next question.]

Others[132] however argue on this and hold that even in such a way that the ends of the tape are on ones skin it is still forbidden being that the bandage will permanently remain attached to the tape after removing it.

Opinion of Admur: According to Admur seemingly it would be forbidden due to sewing even if one were able to remove the bandage from the tape, as Admur holds[133] that only when the tape is place unintentionally may it be removed, and here it is placed intentionally. Vetzaruch Iyun.

May one cut a piece of tape?[134]
Even according to those which permit in times of need the use of tape to attach a bandage to ones wound, this only applies if the piece of tape was cut from before Shabbos, as cutting it on Shabbos poses a "Tikkun Keli prohibition.[135]

May one tie the bandage onto his body, such as his arm or leg?[136]
One is to do so through making a bow over a single knot, and not through a double knot, as doing so may involve the tying prohibition. If, however, it is not possible to make a single knot with a bow then if one is in pain one may make a double knot with intent to remove that day[137], or at the very least in a time of need within seven days.[138]

May one place a band-aid on a wound on Shabbos?[139]
Doing so may involve the tearing prohibition when opening it and the sewing prohibition when applying it.
Opening the band-aid: Some Poskim rule that the band-aid must have its wrapping as well as its white plastic sheet which covers over the tape, removed from before Shabbos. Removing it on Shabbos involves the tearing prohibition.[140] However other Poskim[141] hold that the band-aid may even be opened on Shabbos, and doing so involves no suspicion at all of a prohibition. [Seemingly according to Admur it must be removed from before Shabbos]
Applying the band-aid to the wound: May be done if both sides of the band-aid are fastened to one's skin[142] as opposed to one's clothing or to the other end of the band-aid. [143]

May one remove a bandage that is taped onto his skin, such as a typical band-aid?[144]
If doing so will remove one's hair, then it should not be removed due to a possible shearing prohibition. However, if one is in pain then he may remove it even if it will remove hairs with it.[145]

---

[132] SS"K 34:25 and footnote 64 in name of Rav SZ"A
[133] Admur 340:17
[134] Piskeiy Teshuvos 328:21
[135] Tzitz Eliezer 8:15-14-6
[136] Piskeiy Teshuvos 328:21, see also Tzitz Eliezer ibid which writes that a bow knot is to be made.
[137] However there in Piskeiy Teshuvos he writes "if the bandage is a type which is meant to be removed that day." However, based on chapter 317:1 -2 it makes no difference if the bandage usually is made to last more than one day so long as one's intent is for it to last less than one day.
[138] So is implied from Admur 317:1-2. See "The Laws of tying and untying knots"
[139] Piskeiy Teshuvos 328:21
[140] Minchas Yitzchak 5:39
[141] Beir Moshe 1:36
[142] As there is no sewing prohibition relevant to sticking something to one's skin.
[143] Beir Moshe 1:36
[144] SSH"K 35:29 footnote 73; Piskeiy Teshuvos 328:22
[145] Being that this is a Pesik Reishei that is not beneficial, as well as that the removal of the hair is being done with a Shinui, and thus is permitted in a case of pain.

I. Placing pieces of cotton and the like on a wound:[146]
Designating combed flax and spun wool as a bandage: Combed flax and spun wool that are [common to be] placed on a wound, even if one did not think about designating them for his wound, but rather happened by chance to place it on his wound from before Shabbos, and then immediately removed it, [nevertheless] it is permitted to be moved on Shabbos to place on his wound or for another use, being that these materials are common to be designated for a wound, and therefore have become designated for this use by merely placing them on [his wound], and have thus received the status of a vessel.

It [thus] goes without saying that if one thought about them from before Shabbos, that they be designated to be used to place on wounds, even though one has never actually placed them on a wound [that they may be moved]. Furthermore, even if one did not think about them that they be designated and prepared for wounds, but rather just thought from before Shabbos to place them on [his wound] the next day, on Shabbos alone, while after Shabbos he plans to throw them out [then even so they may be moved on Shabbos].

It [also] goes without saying that if one did an action to them from before Shabbos to prepare them [to be used for wounds], such as for example he dyed them with oil and bound them with a cord [then they may be moved on Shabbos].

Why is the above not prohibited due to that it is forbidden to place medicine on Shabbos? There is no transgression involved in placing this on top of a wound on Shabbos, regarding [the prohibition of] healing [on Shabbos] which was decreed against due to that one may come to grind herbs, as these [materials] do not heal, and they are only placed on [wounds] in order to prevent one's clothing from irritating the wound.

J. Applying oil or water to a bandage:[147]
(As well it is permitted to place plain oil) over a pad which will be placed on [the wound]. (However hot water even plain, may not be placed (if the pad is not designated for this purpose) due to a decree that one may come to squeeze it [and be liable for the laundering prohibition], although by oil there is no decree made that one may come to squeeze it as was explained in chapter 320 [Halacha 21].

Summary-Applying water or oil to the bandage:[148]
One may place oil [and all other liquids which do not contain a smearing or a laundering prohibition] on the bandage and then place it on the wound [in those areas that applying oil is common even for pleasure]. However, water may not be placed on the cloth, unless it is designated to be used as a bandage.

Q&A
May one apply water to a bandage to treat fever? [149]
Yes. However, one must be careful to avoid the laundering prohibition. Thus, one is to only dip a very white and clean cloth into water which had wine or other colored liquid poured into it before Shabbos [or on Shabbos if one did not do so before hand]. As well one may not squeeze the water out of the cloth.

---

[146] Admur 308:56
[147] Admur 328:28
[148] Admur 328:28
[149] Based on Ketzos Hashulchan 136 footnote 2 and 138 footnote 31

K. Placing a poultice [a bandage that contains ointment] on a wound[150]:

Placing leaves on a wound on Shabbos: One may place a [non-Muktzah] leaf over a wound on Shabbos, as it is only placed as a safeguard [from irritation], with exception to grape leaves being that they are used for healing. The same applies for all leaves which heal [that they may not be placed on wounds].

If one placed them [on the wound] from before Shabbos and removed them from it after dark [i.e. after Shabbos already began] even purposely then it is permitted to replace them.

The reason for this is: As [the Sages] only forbade all healing treatments [from being done] due to a decree that one may come to grind herbs, when [the treatment] is being given on Shabbos for its first time, however not when one already began the treatment from before Shabbos and is only returning it on Shabbos.

Removed purposely: However, a poultice[151] which one removed from his wound purposely, even while still being held in his hand, is forbidden to be replaced due to a decree that one may come to smear and smoothen the bumps that are in it and will come to be liable for the smoothening prohibition as was explained in chapter 314 [Halacha 21]. [**See footnote regarding placing a poultice on a wound which causes pain[152]**]

Fell off wound but did not hit ground: However, if it slipped off the wound on its own after dark [but still remained attached to one's skin] then the Sages did not make a decree in such a case and it is permitted for him to return it. [Furthermore] even if it fell off of him completely it has the same status as if it had slipped away [from only the wound and has remained on his skin].

If fell onto the ground: However, this only applies if it fell onto a vessel. However, if it fell onto the floor then if he wishes to return it [to the wound] it is as if he is placing it on Shabbos for its first time and is forbidden due to a decree that he may come to smoothen it and due to the decree that he may come to grind herbs.

Replacing it through a gentile: Through a gentile it is permitted to place it on the wound even initially if it is causing him pain and slight illness as was explained above. However, it is forbidden to tell the gentile to initially make the dressing on Shabbos [by smearing ointment on the bandage], as smearing onto the bandage is a Biblical prohibition and doing so through a gentile is a complete Rabbinical prohibition which was only permitted [to be done] if one's entire body has fallen ill or if a limb is in danger [of being destroyed] as was explained above [in 328/19].

Removing the poultice to clean the wound: One may open part of the poultice and clean the mouth of the wound and then return it, and then go and open its other side and clean the mouth of the wound and then return it as since he does not remove the entire poultice [in the process] therefore he may return it. However, he may not clean the bandage [of the ointment] being that doing so [transgresses the] smearing [prohibition].

Applying a poultice on Shabbos to a healed wound:[153]

A wound which has healed one is allowed to place on it a poultice initially on Shabbos being that it merely protects it from getting irritated by his clothes.

The Reason: [The Sages] were not worried that one may come to smear it or [come to] grind herbs as since it has already healed the person is not so nervous regarding it that he will come to smear and grind herbs [to cure it more].

---

[150] Admur 328:30

[151] This refers to a dressing or pad which has ointment smeared over it which is then placed on the wound

[152] However there are Poskim [brought in Tzitz Eliezer] which say that in a case of pain one may place a poultice that was prepared from before Shabbos onto a wound, and it is only regarding a mere painless wound that they did not allow it to be placed due to suspicion that one may come to smoothen it. [See Tzitz Eliezer 8:15-14-3, So rules Piskeiy Teshuvos 328:20. Vetzaruch Iyun Gadol as from the Shulchan Aruch it is implied that it is forbidden in all cases, unless one is in so much pain that Rabbinical prohibitions may be done, as asks the Tzitz Eliezer himself in his Teshuvos. [although he himself concludes finding a defense for the ruling, although the question still remains].

[153] Admur 328:31

Placing a poultice [a bandage that contains ointment]:[154]
Is forbidden to be initially placed on the wound on Shabbos due to the healing prohibition. If it was placed on before Shabbos and fell off, then if it fell on the ground, it may not be replaced. If it fell on a vessel, it may be replaced. However, if it was removed purposely, then it may never be replaced, although one may open up part of it in order to clean the wound.
One may ask a gentile to place on ones wound an already prepared poultice in all cases that Rabbinical action may be done through a gentile; however, he may not initially prepare the poultice by smearing the [creamy] ointment on the bandage.
A poultice may be placed on a healed wound.[155]

Q&A
May one dab an ointment onto the wound and then place the bandage over it?[156]
Medical ointment: Doing so does not involve a smearing prohibition even though that the cream will inevitably smear upon placing the bandage over it[157], however it does involve the healing prohibition and thus may only be done by a gentile if one is slightly ill, or by a Jew if one is bedridden or feels weak in his entire body.
Ointment which is commonly used for pleasure: May be dabbed on.

L. Switching the bandage of a wound:[158]
By an Apturah or other wound with a hole: It is permitted to switch the current [garment which is covering the Apturah with] a different garment, as if one will not do so then it will smell, and [thus we allow it to be done as we take great precaution] to insure the dignity of people as well as that there is pain from it.
By a wound without a hole: However the above [allowance] only refers to this type of wound [called Apturah] being that it has a hole, however a wound which does not have a hole it is forbidden to change the garment or paper [for another] (because) one draws out puss from the wound (through removing [the cloth] from on it) and it is forbidden due to the "detaching" prohibition, as will be explained.

Summary-Removing a bandage on Shabbos:[159]
One may not remove the bandage on Shabbos if doing so will cause puss [or blood] to come out, due to the detaching prohibition.

M. Removing scabs:[160]
One may remove the scab of a wound [with one's hands[161]]. [However, this may only be done if it will not cause blood to be extracted.[162]]
Final stage of the wound: Even in the final stage of the wound, which is defined as when it has already healed and one feels no pain from it, it is permitted to remove the scab.

---

[154] Admur 328:30
[155] Admur 328:31
[156] Piskeiy Teshuvos 328:20
[157] SSH"K 31:14
[158] Admur 328:34
[159] Admur 328:34
[160] Admur 328:28
[161] However, with a vessel is forbidden [Ketzos Hashulchan 136 footnote 22]
[162] Admur 328:33

Removing scabs:[163]

Is permitted to do with one's hands [so long as doing so does not release blood].

N. Removing a splinter?[164]

Using a needle: A whole needle, [meaning that it is undamaged[165]] is permitted to be moved to take out a splinter, as is the law regarding a vessel which is designated for a forbidden use, which is permitted to be moved in order to use it.

How may one remove a splinter on Shabbos: One needs however to be careful when removing the splinter to do it in a way that it will not for certain cause blood to come out in the process of removing it, as doing so [in a way that will for certain extract blood, transgresses the Melacha of] *Chovel* even if one did not intend to extract the blood, as one is removing it out in a way that it is inevitable for blood not to come out[166]. [Thus] for example, if the thorn turned upside down while trying to remove it and it is [now] impossible to take it out without extracting blood, then it is forbidden to remove it.

Summary-May one remove a splinter?[167]

This may only be done so long as no blood is extracted in the process.

Compilation-May one remove a splinter on Shabbos?[168]

It is permitted to remove a splinter on Shabbos [with one's hands, tweezer, or needle as will be explained].[169] However, one needs to beware upon removing the splinter to do it in a way that it will not inevitably cause blood to come out in the process of removing it.[170] [Thus,] for example, if the thorn turned upside down while trying to remove it and it is [now] impossible to take it out without extracting blood, then it is forbidden to remove it.[171] [Likewise, if the splinter is very deep in the skin and will cause

---

[163] Admur 328:28

[164] Admur 308:38

[165] Admur 308:39

[166] Lit. "Can you cut off its head and have it not die"

[167] Admur 308:38; M"B 328:88 in name of Magen Avraham. Vetzaruch Iyun why this was not mentioned by Admur in 328 which deals with the laws of medical treatments!

[168] Admur 308:38; Michaber 308:11; Rambam Shabbos 25:8; Mishneh Shabbos 122b; M"A 328:32; Vetzaruch Iyun why this law was not mentioned by Admur in 328 which deals with the laws of medical treatments!

[169] Admur ibid; Michaber ibid; Mishneh ibid; M"A ibid

[170] Admur ibid; M"A 328:32 based on Tosafus Sanhedrin 85a; M"B 328:88 in name of Magen Avraham; Kaf Hachaim 308:96
The reason it is forbidden if the removal of blood is inevitable: As doing so [in a way that will for certain extract blood, transgresses the Melacha of] *Chovel* [which according to Admur is a Tolda of the Av Melacha of killing, as explained in Admur 316:14, however, according to the Rambam 8:7 it is a Tolda of Mifareik, see also Admur 328:54 who implies that it contains both Chovel and Mifareik] even if one did not intend to extract the blood, as one is removing it out in a way that it is inevitable for blood not to come out [i.e. Pesik Reishei; Lit. "Can you cut off its head and have it not die"] [Admur ibid; Regarding the prohibition of Pesik Reishei, see Admur 337:1; 253:10-11; 28; 259:7; 277:1-5; 278:4; 302:4; 308:38; 314:3; 316:4-5; 21-22; 318:21; 319:29; 320:17; 20, 22-24; 323:11; 324:1; 326:8; 334:24; 336:9 and 17; 337:1; 340:4; 357:3; 646:13] Nonetheless, according to those Poskim who rule that one is exempt for a Melacha Sheiyno Tzericha Legufa [See Admur 316:16], then here too one would be exempt if he transgressed and did so, as it is merely a Rabbinical prohibition of Pesik Reishei Derabanon. Furthermore, even according to those Poskim who rule that Melacha Sheiyno Tzericha Legufo one is liable for, one can argue that here they would all agree that one is Biblically exempt, as it is Mikalkel. [See Sanhedrin 84b; P"M 328 A"A 33; Machatzis Hashekel on M"A ibid; Tehila Ledavid 328:47; M"B 328:88 and Biur Halacha 308:11 "Hakotz"] Nonetheless, this would remain forbidden as we rule that a Pesik Reishei is forbidden even by a Rabbinical prohibition. [Implication of Admur ibid who rules stringently here unlike the other opinions brought below; Admur 337:1; 320:20 regarding walking on snow; 320:24 regarding a cloth on a Barza; 302:20 regarding squeezing; 316:4 regarding closing container on flies; M"A 314:5; 316:9; Taz 315:3; M"B 316:17 regarding bees; However, see the following case in which Admur is lenient by a Rabbinical Pesik Reishei, Vetzaruch Iyun: Admur 314:3, although in that case we have added reasons for leniency, including: a) Ein Boneh Vesoser Bekeilim. B) mikalkel; c) Kilacher Yad. Even there Admur concludes Lechatchila to be stringent.]
The reason it is permitted if the removal of blood is not inevitable: As in such a case the Melacha of extracting blood is being done without intent, and an action that will not inevitably cause a Melacha to happen is permitted even initially to be done on Shabbos so long as one has no intent for the Melacha to occur. [See Admur 320:20; 324:1; 337:1]

[171] Admur ibid; Implication of Tosafus Sanhedrin 85a that if it will be a Pesik Reishei then it is forbidden; Possible implication of M"A ibid

blood to be extracted upon its removal, then it may not be removed. This follows the ruling of Admur. However, many other Poskim[172] rule that when there is no alternative, it is permitted to remove the splinter even if it will inevitably cause bleeding. Practically, those who follow the rulings of Admur should only be lenient if there is worry of infection and the like, and not due to mere pain, even if it is very painful.]

Using a needle:[173] A whole and working non-damaged needle[174] is permitted to be used on Shabbos for the sake of removing a splinter.[175] [However, if one has a non-Muktzah needle available, such as the needle of a safety pin, then it is preferable to use it over a sewing needle.[176]]

Summary:
It is permitted to remove a needle on Shabbos so long as it will not inevitably cause it to bleed in the process. If its removal will inevitably cause bleeding, then it may not be removed unless it will be prone to infection due to it.

Q&A
May one ask a gentile to remove a splinter that will cause inevitable bleeding when removed?[177]
Yes, if he is in a lot of pain.

May one pluck away pieces of skin with the needle in the process of removing the splinter?[178]
One may puncture and cut through external pieces of skin for the sake of reaching the splinter so long as blood will not inevitably be released as a result.[179] However, one may not cut off pieces of skin due to the Gozez/Shearing prohibition.[180]

Other opinions: Some Poskim rule that it is permitted to remove the splinter even if it will inevitably cause blood to be extracted, as this is a case of Pesik Reishei Derabanon [being that removing the blood is Mikalkel, as explained in footnote above based on conclusion of Sanhedrin ibid] which the Sages permitted to be transgressed for the sake of relieving pain. [Sefer Hateruma 254; Tosafus Shabbos 107b; Biur Halacha 308:11 "Hakotz" and Shaar Hatziyin 328:63 in name of Chemed Moshe; Machatzis Hashekel on M"A ibid *"The M"A wrote that one is initially to be careful in this as much as possible...although certainly if he is unable to then it is permitted as it's a mere Rabbinical prohibition in a case of pain"*; Tehila Ledavid 328:47; Implication of M"B 328:88 and so he rules in Shaar Hatziyon 328:63; Kaf Hachaim 308:96; Piskeiy Teshuvos 328:51; Possible understanding of M"A ibid that even he agrees to this allowance and simply stated that if possible one should try to extract it without it inevitably extracting blood, although if this is not possible, then he too agrees that it is allowed, as he rules in 328:33 that the Sages were lenient by a Melacha Sheyno Tzericha Legufa in a time of pain, and so understands in M"A: Machatzis Hashekel ibid; Tehila Ledavid ibid; Biur Halacha 308:11 "Hakotz" and Shaar Hatziyin 328:63] Furthermore, some Poskim rule that a Pesik Reishei is always permitted by a mere Rabbinical prohibition. [Terumos Hadeshen, brought in M"A 314:5; Shaar Hatziyon 316:21; See Beis Yosef brought in Taz 316:3; Admur 314:3 regarding bees]
[172] Sefer Hateruma 254; Tosafus Shabbos 107b; Biur Halacha 308:11 "Hakotz" and Shaar Hatziyin 328:63 in name of Chemed Moshe; Machatzis Hashekel on M"A ibid *"The M"A wrote that one is initially to be careful in this as much as possible...although certainly if he is unable to then it is permitted as it's a mere Rabbinical prohibition in a case of pain"*; Tehila Ledavid 328:47; Implication of M"B 328:88 and so he rules in Shaar Hatziyon 328:63 and Biur Halacha ibid; Kaf Hachaim 308:96; Piskeiy Teshuvos 328:51; Possible understanding of M"A ibid, and so understands in M"A: Machatzis Hashekel ibid; Tehila Ledavid ibid; Biur Halacha 308:11 "Hakotz" and Shaar Hatziyin 328:63; See other opinions in previous footnote!
[173] Admur ibid; Michaber ibid; Mishneh ibid
[174] See Admur 308:39 and Michaber ibid
[175] The reason: Although a needle is considered Muktzah due to being a Keli Shemilachto Lissur, nevertheless it may be moved as is the law regarding a vessel which is designated for a forbidden use, which is permitted to be moved in order to use it. [Admur ibid]
[176] Piskeiy Teshuvos 328 footnote 417; 308:8
[177] Piskeiy Teshuvos 328 footnote 416; See Admur 328:20 that a Rabbinical prohibition may be done through a gentile to relieve a severe pain, and hence since in conclusion we rule that the inevitable removal of blood is only Rabbinical due to it being Eino Tzericha Legufa and Mikalkel, therefore it falls under the allowance to be done by a gentile in the event that he is in a lot of pain
[178] See Piskeiy Teshuvos 328:51
[179] See Michaber 328:28 and Admur 328:32 that one may pop a boil for the sake of releasing pus
[180] See Biur Halacha 328:28 "Kdei" and Admur 328:37 and 340:3

8. Sobering up on Shabbos using different tactics:[181]

Using an oil and salt mixture: Similarly, one who is drunk of which his cure [to make him sober] is to smear [a mixture of[182]] oil and salt on the palms of his hands and feet, it is permitted to smear [the oil] on them on Shabbos for the above-mentioned reason [that normally there is no medication administered for this ailment].

Sniffing ash: One may not learn from this the allowance that some places have accustomed themselves to sniff ash of a grinded herb into one's nostrils in order to sober up from ones drunken state, because this ash has similar affects to medication regarding other matters as well, and it is thus relevant to decree upon it that one may come to grind herbs.

Summary-Sobering up on Shabbos using different tactics:
One who is drunk may sober himself up by smearing a mixture of oil and salt on the palms of his hands and feet. However, one may not sniff a medicinal ash to sober himself up.

---

9. Sucking the milk from the breast of an animal to cure heart pain:

See "The Laws of Squeezing/Sechitah" Chapter 1 Halacha 9!

10. Pumping/ squeezing breast milk in order to relieve breast pain caused by the milk:

See below chapter 3 Halacha 10

11. Exercising on Shabbos:[183]

Just as it is forbidden to massage one's body in order to exercise and sweat, similarly it is forbidden to exercise in other forms in order so one sweats for healing purposes.

The reason for this is: due to a decree that one may come to grind and drink herbs which cause one to sweat.

Summary:
Is forbidden to be done in order to sweat for healing purposes. [Thus, it is forbidden to be done in order to lose weight and be in shape].

Q&A

May one do pushups, sit-ups, weightlifting and other forms of work outs?
No[184]. Although there are Poskim[185] which allow this to be done if one has pleasure from doing so.

May one do physiotherapy?[186]
No, unless one is bedridden or weak in his entire body due to lack of doing so.

May one exercise his hands?[187]
Yes. This may be done even to relieve pain as there are no exercises done in this area in order to sweat.[188]

---

[181] Admur 328:46
[182] Mishneh Berurah 128
[183] Admur 328:47
[184] Tzitz Eliezer 12:45. See next note regarding opinion of Admur
[185] SSH"K 16 footnote 99. Vetzaruch Iyun from that Admur forbids giving a hard massage even for pleasure, although one has no intent to sweat.
[186] Piskeiy Teshuvos 328:34
[187] Piskeiy Teshuvos 328:34
[188] Tzitz Eliezer ibid

May one exercise his voice box through different breathing forms?[189]
Yes, as there is no concept of exercising to sweat in the inner limbs.[190]

May one cause himself to sweat by covering himself with blankets?[191]
Yes.[192]

May one take a suntan on Shabbos?
The answer to this question is disputed amongst Poskim. Some rule[193] that it is forbidden even when done for mere pleasure.[194] Other Poskim[195] however rule that it is allowed when done for mere pleasure[196], and is done in private, and one has no intent to tan his skin. However according to others[197] it is even allowed if he intends to tan the skin being that he himself is not adding any dye.

**Compilation-May one go walking on Shabbos for weight loss and exercise purposes?[198]**
A. Background:
Going for an exercise walk on Shabbos touches upon two possible prohibitions; 1) Perhaps it transgresses the Rabbinical command that requires for one to change his walking habits on Shabbos. 2) Perhaps it transgresses the Rabbinical prohibition of causing oneself to sweat which was enacted due to the general medicine prohibition on Shabbos. The following is the background of these two prohibitions.
The Shabbos walking restriction:[199] The verse[200] states "Im Tashiv Mishabbos Raglecha…Vechibadeto Meiasos Derachecha etc/If from walking you will rest and honor Shabbos by not doing weekday activity." From here the Sages[201] learned that one's walking on Shabbos should not be like one's walking during the week. Thus, it is forbidden to run on Shabbos.[202] Likewise, one is not to walk more than necessary in order to get to a certain location. Hence, if there are two ways to walk, the shorter route should always be chosen. Nonetheless, it is permitted to go for a Shabbos walk [and take a longer route for that purpose].[203]
The Shabbos exercise restriction:[204] Just as it is forbidden to massage one's body in order to exercise and sweat, similarly it is forbidden to exercise in other forms in order so one sweats for healing purposes. The reason for this is due to a decree that one may come to grind and drink herbs which cause one to sweat. [Accordingly, it is certainly forbidden to run for the sake of exercise and health purposes on Shabbos.[205] This applies even if one runs in small strides.[206]]

---

[189] Piskeiy Teshuvos 328:34

[190] Tzitz Eliezer ibid

[191] Piskeiy Teshuvos 328:34

[192] Yad Halevy 60

[193] Minchas Yitzchak 5:32

[194] Due to a dyeing prohibition, and a possible pain afflicting prohibition [if it is very hot], and it being a degrading act which does not keep with the spirit of Shabbos, and it may coming to cause one to smear creams on him, and if done for healing, then due to a healing prohibition as one may come to try to heal himself with herbs. [Minchas Yitzchak ibid-Vetzaruch Iyun Gadol as since people sunbathes for mere pleasure the healing is not recognizable and should be allowed.]

[195] Az Nidbaru 2:30

[196] As if done for healing it is questionable whether it contains the healing prohibition.

[197] SSH"K 18 footnote 70

[198] See Piskeiy Teshuvos 301:4

[199] Admur 301:1-2 [printed in the new Edition of the Shulchan Aruch, based on manuscript of Maharil, first published in Yagdil Torah N.Y. 10]; Michaber 301:1-3; Shabbos 113; Ketzos Hashulchan 117:2-3

[200] Yeshaya 58:13

[201] Shabbos 113a; Tur 301; Levush 301

[202] Admur ibid; Michaber 301:1; Tosefta Shabbos 17:16

[203] Rama 301:2; Beis Yosef in name of Tosefta; Igros Moshe 5:18; Piskeiy Teshuvos 301:5

[204] Admur 328:47

[205] M"A 301:5; Beis Yosef in name of Tosefta; Admur 328:47 regarding sweating for exercise
The reason: It is forbidden to exercise in order so one sweats for healing purposes due to a decree that one may come to grind and drink herbs which cause one to sweat. [Admur ibid] This is in addition to the prohibition against running on Shabbos due to the above quoted verse.

[206] P"M 301 A"A 1

B. The law by walking:

<u>Plain and regular walking</u>: Some Poskim[207] rule that it is permitted for one to go for a walk in a normal pace on Shabbos without limitation[208] even if he intends to do so for the sake of exercise purposes and to sweat.[209] Accordingly, one who takes a daily walk for weight loss and exercise purposes, may do so even on Shabbos. However, other Poskim[210] rule that it is forbidden to even walk on Shabbos if his intent is to sweat or exercise, and hence one may not go for his daily walk on Shabbos unless it is being done for a different purpose, and not simply for the sake of exercise. Practically, from the letter of the law one may choose to be lenient, and so should be done when medically required. However, it is proper to be stringent and push off the daily walk for Motzei Shabbos and the like, especially in light of the fact that one should use his time on Shabbos for Torah learning.

<u>Power walking/Running/Jugging for exercise</u>:[211] All the above discussion is only regarding walking a normal pace in which it is not recognizable that one is doing so for exercise purposes. However, according to all it is forbidden for one to run or jog or even power walk for the sake of exercise on Shabbos, as in such a case it is apparent to all that he is doing so for exercise purposes[212], and is likewise forbidden due to the Rabbinical restrictions against running on Shabbos.[213] Likewise, even when walking a normal pace, if ones hand movements or dress make it evident that he is doing an exercise walk, then it is forbidden to do so.

Summary:
From the letter of the law, it is permitted for one to go on a regular walk on Shabbos even if he intends to do so as part of his daily exercise, so long as his form of walking is not recognizable that it is being done for an exercise purpose. Nonetheless, it is proper to be stringent to push off such activities until after Shabbos. According to all, only plain walking is allowed, while jogging and power walking remains forbidden.

---

12. Massages:[214]

It is forbidden to massage one's body with force even for mere pleasure.[215] It goes without saying [that this is forbidden to be done] in order to exercise and sweat.[216]

<u>*With oil*</u>:[217] It is permitted to smear [oil] [**See "The laws of oiling one's body" regarding using scented oils**] and massage [it] with ones hand over ones entire body for pleasure so long as it is done differently

---

[207] M"A 301:5; P"M 301 A"A 5 in negation of Elya Raba; Tosefes Shabbos 301:5; Pesach Hadvir 301:3; 1st and Stam opinion in M"B 301:7; Kaf Hachaim 301:13; Shaar Hatziyon 301:8 that so is the implication of Tosefta ibid; Orchos Rabbeinu 3:246 that the Chazon Ish took his daily walk for exercise purposes also on Shabbos

[208] See Beis Yosef 301, brought in Taz 301:1, that he may walk even for the entire day

[209] <u>The reason</u>: As the Sages did not restrict pleasure walking on Shabbos [Rama ibid] and the exercise and sweat prohibition only applies if it is apparent to others that the activity that one is doing is for this purpose. Thus, since going for a regular walk does not appear to onlookers as exercise, therefore it is permitted to be done even if in truth he is doing so for exercise. [P"M 301 A"A 5; Machatzis Hashekel ibid; M"B 301:7; See Admur 327:1; 328:28 and 43]

[210] Elya Raba 301:7 in implication of Levush 301:2 and that so is implied from the Tosefta and Rama ibid, brought, and negated, in P"M 301 A"A 5; 2nd opinion in M"B ibid

[211] See M"A ibid; Piskeiy Teshuvos ibid

<u>Other opinions</u>: See Shut Milameid Lehoil 53 and SSH"K 16 footnote 106 in name of Rav SZ"A and Or Letziyon 3:36-12 that if he enjoys the actual exercise and is not intending do so in order to sweat, then it is permitted

[212] M"A ibid

[213] Taz 301:1 that whenever the purpose of the run is not intrinsically pleasurable, then it is forbidden due to the Rabbinical running restriction; However, from the M"A ibid it is evident that whenever there is a purpose of pleasure involved in doing so, then it is permitted to be done, if not for the secondary prohibition against exercise which is applicable in such a case; See Machatzis Hashekel on M"A ibid

[214] Admur 328:47 and 327:2; Michaber 328:42; Shabbos 147a

[215] Admur 328:47 and 327:2; Michaber 327:2; Shabbos 147a as explains Rashi

<u>Other opinions</u>: Some Poskim rule it is permitted to massage the body regularly for mere pleasure, even strongly. [Rambam as brought in M"A 328:46; M"B 327:7 and Biur Halacha 328:42 "Kdei"]

[216] Admur 328:47; Michaber 328:42; Shabbos 147a as explains Ramabam, and certainly this would apply according to Rashi

[217] Admur 327:2; Michaber 327:2; Mishneh Shabbos 147a as explains Rashi

than how it is done during the week, meaning that he is to oil and massage simultaneously [as opposed to first smearing the oil and then massaging it], [as well as that] he is to not apply force [with his hands] but rather is to do it with his hands gently.

Giving a massage:
Is only allowed to be done gently, and not for purpose of sweating or exercise, and if oil is being used one may only do so by smearing the oil simultaneously to giving the massage.

May one give a massage for healing purposes?
It is questionable whether one may do so gently, without force.[218] Practically, some[219] write that one may not do so at all, even gently.

May one who feels weak and stressed out receive a massage to give him strength?
It is questionable whether this is considered for healing or for pleasure.[220] Even if this is considered healing, it is questionable whether one may do so gently, without force.[221] However some[222] write that doing so is considered healing and hence may not be done at all, even gently.

---

13. Bathing for healing purposes:
See "The Laws of Bathing" Halacha 3!

14. Smearing oil for medication purposes:
See "The Laws of smearing oil on one's skin and leather"

List of illnesses and their status which are not mentioned in Shulchan Aruch:

One who has a standard fever [not lethal]:[223]
One whose temperature is slightly high [i.e. 100.4 F, 38C] is considered like one whose entire body is ill, which thus may take medicine, and have other actions done for him as explained above under that category.[224] If his fever is lower than 100.4 F, 38C, then medicine may not be taken unless he feels weak in his entire body.
A fever that is not the result of the common cold or virus: If the fever is above 39C [102.2 F] then it may be lethal as it may be coming from some inner illness and one may thus even desecrate Shabbos for it.
A Fever above 40 C [104 F]: Is considered life threatening which one may desecrate Shabbos for.
A baby: May be given medicine for even a slight fever below 100.4 F.
Measuring one's temperature: Is allowed with all non-digital thermometers when done to check for fever or other health purposes.[225]

---

[218] Implication of Michaber 328:42 and M"A 328:46 that even when done for healing, such as for sweating, it may be done gently; It is unclear from Admur 328:47 if even when done for healing, such as for sweating, it may be done gently. Another reason to permit doing so gently is because any matter that is done by majority of healthy people may be done for purposes of healing being it does not appear like healing. [P"M 328 A"A 46] Vetzaruch Iyun

[219] Piskeiy Teshuvos 327:2; See M"B 328:130 in which it is not clear if he means to forbid it completely or only forbids doing so with force

[220] Shiltei Giborim brought in M"A 328:46; M"B 328:130

[221] See previous Q&A!

[222] Piskeiy Teshuvos 327:2; See M"B 328:130 in which it is not clear if he means to forbid it completely or only forbids doing so with force

[223] Piskeiy Teshuvos 328:6, based on Ketzos Hashulchan 138 footnote 31

[224] Ketzos Hashulchan chapter 138 footnote 31

[225] Igros Moshe 1:128

Placing a wet cloth on one's forehead: See Chapter 2 Halacha 7 Q&A there!
May one soak in a bath to reduce the fever? Yes[226]

One who has a headache:[227]
The allowance to take medicine depends on the amount of pain he is in. If his headache is very painful but his entire body does not feel weakened and is not bedridden, then he may not take medicine. Although if it does pain him to this point then medicine is allowed. [**However, see footnote below for other opinions.[228]**]
Placing a wet cloth on one's forehead: See Chapter 2 Halacha 7 Q&A there!

One who has heartburn:[229]
One may drink water which had Alka- seltzer[230] or baking soda[231] dissolved in it from before Shabbos, being that at the time that one drinks the water mixture it is not recognizable to others that one is drinking Alka-seltzer.
If one did not prepare the water mixture seltzer from before Shabbos, then he may prepare it an irregular fashion, such as to place the pill in a cup of tea and drink it down slowly.

May one measure one's temperature to see if he is sick?[232]
Is allowed with all non-digital thermometers.[233]

May one measure one's pulse to see if he is sick?[234]
Is allowed with all non-digital thermometers when done to for health purposes.[235]

May one get a shot on Shabbos?[236]
This may be done only if he is bedridden or weak in his entire body [or if he is even slightly ill but is done by a gentile[237]], but only in an area where blood will not for certain be visibly extracted, such as doing so into one's skin or a nerve as opposed to into a vein.
One may not use cotton soaked with alcohol to place over the area of skin. Rather one is to spill some alcohol on it. [However, a gentile may do so for him.]

---

[226] Admur 328:48, and so rules Piskeiy Teshuvos 328:35
[227] Ketzos Hashulchan 138 footnote 31; SSH"K 34:6
[228] Minchas Yitzchak 3:35 rules that aspirin [and other painkillers] may not be taken for a mere ache. However, if one is in great pain he leans to allow it. [Seemingly even if he is not weak in his entire body-so learns Piskeiy Teshuvos 328:2. However SSH"K ibid seems to learn him differently].
Regarding those Poskim which allow aspirin to be taken even by a mere pain-see above "May one take aspirin". However as stated there this does not seem to be the opinion of Admur!
[229] Ketzos Hashulchan chapter 138 footnote 31; Piskeiy Teshuvos 328:29
[230] This refers to the brand-named medicine which is used for heartburn. It is a pill which is dissolved in water and then drunk.
[231] *Dissolve a teaspoon of baking soda into a cup of water. Baking soda will neutralize the acids as soon as it is consumed. It does have a couple of side effects. The first is that it does not have a pleasant taste. Those who use this method of indigestion relief recommend drinking it quickly through a straw. The second side effect is that it will instantly release gas from the acid buildup, causing you to inevitably belch.*
[232] Piskeiy Teshuvos 306:7
[233] Igros Moshe 1:128
[234] Piskeiy Teshuvos 306:7
[235] Igros Moshe 1:128 brought in Piskeiy Teshuvos 306:7
[236] Sheivet Halevy 1:61 brought in Piskeiy Teshuvos 328:22
[237] As explained above in chapter 2 Halacha 4

May one add water to a humidifier or vaporizer on Shabbos?[238]

Some Poskim[239] rule it is forbidden to add water to any vaporizer or humidifier.[240]

Other Poskim[241] rule it is permitted to add water to a vaporizer if certain conditions are met.[242] The following is the law of cold and hot humidifiers according to these Poskim that are lenient:

Cold humidifier: If the humidifier expels only cold air according to this opinion it is permitted to add water to it if the following conditions are met: 1. The machine is still on and will not turn on due to the added water. 2. No lights in the machine will turn on or off due to the added water. 3. The lights in the house will not decrease their quality of light due to this.[243] 4. One may not remove any part of the humidifier in order to enter the water if doing so causes the humidifier to shut off until the part is reinserted.[244]

Hot humidifier: If the humidifier expels hot air it is forbidden to add water to it on Shabbos due to the cooking prohibition. However, it is permitted to add hot water directly from an urn into the humidifier, fulfilling all the Chazara conditions[245], and provided that all the above-mentioned conditions [of a cold humidifier] are fulfilled. Likewise, this may only be done if the water that remains in the container is already cooked.[246]

---

[238] See Shabbos Kehalacha Vol. 1 6:21-22; Piskeiy Teshuvos 318:28; Minchas Yitzchak 7:21; 8:28;

The possible issues involved in adding water to a vaporizer:

    1.   Cooking
    2.   Zoreh
    3.   Nolad
    4.   Increasing or decreasing current of electricity [problem of Molid or Kibuiy of the lights which have their current diminished]
    5.   Causing light on machine to turn on or off.

[239] Minchas Yitzchak 7:21

[240] The Minchas Yitzchak ibid forbids adding even cooked hot water to a hot vaporizer being that in his opinion this is considered cooking. Likewise, he leans to forbid even cold vaporizers due to Nolad and possibly causing change of current in electricity.

[241] Shabbos Kehalacha Vol. 1 6:21-22; Hilchos Shabbos Zoreh footnote 64 in name of Rav Moshe Feinstien allows doing so for an ill person; Beir Moshe 6:52 allows doing so through a gentile for the sake of an ill person; Shalmei Yehuda 2:14 in name of Rav SZ"A permits doing so for the sake of an ill person.

[242] According to them there is no problem of increasing or decreasing the electricity as what Melacha is there involved in making a greater current of electricity. Likewise, the electric current does not decree the quality if the lights in the house due to a mere amount of added electricity. If, however, adding more water to the machine takes a lot of electricity then even in their opinion it would be forbidden to add more water if it causes the quality of light in the house to diminish. [Shabbos Kehalacha ibid footnote 33]

[243] See previous footnote

[244] Hilchos Shabbos Zoreh footnote 64 in name of Rav Moshe Feinstien and Shalmei Yehuda 2:14 in name of Rav SZ"A permit adding water only through a water hole and do not allow one to remove any parts to enter the water. Vetzaruch Iyun as the logic of this ruling. Seemingly those machines that they referred to would shut off when the water container was removed and hence if removing the container will not hut off the machine then it is allowed to be done. [Shabbos Kehalacha ibid footnote 33]

[245] Thus, one must pour the water directly from an urn without removing it with a utensil. [Shabbos Kehalacha ibid]

[246] Otherwise adding removing it and then reinserting it is considered cooking the water. [Shabbos Kehalacha ibid] Likewise one may not pour from a Keli Rishon on to such water. [Shalmeiu Yehuda ibid; However, see Shabbos Kehalacha ibid Biurim 6]

CHAPTER 4: THE LAW OF A YOLEDES/WOMEN DURING AND AFTER CHILDBIRTH

1. Desecrating Shabbos on behalf of a Yoledes: [1]

Like a dangerously ill person: A Yoledes [see exact Halachic definition in Halacha 3] is [considered] like a dangerously ill person and one [thus] is to desecrate Shabbos on her behalf for all of her needs. [See Halacha 2 for a list of her needs]

The requirement to use an irregularity upon desecration: Nevertheless [despite the fact that she is considered like a dangerously ill patient], since the pain of a Yoledes is natural and not [even] 1 of 1000 die from childbirth, therefore the Sages were stringent to require one to change [from his way of normally doing the action needed of desecrating Shabbos] in whatever he is able to change in it.

For example: If one needs to bring the woman a vessel through a public area then her assistant should bring it through tying it to her hair which is carrying in an irregular way and does not contain a Biblical prohibition. The same applies for all cases of the like.

If she [the Yoledes] needs oil then her friend should not smear oil on her hair and then come to her [the Yoledes] and squeeze the oil out, rather she should bring it in a vessel which is hanging on her hair, as it is better to carry [the oil] with a vessel in an irregular way, without any other prohibition, then to add in doing the squeezing prohibition, even though that squeezing hair is only Rabbinically forbidden as was explained in chapter 326 [Halacha 5].

Summary:
A woman which has reached a state in labor in which she is defined as a Yoledes [see Halacha 3] may have Shabbos desecrated on her behalf for of all her needs. However, whenever a desecration is done it is to be done in an irregular manner, in whatever way one is able to change from the normal method that the act is done during the week.

Q&A
May one desecrate Shabbos on behalf of treating or preventing a miscarriage?[2]
Yes[3]. This applies even if she is less than 40 days pregnant and even if there is no danger to her but there is possibility of saving the pregnancy.

Davening for a woman not to give birth on Shabbos:
Sefer Chassidim 793; Toras Hayoledes p. 11

---

2. Preparing matters from before Shabbos:[4]

It is proper to beware that when the 9th month arrives one prepares all [the matters that would require desecration in the event she was to give birth on Shabbos] from before Shabbos in order so they will not be required to desecrate Shabbos. [**See Q&A**]

Summary
Once a pregnant woman has reached her ninth month she is to prepare as much as possible before Shabbos in order to diminish Shabbos desecration if need be.

---

[1] Admur 330:1
[2] Piskeiy Teshuvos 330:4 and 6
[3] As during a miscarriage she is considered like a dangerously ill person.
[4] Admur 330:3

What matters are to be prepared from before Shabbos within the 9ᵗʰ month?[5]

The following is to be taken care of prior to the 1ˢᵗ Shabbos within ones entering of the 9ᵗʰ month:

1. Registration to the hospital and all the matters which pertain to her giving birth there such as the identification tags, and the testing of her type of blood.
2. Remove any hair interfering with the birth from before Shabbos [if this is standard procedure in the hospital[6]].
3. Leave a light on in the house throughout the night.
4. If one will be traveling in their private car then one is to: disengage the inner car lights from turning on upon opening the car doors; remove Muktzah items from the car seats and in case one will be traveling past the Techum to remove all unnecessary items.
5. One who lives far from the hospital it is proper for them to set up to stay for Shabbos in an area near the Hospital. However, if there is difficulty in doing so she is not obligated to do it, especially if there is a gentile ambulance driver available in her place.
6. If before Shabbos she begins to feel ready to give birth she should already go before Shabbos to the hospital and not wait for things to pick up and then go on Shabbos.[7]

May one induce labor on Shabbos?[8]

One must avoid doing so due to causing unnecessary desecration of Shabbos, unless the matter involves a medical emergency. In a case of great pain, one is to contact a Rav.

3. List of matters that may be done for a Yoledes:

A. Calling a midwife:

One may call a midwife for her from one place to another. [**See Halacha 4 regarding when it becomes permitted to call a midwife**]

Helping her give birth: One may help her give birth.

B. Desecrating Shabbos for non-essential matters which will calm her down:

Turning on the light: At night one may light a candle for her. [Furthermore] even if she is blind and even if the other women which are assisting her do not require this candle, as they are able to fully assist her without a candle, [nevertheless] one lights a candle for her.

The reason: as although she [the patient] cannot see she becomes calmer upon knowing that there is light here, as she tells herself that if there is anything that she needs my friends can see and can do so for me. However, if she were to know that there is no candle here then there is worry that she will become endangered due to fear in her heart, as she will fear that perhaps the assistors are not doing properly what she needs done.

Q&A

May a relative or friend accompany the Yoledes to the hospital?[9]

First Opinion: Any relative or friend who will help the Yoledes keep calm may travel with them. This applies even if there are other people in the car, such as a medic or EMT, and even if the Yoledes says that he/she does not need the escort of the relative or friend.[10] [However care must be taken to

---

[5] Piskeiy Teshuvos 330

[6] This used to be standard birth procedures in hospitals due to hygienic reasons. In most Modern countries this is no longer practiced.

[7] Ketzos Hashulchan 140:3

[8] Toras Hayoledes chapter 2

[9] See Piskeiy Teshuvos 330:1

[10] So rules Chazon Ish and Az Nidbaru 1:29

avoid Chilul Shabbos in the process, such as not to carry items with him/her if there is no Eiruv.]

Second Opinion: However, there are Poskim[11] which are less lenient and only allow an escort in a case that the Yoledes is asking for one.

Third Opinion: Others[12] allow it in the following cases: a) A first birth even if she says she does not need an escort. B) A 2nd birth and onwards so long as she does not say that she does not need it. C) Even if she says she does not need it by a 2nd birth and on, but she will be left in the ambulance in the care of gentiles. Thus, only if it is her 2nd or subsequent birth, and there is a Jewish driver or Medic with her, and she says that she does not need an escort should a friend or relative refrain from escorting her.

May more than one person accompany the Yoledes to the hospital, such as her mother and husband?

Seemingly this should depend on how badly the Yoledes wants their company.

May one travel to a hospital of their choice or must it be the closest available hospital?[13]

One may travel to whichever hospital he/she feels that they will receive the best medical treatment or care. However, one may not travel to a further hospital simply to save money.

May one who traveled to the hospital to give birth and was then released on Shabbos, due to being told that she is not ready to give birth, return home on Shabbos?[14]

It is forbidden for her to drive back home. Although if there is no comfortable area where she can wait until after Shabbos[15] there is room to allow her to have a gentile drive her home, so long as her house is within Techum Shabbos.[16]

If on Shabbos one traveled to a hospital outside of Techum Shabbos as an escort for a Yoledes, may he/she walk out of the hospital?[17]

Yes.[18] One may walk within 2000 cubits from his destination. If he arrived in a city, he has the same Techum as do the city inhabitants.

When traveling to the hospital on Shabbos what items may one bring with him?

All items which the Yoledes will need for the actual birth, even if it is merely to help her feel relaxed and calm, may be brought in all cases. All other items may only be brought if:

1. The item is not Muktzah and,
2. One is traveling within the city [i.e. within Techum Shabbos] and,
3. There is an Eiruv in the city and,
4. The item is needed on Shabbos.

- **If one prepared their bag before Shabbos with items that may not be brought, must they remove it on Shabbos prior to leaving?**

  If there is no time to do so, such as that the Yoledes must immediately go to the hospital, then there is no need to clear the bag. If, however, time does remain then the Muktzah and other

---

[11] So is implied from Igros Moshe 1:132

[12] Teshuvos Vehanhagos 2:177

[13] Piskeiy Teshuvos 330:3

[14] Piskeiy Teshuvos 330:1

[15] This includes if one will not be able to pray with a Minyan or eat the Shabbos meals. [Teshuvos Vehanhagos ibid]

[16] SSH"K 36:10; Teshuvos Vehanhagos 2:174-However there the allowance is only if the gentile is any ways traveling to their area, or one hints to a gentile ambulance driver to do so. However, to ask a regular gentile to drive them back he does not allow.

[17] Based on 407:1

[18] As this is similar to a midwife which has traveled to help a woman give birth. Likewise, the escorts are also considered to have traveled due to Pikuach Nefesh. Now although in 405:5 Admur rules that *"when one left the Techum due to Ones then if there is a Kosher Eiruv in the city one may walk anywhere in the city. If there isn't a Kosher Eiruv in the city, then one may not leave the hospital building for any purpose."* Nevertheless, in a case that one left to help save a life the Sages did not limit them to their 4 cubits even if there is no Eiruv in the city.

unnecessary item are to be shaken out.

If one is traveling outside of Techum Shabbos must the escorts diminish in the amount of clothing they wear? Such as may the husband take his hat, gartel, kapata?
No.[19]

Advice to be able to carry items out of Techum:[20]
Those traveling on Shabbos and Yom Tov to a hospital that is outside of the Techum may only bring with them items that are of absolute necessity for the birth, as explained above. If, however, one makes the item Hefker before Shabbos/Yom Tov then it is permitted to bring the item outside of the techum. Hence, it is advised that the wife and escort make Hefker all items that they desire to bring with them to the hospital [and are not needed for the actual birth]. Initially, the items are to be made Hefker in front of three people. If this is not possible, it is to be made Hefker even amongst oneself.

4. From when does a woman carry the Halachic definition of a Yoledes:[21]

From when is a [woman] defined as a Yoledes [in the process of giving birth] to be allowed to desecrate Shabbos [on her behalf]? From when she sits on the birthing stool[22] [**See Q&A for practical definition today**], or from the time that the blood is drooling out [**See Q&A for definition, and regarding breaking of the waters**], or from the time that her friends [have to] carry her by her arms due to her not having strength to walk. Once any of the above has begun to occur one is [allowed] to desecrate Shabbos on her behalf for all her needs which are able to be done now without delay[23].

---

[19] Tzchebiner Rav answer to Rav Gerelick of Kfar Chabad [brought in Yagdil Torah Tzemach Tzedek]; Toras Hayoledes p. 32
[20] See Toras Hayoledes p. 36; See Admur 246:9; Kuntrus Achron 445:1
[21] Admur 330:3
[22] A birthing stool is a stool which has been specifically designed for use during childbirth. It allows a woman to sit or squat while giving birth with support to help her if she begins to feel fatigued.
[23] Meaning that those matters which do not take time to do may only be done from when she reaches this state.

Q&A

What is the practical definition today of sitting on the birthing stool? [24]

This refers to contractions[25]. Some[26] explain this to refer to the consistent set of contractions which occur before birth to open up the cervix, in which case one may desecrate Shabbos even if it is questionable if this will lead her to giving birth. Others[27] question however if perhaps the contractions refer to those which come when one is ready to push the baby out, after the cervix has already successfully opened.

What is the definition of blood coming out? [28]

This does not refer to a mere few drops but rather to a nice surge of blood.[29]

May one desecrate Shabbos if the woman's water broke?[30]

Some[31] have written that this is considered like a gush of blood coming out which defines her as a Yoledes, and one may thus desecrate Shabbos on her behalf from that time and on. Others[32] however argue this claim and say it has no source, and it happens that the water breaks much time prior to the birth. Others[33] say that if the breaking of the waters is accompanied by contractions then she is considered a Yoledes.

If one has not yet reached the above stage but a Doctor says that Shabbos must be desecrated for her may one do so?[34]

Yes.

---

5. Matters which take time may be done before she reaches the Halachic state of a Yoledes: [35]

Calling a midwife: However, to call a midwife from place to place which is a matter which takes time and delay is permitted to be done prior to this [i.e. to her reaching the above mentioned state of a Yoledes] from the time that she feels a little [need to give birth], even if she is in doubt.

Q&A

When may one call an ambulance or drive to the hospital if he suspects his wife may need to give birth?

From the time one suspects his wife needs to give birth, even if she has not yet reached the Halachic state of a Yoledes, one may call an ambulance or drive her to the hospital.

---

[24] Piskeiy Teshuvos 330:3
[25] Aruch Hashulchan 330:4
[26] SSH"K 36:8
[27] Toras Hayoledes 29
[28] Piskeiy Teshuvos 330:3
[29] Toras Hayoledes
[30] Piskeiy Teshuvos 330:3
[31] SSH"K 36:9
[32] Toras Hayoledes
[33] In name of Sheivet Halevy
[34] Piskeiy Teshuvos 330:3
[35] Admur 330:3

6. Assisting a gentile woman give birth:[36]

Is forbidden even for reward as one can excuse herself without causing enmity: One may not assist a gentile to give birth even if the needed assistance does not involve desecrating Shabbos, such as [in a case that] the baby has already detached [from the womb and begun] to exit, in which case removing it does not involve [the prohibition of] uprooting an item from its area of growth. Furthermore, [even] if the Jewish woman is a known midwife and she receives payment [for assisting in birth], in which case it is permitted for her during weekdays to assist gentile women in giving birth due to [that refusing to do so will cause] enmity, nevertheless on Shabbos [since] there is no enmity [involved in refusing to assist, and thus it remains forbidden to help a gentile woman give birth].

The reason that there is no enmity on Shabbos is because: the Jewish midwife is able to excuse herself [from assisting without causing hatred] by saying "Our women which keep Shabbos are permitted to be assisted in giving birth on Shabbos, however your women which do not keep Shabbos it is forbidden for us to assist them in giving birth".

The Law by an Arab woman: [Furthermore] even an Arab woman, which is not an idolater, (and there is thus no prohibition to assist them in giving birth during the week as there is by idolatress gentiles in which it was forbidden due to that she is assisting a idolatress child to be born, nevertheless on Shabbos) it is forbidden [to assist her] due to it being an unnecessary act, as will be explained in Chapter 332 [Halacha 1], (being that it is possible to excuse oneself from giving assistance without causing hatred).

The law by Karite women: However, the Karaim since they keep Shabbos it is permitted to assist them in giving birth (in exchange for reward [and only] in matters that do not contain desecration of Shabbos. [This may be done] due to enmity)

If one is not able to excuse herself without causing enmity: Even by idolatress gentile women if it is impossible to excuse oneself [from assisting] without causing enmity, it is permitted [to assist] in matters that do not contain desecration of Shabbos.

Summary- Assisting a gentile woman give birth:
It is forbidden to assist any[37] gentile women to give birth on Shabbos in any way even if it does not involve a Shabbos desecration[38]. However, if one is unable to excuse herself from assisting without causing enmity, then it is allowed to assist her in matters that involve no Shabbos desecration.

Q&A

Practically today may one assist a gentile woman in giving birth, and may he desecrate Shabbos on her behalf?[39]

Yes[40], as due to advanced communication and the constant anticipation of reasons to use to hate and attack Jews the matter can lead to actual danger for other Jews if one were to refuse to treat them. It is thus allowed to even do Biblical transgressions. However, some have written[41] that while doing so one is to constantly think that he is doing so simply to save himself or other Jews from danger, and then it is considered like a Melacha Sheiyna Tzarich Legufa which many Poskim allow to help save a gentile.

---

[36] Admur 330:2
[37] Even one who does not sever idols, such as a Muslim
[38] due to it being an unnecessary act, as well as if she is an idol worshiper it is forbidden even during the week due to that she is assisting a idolatress child to be born.
[39] Piskeiy Teshuvos 330:2
[40] So rules: Chasam Sofer [2] Yoreh Deah 131; Divrei Chayim 2:25; Igros Moshe 4:49; Chelkas Yaakov 2:54; Minchas Yitzchak 1:53, 3:20
[41] Shearim Hametzuyanim Behalacha 92:1; Titz Eliezer 8:15-6

7. Desecrating Shabbos for a woman who is after birth:

A. First three days after birth:[42]

Throughout the entire first three days after birth the Yoledes is considered like a definite dangerously ill person.

The reason for this is because: her limbs are loose and she is physically crushed.

The allowance to desecrate Shabbos without an experts orders: Therefore one is to desecrate Shabbos on her behalf even if she claims that it is unnecessary but her comrades claim that she needs it. Even if there is no midwife or doctor amongst them one is to do for her all her needs, as the matters that are done for a Yoledes during the week are well known to all. Even if she eats the foods of other [healthy] people [and thus it appears that she is healthy] we say that [this is because] she temporarily does not feel [her ill state], but [in truth] if she were to eat cold foods or other foods that a dangerously ill person refrains from eating, she would fall in danger.

Not to desecrate Shabbos if medical experts say it's unnecessary: However, if a midwife or a doctor say that there is no need to desecrate Shabbos, [the comrades] are to listen to them.

The reason for this is: because there are many Yoldos which do not have hot food made for them daily, and so is the custom today in some places that they eat on Shabbos the foods heated from the day before.

B. After 3 days but before 7 days after birth:[43]

From [after] three [days after birth] until the end of the seventh [day], if she says "I do not need [Shabbos desecrated]" then it is not to be desecrated even if her comrades claim that she does need [it done].

The reason for this is: because she is no longer considered endangered with regards to those matters which her comrades commonly do for her during the week, and it is [thus] possible for her to wait until the night [after Shabbos to have those things done].

If a midwife or doctor say she needs an action done: The above is with exception to if a midwife or doctor say that she needs [Shabbos desecrated for her], in which case Shabbos is likewise desecrated for other ill patients, as was written in chapter 328 [Halacha 10].

If the Yoledes does not voice an opinion: All the above is when she claims that she does not need Shabbos desecrated, however ordinarily when she does not voice an opinion and her comrades do not know [if she needs it done or not], then Shabbos is desecrated [for her]. However, if her comrades say that she does not need [Shabbos desecrated], then it is not to be desecrated.

If the Yoledes claims she needs Shabbos desecrated: However, the above is with exception to if she says "I do need [Shabbos desecrated]," in which case even if 100 doctors say she does not need Shabbos desecrated, [nevertheless] it is to be desecrated.

The reason for why she is believed over the doctors is: because one's own heart knows the bitterness of his soul, and as will be explained in chapter 618 [Halacha 1] regarding other ill patients.

C. From after seven days:[44]

From the end of seven days and onwards, even if she says she needs [Shabbos desecrated], it is not to be desecrated for her behalf. Rather she is considered until thirty days like a non-dangerously ill person, of which all their needs may be done by a gentile, with exception to the matter of a heater of which if she needs it, it is to be done by a Jew being that feeling cold is a danger for her for the entire duration of the thirty days, and even in the time of Tamuz. Regarding if others are allowed to warm up opposite this bonfire [which was heated for her] was explained in Chapter 276 [Halacha 13].

---

[42] Admur 330:4; See Toras Hayoledes chapter 35
[43] Admur 330:5
[44] Admur 330:5

D. How to calculate the 7 days:[45]

These [above mentioned] days are not counted through 24 hours [per day], but rather if she gave birth on Wednesday close to night, then when the entrance of night of Shabbos arrives, it is already the fourth day from her birth, even though she had not completed three 24 hour days until close to the night of Shabbos. The same applies for [calculating] the seven days and thirty days.

Summary-Desecrating Shabbos for a woman which is after birth

A. First three days after birth: [46]

Throughout the entire first three days after birth the Yoledes is considered like a definite dangerously ill person. Therefore, one is to desecrate Shabbos on her behalf even if she claims that it is unnecessary, but her comrades claim that she needs it. Even if there is no midwife or doctor amongst them one is to do for her all her needs,

Not to desecrate Shabbos if medical experts say it's unnecessary: However, if a midwife or a doctor say that there is no need to desecrate Shabbos, [the comrades] are to listen to them.

B. After 3 days but before 7 days after birth:[47]

From after three days after birth until the end of the seventh day, if she says "I does not need [Shabbos desecrated]" then it is not to be desecrated even if her comrades claim that she does need [it done].

If a midwife or doctor say she needs an action done: If a midwife or doctor say that she needs Shabbos desecrated for her then Shabbos is to be desecrated.

If the Yoledes does not voice an opinion: When she does not voice an opinion and her comrades do not know [if she needs it done or not], then Shabbos is desecrated [for her]. However, if her comrades say that she does not need [Shabbos desecrated], then it is not to be desecrated.

If the Yoledes claims she needs Shabbos desecrated: If she says "I do need [Shabbos desecrated] ", then even if 100 doctors say she does not need Shabbos desecrated, [nevertheless] it is to be desecrated.

C. From after seven days:[48]

From the end of seven days and onwards, even if she says she needs [Shabbos desecrated], it is not to be desecrated for her behalf. Rather she is considered until thirty days like a non-dangerously ill person, of which all their needs may be done by a gentile. This is with exception to igniting a heater that if she needs it, it is to be done by a Jew being that feeling cold is a danger for her for the entire duration of the thirty days, and even in the time of Tamuz.

D. How to calculate the 7 days:[49]

The above-mentioned days are not counted through 24 hours [per day]. Thus, if she gave birth on Wednesday close to night, then when the entrance of night of Shabbos arrives, it is already the fourth day from her birth, even though she had not completed three 24-hour days until close to the night of Shabbos. The same applies for [calculating] the seven days and thirty days.

Q&A

If a woman had a miscarriage does she have the same status as a Yoledes in the above laws? [50]

Yes[51], so long as the fetus was 40 days into the pregnancy.

---

[45] Admur 330:6
[46] Admur 330:4
[47] Admur 330:5
[48] Admur 330:5
[49] Admur 330:6
[50] Piskeiy Teshuvos 330:4
[51] So rules M"B 617 in Biur Halacha, and Kaf Hachayim 330:2

May a Yoledes take a hot shower on Shabbos?
Toras Hayoledes writes that yes within three days from birth. Best ask gentile. If no gentile than do with shinuiy.

8. The law if a woman died r"l during childbirth:[52]

A woman which sat on the birthing stool and died, one is to bring a knife on Shabbos even through a public property, and tear her stomach and take out the baby as perhaps [the baby] will be found alive.
The reason for why we suspect that he is alive: Now, although majority of times the infant dies prior to the mother, nevertheless by the danger of a life we do not follow the majority, and at times it is able to live after its mother's death. Now, although this infant never had a living status, Shabbos is to be desecrated due to doubt just as one who did have a living status.
The reason for why today we are no longer accustomed to tear the mothers stomach: The reason that [cutting the mother's stomach] is not in practice today even during the week is because we are no longer expert in the mother's death to such close proximity that the child still can live, as [we suspect that] perhaps she fainted and if her stomach were to be torn she will die, and thus one needs to wait [to verify whether she has died or merely fainted] and until then the child has certainly died. [**See Q&A for Halacha today**]

Summary: The law if a woman died r"l during childbirth:[53]

If a woman died during labor r"l, one is to bring a knife on Shabbos even through a public property, and tear her stomach and take out the baby, as perhaps [the baby] will be found alive. Today however this in no longer in practice being that by the time we determine her death the baby has certainly died.

Q&A

Practically today is one to desecrate Shabbos to remove the baby if the mother died?[54]
Being that today there are machines which determine the exact time of death for the mother, as well as whether the baby is still alive, one may obviously desecrate Shabbos to help save the baby in accordance to the readings of these machines.

---

9. What may be done for the new born on Shabbos?[55]

The child which is born on Shabbos may have all of his needs done for him.
One may:

1. **Bathe him**,
2. **Salt him** in order so his flesh harden,
3. **Bury the placenta** in order to warm the infant[56],
4. **Cut the umbilical cord**,

As all these matters the infant has pain from them if they are not done for him, and since they do not contain any Biblical work the Sages allowed it [to be done].

---

[52] Admur 330:7
[53] Admur 330:7
[54] Piskeiy Teshuvos 330:5
[55] Admur 330:8
[56] This had a supernatural effect in warming the child [M"B]

5. **Straightening the child's limbs:**[57]

One may straighten the limbs of a livable child which have dislocated due to the pain of the birth. However, this is only allowed to be done on the day of the birth, however afterwards it is forbidden.

The reason for this is: because it appears like building.

To wrap him in his clothing: However, to wrap him in his clothing in order to straighten his limbs is always permitted as this is the ordinary way of doing things during the week and it does not appear like building on Shabbos. However, an infant which is not wrapped during the week and his limbs have bent on Shabbos, it is forbidden to wrap him in order to straighten them.

6. **Lifting up the foreskin of the throat:**[58]

If the foreskin of the throat of the infant fell it is permitted to place a finger into his mouth and remove the foreskin to its place even though that at times this will cause him to vomit.

If the child was born prematurely:[59]

Certainly born in 7th or 9th: The above allowance applies by a livable baby, which is defined as a baby which was for certain born in the ninth [i.e. after the end of the 9th month, which is approximately after week 38[60]] or seventh [month] (such as if the husband separated from her after [the original] marital relations [which got her pregnant]).

Questionably or Certainly born in 8th: However if the child was born in the eighth month, or if it is questionable whether it was born after seventh or eighth, then one does not desecrate Shabbos for him whether for the above matters, whether for matters which lack of performing can endanger him, such as to undo a mound that is over him, unless his hair and nails have completed growing, in which case he certainly was fully developed by the seventh months and it just delayed leaving his mother's womb after having been fully developed. Therefore, even if he is for certain born in the eighth, such as if her husband separated from her after having marital relations, his status is like one who was born in the seventh month for all matters and he is [thus] to be circumcised on Shabbos.

However, if his hair was smitten and his nails are not complete as [are to be] when born, then even if he is questionably a child of the eighth month, his ruling is like one who is for certain of the eighth month for all matters. Furthermore even regarding life threatening matters in which one [is ordinarily allowed to] desecrate [even] when there is a doubt, even by a fetus which never had a living status due that we suspect that perhaps he has developed enough months and his hair and nails are complete, nevertheless here where we see that [his nails and hair] are not complete it is close to certain that he was born in the eighth [month], [and he] would not have been complete until the ninth month, and he hurried to be born prior to the time and he is a stillborn.

Moving the eighth month baby who did not complete his nails/hair: Even to move such a baby is forbidden the same way it is forbidden to move a stone. Therefore, one does not circumcise this child on Shabbos.[61]

The reason he is not allowed to be circumcised on Shabbos: We do not say let us circumcise the child in any event as if the child is a seventh month old then his circumcision overrules Shabbos and if he is an eighth month child then there is no Shabbos desecration here in the circumcision, as it is like merely cutting meat. [The reason for this is] as since it is close to certain that it is an eighth month child the Sages

---

[57] Admur 330:10

[58] Admur 330:11

[59] Admur 330:8

[60] The child is only considered a Ben Tesha Chodesh after a full 9 months have passed, and has now entered into the 10th month. [See Y.D. 374:8] We follow the Hebrew months in this regard, and not an amount of weeks or days. Thus, since the months vary between 29 and 30 days, determining how many weeks/days need to pass depends on how many days were in each of the nine months of her pregnancy. If, for example, there were five 30 day months and four 29 day months, then it is exactly 38 weeks, which is 266 days. If, however, there were more or less than five 30 day months, then it would be more or less than 38 weeks. Thus, we determine the completion of nine months based on the passing of Hebrew months, and not based on weeks or days. [See Meil Tzedaka 5, brought in Pischeiy Teshuvah 374:9]

[61] This follows the opinion of the Michaber in Yoreh Deah 266:11

did not want to allow moving him on behalf of his circumcision in a scenario where it is close to certain that his circumcision is meaningless.

Other Opinions: There are those[62] who argue on this and say that since it is possible that he is a seventh month child and all seventh month children are not stillborns despite that their hair and nails have not fully developed, therefore there is no prohibition at all to carry him on Shabbos, and so too he is to be circumcised on Shabbos in any event.

According to all cannot desecrate Shabbos for this child: However, one may not desecrate Shabbos for him according to all whether for matters in which there is danger [for the child] if they are not done, whether for matters that [the Sages] permitted to do for the child on the day that he was born due to his pain even though that [doing these actions] do not contain a Biblical prohibition.

The custom today-To circumcise and move babies born in eighth: Based on this [latter] opinion today we circumcise all children even if he was born in the eighth month as we are not expert in the months of pregnancy as at times a woman conceives near her immersion and at times she does not conceive until later and it is possible that the child is a seventh month child, and even though that his hair and nails have not fully developed he is to be circumcised, and so too it is permitted to move him on Shabbos.

The Final Ruling: (Regarding the final ruling in a Rabbinical matter one follows the lenient opinion and therefore one who is lenient to move the child like the latter opinion does not lose [following religious law], however with regards to circumcision on Shabbos it is better to sit and do nothing, as it is proper to suspect for the words of the forbidding opinions, [as] although there is no prohibition in moving the child there is a prohibition in circumcising the child on Shabbos for no need as similarly there is a prohibition in cutting the umbilical cord on Shabbos even according to the latter opinion as was explained [above].) [In 331/3 Admur plainly rules that an 8th month child who has not fully developed his hair and nails is not to be circumcised.]

Summary:
If the baby's hair or nails are not completely developed <u>and</u> it is questionable whether the baby was born in its eighth month, and certainly if one knows that it was born in the eighth month, then one may not desecrate Shabbos even for Rabbinical matters, even to help save this child. However, one may be lenient to move the baby, and some are accustomed to even circumcise the baby on Shabbos, although regarding circumcision it is better to abstain from doing so on Shabbos.[63]
If the child has complete hair and nails, or it does not but one knows for certain that it is a ninth- or seventh-month baby then Shabbos is to be desecrated to help save him.

Q&A

Practically, may one today desecrate Shabbos to help save a premature baby if it is in the eighth month?[64]
Yes, as today we have incubators and other forms of technology which highly raise the child's ability of survival and it is thus no longer considered like a stillborn.[65]

May one desecrate Shabbos to help save a test tube baby [IVF]?[66]
While the egg is in the stage of being fertilized in the tube one may not desecrate Shabbos to help save it, as only a fetus in its mother's womb is considered a livable entity.[67]

---

[62] This follows the opinion of the Rama in Yoreh Deah 266:11
[63] To note in 331:3 Admur writes plainly that he may not be circumcised on Shabbos.
[64] Piskeiy Teshuvos 330:6
[65] So rules Minchas Yitzchak 4:123; Kinyan Torah 3:42; Chazon Ish Yoreh Deah 155
[66] Piskeiy Teshuvos 330:7
[67] So rules Sheivet Halevy 5:47

10. Pumping and squeezing breast milk on Shabbos:[68]

Into a cup and the like: A woman may not squeeze milk from her breasts into a cup or into a pot in order to nurse [the milk] to her child. [**See Q&A regarding if the child refuses to nurse and there is danger involved**]

The reason for this is: because one who milks into a vessel is completely detaching and is liable for the threshing prohibition, and it was only permitted to do a Biblical prohibition in a case of life-threatening danger.

Trickling milk in order to stimulate her child to nurse: However, it is permitted for a woman to squeeze out some milk [and have it trickle down her skin and the like[69]] in order to stimulate her child to take hold of her breast and nurse. [However, she may not squeeze the milk into his mouth in order to stimulate him -**See Q&A below**]

The reason for this is because: as since this milk [that is squeezed] is going to waste it does not contain a Biblical "detaching" prohibition, but rather a Rabbinical prohibition as explained in chapter 320 [Halacha 21] and for the need of a child [the Sages] did not apply their decree.

Squirting milk onto one who is spellbound: However it is forbidden to squirt from her milk onto one who has been overtaken by an evil spell, as he is not in any danger and is not in great pain for us to rescind for him a Rabbinical prohibition to be done through a Jew, as [opposed to] what was permitted by one who has heart ache and the like. See chapter 330 [Halacha 9].

Is it permitted for a woman to squeeze out milk from her breast to relieve pain?[70] Even a child which is for certain an eighth month [child], which is [therefore] forbidden to move according to all, his mother may bend over him and nurse him due to the pain of the milk which pains her.

Similarly, she herself may remove with her hands the milk which is causing her pain. [**See Q&A regarding using a pump**]

The reason for this allowance is: as since this milk is going to waste it does not contain the [Biblical] detaching prohibition but rather [only] the Rabbinical, and due to her pain, they did not decree [against removing it].

Summary-Pumping milk from a woman's breast on Shabbos:
Is forbidden to be done into a vessel due to the Biblical detaching prohibition. However, it is permitted for a woman to squeeze out some milk and have it trickle down her skin in order to stimulate her child to take hold of her breast and nurse. As well it is permitted for her to squeeze milk from her breast onto the ground in order to relieve breast pain caused by the milk.

Q&A
May a woman pump milk out to feed her baby if he refuses to suck from the breast?[71]
If there is nothing else available for the child to eat [such as formula] and there is thus possible danger involved then she may pump out less than a Grogeres[72] worth of milk at a time and feed him it, and then pump out another Grogeres worth and feed him it. She may not pump out more milk until the child is fed the previous milk that was pumped.

May one squeeze the milk into the baby's mouth to stimulate it to eat?[73]
No! One may **not** squirt the milk into the mouth of the baby as in such a case it is not going to waste and thus squeezing it contains a Biblical prohibition. [**See footnote for opinion of M"B[74]**]

---

[68] Admur 328:41
[69] See reason and footnote below.
[70] Admur 330:9
[71] Har Tzevi 201
[72] A Grogeres is 19.2 milliliters [Shiurei Torah 3:17], thus one is to squeeze less than this amount at a time.
[73] Ketzos Hashulchan 138 footnote 30
[74] This is unlike the understanding of the Mishneh Berurah [112] based on the Shevulay Haleket that one may squirt into the baby's mouth. In the Sharreiy Tziyon the Mishneh Berurah queries how come this is allowed. According to the Alter Rebbe the query does not apply as in truth it is

May a woman use a pump to release milk in order to relieve breast pain?[75]

<u>If plans to store this milk</u>: If the pump contains a bottle which will store the milk, then it is forbidden to be done if she plans to use the milk.

<u>If plans to throw out the milk</u>: If she plans to throw out the milk from the bottle some Poskim[76] rule it is nevertheless forbidden. Others[77] however rule that this is allowed to be done. The Ketzos Hashulchan[78] rules that one may be lenient like these opinions to pump out less than a Grogeres[79] worth of milk at a time and then spill it out prior to pumping again.[80]

<u>If the milk goes directly to waste from the pump</u>: It is allowed according to all opinions to use a pump to release the milk, in order to relieve pain, if the pump squeezes out the milk directly onto the floor or garbage.

---

not allowed.

[75] Piskeiy Teshuvos 330:8

[76] Bris Olam

[77] Avnei Nezer 47

[78] 138 footnote 30

[79] A Grogeres is 19.2 milliliters [Shiurei Torah 3:17], thus one is to squeeze less than this amount at a time.

[80] As one is only liable for the Detaching prohibition if he pumps the minimum measurement of a Grogeres.

CHAPTER 5: LAWS RELATING TO A FIRE ON SHABBOS

1. The law if the fire poses a danger:[1]

It is permitted and praiseworthy to extinguish any fire which has even a remote doubt[2] as to if it can be life threatening. Thus, any fire which has the ability to reach people who will be unable to escape from it, such as old and sick people as well as children, then one is to extinguish the fire on Shabbos. [Hence practically today, fires which occur in homes, offices and the like may be extinguished due to fear they may spread to a home that contains people which will be unable to escape. In such cases one may phone the fire department and do all that he can to extinguish the fire. Thus, only if the house is sitting alone in a large plane of land, and hence there is no suspicion of the fire spreading to others, does it remain forbidden to extinguish the fire, if all the inhabitants are able to escape the house.[3]]

No need for atonement:[4] Anyone which extinguished a fire which posed a possible danger does not need atonement, and is not allowed to be stringent on himself and do acts of repentance on it even if he so wishes.[5] [One is not to have any worry or sadness over the fact he had to desecrate Shabbos.[6]]

Practically what is one to do if there is a small fire in one's home such as Shabbos candles?
Seemingly it is best to try to first extinguish the fire in indirect ways, such as by placing bags of water around it. If this is not possible and there is fear the fire may spread, then one is to spill water around the fire. If this too does not help one may extinguish the fire directly.

---

2. Extinguishing a fire which merely poses a safety hazard:[7]

It is permitted to extinguish a fiery metal coal if it is found in an area which poses a public safety hazard, even if it is not life threatening.[8] Furthermore, even by a wood coal it is permitted for one to be lenient to extinguished it if it poses a public safety hazard, even if it is not life threatening.[9] Nevertheless every Baal Nefesh should be stringent and avoid extinguishing wood coals even if they pose a safety hazard, so long as they are not life threatening.[10]

---

[1] Admur 329:1

[2] Admur 329:3

[3] SSH"K 41:1

[4] Admur 334:28; Darkei Moshe 334:7; Or Zarua 2:38; Chavos Yair 236; Shaareiy Teshuvah 334:2; M"B 334:78 in name of Nezer Yisrael in name of Zechor Leavraham;

Other opinions: Some Poskim rule that an individual may choose to fast for atonement if he desecrated Shabbos Biblically, although we do not rule this way to anyone who asks. [Chavos Yair ibid; see Piskeiy Teshuvos 3287 footnote 61]

[5] The reason: As this can cause himself [or others] to be lax in extinguishing a fire the next time it occurs. [ibid]

[6] Tashbatz 1:54; Shulchan Shlomo 334:4; Chasam Sofer 85 "Just as one is not to be pained for doing Mila on Shabbos, so too regarding Pikuach Nefesh"

[7] Admur 334:29

[8] As extinguishing a metal coal is merely Rabbinically forbidden, and in a case of a public safety hazard the Sages did not uphold their decree. [ibid]

[9] As according to the opinions which rules a Melacha which is not needed Legufa is not Biblically forbidden, then extinguishing this coal is only a Rabbinical prohibition, and is thus permitted to be done in a case of safety hazard. The reason for this is because the Sages did not uphold their Rabbinical decrees in a case of public safety hazard despite the fact that they uphold it even in a case of money loss. Now although there is a dissenting opinion that rules a Melacha which is not needed Legufa is nevertheless Biblically forbidden, and hence extinguishing this coal is a Biblical prohibition, nevertheless the main ruling is like the lenient opinions. [ibid]

[10] As according to the opinion which rules a Melacha which is not needed Legufa is nevertheless Biblically forbidden, then extinguishing this coal is a Biblical prohibition, and is only permitted in a life-threatening scenario. Now although we rule like the dissenting opinion that it is not Biblical, nevertheless a meticulous person is to be stringent. [ibid]

To note that in 316:22 in which a similar dispute is brought Admur there concludes that a Baal Nefesh should only be meticulous if he is able to avoid the danger and is able to warn others to avoid it. Vetzaruch Iyun why a similar conclusion was not brought here. Perhaps one can explain that there it is more difficult to avoid the danger as the damaging creature moves, however here with a coal it does not move and can be easily avoided. However, Tzaruch Iyun nevertheless why this law was placed in parentheses.

Summary:
It is permitted to extinguish any fire that poses a safety hazard even if it is not life threatening. Nevertheless, one who is meticulous should be stringent against doing so.

---

3. Preventing a non-lethal fire from spreading:[11]

Spreading non-flammable material onto the area near the fire: If a vessel has caught fire it is permitted for one to spread a non-flammable material, such as non-Muktzah goatskin, near the fire, over the untouched area, in order to prevent the fire from spreading.[12]

Placing jugs of water near the fire: One may surround the fire with vessels filled with water, hence having the fire break through the vessel, causing the water to spill, extinguishing the fire.[13] [It is however forbidden to spill water around the fire, having it extinguish when it reaches the water.[14]]

Pouring liquid on a cloth:[15] If a cloth has caught fire, it is permitted to pour colored liquids, such as red wine, onto the cloth a short distance from the fire, in order for it to extinguish the fire when it reaches the water.[16] It is however forbidden to pour water or white/clear colored liquids onto the cloth due to the whitening prohibition.[17]

Shaking a cloth that has caught fire:[18] It is forbidden to shake a cloth that has caught fire in order to extinguish it. One however may use the cloth for its intended purposes, and if doing so causes the fire to extinguish, so be it.

Placing a vessel of water under a candle to catch the falling sparks:[19] It is forbidden to place a vessel of liquid under a flame in order to catch falling sparks.[20] Furthermore even before Shabbos it is forbidden to set up this vessel with liquid to catch the falling sparks on Shabbos.[21]

Q&A
May one shake on to the floor a lit match or candle which has fallen onto one's tablecloth?[22]
Yes.

May one extinguish a spark?
No.[23] However some Poskim[24] rule this is allowed in a case of great loss.[25]

---

[11] Admur 334:22

[12] Goat skin prevents fire from spreading as it itself becomes scorched but does not catch fire and it hence protects the object under it. [ibid]

[13] The Sages did not decree against causing the fire to extinguish in this manner in a case of loss, as in truth it is only a grama, indirect, form of extinguishing, as it is the fire itself which causes the vessels to break and the water to spill. [ibid]

[14] As this is not considered indirect [grama] as in the previous case when there was an interval between the fire and the water, and it was the fire that destroyed the interval. [ibid and 265:8]

[15] Admur 334:23

[16] Now although in this case there is no interval between the fire and the water, and thus should be forbidden as explained in the previous case, nevertheless since it does not actually extinguish the fire but simply prevents it from spreading on the wet area, hence causing the fire to extinguish on its own, therefore it is allowed. [ibid]

[17] As soaking a cloth constitutes laundering it. Alternatively, it is due to a decree one may come to squeeze the water from it. [ibid]

[18] Admur 334:24

[19] Admur 265:8

[20] As the liquid hastens the extinguishing of the sparks and by doing so this is considered as if one is directly extinguishing the flame. Even by an actual fire the Sages only permitted placing liquid in a vessel and having the fire break through the vessel, as the vessel separates between the fire and the water, hence considered the person's action an indirect cause. Alternatively, they allowed wetting the other side of a cloth hence preventing the fire from spreading. However, to pour water in the path of the fire is not considered indirect and is forbidden. [ibid]

[21] Now, although all actions are permitted to be done before Shabbos, despite this causing a Melacha to occur on Shabbos, nevertheless in this case the Sages were stringent as not all know of the prohibition in hastening the extinguishing of a spark and if it were to be allowed to be done before Shabbos people may come to do so on Shabbos. [ibid]

[22] Ashel Avraham Mahadurah Tinyana 23

[23] As is evident from above 265:8

[24] Bashamayim Eish 194

4. Asking a gentile to extinguish a non-lethal fire:[26]

Asking a gentile to extinguish a fire from within one's own home: It is forbidden to ask a gentile to extinguish a fire in one's home [that does not pose any bodily danger[27]] even if not doing so will cause one great loss.[28] It is however permitted to ask a gentile to extinguish a fire in order to save Sefarim from being burnt if there is no other way for them to be saved. [Based on this if one's Mezuzas are hammered into the door post one may always ask a gentile to extinguish a fire in order to save the Mezuzos from getting burned.[29]] Furthermore, although one may not ask a gentile to extinguish the fire, as explained above, one may however announce that whoever extinguishes the fire will not lose out [compensation]. One may even call a gentile to come with him to the area of the fire and then make this announcement.[30]

If the gentile decided to extinguish the fire on his own:[31] If a gentile has come to extinguish the fire on his own accord, there is no need to protest his actions.[32]

May one tell a gentile to extinguish a fire from within another person's home? [33] It is permitted to ask a gentile to extinguish a fire within a <u>gentile's</u> home even in order to prevent the fire from reaching one's own home. [Furthermore, if one is doing so to prevent the fire from reaching his own home, then it is allowed even if the fire is in another Jews home.[34] Furthermore, even if there is no worry of damage to one's own belongings some Poskim[35] rule one may nevertheless ask a gentile to extinguish the fire in another Jews home.[36] Vetzaruch Iyun.[37]]

5. A child which has come to extinguish the fire, must he be protested?[38]

One must protest against a child which has come to extinguish a fire, as certainly he is doing so or the benefit of the adult owner and not for his own benefit.

6. Extinguishing a metal coal:[39]

It is Rabbinically[40] forbidden to extinguish a metal coal which does not pose danger for the public.

---

[25] As they claim a spark has no real tangibility and hence in a case of great loss is allowed. No inference can be brought from Admur ibid that doing so is forbidden in a case of great loss, as Admur is discussing a case that the fire would in any event definitely extinguish in the vessel, and one simply desires to hasten it, in which he rules it is forbidden.

[26] Admur 334:25

[27] If however it poses bodily danger, even if it is not lethal, nevertheless even a Jew himself may extinguish the fire as explained above.

[28] Although all Rabbinical prohibitions may be done through a gentile in a case of great loss, and hence here too extinguishing [which is merely Rabbinical according to those which say one is exempt from a Melacha done not Legufa] should be allowed according to those opinions that it is Rabbinical, nevertheless it was prohibited by the Sages, lest one come due to panic to extinguish the fire himself. Meaning, that since such a person is naturally in a state of panic and is unable to think clear, if we allow him to save his valuables in any way he may come to do so himself. [ibid]

[29] Misgeres Hashulchan 85:2

[30] Admur 334:27

[31] Admur 334:26

[32] As when a gentile does so, he has certainly calculated the benefits he will receive from his actions either now or later, and thus he intends on doing so for his own benefit. [ibid]

[33] Admur 307:35

[34] As it is Amirah Lenachri in a case of great loss, and the Jew is not panicky that we should decree against him doing so. Nevertheless, Tzaruch Iyun from 307:35 where Admur only mentions an allowance to ask a gentile to extinguish his own fire, or another gentiles fire, and does not mention the fire of a Jew.

[35] Rav SZ"A in SSH"K, brought in Piskeiy Teshuvos 334:6.

[36] As the entire reason it is forbidden for one to tell a gentile to extinguish his own fire is because one is panicky and if we were to allow him to so he may come to extinguish the fire himself. This reason however does not apply to another person, which his belongings are not in jeopardy.

[37] As why should Amirah Lenachri be allowed to this person if he has no great personal need for it to be done. This is besides for the fact that according to some extinguishing a fire is Biblically forbidden [as Melacha Sheiyno Tzarich Legufa is Chayav], and hence it is not allowed even in a case of loss.

[38] Admur 334:26

[39] Admur 334:29

[40] There is no Biblical prohibition involved in extinguishing a metal coal being that it does not burn. It is however Rabbinically forbidden to extinguish it. [ibid]

7. What may one save from a fire in one's home in a case that the fire does not pose a danger?[41]

A. The general rules:

The Sages decreed that one is forbidden from saving anything from a fire[42] which is in his house [or building or courtyard[43]] with exception to the amount of food he needs for the remaining meals of Shabbos, clothing and Sefarim as will be explained.

Saving items into one's own courtyard ,neighbors house, other room in same house:[44] It is disputed whether the above restriction of the Sages apply in all cases, even if one desires to save the objects into his own private courtyard, or only when he desires to save them into a courtyard which is jointly owned[45]. [However according to all it is permitted to save the items from one room to another.[46]] Practically one is to be stringent [to save the items into another room rather than to outside his house. If, however, this is not possible, one may be lenient to save all his items into his own courtyard or into a next door neighbor's home with which there is an established Eiruv[47].[48]]

Asking a gentile to save items from a fire:[49] It is forbidden to ask a gentile to save one's items from the fire if those items are forbidden for the Jew himself to save.[50] Thus, only those items to be mentioned that may be saved by a Jew, may be saved through a gentile. Nevertheless, although one may not ask a gentile to save items from the fire, as explained above, one may however announce that whoever saves items from the fire will not lose out. One may even call a gentile to come with him to the area of the fire and then make this announcement.[51]

If the gentile decided to save items from the fire on his own:[52] If a gentile has come to save one's belongings from the fire on his own accord, there is no need to protest his actions.[53]

B. Saving food:

It is permitted for one to save the amount of food he needs for the remaining meals of Shabbos. Hence if the fire occurred Friday night prior to the meal one may save three meals worth of food. If the fire occurred Shabbos day before the meal one may save two meals worth. If the fire occurred Shabbos afternoon before Mincha he may save one meals worth. One may save enough food for the remainder of Shabbos for oneself, and animals. The above allowance applies even if one has food to eat elsewhere.[54]

Taking out in a single vessel:[55] It was only prohibited to take out more than one's need for his remaining meals if one will be making more than one trip to and from the house. One may however take out as much food as he can fit into a single vessel in a single trip, even if the vessel will contain a lot more than three meals worth. Hence one may spread his Tallis and pile into it as much food as he can fit. [This allowance

---

[41] Admur 334:1

[42] This includes food, drink, and all items even if they are not Muktzah and there is an Eiruv in the city, or even if one desires to bring the items to another room away from the fire. [ibid]
The reason for this decree is because they suspected that if one were to be allowed to save all of one's belongings he may come, due to the panic and hastiness of saving the items, to forget that it is Shabbos and extinguish the fire. [ibid]

[43] Aruch Hashulchan 334:17; Kaf Hachayim 334:6

[44] Admur 334:11

[45] Thus, to save them to a next door neighbor's house if an eiruv is established between the two houses, or to save the items into one's own courtyard some hold is permitted. [ibid]

[46] Ketzos Hashulchan 141:8 in name of M"B

[47] What does this mean? Is there space between the two houses? Wouldn't this mean that he is taking it to a joint courtyard which is forbidden to all?

[48] Ketzos Hashulchan 141 footnote 13. M"B rules one may be lenient in a Rabbinical dispute.

[49] Admur 334:25

[50] Although all Rabbinical prohibitions may be done through a gentile in a case of great loss, and hence here too saving the objects through a gentile should be allowed, nevertheless it was prohibited by the Sages, lest one come due to panic to extinguish the fire himself. Meaning, that since such a person is naturally in a state of panic and is unable to think clear, if we allow him to save his valuables in any way he may come to do so himself. [ibid]

[51] Admur 334:27

[52] Based on 334:26 regarding him coming to extinguish the fire.

[53] As when a gentile does so, he has certainly calculated the benefits he will receive from his actions either now or later, and thus he intends on doing so for his own benefit. [ibid]

[54] Admur 334:3

[55] Admur 334:6

applies each time one returns to the house to take out items that he is permitted to remove. This allowance however is limited only to items that are needed for the meal. It is however forbidden to take out items not needed for the meal even in a single vessel.[56]]

Saving for household members:[57] All household members must save for themselves and may not have others save for them. One may however save for the sick, weak and old.

How much food may one save per meal:[58] Through using Harama[59] one may save as many types of dishes and foods as he desires. For example, if one took enough meat for the remaining meals, he may now return and take fish for the remaining meals, saying that he currently enjoys fish more. The same applies with regards to different types of breads. It is however forbidden for one to save more than one dish per meal without using this method of Harama.[60]

May one save vessels needed for the meal?[61] One may save all the utensils that will be needed for the remaining meals. [However, one may not save many vessels within one vessel, or do Harama, as is permitted by food.[62]]

May other people save items from one's fire?[63] It is forbidden for neighbors and friends to save any item from another person's fire, on behalf of that person.[64] However the neighbors and friends may save for themselves enough food for their own remaining meals, if the owner asked them to do so. If they were not asked to do so, then they may not save anything from the fire. In all cases it is forbidden for others to save items not needed for their remaining meals.

May one carry the saved items outside if there is no Eiruv?[65] It is forbidden for one to carry the items into an area that does not have an Eiruv. This prohibition includes even saving them to another courtyard that is lacking Eiruv Chatzeiros.

Saving a box which contains food:[66] If food (or a ring) is inside of a vessel which contains valuables, it is forbidden to save the entire vessel together with the food (or ring).[67] Nevertheless in a case of great loss it is permitted to place any item which may be saved on top of any other item, and then save them to another courtyard which has an Eiruv even if they contain Muktzah items. Thus, in a case of great loss one may place bread on top of his wallet and then carry out the wallet together with the bread on top of it.

Q&A

May one save Lechem Mishneh for each meal?[68]
Yes.

May one save foods for dessert?[69]
Yes. One may take out one dish for desert unless he uses Harama in which cases he may take out as many dishes as he wishes for that meal, using this method.

---

[56] Ketzos Hashulchan 141 footnote 5
[57] So is implied from 334:4-5
[58] Admur 334:3
[59] Trickery as will be explained next
[60] So is implied from Admur ibid and so rules Ketzos Hashulchan 141 footnote 2, nevertheless he concludes that the reason behind this matter requires further analysis, as in truth one should be able to save as many dishes as he feels he will eat during the meal.
[61] Admur 334:8
[62] Ketzos Hashulchan 141 footnote 7
[63] Admur 334:7
[64] As although they are not in a state of panic and hence there is no worry that they will come to extinguish the fire, nevertheless it is forbidden as the Sages did not differentiate in their decree. [ibid]
Other Opinions: The Chayeh Adam, brought in M"B rules they may save for the owner any item in the house, including money. Clearly this is not the opinion of Admur as is evident from 334:7. According to all it is forbidden for others to save items for themselves that are not needed for their remaining meals. [Ketzos Hashulchan 141 footnote 8]
[65] Admur 334:9
[66] Admur 334:18
[67] As the food or ring are nullified to the valuables.
[68] Ketzos Hashulchan 141 footnote 2 in name of Biur Halacha
[69] Ketzos Hashulchan 141 footnote 2

How much liquid may one save?[70]
One may save as much liquid as one will need throughout the remainder of Shabbos.

C. Saving clothing:[71]
One may save as many pairs of clothing as he wishes by wearing them. One may make many trips back and forth and even ask others to do the same. One may wear various clothing on top of each other even into an area without an Eiruv. [Those clothing which one needs to wear that day one may save in hands, without wearing them.[72]]

D. Saving Sefarim:[73]
Today all Torah Sefarim may be saved from a fire, irrelevant of what language they are written in.[74] It is even permitted to ask a gentile to extinguish a fire in order to save Sefarim from being burnt if there is no other way for them to be saved.[75] [Based on this if one's Mezuzas are hammered into the door post one may always ask a gentile to extinguish a fire in order to save the Mezuzos from getting burned.[76]]

Saving a Pasul Sefer Torah:[77] One may save a Pasul Sefer Torah so long as it has intact enough complete words which in total account to 85 letters, or contains Hashem's name. The same law applies to single pages of a Sefer Torah that they may only be saved if they contain the above-mentioned amount of words or G-d's name.[78]

Saving above items to area without an Eiruv:[79] It is forbidden to save Sefarim, or even a Sefer Torah to an area without an Eiruv. If, however, it has an Eiruv and is merely lacking Eiruv Chatzeiros or Muvaos then it is allowed. Some opinions allow asking a gentile to save Sefarim even to a Reshus Harabim.[80]

Saving a box which contains books:[81] If Sefarim, Tefillin, Mezuzas are inside of a vessel, it is permitted to save the entire vessel together with them, even they contain Muktzah items. Nevertheless, it is forbidden on Shabbos to initially place those items in the vessel in order to be allowed to do so in case of a fire.

Summary list of items that may be saved:
- One may save <u>all</u> items [including expensive Muktzah] from one room to another, or even from inside to his back or front yard.
- Foods, liquid and vessels for the remaining meals may be saved. Unlimited amount of foods may be saved in a single vessel.
- Valuables: All valuables that have great loss, even if Muktzah, may be saved by placing needed meal foods on them
- Clothing: All clothing needed for that day may be taken in hand and all other clothing may be worn, even in many trips.

---

[70] Ketzos Hashulchan 141 footnote 2 in name of Biur Halacha
[71] Admur 334:9
[72] Ketzos Hashulchan 141 footnote 9
[73] Admur 334:12-13
[74] The concept of a Sefer written in a language that one's country does not understand no longer applies today as with mail or countries can receive the products of other countries and if it can't be read in this country it can be read in the next country. Thus, all books written in languages spoken today have holiness and may be saved irrelevant of where they are written [Ketzos Hashulchan 141 footnote 18]
[75] Admur 334:25
[76] Misgeres Hashulchan 85:2
[77] Admur 334:15
[78] Admur 334:20
[79] Admur 334:17
[80] Admur 334:19
[81] Admur 334:18

- Sefarim: All Sefarim may be saved.

Q&A

May one remove a Mezuzah from a door to save it from a fire?[82]

No.[83] One may however ask a gentile to extinguish the fire to prevent them from getting burned. Based on this if one's Mezuzas are hammered into the door post one may always ask a gentile to extinguish a fire in order to save the Mezuzos from getting burned.[84]

8. May one save his items from an approaching fire that is in his neighbor's home?[85]

If the fire is in a neighbor's home [that is not within the same building or courtyard[86]], there is no limit given in terms of items that one may save from the potential fire that may spread into his home.[87]

May one save Muktzah objects? It is permitted for one to save from a neighbor's oncoming fire[88] valuable Muktzah items[89]. [Nevertheless, it is best to place on the Muktzah items a non-Muktzah object and then carry them together.[90]] It is forbidden according to all to move Muktzah items which are not of much value.[91]

May one carry the items outside if there is no Eiruv? It is forbidden for one to carry the items into a Karmalis.[92] Hence one may only save the items into an area that has an Eiruv.

9. Saving items from robbers: [93]

If robbers are coming to search and rob from one's home, it is permitted for one to move valuable Muktzah items[94], in order to save them from the robbers. It is forbidden according to all to move Muktzah items which are not of much value.[95]

May one carry the items outside if there is no Eiruv? It is forbidden for one to carry the items into a Karmalis.[96] Hence one may only save the items into an area that has an Eiruv.

---

[82] Misgeres Hashulchan 85:2

[83] This is forbidden to be done due to the destroying prohibition.

[84] Misgeres Hashulchan 85:2

[85] Admur 334:2; 301:40

[86] Aruch Hashulchan 334:17; Kaf Hachayim 334:6

[87] As so long as the fire has not yet reached one's home one is not in a state of panic to the point that he will forget it is Shabbos. [ibid]

[88] However, if the fire is in one's own home, it is forbidden for him to even food more than 3 meals worth, let alone Muktzah items. [ibid] Hence even according o the opinion that moving Muktzah was allowed in a case of great loss or in a case of fire, certainly they agree that when the fire is within one's own home it is forbidden.

[89] As there are opinions which rule one may move Muktzah in a case of great loss. Furthermore, even according to those which rule Muktzah is forbidden to be moved even in a case of great loss, there are opinions which say in such a case moving Muktzah is allowed, as if it were to be forbidden, out of panic, one may come to transgress an even more severe sin, such as extinguishing the fire. Practically with the joint of these two opinions one may be lenient to move out his Muktzah items from the fire. [ibid]

[90] As in such a case there are those which allow doing so even in one's own home fire. [Ketzos Hashulchan 141 footnote 15]

[91] As in such a case there is no great loss, and one is not panicky about it.

[92] There are opinions which rule that it is even permitted to carry into a Karmalis the items which one desires to save, as if we were to forbid this, they may come, due to panic, to transgress a more sever sin such as extinguishing the fire. Nevertheless, many Poskim argue on this opinion and practically one may not be lenient, and it is only by Muktzah that some Poskim also rule that Muktzah is permitted to be moved in a case of great loss, that we combine the opinions and allow one to be lenient. [ibid]

[93] Admur 334:2; 301:40

[94] As there are opinions which rule one may move Muktzah in a case of great loss. Furthermore, even according to those which rule Muktzah is forbidden to be moved even in a case of great loss, there are opinions which say in such a case moving Muktzah is allowed, as if it were to be forbidden, out of panic, one may come to transgress an even more severe sin, such as extinguishing the fire. Practically with the joint of these two opinions one may be lenient to move out his Muktzah items from the fire. [ibid]

[95] As in such a case there is no great loss, and one is not panicky about it.

[96] There are opinions which rule that it is even permitted to carry into a Karmalis the items which one desires to save, as if we were to forbid this, they may come, due to panic, to transgress a more sever sin such as burying the money. Nevertheless, many Poskim argue on this opinion and practically one may not be lenient, and it is only by Muktzah that some Poskim also rule that Muktzah is permitted to be moved in a case of great loss, that we combine the opinions and allow one to be lenient. [ibid]

10. Atonement for desecrating Shabbos for sake of saving belongings:[97]

If one transgressed and extinguished a fire in a case that doing so posed no safety hazard, then he is in need of atonement. This is accomplished through fasting a certain set of fasts and donating a certain amount of money to charity.

General summary

1. <u>One may extinguish a fire in any of the following cases:</u>
   - It poses danger to anyone's life, or can potentially pose danger if not extinguished. Practically today that we live in populated areas with houses very close to each other, it is almost always allowed to extinguish a fire in such cases. In such a case one may extinguish the fire and do any Melacha necessary to have the fire put out.
   - The fire does not pose any danger of life but can cause injury. In such a case one may extinguish a fire but <u>may not do any other Biblical Melacha</u>.

2. <u>One may ask a gentile to extinguish a fire in any of the following cases:</u>
   - Poses bodily danger or injury.
   - The fire is in someone else's home [although not within one's building].
   - There are Sefarim that need to be saved and cannot be saved in another way.
   - There are Mezuzas attached to the doors and cannot be taken down without transgressing the destroying prohibition.

---

[97] Admur 334:28

TRANSLATION OF CHAPTER 340

A detailed compilation on this chapter complete with Summaries and Q&A is provided in the sections that follow the translation.

Chapter 340
Miscellaneous Shabbos Prohibitions
18 Halachos

Gozez/Shearing:

Halacha 1:

The Av Melacha-Shearing wool from skin: One who shears [hair/wool] whether from alive or dead animal, whether from a domestic and wild animal, even from skin that has been removed, is liable [for a sin offering]. Doing so is amongst the principle Shabbos Melachas as in the Tabernacle they would shear the skin of the Techashim and rams.

Using one's hands to remove the wool: However, one who removes wool with his <u>hand</u> from an animal or from its skin is exempt [from a sin offering] as this is not the common form of shearing. [However, it is Rabbinically forbidden as will be explained next]

Removing one's hair/nails with fingers/teeth: Similarly, one who removes his hair and nails with his hands or teeth is exempt [from liability]. However, it is Rabbinically forbidden to remove [hair or nails] with ones hand even from another person, despite the fact that one is unable to train his hands to skillfully remove [the hair/nail] with his hands, without use of a vessel, when removing them from another person.

Cutting one's hair with a vessel: However, if one cut them with a vessel, he is liable even on only two hairs. On one [hair] he is exempt [from a Sin offering] although doing so is Biblically forbidden as [is the law by all] other half measurements [that they are Biblically forbidden].

One who removes a white hair from amongst black hairs: One who gathers white [hairs] from amongst black hairs so he does not appear old, even for [removing] one [hair] he is liable [for a sin offering]. Doing so is even forbidden during the week due to the prohibition against "a man wearing the garment of a woman" which is defined as a man may not adorn himself like the adornments of women.

Halacha 2:

One who cuts not for the need of the cut item: One who shears and cuts nails with a vessel is liable [for a sin offering] unless he needs the wool or the hair or the nails which he cut. However, if he does not need them then this is a Melacha which is not needed for its own sake [which is only Rabbinically prohibited according to some opinions].

Asking a gentile to cut ones nails for Mikveh

First opinion-Gentile may cut with vessel: [Based on the above] therefore a woman which forgot from before Shabbos to remove her nails and on Shabbos is her night of immersion there is an opinion which permits her to tell a gentile woman to cut it for her, as all matters which are only Rabbinically forbidden are permitted to be done through a gentile for the need of a Mitzvah as is written in chapter 307 [Halacha 12] and 325 [Halacha 5].

Second Opinion-Gentile may not cut with vessel: However, there are opinions which say that even if one does not need the wool, hair and nails he is liable [for a sin offering]

The reason for this is: (as the principal Melacha [of shearing] is removing the hair and wool from the skin and the nails from the fingers, and he does need this removal in it of itself, and furthermore) also in the Tabernacle they would shear the skins of the Techashim even though they did not need their hair.

Therefore, one may not allow to ask a gentile woman to cut the nails being that this is a complete Rabbinical prohibition which was not permitted [even] for the need of a Mitzvah as was explained in chapter 276 [Halacha 8]. Rather one may tell her to remove them with her hands or with her teeth which is a Rabbinical prohibition upon a Rabbinical prohibition.

The reason that assisting is permitted: Now, although she tilts her fingers towards the gentile and [thus] slightly assists her, this is [Halachicly] meaningless as one who assists does not carry [Halachic] weight (and is completely permitted Biblically, and even Rabbinically there is no prohibition against assisting with exception to one who is doing a complete Melacha or a matter which is forbidden due to a Rabbinical prohibition not in the place of a Mitzvah. However, in the case of a Mitzvah there was no decree made on the assisting just like they did not decree against telling the gentile [to do the Rabbinical prohibition] as he [the Jew] is not doing anything, and as well by assisting he is not doing anything as assistance truly carries no [Halachic] weight and it is just that the Sages decreed a decree upon doing so due to that one may come to do so himself. However, one who does an [actual] action is forbidden even if it is a Rabbinical prohibition upon a Rabbinical prohibition in a Mitzvah scenario, as was explained in chapter 331 [Halacha 8].)

Halacha 3:
Cutting off a blister
It is forbidden to cut a blister from one's body whether with ones hand whether with a vessel, whether for himself whether for others, whether it is [filled with] puss [blister] whether it is dry. And if one cut a puss [filled] blister with a vessel he is liable for shearing according to those which hold one liable for shearing even if he does not require that which is being sheared.

The laws of writing and erasing:

Halacha 4:
The Av Melacha-To write, or erase with intent to write: One who writes, and erases in order to write in the erased area, is one of the primary Melachas. [This is derived from the work done in the Mishkan] as [in the Mishkan] they would write on the beams of the Tabernacle as signs to know which beam corresponds to it, and at times they would make a mistake and erase what they wrote and then return and write in that place [the correct signs].

To erase without intent to write: However, to erase not in order to write within that space was not done in the Tabernacle, and is not similar to a Melacha at all.

Liability for erasing ink splotches and removing wax in order to write: Since the liability for erasing is due to him doing so on behalf of writing, which means that he is fixing the area to write on, therefore even if he did not erase letters but rather erased mere splotches of ink, or wax which fell on the tablet [he is liable]. [This tablet] refers to a wooden writing board which is smeared with wax and inscribed onto using a metal pen. [Thus, if it were to happen that] external[1] wax fell on this board and one erased this wax and removed it from there in order to engrave in its place on the wax that is under it which was smeared on the board [to begin with], then he is liable.

Liability is only on two letters: [However the above liability] is when there is enough space [in the erased area] to write or inscribe two letters, and similarly one who writes or erases letters is only liable on two letters, however on one letter he is exempt, although this is [still] Biblically forbidden as are other half measurements.

Removing wax from parchment in order to write: This law similarly applies to one who erases and removes wax from the parchment in order to write in its space.

Removing wax from letters to see better the letters: As well this is the law for one who removes wax which dripped on the letters, as what is the difference if one fixes a place for writing or if one fixes already written letters, and on the contrary this [latter erasing of wax to see the current letters] is more of a fixing [than the erasing of wax merely to write on it in the future]. [However] there are those[2] which are lenient in this.

Rabbinically forbidden to erase even without intent to write: Rabbinically it is forbidden to even erase not for the sake of writing [in its space].

---

[1] Meaning that wax from the outside fell onto the original wax layer, thus making a further wax layer on that part of the board and making it uneven.
[2] Shvus Yaakov 2:4

Forbidden to eat cake with letterings: It is therefore forbidden to break a cake which has on it forms of letters, even though ones intent is simply to eat [the cake] as he is [nevertheless] erasing [these letters].

Permitted to give a child the cake to eat: However, it is permitted to give the cake to a young child, as a child which does [transgressions] for his own benefit does not need to be separated [from the act] as is will be explained in chapter 343[Halacha 1 and 10]

Closing and opening books with writing on their side pages:

First Opinion-Is forbidden: [Regarding] those books which have letters written on the top edges of the pages there are those[3] which prohibit opening them on Shabbos due to the erasing prohibition. As well as [they forbid] to close them due to the writing prohibition.

The reason for this prohibition: Now, although they have no intent to do this [writing or erasing, nevertheless it is forbidden as] it is an inevitable occurrence.

Other Opinions-Is permitted: [However] there are those opinions[4] which permit to close [the books] as since the letters are already written and it is just that they are lacking proximity, this does not contain a writing prohibition, as since it is possible to bring them close together easily without doing any new action, they are considered like they are close and standing and one is doing nothing with this proximity. Similarly, it is permitted to open them for this reason and one is not considered like he is erasing them as their writing [remains] intact and it is possible to near them to each other easily and they are [thus] considered already now to be] as if [they are] close.

The final ruling: And so is the custom [like the latter opinion].

Halacha 5:
One who edits letters:

One who edits one letter such as he removed the roof of the "Ches" and turned it to two "Zayins" is liable. (And one who edits another single letter such as he removed the roof of the "Daled" and turned it into a "Reish" is exempt [from liability of a bringing a sin offering] although doing so is Biblically forbidden).

Halacha 6:

One is only liable for a permanent writing: One is only liable [for a sin offering] when he writes with an item [whose mark is] permanent on top of a material [which the writing on it will remain] permanent.

Rabbinically even a temporary writing is forbidden: However it is Rabbinically forbidden [to write] even with an item [whose mark is] not permanent on top of a material [which the writing on it will] not [remain] permanent, such as to write with liquids and fruits juices on top of vegetable leaves and the like, and therefore one must beware not to write with his fingers on the liquid that is on the table or to engrave in ash or congealed fat or honey.

Writing in the air or on a clear table: It is permitted to write in the air forms of letters being that their mark is not at all recognizable. The same law as well applies to [that one may write figuratively] on a table that does not have liquid [in that area], as well in this case the mark is not at all recognizable.

Now although through doing so one trains and builds his hands for writing, this is [Halachically] meaningless.

It is as well permitted to view a craftsmanship on Shabbos even though he is learning it in the process.

Halacha 7:

Tearing letters into leather: One who <u>tears</u> onto leather [letters which shape] the form of writing is liable, as engraving is a form of writing.

Marking letters on leather: However, one who <u>marks</u> [with his finger] on the leather the form of writing is exempt [from liability to bring a sin offering] as this is not something which will last. Nevertheless, this is Rabbinically forbidden due to a decree against [writing in a] permanent [method].

---

[3] Levush
[4] Shut Rama:Taz

Making a mark on leather as a reminder: However, if [the writing] does not have the form of writing and he is making a mark as a mere symbol, and it does not have the form of letters [or recognized symbols[5], such as a mere indentation], it is allowed even initially.

Making a mark in a book as a symbol for editing It is therefore permitted to mark with one's nail on [the page of] a book [made of parchment], like those which make a mark as a sign in a place where there is a mistake.

Making a mark on paper: However, this only applies by parchment which is hard, and its mark thus does not last, however on paper it is forbidden to mark being that its mark lasts for a long time.

Now although [the mark] is not a form of writing it is [nevertheless] Rabbinically forbidden due to a decree against [coming to mark] a form of writing on which one is liable on when it lasts.

Other Opinions by making marks on parchment: There are those which prohibit [making marks] even on parchment. *Their Reasoning*: as they hold that even one who makes a mark for a mere symbol and not like a form of writing is liable [to bring a sin offering] if it is a permanent mark, as they too [in the times of the building of the Tabernacle] would make marks on the boards of the Tabernacle to know which [board] corresponds to it. Therefore, if one marked one marking on top of two boards, or two lines on one board, as a symbol as was done with the beams of the Tabernacle, is liable [to bring a sin offering]. [However] one marking on one board is exempt [from liability to bring a sin offering] although is [nevertheless] Biblically forbidden, being that it is a permanent matter [mark]. [Therefore] one who makes a mark on parchment in which [the mark] will not last is Rabbinically forbidden due to a decree against [coming to make a mark which] permanent.

The final ruling: A G-d fearing [person] is to be stringent upon himself like their words [to avoid making marks on even parchment].

Halacha 8:

Writing symbols: All the above is when [the mark] is not at all in the form of writing, however so long as [the mark] is in the form of any writing, even if it is not the Ashury writing, even if they are unknown letters which are only used for symbols, such as the symbols which are commonly used to refer to the numbers, then it is considered the form of writing and one is liable [to bring a sin offering] on doing so if it was done on a item [in which the writing will be] permanent. If it was done on an item which [its writing will] not [remain] permanent] it is Rabbinically forbidden according to all.

Writing שעטנז גץ without the Zayins: One who writes in Ashuris and omitted the זיונין[6] from the letters of שעטנז גץ is exempt on [liability to bring a sin offering] over them being that their work is incomplete.[7]

Writing an incomplete letter: Similarly, all writings from any language which its letters were not completely written one is exempt [from liability to bring a sin offering in having written them]. However, it is Rabbinically forbidden [to do so].

Writing in Rashi Script: Therefore, one who writes a fine print called "Meshita" [i.e. Rashi script] there are those which say that he is exempt from [liability of bringing a sin offering] over it, due to that this script was taken from the Ashuri script, and it is thus similar to an incomplete Ashuri script [of which one is not liable on] as will be explained in chapter 545.

Halacha 9:

Making letter necklaces: If one inserts silver letters into a clothing, it is considered writing and is forbidden to be done on Shabbos.

Halacha 10:

Drawings and designs: One who makes marks and designs on a document and the like, in the way that the artists design, is liable to an offshoot of the writing prohibition. The same applies for one who erases it.

---

[5] See Halacha 8
[6] This refers to the small Zayin letters which protrude on the very top of each of the letters in the grouping of Shatnez Gatz.
[7] Other Opinions: The M"B 340:22 rules that one is liable even in such a case being that Halachically the Zayins do not invalidate the letters.

Halacha 11:
Making lines on skin and paper:
The Av Melacha-On skins: It is common for the leather makers that when they come to cut the leather they first scratch a line into it in accordance to how he wants to lengthen, widen and shorten the cut, and afterwards he passes the knife over the marked line. This was also done by the skins of the Tabernacle when they were cut, and therefore this line marking is one of the Principal Melachas.

Making lines on paper and parchment: Similarly, one who imprints a line into even parchment or paper in order to write straight is liable [for a sin offering].

The Laws of Sewing and Tearing
Halacha 12:
The Biblical prohibition: One who sews two stitches and [makes] a knot [at its end], or three stitches even if he does not make a knot [at its end] is liable [to bring a sin offering].

However [one who sews] two stitches and does not make a knot is exempt [from Biblical liability].

The reason for this is: because [in such a case the sewing] does not last.

Rabbinically forbidden to make two stitches without a knot: However it is [nevertheless] Rabbinically forbidden.

Tying prohibition: One who makes a knot [in any of the above cases] is also liable for the tying prohibition.

Halacha 13:
Pulling a thread to tighten the connection between the parts of a clothing:
A clothing which was sturdily sewed and its thread was left sticking out[8], and two parts of the clothing slightly split apart from each other, and the threads of the sewing are sticking out, then if one pulls the head of the threads in order to tighten and connect the two sides, this is considered sewing and one is liable [to bring a sin offering]. [This applies] even if one has not made a knot [at its end] if [the amount that the clothing have reconnected] is like the amount of three stitches.

Pulling the thread that tightens the sleeves of shirts: Those [people] who tighten their clothing around their arms through [pulling] a thread which pulls and tightens it, [are forbidden to do so as it] is forbidden to pull [such a thread] on Shabbos due to the sewing prohibition.

The reason it is forbidden: (Now, although the sewing is not one that will last being that one only tightens it at the time that he wears it while at the time that he removes it he loosens it, nevertheless it is Rabbinically forbidden being that it is similar to sewing.)

If the holes are wide, round, and sewed: It is only allowed if [the shirt] has slightly wide holes which are fixed in with sewing and [the hole is] round in circumference, in which case it is no longer similar to sewing[9].

Walking into a public domain with a needle attached to this thread: [In the above circumstance that the holes are wide, round and fixed with sewing] then even if the thread is inserted into a sewing needle [a needle with a hole] it is permitted to go out with it [into a public domain] since it is always connected to the thread, and the thread [is always connected] to the clothing, and it is thus an accessory to the clothing.

If one is able to remove the clothing without loosening the tightened thread: If the clothing is not very much tightened by this thread to the point that one must loosen it when he removes [the clothing in order so it come off], but rather at times he changes his mind and decides to leave it this way eternally being that he is [anyways] able to remove it this way with it remaining slightly tightened, then it is forbidden to tighten it on Shabbos in all cases [even if the holes are wide and round and are fixed with sewing, and even if he does plan to loosen it].

The reason for this is: because perhaps one will change his mind and decide to leave it this way forever,

---

[8] Lit. Long

[9] As this is like placing hooks into loops which has no resemblance of a Melacha. [M"B 29]

and it is thus found that he made a sewing which will last, and by a permanent sewing it does not help the fact that the holes are wide and are fixed with sewing and are round.

Tikkun Keli

Halacha 14:
Placing stuffing into a pillow:
Mochin [which is a general term for any soft material such as cotton and strings [made] of soft wool of an animal, and the scrapes of worn-out clothing[10]] which fell out from a pillow are permitted to be returned. However, they are forbidden to be initially placed there on Shabbos due to that by doing so he is now turning it into a vessel. See chapter 317 [Halacha 5][11]

Meameir-Gathering produce

Halacha 15:
The Av Melacha: The action of Meameir [gathering stalks] is one of the principal Shabbos prohibitions which occurred in the Tabernacle with the planted herbs.
Gathering in area of growth-First Opinion: It is only considered [the Melacha of] Meameir when one gathers [the produce] in the area of its growth, similar to a harvested stalk of which the ears of grain are gathered in their area of growth.
Gathering fruits: Similarly one who gathers fruits and joins them together in the area where they fell off the tree [has transgressed the Meameir prohibition].
Gathering from area not of growth-Permitted: However, if the [fruits] have dispersed into another area [out from its original place of growth] then it is permitted to gather them as written in chapter 335 [Halacha 5].
Items that grow from the ground: The [Biblical] Meameir prohibition only applies with [the gathering of] items which grow from the ground.
The Rabbinical prohibition-Items that do not grow from ground: However Rabbinically it is forbidden to be done even with items that do not grow from the ground to gather them in their area of growth, such as to gather salt from the evaporated deposits of water, which evaporates the water and creates the salt and so too with all cases of the like.
Second Opinion-Making items into one mass out from their area of growth: ([However] there are opinions which say that one who presses fruits [together] until they form one mass is liable for Meameir even when he does so not in the place of its growth such as) one who gathers figs and makes from it a round cake [of pressed figs] or punctures the figs and enters a rope through them until they gather and form one mass, then this is an offshoot of the Meameir prohibition and one is liable, and so too any cases of the like.
The Final Ruling: (One must be stringent like their words [of the latter opinion])

Lisha-Kneading

Halacha 16:
Placing sesame seeds into liquids on Shabbos:
One who places flax or sesame seeds into water and the like is liable for kneading [**according to all opinions[12]**] being that they [the water and the seed] mix and stick to each other.

---

[10] 257:5
[11] There it is explained that it is forbidden to place a lace permanently through a hole [even if wide] when being done for its first time due to that doing so is considered fixing a vessel.

[12] Meaning even according to the first opinion mentioned in 321:16, as stated explicitly in Rambam that one is liable for kneading in such a case despite that he himself rules like the first opinion.

Tikkun Keli in cutting an item:

Halacha 17:

Cutting an item with a knife to make a use with it: Although cutting items detached [from the ground] is initially permitted when one is not particular to cut it in a specific measurement, as explained in chapter 314 [Halacha 16[13]] nevertheless if through doing so one fixes the item to be used for a certain use, then he is liable for [the] "fixing a vessel" [prohibition] if he cut it using a knife as was explained in chapter 322 [Michaber Halacha 4] regarding the cutting of a twig[14].

Tearing it with ones hands to make a use of it: If it was done without a knife then one is exempt [from Biblical liability], although it is [Rabbinically] forbidden.

Breaking earthenware and tearing paper for a use: Therefore, one may not break earthenware and may not tear [a kind of] paper which is permitted to move [i.e. is not Muktzah] in order to use the [torn or broken piece] for a use due to that doing so is similar to him fixing a vessel. See Chapter 508 [Halacha 2[15]]

The tearing prohibition:

Only applies by tearing apart many entities: (However regarding [the] tearing [prohibition] there is only a prohibition [involved] when one tears and separates many entities which have [become] attached, such as one who tears a garment woven from many threads; however, paper which is a single entity does not contain within tearing it or cutting it the tearing prohibition. [**For other opinions see footnote[16]**]

Tearing leather: It is for this reason that it is permitted to tear leather that covers the mouth of a barrel of wine as explained in chapter 314 [Halacha 12] being that the leather is a single entity and [thus] the tearing prohibition is not applicable to it, but rather only the prohibition to cut it, if he is particular to cut it to a specific measurement as explained there [in chapter 314/16].)

Separates papers that are attached: However, one who separates papers that are attached is [liable for doing] an offshoot of [the] tearing [prohibition].

Gluing things together: One who attaches papers or skins with glue of the scribes and the like is [doing] an offshoot of the sewing [prohibition] and is liable.

Separating items which were accidently attached: However, this only applies when the attachment was done for it to last, however pages of books which have attached to each other through wax [which fell on them] or at the time of their binding, are permitted to be opened on Shabbos.

The reason for this is: as since [this attachment] was not made to last and furthermore it was done on its own without intent, therefore it is not at all similar to sewing, and it does not contain [the] tearing [prohibition].

Halacha 18:

Fixing a needle: A needle which has become bent, even slightly, is forbidden to be straightened.

The reason for this is: (due to [the prohibition of] fixing a vessel.)

---

[13] There it is explained that cutting wood to a desired measurement is Biblically forbidden.

[14] Evidently this refers to the law that if one were to cut a twig with a knife for a use then he is Biblically liable.

[15] There Admur brings different cases that tearing or breaking an item is forbidden due to one making it now fit for a use.

[16] The Mishneh Berurah in Biur Halacha "Eiyn Shovrin" says that the prohibition applies even when tearing a single entity.

CHAPTER 1: THE LAWS OF GOZEIZ-SHEARING
Removing hair, skin, and nails

1. The Av Melacha-Shearing wool from skin:[1]
One who shears hair or wool from a living or dead animal, whether the animal is domestic or wild, or even [if he shears wool/hair] from removed skin, he is liable [for a sin offering]. Doing so is amongst the principle Shabbos Melachas as in the Tabernacle they would shear the skin of the Techashim and rams.

2. Using one's hands to remove the wool:[2]
One who removes wool with his hand from an animal or from its skin is exempt [from a sin offering] as this is not the common form of shearing. [However, it is Rabbinically forbidden as will be explained next]

Summary- Shearing hair/wool:

Using a Vessel: It is a Biblical prohibition to shear hair/wool **using a vessel**, whether from alive or dead animal, whether from a domestic and wild animal, even from removed skin. Doing so is amongst the principle Shabbos Melachas as in the Tabernacle they would shear the skin of the Techashim and rams.

Using one's hands: It is Rabbinically forbidden to remove wool with one's hand.

Q&A
May one pluck a feather from his piece of chicken?[3]
This matter is disputed amongst Poskim.[4] The dispute applies even if one intends to eat the chicken right away after removing the feathers, due to a question of whether this involves the "Shearing" prohibition. Practically one should initially avoid removing feathers from chicken[5], [although those that do so have upon whom to rely on if they eat the chicken right away[6]]. This prohibition certainly applies if one desires to remove the feathers in order to make the chicken more presentable to the guests in which case one must take great care not to remove those feathers.
For later use: According to all it is forbidden to remove the feathers for later use due to the Borer restrictions.[7]

---

3. Removing one's hair and nails:[8]
A. The general rules:
Cutting one's hair or nails with a vessel: If one cuts his hair or nails with a vessel, he is liable. By hair he is liable even if he only cuts two hairs. If he cut only one hair, he is exempt [from a Sin offering] although doing so is Biblically forbidden as is the law regarding all half measurements [i.e. that if one transgresses less than the measurement of liability he has nevertheless transgressed a Biblical command].
One who does not need to use the hair or nails:[9] One who shears [hair] and cuts nails with a vessel is only liable [for a sin offering] if he needs the wool or the hair or the nails which he cut. However if he does not

---

[1] Admur 340:1
[2] Admur 340:1
[3] Shabbos Kihalacha Vol. 2 p. 229
[4] The stringent opinion: Is brought in Ketzos Hashulchan 143 footnote 1 in name of the Yeshuos Chachma, and so plainly rules SSH"K 3:30.
The lenient opinions: The Ketzos Hashulchan [ibid] himself says that the world is not accustomed to be stringent in this and he goes on to be Melamed Zechus through four different reasons for why removing feathers of cooked chicken does not contain a prohibition of "Shearing", and he thus concludes that one should "leave the Jews to do so". So rules also that it is allowed: Shut Har Tzevi, Yalkut Yosef, Igros Moshe.
[5] So rules Rav Farkash ibid, however the Ketzos Hashulchan rules that the world is lenient in this, and so rules Piskeiy Teshuvos [340:2].
[6] Ketzos Hashulchan 143 footnote 1
[7] As this is similar to the removing of the skin or peal of a fruit which is only allowed to be done prior to the meal. [Piskeiy Teshuvos 340:2]
[8] Admur 340:1
[9] Admur 340:2
This concept is called a "Melacha Sheiyno Tzarich Legufa"

need them then this is a Melacha which is not needed for its own use ["Eino Tzarich Legufa", which is only Rabbinically prohibited according to some opinions].

However there are opinions which say that even if one does not need the wool, hair and nails he is liable [for a sin offering] (as the principal Melacha [of shearing] is removing the hair and wool from the skin and the nails from the fingers, and he does need this removal in it of itself, and furthermore) also in the Tabernacle they would shear the skins of the Techashim even though they did not need their hair.

Removing ones hair/nails with fingers/teeth: One who removes his hair and nails with his hands or teeth is exempt [from liability]. However, it is Rabbinically forbidden to remove [hair or nails] with one's hand even from another person, despite the fact that one is unable to train his hands to skillfully remove [the hair/nail] with his hands from another person, without use of a vessel.

One who removes a white hair from amongst black: One who gathers white [hairs] from amongst black hairs so he does not appear old, even if he removes one hair, is liable [for a sin offering]. Doing so is even forbidden during the week due to the prohibition against "a man wearing the garment of a woman" which is defined as a man may not adorn himself with the adornments of women.

[See Q&A regarding cleaning out dirt from under ones nails]

Summary-cutting hair and nails on Shabbos:

Cutting one's hair or nail with a vessel: It is Biblically forbidden to cut with a vessel even one hair [from anywhere on one's body[10]] or nail. However, if one is cutting not in order to use the cut item, then there is a dispute as to whether this is Biblically or Rabbinically forbidden.

Removing one's hair/nails with fingers/teeth: It is Rabbinically forbidden to remove with one's finger or teeth even one hair [from anywhere on one's body[11]]. It is Rabbinically forbidden to peel or bite off a nail.

One who removes a white hair from amongst black: Is liable for a sin offering and doing so is forbidden even during the week due to the prohibition of "Beged Isha".

Q&A
May one scrape dirt from under his nail on Shabbos?[12]
Yes, although when doing so one must beware to press down the flesh under the nail in order to avoid scraping the nail in the process of removing the dirt.[13]

May one scrape off the inside of his nail?
No, as explained above.

May one brush their hair on Shabbos?
See below!

May one pluck hairs out from a garment made of animal skin?[14]
No. Doing so involves the Shearing prohibition.

---

[10] Ketzos Hashulchan 143:1
[11] Ketzos Hashulchan 143:1
[12] Admur 161:3, so rules also Biur Halacha there
[13] As scraping the nail is problematic due to the shearing prohibition.
[14] Ketzos Hashulchan 143:4 in name of Taz in end of 337

B. May one ask a gentile to cut ones nails for Mikveh if they forgot to do so before Shabbos?[15]

First opinion[16]-Gentile may cut even with vessel: One who shears [hair] and cuts nails with a vessel is only liable [for a sin offering] if he needs the wool or the hair or the nails which he cut. However, if he does not need them for this purpose then this is a Melacha which is not needed for its own use [which is only Rabbinically prohibited according to some opinions].

Therefore, a woman which forgot to remove her nails before Shabbos and Shabbos is her night of immersion there is an opinion which permits her to tell a gentile woman to cut the nails for her, as all matters which are only Rabbinically forbidden are permitted to be done through a gentile for the need of a Mitzvah as is written in chapter 307 [Halacha 12] and 325 [Halacha 5].

Second Opinion[17]-Gentile may not cut with vessel but may cut with teeth hands: However there are opinions which say that even if one does not need the wool, hair and nails he is liable [for a sin offering] (as the principal Melacha [of shearing] is removing the hair and wool from the skin and the nails from the fingers, and he does need this removal in it of itself, and furthermore) also in the Tabernacle they would shear the skins of the Techashim even though they did not need their hair.

Therefore, one may not allow to ask a gentile woman to cut the nails being that this is a complete Rabbinical prohibition which was not permitted [even] for the need of a Mitzvah as was explained in chapter 276 [Halacha 8]. Rather one may tell the gentile woman to remove the nails with her hands or with her teeth which is a Rabbinical prohibition upon a Rabbinical prohibition. **[See Q&A for the final ruling]**

The reason why the above is not prohibited due to that she is assisting the gentile to cut the nails: Now, although she tilts her fingers towards the gentile and [thus] slightly assists her, this is [Halachically] meaningless as one who assists does not carry [Halachic] weight (and is completely permitted Biblically. Even Rabbinically there is no prohibition against assisting, with exception to one who is doing a complete Melacha or a matter which is forbidden due to a Rabbinical prohibition not in the place of a Mitzvah. However, in the case of a Mitzvah there was no decree made on the assistance just like they did not decree against telling the gentile [to do the Rabbinical prohibition] as he [the Jew] is not doing anything, and as well by assisting he is not doing anything as assistance truly carries no [Halachic] weight and it is just that the Sages decreed a decree against doing so due to that one may come to do so himself. However, one who does an [actual] action is forbidden even if it is a Rabbinical prohibition upon a Rabbinical prohibition in a Mitzvah scenario, as was explained in chapter 331 [Halacha 8].)

---

[15] 340:2
[16] Shach Nekudos Hakesef Yorah Deah 198
[17] Taz Yorah Deah 198:23

Summary- May one ask a gentile to cut her nails for Mikveh if she forgot to do so before Shabbos?

A woman who needs to immerse on Friday night and forgot to cut her nails before Shabbos may ask a Gentile to cut her nails using her teeth or hands. Regarding if the gentile may use a vessel to cut them, this matter is disputed in Admur, see Q&A below regarding the final ruling.

Q&A

Practically may one ask a gentile to cut the nails using a vessel or not? [18]

Rav Farkash rules[19] that although Admur does not explicitly write to be stringent, nevertheless based on the rules of the Poskim, it is implied that he holds of the second, stringent, opinion, and one is to thus be stringent to forbid asking a gentile to cut the nails using a vessel even if she cannot do so otherwise.[20] [**For ruling of Mishneh Berurah and others see footnote[21]**]

What is the woman to do if a gentile is unable to remove the nails with her teeth or hands?[22]

She is to clean out very well all dirt from under her nail and verify that there is no dirt left there.[23] Care must be taken that she does not scrape off part of the nail in the process. Thus, she should press her finger downwards to open more space for the cleaning and thus prevent scraping.[24]

May one ask a gentile to also remove the woman's toe nails?[25]

No.[26] Rather she is to clean out from under her nail very well and verify that there is no dirt left there. Care must be taken that she does not scrape off part of the nail in the process. Thus, she should press her finger downwards to open more space up for the cleaning and thus prevent scraping.[27]

C. Removing a nail or piece of skin which is irritating:[28]

If majority of it has begun peeling off: A nail which is in the process of peeling off and cuticles, which are thin strings [of skin] which have [begun] separating off of the skin of the finger that surrounds the nail, then if majority of it has peeled off, since they are close to becoming [completely] disconnected there is no Biblical shearing prohibition applicable to removing it even if one cuts it off with a vessel. However, it is Rabbinically forbidden [to do so with a vessel].

Removing it with ones hands: However to remove it with one's hand [or teeth[29]], [being that it] is not the common way of shearing, is permitted to be done even initially if they are irritating him, so long as they have peeled off towards the top, meaning that it had begun to peel off on the side of the nail [as opposed to under the nail].

Other Opinions[30]: [However] there are opinions which say that towards the top means towards the body and not towards the nail.

---

[18] Tahara Kehalacha chapter 19:79-3 footnote 202

[19] ibid

[20] Vetzaruch Iyun as to why Admur did not rule this way explicitly as he does by other disputes?

[21] The Magen Avraham 340:1 rules that initially one is to have a gentile do so without using a vessel. However, if this is not possible then the gentile may use a vessel to do so.
The Mishneh Berurah 340:3 rules like the Magen Avraham, although adding that the woman is to not assist at all in the removal of the nails, and the gentile is to be taught to take the woman's hand herself.

[22] Taharah Kehalacha 19:79-3

[23] Taharah Kehalacha ibid in name of many Poskim

[24] Admur 161:3

[25] Taharah Kehalacha ibid in name of Mishneh Berurah in Biur Halacha

[26] As people are less particular regarding the cleanliness of the toenails.

[27] Admur 161:3

[28] Admur 328:37

[29] Taharah Kehalacha 19:79, and so seems Pashut from 340:2

[30] Rabeinu Tam. The former opinion is that of Rashi.

The Final Ruling: One needs to suspect for both explanations [and thus it is never permitted to peel the skin off even when majority of it has begun to peel off.[31] [**Regarding the nail-See Q&A**].

If only minority of the nail or skin has peeled off: If majority of [the skin or nail] did not peel off and one took it off with his hand then he is exempt [from Biblical liability] although he has done a [Rabbinical] prohibition. [However] if one cut it with a vessel then he is liable for shearing. [Furthermore] even according to those opinions that say that an action which is not done for its own use one is not liable on, [nevertheless] there are opinions which say that by shearing one is liable according to everyone for the reason to be explained above.

Summary-Removing a nail or pieces of skin on Shabbos:[32]

If they are not irritating him: Then it is forbidden in all cases to peel off a nail or skin.

If they are irritating him:

1. Pieces of skin: It is forbidden to remove pieces of skin whether with one's hands or with a vessel, even if it is irritating him and majority of it has peeled off. When done with a vessel and majority has not yet peeled off it is Biblically forbidden due to shearing.

2. A Nail: When done with a vessel and majority has not yet peeled off then it is Biblically forbidden due to shearing. If majority has peeled off, then it is Rabbinically forbidden to remove it with a vessel. Regarding removing it by hand-see Q&A.

Q&A

May one remove a nail which has peeled off in its majority?[33]

Some Poskim[34] rule that it is allowed to be removed by hand [or teeth[35]] if they are irritating him, as the dispute with regards to what is considered going upwards and downwards was only with regards to pieces of skin and not with regards to the nail. Whatever the case one must beware that no blood gets extracted in the process.[36]

How is one to wash his hands for bread if he has a nail that has partially peeled off?

See Piskeiy Teshuvos 161; Taharah Kehalacha chapter 20 in laws of tevila.

---

[31] Ketzos Hashulchan 143:1; Mishneh Berurah 99
[32] 328:37
[33] Piskeiy Teshuvos 328:25
[34] Ketzos Hashulchan 143:1 and footnote 3; Piskeiy Teshuvos 161:5; Az Nidbaru
[35] Taharah Kehalacha 19:79, and so seems Pashut from 340:2
[36] So rules Peri Megadim M"Z 328:23, brought in Taharah Kihalacha 19:79-2, Upashut!

4. May one style their hair or undo the style on Shabbos?[37]
A. May one make or undo a hair braid ["Tzama" in Hebrew] on Shabbos?[38]
It is [Rabbinically[39]] forbidden for a woman to braid her hair [or another women's hair or child's hair] on Shabbos.[40] It is likewise forbidden for her to undo a braid on Shabbos [even if it was made before Shabbos].[41] [Some Poskim[42] rule it is even Biblically forbidden to do so.[43] Those women who are lenient to do so are to be protested.[44] This prohibition applies even if one will make a weak braid, and will use a soft brush that does not pull out hair.]

Summary:
It is forbidden to make a braid or undo a braid on Shabbos.

Q&A
May one make or undo a braid on a Sheital on Shabbos?[45]
No.[46] Nevertheless, it is not required to protest those who do so if they in any event will not listen.[47]

May one simply remove the elastic from the braid, without actually undoing it?
Some[48] write it is permitted to do so, even though it will eventually become undone on its own without the elastic.

B. Splitting the hair "down the middle":
However, she may split the hair[49] [through the middle having the hair on the right part of the head brushed to the right and the hair on the left part of the head brushed to the left, thus having an empty path in the middle of the head[50]].

---

[37] 303:26
[38] Michaber 303:26
[39] P"M 303 A"A 20; M"B 303:82; Rambam 20; Chachamim in Mishneh ibid; The following Poskim rule like Chachomim regarding makeup, and the same applies to a braid: Implication of Michaber 303:25 and Admur 320:27; M"A 303:19; Olas Shabbos 303:19; M"B 303:79; See Biur Halacha 303:25 "Mishum Tzoveia"; Kaf Hachaim 303:115-116
[40] Michaber ibid; Mishneh Shabbos 94b "Hagodeles"
The reason: This is forbidden due to the building prohibition, as it is similar to building and hence the Sages prohibited it. [M"A 303:20; M"B ibid; based on Shabbos 95a] This is supported in the Torah, as the verse states "Vayiven Hashem Elokim Es Hatzela" and the Sages teach that Hashem made a braid for Chava and presented her to Adam Harishon, and thus we see that a braid in the Torah is referred to as building. [Shabbos 95a; Machatzis Hashekel 303:20; M"B 303:82] It is not Biblically forbidden due to building, as the building prohibition only applies to structures. It is also not Biblically forbidden due to weaving, as this prohibition only applies a) To matters that are not attached to a person or the ground, and b) To a weaving that lasts and is permanent. [M"A 303:20; M"B 303:82; Tosafus Shabbos 94b] Regarding why it does not transgress the tying prohibition-see Or Sameach on Rambam 10:8 and Shevet Halevi 1:101
[41] Michaber ibid; Tosafus Shabbos 57a "Bema"
The reason: This is forbidden due to the destroying prohibition, as it is similar to destroying and hence the Sages prohibited it. [P"M 303 A"A 20; M"B 303:83; Tosafus ibid]
[42] Rebbe Eliezer in Mishneh ibid, brought in Shaar Hatziyon 303:66; The following Poskim rule like Rebbe Eliezer regarding makeup, and the same applies to a braid: Elya Raba 303:40 in name of Rishonim who rule like Rebbe Eliezer in Mishneh ibid; Yireim, brought in Nishmas Adam; Semag; Ran; Ravan; See Biur Halacha ibid and Kaf Hachaim ibid
Difference between doing it to a friend and to oneself: The Gemara Shabbos 95a differentiates between if a woman makes a braid on her own hair, in which case she is exempt [even according to the approach of Rebbe Eliezer, and only when she makes a braid on her friends' hair is she liable, as only then is the braid nice and beautiful.
[43] The reason: Although it is farfetched to consider a hair braid similar to building a building, nevertheless, the Torah itself testifies that it is considered a category of building, as the verse states "Vayiven Hashem Elokim Es Hatzela" and the Sages teach that Hashem made a braid for Chava and presented her to Adam Harishon, and thus we see that a braid in the Torah is referred to as building. [Shabbos 95a; M"B 303:82]
[44] Darkei Moshe 303:7; Bedek Habayis; See Beis Yosef 303:26; Kol Bo 31
[45] M"B 303:82
[46] The reason: Although doing so does not transgress the building prohibition [as a braid is only considered building when attached to the body, just like Chava], nevertheless, it is forbidden due to the weaving prohibition. Now, although the braid is temporary, it is nevertheless Rabbinically forbidden. [M"B ibid] It is likewise forbidden to undo the braid due to the prohibition of Potzeia, which is undoing the weaving. [Shaar Hatziyon 303:71]
[47] M"B ibid; See Kol Bo 31, brought in Beis Yosef 303:26
[48] Chut Shani 36:15, brought in Piskeiy Teshuvos 303 footnote 87

Other Opinions:[51] However, there are opinions which forbid to split the hair[52] [in the way explained above], which means to make the Sheitel, and so is the custom to forbid doing so using a vessel, however with a mere finger the custom is to be lenient.

Summary:
Braid: It is forbidden to make a braid or undo a braid on Shabbos.
Split: Splitting the hair down the middle having the hair on the right part of the head brushed to the right and the hair on the left part of the head brushed to the left, thus having an empty path in the middle of the head, may be done only with a mere finger [as opposed to one's hand[53]].

Q&A
May one make a hair do on Shabbos?[54]
It is forbidden to make a hair do having it hold in place using clips and bobby pins. However, one may enter bobby pins into the hair for mere orderliness and not for the sake of a design.

May one use a soft brush to make the above-mentioned hair split?[55]
Some Poskim[56] rule it is forbidden to do so.[57] Other Poskim[58] rule it is permitted if no hair will be removed in the process.[59] Practically one should be stringent.

May one use his hands to make the split?[60]
No. One may only use a mere a finger.

May one use a comb to gather the hair and make it into a ponytail and the like?[61]
No, one may only do so by hand.

Do the above laws of braiding and hair do's apply equally to a Sheitel?
Yes, it thus may not be designed on Shabbos.

Does the hair design prohibition apply to men as well?
Yes.

May one twirl his Peiyos on Shabbos?[62]
It is best to avoid doing so.[63]
Nevertheless, some Poskim[64] write that if they were already twirled before Shabbos then doing so does not involve a building prohibition. However, one must take care to only do so with his hands while the Peiyos are dry[65] and to not remove any hairs in the process.

---

[49] Michaber ibid
[50] Ketzos Hashulchan 146:11
[51] Rama ibid
[52] Due to the building prohibition. [Ketzos Hashulchan 146 page 39] However others explain that this is due to a suspicion that one may come to tear out hair. [Mishneh Berurah 303:84]
[53] Ketzos Hashulchan 146 page 40
[54] Piskeiy Teshuvos 303:8 in name of Minchas Yitzchak 1:80
[55] Piskeiy Teshuvos 303:8 and footnote 27
[56] Ketzos Hashulchan ibid
[57] As doing so even with a soft brush still contains the building prohibition.
[58] M"B 303:84
[59] As there is no building prohibition involved in splitting the hair and it was only forbidden due to suspicion that it may come to remove hairs.
[60] Ketzos Hashulchan 146 page 40
[61] Piskeiy Teshuvos 303:8 in name of Ketzos Hashulchan 146 footnote 21 [I have not found the source for this in the Ketzos Hashulchan there!]
[62] Piskeiy Teshuvos 303:9
[63] So writes Piskeiy Teshuvos ibid, and so is implied also from Ketzos Hashulchan ibid

Others[66] rule that twirling the Peiyos is not at all within the building prohibition and may thus be done in all cases, so long as it is done softly with one's hands while the Peiyos are dry.

May one fold his beard on Shabbos?[67]
Yes.[68]

5. May one brush his/her hair on Shabbos?[69]

Using a brush:[70] It is forbidden to brush [hair] with a brush on Shabbos, even with those [brushes] made of swine hair.
The reason for this is because: it is impossible to avoid removing hairs in the process.
Using ones hands:[71] However it is permitted to separate the hairs apart with ones hands.

Summary:
One may not use a brush to brush one's hair on Shabbos as it causes hair to come out. However, one may use one's fingers.

Q&A

May one use a soft brush to brush their hair on Shabbos?[72]
To straighten out the hair: One may use a soft brush to gently brush hair on Shabbos. One may not brush with force is this can lead to pulling out any hair. As well it is proper that the brush be designated for use only on Shabbos.
To make a design: See above!

May one brush their Sheitel on Shabbos?[73]
If the Sheitel is wearable without the brushing: One may brush a Sheitel using a soft brush and doing so softly in order to avoid pulling out any hair. As well it is proper that the brush be designated for only Shabbos use.[74]
If the Sheitel is not wearable without the brushing: Then it is forbidden to be brushed even in the above method due to the Fixing prohibition.

6. Cutting off a blister:[75]

It is forbidden to cut a blister from one's body whether with ones hand [or teeth[76]] whether with a vessel, whether for himself whether for others, whether it is [filled with] puss [blister] whether it is dry. If one does cut a puss [filled] blister with a vessel he is liable for the shearing prohibition according to those which hold one is liable for shearing even if he does not require that which is being sheared.

---

[64] The Ketzos Hashulchan 146 p. 42 is Milamed Zechus that it does not involve a building prohibition as one is merely adjusting an already twirled Peiyos.
[65] So rules Beir Moshe 1:19 and 5:74
[66] Beir Moshe Ibid
[67] Ketzos Hashulchan 146 page 41
[68] As doing so is not considered a form of design. [ibid]
[69] 303:27
[70] Michaber ibid
[71] Rama ibid
[72] Kitzur Shulchan Aruch 80:31
[73] Ketzos Hashulchan 143 footnote 6; Piskeiy Teshuvos 303:10
[74] The Minchas Shabbos [80:117] concludes that it is forbidden to do so, although he brings that there are those which are lenient and a Baal Nefesh is to only do so in the way described above.
[75] Admur 340:3
[76] Ketzos Hashulchan 143 in name of Mishneh Berurah.

Summary

It is a Biblical prohibition according to some opinions to cut off a blister with a vessel, if the blister is filled with puss. It is Rabbinically forbidden to remove it with one's hands [or teeth] even if it is dry.

---

7. Removing scabs:[77]

One may remove the scab of a wound [with one's hands[78]]. [However, this may only be done if it will not cause blood to be extracted.[79]]

Final stage of the wound: Even in the final stage of the wound, which is defined as when it has already healed and one feels no pain from it, it is permitted to remove the scab.

Summary:[80]

It is permitted to remove scabs with one's hands [so long as doing so does not release blood in the process].

Q&A

May one remove a bandage that is taped onto his skin, such as a typical band-aid?[81]

If doing so will remove in the process hair, then it should not be removed due to a possible shearing prohibition. However, if one is in pain he may be lenient to remove it even if hairs will be removed through doing so.[82]

---

8. Removing lice from skins:[83]

One may not remove lice from the skins of fox and the like being that [in the process] one removes hair from the skin which contains the sheering prohibition, and although it is done unintentionally, nevertheless it is an inevitable occurrence [and is thus forbidden].

---

[77] Admur 328:28

[78] However, with a vessel is forbidden [Ketzos Hashulchan 136 footnote 22]

[79] Admur 328:33

[80] Admur 328:28

[81] SSH"K 35:29 footnote 73; Piskeiy Teshuvos 328:22

[82] Being that this is a Pesik Reishei that is not beneficial, as well as that the removal of the hair is being done with a Shinui, and thus is permitted in a case of pain.

[83] Admur 316:21

CHAPTER 2: THE LAWS OF WRITING

Writing letters, symbols, marks, pictures [Halacha's 1-

1. The Av Melacha[1]
To write or erase with intent to write: One who writes[2], and erases in order to write in the erased area, has performed one of the primary Melachas. [This is derived from the work done in the Mishkan] as [in the Mishkan] they would write on the beams of the Tabernacle to know which beam corresponds to it, and at times they would make a mistake and erase what they wrote and then return and write in that place [the correct signs].

2. The Biblical and Rabbinical Prohibitions
Liability for sin offering is only on two letters:[3] One who writes .... letters is only liable on two letters, however on one letter he is exempt, although this is [still] Biblically forbidden as are other half measurements.

One is only liable for a permanent writing:[4] One is only liable [for a sin offering] when he writes with an item [whose mark is] permanent on top of a material [which the writing on it will remain] permanent.

Rabbinically even a temporary writing is forbidden:[5] However it is Rabbinically forbidden [to write] even with an item [whose mark is] not permanent on top of a material [which the writing on it will] not [remain] permanent, such as to write with liquids and fruits juices on top of vegetable leaves and the like, and therefore one must beware not to write with his fingers on the liquid that is on the table or to engrave in ash [or earth[6]] or congealed fat or honey.

Writing שעטנז גץ without the Zayins:[7] One who writes in Ashuris and omitted the זוי"ן[8] from the letters of שעטנז גץ is exempt from [liability to bring a sin offering] for doing so being that this work is incomplete.[9]

Writing an incomplete letter:[10] One who writes an incomplete letter of any language is exempt on them [from liability to bring a sin offering]. However, it is Rabbinically forbidden [to do so].

Writing in Rashi Script:[11] Therefore one who writes a fine print called "Meshita" [i.e. Rashi script] there are those which say that he is exempt from [liability of bringing a sin offering] over it, due to that this script was taken from the Ashuri script, and it is thus similar to an incomplete Ashuri script [of which one is not liable on] as will be explained in chapter 545.

3. Writing on condensation of fruits, windows, engraving in sand earth: 12
It is Rabbinically forbidden [to write] even with an item [whose mark is] not permanent on top of a material [which the writing on it will] not [remain] permanent, such as to write with liquids and fruits juices on top of vegetable leaves and the like, and therefore one must beware not to write with his fingers on the liquid that is on the table or to engrave in ash [or earth[13]] or congealed fat or honey.

---

[1] Admur 340:4

[2] The Minchas Chinuch explains that one is not liable until the ink dries. [Ketzos Hashulchan 144 footnote 1]

[3] Admur 340:4

[4] Admur 340:6

[5] Admur 340:6

[6] Ketzos Hashulchan 144:4

[7] Admur 340:8

[8] This refers to the small Zayin letters which protrude on the very top of each of the letters in the grouping of Shatnez Gatz.

[9] However the M"B 340:22 rules that one is liable even in such a case being that Halachically the Zayins do not invalidate the letters.

[10] Admur 340:8

[11] Admur 340:8

[12] Admur 340:6

[13] Ketzos Hashulchan 144:4

Summary:

Biblical: One is only Biblically liable to bring a sin offering for writing on Shabbos if <u>all</u> the following conditions are fulfilled:

1. He wrote two letters [by one it is Biblically forbidden but does not carry liability]
2. He wrote complete letters.
3. The letters are permanent and will hence not fade out.

Rabbinical: It is Rabbinically forbidden to write even if a) the writing will not last at all and b) even if the letters are incomplete in their form.

Based on the above it is forbidden to write the following:

1. It is forbidden to mark letters on liquids that are on a table.
2. It is forbidden to form words within condensation of a fruit [or condensation of a window].
3. It is forbidden to engrave words within sand or congealed fat.

Q&A

May one place toy letters next to each other thus forming a word?[14]

So long as one does not fasten the letters to each other or to a background in a way that the word will last, it is permitted.[15] Regarding puzzles-See Halacha 3 Q&A there!

May one place plastic letters onto a cake thus forming a word?

Seemingly this is allowed, as explained above.

What is the definition of permanent writing? How long must the writing last for it to be Biblically forbidden?[16]

Some[17] write that so long as it can last one day it is Biblically forbidden. Others[18] however write that it is only Biblically forbidden if it is written to last much longer than one day as is common for writers to do.

Is writing with a pencil Biblically forbidden?[19]

Yes.

May one use a rubber stamp on Shabbos?[20]

Doing so is Biblically forbidden.

Is typing on a computer also forbidden due to writing?[21]

Some Poskim[22] rule that doing so is considered like writing, and is thus Biblically forbidden due to the writing prohibition.

To note that according to all typing is in any event forbidden due to its use of electricity.

---

[14] Ketzos Hashulchan 144 footnote 10

[15] So rules Chayeh Adam [37] and Ketzos Hashulchan ibid regarding cases brought there [to sew letters onto a peroches, that if they are weekly sewn they contain no writing prohibition]. So rules also Igros Moshe 1:135; Piskeiy Teshuvos 340:7 and 16.
Avnei Neizer, brought in Ketzos Hashulchan 144 footnote 4, rules that placing letters near each other has no prohibition

[16] Piskeiy Teshuvos 340:11

[17] Minchas Yitzchak 7:13

[18] Ketzos Hashulchan in additions on Chapter 146, mentioned in Piskeiy Teshuvos 340 footnote 38

[19] Biur Halacha 340 in name of Rashba

[20] Piskeiy Teshuvos 340:11

[21] Piskeiy Teshuvos 340:12

[22] Sheivet Haleivi 6:36

May one write on carbon paper?[23]

Doing so is Biblically forbidden. It is thus forbidden to ask a gentile which is writing to write on such paper, so the person also remains with a copy.

Regarding writing numbers and other symbols-See Halacha 5C and Q&A there!

---

3. Drawings, pictures, and designs:[24]

One who makes marks and designs on a document and the like, in the way that the artists design, is liable due to an offshoot of the writing prohibition. The same applies for one who erases it.

Summary:
Is forbidden just like writing letters.

Q&A

May one put together puzzles on Shabbos?[25]
See General Q&A!

May one engrave designs and pictures onto his food, cake, non-Muktzah sand?
No.[26]

Does taking a picture with a camera, scanner, x-ray also involve the writing prohibition?[27]
Yes. Doing so is Biblically forbidden due to writing[28], in addition to the prohibition of using electricity.[29]

---

4. Figuratively writing in the air or on a table and the like:[30]

Although it is Rabbinically forbidden [to write] even with an item [whose mark is] not permanent on top of a material [which the writing on it will] not [remain] permanent, {such as to write with liquids and fruits juices on top of vegetable leaves and the like, and therefore one must beware not to write with his

---

[23] Piskeiy Teshuvos 340:13

[24] Admur 340:10; 519:6; M"A 340:6; Rambam Shabbos 11:17; Degul Merivava 340; Tehila Ledavid 340:3
Ruling of Admur in 302:5: See Admur 302:5 who writes "For example one who designs a [picture of a] figure on a vessel which is waiting to be designed on, even if he only designed part of the figure, he has done part of the finishing touch of the vessel and is liable [for a sin offering]. As although the figure on its own is not considered a [Biblically] forbidden form of work , nevertheless now that the vessel is complete and fixed through his action it is considered [a Biblically forbidden form of] work." However, perhaps this is referring to an incomplete figure, in which case there is no writing prohibition involved as explained in chapter 340:8, or perhaps this is referring to the building prohibition, that in it of itself it does not apply to a drawing. However, the writing prohibition does apply to a complete drawing as explained in chapter 340:10; See also Tehila Ledavid 340:3 who suggests in Rambam that one who engraves a picture on a vessel is not liable for writing, but only for Maka Bepatish. Now, although Admur 340:6 explicitly rules that one may not engrave into ash, perhaps that refers only to letters and not pictures. Now, although the Poskim do not differentiate between pictures and letters and rather rule that making a drawing is a Tolda of writing [See Admur 340:10; M"A 340:6; Rambam Shabbos 11:17; Degul Merivava 340; Tehila Ledavid 340:3] perhaps Admur holds that when it comes to pictures, there is a difference between writing and engraving. See Admur 340:10 who writes "One who makes marks and designs on a document and the like, in the way that the artists design, is liable due to an offshoot of the writing prohibition. The same applies for one who erases it." Admur does not simply write that pictures have the same status as writing, and qualifies the case with **"on a document..in the way that artists design.."** This extra wording of Admur seems to imply that there are cases that the writing prohibition does not apply to making a picture, and perhaps an engraved drawing is one of those cases. If the above is correct, then there would be no prohibition to engrave pictures into non-Muktzah sand, a cake and the like. Vetzaruch Iyun, as I have not found any Poskim who suggest such a ruling. Likewise, from Admur 519:6 it is clearly implied that the prohibition applies even to an engraved picture.

[25] Piskeiy Teshuvos 340:16-footnote 51

[26] The reason: As engraving is similar to writing as explained in Halacha 5. Vetzaruch Iyun from the wording of Admur ibid as well as Admur 302:5. See previous footnote

[27] Piskeiy Teshuvos 340:15

[28] So rules Keren Ledavid 102; Minchas Yitzchak 2:20

[29] However, the Beir Moshe [7:50] rules that x-rays involve only a Rabbinical writing prohibition being that the x-ray is only understandable by experts.

[30] 340:6

fingers on the liquid that is on the table or to engrave in ash or congealed fat or honey} nevertheless it is permitted to write in the air forms of letters being that their mark is not at all recognizable.

The same law applies to [that one may write figuratively, in order to hint something to a friend[31],] on a table that does not have liquid [in that area], being that in this case too the mark is not at all recognizable.

The Reason this does not contain a prohibition of training one's hands: Now although through doing so one trains and builds his hands for writing, this is [Halachicly] meaningless. It is as well permitted to view a craftsmanship on Shabbos even though he is learning it in the process.

Summary:
It is permitted to figuratively write letters in the air or on a clear table being that the letters are completely not noticeable. However, to engrave letters in sand or food, or to write using liquid on a table is Rabbinically forbidden being that the letters are noticeable.

Q&A

May one write using a magnetic board?[32]
Doing so is [Rabbinically] forbidden.

May one use a thermometer strap which reveals letters or numbers upon being heated?[33]
Some Poskim[34] rule it is Rabbinically forbidden to place on such a strap to measure fever. It is likewise forbidden to remove it once if it is already on.[35]
Other Poskim[36] rule that one may be lenient to use it to measure temperature[37] if one is unable to use a regular mercury thermometer.
If the letters were originally visible without the heat, or if there are no letters which become revealed but rather a mere color, then it is permitted to be used.[38]

May one take a pregnancy test on Shabbos?
If letters are revealed to reveal whether she is pregnant then it is forbidden to use on Shabbos. If no letters are revealed but rather a mere line it requires further analyses whether it may be used.[39]

May one design letters and words using sticks or threads?[40]
No.

May one form letters and pictures using his fingers [meaning by placing them in positions that form an item or symbol]?[41]
Some[42] prohibit doing so.

---

[31] Ketzos Hashulchan 144:4
[32] Writing on a magnetic board involves placing a magnetic pen on the board to lift small pieces of metal and thus form a word.
[33] Piskeiy Teshuvos 340:6
[34] Minchas Yitzchak 7:22
[35] As the letters are not considered written until they are brightened through the heat, and thus revealing them or concealing them involves the writing and erasing prohibition.
[36] Tzitz Eliezer 14:30 and Kinyan Torah 3:39
[37] As this involves a Shvus Deshvus [a Rabbinical prohibition upon a Rabbinical prohibition] 1) Temporary writing and 2) Being written through heat. [ibid]
[38] SSH"K 40:20
[39] Seemingly it should nevertheless be forbidden due to it being considered a design or symbol. [340:7-8]
[40] Piskeiy Teshuvos 340:16 Upashut
[41] Piskeiy Teshuvos 340:16
[42] Mekor Chaim [of Chavos Yair] 340:4.

5. *Engraving letters [or pictures]:*
A. Onto leather:[43]

Tearing letters into leather: One who tears onto leather letters of writing is liable, as engraving is a form of writing.

Marks letters on leather with one's finger: However, one who marks [with his finger] on the leather the form of writing is exempt from liability [to bring a sin offering] as this is not something which will last. Nevertheless, this is Rabbinically forbidden due to a decree that one may come to [write in a] permanent [method].

B. Engraving on earth, sand, fat, honey, water: 44

One must beware not to write with his fingers on the liquid that is on the table or engrave in ash [or earth[45]] or congealed fat or honey.

The reason for this is because: It is Rabbinically forbidden [to write] even with an item [whose mark is] not permanent on top of a material [which the writing on it will] not [remain] permanent.

Summary:

Leather: It is forbidden to engrave letters either through tearing them into the item [Biblically] or pressing them into it [Rabbinically].

Earth, sand/water: It is forbidden to engrave letters into earth, ash or any food.

Q&A

May one engrave or protrude letters into or out of a rubber stamp or signet ring?[46]

Doing so is Biblically forbidden.

May one engrave letters on a window with condensation?[47]

No. It is forbidden to engrave on it either letters or pictures.

May one engrave letters into a cake?

No. See General Q&A Below.

May one walk on Shabbos on sand, mud, or snow with shoes or sneakers which cause imprints of letters or pictures on them?[48]

Yes[49], although some Tzaddikim have been careful to avoid doing so.

---

[43] Admur 340:7
[44] Admur 340:6
[45] Ketzos Hashulchan 144:4
[46] Piskeiy Teshuvos 340:11
[47] Ketzos Hashulchan 144 footnote 5
[48] Piskeiy Teshuvos 340:9
[49] So rules Chelkas Yaakov 2:132 as doing so involves a two Rabbinical prohibitions which is permitted in a case of Piseik Reisha Shelo Nicha Lei.

6. Making marks on books/parchment and the like:

A. On leather and parchment:[50]

*Making a mark on **leather** as a reminder:* [Although it is forbidden to mark letters onto leather], if [the mark] does not have the form of writing and he is making a mark as a mere symbol, and it does not have the form of letters [or recognized symbols[51]], [such as a mere indentation] it is allowed even initially.

*Making a mark on **parchment** as a symbol that it needs editing:* It is therefore permitted to mark with ones nail on the page of a book [made of parchment] like those who make a mark as a sign in a place where there is a mistake. However, this only applies by parchment which is hard, and its mark thus does not last, however on paper it is forbidden to mark being that its mark lasts for a long time.

Other Opinions by making marks on parchment: There are those who prohibit [making marks] even on parchment [and certainly leather].

Their Reasoning: as they hold that even one who makes a mark for a mere symbol and not like a form of writing is liable [to bring a sin offering] if it is a permanent mark, as they too [in the times of the building of the Tabernacle] would make marks on the boards of the Tabernacle to know which [board] corresponds to it. Therefore, if one marked one marking on top of two boards, or two lines on one board, as a symbol as was done with the beams of the Tabernacle, is liable [to bring a sin offering]. [However] one marking on one board is exempt [from liability to bring a sin offering] although is [nevertheless] Biblically forbidden, being that it is a permanent matter [mark]. [Therefore] making a mark on parchment in which [the mark] will not last is Rabbinically forbidden due to a decree against [coming to make a mark which] permanent.

The final ruling:[52] A G-d fearing [person] is to be stringent upon himself like their words [to avoid making marks on even parchment].

Regarding writing symbols- See C below!

B. Making a mark on Paper:[53]

[The above leniency according to the first opinion] only applies by parchment which is hard, and its mark thus does not last, however on paper it is forbidden to make a mark being that its mark lasts for a long time.

The Reason: Now although [the mark] is not a form of writing it is [nevertheless] Rabbinically forbidden due to a decree against [coming to mark] a form of writing which one is liable for when it lasts.

C. Writing symbols:[54]

All the above is when [the mark] is not at all in the form of writing, however so long as [the mark] is in the form of a any writing, even if it is not the Ashury writing, even if they are unknown letters which are only used for symbols, such as the symbols which are commonly used to refer to the numbers, then it is considered the form of writing and one is liable [to bring a sin offering] on doing so if it was done on a item [in which the writing will be] permanent. If it was done on an item which [its writing will] not [remain] permanent] it is Rabbinically forbidden according to all.

D. Making lines on skin and paper:[55]

The Av Melacha-On skins: It is common for the leather makers that when they come to cut the leather they first scratch a line into it in accordance to how he wants to lengthen, widen and shorten the cut, and afterwards he passes the knife over the marked line. This was also done by the skins of the Tabernacle when they were cut, and therefore this line marking is one of the Principal Melachas.

---

[50] Admur 340:7
[51] See C below
[52] Admur ibid; Kneses Hagedola; Birkeiy Yosef; Mor Uketzia 340; Biur Halacha 340 "Mutar"
[53] Admur 340:7
[54] Admur 340:8
[55] Admur 340:11

Making lines on paper and parchment: Similarly, one who imprints a line into even parchment or paper in order to write straight is liable [for a sin offering].

Summary:

Symbols: According to all it is forbidden to mark recognized symbols on any material whether the symbol will be permanent [Biblically prohibited] or temporary [Rabbinically forbidden].

Lines: Lines are Biblically forbidden to be indented onto any material, whether leather, *parchment or paper.*

Mere marks such as indentations:

1. On leather/Parchment: It is disputed whether it is allowed to make mere marks, such as indentations, as reminders and symbols on leather and parchment. A G-d fearing [person] is to be stringent upon himself to avoid doing so.
2. On paper: Is forbidden according to all.

Q&A

May one write numbers?[56]

Doing so is Biblically forbidden as it carries the same laws as does writing letters.

May one take a fingerprint on Shabbos?[57]

Doing so is Biblically forbidden, as it is considered a complete picture.

May one bend a page in a book as a reminder?[58]

Yes[59], as one has no intent to make an indentation.

---

7. Entering letters into clothing:[60]

If one [firmly[61]] inserts silver letters into clothing, it is considered writing and is [thus] forbidden to do on Shabbos.

Summary:

Is forbidden.

Q&A

May one enter letters into a necklace or bracelet?[62]

This is forbidden due to the prohibition against fixing a vessel[63], and according to others[64] also due to the "Meameir" prohibition. Some[65] however permit it to be done, as they say that the Meameir prohibition only applies by gathering items that grow from the ground, and they do not hold that doing so involves the fixing prohibition.[66]

---

[56] Piskeiy Teshuvos 340:14, Upashut.
[57] Piskeiy Teshuvos 340:18 in name of many Poskim
[58] Piskeiy Teshuvos 340:19
[59] So rules Sheivet Hakehasy 1:130 and Kinyan Torah 2:115
[60] Admur 340:9
[61] See Ketzos Hashulchan 144 footnote 10
[62] Ketzos Hashulchan 146 footnote 49-25; Piskeiy Teshuvos 340:26
[63] Ketzos Hashulchan 146 footnote 49-25
[64] Orchos Chayim 13
[65] Shevisas Hashabbos Meameir
[66] According to all it does not involve the writing prohibition as there is no prohibition in forming a word as explained above.

8. Closing and opening books with writing [or designs[67]] on their side pages:[68]

First Opinion-Is forbidden: [Regarding] those books which have letters written on the top edges of the pages there are those[69] which prohibit opening them on Shabbos due to the erasing prohibition. As well as [they forbid] to close them due to the writing prohibition.

The reason for this prohibition: Now, although they have no intent to do this [writing or erasing, nevertheless it is forbidden as] it is an inevitable occurrence.

Other Opinions-Is permitted: [However] there are those[70] which permit to close [the books] as since the letters are already written and it is just that they are lacking proximity, this does not contain a writing prohibition. As since it is possible to bring them close together easily without doing any new action they are considered like they are close and standing and one is doing nothing with this proximity. Similarly, it is permitted to open them for this reason and one is not considered like he is erasing them as their writing [remains] intact and it is possible to near them to each other easily and they are [thus] considered already now to be] as if [they were] close.

The final ruling: And so is the custom [like the latter opinion]. [**See footnote for other Opinions**[71]][However initially one must beware to avoid writing letters or designs on the edges of a book, and if one did so then one should cut off the edges until the letters are no longer recognizable.[72]]

General Q&A

May one use a combination lock on Shabbos?[73]

Yes[74]. Combination locks may be used whether they include numbers or letters.[75] However, there are opinions[76] which question this allowance and rule that a meticulous person should be stringent.

May one play scrabble?[77]

This is allowed as the letters can be easily moved around, and are thus not considered set within a frame.

May one engrave designs onto his food or cake?

No, as engraving is similar to writing as explained in Halacha 4.

Compilation-Closing and opening books with writing [or designs] on their side pages:[78]

Books that have [words or] letters [or designs[79]] written on the top edges of the pages [i.e. the sides of the pages] some Poskim[80] rule it is forbidden to open or close them on Shabbos due to the writing and erasing

---

[67] Ketzos Hashulchan 144 footnote 4

[68] Admur 340:4

[69] Levush

[70] Shut Rama:Taz

[71] So rules also Tzemach Tzedek in Mishnayos Shabbos 12:44; Igros Moshe 2:40.
However, the Avnei Neizer 210 rules stringently in this, that it is forbidden to be opened or closed. This would apply as well if there are designs on the edges of the papers.
The Mishneh Berurah 340:17 rules like Admur although says that when one has another of that same Sefer available then it is better to be stringent.

[72] Ketzos Hashulchan 144:3; Sharreiy Tziyon in Biur Halacha 25

[73] Piskeiy Teshuvos 340:8

[74] So rules Tzitz Eliezer 13:44; Mishneh Halachos 5:48; Bitzeil Hachamah 1:40

[75] Doing so does not involve a writing prohibition, as placing letters or numbers near each other is not considered writing.

[76] Tiferes Adam 33; Chelkas Yaakov 3:150

[77] Beir Moshe 6:26, based on ruling brought above that there is no prohibition to form words.

[78] Admur 340:4

[79] Ketzos Hashulchan 144 footnote 4; See Piskeiy Teshuvos 340:9 footnote 99 that this refers to designs of figures, such as people and animals, and not a mere circle or square and the like. It certainly does not include a mere splash of ink as is common in many Sefarim. See also Ashel Avraham of Butchach 340 who is very lenient in this matter, saying perhaps the stringency only applies to letters.

[80] 1st opinion in Admur 340:4; M"A 340:6; Levush 340:4; Menorah Hatehora 340:4

prohibition.[81] However other Poskim[82] rule it is permitted to close and open [the books].[83] Practically, the custom is to be lenient like the latter opinion.[84] [However, initially, one must beware to avoid writing letters or designs on the edges of a book, and if one did so then one should cut off the edges until the letters are no longer recognizable.[85] Likewise, if one has another Sefer available of that type then it is best to be stringent.[86]]

Summary:
This matter is disputed in Poskim and the custom is to be lenient. [However initially one must beware to avoid writing letters or designs on the edges of a book, and if one did so then one should cut off the edges until the letters are no longer recognizable.[87]]

Q&A

If the page of a book is torn may one place the torn halves together in order to read it?[88]

Still bound to book: [If the ripped page is still attached to the book, then seemingly this is permitted, being that we rule like the latter opinion.[89]]

Individual papers: If the page was completely ripped out of the book some Poskim[90] rule that if the tear has occurred within the letters it is forbidden to place the pages together even according to the lenient opinion mentioned above[91]. If, however, the tear is between the letters and no letters have been torn, then one may place the pieces together.[92] Other Poskim[93] permit this even when the tear occurred within the letters, if one is doing so for learning Torah. Practically, from Admur it is implied like the latter approach, that the leniency applies in this case as well.[94]

May one open or close curtains or doors which form words, letters or pictures upon opening or closing them?[95]

Yes, as this is similar to books with writing on their sides of which Admur rules that it is permitted to open and close.[96]

---

[81] The reason: They prohibit opening them on Shabbos due to the erasing prohibition and as well [they forbid] to close them due to the writing prohibition. Now, although they have no intent to do this [writing or erasing, nevertheless it is forbidden as] it is an inevitable occurrence. [Admur ibid]

[82] 2nd opinion in Admur 340:4; Taz 340:2; Shut Rama 119; Maharash Halevi 27

[83] The reason: As since the letters are already written and it is just that they are lacking proximity, this does not contain a writing prohibition. As since it is possible to bring them close together easily without doing any new action, they are considered like they are close and standing and one is doing nothing with this proximity. Similarly, it is permitted to open them for this reason and one is not considered like he is erasing them as their writing [remains] intact and it is possible to near them to each other easily and they are [thus] considered already now to be] as if [they were] close. [Admur ibid; Taz ibid; Nishmas Adam 37:2; See Shut Rama ibid for other reasons mentioned; See Piskeiy Teshuvos 340 footnote 97]

[84] Admur ibid; Kneses Hagedola, brought in M"A 340:6; Tzemach Tzedek in Mishnayos Shabbos 12:4; Tosefes Shabbos 340:9; Birkeiy Yosef 340:5; Mor Uketzia 340; Chayeh Adam 38:5; Levushei Mordechai 1:59; Aruch Hashulchan 340:27; Mishneh Berurah 340:17; Poskim in Kaf Hachaim 340:30 and so concludes Kaf Hachaim ibid; Igros Moshe 2:40; Minchas Yitzchak 7:15; Poskim in Piskeiy Teshuvos 340:10 footnote 98
Other opinions: Some Poskim rule like the stringent opinion, that it is forbidden for the book to be opened or closed. This would likewise apply if there are designs on the edges of the papers. [Avnei Neizer 210]

[85] Ketzos Hashulchan 144:3; Shaar Hatziyon 340:25 in name of Achronim; Sefer Hachaim; Poskim brought in Piskeiy Teshuvos 340 footnote 98]

[86] Chayeh Adam ibid; Mishneh Berurah 340:17

[87] Ketzos Hashulchan 144:3; Sharreiy Tziyon in Biur Halacha 25

[88] Piskeiy Teshuvos 140:7

[89] So is implied from Az Nidbaru 5:18, as well as that it seems no different than a book with letters at its edge.

[90] Bris Olam Mocheik 8; Az Nidbaru 5:18; Igros Moshe Yoreh Deah 2:75

[91] The reason: As in this case it is lacking the mere closeness, and opening and closing of a book.

[92] As merely bringing letters together to form a word is permitted, as brought from Poskim in Halacha 1 above.

[93] Mishneh Halachos 6:89; Beir Moshe 6:125

[94] See Admur ibid who only records the 2nd reason in Teshuvos Harama, "As since the letters are already written and it is just that they are lacking proximity, this does not contain a writing prohibition. As since it is possible to bring them close together easily without doing any new action, they are considered like they are close and standing and one is doing nothing with this proximity." This is opposed to the 1st reason in Rama ibid who states the allowance is due to that the book is bound and meant for opening and closing. Thus, we see that Admur ibid negated this reason and accepted the reason that applies equally to jigsaw puzzles.

[95] Piskeiy Teshuvos 340:17

Compilation-Playing with jigsaw puzzles on Shabbos:

Puzzles are made up of various pieces, each piece containing some part of the picture or letter/word that the puzzle desires to portray. Putting a puzzle together on Shabbos touches upon the question of whether it transgresses the prohibition of writing on Shabbos, and taking apart a puzzle raises the question of whether it transgresses the prohibition of erasing on Shabbos. The following is an analysis on this subject:

The general law: It is forbidden to write or erase the letters of a word on Shabbos.[97] Likewise, it is forbidden to draw or erase pictures on Shabbos.[98] It is Rabbinically forbidden to do so even if the letter or picture will not last a long time.[99] It is however disputed as to whether the prohibition applies even in a case that the parts of the letter or picture already exist, and one simply places them near each other, or distances them from each other on a temporary basis.[100] An example of such a case is opening or closing a book that had letters or pictures written/drawn on the side pages of a book. Practically, the custom is to be lenient to allow opening and closing such books on Shabbos [although it should initially be avoided[101]].[102] The question of whether it is permitted to put together, or take apart jigsaw puzzles, on Shabbos, is dependent on how one understands the above dispute, as will now be explained.

The law by jigsaw puzzles:[103] Some Poskim[104] rule that even according to the lenient opinion, and custom, brought above, it is forbidden to put together, or take apart, jigsaw puzzles which contain pieces that create letters or pictures.[105] Other Poskim[106] however rule that this case follows the same leniency brought above, and hence it is permitted to build or take apart a puzzle on Shabbos even if it creates letters and pictures.[107] Practically, from Admur it is implied like the latter approach, that the leniency applies in this case as well.[108] Nonetheless, as stated above, initially one is to avoid entering the dispute and hence should not build, or take apart such puzzles on Shabbos, although one does not need to protest those who do so.[109] Likewise, one may be lenient to allow children below Bar/Bas Mitzvah to play with such puzzles

---

[96] Even according to those Poskim [Avnei Nezer] which are stringent, this only applies if the doors or curtains form a picture or letter, if however, they simply form a word then according to all it is allowed.

[97] Admur 340:4

[98] Admur 340:10; M"A 340:6; Rambam Shabbos 11:17; Degul Merivava 340; Tehila Ledavid 340:3

[99] Admur 340:6

[100] Some Poskim rule it is forbidden to open or close them on Shabbos due to the writing and erasing prohibition. [1st opinion in Admur 340:4; M"A 340:6; Levush 340:4; Menorah Hatehora 340:4] However other Poskim rule it is permitted to close and open [the books]. [2nd opinion in Admur 340:4; Taz 340:2; Shut Rama 119; Maharash Halevi 27] The reason for this lenient opinion is as follows: As since the letters are already written and it is just that they are lacking proximity, this does not contain a writing prohibition. As since it is possible to bring them close together easily without doing any new action they are considered like they are close and standing and one is doing nothing with this proximity. Similarly, it is permitted to open them for this reason and one is not considered like he is erasing them as their writing [remains] intact and it is possible to near them to each other easily and they are [thus] considered already now to be] as if [they were] close. [Admur ibid; Taz ibid; Nishmas Adam 37:2; See Shut Rama ibid for other reasons mentioned; See Piskeiy Teshuvos 340 footnote 97]

[101] Admur ibid; Kneses Hagedola, brought in M"A 340:6; Tzemach Tzedek in Mishnayos Shabbos 12:4; Tosefes Shabbos 340:9; Birkeiy Yosef 340:5; Mor Uketzia 340; Chayeh Adam 38:5; Levushei Mordechai 1:59; Aruch Hashulchan 340:27; Mishneh Berurah 340:17; Poskim in Kaf Hachaim 340:30 and so concludes Kaf Hachaim ibid; Igros Moshe 2:40; Minchas Yitzchak 7:15; Poskim in Piskeiy Teshuvos 340:10 footnote 98
Other opinions: Some Poskim rule like the stringent opinion, that it is forbidden for the book to be opened or closed. This would likewise apply if there are designs on the edges of the papers. [Avnei Neizer 210]

[102] Ketzos Hashulchan 144:3; Shaar Hatziyon 340:25 in name of Achronim; Sefer Hachaim; Poskim brought in Piskeiy Teshuvos 340 footnote 98]

[103] Piskeiy Teshuvos 340:16-footnote 51 [old] 340:19 [new]

[104] Shalmeiy Yehuda 5:3 in name of Rav Elyashiv; Bris Olam Mocheik 8, Az Nidbaru 5:18; Igros Moshe Yoreh Deah 2:75 regarding the prohibition in placing torn pages together

[105] The reason: This is Rabbinically forbidden due to the writing prohibition. It is not similar to the allowance of closing a book with letters written on its pages, being that by a book, the pages are bound together and is already considered to be very close. [Az Nidbaru ibid based on 1st reason in Teshuvas Harama ibid] Likewise, here one has intent to create a letter or picture.

[106] Beir Moshe 6:26; Yesod Yeshurun 1:53; SSH"K 16:23; Mishneh Halachos 6:89 and Beir Moshe 6:125 regarding the allowance to place torn pages.

[107] The reason: As this is similar to closing a book with writing on its edges which is allowed, as so long as the pieces of the letter were made before Shabbos, and it is merely lacking approximation, there is no writing prohibition relevant.

[108] See Admur ibid who only records the 2nd reason in Teshuvos Harama, "As since the letters are already written and it is just that they are lacking proximity, this does not contain a writing prohibition. As since it is possible to bring them close together easily without doing any new action they are considered like they are close and standing and one is doing nothing with this proximity." This is opposed to the 1st reason in Rama ibid who states the allowance is due to that the book is bound and meant for opening and closing. Thus, we see that Admur ibid negated this reason and accepted the reason that applies equally to jigsaw puzzles.

[109] See Ketzos Hashulchan 144:3

on Shabbos.[110] If placing the pieces together does not create new letters or pictures, it is permitted according to all to put together or take apart, even if it creates a word, such as if each piece contains a complete letter.[111]

Summary:

It is disputed whether one may play with jigsaw puzzles on Shabbos. Practically, one is to avoid doing so, although those who are lenient have upon whom to rely. This leniency especially applies to young children.

---

[110] Piskeiy Teshuvos ibid
[111] Chayeh Adam; Ketzos Hashulchan 144:10 regarding cases brought there [to sew letters onto a peroches, that if they are weekly sewn they contain no writing prohibition]; Igros Moshe 1:135; Piskeiy Teshuvos 340:7 and 16; Beir Moshe 6:26; Avnei Neizer, brought in Ketzos Hashulchan 144 footnote 4, rules that placing letters near each other has no prohibition.

CHAPTER 3: THE LAWS OF ERASING

General rule:
Whenever something is forbidden to be written on Shabbos, as explained in the previous chapter, it is likewise forbidden to be erased unless stated otherwise[112]. Refer to the previous chapter for all cases that contain the writing prohibition.

---

1. The Biblical Prohibition[113]

To write or erase with intent to write: One who writes, and erases in order to write in the erased area, is one of the primary Melachas. [This is derived from the work done in the Mishkan] as [in the Mishkan] they would write on the beams of the Tabernacle as signs to know which beam corresponds to it, and at times they would make a mistake and erase what they wrote and then return and write in that place [the correct signs].

Liability is only on two letters: [However the above liability] is when there is enough space [in the erased area] to write or inscribe two letters, and similarly one who writes or erases letters is only liable on two letters, however on one letter he is exempt, although this is [still] Biblically forbidden as are other half measurements.

Summary:
One is only liable for a sin offering when one erases an area in which he plans to write two letters. If there is only space to write one letter although it is Biblically forbidden it does not carry liability for a sin offering.

Q&A

May one separate letters from a word if the letters will remain intact?[114]
Yes, as there are no letters being erased.[115]

May one erase engraved letters?[116]
No.

---

2. To erase without intent to write:[117]

Erasing without intent to write within that space, was not done in the Tabernacle, and is not similar to a Melacha at all.

Rabbinically forbidden to erase even without intent to write: Rabbinically it is forbidden to erase even if it is not being done for the sake of writing [in its space]

---

[112] The one exception to this rule is regarding engraving letters into cake which although is forbidden to be done is permitted to be erased within the process of eating as will be explained here.
[113] Admur 340:4
[114] SSH"K 9 footnote 48 in name of Rav SZ"A; Ketzos Hashulchan 144 footnote 4
[115] As there is no prohibition of erasing by ruining a word and leaving all the letters intact at the same time. Regarding the dispute in the case of opening and closing a Sefer with letters on its edges, there the dispute is due to the fact that one is creating/erasing the actual letter by closing and opening the book, and not that he is separating letters from a word. [based on Avnei Neizer brought in Ketzos Hashulchan 144 footnote 4]
[116] See chapter 1 Halacha 5 that the Biblical and Rabbinical writing prohibition applies if one engraves, and consequently it would be forbidden to erase it; See
[117] Admur 340:4

Summary:
Is Rabbinically forbidden.

---

3. To erase drawings and designs:[118]

One who makes marks and designs on a document and the like, in the way that the artists design, is liable due to an offshoot of the writing prohibition. The same applies for one who erases it.

Summary:
Is forbidden just like erasing letters.

Q&A

May one erase drawings and designs that were made in condensation of one's window?[119]
No.

May one erase engraved drawings or designs, such as on sand?
No.

---

4. Erasing ink/dye splotches and removing wax in order to write:[120]

Liability for erasing ink splotches and removing wax in order to write: Since the liability for erasing is due to him doing so on behalf of writing, which means that he is fixing the area to write on, therefore even if he did not erase letters but rather erased mere splotches of ink [or dye[121]], or wax which fell on a tablet [he is liable]. [This tablet] refers to a wooden writing board which is smeared with wax and inscribed onto using a metal pen. [Thus, if it were to happen that] external[122] wax fell on this board and one erased this wax and removed it from there in order to engrave in its place on the wax that is under it which was smeared on the board [to begin with], then he is liable. [However, the above liability] is when there is enough space [in the erased area] to write or inscribe two letters, and similarly one who writes or erases letters is only liable on two letters, however on one letter he is exempt, although this is [still] Biblically forbidden as are other half measurements.

Removing wax from parchment in order to write: This law similarly applies by one who erases and removes wax from the parchment in order to write in its place.

---

[118] Admur 340:10; 519:6 regaridng a Chosem; M"A 340:6; Rambam Shabbos 11:17; Degul Merivava 340
[119] Implication of Admur 519:6; See chapter 1 Halacha 5 that the Biblical and Rabbinical writing prohibition applies if one engraves, and consequently it would be forbidden to erase it; Vetzaruch Iyun from the wording in Admur ibid and Admur 302:5, as explained in Chapter 1 Halacha 3 in footnotes.
[120] Admur 340:4
[121] Ketzos Hashulchan 144:1
[122] Meaning that wax from the outside fell onto the original wax layer, thus making a further wax layer on that part of the board and making it uneven.

Summary:
Is Biblically forbidden.

Q&A

May one erase ink splotches without intent to write in its place?[123]
No, doing so is Rabbinically forbidden [as one is preparing the area for writing by doing so].

May one remove a fresh ink splotch which is not yet dry?[124]
No, it may not be wiped off in any way, just like the ruling by dry ink.

May one remove food splotches or other splotches from a book, such as a bentcher?[125]
If the splotch is not covering letters and one is able to write over it, then this is allowed. If, however, one cannot write over it, then it is forbidden. If the splotches are covering letters-see next Halacha.

May one remove ink or dye blotches from one's table or other non-writing surfaces?[126]
Yes.[127] Regarding washing them off one's skin-see General Q&A!

May one wash ink blotches, letters, or drawings off his skin?[128]
Ink or paint blotches: Many Poskim[129] rule it is forbidden to erase dye from the skin due to the erasing prohibition. According to these Poskim one must be careful when washing hands to avoid erasing the ink, and is to bind a cloth around the hand prior to washing it. Other Poskim[130] however rule ink or paint blotches may be washed off one's skin and so is the worldly custom.[131] [However according to all one must avoid wiping the ink on a towel and the like due to a dying prohibition.[132]]
Letters: It is forbidden to erase letters from ones skin.[133] Thus if one has letters on his skin he must beware not to erase them while washing his hands. One is to therefore avoid drying his hands after washing[134]. Some[135] go as far to say that one must cover the area of the letter with a towel while washing.

---

[123] Ketzos Hashulchan 144:1, as he understands from Admur 340:4

[124] Ketzos Hashulchan 144 footnote 1

[125] So is implied from Ketzos Hashulchan 144 footnote 1

[126] Ketzos Hashulchan 144 footnote 10

[127] As by doing so one is not preparing the area for writing as it is not common to write on a table.

[128] Ketzos Hashulchan 144 footnote 10; Piskeiy Teshuvos 340:3

[129] Chayeh Adam [Laws of Netilas Yadayim]40:8; Minchas Shabbos 80:199; Peri Haaretz 2:4; Ikkarei Dinim 14:70; Kaf Hachaim [Falagi] 30:57; Vayaan Avraham 31; Ben Ish Chaiy Pekudeiy 2:1; Tal Oros p. 334

[130] Ketzos Hashulchan 144 footnote 10; Kaf Hachayim 161:27 in name of Pischeiy Teshuvah; Meged Yehuda 2; Minchas Shlomo 2:10; Beir Moshe 8:25; SSH"K 14 footnote 83 in name of Rav SZ"A; Piskeiy Teshuvos 340:5

[131] The reason: Since the blotches of ink was not the Melacha in Mishkan and since the skin is not an area of writing and thus one is not fixing the area for writing by erasing the ink, the Sages therefore did not prohibit erasing ink from one's skin. This can be proven from fact a) One may wash off the pomegranate and strawberry dye from his hands and it does not involve a erasing prohibition. And b) One may clean a spill of an item off a table and doing so does not involve an erasing prohibition. Therefore, since it is embarrassing to walk around with dirty hands and it is as well a Mitzvah to dry one's hands after washing for bread and the like, one should not protest those that are lenient in this. So rules also Kaf Hachayim 161:27

[132] Kaf Hachayim 340

[133] As erasing letters was the Melacha done in the Tabernacle and thus it has enough resemblance for the Sages to decree against doing so even on a surface that is not meant for writing.

[134] So rules Peri Haaretz and Chayeh Adam. [ibid]

[135] Minchas Shabbos ibid

May one wash his hands for bread or prayer if they have ink blotches, letters or drawings on them?

See above Q&A.

May one wash his hands from soot, as is common to occur when moving pots?

This has the same ruling as washing off ink blotches from one's hands. See above Q&A!

May one remove glue from one's skin on Shabbos?[136]

Yes.[137] However there are Poskim which are stringent in this just as they are in regards to removing ink blotches.

Q&A on removing makeup

May one remove dye from an item on Shabbos?

The Melacha of dyeing in the Mishkan does not contain an opposite Melacha against erasing the dye. Likewise, in the Talmud and Shulchan Aruch, we do not find any attribution of a prohibition against erasing dye on Shabbos. Nevertheless, the later Poskim question whether the erasing of dye contains the erasing prohibition, which corresponds to the writing prohibition on Shabbos. Many Poskim[138] rule it is forbidden to erase dye from the skin due to the erasing prohibition. Other Poskim[139] rule it is permitted to erase dye from one's skin and practically so is the custom.[140]

May one remove makeup from the face on Shabbos?[141]

This matter is relevant to the same dispute in Poskim regarding erasing ink blotches from one's skin, in which the custom is to be lenient. Nevertheless, some[142] write one is to be stringent not to remove makeup on Shabbos even according to the lenient opinion mentioned above. Practically, those who are lenient have upon whom to rely.[143]

---

[136] Piskeiy Teshuvos 140:3

[137] So rules Tzitz Eliezer 8:15 and others. Doing so does not contain the Mimacheik prohibition, as the Mimacheik prohibition does not apply to one's skin.

[138] Chayeh Adam [Laws of Netilas Yadayim]40:8; Minchas Shabbos 80:199; Peri Haaretz 2:4; Ikkarei Dinim 14:70; Kaf Hachaim [Falagi] 30:57; Vayaan Avraham 31; Ben Ish Chaiy Pekudeiy 2:1; Tal Oros p. 334

[139] Ketzos Hashulchan 144 footnote 10; Kaf Hachayim 161:27 in name of Pischeiy Teshuvah; Meged Yehuda 2; Minchas Shlomo 2:10; Beir Moshe 8:25; SSH"K 14 footnote 83 in name of Rav SZ"A; Piskeiy Teshuvos 340:5

[140] The reason: Since the blotches of ink was not the Melacha in Mishkan and since the skin is not an area of writing and thus one is not fixing the area for writing by erasing the ink, the Sages therefore did not prohibit erasing ink from one's skin. This can be proven from fact a) One may wash off the pomegranate and strawberry dye from his hands and it does not involve a erasing prohibition. And b) One may clean a spill of an item off a table and doing so does not involve an erasing prohibition. Therefore, since it is embarrassing to walk around with dirty hands and it is as well a Mitzvah to dry one's hands after washing for bread and the like, one should not protest those that are lenient in this. [Ketzos Hasulchan ibid]

[141] SSH"K 14:61; Orchos Shabbos 15:85 in name of many Poskim; Based on 320:27 that one may wash off the pomegranate and strawberry dye from his hands and it does not involve a erasing prohibition.

[142] Piskeiy Teshuvos 340:5; SSH"K 14:66 writes initially to remove the nail polish with a gentile, if a gentile is available; So rules also Shabbos Kehalacha 18:27 [Volume 3 p. 179] that one may only remove the nail polish in times of great need, such as to go to Mikveh; See also Ketzos Hashulchan ibid which concludes "since it is shameful to walk with stained hands, one is not to protest against those that are lenient"

The reason: This case is more severe than the case of removing ink blotches from the skin, as in this case one intends to eventually redye the skin after removing the makeup, and it is similar to the Biblical prohibition against erasing with intent to write.

[143] Beir Moshe 8:25 rules one may remove makeup on Shabbos prior to Mikveh; See SSH"K ibid; Orchos Shabbos 15 footnote 85; Shabbos Kehalacha footnote 55

The reason: As although one intends to eventually redye the skin after removing the makeup, and it is similar to the Biblical prohibition against erasing with intent to write, nevertheless, we rule that erasing dye from the skin is not relevant at all to the erasing prohibition, and there is no prohibition of erasing dye which corresponds to the prohibition of dyeing, and hence there is no source in Halacha to prohibit this [ibid]

May one remove nail polish on Shabbos?[144]

This matter is relevant to the same dispute in Poskim regarding erasing ink blotches from one's skin, in which the custom is to be lenient. Nevertheless, some[145] write one is to be stringent not to remove nail polish on Shabbos even according to the lenient opinion mentioned above. Practically, those who are lenient have upon whom to rely.[146]

If a woman forgot to remove her nail polish from her nails before Shabbos, may she do so on Shabbos in order to immerse in a Mikveh?

Some Poskim[147] rule she is allowed to remove the nail polish herself, following the lenient opinion stated above. Others[148] rule that she should ask a gentile to remove it for her, and only in the event that a gentile is not available may she do so herself. Others[149] rule that if the polish is complete on all the nails, it is better to immerse with the polished nails then to remove it on Shabbos.[150] If, however, the polish has begun coming off, then she should ask a gentile to remove it. If no gentile is available, she may remove it herself. Others[151] write it is best for her to puch off her immersion until the next night. [When removing the nail polish, one may use nail polish remover, although she may not soak a cotton ball in the liquid. She may however rub the polish off using a dry cotton ball.[152]]

___

5. Removing wax [and the like] from letters in order to see the letters more clearly:[153]

Following the above ruling in Halacha 4 it is likewise forbidden for one to remove wax which dripped onto letters. The reason for this is because what is the difference if one fixes a place for writing or if one fixes already written letters? On the contrary this [latter erasing of wax to see the current letters] is more of a fixing [then the erasing of wax merely to write on it in the future].

Other Opinions: [However] there are those[154] which are lenient in this matter.

See Q&A regarding removing food splotches from letters and regarding a Sefer Torah which has blotches on its letters.

___

[144] SSH"K 14:61

[145] Piskeiy Teshuvos 340:5; SSH"K 14:66 writes initially to remove the nail polish with a gentile, if a gentile is available; So rules also Shabbos Kehalacha 18:27 [Volume 3 p. 179] that one may only remove the nail polish in times of great need, such as to go to Mikveh.

The reason: This case is more severe than the case of removing ink blotches from the skin, as in this case one intends to eventually redye the skin after removing the makeup, and it is similar to the Biblical prohibition against erasing with intent to write.

[146] Beir Moshe 8:25 rules one may remove makeup on Shabbos prior to Mikveh; See SSH"K ibid; Orchos Shabbos 15 footnote 85; Shabbos Kehalacha footnote 55

The reason: As although one intends to eventually redye the skin after removing the makeup, and it is similar to the Biblical prohibition against erasing with intent to write, nevertheless, we rule that erasing dye from the skin is not relevnt at all to the erasing prohibition, and there is no prohibition of erasing dye which corresponds to the prohibition of dyeing, and hence there is no source in Halacha to prohibit this [ibid]

[147] Yesod Yeshurun brought in Piskeiy Teshuvos 340 footnote 7; Beir Moshe 8:25 rules one may remove makeup on Shabbos prior to Mikveh; See SSH"K ibid; Orchos Shabbos 15 footnote 85; Shabbos Kehalacha footnote 55

[148] SSH"K 14:66; Ateres Moshe 1:94; Piskeiy Teshuvos 340:5

[149] Taharah Kehalacha 15:79 p. 505 based on Rav SZ"A; However see what he writes in Shabbos Kehalacha 18:27 [vol. 3 p. 179]

[150] As RSZ"A questions whether removing nail polish is similar to erasing with intent to write, as she does have in mind to repaint it later on.

[151] Pischeiy Daas in name of Rav Elyashiv, brought in Piskeiy Teshuvos 340:5

[152] As dyeing is not relevant to cotton balls as they are designated for this purpose to become dirty and be discarded. It is hence similar to all items which are designated specifically for a dirty use which does not contain the dying prohibition. This follows the ruling written in "The Laws of Dyeing" regarding using a tissue to clean a wound, which is allowed based that it is designated for this purpose. [Admur Kuntrus Achron 302; SSH"K 14:19; Piskeiy Teshuvos 320:11] This ruling is unlike the ruling of Rav Farkash in Taharah Kehalacha ibid which prohibits the use of a cotton ball in all cases. Vetzaruch Iyun Gadol on his opinion.

[153] 340:4

[154] Shvus Yaakov 2:4

Summary:

Is Biblically forbidden, although there are those which are lenient. [**see footnote for summary of Ketzos Hashulchan**[155]]

Q&A

May one remove food splotches or other splotches from letters in order to see the letters better?[156]

No. [Thus one may not remove food stains from the letters of a Bentcher. If, however, the splotches are clear color and thus is not concealing the letter, seemingly this may be done[157].]

Regarding if one may remove splotches from blank areas see previous Halacha.

On Shabbos, may one remove wax blotches [as well as other forms of blotches] from letters of a Sefer Torah and does it invalidate the Torah?[158]

If there is wax [or other blotch] on a letter and the letter is not recognizable due to this then the Sefer is invalid and another Sefer Torah must be taken out.[159] However if the wax is dry enough that folding the parchment between the wax will cause the wax to flick off, then this may be done, and one may continue reading from this Sefer.[160] However, one may not remove the wax with his hands due to the Mimachek/smoothening prohibition.[161] Other Poskim[162], however, rule that one should never remove the wax in any case and should rather read that letter orally and continue with the reading.

6. Editing letters:[163]

One who edits one letter such as he removed the roof of the "Ches" and turned it to two "Zayins" is liable. (And one who edits another single letter such as he removed the roof of the "Daled" and turned it into a "Reish" is exempt [from liability of a bringing a sin offering] although doing so is Biblically forbidden).

Summary:

Is Biblically forbidden if by editing them one created a new letter.

---

[155] The Ketzos Hashulchan [144:1] summarizes this Halacha as follows: It is forbidden to remove the wax and there are those which say that one is liable for doing so. Vetzaruch Iyun Gadol, as this implies that the entire dispute is if it's a Biblical or Rabbinical prohibition and not whether its allowed or not. However after reading the source of the more lenient opinion, the Shvus Yaakov, one sees it clearly written that it is permitted to be done, and so is the simple meaning of the words of Admur "And there are those that are lenient", that there are those which even initially permit this, and so writes the Ketzos Hashulchan himself in Badei Hashulchan 144:2. Furthermore the Ketzos Hashulchan goes on to say there that Admur did not rule in this dispute as he normally does, and he then goes on to rely on the lenient opinion in certain cases [see the case of a Sefer Torah in Q&A]. It is thus not understood why he mentions the dispute the way he does without mentioning at all a lenient opinion.

[156] Ketzos Hashulchan 144 footnote 1, brought also in Elyah Raba, Chayeh Adam and Mishneh Berurah. [ibid]

[157] So is implied from Ketzos Hashulchan ibid

[158] See Ketzos Hashulchan 87:7; 144 footnote 2

[159] Shaareiy Efrayim 6:7; Ketzos Hashulchan ibid in name of Shaareiy Efrayim and Rav Akiva Eiger.

[160] Shvus Yaakov 2:4; Sharreiy Efrayim ibid; Kitzur Shulchan Aruch 24; Ketzos Hashulchan ibid and ibid

The reason: As this proves that the wax never really covered the letter. [Shvus Yaakov ibid]

[161] Shvus Yaakov ibid; Shaareiy Efraim ibid; Ketzos Hashulchan ibid. However, Rav Akivah Eiger writes that the reason is because of Tikkun Keli. See Ketzos Hashulchan ibid which argues that in this case there is no problem of Tikkun Keli.

[162] M"B 340:10

[163] Admur 340:5

7. Eating cake with letterings:[164]

[Based on above] it is therefore forbidden to break a cake which has on it forms of letters, even though one's intent is simply to eat [the cake] as he is [nevertheless] erasing [these letters]. [It is thus forbidden to eat this cake on Shabbos.[165]] [**See Q&A for letters made from fruit juice, engraved letters, designs, and chopping off the entire layer of the letters**]

Permitted to give child the cake to eat: However, it is permitted to give this cake to a child [below the age of Chinuch[166], even though one knows for certain that the child will eat it[167]], as a child who does [transgressions] for his own benefit does not need to be separated [from the act].

Forbidden to place the cake in the child's mouth:[168] However, one may not place the cake directly into the mouth of the child. [Likewise, it is forbidden for one to tell the baby to eat it.[169]]

Not to break cakes with engraved lettering:[170] The symbols which are made on the Matzos should not be made through forms of letters using a molded imprint [i.e. cookie cutter], or with one's hands (for the reason explained in chapter 470 and others) being that one is required to break them on Yom Tov, and there are opinions[171] which prohibit to break a cake which has forms of letters on it even though he does not intend to erase the letters, but rather to eat them on Yom Tov, as was explained in chapter 340. [**See footnote for other opinions[172]**] Rather these symbols are to be made through holes or grooves, as long as one is careful to extremely speed their process, as was explained in chapter 460, see there.

The allowance to break cakes with engraved pictures: Admur 460:7-9

Summary:

Cake which has lettering written on it is forbidden to be eaten on Shabbos or Yom Tov if by doing so the letters will break. It is permitted to give it to a child below the age of Chinuch for him to eat, although one may not place it directly into the child's mouth. If the cake has letters engraved into it, it is likewise forbidden to be broken [although regarding placing it directly into one's mouth see Q&A.]

Q&A
May one eat a cake that has designs or pictures?[173]

If the designs are **engraved** into the cake, then one may even break a piece and eat it if there are no letters on the cake.[174] If, however, the designs are formed through icing or any other external item, such as chocolate chips etc, [as opposed to engraving which is within the cake itself] then it has the same laws as does a cake with letters.

---

[164] Admur 340:4

Other opinions: Some Poskim rule that it is always permitted to break letters of a cake. [Degul Merevava 340]

[165] Admur 343:10; Chazon Ish 61:1; This comes to teach that even within the process of eating it is forbidden, unlike the ruling of the M"B in next footnote. The Chazon Ish ibid rules like Admur that even within the process of eating this is forbidden.

Other opinions: Some Poskim rule that it is always permitted to break letters of a cake. [Degul Merevava 340] The M"B 340:16 thus rules based on this that one may be lenient to break the letters **within the process of eating** [meaning upon chewing it] as opposed to breaking off a piece with letters and then eating it.

[166] If the child is below the age of Chinuch it is obviously forbidden to give him the cake and have him do a prohibition as rules Admur in 343:2

[167] Admur 343:10

[168] Admur 343:10

[169] Ketzos Hashulchan 147 footnote 11

[170] Admur 458:8; Teshuvaas Rama; Chok Yaakov 475; Levush

[171] Tzaruch Iyun why Admur simply states here that "there are opinions that forbid" when in truth there is no argument on this matter.

[172] So rules stringently Levush and Chok Yaakov chapter 475.

However other Poskim rule that by cakes with engraved letters one is allowed to even break off a piece and then eat it. So rules: M"B 340:15; SSH"K 11:8. Ra"sh Haleivi brought in Magen Avraham 340:6, although he himself concludes with Tzaruch Iyun; Mahril.

[173] Ketzos Hashulchan 144 footnote 3

[174] Implication of Admur 460:7, 9; Beis Yosef 460 in name of Rabbeinu Yerucham

May one break letters on cakes/food if the letters/pictures are made from fruit juice and the like?[175]
This may be done[176] if the letters are made from a liquidly substance in which case the letters will not last [such as when made from water and honey].[177] However if the letters are made from a thick substance that hardens, such as today's icings, then it may not be eaten [even within the process of eating.[178]]

May one break letters/pictures made from candies, such as chocolate chips and the like?
No, this has the same status as all letters. It is thus forbidden to remove a candy from the letter, as doing so ruins the letter.[179]

May one slice off the layer of the letterings/pictures and then eat the cake?[180]
Yes, this may be done even if a letter may break in the process, so long as it is not inevitable. Furthermore, one may even slice off each individual letter [even though the word will be broken by doing so, as explained in Halacha 2 Q&A there!].

May one remove plastic letters from a cake thus ruining the word?
Seemingly this is allowed.

If the pieces were cut from before Shabbos may one remove a piece from the cake if doing so will ruin the letters?[181]
Yes. This may be done even if by doing so it will ruin the letter or picture, as since it was already cut before Shabbos the letter or picture was already considered ruined.

May one eat biscuits, cakes and the like which have words/letters engraved on them?[182]
To break it and then eat it: According to Admur[183] it is forbidden to break off a piece and then eat it. [Other Poskim[184] however allow even this to be done. Regarding non-food items that have letters engraved in them-see general Q&A below!]
To take a bite out from it: Some Poskim[185] rule that even according to Admur one may break engraved letters within the process of eating. Meaning, that one may break the letters in the process of taking a bite from the food but not by breaking it and then placing it into one's mouth.[186] However other

---

[175] Ketzos Hashulchan 144 footnote 3 towards end; Bear Moshe 6:94; Piskeiy Teshuvos 340:4; SSH"K 11:7 which only allows breaking it in ones mouth, based on the Mishneh Berurah mentioned above, although to break with one's hands he agrees that it is forbidden.
[176] So rules Mishneh Berurah 340:15, SSH"K, taken from Agudah brought in Magen Avraham.
[177] So explains the Elyah Raba
[178] According to Admur, while according to the M"B 340:15 [and so rules SSH"K 11:8] it is allowed in the process of eating.
[179] However according to Taz brought in M"B 340:16 [and so rules SSH"K 11:7] one may break the letter within the process of taking a bite from the piece.
[180] Ketzos Hashulchan 144 footnote 3 towards end.
[181] SSH"K 11:7
[182] Ketzos Hashulchan 144 footnote 3
[183] 458:8
[184] M"B 340:15; SSH"K 11:8. Ra"sh Haleivi brought in Magen Avraham, although he himself concludes with Tzaruch Iyun.
[185] Ketzos Hashulchan 144 footnote 3 [His final ruling is written on page 151 at the end of the paragraph]; Shabbos Kehalacha Volume 3 p. 369; 20:73
[186] The reason: The basis of this ruling is that a) There are Poskim [Degul Merivava] who always allow breaking letters within the process of eating [chewing it] and b) There are Poskim which allow even to break engraved letters. Thus, although Admur rules stringently on breaking within process of eating [with regards to letters written with icing] while the Magen Avraham leaves in question braking engraved letters, when both leniencies are combined, such as breaking within the process of eating letters engraved on a biscuit, one may be lenient. [Ketzos Hashulchan there] This seemingly holds true as well in accordance to the ruling of Admur in Hilchos Pesach [brought above] which simply forbids breaking the Matzah with engraved letters, implying that taking a bite from it is allowed. [To note that the Ketzos Hashulchan did not mention this ruling in chapter 144 and only later was it mentioned by him in the glosses to the end of the 7th volume, nevertheless it is implied from there that his conclusion to allow breaking them while eating remains the same.] See however the next case of a bottle cap with engraved letters that the Ketzos Hashulchan allows one to break it on Shabbos, although contradicts himself in the glosses to the end of volume 7. Vetzaruch Iyun.
The reason behind the leniency of engraved letters over external letters: Engraved letters are not common today, and thus since here one has no intent to write in the area that the letters are erased, and it is thus only a Rabbinical prohibition, in this case we allow it being that in non-common

Poskim[187] rule that according to Admur they may not be broken even within the process of eating.[188] According to this latter opinion, one may not give these such foods to children that have reached the age of Chinuch.

<u>Dipping the biscuit into tea</u>: One may dip the biscuit that contains engraved letters into tea if doing so will not inevitably cause the biscuit to break in the area of the letters. If, however, the biscuit will break in the area of the letters then doing so is forbidden. [One must beware to wash his hands without a blessing prior to eating biscuits dipped in coffee or tea and the like prior to eating them.[189]]

May one make cheesecake using whole biscuits that contain engraved words?

It is not advised to do so due to the eating restriction to be explained. If one did so then care must be taken not to break the biscuits in a way that the letters will break.[190] One may however eat the biscuits whole, having them break in his mouth, according to some Poskim.[191]

May one eat a cake or pastry which was made in the form of a letter or picture?[192]

Yes.

Does washing one's hands with a bar of soap which contains engraved lettering contain the "erasing" prohibition?[193]

The Ketzos Hashulchan leaves this matter in doubt[194] although in any event the custom is not to wash at all with a bar of soap as explained above. Irrelevant of the above, it is forbidden to wash with a bar of soap due to the Molid prohibition, as explained in Volume 2 "The Laws of Nolad" Halacha 4!

---

cases the Sages did not make their decree. Hence here since engraving is uncommon, they did not suspect that one may come to erase engraving with intent to write in its place. [Ketzos Hashulchan ibid]

[187] Rav Bitstritzky in Shut Ara Degalil p. 35; Piskeiy Teshuvos 340 that from Admur ibid it is implied that this too is forbidden; Rav Eliyahu Landa that the custom is to be careful not to eat such foods on Shabbos.

[188] Rav Bistritzky does not make mention of the ruling of the Ketzos Hashulchan throughout his entire ruling. However, at the end in a footnote he mentions that he found a ruling of the Ketzos Hashulchan which contradicts his ruling, and he writes that seemingly the Ketzos Hashulchan forgot the ruling of Admur in 458:8. However in truth the Ketzos Hashulchan in his Hosafos does add the ruling of Admur there and nevertheless does not retract his final ruling said above.

[189] 158:3

[190] Admur 458:8 regarding Matzah on Pesach
<u>Other opinions</u>: Some Poskim allow breaking engraved letters that is on food. [M"B 340:15; SSH"K 11:8. Ra"sh Haleivi brought in Magen Avraham, although he himself concludes with Tzaruch Iyun]

[191] Ketzos Hashulchan 144 footnote 3; Shabbos Kehalacha Volume 3 p. 369; 20:73

[192] So rules Chazon Ish 61:1, brought in Piskeiy Teshuvos 140:4

[193] Ketzos Hashulchan 146 footnote 32

[194] As the Magen Avraham concludes with a Tzarich Iyun regarding the stringency of Avraham Halevy by engraved letters. [ibid] Now although Admur rules in 458:8 that engraved letters are forbidden to be broken, nevertheless see Ketzos Hashulchan 144 footnote 3 that this is only forbidden when one breaks it and then eats it, if however one breaks it within the process of eating it is allowed. Thus perhaps here too there is room to question whether erasing the letters in the process of using the soap is truly forbidden.

Compilation-May one eat biscuits, cakes, and the like, which have words/letters/pictures engraved on them?[195]

To break it and then eat it:[196] It is forbidden to break the letters that are on a food, even if the letters are engraved.[197] Accordingly, one may not break a piece off from the cake or biscuit if doing so entails breaking one of the letters.

To take a bite out from it: Some Poskim[198] rule that one may break engraved letters within the process of eating. Meaning, that one may break the letters in the process of taking a bite from the food, and the prohibition is only against breaking it with one's hands and then placing it into one's mouth.[199] However, other Poskim[200] rule they may not be broken even within the process of eating. According to this latter opinion, one may not give such foods to children that have reached the age of Chinuch. Practically, one is to speak to his Rav for a final ruling.

Engraved pictures:[201] Pictures and designs that are engraved onto a cake, biscuit and the like, may be eaten as normal on Shabbos.[202] One may even break a piece off and eat it, so long as there are no letters

---

[195] Ketzos Hashulchan 144 footnote 3

[196] Admur 458:8 "The symbols which are made on the Matzos should not be made through forms of letters using a molded imprint [i.e. cookie cutter], or with one's hands (for the reason explained in chapter 470 and others) **being that one is required to break them on Yom Tov, and there are opinions who prohibit to break a cake which has forms of letters on it even though he does not intend to erase the letters**, but rather to eat them on Yom Tov, as was explained in chapter 340. Rather these symbols are to be made through holes or grooves, as long as one is careful to extremely speed their process, as was explained in chapter 460, see there."; Teshuvas Rama 119; Chok Yaakov 475; Levush 473; Magen Avraham 340:6 leaves this matter with a Tzaruch Iyun

Other opinions: Some Poskim rule the erasing prohibition does not apply to the engraved letters that are on a food. [Ra"sh Haleivi brought in Magen Avraham 340:6, although he himself concludes with Tzaruch Iyun; Maharil; Degul Merivava 340; M"B 340:15; SSH"K 11:8]

[197] The reason: It is Rabbinically forbidden to erase letters on Shabbos even if one does not plan to write any letters in its place. [Admur 340:4]

[198] Ketzos Hashulchan 144 footnote 3 [His final ruling is written on page 151 at the end of the paragraph]; Shabbos Kehalacha Volume 3 p. 369; 20:73 [To note that the Ketzos Hashulchan did not mention this ruling in chapter 144 and only later was it mentioned by him in the glosses to the end of the 7th volume, nevertheless, it is implied from there that his conclusion is to allow breaking the letters in the process of eating. See however the case of a bottle cap with engraved letters that the Ketzos Hashulchan allows one to break it on Shabbos, although contradicts himself in the glosses to the end of volume 7. Vetzaruch Iyun. The Rebbe was once addressed this question of whether one may break engraved letters according to Admur, and the Rebbe answered that no conclusive stance can be taken on this issue. Vetzaruch Iyun, being that this matter is explicitly ruled on in Admur 458:8]

[199] The reason: The basis of this ruling is that a) There are Poskim [Degul Merivava 340; M"B 340:15] who always allow breaking all letters within the process of eating [chewing it] and b) There are Poskim [See Poskim ibid in other opinions] who allow breaking engraved letters even with one's hands. Thus, although Admur rules stringently regarding on breaking within process of eating [with regards to letters written with icing], while the Magen Avraham leaves in question regarding breaking engraved letters, when both leniencies are combined, such as breaking engraved letters of a biscuit within the process of eating, then one may be lenient. [Ketzos Hashulchan ibid] This seemingly holds true as well in accordance to the ruling of Admur in Hilchos Pesach 458:8, as there he writes that a) **some** opinions rule and b) it is forbidden to **break** the Matzah with engraved letters. This implied that taking a bite from it is allowed, as in such a case there are two reasons to assume the Sages would not make a decree, and one may rely on those opinions who argue on the "some opinions rule". Likewise, we similarly see in Admur 460:9 in which he implies that it is permitted to break Matzahs that contain engraved **pictures**. So is also the implied ruling of M"A 340:6 as he understood from the Mordechai [see Ketzos Hashulchan ibid] Now, in truth, pictures have the same status as letters regarding writing and erasing on Shabbos, as rules Admur 340:10, rather one must say that the Rabbinical decree against erasing was not made in all cases, and so too here, since there are two reasons to be lenient, it is permitted to be done.

The reason behind the leniency of engraved letters over external letters: The above allowance only applies to engraved letters, while external letters are prohibited to be broken even within the midst of eating. [Admur 343:10] Vetzaruch Iyun as why by engraved letters we are more lenient, as engraving is also prohibited due to writing. Some Poskim suggest that engraving letters is no longer common today, and thus, since one has no intent to write in the area that the letters are erased, in which case it is at the very most only a Rabbinical prohibition, therefore, the Sages did not make their decree, as they do not decree against uncommon cases, if it will prevent Oneg Shabbos. Now, although we see that Admur ibid and other Poskim ibid were stringent even regarding erasing engraved letters on foods, nonetheless, one can suggest that they did not extend the prohibition to a case of breaking them even within the process of eating, in contrast to external letters, which Admur forbids breaking even within the process of eating. [Ketzos Hashulchan 144 footnote 3]

[200] Rav Bitstritzky in Shut Ara Degalil p. 35; Piskeiy Teshuvos 340 that from Admur ibid it is implied that this too is forbidden; Rav Eliyahu Landa that the custom is to be careful not to eat such foods on Shabbos; See article of Rav Shalom Dovber Hertzel in Koveitz Ohalei Torah 1083 p. 108 [Rav Bistritzky does not make mention of the ruling of the Ketzos Hashulchan throughout his entire ruling. However, at the end in a footnote he mentions that he found a ruling of the Ketzos Hashulchan which contradicts his ruling, and he writes that seemingly the Ketzos Hashulchan forgot the ruling of Admur in 458:8. However, in truth the Ketzos Hashulchan in his Hosafos does add the ruling of Admur there and nevertheless does not retract his final ruling said above.]

[201] Implication of Admur 460:9; Beis Yosef 460 in name of Rabbeinu Yerucham; M"A 340:6 in his understanding of Mordechai; Ketzos Hashulchan 144 footnote 3

[202] The reason: It is unclear as to why Admur, and the Poskim ibid, are more lenient by engraved pictures than engraved letters, if they both are part of the same writing and erasing prohibition. However, perhaps the Sages did not apply their decree against erasing an engraved picture in such a situation, being it is not as common as erasing an engraved letter. [See Ketzos Hashulchan ibid] Alternatively, some suggest that there is no writing or erasing prohibition involved in **engraved pictures** [See Tehila Ledavid 340:3 in his initial understanding of Rambam-See Koveitz

on the cake.

Summary:
One may not break the engraved letters found on a food, although some are lenient to do so in the process of eating, through taking a bite, as opposed to breaking a piece off with one's hands. One may break the engraved picture of a food even with one's hands.

Q&A

May one dip a biscuit with engraved letters into a tea?
One may dip a biscuit that contains engraved letters into tea if doing so will not inevitably cause the biscuit to break in the area of the letters. If, however, the biscuit will break in the area of the letters then doing so is forbidden. [One must beware to wash his hands without a blessing prior to eating biscuits dipped in coffee or tea and the like, prior to eating them.[203]]

May one make cheesecake using whole biscuits that contain engraved words?
It is not advised to do so due to the eating restriction to be explained. If one did so, then care must be taken not to break the biscuits in a way that the letters will break.[204] According to some Poskim[205], however, one may eat the biscuits whole, having them break in his mouth.

---

8. Closing and opening books with writing on their side pages:
See above Chapter 1 Halacha 8

Practical Q&A

May one wash ink blotches or letters and drawings off his skin?[206]
See above Halacha 4 Q&A for all Q&A which relate to this!

May one open a cap of a bottle and the like which has engraved letters which will break upon opening it?[207]
This is to be done before Shabbos, however if one forgot to do so, some rule one may be lenient to open it on Shabbos being that the letters are engraved. [It however requires further analyses if this

---

Ohalei Torah 1083 p. 108] Now, although Admur 340:6 explicitly rules that one may not engrave into ash, perhaps that refers only to letters and not pictures. Now, although the Poskim do not differentiate between pictures and letters and rather rule that making a drawing is a Tolda of writing [See Admur 340:10; M"A 340:6; Rambam Shabbos 11:17; Degul Merivava 340; Tehila Ledavid 340:3] perhaps Admur holds that when it comes to pictures, there is a difference between writing and engraving. See Admur 340:10 who writes "One who makes marks and designs on a document and the like, in the way that the artists design, is liable due to an offshoot of the writing prohibition. The same applies for one who erases it." Admur does not simply write that pictures have the same status as writing, and qualifies the case with "**on a document..in the way that artists design..**" This extra wording of Admur seems to imply that there are cases that the writing prohibition does not apply to making a picture, and perhaps an engraved drawing is one of those cases. See also Admur 302:5 who writes "For example one who designs a [picture of a] figure on a vessel which is waiting to be designed on, even if he only designed part of the figure, he has done part of the finishing touch of the vessel and is liable [for a sin offering]. **As although the figure on its own is not considered a [Biblically] forbidden form of work**, nevertheless now that the vessel is complete and fixed through his action it is considered [a Biblically forbidden form of] work." If the above is correct, then there would be no prohibition to engrave pictures into non-Muktzah sand, a cake and the like. Vetzaruch Iyun, as I have not found any Poskim who suggest such a ruling.
[203] Admur 158:3
[204] Admur 458:8 regarding Matzah on Pesach
Other opinions: Some Poskim allow breaking engraved letters that is on food. [M"B 340:15; SSH"K 11:8. Ra"sh Haleivi brought in Magen Avraham, although he himself concludes with Tzaruch Iyun]
[205] Ketzos Hashulchan 144 footnote 3; Shabbos Kehalacha Volume 3 p. 369; 20:73
[206] Ketzos Hashulchan 144 footnote 10
[207] Ketzos Hashulchan 144 end of footnote 3. Vetzaruch Iyun from the glosses written at the end of volume 7 in which he writes that one may not [according to all opinions] break the engraved letters of a stationary being that in this case the letters have a change of color and **being that the allowance was only said regarding food products.**

allowance applies even according to the ruling of Admur that one is not to engrave letters on the Matzos.[208]]

May one break an egg that contains pink lettering?[209]

One may not break it within the letter area. This transgresses the prohibition of Mechikah/erasing. One however need not be hesitant against breaking it in the non-lettered area as even if it does accidently break the letters, one has not transgressed being that the breaking of the letters was not inevitable.

May one cut Chalah together with its label on Shabbos?[210]

One must beware not to cut the letters of the label. [One may only remove the label directly prior to the meal due to the Borer prohibition, and if one is using it for Lechem Mishna one is to only remove it after cutting the challah in order so it remain complete.]

May one tear the wrapper of a food that contains words or pictures on it?[211]

One must beware not to cut the wrapper in a way that the letters will inevitably be torn. [One however need not be hesitant against tearing it in the non-lettered area as even if it does accidently break the letters, one has not transgressed being that the breaking of the letters was not inevitable.] If it is not possible to avoid cutting the letters, then in a time of need some Poskim[212] allow one to do so with an irregularity.[213]

May one use tissues or toilet paper that has letters or pictures on them?

This matter is disputed amongst Poskim. Some Poskim[214] rule that it is Rabbinically forbidden to use such tissues or toilet paper, as is always the law regarding tearing letters and pictures. However other Poskim[215] rule that it is permitted to use them being that one is destroying the paper in the process and thus it is no longer possible to now write on the item. Practically if one has nothing else available this may be used.[216]

May one erase letters or pictures on a magnetic board?[217]

Doing so is [Rabbinically] forbidden.

---

[208] Perhaps this ruling of Admur regarding matzos is only Lechatchilah. Meaning that initially one is not to enter himself into a situation that he will be required to break the engraved letters. After the fact however perhaps Admur agrees that one may be lenient. Vetzaruch Iyun.

[209] Ketzos Hashulchan 144 footnote 10; Kaf Hachayim 340:34; Shabbos Kihalacha Vol. 1 p. 288

[210] Ketzos Hashulchan 144 footnote 3 towards end.

[211] Piskeiy Teshuvos 140:4

[212] Az Nidbaru 10:8

[213] As this is considered a Rabbinical prohibition within a Rabbinical prohibition [1) irregularity and 2) erasing not with intent to write] which is permitted in a case of Pisek Reisha.

[214] Daas Torah 340:3; Bris Olam Mocheik 5

[215] Mahrshag 2:41

[216] As it is being ruined with an irregularity which makes it a double Dirabanan of Piseik Reishei as well as that there are Poskim which always permit this.

[217] A magnetic board is used by using a magnetic pen to lift the small pieces of metal and one can thus form a word.

CHAPTER 4: THE LAWS OF MEAMEIR
Gathering Scattered items on Shabbos.

1. The Av Melacha:[1]
The action of Meameir [gathering stalks] is one of the principal Shabbos prohibitions which occurred in the Tabernacle with the planted herbs.

2. The Biblical Prohibition:[2]
A. The Gathering is being done in area of growth unless being pressed into one mass
First Opinion: It is only considered [the Melacha of] Meameir when one gathers [the produce] in the area of its growth, similar to the harvesting of stalks of which the ears of grain are gathered in their area of growth.
Second Opinion-Making items into one mass: ([However] there are opinions which say that one who presses fruits [together] until they form one mass is liable for Meameir even when he does so not in the place of its growth such as) one who gathers figs and makes from it a round cake [of pressed figs] or punctures the figs and enters a rope through them until they gather and form one mass, then this is an offshoot of the Meameir prohibition and one is liable, and so too any cases of the like.
The Final Ruling: (One must be stringent like their words [of the latter opinion).

B. Items that grow from the ground:
The [Biblical] Meameir prohibition only applies with [the gathering of] items which grow from the ground. [However, Rabbinically it applies to all items as will be explained next.]

3. The Rabbinical prohibition-Gathering items that do not grow from ground in their area of growth:[3]
Rabbinically gathering is forbidden to be done even with items that do not grow on the ground, [meaning that it is forbidden] to gather them in their area of growth.
Example-Gathering salt from their deposits: For example [it is Rabbinically forbidden] to gather salt from the evaporated deposits of water, [these deposits] evaporates the water and create the salt and so too with all cases of the like.

4. Permitted form of gathering-Gathering from out of the area of growth:[4]
First Opinion: If the [fruits] have dispersed into another area [out from its original place of growth] then it is permitted to gather them as written in chapter 335 [Halacha 5].
Second Opinion-Making items into one mass out from their area of growth: ([However] there are opinions which say that one who presses fruits [together] until they form one mass is liable for Meameir even when he does so not in the place of its growth such as) one who gathers figs and makes from it a round cake [of pressed figs] or punctures the figs and enters a rope through them until they gather and form one mass, then this is an offshoot of the Meameir prohibition and one is liable, and so too any cases of the like.
The Final Ruling: (One must be stringent like the words [of the latter opinion and thus not turn into one mass, items that are gathered even out of their area of growth].)
Gathering all the food together versus a little at a time: Scattered fruits: See Halacha 5. Other items: See Halacha 5 Q&A there!
Placing the gathered item into a basket: Scattered fruits: See Halacha 5 Other items: See Halacha 5 Q&A there!

---

[1] Admur 340:15
[2] Admur 340:15
[3] Admur 340:15
[4] Admur 340:15

Summary of Gathering items on Shabbos [1-4]:

In area of growth: It is forbidden to gather items together within their area of growth. This applies to both items which grow from the ground [in which case gathering them in their area of growth is Biblically forbidden] and items that do not grow from the ground such as salt [in which case gathering them there consists of a Rabbinical prohibition].

Out of area of growth: It is forbidden [according to some Biblically] to gather items together and press them into one mass, such as a fig ring, even out of their area of growth.

It is permitted to gather items out of their area of growth if one does not press it into one mass.[5] Regarding gathering the items into one basket and gathering them all together in one time-see the next Halacha!

---

5. Gathering scattered fruits:

A. From under the tree which they grew on:[6]

One who gathers fruits and joins them together in the area where they fell off the tree [has transgressed the Meameir prohibition].

B. From an area which they have not grown in:[7]

Gathering fruits which scattered in courtyard: One's whose fruits scattered in his courtyard, one [fruit going] to one area and another to another area, may gather a small amount of them at a time and eat [them]. However, he may not place [the gathered fruits] into a basket or into a box.

The reason for this: Is so one not [gather the fruits] in the same way that he does so during the week [which is considered a mundane act[8]].

Gathering fruits which have fallen into one area: However, if the fruits have fallen into one area [and did not scatter] then one may place them even into a basket or box.

If they fell into one area but is amongst pebbles and dust: However, one whose fruits have [fallen] into pebbles and dust, may only be gathered one at a time [in order] to eat [right away[9]]. However, he may not place them into a basket or box. [**See Q&A regarding if this applies to other foods**]

The reason for this is:[10] So he does not do a mundane act [which resembles Borer[11]].

---

[5] So is implied from Admur and so rules M"B 340:37. However Piskeiy Teshuvos 340:24 brings from Bris Olam that gathering items even out of their place of growth is forbidden due to Meameir. Vetzaruch Iyun Gadol on his source.

[6] Admur 340:15

[7] Admur 335:5

[8] Some explain that the intent of this mundane act prohibition is due to it being troublesome to gather all the fruits. [Bris Olam Meameir 7] According to this all-scattered items which are troublesome to be gathered would carry the same restrictions as gathering fruits and it would thus be forbidden to gather them a lot at a time and place them into a basket. [Az Nidbaru 14:17 brought in Piskeiy Teshuvos 335:1]

[9] Shabbos Kehalacha 14:45

This requirement for it to be done for right away use is due to the Borer restrictions, and is irrelevant to the laws of Meameir. Thus, in a case that the fruits scattered on a clear floor in which the fruits are not mixed with any other items, it may be gathered for even later on use, so long as it is done for a Shabbos need. [Compiler]

[10] 335:5

[11] Ketzos Hashulchan 146 p. 98 number 2; However the M"B explains that this is forbidden simply because of Uvdin Dichol. The Ketzos Hashulchan ibid questions this explanation of the M"B and thus gives his alternative explanation mentioned above.

Summary-Gathering scattered fruits:

From area of growth: Is always forbidden.

Out of area of growth:

- Scattered to different directions: Fruits which have scattered to different directions, not within their area of growth, may only be gathered a small amount at a time in order to eat and may not be placed into a basket or box.

- Fell into same area: Fruits which have fallen into the same area, then if the area does not contain dust and pebbles, one may gather the fruits in order to eat and he may place them into a basket or box. However, fruits which have fallen into pebbles and dust may only be gathered one at a time in order to eat but may not be placed into a basket or box even if they have fallen into the same area.

Q&A

May one gather the fruit into his pocket or shirt in a case that it may not be gathered into a basket?

Some rule[12] that this has the same ruling as does a basket, and is thus forbidden. Others[13] rule that in a case that the fruits scattered and are **not** mixed with pebbles and dirt then they may be gathered into ones shirt.

If the fruits are in danger of being ruined if left un-gathered may one be lenient to gather them into a basket?[14]

Seemingly one may be lenient in such a case. Certainly, one may be lenient to gather them into one's shirt.

Does the above restriction to only gather items a little at a time and not to place them in a basket apply by all scattered items or only by fruit?[15]

Some[16] learn that if it is troublesome to gather the items then it has the same restrictions as fruits.

Does this restriction against placing a selected food into a basket apply to other foods as well or only to fruits that have fallen into earth?[17]

From the letter of the law, it does not apply to any other situation other than the one listed above, and thus so long as one plans to eat the selected item right away, he may place it anywhere he wishes.[18] However, there are opinions[19] which are stringent in this with regards to all cases to restrict one from placing the selected food in one's pocket or designated basket even if he plans to eat it right away. Nevertheless, even according to them it is allowed to place the food on the eating table or one's plate and he does not have to literally place it his mouth directly following the separation.

---

[12] M"B 335:18; See Shabbos Kehalacha 12:45 in the stringent opinion there!

[13] Ketzos Hashulchan 146 footnote 50 -7

[14] Ketzos Hashulchan 146 footnote 50 -7, brought in Piskeiy Teshuvos 340:24

[15] Piskeiy Teshuvos 340:24 and 335:1

[16] Az Nidbaru ibid

[17] Shabbos Kehalacha 12:45

[18] So rules the Beis Yosef and Tosefas Rid, and so rules Rav Farkash proving that this too is the opinion of Admur.

[19] So rules the Igleiy Tal, brought in Ketzos Hashulchan 125 footnote 8

General Q&A

May one gather eggs from a chicken coop on Shabbos? [20]
It is forbidden to be done even if the eggs were laid before Shabbos and are not Muktzah as gathering items that do not grow from the ground.[21] However, if delaying their gathering will cause a great loss one may be lenient to ask a gentile to gather them.[22]

May one gather non-Muktzah papers which have scattered on the floor? [23]
According to some opinions if it is troublesome to gather them then this would have the same restrictions as do fruits and may thus only be gathered a little at a time and may not be entered into a basket.

May one gather apples which fell and scattered on one's floor?
See summary of gathering scattered fruits.

May one make a necklace or bracelet by entering items into them? [24]
This is forbidden due to the prohibition against fixing a vessel[25], and according to others[26] also due to the "Meameir" prohibition. Some[27] however permit it to be done, as they say that the Meameir prohibition only applies by gathering items that grow from the ground, and they do not hold that doing so involves the fixing prohibition.[28]

May one make a flower bouquet on Shabbos?
Some Poskim[29] rule it is forbidden to do so.[30] According to these Poskim it is forbidden to be done even if one does not tie the flowers together and simply places them in the same vase.

---

[20] Ketzos Hashulchan 146 footnote 49-22.

[21] As gathering items that do not grow from the ground in their area of growth [which in this case is the coop] is Rabbinically forbidden.

[22] Sheivet Haleivi 4:39 As is always the ruling regarding asking a gentile to do a Rabbinical prohibition in a time of great need.

[23] Piskeiy Teshuvos 340:24

[24] Ketzos Hashulchan 146 footnote 49-25; Piskeiy Teshuvos 340:26

[25] Ketzos Hashulchan 146 footnote 49-25

[26] Orchos Chayim 13

[27] Shevisas Hashabbos Meameir

[28] According to all it does not involve the writing prohibition as there is no prohibition in forming a word as explained above.

[29] Igros Moshe 4:73

[30] This is forbidden due to fixing a vessel, as the gathering of the different flowers to make a bouquet are considered making a nice vessel out of the flowers. [ibid] However see Ketzos Hashulchan 8 p. 92 which seems to imply that the only question involved in gathering the flowers together is the prohibition of Miameir. However, when done outside of the area of growth, such as in one's home, it is permitted. Hence implying doing so does not carry the Tikkun Keli prohibition. Vetzaruch Iyun on the essence of the logic itself to consider simply placing flowers near each other as Tikkun Keli. It does not appear at all like one is making a Keli. This is unlike a necklace which when one enters the beads it is clearly apparent as if one is making a Keli. Vetzaruch Iyun.

CHAPTER 5: THE LAWS OF SEWING, GLUING AND TAPING ITEMS TOGETHER ON SHABBOS

1. The Biblical prohibition-Sewing a stable set of stitches:[1]
One who sews two stitches and [makes] a knot [at its end], or three stitches even if he does not make a knot [at its end] is liable [to bring a sin offering]. However [one who sews] two stitches and does not make a knot is exempt [from Biblical liability, although it is Rabbinically forbidden].
The reason for this is: because [in such a case the sewing] does not last.
Tying prohibition: One who makes a knot [in any of the above cases] is also liable for the tying prohibition.

2. The Rabbinical prohibition-sewing an unstable set of stitches:[2]
Rabbinically forbidden to make two stitches without a knot: Although [one who sews] two stitches which is defined as sewing is not meant to last forever and does not make a knot is exempt [from Biblical liability], it is [nevertheless] Rabbinically forbidden.

Summary-Sewing:
It is forbidden to stitch threads into an item even the threads will not last[3].

Practical Q&A on Sewing
Is sewing permitted if it will only last temporarily, or will not last at all?
It is clear from the above ruling, that even temporary sewing, which is defined as sewing that is not meant to last forever, is at the very least Rabbinically forbidden to be done on Shabbos. It is unclear however if this Rabbinical prohibition applies even if the sewing is not meant to last at all, not even for 24 hours.[4]

---

[1] Admur 340:12
[2] Admur 340:12
[3] If it will not last, such as if he made two stitches without a knot at its end, it is Rabbinically forbidden. If it will last, such as three stitches or two with a knot at its end, then it is Biblically forbidden.
[4] Regarding other prohibitions we find that although the sages forbade doing even temporary Melacha, such as to make an act that is only meant to last temporarily, or attach the parts of a vessel even if it's only meant to last temporarily, nonetheless, they permit it if it's not meant to last anytime at all, which is defined as less than 24 hours or within that day. The question therefore is raised as to whether we apply the same leniency as well to the laws of sewing. Vetzaruch Iyun! Indeed, the Poskim of today debate this matter in their discussion of whether or not it's permitted to use diapers that contain an adhesive sticker being that is not meant to last even for a day.

May one attach two sides of his clothing using a safety pin?[5]

Regarding making it into a double stitch: Some Poskim[6] rule that this should not be done. Others[7] rule that so long as it is not meant to be placed there for permanent use [as is usually the case] it is allowed.[8] The Rebbe[9] defends the practice of making even double and triple stitches for use on Shabbos, however he forbids making more than three stitches.

A single stitch:[10]: According to all[11] one may enter the pin into a single stitch, which means that he enters it on one side and has it lift out on the other side.

May one staple papers together or remove staples from papers on Shabbos?[12]

It is forbidden to staple paper or other items together due to the sewing prohibition. This is prohibited from being done even if one plans to leave the items attached with the staple for a very short while.[13]

As well it is forbidden to remove staples from items which have been stapled to last there permanently.[14] However by items which their staple will eventually be removed, as is the case by a stapled envelope, some opinions[15] allow one to remove the staple, while others[16] are stringent.

May one place a clasp on an ace bandage to fasten it together?[17]

Yes, as explained above regarding safety pins.

May one enter or remove papers from a metal binder on Shabbos?[18]

Yes. However, there are Poskim[19] which are stringent regarding binders that use a flexible metal strip to folds over the papers in order to bind them.

Is zippering two items together forbidden due to the sewing prohibition?

Some opinions[20] rule that this is forbidden when done with intention to leave the item attached for a

---

[5] Piskeiy Teshuvos 340:22

[6] Mishneh Berurah 340:27, in name of Karban Nisanel; Minchas Yitzchak 2:19; Sheivet Haleivi 4:35; Poseik who wrote to Rebbe about forbidding pinning clothing on Shabbos.

[7] Sharreiy Teshuvah 340:3; Chazon Ish Supplements to Orach Chayim 156; Igros Moshe 4:84; Tzitz Eliezer 13:43

[8] The reason for this leniency is because: a) The concept of sewing does not apply to metal; b) It is not made to last [of which is only Rabbinically forbidden] c) Is being done for a Shabbos use. It is thus permitted as by a Rabbinical prohibition within a Rabbinical prohibition we are lenient.

for a Shabbos use. [Rebbe in Shaareiy Halacha Uminhag 2:164]

[9] Shaareiy Halacha Uminhag 2:164

[10] So is implied from M"B 340:27, and so rules Minchas Yitzchak ibid, Rebbe in Shaareiy Halacha Uminhag Ibid and the other stringent opinions regarding making two stitches, that by one stitch it is permitted according to all.

[11] So writes Rebbe in Shaareiy Halacha Uminhag ibid

[12] Piskeiy Teshuvos 340:20

[13] Bris Olam Tofer 8; SSH"K 28 Footnote 17

[14] Az Nidbaru 1:58

[15] SSH"K 28:5

[16] Az Nidbaru Ibid

[17] SSH"K 35:22

[18] Piskeiy Teshuvos 340:20

[19] Yesodeiy Yeshurun 1:201

[20] Sheivet Haleivi Vol. 3 chapter 51

long period of time.[21] Others[22] however rule that it is allowed.

May one zipper the wool lining on to a coat?
If done with intent to only leave on for a short amount of time it is permitted according to all. If, however, one intends to leave the lining in the coat for a long period of time then some opinions rule it is forbidden to do so, as this is similar to fixing a vessel[23], as well as that doing so resembles sewing.[24] Others[25] however rule it is allowed even in such a case.

May one attach items together using Velcro?
Yes, as there is no sewing involved here at all but rather just placing of strings onto hoops.

May magnets be used on Shabbos?[26]
Yes.[27] One may thus play with games that involve magnets and may attach a non-Muktzah magnet to a fridge.[28]

---

3. Pulling a thread to tighten the connection between the parts of clothing:[29]
A clothing which was sturdily sewed and its thread was left sticking out[30], and two parts of the clothing slightly split apart from each other with the threads of the sewing sticking out, then if one pulls the head of the threads in order to tighten and connect the two sides, it is considered sewing and one is liable [to bring a sin offering]. [This applies] even if one has not made a knot [at its end] if [the amount that the clothing have reconnected] is like the amount of three stitches.
Pulling the thread that tightens the sleeves of shirts: Those [people] who tighten their clothing around their arms through [pulling] a thread which pulls and tightens it, [are forbidden to do so as it] is forbidden to pull [such a thread] on Shabbos due to the sewing prohibition.
The reason it is forbidden: (Now, although the sewing is not one that will last being that one only tightens it at the time that he wears it while at the time that he removes it he loosens it, nevertheless it is Rabbinically forbidden being that it is similar to sewing.)
If the holes are wide, round, and sewed: It is only allowed if [the shirt] has slightly wide holes which are fixed in with sewing and [the hole is] round in circumference, in which case it is no longer similar to sewing[31].
Walking into a public domain with a needle attached to this thread: [In the above circumstance that the holes are wide, round and fixed with sewing] then even if the thread is inserted into a sewing needle [a needle with a hole] it is permitted to go out with it [into a public domain] since it is always connected to the thread, and the thread [is always connected] to the clothing, and it is thus an accessory to the clothing.
If one is able to remove the clothing without loosening the tightened thread: If the clothing is not greatly tightened by this thread to the point that one must loosen it when he removes [the clothing in order so it

---

[21] As this is similar to fixing a vessel, as well as that doing so is like sewing. [ibid]
[22] SS"K 15:74 based on a ruling of Rav Shlomo Zalman Aurbauch.
[23] Chelkas Yaakov 4:24
[24] Sheivet Halevy Vol. 3 chapter 51
[25] Beir Moshe and SS"K 15:74 based on a ruling of Rav Shlomo Zalman Aurbauch.
[26] See Shulchan Shlomo 2:314 [One may play with games that have magnets]
Other opinions: Some rule that if the magnet will be left in place for some time as is common by magnets of a fridge then it is forbidden. [SSH"K 46 [new print]; Rav Elyashiv in Migdal David p. 599 footnote 28]
[27] It is not considered Tofer as there is no third item that attaches the two things together but rather a magnetic pull. [see Beir Moshe 29]
[28] It is not forbidden due to Boneh even if one decides to leave the magnet in place for a long time being that placing the magnet on the surface is not considered that one is building on the surface [as would be hammering a nail and the like] and it serves the fridge no benefit. Furthermore, perhaps a magnetic pull is not viewed as any real attachment and hence it is no different than resting a piece of paper on a fridge which certainly is not considered building. See also 315:6 that it is permitted to even permanently hang a decorative sheet on a wall.
[29] Admur 340:13
[30] Lit. Long
[31] As this is like placing hooks into loops which has no resemblance of a Melacha. [M"B 29]

come off], but rather at times he changes his mind and decides to leave it this way eternally being that he is [anyways] able to remove it this way with it remaining slightly tightened, then it is forbidden to tighten it on Shabbos in all cases [even if the holes are wide and round and are fixed with sewing, and even if he does plan to loosen it].

The reason for this is: because perhaps one will change his mind and decide to leave it this way for ever, and it is thus found that he made a sewing which will last, and by a permanent sewing it does not help the fact that the holes are wide and are fixed with sewing and are round.

Summary:
It is forbidden to tighten two loose parts of a cloth by pulling at the thread that is sticking out, even if one is doing so for temporary use, like to undo that day.[32] Thus the sleeves of a shirt which have a thread which is pulled on in order to tighten may not be used unless a) the hole from where the thread protrudes is round and b) the hole is fixed in by having been stitched around its circumference, and c) One is unable to remove the sleeve without loosening the thread, thus guaranteeing that one will not leave it permanently in its tightened state.

Q&A

May one pull the drawstring[33] of a garbage bag or sweatpants to tighten it?
Yes. This may be done even if one plans to leave it tightened permanently, as the above is not similar at all to sewing being that its holes [which contain the draw strings] are large and the string itself is not at all similar to a thread.

May one tighten a loose button through pulling on one of its threads?[34]
Doing so is forbidden due to the sewing prohibition.

---

4. Weaving and unraveling ropes and wicks:[35]
See Volume 2 "The Laws of Tying and Untying on Shabbos"!

5. Gluing things together:[36]
One who attaches papers or skins with glue of the scribes and the like is [doing] an offshoot of the sewing [prohibition] and is liable.

Summary:
It is forbidden to glue items together on Shabbos.

Q&A

Is gluing permitted for temporary purpose, or if it will not last at all?
The ruling regarding sewing is that even temporary sewing, which is defined as sewing that is not meant to last forever, is at the very least Rabbinically forbidden to be done on Shabbos. It is unclear however if this Rabbinical prohibition applies even if the sewing is not meant to last at all, not even for 24 hours.[37] Seemingly, this same law and its subsequent doubt would apply likewise to gluing, and

---

[32] If the amount that the clothing have reconnected is like the amount of three stitches then one is Biblically liable even if he does not make a knot at its end.

[33] This refers to a string or cord that is placed in garbage bags, sweatpants and the like to serve easy fastening.

[34] SSH"K 15:8; Piskeiy Teshuvos 340:20

[35] Admur 317:11

[36] Admur 340:17

[37] Regarding other prohibitions we find that although the sages forbade doing even temporary Melacha, such as to make an act that is only meant to last temporarily, or attach the parts of a vessel even if it's only meant to last temporarily, nonetheless, they permit it if it's not meant to last anytime at all, which is defined as less than 24 hours or within that day. The question therefore is raised as to whether we apply the same leniency

thus it is forbidden to glue things together even for a temporary purpose however if it is not meant to last at all then this matter would be under question.

May one use scotch tape on Shabbos to tape things together?
Doing so is forbidden even when done for temporary use. In addition, cutting the piece of tape from the role contains a fixing prohibition.

May one use a piece of tape to tape a bandage onto one's skin?[38]
One may not do so due to the sewing prohibition.[39] However, if there is no other option of attaching the bandage to the wound then there is an opinion[40] which allows one to tape the bandage to one's skin if both ends of the tape are on one's skin. [Meaning the bandage is in the middle of the tape.] [However, the tape must be cut before Shabbos as will be explained in next question.] Others[41] however argue on this and hold that even in such a way that the ends of the tape are on one's skin it is still forbidden being that the bandage will permanently remain attached to the tape after removing it. **[For Opinion of Admur see footnote.[42]]**

May one place pictures into an album which contains cellophane to keep the picture in place?
No, as this is similar to gluing the picture to the album background, which is forbidden due to the sewing prohibition.

May one use "post it" notes on Shabbos?
No, as this is similar to sewing something temporarily.

May one seal an envelope on Shabbos through wetting the top lining and pressing it down?
No.

May one reattach the tape of the binding of a Sefer which is beginning to peel off?
No.

May children play with stickers on Shabbos?
Based on the ruling above that even temporary sticking of items is forbidden onShabbos, children who are above the age of Chinuch are to be educated not to play with stickers on Shabbos.

May one use sticker jewelry [earrings] on Shabbos?
Although there is seemingly no issue with placing it on one's skin[43], removing the plastic covering from the sticky surface could be an issue of Koreia, as explained regarding diapers.

---

as well to the laws of sewing. Vetzaruch Iyun! Indeed, the Poskim of today debate this matter in their discussion of whether or not it's permitted to use diapers that contain an adhesive sticker being that is not meant to last even for a day.
[38] Piskeiy Teshuvos 328:21
[39] As one is sewing the tape onto the bandage. Tzitz Eliezer 8:15-14-6-unless is a time of need, as will be explained; SSH"K 34:25 in all cases even in a time of need.
[40] Tzitz Eliezer 8:15-14-6
[41] SS"K 34:25 and footnote 64 in name of Rav SZ"A
[42] According to Admur [340:17] seemingly it would be forbidden due to sewing even if one were able to remove the bandage from the tape as Admur holds that only when the tape is place unintentionally may it be removed, and here it is placed intentionally. Vetzaruch Iyun.
[43] See Tzitz Eliezer 8:15-14-6

6. The Tearing prohibition- Tearing sewed items and separating items that were glued together?

See Volume 2 "The Laws of Cutting and Tearing items on Shabbos" for the full elaboration on this subject.

Below [in the gray table] is a brief summary which relates to the tearing prohibition that corresponds to the sewing prohibition. It does not relate to the cutting and fixing prohibition which may also apply.

Summary:

<u>Cutting and tearing sewn threads:</u> The tearing prohibition applies when one tears or separates two entities from each other, even if one does not have intent to reattach them[44], if the attachment was meant to last. The tearing prohibition does not apply by tearing a single entity. If the sewn items were meant to be eventually torn then it may be torn not in the presence of an ignoramus.

In all cases that there is no tearing prohibition involved in tearing an item one must verify that there is likewise no cutting or fixing prohibition involved in doing so.

<u>Separating glued items:</u> It is forbidden to separate glued items if the items were glued to be permanently attached. If they are not meant to be attached and were accidently glued on their own, as at times occurs during book binding that glue or wax attaches pages together, than they may be separated on Shabbos. [**See Q&A regarding if they were intentionally glued to last a very short time!**]

Q&A

May one separate items that were intentionally glued for temporary purpose?[45]

This may be done not in the presence of an ignoramus.[46]

May one place a band-aid on a wound on Shabbos?[47]

Doing so may involve the tearing prohibition when opening it and the sewing prohibition when applying it.

<u>Opening the band-aid:</u> Some Poskim[48] rule that the band-aid must have its wrapping as well as its white plastic sheet which covers over the tape, removed from before Shabbos. Removing it on Shabbos involves the tearing prohibition. However other Poskim[49] hold that the band-aid may even be opened on Shabbos, and doing so involves no suspicion at all of a prohibition. [Seemingly according to Admur it must be removed from before Shabbos.]

<u>Applying the band-aid to the wound:</u> May be done if both sides of the band-aid are fastened to one's skin[50] as opposed to one's clothing or to the other end of the band-aid. [51]

May one use diapers on Shabbos which are fastened using a piece of tape or Velcro which is attached to the diaper?

<u>Velcro diapers:</u> May be used in all cases.

<u>Adhesive tape:</u> This matter is disputed amongst Poskim in whether it is allowed. Some are stringent to prohibit using it even if one opened the tape from before Shabbos. Others are lenient even if he forgot to open it from before Shabbos.

<u>Below is a full analysis on the subject:</u>

The following "Sewing" and "Tearing" related questions apply by diapers which are attached using tape:

---

[44] In such a case it is Rabbinically forbidden. It is Biblically forbidden if torn with intent to re-sew.

[45] Minchas Yitzchak 8:31

[46] As rules Admur regarding tearing a temporary stitch.

[47] Piskeiy Teshuvos 328:21

[48] Minchas Yitzchak 5:39

[49] Beir Moshe 1:36; See Beir Moshe 2:29:2 that it only applies when a third item is sticking two items together.

[50] As there is no sewing prohibition relevant to sticking something to ones skin.

[51] Beir Moshe 1:36

1) Opening up the tape which involves removing the tape from the plastic covering. 2) Placing the tape onto the diaper when fastening it onto the child. 3) Removing the tape from the fastened diaper upon changing it. The following is the Halachic rulings in the above.

-Removing the protective covering from the tape: Many Poskim[52] hold that opening the tape is forbidden due to the tearing prohibition[53] and thus may only be done if one had previously opened it before Shabbos. Other Poskim[54] hold that if this was not done then it is allowed to open it on Shabbos[55].

-Attaching the diaper to the child: Some Poskim[56] hold that placing the tape on the diaper to fasten it is forbidden due to sewing[57]. Many others[58] however rule that this is allowed being that it is not made to last at all.

-Removing the Diaper from the child: Some Poskim[59] hold that removing the tape from the diaper in the process of changing the baby may only be done in private and not in the presence of an ignoramus[60]. Other Poskim[61] rule that one may remove the tape without restriction. According to all one is to avoid re-taping the diaper up after having removed it and then throw it out as is commonly done during the week.

Question:
May sticky note placeholders be used on Shabbos? Basically, I have little sticky notes that I used as page holders in my Sefarim, and I would like to know if it's permitted for me to take them off and put them on another page, as a placeholder. I don't know if it makes a difference, but the sticky notes are actually manufactured for this purpose to be used as page holders.

Answer:
It is forbidden to be used on Shabbos whether to remove them from a page or to stick them back onto a page. Their manufacturing purpose is irrelevant.

Explanation: It is forbidden to glue stuff together on Shabbos due to a sewing prohibition, and it is rabbinically forbidden to do so even if it is only meant to last temporarily. It is likewise forbidden to remove even temporary glued items from a page due to the tearing prohibition, with exception to certain circumstances.

Sources: See Admur 340:12 and 17; 317:7 [permitted for scholar to remove temporary sewing not in the face of an ignoramus]; See the following Sefarim regarding the similar discussion if the sewing and tearing prohibition applies to the adhesive part of a diaper, however in this case that the placeholder is meant to last for as long as needed it would be forbidden according to all: Minchas Yitzchak 8:31; 9:41; Mishneh Halachos 8:60; Kinyan Torah 5:26; Lehoros Nasan brought in Piskeiy Teshuvos 340 footnote 101; Sheivet Halevy 5:31; Az Nidbaru 6:31; Yechaveh Daas 6:25, Tzitz Eliezer 16:6; Beir

[52] Tzitz Eliezer 16:6; see Minchas Yitzchak 5:39 regarding removing the plastic cover from a band aid in which he rules it is forbidden. Shemiras Shabbos K'hilchoso 15:81, Az Nidberu 13:25, Shevet Ha'Levi 5:78, Yechaveh Da'as 6:24, Machzei Eliyahu 71, Be'er Moshe 6:14, Chut Shuni Shabbos 1:17: page 137
[53] As it is meant to be attached to the plastic part so long as it is not used. It is thus an attachment that is meant to last some time.
[54] Az Nidberu 7:34; Yechaveh Daas 6:25
[55] As they hold that if one were to buy the diaper that day then it would be meant to be opened that same day,, and thus the attachment of the tape to the plastic part is not really meant to last.
[56] Minchas Yitzchak 8:31; 9:41; Mishneh Halachos 8:60; Kinyan Torah 5:26; Lehoros Nasan brought in Piskeiy Teshuvos 340 footnote 101
[57] As a) The attachment is at the very least considered temporary which is also forbidden in the laws of sewing. [Minchas Yitzchak ibid]. b) Because the tape never gets removed from the diaper as it tears part of the diaper off with it upon opening the tape, and thus regarding that part which gets removed with the tape it is considered a permanent attachment. [Lehoros Nasan, and so ruled to me Rav Asher Lemel Kohen]
[58] Sheivet Halevy 5:31; Az Nidbaru 6:31; Yechaveh Daas 6:25, Tzitz Eliezer 16:6; Beir Moshe 6:14; SSH"K 15:81.
[59] Minchas Yitzchak ibid.
[60] As rules Rama and Admur in 317 regarding tearing the sewn stitches of the collar done by the laundry mat to keep it temporarily in place.
[61] Sheivet Halevy 5:31; Az Nidbaru 6:31; Yechaveh Daas 6:25, Tzitz Eliezer 16:6; Beir Moshe 6:14; SSH"K 15:81.

Moshe 6:14; SSH"K 15:81

CHAPTER 6: READING ON SHABBOS
The laws pertaining to reading books, papers, documents and other forms of writing, on Shabbos

1. Reading business documents and contracts:[1]
Laymen documents, such as loan, business, collateral, and accounting documents, and the like of matters which are forbidden to be done on Shabbos, are forbidden to be read on Shabbos due to the decree of "Mimtzoe Cheftzecha".

Reading them in ones thought without verbalizing: Furthermore, even to read in ones thought without verbalizing [the words] is forbidden.

The reason why even in thought it is forbidden: It was only said that speech is forbidden while thought is permitted when it is not evident [to others] that one is thinking about forbidden matters. However here that it is evident to all that one is thinking of the forbidden matters which are written in the document, it is thus included in the prohibition of "Mimtzoe Cheftzacha" just as was included in this [decree against] one who is strolling in his field to see what it requires. As although strolling in a field is a permitted matter in it of itself, as well as thinking about the needs of one's field is a permitted matter, nevertheless since it is apparent to all that he is strolling there for this purpose, it is therefore forbidden due to "Mimtzoe Cheftzecha", as was written in chapter 306 [Halacha 1-2].

Summary:
It is forbidden to read, whether verbally or in one's mind, business documents such as loans, contracts and all matters of the like which are forbidden to be done on Shabbos. This is due to the decree of Mimtzo Cheftzecha, that one is not to do weekday activity on Shabbos.

2. Reading non-business related writings:[2]
[In addition to the above decree against business documents] they decreed against reading any type of writing, even if it does not contain matters which are forbidden [to do on Shabbos]. Even to read it without verbalizing is forbidden.

The reason for this is: due to a decree that one may come to read, either verbally or in ones thought, layman documents.

Summary:
It is forbidden to read, whether verbally or in one's mind, even non-business related writings due to a decree that this may lead one to come to read business documents.

3. Reading the guest list for one's meal:
The letter of the law:[3] Based on the above, one who invited guests and prepared for them delicacies and wrote before Shabbos the names of the guests which were invited so he not forget to call them on Shabbos, or he wrote the name of delicacies which he prepared for them, it is forbidden to read this writing on Shabbos. Even to read in ones thought without verbalizing is forbidden.

The custom today:[4] In today's time it is accustomed that the servant calls for the meal from the writing which has the names of the meal guests written on it.

The reason it is permitted: There are those which have learned merit on this custom being that this is only

---
[1] Admur 307:21
[2] Admur 307:22
[3] Admur 307:22
[4] Admur 307:23

accustomed to be done by feasts of a Mitzvah, and for the need of a Mitzvah there is not to be decreed [against reading non-document related material] due to that one may come to read laymen documents, being that the prohibition against reading laymen documents , is itself only because of "Mimtzo Cheftzecha", and the prohibition of Mimtzo Cheftzecha does not apply by the matter of a Mitzvah. As matters of heaven which are forbidden to be done on Shabbos are permitted to be spoken of, and no decree was made by heavenly matters that one may come to also permit mundane matters. Thus, certainly there is not to decree by a Mitzvah matter against permitted matters due to that one may come to read laymen documents, and will transgress the prohibition of Mimtzo Cheftzecha.

Furthermore, it should not be prohibited here due to a decree that one may come to erase [a name from the list], as this [decree] is only relevant to decree against the host himself, which has the power to erase and diminish the number of guests. However, the servant has no power to remove [a guest] and thus there is no reason to forbid him [from reading the guest list] if not for that he may come to read laymen documents if it is not a meal of a Mitzvah[5].

([Thus] the Sages only prohibited the host himself from counting the guests from the writing due to a decree that he may come to erase [a guest]. In this decree they decreed even in a scenario involving hosting guests [of another city], despite it being a great Mitzvah. [However] the prohibition [against reading the list of guests] engraved on the board and pad due to a decree that one may come to read layman documents was only applied regarding guests which are not from another city, such as he invited local friends of his city for a friendly feast which is not a feast of a Mitzvah. Look in chapter 333 [Halacha 6[6]])

Summary:
It is forbidden for the host to read the guest list or to read the menu, even if it is a Mitzvah related feast, due to worry that the host may come to erase a guest name or a delicacy from the list. It is however accustomed to allowing the servant to read the list by a Mitzvah related feast, as by a Mitzvah the Sages did not uphold their decree of "Mimtzo Cheftzecha".

---

4. Reading engraved writings:[7]
Reading writing engraved on a board or pad: Even if the names [of the guests] are engraved on a board or pad and are not written, it is forbidden to be read, as perhaps they will mistakenly come to allow [reading] even laymen documents, as the board and pad are confused with documents.
Reading writings engraved on a wall: However, if it is engraved on a wall it is permitted to read it on Shabbos, as the engraving on a wall is not confused with a document. However this only applies if they are engraved concavely, however if they are protruding then it is forbidden even to read them in one's mind, due to a decree that one may come to erase one of the guests after seeing that he has not prepared for them all their needs, and he will regret that he invited more guests then he is able to [cater for], and he will scrape and remove the protruding names from the wall in order so the servant not read them. This is in contrast to concaved engravings which are difficult to erase, and due to this he will thus remember that it is Shabbos and will not come to erase. Furthermore, even if the protruding engraving is very high up on the head of the wall to which one is unable to reach to erase it, it is forbidden [to be read on Shabbos], because the Sages did not differentiate in their decree between [writing which is] high or low, as is written in chapter 275 [Halacha 2[8]]. *Reading writing written on a wall*: It goes without saying that if one

---

[5] Meaning that by a non-Mitzvah meal it is forbidden for the servant to read the guests list solely because he may come to read layman documents, and not because he may come to erase.
[6] There is explained that only when one is hosting a guest of another city is it defined as a Mitzvah and when not.
[7] Admur 307:22
[8] There it is explained that it is forbidden to read by the light of a candle even if it is high up on a wall and thus cannot be reached, in which case no worry exists that one may come to tilt it, as nevertheless the Sages

wrote with writing [in contrast to engraving] on the head of the wall, it is also forbidden [to read] due to the decree that one may come to read laymen documents, as the writing on a wall gets confused with the writing on a document.

Summary:
On a pad and the like: Just as it is forbidden to read writings, likewise it is forbidden to read words which have been engraved on a pad or board, due to that one may come to read business documents.
On a wall: Words engraved[9] on a wall are permitted to be read. This however is with exception to a list of guests or menu foods which are engraved in the wall in a protruding way as opposed to concaved, in which case it is forbidden to be read by the leader of the household due to a decree that he may come to erase a name.[10]

---

5. Reading Mitzvah related matters:[11]
The prohibition against reading laymen documents, is itself only because of "Mimtzo Cheftzecha", and the prohibition of Mimtzo Cheftzecha does not apply by the matter of a Mitzvah. As matters of heaven which are forbidden to be done on Shabbos are permitted to be spoken of, and no decree was made by heavenly matters that one may come to also permit mundane matters. Thus, certainly there is not to be decreed by a Mitzvah matter against permitted matters due to that one may come to read laymen documents, and will transgress the prohibition of Mimtzo Cheftzecha.
Reading the names of the souls by Yizkor:[12] (Similarly that which is accustomed to read the [names of those] souls [which have passed away] from writing is considered like a Mitzvah matter, [as] they vow to charity for the sake of mentioning the deceased. Look in chapter 306 [Halacha 14/15[13]]

Summary:
It is permitted to read Mitzvah related matters, as such matters were never given the decree of "Mimtzo Cheftzecha".

Q&A
May one read the words written on the Peroches; Bimah etc?[14]
Yes.[15]

May one read the names of the deceased when no charity is being given in connection with it?[16]
No.

May one read names for a Mi Shebeirach for the sick on Shabbos?
Yes.[17]

---

[9] This applies whether the words are engraved protruding or concavely. [So is implied from Admur that this differentiation is only relevant in a case of guest lists being there is a worry that a guest name may get erased. So rules also **Ketzos Hashulchan** 107:23 footnote 38]

[10] However, in other cases there is no suspicion that one may come to erase the writing. [See previous footnote]

[11] Admur 307:23

[12] Admur 307:24

[13] There it discusses when and how giving a donation on Shabbos is permitted.

[14] Ketzos Hashulchan 107 footnote 40

[15] As matters of holiness will not come to be confused with business documents. [ibid]

[16] Ketzos Hashulchan 107 footnote 41

[17] As charity is donated on behalf of the sick. Furthermore, it is a matter of the body [health] of which it is ruled that even to read letters which their content is questionable is allowed due to it perhaps containing matters of the body. Now, although there Admur concludes one is to only read it in his mind and not verbalize, perhaps that is only because one does not know the letters content. However, if one knows its content of bodily matters then it is allowed. In any event reading the name of the sick is certainly no worse than reading the Mi Shebeirach itself which is allowed.

May one read a wedding or Bar Mitzvah invitation on Shabbos?[18]

Yes.

<u>Distributing the invitations on Shabbos</u>: It is permitted to distribute an invitation on Shabbos. However, some Poskim[19] rule that if the invitation is sealed closed it is Muktzah, and even if not, one may not distribute it if he will see the people during week.[20]

---

6. Reading to the public, matters which pertain to the community:[21]

Similarly, that which is accustomed that the servant read the approbations or excommunications from writing is not to be forbidden due to that one may come to read layman documents, being that [the above writings] are for the need of the public, and the needs of the public have the legal status of a Mitzvah matter, as written in chapter 306 [Halacha 12[22]]

Summary:

It is permitted for communal matters to be read before the community, as matters pertaining to the public have the status of a Mitzvah.

---

7. Reading mail:

A. Which letters are permitted for one to read?[23]

Reading a letter from a friend: A [common] letter [of a friend or relative] inquiring one's wellbeing is forbidden to read [verbally], and even to read in one's mind without verbalization [is forbidden] due to a decree [that one may come to read] layman documents.[24]

Letters regarding finding objects: (It goes without saying regarding letters sent to inquire about a certain matter, even if it is a matter which is permitted to do on Shabbos, [that it is forbidden to be read] as they are to be decreed against due to [one may come to read about] matters which are forbidden).

Other Opinions: There are those opinions[25] which permit reading a letter which is sent to him of which its content is unknown, as perhaps it contains matters which pertain to his body[26], and it is thus not similar to layman documents which have no pertinence to one's bodily [health and security], but rather pertain to one's money.

The Final Ruling:[27] One may rely on their words to be lenient on a Rabbinical matter. Nevertheless, one is not to read it verbally but rather in his mind, without verbalization, as there is an opinion who is lenient regarding reading [in one's mind] without verbalizing even writings which are forbidden to read according to all.

B. Are forbidden letters Muktzah?[28]

Letters are not Muktzah: It is permitted to move the letter on Shabbos, and it is not forbidden due to Muktzah even if it is not fit on Shabbos for its main benefit, which is to be read, such as when one knows

---

[18] Piskeiy Teshuvos 307:19; Minchas David 2:40

[19] Piskeiy Teshuvos ibid

[20] Vetzaruch Iyun as a) There is no Issur of Tircha on Shabbos when a person will benefit from it on Shabbos and it can read it on Shabbos. B) One may ask a gentile to open it and hence why should it be Muktzah.

[21] Admur 307:24

[22] There it is explained that even mundane communal matters may be talked of and overseen by the appointed public workers, as matters of the public are like a matter of a Mitzvah which does not contain the prohibition of Mimtzo Cheftzecha or Daber Davar.

[23] Admur 307:25; Michaber 307:14

[24] So rules Rashi Shabbos 116b

[25] Tosafos Shabbos 116b

[26] Meaning his health, or security. [See Tosafos there]

[27] Admur ibid; Michaber ibid

[28] Admur 307:26

it does not contain matters pertaining to ones bodily [health and security], in which case it is forbidden to even read it in one's mind.

The reason for why it is not Muktzah is because: Nevertheless, it is fit for another benefit, such as to cap a bottle with and matters of the like.

If the letter arrived from outside the city boundaries: Even if the letter was brought from outside the Shabbos parameter on Shabbos it is not Muktzah, as is written in chapter 515 [Halacha 14[29]], and even the person for whom the letter was brought for is permitted to benefit from it even from its main benefit, which is to read it if he is unaware of its content.

The reason it is permitted even when arrived from outside city limits: It is not similar to other items brought from outside the city limits which is forbidden for the person to whom it was brought for to benefit from until after Shabbos, as the reason [there is] due to a decree that one may tell a gentile to bring him an item from outside the city limits, however by a letter this is not relevant [as one does not know when a letter is arriving]. Furthermore, this letter was not brought on his behalf at all being that the sender sent it for himself and not on behalf of the one it is being sent to. (Furthermore, even if it was sent on his behalf, nevertheless the gentile which is bringing the letter from outside the city limits intends on doing the task of the sender and not on behalf of the person it is being sent to. It is not similar to a Jew which sent fruits to his friend before Shabbos through a gentile and he was delayed and brought them on Shabbos, in which they are forbidden for the person to whom it was sent to, as written in chapter 515 [Halacha 22], as since the gentile knows that this Jew which he is bringing them to will eat on Shabbos these fruits and therefore he is bringing them to him, if so he is then intending in his bringing them from outside the city limits on behalf of the bodily benefit of the receiver, and for this reason even if the gentile intends on doing his task for the sake of himself, in order to receive payment, it is forbidden as is written in chapter 515 [Halacha 21]. This is in contrast to a letter in which the body of the recipient does not benefit from the body of the letter, and the gentile only intent in bringing the letter from outside the city limits is to fulfill the will of the Jewish sender, or for his own benefit to receive payment, and not for the sake of whom it is being sent for.)

C. Not to take the mail from the postman's hand:[30]

It is accustomed not to accept a letter from the hands of a gentile which brought it on Shabbos, but rather the gentile is told to place it on the ground or on the table, as we suspect that perhaps prior to the gentile standing to rest [upon arriving] the Jew will take the letter from his hands, and it is thus found that the Jew has done the "Hanacha" [placing down part of the carrying], which is Rabbinically forbidden even in these times that there are those which say that we do not have a public domain, as is written in chapter 325 [Halacha 2, 16]

D. May one open an envelope in order to remove its letter?[31]

It is forbidden to open an envelope on Shabbos.[32] [This applies even in a case of great need.[33] However some Poskim[34] rule one may do so in a time of great need, if he destroys the envelope in the process.]

---

[29] There it is explained that matters brought from outside the Techum on Shabbos are only forbidden for that person to who it was brought to and not to others. Thus, it cannot become Muktzah, as a matter which is not Muktzah for others is not Muktzah for any. [See 308:89]

[30] Admur 307:27

[31] Admur 307:7; 519:6; So also rules: M"A 307:20 based on Aguda; Peri Chadash Y.D. 118 [brought in Biur Halacha 340:13 "Haneyar"]; Chacham Tzvi 39; M"B 340:41 forbids according to all opinions, see Biur Halacha "Haniyar"; Ketzos Hashulchan 119 note 34; SSH"K 28:4; See Piskeiy Teshuvos 340:29

[32] The reason: This is due to a Rabbinical prohibition of Soser:destroying. [Admur 519:6] The reason for this is because although the envelope is considered an un-sturdy structure, nevertheless since there is no Shabbos need involved in opening it, meaning that reading the letter is not a Shabbos necessity, therefore it is forbidden, as destroying a non-sturdy vessel was only allowed in order to remove what is inside for a Shabbos need, as explained in 314:1. [Ketzos Hashulchan ibid]

Other reasons: Some Poskim rule that it contains a Biblical prohibition of Soser being one is tearing the enevelope with intent to fix a certain matter, which is the reading of the letter. [Peri Chadash ibid] Others maintain that it contains a Rabbinical prohibition. [Admur ibid; Chacham Tzvi ibid, brought in Biur Halacha ibid; Igros Moshe 1:122 argues on the Peri Chadash]

[33] Ketzos Hashulchan ibid; M"B ibid

[34] Bris Olam Koreia 7; based on Chazon Ish 61:2, and so leans to rule Rav SZ"A in SSH"K 28 footnote 15, Shut Even Yisrael 16

Asking a gentile:[35] One may not ask a gentile directly to open the letter. However it is permitted to tell the gentile mail man that he cannot read the letter until it is opened, and have the mailman understand that he wants him to open it.[36] [This allowance applies only for the mailman who delivered the letter, and not to another gentile, in which case one must protest if he sees him opening the letter.[37] Likewise some Poskim[38] rule this allowance only applies if one personally asked the mailman to deliver the letter, and not by the state appointed mailman. However, in a time of great need one may ask the gentile to open it.[39]]

On Yom Tov:[40] One may tear open an envelope on Yom Tov. [According to those who hold that opening cans on Shabbos is forbidden due to Tikkun Keli, it is to be opened in a destructive manner, just as they rule by cans.[41] However according to those who hold that cans may be opened in a non-destructive manner then seemingly it is permitted to open an envelope even in the area of the glue, by separating the two parts.[42]]

Summary-Reading mail:

Letters [which have had their envelope opened from before Shabbos[43]] of which their content are unknown, and it is thus possible that in them are matters pertaining to one's health and security, are permitted to be read in one's mind without verbalization.[44] If, however, one knows that it does not contain content relevant to one's health and security, then it is forbidden to read their content even in one's mind without verbalization. Nevertheless, the letter is not Muktzah, as it is still fit to be used as a bottle stopper. Furthermore, even if the letter arrived on Shabbos from out of city limits it is not Muktzah.[45]

Taking mail from the mailman:[46] One is not to take mail from the mailman, but is rather to have him put it down, in order so one not come to take any part in the gentile's act of carrying.

---

8. Reading descriptions written under designs, portraits and paintings:[47]

A wall or curtain which contains designs of different animals or sketches of people [portraying] historical events, such as the battle of David and Goliath, and it is written under [these portraits] "this is the figure of this animal" and "this is the portrait of this person", it is forbidden to read this writing on Shabbos due to a decree that one may come to read layman documents. Even to read them in one's mind without verbalization is forbidden. [See footnote[48]]

---

[35] Admur 307:7; M"A 307:20 based on Aguda; M"B ibid

[36] The reason: As the gentile is doing so to simply complete the job he was paid to perform by delivering the letter, and hence one is not required to protest against him doing so. [Admur ibid in parentheses; See Ketzos Hashulchan ibid]

[37] Ketzos Hashulchan ibid

[38] Ketzos Hashulchan ibid based on Admur ibid that states the reason for the allowance is because he is doing so to complete

[39] M"B ibid as explained in Biur Halacha ibid; Ketzos Hashulchan ibid

[40] Admur 519:6

[41] See Piskeiy Teshuvos ibid; Bris Olam Koreia 7; based on Chazon Ish 61:2; SSH"K 28 footnote 14-15

[42] Ketzos Hashulchan ibid

The reason: Although on the onset it seems that doing so should be forbidden due to Koreia, as it is forbidden to separate glued items, as written in 340:17, nevertheless in truth one can argue that in this case it is permitted to do so as a) the prohibition only applies by two entities that are glued together as opposed to a single entity, and b) It was sealed with intent to be opened, and is hence a temporary sealing. [Ketzos Hashulchan ibid]

[43] See Q&A below

[44] Admur 307:25

[45] Admur 307:26

[46] Admur 307:27

[47] Admur 307:29

[48] The Magen Avraham 301:4 allows to read captions written under pictures for the sake of pleasure. However other Poskim argue on this. [See Beir Moshe 6:66, and Ketzos Hashulchan 107:2 how he learns this Halacha.]

Summary:
It is forbidden to read even in one's mind, without verbalization, the information written under portraits, pictures and the like, due to a decree that one may come to read business documents. [However, if the information is engraved on the wall, then it is permitted to be read.[49]]

Compilation-Looking at pictures, or illustrations, on Shabbos and reading the captions that describe it:
It is permitted to look at pictures on Shabbos.[50] [Nonetheless, it is not proper to use one's time on Shabbos for looking at pictures, if he can use it for Torah learning.[51]]

Reading the descriptions under the pictures:[52] It is forbidden to read the captions that are under a picture and describe the people, or events associated with it.[53] This applies to [all] pictures [whether on] a wall, curtain [or in a book[54]]. It is forbidden to read the caption even in one's mind, without verbalizing the words.[55] This prohibition applies even if one derives pleasure and excitement from reading the captions under the pictures.[56] This prohibition applies even if the picture is of matters discussed in Tanach, such as the battle between Dovid and Goliath [or Akeidas Yitzchak[57]].[58] This prohibition applies even if the caption is engraved onto the picture, and not written, [with exception to if it is engraved on a wall, in which case a concave engraving may be read].[59]

The cases of exception: In the following cases, it is permitted to read the captions that are found under a picture:

1. One is reading it for the sake of a Mitzvah or for the sake of learning Torah [such as pictures found in Torah books for the sake of illustrating a Halacha or Sugya[60]].[61]
2. The caption discusses a matter that pertains to the public.[62]

---

[49] Admur 307:22

[50] Admur Kuntrus Achron 301:2 "If even during the week its permitted, from where would we get to prohibit it on Shabbos?"; [Now, although Admur ibid records a dispute regarding if one may look at pictures [Diyoknos] even during the week [see Shabbos 149a], that is only in his analyzation of the opinion of the M"A 301:5, however, in truth we rule that one may look at pictures during the week, so long as they were not made for purposes of idolatry. (Michaber Y.D. 142:15; Shach 142:33; Rosh 23:2; Tosafus Shabbos ibid)] P"M 301 A"A 5; Chemed Moshe 3012; Mamar Mordechai 301:2; Piskeiy Teshuvos 307:22
Other opinions: Some Poskim rule it is forbidden to look at pictures on Shabbos. [Chazon Ish, brought in Orchos Rabbeinu 3:238]

[51] See Admur 307:2 and 290:5

[52] Admur 307:29 *"A wall or curtain which contains designs of different animals or sketches of people [portraying] historical events, such as the battle of David and Goliath, and it is written under [these portraits] "this is the figure of this animal" and "this is the portrait of this person", it is forbidden to read this writing on Shabbos due to a decree that one may come to read layman documents."*; Michaber 307:15; Shabbos 149a as explained in Rashi
Other opinions: Some Poskim rule it is permitted to read the captions written under pictures for the sake of pleasure, as will be explained in coming footnotes.

[53] The reason: This is due to a decree that one may come to read layman documents. [Admur ibid; Kuntrus Achron ibid; Rashi ibid; Rosh 23:1; Beis Yosef 307; Levush 307; M"B 307:57] Alternatively, the reason is due to worry that one may come to erase the words. [Rambam, brought in Kuntrus Achron ibid; Semak and Ran, brought in Elya Raba 307:37 and Kaf Hachaim 307:109] The practical ramification between the two reasons is if one may read engraved captions. [Elya Raba ibid]

[54] Makor Chaim 307; Piskeiy Teshuvos 307:22

[55] Admur ibid; Rabbeinu Yonah, brought in Rosh ibid; Olas Shabbos 307:19; Kaf Hachaim 307:108

[56] Admur Kuntrus Achron 301:2 "If the M"A intended to permit the reading of the captions, this requires great analysis, as how can we permit a Rabbinical decree simply due to pleasure. Should we permit doing business on Shabbos due to pleasure? Chas Veshalom to suggest such a thing, and it is obvious that we do not push off a prohibition due to the Mitzvah of Oneg, as this is a Mitzvah Haba Baveira."; Elya Raba 301:6; Chemed Moshe 3012; Mamar Mordechai 301:2; Menorah Hatehora 301:4; Aruch Hashulchan 301:44; Kaf Hachaim 301:12; Shaar Hatziyon 301:7; Piskeiy Teshuvos 307:22; See Beir Moshe 6:66, and Ketzos Hashulchan 107:2
Other opinions: Some Poskim rule it is permitted to read the captions written under pictures for the sake of pleasure. [Possible way of understanding M"A 301:4, and so understands P"M 301 A"A 5; See Admur in Kuntrus Achron ibid who questions the understanding in the M"A ibid]

[57] Olas Shabbos 307:18; Elya Raba 307:36; P"M 307 A"A 21; Kaf Hachaim 307:107

[58] Admur ibid; Michaber ibid; Rashi ibid

[59] Admur 307:22; Kaf Hachaim 307:109

[60] Orchos Rabbeinu 1:140; Piskeiy Teshuvos 307:22 footnote 187

[61] Admur 307:23

[62] Admur 307:24

3. The caption discusses matters that pertains to one's health [such as a safety sign]. In such a case one may read it in one's mind.[63]
4. The caption is engraved in a wall.[64]

Summary:
Although it is permitted to look at pictures on Shabbos, nevertheless, it is forbidden to read the captions even in one's mind, without verbalization, unless the matter pertains to a Mitzvah, Torah learning, or a public matter. If it pertains to a health matter, one may read it without verbalization.

Q&A
May one read the captions under pictures found in a Sefer, such as a Chumash, Gemara, Mishnayos, and the like?
One may do so in the process of learning Torah, and for the purpose of learning.[65] Furthermore, some learn that one may do so even out of curiosity [not in the midst of learning] as the pictures in Torah Sefarim bring one to learn from the Sefer.

May one read the captions on sports cards and the like?
No.

May one read the captions on pictures of Tzadikim?
Some[66] write that it is permitted to do so, as it purpose is to bring one closer to fear of Heaven, and is hence considered done for the sake of a Mitzvah.

---

9. Reading books:
A. History books and novels:[67]
Similarly [history] books of wars (and the history of gentile kings) and parables and metaphors regarding mundane talk, such as the book Emanuel, and it goes without saying books of romance are forbidden to be read on Shabbos. Even to read them in one's mind without verbalization [is forbidden], due to a decree against [coming to read] laymen documents.
During the week: Furthermore, even during the week it is forbidden to be read [the above books] due to " Moshav Leitzim/A setting of scoffers", even if they are written in Hebrew.[68]Regarding books of romance there is an additional prohibition even if they are written in Hebrew, as one entices the evil inclination on himself, and those which compiled it and those which copied them ,and it goes without saying those which published them are included within those which cause the public to sin.
Ethical history books: However, those history books which bring out ethics and fear of heaven, such as the book of Josephus and the like, are permitted to be read even on Shabbos even if they are written in a foreign language [not Hebrew]. (Nevertheless, it is not proper for people to spend much time reading them.)

---

[63] Admur 307:25
[64] Admur 307:22
[65] Orchos Rabbeinu 1:140
[66] Mishnas Yosef 7:72; Chazon Ovadia 6:45; Migdanos Eliyahu; Piskeiy Teshuvos 307 footnote 187
[67] Admur 307:30
[68] However, the Rama rules that history books and novels written in Hebrew are permitted to be read on Shabbos, and certainly during the week. [Rama 307:16]

B. Books of wisdoms, such as Medical books and the like:[69]
Some opinions say that it is forbidden to study [any book] on Shabbos and Yom Tov with exception to [books with] words of Torah and fear of heaven. Even books of wisdoms are forbidden [to study]. The reason for this is because any book which does not have a remnant of holiness one is decree against [reading it] due to laypersons documents [which one may come to read].
Are these books Muktzah: According to this even to move these books is forbidden.
Other Opinions: There are those which permit [to read] all books of wisdom and books of medicine being that matters of wisdom will not be confused[70] with a laypersons document and [thus] one is not to decree on this [type of writing] due to the other [type of writing].
The final ruling: The custom is to be lenient [like the second opinion].

Summary:
History books and novels:[71] Books of history and novels which do not contain themes involving morals and fear of heaven are forbidden to be read on Shabbos, even in one's mind without verbalization, due to Mimtzo Cheftzecha. Furthermore, even during the week they are forbidden to be read due to Moshav Leitzim. Those history books and novels which do contain morale messages are permitted to be read on Shabbos.
Medical books and other books of wisdom:[72] The custom is to allow reading books of wisdom and medicine on Shabbos.

Q&A
May one read a book on Shabbos for the purpose of editing it after Shabbos?[73]
It is forbidden to read any book for the purpose of editing it after Shabbos[74].

May one read from the manuscript of a Sefer[75] which is meant for editing?
If it is designated only for editing and not learning: It is permitted to be read such a book on Shabbos for learning purposes[76], although for editing purposes it is forbidden to read it[77].[78] However there are some Poskim[79] which are stringent and rule that one should not read such manuscripts at all on Shabbos. [According to all] this manuscript is considered Muktzah Machmas Issur on Shabbos as it is designated only for writing on.[80]
If it is designated for both learning and editing:[81] Then it is not Muktzah at all. Although it is forbidden to read it for editing purposes.

May one read a Torah book on Shabbos for the purpose of writing about it after Shabbos, as is common with Chidushei Torah, or homework of Limudei Kodesh?
Some Poskim[82] rule that doing so is permitted[83]. However other Poskim[84] have written that one is to

---

[69] Admur 307:31
[70] Lit. switched
[71] Admur 307:30
[72] Admur 307:31
[73] Based on Shut Radbaz brought in Sharreiy Teshuva 307:1; so rules SSH"K 20:18; Hisorerus Teshuva 2:165; Tzitz Eliezer 10:21; Az Nidbaru 7:8
[74] As it is forbidden to prepare on Shabbos for matters that may only be done after Shabbos.
[75] The same applies for all other books which are permitted to be read on Shabbos which have been designated for editing. See Halacha 5 1
[76] As we do not suspect that one may come to find an area that needs editing and come to edit it.
[77] As it is forbidden to prepare on Shabbos for matters that may only be done after Shabbos.
[78] Based on Shut Radbaz brought in Sharreiy Teshuva 307:1; so rules SSH"K 20:18; Hisorerus Teshuva 2:165; Tzitz Eliezer 10:21; Az Nidbaru 7:8
[79] Kinyan Torah 2:115 and other Poskim brought in Piskeiy Teshuvos 307:1
[80] Toldos Shmuel 3:99-16, brought in SSH"K 20 footnote 44; Piskeiy Teshuvos 310:1.
[81] Pashut, and so rules Piskeiy Teshuvos 307 footnote 2
[82] Kinyan Torah 2:115; Az Nidbaru 7:8; Piskeiy Teshuvos 307:1
[83] As a) It is not recognizable that one is doing so for the purpose of writing it down. b) In any event one is also doing it for the purpose of learning it now. [Az Nidbaru ibid]; and c) It is for the purpose of a Mitzvah. [Kinyan Torah ibid]

refrain from doing so.

On Shabbos may one prepare next week's Shabbos Torah reading?[85]
Yes.[86]

On Shabbos Erev purim may the Baal Korei prepare the reading for the night?[87]
Yes.
<u>May he use a Kosher Megillah to prepare the reading?</u> Yes. However, some Poskim[88] rule that beginning from Plag Hamincha the Megillah is Mukztah and may not be used.

May one make a marking on a book in order to remember a place that needs correction, or the page that he is on?
It is forbidden to make an indentation on the book due to the writing prohibition.[89] However [according to some opinions[90]] one may bend the corner of a page as a reminder of where he is holding or as a sign that it needs correction. [91] See "The laws of Writing and Erasing on Shabbos" for the full details of this subject!

Question:
I have a big midterm coming up this Sunday on the subject of the history of World War II. It mainly focuses on the history of Hitler and the rise of Hitler YIM"Sh to power and the anti-Semitic laws passed in Germany prior to the start of the war. My question is whether I'm allowed to study this material on Shabbos or not.

Answer:
You may not read this material on Shabbos whether to study for a test or for mere personal knowledge.

<u>Explanation:</u> There are three halachic issues that come into play in this question: 1) Does reading history books transgress the Shabbos reading restrictions? 2) Does reading subjects associated with tragedies of the Jewish people transgress a prohibition against being sad and possibly crying unnecessarily on Shabbos. 3) Does preparing for a test on Shabbos transgress the prohibition against preparing on Shabbos for the weekday. Practically, while this last issue can find halachic leniency, the former two issues seem to be a real problem in this case and therefore we concluded that it may not be done. The following is an analysis on the subjects: The sages prohibited one from reading materials on Shabbos that are not Torah related and that do not relate to wisdom. Practically, it is explicitly ruled that history is not a field of wisdom and that therefore it is forbidden to read history books dealing with the wars of the Gentiles on Shabbos and only history books dealing with Jewish history that contain a moral and ethical lesson, such as the book of Josephus or Shevet Yehuda, may be read on Shabbos. The Achronim further stipulate that even by these books one may only read the joyful subjects, such as the miracles that G-d did for us, and not read the chapters dealing with tragedies as one is not allowed to be sad on Shabbos. Accordingly, there is no room to allow studying World War

---

[84] Ashel Avraham Butshach 306 writes that one is to refrain from thinking of writing Chidushei Torah on Shabbos; Minchas Shabbos 90:9 learns to say that it is forbidden to look up a Torah subject on Shabbos if one plans to write it down.

[85] Az Nidbaru 7:8

[86] As there is no prohibition in reading the Torah on Shabbos, and thus Mimtzo Cheftzecha does not apply.

[87] Sdei Chemed Mareches Purim 5 in name of Ikarei Daat; Piskeiy Teshuvos 688:18; Nitei Gavriel Purim 28:4; See Az Nidbaru 7:8

[88] Rebbe in Sichas 13th Adar 1956; Nitei Gavriel 28:6
<u>Other Opinions:</u> See Sdei Chemed ibid that explains why that the Megillah is not Muktzah from Plag Hamincha even according to the Peri Chadash.

[89] 340:7

[90] Kinyan Torah mentioned above in the previous question. However according to the Minchas Shabbos, seemingly this would be forbidden.

[91] So rules Sheivet Hakehasy 1:130 and Kinyan Torah 2:115

II history on Shabbos as if it does not include the aspects of Jewish history then it is forbidden under the prohibition of history books of the wars of the Gentiles. Furthermore, even if it does contain sections of history of the Jewish people, it remains forbidden either due to a dealing with tragedies and sad content, or due to it not containing any moral and ethical lesson, or due to both reasons. However, there is seemingly no prohibition against reading permitted material on Shabbos in preparation for a test and hence it is prohibited simply because it is prohibited material and may not be read whether for a test or for individual knowledge.

Sources: See regarding the reading prohibition: Admur 307:30; Michaber 307:16; Mur Uketzia 307; M"B 307:58; Piskeiy Teshuvos 307:24; see regarding reading in preparation for a test: Piskeiy Teshuvos 290:5; SSH"K 28:92 footnote 220 in name of Rav SZ"A

10. Are writings which are forbidden to be read on Shabbos Muktzah?[92]

One is particular about the writing: Any writing which is forbidden for one to read on Shabbos, is [Muktzah Machmas Gufo and is hence] forbidden to be moved if it is of importance in one's eyes, and he is thus particular against using it as a bottle stopper and the like. [The reason for this is] because it is not fit for any use on Shabbos.

Bills of divorce: Therefore, there are opinions which prohibit moving a Kosher bill of divorce [Get"] which one plans to divorce with, as is written in Even Haezer chapter 136 [Halacha 7] look there. However, an invalid bill of divorce ["Get"] or a Bill of divorce which was already used to divorce the woman with, is permitted to be moved, as one is no longer particular against using it to stop up a bottle.

One is not particular about the writing:[93] It is permitted to move the letter on Shabbos, and it is not forbidden due to Muktzah even if it is not fit on Shabbos for its main benefit, which is to be read, such as when one knows it does not contain matters pertaining to ones bodily [health and security], in which case it is forbidden to even read it in one's mind. The reason for why it is not Muktzah is because nevertheless it is fit for another benefit, such as to cap a bottle with and matters of the like.

Summary:
All writings which are forbidden to be read on Shabbos, are considered Muktzah Machmas Issur if they are not of importance for oneself. If however they are of importance, and one would thus refrain from using the paper for purposes which will destroy it in the process, then they are completely Muktzah. [Thus, books which are forbidden to be read on Shabbos are Muktzah.[94]]

Letters: Even those letters which are forbidden to be read on Shabbos are not [completely] Muktzah, as it is still fit to be used as a bottle stopper, [rather they are considered MM"I]. Furthermore, even if the letter arrived on Shabbos from out of city limits it is not Muktzah.[95]

Q&A
Are newspapers which are forbidden to be read Muktzah? [96]
They are MM"I, and if they are forbidden to be read even during the week due to them containing matters of heresy and promiscuity, then they are MM"G.

---

[92] Admur 307:28
[93] Admur 307:26
[94] Taz brought in M"B 307:62
[95] Admur 307:26
[96] Beir Moshe 6:66

General Summary on Books:

In general, all non-Torah related books may not be read on Shabbos, unless they contain a moral message, or [according to our custom it is also allowed if they] are books of wisdom, such as healing and science and the like.

Practical Q&A

May one read a newspaper?[97]

Newspapers which contain matters relating to business, economy, and advertisements, are forbidden to be read, even with intent to read only the non-business related sections and articles, being that it is very difficult for one to prevent oneself from reading the other sections.[98] However there are some Poskim[99] which permit reading the news sections, so long as one does not read the business sections. However even to them it is proper for every G-d fearing Jew to avoid reading newspapers on Shabbos.

Newspapers which do not contain any business related matters: Are permitted to be read[100], although one is to avoid doing so as many times the articles contain content which cause one to be saddened, which is forbidden on Shabbos.[101]

Newspapers with pages designated for words of Torah and other pages designated for business: It is permitted to read the Torah sections[102], although some are stringent to require one to only read them in his mind, without verbalization[103].

Magazines and newspapers with advertisements: Seemingly advertisements have the status of business-related matters.[104] However, this matter requires further clarification as the world is accustomed to be lenient to read pamphlets and magazines etc which contain advertisements, despite the above accepted ruling not to read papers which contain business related matters.

May one read the captions under the pictures in a newspapers or magazine? Seemingly this is forbidden, as explained above in Halacha 7, however the world is lenient to do so[105].

Are newspapers which are forbidden to be read Muktzah? They are MM"I, and if they are forbidden to be read even during the week due to them containing matters of heresy and promiscuity, then they are MM"G.[106]

May one order newspapers from the company if they will also be printed and delivered on Shabbos on his behalf?[107] No. It is strictly forbidden to allow the newspapers to be delivered for him on Shabbos as the gentile is transgressing a prohibition on behalf of the Jew in delivering it. This is aside for the fact that the printing press is printing an extra newspaper on Shabbos on his behalf. [It is however permitted for one to order a daily paper from the company telling them that he is not interested in receiving any newspapers on Shabbos or holidays. In such a case, even if the company chooses to still send the newspapers, this has no Halachic impact for the Jew.[108]]

---

[97] Piskeiy Teshuvos 307:9

[98] Yaavetz 162; Ketzos Hashulchan 107 footnote 53, Mishneh Berurah 307:63.

[99] SSH"K 29:46; Beir Moshe 6:66 allows reading them in the bathroom. The Shevus Yaakov is lenient and rules that it is permitted to read newspapers.

[100] Reading news is not within the category of words of vanity as there is necessity to know the news items, as well as that one receives pleasure from the reading, and it is painful to refrain one from doing so. [Yaavetz ibid, brought in Ketzos Hashulchan ibid]

[101] Ketzos Hashulchan ibid

[102] SSH"K 29:46 based on Daas Torah 307:14, there they permit reading articles of Torah in all cases [implies even on same page as business related matters.]

[103] Az Nidbaru 9:7

[104] So is implied from term used by Yaavatz, and so seems logical. So is implied also from SSH"K ibid

[105] See Piskeiy Teshuvos 307 footnote 42. The Magen Avraham 301:4 allows to read captions written under pictures for the sake of pleasure. However other Poskim argue on this. [See Beir Moshe ibid, and Ketzos Hashulchan 107:2 how he learns this Halacha.]

[106] Beir Moshe 6:66

[107] Beir Moshe 6:66, based on Teshuvos Mahrahm Shick 123

[108] Mahrahm Shick ibid.

May one read a cook book?[109]
It is permitted to read it for mere enjoyment, as it is common for women to enjoy reading different ideas of recipes.[110] However it is forbidden to be read as a preparation for preparing a meal in the coming days.[111]

May one read announcements placed on a bulletin board?[112]
Those announcements which do not deal with matters of business, or mourning may be read.

May a list which one wrote before Shabbos be read on Shabbos?[113]
[If they do not involve words of Torah] then they may not be read.

May one read words on a billboard or street sign?
Seemingly it is permitted to read billboards and street signs in one's mind if it is not recognizable to others that he is reading it.[114] However this matter requires further analysis.[115]

May one look up an address in a phone book?
For a Mitzvah purpose:

---

[109] Beir Moshe 6:67

[110] As a) One can view recipes as a matter of wisdom in cooking, and matters of wisdom are permitted to read on Shabbos in accordance to the custom. [Rav SZ"A in SSH"K 29 footnote 116] b) The Magen Avraham 301:4 allows reading matters which give one pleasure.

[111] As in such a case one is preparing for the week to do a forbidden matter. [Beir Moshe ibid, SSH"K 29:46 forbids it in all cases due to this reason].

[112] SSH"K 29:48

[113] SSH"K 29:49

[114] As since it is not recognizable to others that one is reading the signs, it should therefore be permitted, as is always the rule by Mimtzo Cheftzecha, that if it is not recognizable to others it is not forbidden. [306:1-2] So rules also Ketzos Hashulchan 107 footnote 9 that one may look for rent signs on houses on Shabbos. So is also clearly implied from 307:21 that reading in thought is permitted when not recognizable.

[115] Tzaruch Iyun from the ruling that one may not read the captions under paintings and the like [307:29], as in truth how can another person recognize whether he is reading the captions or looking at the picture. Vetzaruch Iyun.

CHAPTER 7: THE LAWS OF MUSIC; NOISEMAKING, CLAPPING AND DANCING ON SHABBOS

1. Making sounds, rhythms or music on Shabbos using an instrument or vessel:[1]

Making sounds of music with an instrument: It is forbidden to make the sound of music, including a mere tune[2], on Shabbos, using any instrument or vessel, even if the instrument or vessel is not a musical instrument[3].[4] Likewise it is forbidden to make sounds of music even using one's body[5], with exception to one's mouth as will be explained in Halacha 3.

Making noise with an instrument: It is permitted to make noise[6] on Shabbos using an item that is not designated for noise making, so long as one does not intent to sound a tone of music with this noise. However, an item which is designated for making noise[7] is not to be used to consciously make any noise.[8]

Moving an item which upon being moved makes noise or music: When permitted to move an item designated for making music[9] or noise [see Halacha 2 below regarding Muktzah], it is permitted to do so even if this music or noise will inevitably occur upon moving it, so long as one has no intent to sound this music or noise[10] [and it is not electrically based].

Asking a gentile to play music:[11] It is forbidden to ask a gentile to play music on Shabbos. However, some allow doing so for the sake of a wedding.[12]

Making music to help an ill person fall asleep: It is permitted to make a tune or beat in order to help a bedridden person fall asleep.[13]

May one sing or whistle? See Halacha 3 below!

Examples:

- *Placing water into a punctured vessel having it drip:* It is forbidden to place water into a punctured vessel, having the drops drip onto an upside-down metal vessel, in order so it form a pleasant sound of "Tif Tif, Tif Tif" to help one fall asleep.[14] It is however permitted to do so for the sake of one who is sick and bedridden[15] in order to help him fall asleep.

---

[1] Admur 338:1

See Rambam Chagiga 3:7 that we delay Hakhel if it falls on Shabbos because of Tekios and Chatzotzros

[2] The definition of a sound of music is any sound which a person intends to make in an even slightly pleasant tone, as is done by music. [Admur ibid]

[3] Meaning even if the vessel is not designated for making music it is forbidden to be used to sound music. [ibid]

[4] The reason: This is forbidden due to a Rabbinical decree that one may come to fix a musical instrument. [Admur ibid]

[5] So is evident from wording of Admur "It is forbidden to make a sound of music with exception to one's mouth, but not with anything else". So is also evident from 339:2 that it is forbidden to snap one's fingers in playing a tone.

[6] This refers to random sounds which have no rhythm or beat such as a simple knocking on a door.

[7] Meaning even if it is not designated to make music, but mere noise, such as a metal door knocker it is not to be used. [ibid]

[8] Admur brings a dispute regarding this matter: The first opinion [Michaber; brought as the Stam opinion] rules that it is permitted to make noise with any instrument if one does not intend to sound a tone, even if the instrument is designated for music. Other opinions [Rama 338:1] however rule one may not make any sound, even a mere noise, using an instrument which is designated to make noise. Practically the custom is like the latter opinion. [ibid]

[9] So is implied from Admur regarding Bells attached to clothing that they are allowed even though they make "sounds of music".

[10] This follows the ruling of M"A 338:1; Shach Yoreh Deah 282:4

Other Opinions: The Taz Yoreh Deah 282:2 rules it is forbidden to make noise using an instrument designated for this purpose even if one does not intend to do so. So rules also: Gr"a; Elya Raba; Shaar Efrayim; M"B 338:6 that one is not to be lenient Lechatchilah in this matter.

[11] Admur 338:3

[12] Some opinions allow one to tell a gentile to play musical instruments by weddings which have continued into Shabbos out of respect for the Chasan and Kalah. This is allowed as the Sages did not decree against doing Rabbinical prohibitions through a gentile in a circumstance which involves a Mitzvah, and having music is the main aspect of Simchas Chasan Vekalah. According to all however it is forbidden to tell the gentile to perform a Biblical prohibition for the sake of playing music, such as telling him to fix the string of a guitar or the like, which involves the Biblical prohibition of Tikkun Keli. [This follows the ruling of M"A, however the Rama 338:1 rules it is permitted.] According to all it is forbidden to ask a gentile to play music for purposes other than a wedding. Nevertheless, today the custom has become to be lenient in this, and they are not to be protested. [ibid]

[13] So is implied from the allowance of Admur to use the "tif taf" water dripping bucket. So is also learned from 328:19 That all Rabbinical prohibitions may be done using an irregularity. Vetzaruch Iyun why here no mention is made of using an irregularity.

[14] A pleasant sound helps one fall asleep. This is forbidden to be done as it is considered similar to an instrument and it thus receives the decree against using it due to fear one may come to fix a musical instrument. [ibid]

[15] Admur writes "sick". Vetzaruch Iyun as there are different gradations of illnesses as explained in chapter 328; Bedridden; slightly sick; in great pain, in slight pain. The Halachas differ in accordance to the ailment. Seemingly however when Admur plainly writes sick he is referring to a Choleh Sheiyn Bo Sakana which is a person which is week in his entire body or is bedridden, and not any of the other gradations of illness.

If, however, the drops are falling with much strength onto the metal, hence making loud noise rather than music, such as for the purpose of waking someone, it is permitted for one to set it up on Shabbos.[16]

- *Knocking on a door*: One is not to use a door knocker to knock on a door on Shabbos, due to opinions which forbid its use.[17] Rather the custom is to knock with one's hands on the door. Some knock with an instrument that is not designated for knocking. [Thus, one may knock using a key, a book, or any item that is not designated for knocking.]

- *Shaking a bell*:[18] One may not shake a bell in order to quiet down a child.

- *Moving a bell*: It is permitted to move a bell even if doing so will cause it to make noise, if one has no intent for this noise to occur.[19]

- *Clothing with a bell attached*: It is permitted [for an adult[20]] to walk with clothing which has a bell attached to it that makes sounds of music being that one has no intent to do so.[21] It is however forbidden to give these clothing to a child to wear[22] [even if the child is below the age of Chinuch[23]], [and certainly it is forbidden to dress the child in these clothes[24]] as certainly the child has intent to make the sounds of the bells while walking with the clothing.[25] Likewise it is even forbidden for an adult to wear such clothing if he consciously intends to make the sounds of the bell.[26]

- *Paroches with bells attached*: It is permitted to connect to the Aron Kodesh a Paroches which has bells attached to it and makes noise upon being opened.[27] This Paroches may be opened [and closed[28]] on Shabbos without hindrance.

- *Alarm clock*:[29] It is permitted to set up an alarm clock before Shabbos for it to set off its alarm on

---

However, Tzaruch Iyun on the entire case, as even for one who is bedridden it is only permitted to do a Rabbinical prohibition with an irregularity. Why then is there no requirement for an irregularity mentioned here?

[16] As the sound it makes is not similar a musical note as it is not a pleasant sound. [ibid]

[17] Admur brings a dispute regarding this matter: The first opinion [brought as the Stam opinion] rules that it is permitted to knock on a door using its knocker. Other opinions however rule one may not do so being it is an instrument which is designated to make noise. Practically the custom is like the latter opinion. [ibid] Vetzaruch Iyun if this ruling is based on Admur's legal conclusion or based on custom. Tzaruch Iyun if when Admur wrote the custom he was intending to give a final ruling like whom we follow and hence we follow the stringent opinion based on custom, or perhaps previously when he wrote "it is forbidden to knock using the door knocker" this was the final ruling, and when he added the custom to knock with one's hand, it was to exclude knocking with an undesignated vessel.

[18] Admur 339:2

[19] This follows the ruling of the M"A 338:1; Shach Yoreh Deah 282:4

Other Opinions: According to the Taz Yoreh Deah 282:2 this would be forbidden. So rules also: Gr"a; Elya Raba; Shaar Efrayim; M"B 338:6 that one is not to be lenient Lechatchilah in this matter.

[20] Admur 301:21 rules that for children it is forbidden to give them such clothing to wear on Shabbos

[21] Admur 338:1

[22] Admur 301:21

[23] So is implied from Admur 301:21 which mentions that doing so is "Feeding the prohibition with one's hands" which is forbidden to be done even to children below the age of Chinuch. So is also implied from Tehila Ledavid 343:2 and so certainly learns Chickrei Halachos 4 p. 54. With regards to the seeming contradiction between this ruling and the ruling in 343:10, see Chikrei Halachos ibid; Haros Ubiurim Ohalei Torah 831 p. 79.

[24] As then certainly it is like one is feeding the child the Issur.

[25] Hence giving these clothing to the child is like feeding a prohibited food with one's hands to a child, which is forbidden to be done.

One must conclude that a child has conscious intent to make the noise with the bells as otherwise this would contradict the ruling in 338:1

[26] As is understood from 338:1

[27] As although the bells make noise when the Peroches is moved and the bells were attached to the Paroches for the sake of letting the congregation hear the bells and know when the ark is being opened so they can stand up for the removal of the Torah scroll, nevertheless since the person opening the Peroches has no intent to make this sound, it is permitted to be done. Furthermore, even if the opener consciously desired to make the sounds, this would remain permitted as it is being done for the sake of a Mitzvah so the congregation hears and stands. Now, if even for an ill person so he fall asleep the Sages allowed even to make a sound of music, then certainly for a Mitzvah one is allowed to make a noise which is not even the sound of music. As the sounding of the bells is not in a pleasant form of tunes but is rather simply an instrument designated to make noise. [ibid]

This follows the ruling of the M"A 338:1; Shach Yoreh Deah 282:4.

Other Opinions: According to the Taz Yoreh Deah 282:2 using such a Peroches would be forbidden. So rules also: Gr"a; Elya Raba; Shaar Efrayim; M"B 338:6 that one is not to be lenient Lechatchilah in this matter.

[28] So long as one has no intent to make the noise of the bells upon closing it, as in this case there is no Mitzvah involved in closing it, as there is when opening it.

[29] Admur 338:4; 252:16

Shabbos.[30] It is however forbidden to set up an alarm clock on Shabbos even if it is mechanical [non-battery operated] being that by doing so one is consciously causing noise to be made.[31]

- *Playing a beat with an almond and the like:*[32] One may not play a beat with an almond [or other item].
- *Shofar:*[33] It is Rabbinically forbidden to blow Shofar on Shabbos due to Uvdin Dechol [a mundane activity]. [It is not forbidden to do so due to a decree of musical instruments.[34]]

Summary:
It is forbidden to play a tune, rhythm or beat using any instrument or vessel. It is forbidden to even make mere noise using an instrument designated for noise making. It is permitted to make mere noise using an item that is not designated for this purpose.

Examples of noise making items that may not be used to intentionally make noise with on Shabbos:
- Bell
- *Gragger; Ratchet*
- Whistle
- Door Knocker

Q&A

May one ring bells or other instruments with an irregularity?[35]
No.[36]

May a child play with toys that make music or noise?
Some Poskim allow giving a child noise[37] making toys for the child to play with up until the age of 6.[38] However according to Admur it is seemingly forbidden to allow a child who has reached the age of Chinuch to play with such objects even if the objects merely make noise and not music.[39] The age of Chinuch in this regard is defined as the age that the child can understand being told not to do something. Practically this is near the age of three.[40] Furthermore, according to Admur, even a child below the age of Chinuch, such as a mere infant, may not be given any toy which is designated for making music[41] or noise[42].

---

[30] This applies even if one desires it to ring for the remainder of the day. [ibid] As although it is a noise making Melacha, of which one is to be stringent against doing even before Shabbos, nevertheless since it is common knowledge that alarms are set up the day before they ring, there is therefore no applicable suspicion that people may think it was set up on Shabbos. [252:16]

[31] This applies even if the alarm clock only sounds noise and not musical tones, as nevertheless it is forbidden to make noise with a vessel that is designated for noise making. It goes without saying that one may not set up the alarm clock if doing so causes tunes to sound and the like. [based on 252:16; 338:4 which states in parentheses that it is forbidden being that it is a vessel which is designated for noise, of which the law is that even for mere noise it is forbidden to be used]

[32] Admur 339:2

[33] Admur 588:4; 596:2; 623:11 "not a Shvus Gamur"; M"A 623:4; See also

[34] Based on Admur ibid; See Michtam Ledavid ibid

[35] Biur Halacha 339 "Ulesapek Kelacher Yad"

[36] The allowance of an irregularity is only applicable to clapping and not to instruments. [ibid]

[37] In contrast to music, see next footnote.

[38] Beir Moshe 6:27; SSH"K 16:3. As the entire reason behind the noisemaking prohibition-in the opinion of M"B- is because of Uvdin Dechol, which is not so applicable by such toys. However according to Admur which rules the reason behind the prohibition is due to a decree one may come to fix the vessel, then it would seemingly be forbidden. Seemingly according to all it would be forbidden to give the child music making toys as it is forbidden due to a Rabbinical decree according to all. [So also concludes Piskeiy Teshuvos 338 footnote 2]

[39] So seems to be the opinion of Admur, as the reason behind the prohibition of intentionally making noise is because one may come to fix the item. Hence this is a typical Rabbinical prohibition which applies to all children above the age of Chinuch. However, Tzaruch Iyun as noise making items are disputed if they are forbidden to be used even by adults and hence perhaps by children there is room to be more lenient.

[40] See Piskeiy Teshuvos 343

[41] 301:21 regarding giving a child clothing with bells to wear. This ruling is based on the understanding of Chikrei Halachos 4 p. 54, and other alternative explanations of this ruling. However according to the explanation of Hearos Ubiurim 831 p. 79 so long as the adult has no intent for

May one make noise with a baby toy in order to lull a baby to sleep?

If the toy makes sounds of <u>music</u> then from the letter of the law this is forbidden to be done.[43] If the toy simply makes noise then in a time of need, such as a screaming child that cannot be comforted, one may use a toy specifically made for babies, such as a rattle, to lull the baby to sleep, if the toy simply makes noise and not music.[44]

May one move a Torah crown with bells on Shabbos?

Yes, even if this will make noise in the process.[45]

May one dress children in clothing that have bells?

No, as explained above in the Examples given from the Shulchan Aruch.

May one knock on the door with his key?

Yes.[46]

May one who is bedridden ring for a nurse using a mechanical bell?[47]

Yes.

May one drum on one's table?

No, one may not do so either using his hands or a spoon and the like. Although if doing so in beat of a Niggun-see Halacha 3 Q&A.

May one ask a gentile to set up one's alarm on Shabbos in order to awaken for Zman Kerias Shema?

No.[48] Some Poskim[49] rule this applies even to a mechanical alarm clock that does not work on electricity.

Compilation-May one use a door knocker on Shabbos?[50]

A. Background-Making noise with an item on Shabbos:

The sages prohibited one from sounding music on Shabbos, due to the crazy one way come to fix musical instruments.[51] Included in this prohibition is sounding any sound with the intent of making it into a tune or melody. However, if one's intent is simply to make a noise and not a melody or tune, then the following law applies:

---

the child to make noise with the object, such as the objects can be used in a different way to entertain the child, then giving him the object is allowed.

[42] Tzaruch Iyun regarding noise making objects as bells can be defined as an item which makes music, as well as that noise making items is a dispute if forbidden even by an adult.

[43] As rules Admur explicitly regarding shaking a bell for a child.

[44] Beir Moshe 6:27; SSH"K 16 footnote 11 in name of RSZ"A.
As there are opinions which allow even an adult to do so.

[45] This is permitted according to all opinions, even those [Taz] which dispute the ruling of M"A:Admur, as these bells make a minimal amount of noise and are placed merely for beauty. [Sheivet Haleivi 1:61]

[46] As it is not designated for this purpose. See M"B 338:4

[47] SSH"K 40:19; So is clearly evident from Admur 338:1 which allows even making musical notes through the drops of water for the sake of a bedridden person.

[48] M"B 252:50 based on P"M 252 M"Z

The reason: As an electric alarm involves a Biblical prohibition of electricity and is hence forbidden due to Amira Lenachri even for the sake of a Mitzvah. [See 307:12; 331:7; 446:6 in Hagah]

[49] M"B ibid; However it is clear from Admur 252:16 and 338:4 that doing so does not involve any Biblical prohibition and hence it is a Shevus Deshvus and hence should be permitted for the sake of a Mitzvah. [See 307:12]

[50] Admur 338:1; See Piskeiy Teshuvos 338:1-2

[51] Admur ibid; Michaber 338:1; Rambam 23:4; Raba Eiruvin 104a

Item not designated for noise making:[52] It is permitted to make noise[53] on Shabbos using an item that is not designated for noise making, so long as one does not intent to sound a tune of music with this noise.

Item designated for noise making: [It is disputed amongst Poskim as to whether an item designated for noisemaking may be used to make noise on Shabbos. Some Poskim[54] rule that it is permitted to make noise with any instrument if one does not intend to sound a tone, even if the instrument is designated for music.] Other Poskim[55], however, rule that it is forbidden to use an item which is designated for noise making[56] to make noise on Shabbos, even though no tune or melody is being sounded, due to a decree that one may come to fix it.[57] Practically, the [Ashkenazi] custom is like the latter opinion.[58] [Furthermore, some Sephardim are also accustomed to be stringent like the latter opinion[59], although others are lenient like the former opinion.[60]]

B. The Law-Using a door knocker:[61]
Based on the final ruling, and custom stated above, one is not to use a door knocker to knock on a door on Shabbos even though one has no intent to sound a tune or melody. Accordingly, it is forbidden for the community Shamash to knock on doors to call people to come to Shul using the set door knocker. Rather, he is to knock on the door with one's hands, and so is the custom.[62] Some communities, however, are accustomed [not to use their hands to knock, but rather] to nock with another instrument that is not designated for knocking.[63] [Thus, one may knock using a key, or any item that is not designated for knocking. The above however only applies for Ashkenazim, however amongst Sephardim, many are lenient to permit knocking on the door with a door knocker.[64]]

Summary:
Ashkenazim may not use a door knocker to knock on a door on Shabbos.

If one cannot enter the home without using the door knocker, such as nobody can hear him knocking with his hand, may he use it?
Some Poskim[65] rule that in such a case one may be lenient to use it, as rules the first opinion stated above. Other Poskim[66], however, question this ruling.

---

[52] Admur ibid; M"A 338:3 as explained in Machatzis Hashekel ibid; Raba Eiruvin ibid
Other opinions: Some Poskim rule it is forbidden to make any noise using a vessel, even if it is not designated for this purpose. [Gr"a; Rabbeinu Chananel brought in Tur 338; Yerushalmi Beitza 5:2; Orchos Rabbeinu 1:168]
[53] This refers to random sounds which have no rhythm or beat, such as a simple knocking on a door.
[54] Implication of Stam ruling in Admur ibid who writes Viyeish Omrim; Implication of Michaber 338:1, as implied from M"A 338:1 and as explains Machatzis Hashekel ibid in his first explanation that the M"A/Michaber he is arguing on Rama ibid; Beis Yosef 338 argues against Iggur; So also learn the following Poskim that the Michaber ibid [and consequently the first Stam opinion in Admur ibid] is arguing on the Rama: Biur Halacha 338:1 "Al Hadelet [explains that a) The Beis Yosef questions the ruling of Iggur, and that from Pirush Hamishnayos of Rambam it implies that it is permitted] "Hoil" in brackets that seemingly the Kalkeles Hashabbos learns that the Michaber ibid argues on Rama [and explains that the fact the Rama did not write Yeish Omrim does not necessarily mean that it is not under debate]; Implication of Aruch Hashulchan 338:2-4; Or Letziyon 2:39-1 concludes that the Michaber argues on Rama and hence permits it for Sephardim; Piskeiy Teshuvos 338:1-2; Rav Yaakov Yosef z"l; See Hagahos Maimanis on Rambam ibid; Ravaya 795; Tur in name of Rabbeinu Tam
[55] 2nd opinion in Admur ibid; Rama 338:1; Iggur 518; Shut Maharil 38; Beis Yosef 338 in name of Iggur
[56] Meaning, even if it is not designated to make music, but mere noise, such as a metal door knocker, it is not to be used. [Admur ibid]
[57] Admur ibid; Levush 338:1; See Kaf Hachaim 338:9
Other reasons: Some Poskim Rule it is forbidden because we may intend to make music with it. [Beis Yosef 338; Olas Shabbos 338:1]
[58] Admur ibid; Rama ibid; Darkei Moshe 338:3; See Kitzur Shelah P. 86; Yifei Laleiv 338:2; Kaf Hachaim 338:10
Other opinions: Some Poskim imply like the former opinion even according to Ashkenazim. [See Aruch Hashulchan 338:2-5 and 9]
[59] Chida in Tov Ayin18:68; See Yifei Laleiv 338:2; Kaf Hachaim 338:10
[60] Or Letziyon 2:39-1
[61] Admur 338:1
[62] Admur ibid; Rama 338:1
[63] Admur ibid; M"A 338:3
[64] Or Letziyon 2:39-1 concludes that the Michaber argues on Rama and hence permits it for Sephardim; Rav Yaakov Yosef z"l
[65] Kalkeles Shabbos, brought Biur Halacha 338:1 "Hoil" and Kaf Hachaim 338:10
[66] See Biur Halacha ibid

2. Are instruments which are designated to make music or noise Muktzah on Shabbos?

Designated for music:[67] Any item which is designated to make musical notes is MM"I on Shabbos, and hence may only be moved for their space or a permitted use, and not to save from damage. [If the item is expensive and one is thus careful not to use them for any other purpose then the item is MMC"K and is forbidden to be moved for any purpose on Shabbos, unless it is moved with an irregularity.[68]]

Designated for noise making Items which are designated for simply making noise and not music are not Muktzah[69][**See footnote for other opinions**], although they may only be moved if one does not consciously intend to make noise while moving them.

Examples of Musical items and their Muktzah status:
- Guitar is MMC"K
- Piano is MMC"K
- Keyboard: MMC"K
- Violin: MMC"K
- Saxophone: MMC"K
- Trumpets: MMC"K
- Xylophone: MMC"K
- Chello: MMC"K
- Harp: MMC"K
- Clarinets and Flutes: MMC"K
- Toys which is meant for playing music: MM"I
- Toys which are meant for making noise: According to some Poskim[70] is MM"I. From Admur it is implied it is not Muktzah.[71]
- Rattle: According to some Poskim[72] is MM"I. From Admur it is implied it is not Muktzah.[73]
- Bell: According to some Poskim[74] is MM"I. From Admur it is implied it is not Muktzah.[75]

Are toys which are not designated specifically for noise or music making, but do so in the process of being used, considered Muktzah?
- Example: A toy train which makes sounds when moving.

If the toys are battery operated they are MM"I. If they are mechanical, then if they make music they are MM"I[76]. If they do not make music, just noise, they are not Muktzah.[77]

---

[67] Admur 308:20

[68] Pashut as explained in "The Laws of Muktzah", and so rules Rav SZ"A in SSH"K 16 footnote 8

[69] Levush brought in Peri Megadim 338:3 and so is implied from Admur [338:1] which allows moving a bell if he does not intend to make noise with it and does not mention any of the Muktzah regulations.

Perhaps the reason for this is because there is a dispute with regards to if even initially one may make noise with this vessel on Shabbos, hence regarding Muktzah we are lenient. [As rules Levush brought in Peri Megadim 338:3 that since it is a mere stringency it is not Muktzah] Now even though he mentions the concept of "sound of music" regarding bells worn on clothing, and hence it seems that bells are defined as designated for actual music and not just noise, in which case according to all it is forbidden to make music with them on Shabbos, nevertheless perhaps Admur there was referring to that specific case of bells on clothing which make musical sounds and not mere noise when walked with. However a typical bell itself is not designated specifically for music but for noise, although it can be used also to make music.

Other Opinions: The Peri Megadim [ibid] leaves this matter in question, as does the Biur Halacha "Asur". Piskeiy Teshuvos 338:1 and SSH"K 16:2 rule these items are Muktzah.

[70] The Peri Megadim [ibid] leaves this matter in question, as does the Biur Halacha "Asur". Piskeiy Teshuvos 338:1 and SSH"K 16:2 rule these items are Muktzah.

[71] See previous footnotes in summary.

[72] The Peri Megadim [ibid] leaves this matter in question, as does the Biur Halacha "Asur". Piskeiy Teshuvos 338:1 and SSH"K 16:2 rule these items are Muktzah.

[73] See previous footnotes in summary.

[74] The Peri Megadim [ibid] leaves this matter in question, as does the Biur Halacha "Asur". Piskeiy Teshuvos 338:1 and SSH"K 16:2 rule these items are Muktzah.

[75] See previous footnotes.

[76] As even children may not to play with such items. [Piskeiy Teshuvos 338 footnote 2]

3. Clapping, dancing and snapping one's finger on Shabbos:[78]
A. May one whistle [or make other musical sounds] with one's mouth on Shabbos?[79]

It is Rabbinically forbidden to play musical instruments, or make music using the movements of one's body[80], on Shabbos.[81] Nevertheless, the Sages limited this prohibition only to the doing of an action [with a bodily limb, such as one's hands or feet] to sound music, however, it remains permitted to sound music using one's mouth.[82] Thus, it is permitted to sing on Shabbos. Furthermore, it is permitted to sound music using one's mouth even if it is not in the form of singing, but is rather similar to the sound of an instrument or the sound of a bird, such as those who call at their friend and whistle like a bird.[83] This allowance applies even if the whistling sound is in the form of a tune.[84] [Thus, it is permitted to whistle on Shabbos for any purpose and to any tune. Likewise, one may sound other forms of musical notes with one's mouth in imitation of a musical instrument, as is commonly done in a Capella.[85] Indeed, based on this, it was an old Ashkenazi custom to sound music using their mouths and make sounds identical to an actual musical instrument. This was done even by the holy Rabbis and Chassidim of Ashkenaz.[86] The Rebbe was accustomed to telling people to whistle on Shabbos during the Niggunim of the Shabbos gatherings.[87]]

Summary:
It is permitted to whistle on Shabbos without restriction.

---

[77] This applies according to all. [Mishneh Halachos 6:74 in name of Rav SZ"A rules they are not Muktzah, as since they are not Muktzah for children they are not Muktzah for adults.

[78] Admur 339:2

[79] See Admur 338:1-2; Aruch Hashulchan 338:6-8; Piskeiy Teshuvos 338:4

[80] Admur 339:2; 338:1 "However, not with another matter"; Michaber 339:3; Mishneh Beitza 36b

[81] Admur ibid; Michaber 338:1; Rambam Shabbos 23:4; Raba Eiruvin 104a
The reason: This is forbidden due to a Rabbinical decree that one may come to fix a musical instrument. [Admur ibid]

[82] Admur 338:2; 338:1 "It is forbidden to make sounds of music, with exception to one's mouth"; Rama 238:1; Darkei Moshe 338:4; M"A 338:2; Shiltei Hagiborim Eiruvin 35b in name of Riaz; Aruch Hashulchan 338:6-8
The reason: As the decree against sounding music is due to worry that one may come to make a musical instrument, and this worry is only applicable when one does an action [with an item or bodily limb] to make musical notes, as then there is room to suspect one may come to fix an instrument. However, when sounding music merely with one's mouth, there is no need to worry that it may lead to fixing instruments. [Admur ibid; See Levush 338]

[83] Admur 338:2; Rama 238:1; Darkei Moshe 338:4; M"A 338:2; Shiltei Hagiborim Eiruvin 35b in name of Riaz; Aruch Hashulchan 338:6-8 [See there that he questions this ruling of Rama, as being obvious and superfluous, as all mouth sounds are permitted, thus concluding that the novelty here is that one may whistle even with his fingers in his mouth]

[84] Admur ibid; M"A ibid [See Machatzis Hashekel 338:2]; P"M 338 A"A 2; Machazik Bracha 338:1 that so is the custom and ruling of Achronim; Aruch Hashulchan 338:6-7 that so is Pashut!; M"B 338:3; Orchos Chaim 338:4; See Kaf Hachaim 338:7; Piskeiy Teshuvos 338:4; Rav Yaakov Yosef and his father Rav Ovadia Yosef rule it is permitted
Other opinions: Some Poskim rule that it is forbidden to whistle to a tune on Shabbos, and only whistling for the sake of getting someone's attention is permitted. [M"A ibid in implication of Shiltei Hagiborim and Darkei Moshe ibid that it is only permitted if a) an action is not done and b) a musical tune is not sounded; Machazik Bracha 338:1 and Birkeiy Yosef Shiyurei Bracha 338:1 in name of Givat Pinchas 1:36 that it is forbidden to whistle like a bird; Implication of Makor Chaim 338 [Chavos Yair]; See Kaf Hachaim 338:7]

[85] Machazik Bracha 338:1 "On this the Ashkenazim rely to sound music using their mouths and make sounds identical to an actual musical instrument, and to the bystander it actually sounds like musical instruments are being played. I heard this is done even by their holy Rabbis and Chassidim, and so is the arbitration of the Achronim, that it may be done"; Kaf Hachaim 338:7; See Aruch Hashulchan 338:6-8
Other opinions: Some Poskim rule that it is forbidden to make musical sounds with one's mouth on Shabbos. [Machazik Bracha 338:1 and Birkeiy Yosef Shiyurei Bracha 338:1 in name of Givat Shaul 1:36]

[86] Machazik Bracha ibid; Kaf Hachaim 338:7

[87] See Hiskashrus 674

Q&A

May one whistle through placing his fingers in his mouth?

Some Poskim[88] rule it is permitted to whistle even through placing one's fingers in his mouth. However, other Poskim[89] negate this allowance, and so is the simple implication of Admur.[90] Practically, one may be lenient to whistle a single sound, and not a tune, with the help of his fingers.[91] [As stated above, the Rebbe would motion to people to whistle on Shabbos with their fingers, although seemingly this was done as a single sound and not a tune. Furthermore, making sounds for the sake of Simcha Shel Mitzvah is customarily permitted even when using the body, and hence no further leniency should be derived from it.[92]]

May one whistle with the help of an instrument, such as a whistle, or fork or spoon?[93]

No.

B. Clapping, Dancing:

Clapping: One may not clap his hands against each other or on his lap in a regular fashion, whether out of joy, even for marriage, or whether out of mourning. However, it is permitted to clap in an irregular fashion.

Snapping one's finger: One may not play a tone through snapping his fingers against each other or against another item.

Dancing: It is likewise forbidden to dance for this reason even by a wedding, however on Simchas Torah it is permitted to dance while singing praise for the Torah, as this is in honor of the Torah.

The reason for the all the above restrictions: All of these matters and the like of them are forbidden due to a decree that one may come to fix himself a musical instrument to sing or lament with.

The custom to be lenient:[94] Now that the populace is accustomed to clap and stamp and dance [without an irregularity] by all forms of joyous occasions, one is to not protest their actions as it is for certain that they will not listen, and it is better that they be negligent transgressors then be advertent transgressors. [However] there are those which have learned merit for them [that it be allowed to clap and dance] being that we are no longer expert in musical instruments, and it is thus not relevant to decree that perhaps one will come to make himself a musical instrument, as it is a completely uncommon occurrence. [It is possibly due to this that the custom has become to be lenient in all the above.[95]]

Summary:

Whistling: It is permitted to sing or whistle on Shabbos.

Thumb snapping: One may not snap his thumb in rhythm of a tune.

Clapping and Dancing: It is disputed if one may dance and clap in the regular way done during the

---

[88] Aruch Hashulchan 338:7; See there that he questions the ruling of Rama who permits whistling, as being obvious and superfluous, as all mouth sounds are permitted, and he thus concludes that the novelty here is that one may whistle even with his fingers in his mouth;

[89] See Mishneh Halachos 4:52 who negates the reasoning of the Aruch Hashulchan; Rav Yaakov Yosef in name of his father Rav Ovadia Yosef rules that one should not do so [in retraction of Rav Ovadias ruling in Yabia Omer in name of Aruch Hashulchan ibid]

[90] It is implied from Admur and Poskim ibid that using one's hands is forbidden due to it being an action, as what difference does it make if one claps his hands or uses his fingers.

[91] See Piskeiy Teshuvos 338:4

[92] See Hiskashrus 674

[93] Aruch Hashulchan 338:8; Piskeiy Teshuvos 338:4

[94] This ruling of Admur follows the ruling of Rama.

Other Opinions: The Aruch Hashulchan 339:9 argues that the form of clapping and dancing done today was never included in the original decree of the Sages and hence it is always permitted to be done on Shabbos.

[95] Rama 339:3; "*All the above*" means clapping and dancing, however ringing bells and other forms of music mentioned here are not allowed even according to the custom. [M"B 339:10]

week. One is to be stringent and avoid doing so, although those which are lenient are not to be protested.[96] [Practically today we are lenient regarding dancing and clapping on behalf of Simchas Shabbos and Yom Tov, although not in other scenarios.[97]] According to all one may clap with an irregularity.

May one snap his fingers in order to wake someone up or get their attention?[98]
Yes.[99] However from some Poskim[100] it is evident that even in such a case one is to be stringent not to snap one's finger.

May one clap in order to wake someone up or to get their attention?[101]
Yes.[102]

May one clap after a speech?[103]
Yes.[104]

Question:
Is it permitted on Shabbos to give a standing ovation? Meaning to clap hands after someone's speech and the like? I believe that I was taught that while you are allowed to clap hands for music and singing, you may not clap hands to applaud someone.

Answer:
In truth, it is the opposite. It is permitted to clap hands the normal way on Shabbos for the sake of an applause or standing ovation. However, it is forbidden to clap hands the normal way for the sake of music or while a song is being sung. However, the widespread custom is to be lenient and permit clapping hands the normal way when one is singing songs for the sake of joy of a mitzvah [i.e. Shabbos Niggunim, singing in shul by Davening and Farbrengen]. Thus, there are three types of clapping:
1) For a standing ovation which is permitted the normal way.
2) Clapping to a tune which does not involve Simcha Shel Mitzvah and is therefore forbidden to be done the normal way.
3) Clapping to a tune which involves Simcha Shel Mitzvah in which case one may do so the normal way.

Explanation: The sages prohibited clapping on Shabbos due to that their general music playing prohibition applies even against using one's body to make music. Now, while in truth this matter is debated amongst the Poskim as to whether it applies today, and the widespread custom is to be lenient, nonetheless the final ruling is to be stringent. Nonetheless, this prohibition was only made against using one's body to make music in the normal way, however, to make music using one's body in an abnormal way was never decreed against and is therefore permitted. Furthermore, the prohibition was only made against clapping towards music or in the form of a tune, however, to clap

---

[96] Other Opinions: The Aruch Hashulchan 339:9 argues that the form of clapping and dancing done today was never included in the original decree of the Sages and hence it is always permitted to be done on Shabbos and is not subject to dispute.
[97] See Q&A below
[98] M"B 339:9; Biur Halacha "Oi Al Haluach".
[99] As only when these noises are made in a way of music were they forbidden. [So is implied from Admur that mentions by clapping "out of joy or mourning".]
[100] Tosefes Shabbos; Peri Megadim brought in M"B ibid
[101] Based on M"B 339:9
[102] As only when these noises are made in a way of music were they forbidden. [So is implied from M"A:Admur that mentions by snapping "as do the singers".]
[103] Az Nidbaru 13:14
[104] As one has no intent to make music. [ibid]

simply in order to make noise without any tune was never decreed against and hence one may clap in order to get someone's attention, or wake someone up, or as a standing ovation. Furthermore, the custom is to allow clapping even the normal way when singing on Simchas Torah being that it is done for the sake of a mitzvah, and from this extended the accustomed allowance to permit clapping the normal way on Shabbos when singing a tune for the sake of Simcha Shel Mitzvah, such as in Shul, or by the meal.

Sources: **See regarding the general restriction against clapping and the dispute relevant in today's times**: *Admur 339:2; 338:1; Michaber 339:3; Rama 339:3; Rambam Shabbos 23:5; Mishneh Beitza 36b; M"B 339:10; Aruch Hashulchan 339:9 [rules that the form of clapping and dancing done today was never included in the original decree of the Sages and hence it is always permitted to be done on Shabbos even not for a Mitzvah purpose.];* **See regarding the allowance to clap in the abnormal way**: *Admur 339:2; Michaber 339:3;* **See regarding the allowance to clap for noisemaking and to applaud someone**: *M"B 339:9; Biur Halacha "Oi Al Haluach"; Az Nidbaru 13:14; Piskeiy Teshuvos 339:5;* **see regarding the allowance to clap the normal way for a song of Simcha shel Mitzvah**: *M"B 339:10; Shaar HaTziyon 339:7; Minchas Elazar 1:29; Nimukei Orach Chayim 339; Ashel Avraham [Butshatsh]; Shaareiy Halacha Uminhag 2:165*

Dancing and clapping for purposes of a Mitzvah
Dancing and clapping on Simchas Torah:[105]
According to all it is permitted to dance and clap on Simchas Torah when the praises of Torah are read.

May one ring bells on Simchas Torah?[106]
No. One may not make noise with any instrument.

May one dance and clap for a Mitzvah purpose?[107]
Those which are lenient to do so need not be discouraged.[108]

May one dance and clap to a Niggun on Shabbos and Yom Tov?[109]
The custom today is to allow doing so.[110] This allowance applies equally for those of Sephardic origin.[111]

May one drum his hands or a vessel on the table in beat of a song or Niggun?
From the letter of the law this is forbidden.[112] However the custom is to allow drumming out of joy when singing a Niggun.[113] Nevertheless seemingly one is not to drum using a vessel but rather only

---

[105] Admur 339:2; M"A 669:1 in name of Darkei Moshe and Mahrik; M"B 339:8
[106] M"B 339:8
[107] M"B 339:10
[108] The Rashal rules that in a case of a Mitzvah one may even initially rely on the opinion brought above that today the decree no longer applies. [Shaar HaTziyon 339:7] From Admur however it is implied that he rules that even for the need of a Mitzvah it is forbidden [Nessuin]. Nevertheless, it is the custom today to be lenient like this opinion.
[109] Minchas Elazar 1:29; Nimukei Orach Chayim 339; Ashel Avraham [Butshatsh]; Shaareiy Halacha Uminhag 2:165; M"B 339:10 that for a Mitzvah purpose no need discourage those which are lenient.
Aruch Hashulchan 339:9 rules that the form of clapping and dancing done today was never included in the original decree of the Sages and hence it is always permitted to be done on Shabbos even not for a Mitzvah purpose. He learns this from the fact dancing was allowed on Simchas Torah and it is difficult to say we would nullify a Rabbinical prohibition for the sake of Simchas Torah. Hence, he concludes that in truth it is allowed. To note however that even according to our custom to allow dancing and clapping for Simcha on Shabbos and Yom Tov this is only because it is for the need of a Mitzvah, as is explained in Minchas Elazar ibid. However, for a non-Mitzvah purpose we would still hold by the original prohibition, unlike the Aruch Hashulchan.
[110] As all have accepted the allowance to dance and clap on Simchas Torah, and there is no reason to differentiate between Simchas Torah and Shabbos or other Holidays. [ibid]
[111] Shaareiy Halacha Uminhag ibid.

with his hands.[114]

4. Making noise to chase away animals and birds:[115]

One should[116] not chase away animals and birds from his orchard through clapping his hands together or against his thigh or by stamping his feet on the ground, if this is done in the normal way that it is done during the week.[117] One may however do so in an irregular form. Possibly in today's times one may even be lenient to do so in the regular fashion.[118]

---

[112] Az Nidbaru 13:14
[113] As explained above regarding clapping and dancing to a Niggun.
[114] Piskeiy Teshuvos 339 footnote 4
[115] Admur 338:5
[116] Ideally this is forbidden due to a Rabbinical decree, however since Admur concludes that today possibly this is allowed, therefore we wrote above that it is proper to avoid doing so and not that it is a complete prohibition. Being Admur does bring down the prohibition and does not plainly rule that one may be lenient, we therefore wrote that one should avoid doing so.
[117] This prohibition is due to a decree that one may come to pick up a stone and throw it at them towards a public area [Reshus Harabim] [ibid]
[118] As since today there are opinions which say the concept of a Reshus Harabim no longer exists, and rather all areas are Rabbinical regarding carrying, therefore the decree no longer applies, as the Sages did not make a decree upon a decree. Nevertheless, one is not to protests against women and children which play these games on the ground, as certainly they will not obey to the prohibition, and it is better they do so unintentionally then intentionally. [ibid]

CHAPTER 8: HOME CLEANLINESS
The laws involved in cleaning and repairing one's home on Shabbos
Compiled from Shulchan Aruch Chapters: 308; 320; 323; 333; 336; 337

Sweeping and Mopping [Halachas 1-4]

1. Sweeping on Shabbos:[1]
A. Using brooms made of hard strands:

Breakable strands:[2] It is forbidden to sweep on Shabbos using a broom made of twigs [or other hard strands] which easily break upon being used.[3] This applies to all types of floors, even tiled floors.[4] [Thus one may not use a straw broom to sweep with on Shabbos.[5]]

Non-breakable strands:[6] It is disputed amongst Poskim whether one may sweep an earth floor on Shabbos even if the material of the broom does not break while sweeping with it.[7] It is further disputed amongst Poskim if one may sweep a tiled floor on Shabbos.[8] Practically, if the material of the broom is hard, then even if it does not break while sweeping with it, it is forbidden to be used on even tiled or wooden floors,

---

[1] Admur 337:2-3

[2] Admur 337:3; Rama 337:2; Shiltei Giborim 36

[3] The reason: This is forbidden for two reasons:

1. When using brooms made of reeds [or other breakable materials], it is inevitable that the reeds will not break in the process, and hence sweeping with them is forbidden due to the prohibition of destroying a vessel. Now, although one who destroys is exempt [from Biblical liability], it is nevertheless Rabbinically forbidden. See 314:17. [Admur 337:3; Rama ibid] (For this reason it is also forbidden to sweep using a broom made of branches of a tree even on a tiled floor, even according to the lenient opinion who generally allows sweeping on a tiled floor. The lenient opinion was only lenient with regards to using a broom made of date leaves which do not break upon sweeping.) [Admur ibid, parentheses in original; M"A 337:5]

2. When using a hard broom on an earth floor, even if the material is not breakable, according to some opinions, it is inevitable for the broom not to smoothen the gaps of the floor which is forbidden due to the building prohibition, and according to some opinions this prohibition applies equally to a tiled floor. Practically the custom is to be stringent. [Admur 337:2, as explained next] Nevertheless in a city that majority of the houses have tiled floors [as is the case in all Western countries], it remains permitted to sweep on tiled floors even using hard material so long as the material does not break. If however the material does break then it is forbidden due to the reason explained next. [Ketzos Hashulchan 146:27]

[4] When using a hard material that is also easily breakable it is forbidden to be used on even tiled floors according to all opinions. Meaning that even according to those which normally allow sweeping on tiled floors they only allow doing so by brooms made of palm which does not break. [Admur ibid]

[5] SSH"K 23:1; Piskeiy Teshuvos 337:4 in name many Poskim, Upashut!

[6] Admur 337:2

Background:
When using a hard broom on an earth floor, even if the material is not breakable, according to some opinions, it is inevitable for the broom not to smoothen the gaps of the floor which is forbidden due to the building prohibition. [First and Stam opinion in Admur ibid; Stam opinion in Michaber 337:2; Rambam 21:3; Rashi Shabbos 124b; See Admur 277 Kuntrus Achron 1 that this is a case of Safek Pesik Reishei] According to some opinions this prohibition applies equally to a tiled floor as we decree against tiled floors due to that one may come to sweep on earth floors, as is the final ruling of Admur. [2nd opinion Admur ibid; Rama 337:2; Sefer Hateruma 254; Hagahos Maimanis on Rambam ibid; Mordechai 414] However other opinions rule that it is permitted to sweep stone floors and certainly wood floors [or floors tiled with other material], as there is no worry that one may come to level the ground. (Now, although this can lead one to sweep on an earth floor, since sweeping is a Shabbos necessity, therefore the Sages did not decree against doing so on tiled floors.) [1st and Stam opinion in Admur ibid; Michaber ibid; Rambam ibid] Furthermore, some opinions rule it is permitted to sweep even on earth floors, as they hold that the smoothening of the gaps is not inevitable. [2nd opinion Admur ibid; 2nd opinion in Michaber ibid; Tosafus Shabbos 95a in name of Bahag; Rif] Practically the custom is to be stringent that even by tiled floors it is forbidden to use a hard material broom. One may not divert from this custom. [Admur 337:2; Rama ibid; Rosh 22:15] Nevertheless, in a city that majority of the houses have tiled floors [as is the case in all Western countries], it remains permitted to sweep on tiled floors even using hard material so long as the material does not break. If, however, the material does break then it is forbidden due to the reason explained next. [Ketzos Hashulchan 146:27]

[7] The dispute: When using a hard broom on an earth floor, even if the material is not breakable, according to some opinions, it is inevitable for the broom not to smoothen the gaps of the floor which is forbidden due to the building prohibition. [First and Stam opinion in Admur ibid; Stam opinion in Michaber 337:2; Rambam 21:3; Rashi Shabbos 124b; See Admur 277 Kuntrus Achron 1 that this is a case of Safek Pesik Reishei] However some opinions rule it is permitted to sweep even on earth floors, as they hold that the smoothening of the gaps is not inevitable. [2nd opinion Admur ibid; 2nd opinion in Michaber ibid; Tosafus Shabbos 95a in name of Bahag; Rif]

[8] The dispute: According to some opinions this prohibition applies equally to a tiled floor as we decree against tiled floors due to that one may come to sweep on earth floors, as is the final ruling of Admur. [2nd opinion Admur ibid; Rama 337:2; Sefer Hateruma 254; Hagahos Maimanis on Rambam ibid; Mordechai 414] However other opinions rule that it is permitted to sweep stone floors and certainly wood floors [or floors tiled with other material], as there is no worry that one may come to level the ground. (Now, although this can lead one to sweep on an earth floor, since sweeping is a Shabbos necessity, therefore the Sages did not decree against doing so on tiled floors.) [1st and Stam opinion in Admur ibid; Michaber ibid; Rambam ibid]

due to a decree that one may come to sweep on an earth floor.[9] [If however majority of the city houses have tiled floors, it is permitted to sweep with hard, unbreakable, material brooms on tiled or wooden floors. It however remains prohibited to sweep with such material on an earth floor, or to sweep with breakable material on even a tiled floor.[10] Thus one may sweep his tiled floor using brooms which are made up of woven hairs, whether the hairs are synthetic or real.[11] However some Poskim[12] rule one is to only rely on this leniency if he had previously swept his floor on Erev Shabbos.]

B. Using brooms made of soft materials:[13]
It is permitted to sweep one's floor using a broom made of soft material, such as cloth, rag, or duck feather.[14] [This allowance applies both to tiled and earth floors.[15]]

C. Asking a gentile to sweep one's floor:[16]
It is permitted to ask a gentile to sweep one's floor in any situation [using any type of broom].[17] [This allowance applies even to sweeping an earth floor using a broom of hard breakable strands.]

D. May one sweep away Muktzah items?[18]
In cases that one is permitted to sweep [as explained above depending on the type of broom] it is permitted to also sweep filth that is Muktzah such as earth clumps, almond peels and other filthy items which are Muktzah.[19] It is however forbidden to use a broom to move Muktzah items that have a use, and are not viewed as filth or garbage.[20]

---

[9] Admur 337:2; Rama ibid; Rosh 22:15; See previous footnotes in the first reason behind the prohibition.

[10] Ketzos Hashulchan 146:27 in name of M"B and Iglei Tal. Biur Halacha "Veyeish Machmirim"

[11] SSH"K ibid; Piskeiy Teshuvos ibid

[12] SSH"K 23:1 in name of Biur Halacha 327 "Veyeish"; This opinion is not made mention of in the Ketzos Hashulchan.

[13] Admur 337:2; Rama 337:2; Igur 517

[14] As such materials are light and will not smooth the gaps of a floor. [ibid]

[15] Ketzos Hashulchan 146:27 and so is implied from Admur and M"B 337:11

The reason: As such materials are light and will not come to smooth the gaps of an earth floor.

Other Opinions: SSH"K 23:1 rules it is only allowed on tiled floors.

[16] Admur 337:2

[17] As any [action forbidden due to an] inevitable occurrence is permitted to be done through a gentile. [ibid]

[18] Admur 337:2; M"A 337:4; Biur Halacha 308:27 "Minaeri"

[19] The reason: It is permitted to sweep them being that they are to the person like a pile of filth, which the Sages permitted one to remove to the garbage, due to one's dignity. [Admur ibid; Rashba and Ran; M"B 337:12] Alternatively the reason is because this is considered Tiltul Min Hatzad which is permitted to be done for a Mutar item, such as to make room on the floor. [Shaar Hatziyon 337:7; Biur Halacha 337:2 "Veyeish Machmirim"; Ramban in Milchamos 48b] Admur negates this reason in 308:60, and 259 Kuntrus Achron 3, based on M"A 259:8.

[20] So is implied from Admur here which depends the allowance on the Muktzah being a Graf Shel Reiy. See also 308:60, and Chapter 259 Halacha 4 and Kuntrus Achron 3. See Volume 1 "The Laws of Muktzah" Chapter 1 Halacha 3C!

Other opinions: According to those that rule one may move Muktzah with a knife for the need of the space [Taz 308:18; M"B 308115] would likewise rule here that it is allowed.

Summary-Sweeping on Shabbos with a broom:

Brooms made of hard materials: If the strands of the broom are easily breakable within the process of sweeping, it is forbidden to be used on any type of floor. If made of hard strands that are not easily breakable in the process of sweeping, it is permitted to be used to sweep tiled or wooden floors, however, not earth floors. [Thus, one may sweep his tiled floor using brooms which are made up of woven hairs, whether the hairs are synthetic or real[21].] If majority of the houses of one's city have earth floors, then it is forbidden to sweep using such brooms even on tiled floors.

Brooms made of soft materials: Are permitted to be used on both tiled and earth[22] floors. Soft material brooms are brooms made of cloth, feathers and the like.

Q&A

May one sweep a carpet?

One may do so using a regular broom.[23] One may not use a specially manufactured carpet broom.[24]

List of brooms and their law:

- Straw broom: Forbidden[25]
- Broom with synthetic hairs: Permitted on tiled floors[26] in cities that majority of floors are tiled.[27]

May one screw in the rod of a broom into a broom?[28]

No. It is forbidden to insert a broom onto a broomstick even if it does not involve using any screws. It is likewise forbidden to tighten the attachment while it is already attached.

Question:

Is it permitted to sweep leaves that have fallen onto my patio on Shabbos and does it make a difference if they fell before Shabbos or on Shabbos?

Answer:

It is permitted to sweep leaves from a **tiled** floor on Shabbos, such as the floor of one's patio, if it is disturbing the cleanliness of the area, just as is allowed regarding sweeping the floor of one's home. This applies irrelevant of when these leaves fell from the tree. It is however forbidden to sweep leaves from an earth floor due to a sweeping prohibition.

Explanation: Sweeping Muktzah on Shabbos poses two halachic issues; 1) a Muktzah prohibition 2) a sweeping prohibition. The Muktzah prohibition is waived in the event that an item is defined as a Geraf Shel Reiy, which means that its presence is considered a disturbance to the people who use the area. Thus, being that a dirty floor is considered a disturbance to a home or other area that one is sitting in, therefore it is permitted to sweep dirt from it on Shabbos. In this regard, there is no difference as to

---

[21] SSH"K ibid; Piskeiy Teshuvos ibid

[22] As such materials are light and will not come to smooth the gaps of an earth floor. So rules Ketzos Hashulchan 146:27 and so is implied from Admur and M"B [337:11].
Other Opinions: However the SSH"K 23:1 rules that it is only allowed on tiled floors.

[23] Minchas Yitzchak 5:39

[24] Minchas Yitzchak ibid; Beir Moshe 1:32
It is forbidden due to it being a mundane act and a belittling of Shabbos, as well as it having a suspicion of the whitening prohibition. [ibid]

[25] SSH"K 23:1; Piskeiy Teshuvos 337:4 in name many Poskim, Upashut!

[26] Piskeiy Teshuvos 337:4 in name many Poskim, Upashut!

[27] As seemingly the hairs of such brooms are considered hard material, and hence would only be allowed a) on tiled floors and b) only if majority of the cities floors are tiled.]

[28] SSH"K 23:1

when the leaves fell from the tree, as either way it is considered Muktzah. [Seemingly this is being confused with the law of a fruit that fell from a tree in which case we differentiate between if it fell before Shabbos, in which case it is not Muktzah, and if it fell on Shabbos, in which case it is Muktzah. This has nothing to do with the question of whether you are allowed to sweep Muktzah which is disturbing the peace of an area.] Now, regarding the sweeping prohibition, although ideally the Rama rules that it applies to both tiled and untitled surfaces, nonetheless, practically today the Achronim conclude that it is permitted to sweep tiled surfaces, and the prohibition remains only with sweeping earth floors.

Sources: See regarding sweeping Muktzah: Admur 337:2; M"A 337:4; M"B 337:12; Biur Halacha 308:27 "Minaeri"; See regarding sweeping in general on a tiled versus an earth floor: Admur 337:2; Rama 337:2; Biur Halacha "Veyeish Machmirim"; Ketzos Hashulchan 146:27

2. Is a broom Muktzah?[29]

Those brooms which are permitted to be used on Shabbos to sweep with, as explained above, are not Muktzah. Those brooms which are forbidden to be used as explained above are considered MM"I.
Practically:[30] A broom made of hard material [which can break such as a straw broom[31]] is MM"I. A broom made of soft material [or hard material that cannot break[32] such as synthetic hair[33]] is not Muktzah.[34]

3. May one brush his clothing using a brush or broom?[35]

It is forbidden to brush one's clothes using a brush which its strands will inevitably break in the process of the brushing.[36] [Furthermore, even if the brush is made of hairs and it will not break in the process, the custom is to forbidden using it on clothing being it appears like fixing a vessel and is considered a mundane act.[37]]

---

[29] Admur 308:87

[30] According to all brooms made of inevitably breakable material are MM"I as they are forbidden to be used.
Regarding brooms made of materials which will not inevitably break:
According to those which permit sweeping tiled floors with such brooms, they are not Muktzah as they are like a vessel which is designated for a permitted use. Now, although that during the week one uses them to sweep also [dirt] floors that are not tiled [and thus since on Shabbos it is not fit for this it should have the status of a vessel designated for prohibited use], nevertheless it is [still] like a vessel that is designated for a permitted and forbidden use, of which the law is that one is permitted to move just like a vessel that is [only] designated for a permitted use.
However according to those which forbid to sweep on Shabbos even floors that are tiled, then it is forbidden to move them unless one is doing so in order to use it [for a permitted use] or in order to use its space, just like [is the law by any] vessel that is designated [for only] forbidden use.
The final ruling: We are accustomed to be stringent, although by cities that majority of the houses have tiled floors we are lenient.
Regarding brooms made of soft materials, such as a cloth:
Are not Muktzah according to all

[31] SSH"K 23:1; Piskeiy Teshuvos 337:4 in name many Poskim, Upashut!

[32] As today we allow sweeping tiled floors being that majority of the houses are tiled. [Ketzos Hashulchan 146:27 in name of M"B and Iglei Tal. Biur Halacha "Veyeish Machmirim"]

[33] SSH"K ibid; Piskeiy Teshuvos ibid

[34] Admur 308:87; 337:3-4

[35] Admur 337:3

[36] When using brooms made of reeds and other breakable materials, it is inevitable that the reeds will not break in the process, and hence sweeping with them is forbidden due to the prohibition of destroying a vessel. Now although one who destroys is exempt [from Biblical liability], it is nevertheless Rabbinically forbidden. [ibid]

[37] Tiferes Yisrael in Kalkeles Shabbos 13; Yearos Devash; Makor Chaim 302; Ketzos Hashulchan 146 footnote 62; Piskeiy Teshuvos 302:2; See however Biur Halacha ibid from whom it is evident that he did not hold of this prohibition

---

Q&A

May one clean furniture?[38]

It is forbidden to clean furniture using a brush or cloth that has been manufactured specifically for this purpose.[39] One may however brush off dust and the like using a broom or standard brush.[40]

Shaking the dust off: One may slightly shake dust off old furniture, however not from new dark furniture. He however may not shake heavily even old furniture.[41]

---

4. Mopping on Shabbos:[42]

Mopping: It is forbidden to pour water over one's floor in order to mop it.[43] This applies equally to all floors, even tiled.[44] [This applies even if one does not use a cloth to mop with but rather a plane Squeegee mop. Using a cloth mop, in addition to containing a mopping prohibition as well contains a laundering prohibition.[45]]

Shining one's floor: It is forbidden to pour oil onto one's floor.[46] This applies equally to all floors, even if tiled.[47]

Ributz-pouring water over an earth floor:[48] It is permitted to pour water[49] over the [earth floor of one's] house [in order to prevent the earth from dusting up the room[50]].[51]

Summary:

It is forbidden to mop one's floor on Shabbos, even with a squeegee mop.

Q&A

If liquid spilled on one's floor may one squeegee the water?[52]

Yes.[53]

---

[38] SSH"K 23:4; Piskeiy Teshuvos 338:2

[39] Due to it being a mundane act and possibly carrying with it the whitening prohibition. [ibid]

[40] So rules the Minchas Yitzchak 5:39 regarding carpets and seemingly the same applies by furniture. Now, although above we brought from the Ketzos Hashulchan that one may not use even a standard brush for clothing due to it being a mundane act, nevertheless this is only because by clothing it appears like one is fixing the clothing, which is Tikkun Keli. However, by furniture, it is similar to a floor of which all agree that soft brushes may be used. [SSH"K 23 footnote 18]

[41] Based on 302:1 regarding shaking water off new clothing. [SSH"K ibid]

[42] Admur 337:4

[43] This prohibition is due to a decree that one may come to smoothen the ditches in the floor, which is a subcategory of the building prohibition. [ibid]

[44] This applies even in accordance to those opinions which allow sweeping a tiled floor on Shabbos, as mopping does not contain as much of a need as does sweeping. Hence, they too agree that by mopping the Sages did not differentiate in their decree between a dirt floor or tiled floor, and they forbade mopping on any of them. [ibid] Thus this prohibition applies even if majority of the city floors are tiled.

[45] M"B 337:17 [If however the cloth is designated for this purpose, it does not contain a laundering prohibition, but is nevertheless prohibited due to squeezing.]

[46] In past times oil was poured on a tiled floor in order so one roll over the oil and enter the oil into his skin. Alternatively, it is done in order to shine the floor. In any event it is forbidden to be done for either reason. [Tosefta 17:10]

[47] As explained in previous footnotes regarding mopping.
Admur adds from the Tosefta that one is not to be "Nofeiach" the floor on Shabbos. Seemingly the meaning of this is that one is not to blow the dust off the floor. Vetzaruch Iyun from Minchas Bikurim on the Tosefta there. See Biur Halacha 337 "Velo Madichin".

[48] Admur 337:2

[49] Lit. Lerabeitz. The above explanation is based on Mishneh Berurah 337:5

[50] M"B 337:5

[51] The reason that doing so does not involve a prohibition is because one does not intend to flatten out the gaps [in the ground] but rather to prevent the dust from rising, and it is not inevitable [that one will consequently fill up the gaps in the floor in the process.] [ibid]

[52] Piskeiy Teshuvos 338:5; SSH"K 23:7

[53] As since one did not place the water on the floor with intent to mop it, it is therefore permitted to sweep it away. [ibid]

May one remove the drain cover of one's floor on Shabbos in order to squeegee spilled water into the hole?[54]

If the cover has a handle, or indentation which forms a handle area, then it is permitted to be removed[55]. If there is no handle at all then it is forbidden and is Muktzah.

If water spilled on one's floor may one place a rag over the water to clean it up?[56]

One may place a designated[57] cloth [i.e. rag] over a spill in order so it absorbs the liquid, whether it is water or other liquid. However, one may not wipe the cloth around the floor due to the mopping [and squeezing] prohibition.

May one clean with water a dirty spot on the ground?

Some Poskim[58] rule it is permitted to place water on a dirty area of the floor and then clean the water it in a permitted way [such as to place a rag over the water without moving it around or to squeegee the water].

May one wash and dry one's counter?[59]

It is permitted to clean one's counter using water, synthetic cloth and a squeegee. If using a cloth to dry one must beware not to squeeze it in the process.

May one ask a gentile to mop his floor?[60]

With a squeegee: Yes.[61]

With a rag: One may not ask a gentile to use a rag to mop.[62] If one asked a gentile to mop without mentioning any specific way and he decided to use a rag to do so, it is best to protest against the gentile even on a tiled floor. However, those which are accustomed to allow the gentile to continue using the rag on a tiled floor without protesting his actions have upon what to rely.

May one polish his floor on Shabbos?[63]

No.

May a hospital mop the floors for hygienic purposes?[64]

Yes. A hospital may be lenient to mop a tiled floor using a squeegee mop [no cloth] for hygienic purposes.[65]

---

[54] Piskeiy Teshuvos 308:13; SSH"K 23 footnote 28

[55] Vetzaruch Iyun as why this is not forbidden being that the cover is attached to the ground and is only removed infrequently. Perhaps however since it is meant for constant removal and insertion it is permitted to be removed, even though one does not constantly remove it.

[56] Az Nidbaru 1:79-97

[57] Meaning that the cloth must be designated for cleaning spills. However, a regular clothing such as a shirt and the like may not be used due to the laundering prohibition.

[58] SSH"K 23 footnote 27 in name of Rav SZ"A

[59] SSH"K 12:40; Piskeiy Teshuvos 338:6

[60] Kaf Hachayim 337:21

[61] Admur 337:2 regarding sweeping and so seemingly applies for mopping, and so is implied from Kaf Hachayim.

[62] This is similar to asking a gentile to remove fish from water which is forbidden to be done due to it being a Pesik Reishei. It is not similar to other cases of Pesik Reishei which are permitted to be done through a gentile [see 253:10] as there the Melacha is not being done to the item desired but rather to a different item.

[63] Admur ibid; SSH"K 23:3

[64] SSH"K

[65] As in such a case the mopping is as much of a need as is sweeping, and hence the Sages would be lenient. [ibid]

Moving Furniture
5. *Dragging furniture across one's floor or ground:* [66]

It is permitted to drag an average size table, chair, or bed over any floor, including an earth floor, so long as one has no intent to form a ditch in the earth[67] and doing so does not inevitably cause the ditch to be formed. This applies even if one has other furniture available and does not need specifically to drag this piece of furniture.

If the furniture is very heavy and dragging it on the ground will certainly cause a ditch to be formed, it is forbidden to be done, even if one has no intention to form the ditch.[68] Furthermore, such furniture may not even be dragged inside one's house over a tiled floor, due to a decree that one may come to drag it on an earth floor.[69] [If however the ground of all[70] the houses of one's city is tiled, whether with tiles, wood, or other material, it is permitted to drag furniture such as a chair, bed or table over the floor.[71] [**Regarding if moving a heavy closet and the like contains a Muktzah prohibition, see Q&A!**]

Summary:
It is permitted to drag furniture over the floor of one's house. It is forbidden to drag furniture over an earth floor if doing so will inevitably cause a ditch to be dug.

Q&A
May one push a baby carriage over an earth floor, such as over the ground outside, in a place where there is an Eiruv?[72]
Yes.[73] This is permitted even if one pushes the carriage to the side and makes a ditch in the earth.[74] It is forbidden to push a stroller in an area that does not have an Eiruv.[75]

May one push a wheelchair over an earth floor?
Yes.

Are closets and bookcases which are designated to a specific area allowed to be moved?
Many Poskim[76] forbid moving closets and bookcases due to considering the closets as Muktzah. However seemingly this matter is subject to the same dispute regarding if items of sentimental value[77] are Muktzah in which some learn[78] that according to Admur it is permitted.

---

[66] Admur 337:1

[67] Which is forbidden due to the prohibition of Choreish/plowing.

[68] As the rule by unintended transgressions is that if the transgression is inevitable occurrence of one's action then it is as if one intended to do so, and is hence forbidden to be done. Now although this inevitable forming of the ditch is being done through an irregularity, as one is only liable for digging when it is done with its proper tools, as well as this formation is not beneficial for one's ground but is rather destructive, as well as that it is a Melacha Sheyino Tzarich Legufa, nevertheless it is Rabinically forbidden to be done. [ibid]

[69] Vetzaruch Iyun, as if even on an earth floor it is a mere Rabbinical prohibition, would it not violate the rule "we do not make decrees upon decrees" to decree that even on tiled floors it may not be dragged?

[70] In Ketzos Hashulchan 146:27 he writes majority of the city houses, and so seems to be also the intent here. Vetzaruch Iyun in why he changed the wording.

[71] Ketzos Hashulchan 146:26; Biur Halacha "Veyeish Machmirim"

[72] Ketzos Hashulchan 146 footnote 52

[73] Doing so does not form ditches within the earth but rather presses it more in. There is likewise no prohibition of "mundane act" involved in pushing a baby carriage outside, as there is with regards to carrying someone in a chair on Yom Tov [522:3], as it is very difficult to carry a baby otherwise, and there is thus no longer worry that doing so belittles Shabbos. [ibid]

[74] SSH"K 28:42

[75] Piskeiy Teshuvos 337:1

[76] M"B 308:8; SSH"K 20:22

[77] See Volume 1 "The Laws of Muktzah" Halacha 4 Q&A!

[78] Piskeiy Teshuvos 308:2. However see footnote there.

Cleaning one's table
6. The laws of removing leftovers from one's table:[79]

Introduction: Certain leftover foods are considered Muktzah and are therefore forbidden to be moved. The question hence arises how is one to clean his table from leftovers after the Shabbos meal. It is always permitted to shake the leftovers off the table as will be explained, although this would cause one's floor to become dirty. Hence the question is asked how is it allowed to move the actual leftovers from the table, or move the tablecloth with the leftovers and throw it in the garbage. There are a few scenarios in which doing so is allowed as will be explained.

What leftover foods are considered Muktzah? All leftover bones, shells and peels which are unfit for animal consumption, or are fit for animal consumption but these animals are not commonly found, are defined as MM"G[80] and are forbidden to be moved with ones hands for any reason. *For the entire details of this subject see Volume 1 "The Laws of Muktzah" Halacha 6B!*

Removing crumbs from one's table: Crumbs are not considered Muktzah and thus may be removed from one's table.[81]

May one remove Muktzah leftovers from one's table using his hands? If the bones and peels are unfit for animal consumption, or they are fit for animal consumption but these animals are not commonly found, then they are defined as MM"G and are forbidden to be moved with ones hands for any reason.

Moving the items with a knife: It is forbidden to move Muktzah leftovers even with using a knife. *See Volume 1 "The Laws of Muktzah" Halacha 3B for the full details on this subject!*

Shaking the Muktzah leftovers off the table: In all cases it is permitted to shake the Muktzah leftovers off the table through shaking the table or tablecloth hence causing the leftovers to fall to the ground. [82]

May one move the tablecloth together with Muktzah leftovers without shaking them off?[83] In general it is forbidden to pick up a table or tablecloth together with Muktzah items and carry them elsewhere. [84] Rather one must first shake off the Muktzah item from the table or tablecloth. Thus, it would likewise be forbidden to carry the tablecloth with the leftovers to throw it in the garbage. Nevertheless, there are three cases in which it is allowed to remove the leftovers. The following are the exceptions:

1. There is bread on the table: Whenever there is bread on the tablecloth it is permitted to remove the tablecloth together with all its leftovers and throw it in the garbage. [85] Likewise, if there is bread on one's plate, he may remove the plate and shake the leftovers into the garbage. [See Q&A]

2. One does not want to shake of the leftovers onto the floor: If one does not want to shake the leftovers onto the floor due to that he needs to use that space in which the leftovers were to fall on, then he is not required to shake them off and may rather carry the table or tablecloth together with the leftovers and discard it in the garbage.

3. The leftovers are considered repulsive: If the presence of the Muktzah leftovers such as bones, shells and peels has become repulsive to the person to the point that he is disgusted by them, then he may even remove the leftovers with his hands.[86] However one is not allowed to initially place the

---

[79] Admur 308:60

[80] Muktzah Machmas Gufo

[81] It is permitted to remove from one's table [onto one's floor] crumbs which are smaller than [the size of a] Kezayis [approximately 27 grams], even though they are not designated to be eaten by humans [being that crumbs that are less than a Kezayis are insignificant for humans] and rather [are now only standing to be eaten] by animals or birds. [ibid]
However, a crumb which is more than a Kezayis is forbidden to throw on the floor even during the week being that doing so is degrading to the food.

[82] As since the table was not a *Basis* by dusk it does not have the law of a Basis and may thus be tilted. The moving of the Muktzah through shaking it off a surface that is not a Basis is permitted as shaking is not considered actually moving. Rather shaking is considered an irregularity [which is permitted by Muktzah]. [ibid] See chapter 309 Halacha 6 that even shaking off is only allowed if one needs to use the base that it is on, or the space. However, for the use of the Muktzah object it is forbidden for one to even shake off with his hands, even though this is considered an irregular way of shaking. However, one is allowed to shake it off using his body.

[83] Admur 308:60-61

[84] As this is considered *Tiltul Gamur* (moving without an irregularity), as moving from the side "Tiltul Min Hatzad" was only permitted when done in an irregular way which is defined as shaking off the Muktzah objects. [ibid]

[85] The reason is because the peels are considered nullified to the bread and it is hence permitted to be moved. [ibid]

[86] M"B 308:115; brought in Ketzos Hashulchan 111 footnote 9; implied from Admur 308:67; This applies even if he threw them there with full intent that they would become repulsive.

leftovers on the table with intent to discard the leftovers on these premises.[87] [Accordingly, if the first two allowances mentioned above are not applicable, and one hence would need to discard the leftovers on the pretense of them being a disgusting item, in such a case he should try not to place the inedible peels of foods on the table with the intention to later throw out the tablecloth in a status of a disgusting item. Rather he should throw them straight in the garbage. [Practically the best advice is to simply place a piece of bread on the plate or tablecloth and then place the peels on the plate or tablecloth, and this will allow him to throw out the plate/tablecloth together with the inedible items.[88]]

Summary-Removing Muktzah leftovers from the table:
If there is bread on one's plate one may remove the plate together with the leftovers. If there is bread on the tablecloth one may remove the entire tablecloth with all its Muktzah leftovers. If there is no bread on the table, and one has no bread available to place on the table, one may carry the tablecloth with its leftovers to the garbage if shaking the contents onto the floor will prevent one from using that space for an intended purpose. If one is repulsed by the leftovers, he may even remove them directly with his hands.

Q&A
May one initially place bread on the table in order to be allowed to remove the tablecloth, or must the bread be there before the inedible foods were placed on the table?
It is permitted to place the bread on the table even after the waste had initially been placed there, in order to be allowed to move it.[89] It goes without saying that one may initially place the bread on the table beforehand and then throw the waste onto it.[90]

Do items other than bread which are placed on the table also allow one to move the tablecloth?
Some Poskim[91] rule that other items, such as a spoon and knife, suffice to allow one to move the tablecloth together with the leftovers. Other Poskim[92] rule that only with bread is this allowed.[93]

Cleaning spills

7. How to clean spills on Shabbos:

Introduction: Cleaning a spill on Shabbos involves two actions which touch upon a number of possible prohibitions. These two actions are: 1) Wetting the cloth with the spill and 2) Moving around the soaked cloth. Wetting a cloth on Shabbos touches upon a possible laundering and dyeing prohibition. Moving a soaked cloth around touches upon a possible squeezing prohibition. The Halachic details of the laundering, squeezing and dyeing prohibitions will be discussed below, and a final summary will be given. Please refer to there for the final ruling.

1. Laundering-The laws involved in wetting a cloth:[94] It is forbidden to wet a cloth with clear liquids due to the laundering prohibition. This however only applies if the cloth is not designated for this

---

[87] Admur 308:67 and 77
[88] Hagahos Chasam Sofer 308:27
[89] M"B 308:116; The M"A [308:51] brings a difference of opinions regarding this matter. The PR"M there learns that the opinion of the M"A himself is to allow one to place the bread on the table even after the inedible foods were placed there. Vetzaruch Iyun if according to Admur one may place the bread just in order to be allowed to move the shells, as how can the shells be nullified to the bread if the entire bringing of the bread is for the purpose of the shells.
[90] Chasam Sofer 308:27 in Otzer Hamifarshim of SH"A-Habahir
[91] Az Nidbaru 9:33
[92] Minchas Yitzchak 7:16
[93] To note that bread is given special importance over other items in the laws dealing with a Basis, that bread is always considered more important than is the Muktzah items. On the other hand, regarding the laws of moving a dead body by placing bread on it, it is explained that all permitted items may be placed.
[94] Admur 302:20; 319:13; 320:21

purpose. If, however, the cloth is designated for a purpose which involves getting it wet, such as to filter water or to clean spills, then the laundering prohibition of wetting a cloth does not apply. [95] The laundering prohibition never applies in wetting a cloth with colored liquids.[96]

2. Dyeing: It is forbidden to dye clothing on Shabbos. It is forbidden to cause clothing to become dyed, even if one does not have intent to dye them, and is simply trying to clean his hands and the like.[97] Not all colored liquids contain the dyeing prohibition, and it depends on the thickness of the color.[98] Clothes that are designated for wiping may be used to clean a spill of any colored liquid.[99] Doing so is not prohibited due to the dyeing prohibition, as the dyeing prohibition only applies when one is intentionally doing so for the purpose of dyeing, or when done to a non-designated cloth which is common to dye.[100]

3. The laws involved in squeezing a cloth: [101] It is forbidden to squeeze liquids out from a cloth due to the Mifarek prohibition[102] and at times also due to the laundering/Milaben prohibition[103]. This

---

[95] If the cloth is not designated for this purpose of cleaning spills it is forbidden to soak it in clear liquids due to the laundering prohibition. As if one intends to soak it in the liquid in order to whiten the cloth, he would be liable for laundering. Likewise, if one would proceed to squeeze the liquid out from the cloth he would be liable for laundering. Hence it is forbidden to use such cloths to clean clear liquid spills. However, if the cloth is designated for this purpose then there is no reason to suspect one may place it on the spill for laundering purposes or come to squeeze the liquid out, as this is the entire purpose of the cloth. [319:13; 320:21]

[96] This is allowed as the laundering/whitening prohibition only applies when using water and white wine and the like.
Likewise it is not forbidden due to a decree that one may come to squeeze it and be liable for "detaching", as one is only liable if he needs the liquids being squeezed, of which there is no remote suspicion [here] that one may squeeze the cloth for the sake of the liquids that will come out from it being that [these liquids] are not of any significance and it is not at all common to do this. [320:21]

[97] 1st opinion and final ruling in Admur 320:27

[98] See regarding wine: Ketzos Hashulchan 146 Badei Hashulchan 16 number 13; Shabbos Kihalacha Vol. 2 page 352 and 384

[99] Kuntrus Achron 302:1; See 319:13; 320:21; M"A 319:11; Ketzos Hashulchan 136 footnote 11; SSH"K 14:19; Piskeiy Teshuvos 320:11 based on Admur Kuntrus Achron 302; Shabbos Kehalacha Vol. 3 20:20 [p. 295]
Other opinions: Some Poskim rule it does not suffice to designate a garment for this purpose, and only by an item which people do not care to dye does the allowance apply. [Avnei Nezer 175, brought in Ketzos Hashulchan 136 footnote 11]

[100] The reason: Seemingly, the reason why a designated cloth helps is because it is evident to all that one is not doing an act of dyeing [or laundering] when using it to clean his hands [or strain liquid through] and it is hence not simailr to the Melacha at all. If however the cloth is not desiganated for this purpose, then it appears as if one is soing an act of dyeing, or laundering, and is hence at least Rabiniclaly forbidden. Alternatively, the reason is because once the cloth has been designated for this purpose it is no longer common to dye it at all, and hence there is no need to decree against dyeing if one has no intent to do so. If however one intends to dye it or launder it, then certainly it is forbidden to do on Shabbos even if one designated the cloth for this purpose. It is only that when it is done Derech Lichluch, and no intent to dye, and is not common to dye that we permit it. The practical ramification would be regarding a urine test sticks, and baby diapers that change color, as explained in Q&A at end of chapter!

[101] Admur 320:24
The Background:
Squeezing white Liquids from undesignated cloths: Is forbidden to be squeezed due to the laundering prohibition even if done unintentionally as the squeezing is inevitable.
Squeezing out colored liquids or from a designated cloth:
It is subject to dispute whether squeezing liquids that will be going to waste is forbidden and practically Admur rules to be stringent.
- First opinion: In 320:23 Admur rules one may not clean using a sponge without a handle even though the squeezed liquid goes to waste and one is doing so unintentionally.
- Second Opinion: However, in 320:24 Admur notes another opinion: *"[However] there are opinions which say that so long as the liquid is going to waste then there is only a Rabbinical prohibition involved if one has intention to squeeze it, however so long as he does not intend to [squeeze] it, even if this is an inevitable occurrence, it is permitted. Their reasoning is because the squeezing [of this cloth] gives one no satisfaction being that one has no benefit from it, and it was only made forbidden to insert Mochin into the opening of the bottle even though he has no intent to squeeze it because the liquid that is being squeezed out from the Mochin into the bottle of which one benefits from this squeezing. However the liquids that are squeezed from the cloth that surrounds the pipe goes to waste if there is no vessel under them, and there is thus nothing to benefit from it for him.*
- *The Final ruling: "The main Halachic opinion is like the former opinion, as a sponge that does not have a handle may not be used to clean with even though he has no intention to squeeze [liquid out] and the liquid which is squeezed from the sponge goes to waste."*

[102] Even cloths which have been soaked in liquids which do not whiten [i.e. have been soaked in colored liquids], are forbidden to be squeezed. The reason for this restriction is due to the prohibition of "detaching" which is an offshoot of [the] threshing [prohibition] just as squeezing fruits is prohibited because of "detaching." However, one is only liable on this squeezing if he needs the liquids being squeezed from the cloth, however if one does not need the liquids squeezed out from the cloth and is only doing so in order to clean the cloth, then this is not similar to threshing at all, as by threshing one needs the grains that he is detaching from the stalks, and therefore this squeezing does not contain a Biblical prohibition but rather Rabbinical. [320:21]

[103] One who squeezes a cloth [which had absorbed clear/white liquids] until its liquids come out is considered as if he has laundered clothing and is thus liable for [the] whitening [prohibition]. [301:56] However if it had absorbed red wine or beer or other liquids which do not whiten then there contains no laundering prohibition in squeezing out these liquids. [320:21] If the cloth is designated to get wet then if one squeezes white liquids from it with intent to launder it, it is Biblically forbidden due to the laundering prohibition. If one squeezes it out for other reasons it is not forbidden due to laundering. [So is implied from 320:21 and 24]

applies in all cases[104] even if the squeezed liquid will be going to waste[105], and one is doing so unintentionally but inevitably.

Practically, in what way is it allowed to clean a spill?
Placing a cloth on the spill: One may drop a rag on the spill and have it absorb the liquid on its own. If the spill involves a clear liquid, such as water or white wine, then only cloths which are designated for cleaning, such as a rag, tissue or napkin may be used. However other clothing, such as a towel or shirt and the like is forbidden to even be placed on the spill. If the spill involves colored liquids then all cloths may be placed on the spill to absorb the liquid.[106]

Moving the cloth around the spill: It is forbidden to clean spills in a way that will cause liquids to be squeezed from the cleaning material. Hence one may not take a cloth or sponge in one's hand and move it around the spill, as doing so will inevitably cause liquid to squeeze from the rag.[107] If however one has a sponge or cloth[108] that is attached to a handle then one may hold it by the handle and [gently[109]] clean the spill.[110] [If however even when using the handle one sees that it causes inevitable squeezing from the cloth then one is not to use it.[111]]

Cleaning a spill of liquid with intent of having the liquid drip back into its vessel:[112] It is forbidden to clean a spill of liquid with any cloth or sponge if one plans to drip the absorbed liquid from the cloth back

---

[104] Meaning even by colored liquids where the Milabein prohibition is inapplicable.

[105] However, in such a case if the liquid is a colored liquid doing so is only Rabbinically forbidden. If it is white liquids it is Biblically forbidden. [320:21] If, however, one is squeezing white liquids from a designated cloth then it is only Rabbinically forbidden if done unintentionally. [320:24] There are opinions which rule that all designated cloths, or even non-designated cloths which have been soaked in colored liquids, may be squeezed even intentionally so long as one does not intend to make use of the liquid as the Mifareik prohibition only applies when one wants to use the liquid. We do not rule like this opinion. [ibid as stated above in background]

[106] Admur 319:13; 320:21
This is allowed as the laundering/whitening prohibition only applies when using water and white wine and the like.
Likewise it is not forbidden due to a decree that one may come to squeeze it and be liable for "detaching", as one is only liable if he needs the liquids being squeezed, of which there is no remote suspicion [here] that one may squeeze the cloth for the sake of the liquids that will come out from it being that [these liquids] are not of any significance and it is not at all common to do this. [320:21]

[107] Admur 320:22-24

[108] This refers to a cloth that does not involve a laundering prohibition in wetting it as explained above.

[109] This is based on the explanation in the next footnote and so rules explicitly Shabbos Kehalacha Vol. 3 18:52

[110] Admur 320:23; SSH"K 12 footnote 37
The dispute behind the reason that it is allowed to use a sponge with a handle: The reason this is allowed is because when using a handle to clean with nothing squeezes out from the sponge in the process. [However] there is an opinion which says that even if [the sponge] has a handle it is impossible to clean with the sponge without squeezing it and nevertheless it is permitted as since the squeezing is being done through the [pressing of] the handle it is [therefore] not [Halachicly] considered squeezing and is rather like emptying water from a flask which does not contain [the] "detaching" [prohibition]. However, when it does not have a handle in which case it gets squeezed in the area that he holds it with his hand, then it is forbidden. [ibid]
The practical ramification between these two reasons is in a case that liquid will certainly be squeezed from the sponge. Thus whether one may apply strength when using a sponge with a handle to clean the liquid, and inevitably cause the liquid to spill, is subject to the above dispute.
Practically: It is implied that Admur rules mainly like the first opinion mentioned there that using a handle is only allowed due to it not being an inevitable occurrence. If, however, one sees the squeezing is inevitable, then it once again becomes prohibited. [So is evident from 320:24 that we do not hold of the 2nd opinion above as the final Halacha, as Admur does not simply allow inserting a barrel pipe with a cloth due to this reason, but adds that one must also make sure the liquid goes to waste. In the words of Admur 320:24: "As many argue on their words." Vetzaruch Iyun if these words are going on the opinion of Raavad that even if it squeezes out it is allowed, or if it's going on opinion of the Melamdim Zechus. Furthermore, Tzaruch Iyun on if one can truly derive anything from the Barza case to a regular sponge case, as seemingly Admur learns that a Barza does not have the same status as a handle of the sponge and that's why the Heter is not so clear, however by an actual handle of a sponge perhaps Admur would be lenient even if the liquid does not go to waste, and certainly if it does. Vetzaruch Iyun. I later however found in Shabbos Kehalacha Vol. 3 p. 211-212 a similar conclusion that it is evident from Admur that one may only use a sponge with a handle if it does not inevitably cause squeezing. He deduces this also from Ketzos Hashulchan [133-end] that a toothbrush, despite it having a handle, is forbidden to be used due to it causing inevitable squeezing.

[111] Shabbos Kehalacha ibid, **Based on what was explained in the previous footnote:** If the liquid will not be going to waste then certainly one may not do so. ["As many argue on the lenient opinion"-320:24] If the liquid is going to waste, then it seems from Michaber/Admur that initially even so one should not do so although those which are lenient have upon what to rely. [As Admur/Michaber rule by the Barza case that it should not be done and it is only that we are Melamed Zechus on those that do. However, Tzaruch Iyun on if one can truly derive anything from the Barza case to a regular sponge case, as seemingly Admur learns that a Barza does not have the same status as a handle of the sponge and that's why the Heter is not so clear, however by an actual handle of a sponge perhaps Admur would be lenient even if the liquid does not go to waste, and certainly if it does. Vetzaruch Iyun.]
See M"B 320:55; SSH"K 12 footnote 37; Minchas Yitzchak 3:50

[112] Admur 335:1

into its vessel.[113] This prohibition applies even if one only desires to clean and save only part of the spill for use on Shabbos.

Summary:
One may place any cloth designated for cleaning spills on any spill. One may not however move it around the spill. Regarding if the cloth has a handle see above. One may not place a cloth which is not designated for cleaning spills onto clear/white liquids. One may place it on colored liquids.

Q&A
May one clean a spill using napkins or tissues?[114]
It is permitted to place the tissue or napkin onto the spill.[115] However one may not rub the napkin or tissue around the spill. However, some Poskim[116] allow doing so.[117] Practically one is not to be lenient.[118]

May one clean a dry table/counter using a wet cloth?[119]
No, one may not rub such a cloth around the counter or surface as one will inevitably cause water to squeeze out. This applies even if the cloth is only slightly wet.

May one rub dry a wet counter or table [that does not contain an absorbent tablecloth] using a dry cloth?[120]
No, one may not rub such a cloth around the counter or surface. Only synthetic material may be used as using an absorbent material to press against the counter/table will inevitably cause liquid to squeeze out which is forbidden.

May one wipe the liquid off a wet tablecloth using a knife and the like? [121]
One may only do so lightly, without pressing against the cloth so as not to cause liquid to squeeze out of it. Regarding if one may use a cloth to clean such a spill.

May one move a wet rag or napkin that was used to clean a spill?
If there is a dry area left on the cloth it is permitted to be lifted and moved from that area.[122] If, however, the entire cloth is soaking wet, it is forbidden to move it as doing so will inevitably cause liquid to squeeze out.[123] Seemingly, in such a case it is permitted to move the cloth through placing a knife under it and lifting it up as it is not certain that this will cause squeezing. According to some Poskim[124] one may always move a wet tissue or napkin and there is no need to suspect for the

---

[113] This applies even if the sponge contains a handle and thus it is not inevitable that one will squeeze liquid upon holding the cloth. The reason for this prohibition is because it is considered a mundane act and a desecration of Shabbos. Furthermore, there is suspicion that if one were allowed to clean the spill and drip out the absorbed liquid as he does during the week he may come to intentionally squeeze out the liquid. [ibid]

[114] Piskeiy Teshuvos 302:10

[115] As they are designated for this purpose

[116] Igros Moshe 2:70

[117] As he claims there is no concept of Sechita [squeezing] by tissue and paper, as it is not truly an absorbent material.

[118] See Az Nidbaru 7:9 which argues on many points of the leniency of the Igros Moshe.

[119] SSH"K 12:40

[120] SSH"K 12:40

[121] SSH"K 12:37

[122] As if there is an area that is not wet it is similar to a sponge with a handle which is allowed to be used being that no water will squeeze out from the area he is holding on to. [320:23] So is also proven from Admur 301:59 [Rama 301:46; M"B 301:172] that it is permitted to lift wet clothing if there is no suspicion one will come to squeeze it. In our case there is no suspicion one will come to squeeze the rag or tissue being they are designated for this purpose of cleaning. [see 301:59]

[123] This is similar to a sponge that does not have a handle which is forbidden to even lift due to inevitably causing squeezing. [320:22] One must thus establish the case in Admur 301:59 to be discussing even if there is a dry area of the cloth. However if the entire cloth is soaked without any area, then it is forbidden to be lifted with one's fingers due to the squeezing prohibition.

[124] Igros Moshe 2:70

squeezing prohibition.

May one use baby wipes on Shabbos to clean a table and the like?
Some Poskim[125] prohibit them from being used due to a suspicion of squeezing. However other Poskim[126] permit using baby wipes.
Regarding the opinion of Admur-see footnote[127]
Regarding scented baby wipes: Some Poskim[128] rule that good scents may be used to remove bad smells, even according to those [such as Admur] that hold of a prohibition on placing a scent on one's skin.

Practical Summary of how to clean a spill using a cloth napkin/tissue?[129]
Any cloth [even if dirty] which is designated for cleaning spills [such as a paper napkin or rag] may be placed over a spill of any liquid including water. [However, one may not rub the cloth along the surface, as explained above. One may only place it over the spill.] However, a cloth which is not designated for cleaning spills [such as a cloth napkin] may only be used to clean spills of colored liquids [which do not contain a dying prohibition-see "The Laws of Dyeing"]. However, to cover spills of white liquids such as water they may not be used. In all the above scenarios one must beware to avoid squeezing liquid from the cloth in the process of cleaning the spill, and certainly may not squeeze it afterwards. As well it is forbidden to clean the spill for a purpose of using the absorbed liquid after Shabbos.

Garbage

8. Removing the garbage:[130]
Although in general one's garbage is considered Muktzah, nevertheless it is permitted to remove it outside if the garbage is full. It is forbidden to remove the garbage if it is not yet full.[131] [*For a detailed elaboration on this subject see Volume 1 "The Laws of Muktzah" Halacha 3L!*]

Cleaning dishes

9. Washing dishes on Shabbos:[132]
All dishes/cutlery needed to be used on Shabbos may be washed anytime on Shabbos, even much time prior to the meal.[133] Thus one may wash the Friday night dishes immediately after the meal on Friday

---

[125] Minchas Yitzchak 10:25, in name of also other Rabbanim.
[126] SSH"K 14:33 in name of Rav SZ"A, Rav Wozner allows it for babies only. The Piskeiy Teshuvos [327:1] and SSH"K learns that the foundation for the allowance is from the M"B:Magen Avraham in 613:9 which allow one to dry his legs:hands:feet from before Shabbos and then use it on Shabbos to clean his eyes. However Tzaruch Iyun on this as baby wipes may have a lot more water absorbed in them than the above mentioned towel used to dry only ones hands:feet and face.
[127] If the reality were to be that no liquid [Tofeich al minas Lehatfiach] can be extracted from the squeezed wipes, as well as that the wipes are dried to this point prior to the beginning of Shabbos, then there should be no reason to prohibit their use.
However Tzaruch Iyun why Admur omitted [in 613: 16] the ruling of the Magen Avraham [brought in previous footnote, which serves as the source for the ruling of the lenient opinions] that if one wiped his hands:legs:face with a towel before Shabbos one may use them for his eyes on Shabbos. Perhaps though it can be said that Admur omitted it as its law is already included in his mentioned rule that if it contains enough water before Shabbos to be "Tofeich Al Minas Lehatfiach" then it may not be used, and if it does not then it may.
[128] Beir Moshe 1:34 [based on Sheleis Yaavetz] rules that good smells may always be applied in order to remove bad odors, and so rules Piskeiy Teshuvos [327:1, 328:26]. SSH"K [ibid] also rules leniently in this, although to note that they hold [unlike Admur] there is never a prohibition to place good smells on ones skin.
[129] Based on Admur 320:21. SSH"K 12:38
[130] 308:72
[131] This applies even if it is found in an area that people are commonly found, such as one's kitchen, being that the garbage has a designated space.
[132] Admur 323:6-7
[133] Such as immediately after the previous meal. [ibid]

night and does not need to wait until the morning. Furthermore, so long as there still remains one meal which he will eat on Shabbos one may wash as many dishes and cutlery as he desires, even if he only needs to use one of those dishes for the meal.[134] If however one will not be eating any more Shabbos meals, such as after Shalosh Seudos [or after the 2nd meal in those homes which do not eat a full Shalosh Seudos meal] then it is forbidden to wash any dishes or cutlery.[135] [If however one decides to eat again after the 2nd/3rd meal then he may wash the dishes for the meal.[136]]

Washing cups: It is permitted to wash cups throughout the entire day of Shabbos, even after the final meal[137], unless one is certain that he will no longer need the cup, in which case it is forbidden to wash it.

Washing dishes with soap:[138] It is forbidden to wash dishes using a bar of soap.[139] [One may however use liquid soap as will be explained in the Q&A]

Washing dishes with salt water:[140] One may not use salty water to scrub the vessels as by doing so one actively dissolves the salt which is forbidden due to the Nolad prohibition.[141] One may however rinse the dishes using salty water [so long as he does not rub it with his hands in the process.[142] Likewise one may place salt in water initially on Shabbos for this purpose even if the water ratio will be less than 1/3 of the mixture.[143]]

Washing off non-Kosher food from a utensil: See the end of the next Halacha!

Summary:
One may wash as many dishes as he desires if there is still one remaining meal left to be eaten on Shabbos. After the final meal dishes may not be washed with exception to cups, unless one knows for certain he will not be needing the cups until after Shabbos.

Q&A on washing Dishes
May one wash dirty dishes even if he has clean dishes available?
Some Poskim[144] rule it is better not to wash the dishes if there are clean dishes available. Others[145] rule it is completely forbidden. Others[146] rule it is even initially permitted to wash dirty dishes for the meal even if one has clean dishes available to use. Practically the custom is to be lenient.

May one wash the dishes after his last meal if they are tarnishing the cleanliness of the house?[147]
Yes, one may clean the dishes in order to reside a clean and tidy atmosphere in one's home. One may do so according to all opinions, even if he does not need them to eat another meal on Shabbos.[148]

---

[134] So rules Admur 323:6 regarding cups and the same applies for all eating utensils. The reason for this is because once the Sages allowed washing a dish for the meal, they no longer restricted how many dishes one may wash as every dish washed can possibly be used on Shabbos. Thus, this is allowed even if one is certain that he will not need to use all the dishes washed. [Ketzos Hashulchan 146 footnote 30 in name of Machatzis Hashekel and Peri Megadim]
[135] As by doing so one is preparing for after Shabbos, and it is forbidden for one to trouble himself on Shabbos for the sake of after Shabbos. [ibid]
[136] Ketzos Hashulchan 146:16
[137] As there is no set time for drinking. [ibid]
[138] Admur 326:10
[139] As by doing so one dissolves the soap which is forbidden due to the Molid [creating new substance] prohibition. Now although there are opinions which rule that there is no prohibition against creating a new substance and the reason behind the prohibition for dissolving ice is due to a decree of fruit juices, which has no relevance to dissolving soaps and the like, and hence according to them it is permitted to dissolve soap. Nevertheless, Admur concludes one is to be stringent like the first opinion. [ibid]
[140] Admur 323:12
[141] See 320:19 which brings a dispute in this matter. Practically, Admur rules to be stringent.
[142] Admur 320:19
[143] Ketzos Hashulchan 146 footnote 33, based on fact Admur omits the opinion of the Taz which rules making more than 2:3 ratio of salt to water is forbidden.
[144] Minchas Shabbos 80:154; Tosefes Shabbos 323:8, Betzeil Hachachmah 4:130; see Sheivet Haleivi 6:42
[145] Beir Moshe 6:82
[146] Bris Olam Ofah 90; Mishneh Halachos 6:80
[147] See Beir Moshe ibid; Piskeiy Teshuvos 323:1
[148] This is similar to the allowance to make the beds on Shabbos morning even though they will not be used until the after Shabbos.

May one wash dishes on Shabbos if he will only be using them the next Shabbos?

No.[149] However there are Poskim[150] which rule this is allowed.

May one soak the dishes in water after his last Shabbos meal?[151]

If one is doing so merely so the food does not stick to the dishes, then soaking it is allowed. If however food is already stuck to the dishes and one desires to soak it in order to remove the food, then doing so is forbidden. It is however permitted to place the dishes in the sink as normal, and then proceed to wash one's hands over it.[152]

May one wash his food pots on Shabbos?

No[153], unless one plans on using the pot on Shabbos for a certain usage.

May one enter water into his food pot in order to let the pot soak?

If there is food stuck to the bottom of the pot, doing so is forbidden, as explained above. However, one may place the pot in the sink and casually wash his hands over it.

May one wash his Kiddush cup out after Kiddush of the day meal?

Seemingly if one is particular to only use the cup for Kiddush and Havdala then it may not be washed after the daytime Kiddush unless one plans on using it.[154] If, however, one is not particular in this respect then it may be washed throughout the day as is the law by other cups.

In all cases one may rinse out the wine and then drink some water out from the cup and place it on the drying rack.

Q&A on Soaps

Which soaps may be used to wash dishes?[155]

- It is forbidden to use a bar of soap.
- Liquid soap: Liquid soap may be used on Shabbos.[156] This includes even if the soap is slightly thick to the point that it cannot be poured like actual liquid but is rather more like a pasty substance. [However, there is an opinion[157] which is stringent against using liquid soap even when the soap is thin like water due to the smoothening prohibition. However, if one added water to the soap and it has thus already been melted down with water then it is permitted to be used according to all[158].] Practically the custom is to avoid using thick liquid soap.[159] *Regarding using scented liquid soaps, see Volume 2 "The Laws of Molid Reiach"*
- Dish detergent:[160] Dish detergent may be used with a large amount of water, so as not to transgress the kneading prohibition. Likewise, one may rub it dry onto the dishes using wet hands and then wash it off.

---

[149] Tehila Ledavid 302:6

[150] See Piskeiy Teshuvos 323:1

[151] SSH"K 12:3

[152] Az Nidbaru 5:36

[153] As pots are not a meal utensil and are rather used for the cooking. Hence cleaning them serves no benefit for the meal.

[154] Since a Kiddush cup is a unique cup which some only use for Kiddush alone therefore once Kiddush has been made, it is similar to plates and dishes which have no use any more on Shabbos after the last meal. It is likewise similar to washing cup when one is certain he will no longer use them on Shabbos, in which case Admur rules washing them is forbidden.

[155] SSH"K 14:16 footnote 49, based on Ketzos Hashulchan 138 footnote 31 with regards to using toothpaste. So rules also Ketzos Hashulchan explicitly in 146 footnote 32; See also Shabbos Kehalacha Volume 3 17:73

[156] As it is already a liquid and the bubbles that it creates have no significance.

[157] Igros Moshe 1:113

[158] So rules Az Nidbaru 1:16 brought in Piskeiy Teshuvos 326:8

[159] Shabbos Kehalacha Vol. 3 17:73

[160] Piskeiy Teshuvos 323:5

May one place soap into a cup of liquid and have it dissolved and then use that to wash dishes?[161]

Yes, as doing so is similar to placing ice in one's drink which is allowed. Furthermore, one may even mix the soap into the water through shaking the vessel.[162] However some are stringent to only enter the bar of soap into the water from before Shabbos.[163]

Q&A on Sponges

Which forms of sponges may be used to wash the dishes?

Regular sponge: It is forbidden to use a sponge[164] on Shabbos due to the squeezing prohibition.[165] This applies even if the sponge has a handle.[166]

Synthetic sponges and steel wool[167]: Some Poskim[168] rule all forms of synthetic or steel wool sponges are forbidden to be used due to it being a mundane act, and due to the squeezing prohibition. Others[169] however permit using synthetic [or metal[170]] sponges which have their threads visibly spread apart from each other, as in such a case using them does not involve the squeezing prohibition. However, they forbid using steel wool[171], and any sponge which has its threads close to each other. Others[172]

---

[161] Ketzos Hashulchan 127 footnote 13; Shabbos Kehalacha Vol. 3 17:75
[162] As explained in Volume 2 "The Laws of Melting ice and Snow" Halacha 2 Q&A there, based on Ketzos Hashulchan 127 Footnote 2. So also rules SSH"K 14:16; Kaf Hachaim 320:60
[163] Ketzos Hashulchan 146 footnote 32

[164]

[165] 320:23

[166] A sponge with a handle may only be used to lightly clean spills, as in such a case it is not inevitable one will come to squeeze. However, when using a sponge to clean dishes it is impossible not to come to squeeze, and the squeezed liquid does not go to waste as one uses it to help clean the dishes. [Regarding the sources for this conclusion: So rules Shabbos Kehalacha Vol. 3 18:52; See also Previous Halacha regarding cleaning spills with a sponge that has a handle and the footnotes there. See M"B 320:55; SSH"K 12 footnote 37; Minchas Yitzchak 3:50]
[167] There are three possible issues discussed in Poskim regarding these forms of sponges:
Squeezing and Uvdin Dechol may apply by all sponges and in addition Mimacheik may also apply by steel wool.
[168] Ketzos Hashulchan 146 footnote 33; Minchas Yitzchak 3:49; Beir Moshe 1:34
The Ketzos Hashulchan ibid prohibits it due to both reasons. The Minchas Yitzchak states that steel wool is forbidden being that it contains a Rabbinical squeezing prohibition similar to hair. Beir Moshe 1:34 states that although doing so does not involve a squeezing prohibition [certainly not by the thick stranded steel wool] it is perhaps forbidden due to Uvdin Dechol. Nevertheless he does not rule this way conclusively and hence leaves room for it being allowed.
[169] SSH"K 12:10; Cheishev Haeifod 2:149 [however see below that he rules the sponge must be designated.]
Beir Moshe ibid in previous footnote rules that possibly no prohibition of squeezing is involved even by closely netted sponges of synthetic or metal materials, although it may be forbidden by all sponges due to Uvdin Dechol. Practically he concludes that by closely knitted sponges it is forbidden, while by others it is unclear due to Uvdin Dechol. SSH"K argues that there is no precedence to claim that there is an issue of Uvdin Dechol involved.

[170] According to this opinion if the metal sponge visibly has its strands distanced from each other then it is permitted to be used. [Piskeiy Teshuvos 323:4]

[171] Due to the Mimacheik prohibition, as ruled similarly regarding silver in 323:11 [SSH"K ibid] However it is clear from Beir Moshe:Ketzos Hashulchan ibid that he does not hold of this. Nevertheless, the Beir Moshe concludes not to use the steel wool on plates which one will have to scrub them for a while.
[172] Beir Moshe ibid

question that perhaps it is permitted to use all types of synthetic or metal sponges[173]. Practically, they rule one is not to be lenient by closely knitted sponges. Others[174] rule that even those sponges which are permitted used, may only be used it if the sponge is designated specifically for Shabbos.

10. Scrubbing, Shining and Polishing dishes and silverware:[175]

One may scrub down, shine and polish all dishes and cutlery needed to be used on Shabbos, even if they are made of silver, so long as the shining agent does not remove any layer of the vessel. Thus, it is forbidden to clean or shine silver using a material which will inevitably remove a layer of the silver from it.[176] [**See Q&A regarding removing tarnish from silver!**]

Summary:
One may polish all vessels on Shabbos if the following two conditions are fulfilled:
1. He is doing so in order to use the vessel that Shabbos.
2. The polishing will not inevitably remove any of the material of the vessel.

Q&A on Polishing

May one polish glass dishes?
Yes.[177] This may be done if one plans to use the dishes on Shabbos. Nevertheless there are Poskim[178] which forbid this in all cases.

May one polish silverware, copperware, and other silver vessels?
It is forbidden to remove tarnish from silverware or copperware on Shabbos.[179] If there is no tarnish and one simply desires to shine the vessel it is permitted to do so even if it is made of silver or copper.[180] However some Poskim[181] rule it is forbidden to polish metal vessels in all cases, even with a dry cloth, and even if there is no tarnish.
Using a silver polish cloth: It requires further research to verify whether silver polishing cloths accomplish the shine through removing the silver material or not. If it does not remove the silver, then according to Admur it may be used. If it removes a layer of the silver it may not be used.
Using silver polish cream: It is forbidden to use any polishing cream to polish vessels due to the smearing prohibition.
Using a wet sponge: When using a sponge with water to polish a vessel one must be careful to only use a permitted type of sponge, as explained in the previous Halacha.

---

[173] Even with steel wool [so long as one does not rub very thoroughly], and even if the strands are close together. [ibid]

[174] Cheishev Haeifod 2:149; Minchas Yitzchak 3:50 regarding a sponge with a handle.

[175] Admur 323:11

[176] Silver is soft and can have layers of it rubbed off during polish. Doing so is forbidden due to the Memacheik/Smoothening prohibition. Now although one has no intention to remove a layer of the silver and smoothen it, but rather simply to shine it, nevertheless this is an inevitable occurrence and is hence forbidden. It is however permitted to polish the silver using soap and the like which do not inevitably remove the silver, as even if it happens to do so, since this is not inevitable and one did not intend to do so, it is therefore permitted. [ibid]

[177] Admur 323:11; SSH"K 12:24

Other Opinions: The Mahril rules it is forbidden to polish glass dishes using oats. The M"A 323:15 questions as to why this should be forbidden and suggests that perhaps only washing dishes from dirt did the Sages allow, however to polish is forbidden. He concludes with a Tzaruch Iyun. Admur completely omitted this ruling of the Mahril hence implying it is allowed. SSH"K 12:24 in name of Rav SZ"A rules it is allowed, as even according to Mahril it was only prohibited to polish using oats. Tehila Ledavid 323:17 however explains it is forbidden to polish all vessels due to Tikkun Keli.

[178] Mahril brought in MA 323:15; Tehila Ledavid 323:17 brought in previous footnote; Toras Shabbos 323:9

[179] As tarnish is an actual layer of the metal which has corroded, and its only form of cleansing is removal.

[180] Admur rules [323:11] that it is permitted to be done so long as one is not using an item which will inevitably remove a layer of silver or copper from the vessel, and is doing so simply to shine the vessel and not remove tarnish, as stated above.

[181] SSH"K 12:24 based on Tehila Ledavid 323:17.

The SSH"K learns as does the Tehila Ledavid in the Mahril brought in M"A that the action of polishing metal vessels is forbidden on Shabbos due to Tikkun Keli. Admur clearly however does not learn this way, and likewise omitted the entire ruling of the Mahril as stated above.

May one remove rust from metal, such as from the blade of a knife?[182]
No.[183]

Tevilas Keilim

11. Immersing vessels in a Mikveh:[184]

It is forbidden to immerse a vessel[185] in a Mikveh on Shabbos if the vessel requires immersion in order to be used.[186] Thus any vessel bought from a gentile and has not yet been immersed may not be immersed on Shabbos. This applies even if one did not have the ability to immerse the vessels before Shabbos.

Giving the vessel to a gentile: Being that one may not immerse the vessel on Shabbos, and it is forbidden to use a vessel without immersion, one's only option is to give the vessel to a gentile as a present and then borrow it back from the gentile. This however may only be done if one needs to use the vessel on Shabbos.[187] In such a case, after borrowing the vessel back from the gentile one may use the vessel without immersion, as it now legally belongs to the gentile. Nevertheless, after Shabbos one must immerse the vessel without a blessing[188] [or immerse together with a vessel that requires a blessing[189]]. [Alternatively, one should ask the gentile after Shabbos to acquire the vessel back to him as a complete present, or the Jew should buy it back with a few coins, in which case one can make a blessing on the immersion of that vessel according to all.[190]]

Immersing the vessel in an inconspicuous manner: It is permitted to immerse the vessel in waters that are Kosher for a Mikveh if it is unnoticeable to the onlooker that he is doing so to purify the vessel. Hence a pitcher and other vessel meant to draw water may be entered into the Mikveh waters to draw out water, hence purifying the vessel in the process.[191] In such a case one may not say a blessing on the immersion,

---

[182] Tehila Ledavid 323:17

[183] This is forbidden possibly due to the Mimacheik and Tochein prohibition. [ibid]

[184] Admur 323:5

[185] Whether made of glass, metal or any other materials which requires immersion. [See M"B 323:32 and so is implied from Admur which does not differentiate between the two]

[186] So concludes Admur in 323:5 ["and if one is unable to do the above, **don't** immerse the vessels" and "if one **transgressed** and immersed the vessels". So also summarizes the Ketzos Hashulchan 146:3 that doing so is forbidden.]
Background: Admur brings a dispute regarding this matter:
6. The first [stam] opinion rules that new vessels may be immersed on Shabbos even if one was able to immerse them before Shabbos. Their reasoning is because according to them immersion is only Rabbinically required for new vessels, while Biblically the vessels may be used without immersion. Hence immersing the vessel is not considered like one is fixing the vessel, as Biblically the vessel is already useable.
7. Others however rule that immersing new vessels is forbidden due to it being considered like one is fixing the vessel. According to them this applies even if one did not have the ability to immerse the vessels before Shabbos.
8. It goes without saying that immersing vessels is forbidden according to the opinion which rules that immersing new vessels is Biblically required. As on this premises by immersing the vessel one is doing it a significant fixture according to all, of which the Sages forbade being that it is exactly similar to fixing a vessel which is a Biblical prohibition.
9. The practical ramification between the 2nd and 3rd opinion is regarding glass vessels, which according to all is only Rabbinically required to be immersed.
10. Practically: One may not immerse vessels in a Mikveh on Shabbos as the main opinion follows the opinion which rules that immersing new vessels is Biblically required. [So concludes Admur in 323:5 and so summarizes the Ketzos Hashulchan 146:3. Vetzaruch Iyun from the wording of Admur prior to this ruling that "A G-d fearing Jew will fulfill his obligation according to all and give the vessel to a gentile…" Hence implying that from the letter of the law one may be lenient like the first opinion and immerse the vessel. So also implies the M"B [323:33] from this similar wording of Michaber, that the Michaber rules mainly like the first opinion that it is permitted. Thus, how can Admur say that one who immersed the vessel has transgressed? Vetzaruch Iyun Gadol!!]

[187] As it is only permitted to give a present to a gentile on Shabbos if it is being done for the sake of Shabbos. [ibid]

[188] Being that this vessel will now remain in the hands of the Jew forever, and is thus similar to him having bought it. Alternatively, it is similar to a borrowed Tallis which required Tzitzis after 30 days even though it is not his. Based on this it should be immersed even with a blessing. Nevertheless, since I have not found the matter explicitly ruled in Poskim I am hesitant to rule this way, and rather one should immerse another vessel that requires a blessing together with it. [Yoreh Deah Taz 120:18]

[189] Taz in previous footnote. This applies even according to Admur, and the reason Admur did not state this explicitly is because he is dealing with a case that one only has this vessel to immerse. [Ketzos Hashulchan 146 footnote 6]

[190] Ketzos Hashulchan 146 footnote 6

[191] This does not appear like one is fixing the vessel, as it is not evident at all that one is intending to purify the vessel. This is because not everyone knows that this vessel has not yet been immersed hence causing the onlooker to say he is doing so in order to use the drawn water. [ibid]

as if he were to do so it would be evident that his intents are in truth to purify the vessel.[192] [Thus one who has other vessels available may not immerse the vessel in this method, as by doing so one is causing it to lose its blessing.[193] Likewise only pitchers and cups may be immersed, as only they are capable of drawing water and hence fooling the onlooker. One however may not immerse cutlery and china in a Mikveh under the disguise that he is simply washing off the dirt from the vessels, as it is not common at all to do so in a Mikveh, and one's true intent is hence evident to all.[194] Based on this **today** that it is no longer common to draw water at all from a Mikveh or any body of water other than one's sink, it would hence be **forbidden to immerse vessels in a Mikveh under all circumstances**, as doing so is always apparent of one's true intention.[195]]

The law if one transgressed and immersed vessels on Shabbos: If one transgressed [even advertently[196]] and immersed a vessel on Shabbos it nevertheless may be used on Shabbos.[197]

The law on Yom Tov:[198] It is forbidden to immerse vessels on Yom Tov just as is forbidden to be done on Shabbos. If, however, one did not have the ability to immerse the vessel at any time prior to Yom Tov and on Yom Tov his first opportunity to immerse them arrived, then he may immerse the vessel.[199] Nevertheless, one may not rule this way when asked this question, [and is rather to tell the asker that immersing vessels is forbidden in all cases].[200] Likewise, one may not immerse the vessels in front of other people.[201]

Washing off non-Kosher food from a utensil:[202] It is permitted to rinse off a vessel that was used to eat non-Kosher food if one plans to use the vessel that day.[203] This applies even if there is remnant of the non-kosher food on the vessel.[204]

---

[192] As for why a woman who immerses on Shabbos may say a blessing, this is because the Sages never originally decreed against women immersing on Shabbos. The reason for this is because at the times of the Sages it was not recognizable as to for what purpose the woman is immersing, and hence the Tikkun was never recognizable. Alternatively, this is because the decree against immersing vessels is because one may come to actually fix a vessel which is Biblically forbidden. The Sages however were not this suspicious regarding a person immersing. [Ketzos Hashulchan 146 footnote 8]

[193] M"B 323:36

[194] Ketzos Hashulchan 146 footnote 7

Other opinions: However, the Kaf Hachaim rules one may immerse all vessels in the Mikveh under the disguise that one is doing so to clean the vessel. The Ketzos Hashulchan argues on this saying that it is never common to wash dirt off vessels in a Mikveh, and hence all will know one's true intents.

[195] So is clearly implied from Ketzos Hashulchan ibid regarding his argument against the Kaf Hachaim, and so is evident from the fact he writes that drawing water with the vessel is allowed because "at times today people do draw water from the Mikveh". Now, although this may have been true in the 1950's, the time of the publishing of this Sefer, today this is certainly not the case, and hence the Halacha likewise changes.

[196] As if Admur is referring to one who did so by mistake, then his ruling carries no novelty, as it is already ruled in 339:7 that no fine was enacted against Rabbinical decrees done inadvertently. Hence one must conclude that Admur includes even the advertent sinner in this ruling, that no fine was applied even to him.

[197] Although in general the Sages fined all transgressors against benefiting from their forbidden actions until after Shabbos, even by a Rabbinical transgression, nevertheless in this case no fine was given being that there are opinions which allow doing so even initially. [ibid]

[198] Admur 509:1

[199] Admur 323:8; 509:15

[200] Admur 509:1

Thus, for oneself to do so is allowed, if he knows this Halacha, while for another, it is not allowed if he does not know this Halacha, and hence one may not tell him that it is allowed. The reason for this is because if they are told it is allowed, they may come to also immerse vessels that could have been immersed before Yom Tov. [ibid]

[201] As this itself is considered as if one is ruling to them that immersing vessels is allowed, and they may come to immerse vessels even in cases that it is not allowed. [ibid]

[202] Admur 323:9

[203] According to all this is not considered as if one is fixing the vessel as the actual vessel is permitted to be used and it is just that the non-Kosher food prohibits its use. Hence rinsing it off is similar to rinsing off feces from it. [ibid]

[204] Although non-Kosher food is Muktzah, nevertheless its remains are nullified completely to the vessel and do not have the ability to prohibit moving it at all. [ibid]

Summary:
It is forbidden on Shabbos to immerse vessels in a Mikveh in all cases. If one needs this vessel for Shabbos and cannot do without it, then he may give the vessel to a gentile as a present and then borrow it back from him and use it without immersion. After Shabbos he is to immerse it without a blessing.

Q&A
May one immerse a vessel on Shabbos if there is a doubt as to whether it requires immersion?
Some Poskim[205] rule that if there are no other vessels available, and one is unable to give it to a gentile, as explained above, then one may be lenient to immerse the questionable vessel whether it is made of glass or metal. Others[206] rule that if the vessel in question is made of glass then it may be used on Shabbos without being immersed[207] and if made of metal it may be immersed. Others[208] however rule it is forbidden to immerse the vessel in all circumstances, and it is likewise forbidden to use the vessel even if made of glass, being that it still requires immersion.[209]

12. May one unplug a drain pipe on Shabbos?[210]
It is forbidden to unplug a stuffed drainage pipe on Shabbos unless lack of doing so will cause flooding to one's house, in which case one may remove the blockage of the pipe with an irregularity.[211]
Example: If one's rain pipes on his roof became stuffed with dirt and twigs and is causing flooding in one's house, one may use his feet to press down the blockage, allowing the water to flow freely.

Q&A
May one unplug a stuffed toilet or sink?
Yes.[212] One may even use a plunger or snake to do so. However, some Poskim[213] limit this allowance to only if the blockage occurs often and only if the sink or toilet is not completely stuffed.[214] Others[215] allow it without difference. If easily available, it is best to unplug the sink or toilet through a gentile.[216]

---

[205] M"B 323:33

[206] Kaf Hachayim 323

[207] As this is a doubt in a Rabbinical case in which the rule allows one to be lenient.

[208] Ketzos Hashulchan 146 footnote 5

[209] As even in a case of doubt we rule all vessels need to be immersed, even if made of glass, as one may not actively enter himself into a Rabbinical doubt by avoiding the immersion. Thus once again since the vessel is forbidden to be used until immersed even in a case of doubt we once again return to the same debate in whether this is allowed due to it appearing as if one is fixing the vessel. [ibid]

[210] Admur 336:15

[211] As since this case involves loss, the Sages did not decree against fixing the pipes in an irregular way. [ibid]

[212] Beir Moshe 1:29; Minchas Yitzchak 5:75; 7:19

[213] Igros Moshe 4:40

[214] As only then is it not considered Tikkun Keli.

[215] Bier Moshe and Minchas Yitzchak ibid.

[216] Minchas Yitzchak 5:75; 7:19

Emptying a storage room

13. May one undo a storage room of non-Muktzah items?[217]

It is forbidden to undo a storage room on Shabbos, as doing so involves a great amount of energy, [and is thus not befitting to the day of rest]. This applies even if the items in the storage room are not Muktzah.

14. Undoing the storage for the sake of a Mitzvah?

It is permitted for one to undo the storage for the sake of a Mitzvah even if doing so involves much toil[218]. This includes if one needs to use the space of the storage for:

1. Using the area as a Beis Midrash.
2. Host a Seudas Mitzvah.
3. Hosting a meal for guests.[219] Nevertheless it is only considered a Seudas Mitzvah if the guests are from out of town, whether they are sleeping and eating by him, or sleeping elsewhere and only eating by him. If, however, the guests are from the same city then hosting them is not considered a Seudas Mitzvah but rather a Seudas Reshus and one thus may not empty the storage for their behalf. If, however, these in town guests were invited in honor of an out-of-town guest which is staying by the host, then he too is considered like an out-of-town guest and may have the storage undone on his behalf.[220]

15. How to undo the storage room, when needed for the sake of a Mitzvah:

Take as much as possible at a time:[221] One is to carry as many items as possible when undoing the storage room in order to lessen the amount of times he will need to go back and forth.

How many people are to empty the storage:[222] Each person may only carry the amount needed for a single person to sit in the area of the storage room. Hence if space is needed for many people each person is to carry out their own area of storage needed to be cleared.

Not to empty the entire storage: [223] Even if all the space in the storage room is needed, one is not to empty the entire room [if the floor is made of earth] due to worry that one may come to smoothen the ground. [If however the floor is tiled it is allowed to empty the entire storage if needed.[224]]

General Q&A
If a Mezuzah fell off the doorpost may one reattach it?

The Mezuzah fell together with its case: A Mezuzah which fell together with its case may never be replaced on Shabbos to the door being that doing so involves nailing or taping the Mezuzah to the doorpost which contains a Building prohibition.

If a Mezuzah fell out of its case: If a Mezuzah slid out of its case, and its case has remained on the doorpost, then some Poskim[225] allow one to return the Mezuzah into its case on Shabbos.[226] Others[227] however rule that one may not do so being that it is similar to fixing a vessel.[228] Practically, seemingly one may be lenient[229] so long as it does not involve a building prohibition.[230]

---

[217] Admur 333:1

[218] Such as lifting the items and sending them down flights of stairs, or bringing them from one roof to another. [ibid]

[219] As having guests for a meal makes the meal considered to be a Seudas Mitzvah. [ibid]

[220] Admur 333:6

[221] Admur 333:3

[222] Admur 333:4

[223] Admur 333:4

[224] Kaf Hachayim 333:9

[225] Tzitz Eliezer 13:53

[226] This does not appear like Tikkun Keli even according to the opinion which rules one may not live in a house without a Mezuzah, as this is an obligation on the person and not on the house.

[227] Sdei Chemed Mareches 40:115

[228] The Sdei Chemed brings that this matter is subject to the same dispute as is immersing vessels in a Mikveh. As according to those which rule one may not live in a house without a Mezuzah, placing the Mezuzah fixes the house for living in. According to those which hold one may live in a house without a Mezuzah, there is no fixing occurring to the house by placing the Mezuzah back.

May one remove cobwebs on Shabbos?[231]

Some Poskim[232] imply that it is permitted to break cobwebs on Shabbos, and doing so does not involve the Muktzah or destroying prohibition, or any other prohibition. Other Poskim[233], however, rule that cobwebs are considered Muktzah, just like earth and twigs and other waste. Accordingly, they may only be removed on Shabbos with an irregularity/Shinuiy [such as using ones elbow or feet].[234] Alternatively, if they have become repulsive to oneself, or to the guests in the room, then they may be removed even regularly.[235] Other Poskim[236], however, rule that one is to completely avoid breaking or removing cobwebs that are attached to a wall altogether, as perhaps doing so transgresses the "uprooting an item from its place of growth" prohibition, or other prohibition. Practically, one may be lenient in a time of need to move the cobwebs in the method stated above.[237] Nevertheless, in all cases one must beware not to kill the spider in the process.[238]

May one spray air freshener in his room or bathroom?

Yes[239] [as one is not creating a new smell in any area, as well as that one is doing so in order to repel the bad smells].

May one use a toilet that contains toilet soap?

One is to avoid using all forms of toilet soaps on Shabbos.[240] Thus one is to remove the soap from

---

[229] As even regarding immersing a vessel a dispute is brought, and certainly here that it is unclear if even according to the stringent opinion there is an issue of Tikkun Keli, one may be lenient.

[230] Meaning the use of tape, as taping something to the ground is like building. Hence the allowance only applies if one is able to simply slide the Mezuzah back into the case without use of any item to attach it there.

[231] See Piskeiy Teshuvos 250:9

[232] Implication of Leket Yosher *"One time a spiders web was made on the faucet and he [the Terumas Hadeshen] said that it is permitted to break it on Shabbos."* [Nonetheless, it is still possible to interpret the allowance only to a vessel, such as a faucet, and not to a wall. However, the Betzeil Hachachmah 5:18 and Rav SZ"A in SSH"K 23 footnote 34 clearly rule that there is no destroying or Toleish prohibition involved by cobwebs, and hence when this is joined with the opinion of the Leket Yosher that it also does not contain a Muktzah prohibition, then it is allowed in all cases to be removed or broken on Shabbos]; See Admur 328:53 [based on 1st opinion in Michaber 328:48; Rokeaich 70; Kol Bo 31] that one may treat a bleeding wound through wrapping a spiders web around it, thus proving that it is not Muktzah. See, however, Tehila Ledavid 328:79 that for the sake of relieving pain, the Sages permitted the moving of Muktzah. However, from Leket Yosher ibid, it is implied that it is permitted even not for the sake of relieving pain, as well as that no such allowance is recorded in Admur regarding Muktzah, and on the contrary, he explicitly mentions the Muktzah prohibition even in a case of pain. [See Admur 308:56 regarding placing raw cloth materials on a wound and 328:51 regarding eye pain] Thus, one must conclude that according to the Poskim ibid, cobwebs are not Muktzah on Shabbos. On the other hand, perhaps one can establish the case to be referring to cobwebs that were already prepared before Shabbos. Vetzaruch Iyun.

[233] Mor Uketzia 328; Tehila Ledavid 328:79; Pesach HaDvir 328:11; See Kaf Hachaim 328:270; Orchos Chaim Spinka 328:36

[234] Betzeil Hachachmah 5:18; Regarding the allowance of moving Muktzah with a Shinuiy-See: Admur 308:15; 311:15; 276:9-10; 266:19

[235] SSH"K 23 footnote 34 in name of Rav SZ"A; Beir Moshe 37; In such a case they may be removed even normally, as then they are considered a Graf Shel Reiy. [SSH"K 23 footnote 34 in name of Rav SZ"A]

[236] Yifei Laleiv 328:3 leaves this matter in question as to if its considered a prohibition of removing an item from its place of growth; Kaf Hachaim 328:270; SSH"K 23:9

[237] Betzeil Hachachmah ibid and Rav SZ"A ibid both argue that this prohibition does not at all apply; Piskeiy Teshuvos 250:9

[238] See Admur 316:23; M"A 316:23; M"B 316:48; Biur Halacha "Veafilu"

[239] Beir Moshe [1:34] [See also Minchas Yitzchak 6:26 which was asked this question amongst others although he does not seem to answer this particular point.]

[240] Orach Yisrael 35

Background of the prohibition:

The use of toilet soaps may involve any of the following three prohibitions: *Molid Reiach and Nolad and Tzoveia [dying]*

1. *Prohibition of Nolad*: Seemingly it is forbidden to use toilet soaps due to the Nolad prohibition being that one is melting the solid soap thru flushing the toilet [which is similar to urinating on snow which was viewed as if one is melting the snow with one's hands]. Thus, even using unscented and non-colored toilet soaps would be problematic. [Orach Yisrael 35 rules based on this reason that initially it is forbidden o use toilet soaps unless it is a case of Shaas Hadchak] However there are Poskim which rule that there is no issue of Nolad with toilet soaps as it is only a minute amount which melts, and that itself is through an indirect action. [Shabbos Kehalacha Vol. 3 17:80]

2. *Prohibition of Tzoveia*: If the toilet soap releases a color into the water, then it may not be used due to the dying prohibition. [SSH"K 23:14] However some Poskim allow its use if one has no interest at all in the coloring of the water. [Shabbos Kehalacha Vol. 3 17:80]

3. *Prohibition of creating new smell*: The prohibition of Molid Reiach does not apply even when using a scented toilet soap. [Practically although Poskim [Sharreiy Teshuvah and Mishneh Berurah in 128:6. Minchas Yitzchak 6:26] rule it is forbidden to create a good smell in water, nevertheless it is allowed to absorb a good smell into the toilet water as the good smell is simply there to remove bad odor. [Beir Moshe 1:34 rules that good smells may always be applied in order to remove bad odors, and so rules Piskeiy Teshuvos [327:1, 328:26] Other Poskim however rule it is only allowed if one has no intent to create a good smell within the water. [Shabbos Kehalacha Vol. 3 17:80]

the toilet before Shabbos. If one did not do so it is permitted to remove the soap on Shabbos. Some are stringent to remove it with an irregularity.[241] Some Poskim however rule it is permitted to use such soaps in cases of discomfort.[242] Furthermore some Poskim[243] rule it is only forbidden to use toilet soaps if one intends that the soap color the water or that it release a good smell. If however one does not have intent for this to occur one may use toilet soaps even if they color the water and release good smell.

Urinating on the soap: In all cases it is permitted to urinate in a toilet that contains toilet soap so long as one does not urinate directly onto the soap.[244]

Is the soap Muktzah? [245] Toilet soap is considered Muktzah Machmas Issur. Some Poskim[246] however consider it Muktzah Machmas Chisaron Kis. According to this latter opinion one may not enter or remove the toilet soap from the toilet on Shabbos due to the Muktzah prohibition. It is however permitted to move it with an irregularity.

May one clean a dirty toilet?[247]

Yes. One may even use the toilet brush to do so.

---

[241] See below and Shabbos Kehalacha Vol. 3 17 footnote 196 for a discussion on the Muktzah status of the soap.

[242] Orach Yisrael 35; Shabbos Kehalacha ibid, there he extends the leniency to even toilet soaps that dye the water.
In Sefer Orach Yisrael 35 he rules that one may be lenient to use such soaps if lack of doing so will cause bad odors and distress, as he rules that in a Shaas Hadchak one may be lenient like the opinion which holds that melting soaps and fats do not contain a Nolad prohibition. Furthermore, he rules that if one forgot to remove it before Shabbos then it may be used on Shabbos being that it is Muktzah and is forbidden to remove and thus this case too is a Shaas Hadchak. Vetzaruch Iyun according to Admur why he rules by melting fats near fire that one is to be stringent unless it is a Shaas Hadchak while here by soaps he plainly rules that one is to be stringent [implying even in Shaas Hadchak].

[243] Shabbos Kehalacha ibid

[244] Shabbos Kehalacha Vol. 3 17:81

[245] Shabbos Kehalacha Vol. 3 17 footnote 196

[246] Igros Moshe 5

[247] SSH"K 23:15

CHAPTER 9: PLAYING GAMES ON SHABBOS

Introduction

The spirit of Shabbos

Due to the holiness of Shabbos, adults should avoid playing games on Shabbos even if the game has no Halachic prohibitions involved. The Talmud states that the city of Tur Shimon was destroyed for the sin of playing ball on Shabbos. Some explain this to mean that the city was destroyed due to the sin of using their time on Shabbos for ball playing instead of learning Torah.[1] The Taz[2] writes in the name of the Rashal that it is a wonderment that playing ball is allowed on Yom Tov when in truth it is a game of children and not meant for adults. Thus, he rules that it is an evil custom for adults to spend their time playing ball, and "if I had the power I would nullify it". The Ketzos Hashulchan[3] explains how even during the week ball playing is to be avoided, as it is a mere women's game, being that they are not obligated in learning Torah. As well it is to be avoided being that some of the games were taken from the gentiles.

In light of the above, the laws to be discussed are to be understood in relation to children below the age of Bar Mitzvah or to adults that are far from the spirit of Torah and Mitzvahs.

Games that involve prohibited actions:

Aside for the question of whether playing games negate the spirit of Shabbos, many games involve actions that are questionable whether they are permitted to be done on Shabbos. The following is a list of issues that may be involved.

List of issues to be aware of when playing games on Shabbos:
- Does it involve having items role into an area without an Eiruv?
- Does it involve rolling items on the ground?
- Does it involve writing, or putting words together?
- Does it involve gambling which is defined as any true loss and gain?
- Does it involve Borer?
- Does the game contain batteries?

The rules involved in determining whether a certain game is allowed or not:
- If the game involves writing it is forbidden to be played even if one chooses to play it without writing due to a decree one may come to write.[4]
- If the game involves rolling items on the ground it is forbidden to be done on a dirt floor, and is disputed if may be done on a tiled floor.[5]
- It is forbidden to play any ball game in an area without an Eiruv.

---

[1] Ketzos Hashulchan 110 footnote 16
[2] Admur 518:12
[3] 110 footnote 16
[4] Chayeh Adam 38:11; SSH"K 16:32
[5] Admur 338:6

1. Playing games on Shabbos:[6]

Games which involve rolling on the ground: One may not play games which involve rolling items[7] on the ground[8], even if the ground is tiled[9]. It is however permitted to play with them on a table. [This applies even if the floor of all the houses of one's city is tiled.[10] However, some Poskim[11] rule one may play these games on the floor of a tiled house, however not on the floor of a courtyard.]

Playing chess/5 stones: It is permitted to play a game using [pre-designated] bones[12] so long as one is not doing so for gambling purposes. [Some[13] explain this to refer to chess. Others[14] explain this to refer to "five stones" or "*Kugalach*".]

Gambling: It is forbidden to play any gambling games on Shabbos due to that this appears like business. A gambling game is defined as any game which involves actual loss and gains.

Those who transgress: Women and children which transgress and play games that are forbidden, such as a game involving rolling items on the floor, are not to be protested, as certainly they will not listen, and it is better they do so out of ignorance then do so advertently.

2. Doing a lottery on Shabbos:[15]

One may not make a lottery to give out items to different people on Shabbos.[16] This applies even amongst one's households, such as to see which member will get which item. It is however permitted to make a lottery for one's household to see what portion of food each person will receive, if the portions are all approximately the same size. If however the portions are of recognizably different sizes then doing so is forbidden even during the week.[17] However there are opinions which rule that amongst one's own family it is permitted to make a lottery of even large portions, as all the portions belong to the head of the household.[18] Practically, we rule stringently.[19]

Making a lottery for the Mitzvahs in Shul: It is permitted to make a lottery in order to give out Mitzvahs in Shul such as who will pray for the Amud, and who will get an Aliya.[20] [However others[21] hold doing so is forbidden even for Mitzvah matters. The main opinion follows the lenient opinion.[22]]

---

[6] Admur 338:6

The M"A 338:8 brings R"A Sasson which forbids playing any games on Shabbos being that they do not bring one to a needed wisdom. Admur omits this opinion from his Shulchan Aruch.

[7] Such as apples and almonds [ibid]

[8] Due to a decree that one may come to consciously smoothen ditches in the ground in order to properly roll the almonds or apple on the ground [ibid]

[9] Other opinions [Aruch Hashulchan 338:12] however rule that on tiled floors it is allowed, and no decree was made due to dirt floors as was done by sweeping, as it is not common to play these games.

[10] Ketzos Hashulchan 146 footnote 60; Shevisas Hashabbos, as these games are also played outside on dirt floors, and hence there is worry if we allow it on tiled floors, one may come to do so on dirt floors. However, regarding sweeping, on Shabbos, it is not common to sweep the courtyard as it was already swept before Shabbos. [ibid]

[11] SSH"K 16:5; Piskeiy Teshuvos 338:9 rules that according to Rav SZ"A it is even permitted to play on a tiled courtyard.

[12] As although they make noise during the form of play, one has no intent to make this noise. [ibid]

[13] Minchas Yitzchak 1:33

[14] Chelkas Yaakov 1:71

[15] 322:6

[16] If the items are not similar to each other then this is forbidden due to the gambling prohibition even during the week. If however the items are similar to each other, then during the week it is permitted as there is no gambling involved. However, on Shabbos it is forbidden due to a decree that due to jealousy one may come to measure the individual portions to see which portion is in truth larger. [Michaber ibid] Gambling is likewise forbidden on Shabbos due to it being similar to business. [338:6]

[17] 1st opinion in Michaber 322:6; Tur 322; Beis Yosef 322 that so rules Rif Shabbos 63b and Rosh 23:3; Bach 322 that so is the final ruling and so is implied to be the ruling of the Michaber ibid; M"B 322:22; Kaf Hachaim 322:31 that so is the final ruling

The reason: Although the father of the home owns all the items and it is not real gambling and worry of stealing, nonetheless it is forbidden as this can lead to gambling with others and in a way that people lose and win. [M"B 322:22]

The reason: Due to the gambling prohibition [ibid]

[18] 2nd opinion in Michaber 322:6; Rambam Shabbos 23:7; Taz 322:4

The reason: The reason for this is because gambling itself is only Rabbinically forbidden and hence there is no need to make an additional decree against this leading to one coming to gamble. [Maggid Mishneh on Rambam ibid; Olas Shabbos 322:10; Elya Raba 322:10; See Taz ibid for his alternative explanation]

[19] Bach 322 that so is the final ruling and so is implied to be the ruling of the Michaber ibid; Kaf Hachaim 322:31 that so is the final ruling

[20] M"A 322:9

[21] Nezer Hakodesh, as he understands Shevus Yaakov, brought in M"B 322:24; Ketzos Hashulchan 146:32

[22] Ketzos Hashulchan 146:32 based on Tzemach Tzedek

3. May one play ball on Shabbos?[23]

Some opinions rule it is forbidden to play with a ball on Shabbos or Yom Tov because a ball is Muktzah, being that it does not have the status of a vessel.

Other Opinions: [However] there are opinions which permit to move a ball and play with it in a private[24] domain.

The final ruling: It is an old custom to be lenient and they were not protested in doing so being that they have upon whom to rely. **See Q&A for practical application!**

4. Running and jumping games:[25]

It is permitted for lads who enjoy running and skipping to run or skip on Shabbos. [Thus, they may play "chase," hop scotch, jump rope and the like.[26]] It is forbidden for adults to run or jump on Shabbos for mundane purposes. See "The Laws of Mimtzo Cheftzecha" for further details on this subject.

5. Reading Books:[27]

Books of history and novels which do not contain themes involving morals and fear of heaven are forbidden to be read on Shabbos, even in one's mind without verbalization, due to Mimtzo Cheftzecha. Furthermore, even during the week they are forbidden to be read due to Moshav Leitzim. Those history books and novels which do contain morale messages are permitted to be read on Shabbos.

Medical books and other books of wisdom:[28] The custom is to allow reading books of wisdom and medicine on Shabbos.

For further details on this topic See "The Laws of Reading on Shabbos"!

Books permitted to be read:
- Chemistry
- Biology
- Encyclopedia
- Math
- Medicine

Books forbidden to be read:
- Novels
- History books

---

[23] Admur 308:83

[24] In other printings it says, "Public domain", however this version makes no sense as it is forbidden to carry in a public domain. Thus, the Rebbe says [in Igeres Hakodesh 3 page 27-28] that the correct version is "private domain". To note that the Ketzos Hashulchan 110 footnote 16 explains: On Shabbos they allow to play ball in a private domain, and on Yom Tov even in a public domain.

[25] Michaber 301:2

[26] Beir Moshe 6:33

[27] Admur 307:30

[28] Admur 307:31

General Q&A

May an adult play games on Shabbos?[29]

Due to the holiness of Shabbos, adults should avoid playing games on Shabbos even if the game has no Halachic issues involved. It is forbidden for anyone over Bar or Bas Mitzvah to play with games that contain possible Shabbos prohibitions.

Are games which adults may not play considered Muktzah?[30]

Games which are permitted for children to play with are not Muktzah for adults.

May one play with play dough on Shabbos?[31]

No. It is forbidden even for children to play with play dough and the like on Shabbos due to the smearing prohibition. It is thus Muktzah.

May one play ball on Shabbos?

Although it is ruled in Shulchan Aruch that one may play ball on Shabbos, nevertheless it is forbidden to do so on a steady basis as part of one's Shabbos schedule, as doing so is a great belittling of Shabbos, and is what caused a great city[32] to be destroyed.[33]

<u>A ball which is inflatable with air</u>: Some Poskim[34] rule that all inflatable balls are forbidden to be played with on Shabbos, due to a decree that one may come to inflate it with air upon noticing its need of air, and he will thus transgress the fixing prohibition. According to other Poskim[35] however it is even initially permitted to inflate a ball with air on Shabbos, and thus it remains permitted to play with such balls. [Furthermore, perhaps today even according to the stringent opinion it would be permitted, as it is not common to inflate the balls with air but rather to purchase new ones.]

<u>Playing on a dirt floor</u>:[36] It is forbidden to play ball on a dirt floor due to a decree that one may come to smoothen holes in the ground and thus come to transgress the building prohibition. Hence playing soccer is forbidden.[37]

<u>Playing in an area without an Eiruv</u>:[38] It is forbidden to play ball in an area without an Eiruv.

May one play ping pong on Shabbos?

Some opinions[39] rule that it is allowed, as the custom is to allow playing with a ball on Shabbos and not to consider it Muktzah.

Others[40] rule that it is forbidden to play ping pong on Shabbos according to all opinions as it is belittling of Shabbos.

---

[29] SSH"K 182

[30] Beir Moshe 6:27

[31] SSH"K 16:13; Piskeiy Teshuvos 314:6; Beir Moshe 6:34

[32] The city of Tur Shimon was destroyed, according to one opinion, for the sin of playing ball on Shabbos, which according to the lenient opinion means due to the sin of using their Shabbos for ball playing instead of learning Torah. [Ketzos Hashulchan 110 footnote 16]

[33] Ketzos Hashulchan 110 footnote 16; Taz 518:2 writes in name of Rashal that it is a wonderment that playing ball is allowed on Yom Tov when in truth it is a game of children and not meant for adults. Thus he rules that it is an evil custom for adults to spend their time playing ball, and "if I had the power I would nullify it".
The Ketzos Hashulchan explains how even during the week ball playing is to be avoided, as it is a mere women's game, being that they are not obligated in learning Torah, as well as that some of the games are taken from the gentiles.

[34] Ketzos Hashulchan 110 footnote 16

[35] Yesod Yeshurun 4 page 270; Betzeil Hachachmah 4:92; Beir Moshe 2:20

[36] Admur 338:6; Ketzos Hashulchan Ibid in name of Mishneh Berurah 308:158.

[37] Due to decree of "Mashveh Gumos". 338:6; SSH"K 16:7. It is forbidden even to play on a concrete court as rules Ketzos Hashulchan 146:60 However SSH"K 16:5; Piskeiy Teshuvos 338:9 rule that according to Rav SZ"A it is permitted to play on a tiled courtyard.

[38] Mishneh Berurah 308:158

[39] SSH"K 16:6

[40] Beir Moshe 2:27; Ketzos Hashulchan 110 footnote 16 that it was only allowed to play ball on Shabbos occasionally and not on a steady basis as doing so is a belittling of Shabbos.

May one inflate a balloon?[41]

Some Poskim[42] rule it is allowed to inflate balloons, even if the balloon contains pictures. Others[43] rule doing so is forbidden. According to all it is forbidden to tie the top of the balloon.[44]

May a child play building games such as Lego and the like?[45]

Some Poskim[46] allow this in all cases[47], as the built structures are not meant to last at all, as they are assembled and disassembled constantly.[48]

However other Poskim[49] forbid playing with Lego and other building games of the like which involve attaching pieces strongly together.

Others[50] forbid it only in cases where the structure forms a roofing [due to the Ohel prohibition[51]] or an actual vessel like a ship and the like.

<u>Assembling structures which are meant to last:</u>[52] According to all opinions those building games which are meant to be left intact [in their built state] for a while are forbidden to be assembled on Shabbos.

<u>Regarding adults playing with the above games:</u> Besides for it not being the spirit of Shabbos[53], it is not considered a Shabbos need and is thus seemingly forbidden, as even building non-temporary structures was only allowed for a Shabbos need.[54]

May one form a ship, plane and the like from [non-Muktzah] paper?[55]

Some opinions[56] allow this to be done. Others[57] are stringent.

May one blow bubbles on Shabbos?[58]

Blowing bubbles on Shabbos enters into the question of whether it transgresses the Molid prohibition due to it changing the form of the water into foam. Practically, the mainstream approach follows that it does not contain a Molid prohibition, and therefore children may blow bubbles on Shabbos.[59] However, it is best for adults to abstain from doing so.[60] Furthermore, some Poskim[61]

---

[41] Piskeiy Teshuvos 340:23

[42] So rules Beir Moshe 2:20; 6:23 that it is allowed.

[43] Sheivet Halevy 9:78

[44] Beir Moshe ibid; As this is considered similar to double knot as one is making a single knot on a single end, as explained in "The Laws of Tying".

[45] Piskeiy Teshuvos 313:4

[46] Beir Moshe 6:25; Tzitz Eliezer 13:30

[47] Even to build ships and vessels of the like.

[48] As well for a child it is considered a Shabbos need and thus fulfills all the conditions required by a not even temporary vessel.

[49] Shalmei Yehuda 85:1

[50] SSH"K 16:20

[51] Michzei Eliyahu 69

[52] SSH"K 16:20

[53] Beir Moshe 6:24

[54] See Volume 2 "The Laws of Building and Destroying".

[55] Piskeiy Teshuvos 313:4

[56] Beir Moshe 6:102

[57] SSH"K 16:20; Sheivet Halevy 5:35

[58] See SSH"K 16:30; Shabbos Kehalacha Vol. 3 17:79; Piskeiy Teshuvos 326:13 footnote 161

[59] Evident from Ketzos Hashulchan 146:32; SSH"K ibid in name of Rav SH"Z Aurbauch; Shabbos Kehalacha ibid; Piskeiy Teshuvos ibid although writes that initially one should not instruct children to do so and it is just that if they do so they do not have to be protested

<u>The reason:</u> Although it is forbidden on Shabbos to change the form of an item, such as to turn ice into water, due to the Molid/Nolad prohibition, nevertheless the Poskim rule that the formation of foam/bubbles that becomes created when using soap to wash hands/dishes does not fall under this prohibition as the foam has no real substance, and does not last at all. [So rules Ketzos Hashulchan 146 footnote 32; Tzitz Eliezer 6:34; -14; in length; Beir Moshe 8:247; SSH"K ibid in name of Rav SZ"A; Piskeiy Teshuvos ibid; However some are stringent in this: See Ginas Veradim [Halevi] O.C. Klall 3:14 regarding hard soap; Shevisas Hashabbos Dash 61; Az Nidbaru 10:16] For this reason, also the placing of toothpaste on one's teeth [without a tooth brush] does not consist of a Nolad prohibition, even though it creates foam in the process, as the foam has no substance. [Ketzos Hashulchan 138 footnote 31]. Accordingly, it would be permitted here as well to blow bubbles, being that the bubbles hold no substance and do not last. However, Tzaruch Iyun, as in the case of blowing bubbles one has intent to create the foam and it is thus unlike the case discussed above in the Poskim regarding soap bubbles, in which case one has no intent for them to be made. [see Shabbos Kehalacha ibid;

rule that even children who have reached the age of Chinuch are to avoid blowing bubbles on Shabbos.[62]

Is snow Muktzah?[63]
Snow retains the same law as rainwater, and is thus not Muktzah [if useable for eating drinking etc, as said above by rainwater].

May one make snowballs and snow men?
It is forbidden to make snowballs on Shabbos.[64]
Children: Some Poskim[65] rule that by children below nine years old one may be lenient to allow them to make snowballs in an area where there is an Eiruv. If however there is no Eiruv then every child above Chinuch is forbidden to throw snowballs. Other Poskim[66] rule it is proper to refrain all children [which have reached the age of Chinuch] from making snowballs on Shabbos.
Snow man: In all cases it is forbidden for even children [above the age of Chinuch] to make snowmen and the like.[67]

May one ride a bicycle on Shabbos?[68]
Children below Chinuch: May ride any bike on Shabbos.
Children above Chinuch: May ride a bike on Shabbos, although it is proper to refrain them from riding a regular bike.[69] They may ride a tricycle without restriction. If the bike contains training wheels there is more room for a father to be lenient to allow his child to ride it on Shabbos.[70]
Adults: May not ride bikes on Shabbos.[71]
Fixing the bike: One may not fix a bike on Shabbos due to the prohibition of "Tikkun Keli". However, some Poskim allow a child to replace the chain onto the wheel as doing so is not really considered like fixing. Nevertheless, an adult should not help a child do so.

Piskeiy Teshuvos ibid] Nevertheless, it is clear that the Ketzos Hashulchan 146 footnote 32 learns it is permitted even a case that one intends to make the bubbles, as he also explains that it is permitted to make seltzer for this reason, even though one certainly has intent to create the bubbles.
[60] SSH"K ibid; Shabbos Kehalacha ibid
The reason: As one intends to make the bubble and it is hence unlike the case discussed regarding soap bubbles in which case one has no intent for them to be made. [SSH"K ibid; Piskeiy Teshuvos ibid]
[61] Shraga Hameir 7:44; Koveitz Mibeiys Halevy 6:44 in name of Rav Shmuel Wozner and Nishmas Shabbos 250, brought in Shabbos Kehalacha ibid footnote 192
[62] The reason: As nevertheless, one has intent to make the bubbles and it is hence similar to Molid Davar Chadash. [ibid]
[63] Beir Moshe 6:30; Har Tzevi Kuntrus of 39 Melachos "Soser", and so is implied from other Poskim which deal with the question of making snowballs on Shabbos.
[64] Makor Chaim [Chavos Yair] 320:9; Shabbos Kehalacha Vol. 3 17:67; SSH"K 16:44 rules that doing so is forbidden due to the building prohibition. Beir Moshe 6:30 argues that doing so contains no building prohibition being that it does not contain the building characteristics and does not last at all. However, he concludes that it is nevertheless forbidden being that doing so causes snow to melt, which is forbidden. Vetzaruch Iyun Gadol as from Admur [320:16 -18] which writes that the prohibition is only when one intends to use the melted water, while by a snowball there is no intent for it to melt at all. Furthermore, the source of the Beir Moshe from 320:19 itself is dealing with crushing snow together within water when washing, and one thus certainly does care about having more melted water.
[65] Beir Moshe ibid
[66] Shabbos Kehalacha ibid. In footnote 167 he writes that in truth there seems to be no reason to prohibit making snowballs, however he nullifies his opinion in face of the Makor Chaim which explicitly chastises those that make lads that make snowballs on Shabbos and throw them at each other.
[67] Beir Moshe ibid; Shabbos Kehalacha ibid
[68] Beir Moshe 6:16-17; See also Rav Poalim 1:25; Yaskil Avdi 3:19; Ketzos Hashulchan 110 footnote 16
There is no explicit prohibition stated in Shulchan Aruch against riding a bike. Nevertheless, Poskim prohibit riding it due to a number of reasons. The issues are as follows: 1. Perhaps the bike may break, and one will come to fix it. This is similar to the prohibition against playing musical instruments. 2. It is a mundane act. 3. Perhaps he will end up going outside the Techum Shabbos. [ibid]
[69] As by a regular bike then all the suspicions applicable to a bike apply. Nevertheless, from the letter of the law a child even below Chinuch may ride it as there is no suspicion that he will come to fix the bike or ride outside the Techum.
[70] As in such a case everyone can tell the bike is meant for children.
[71] For reasons mentioned in previous footnotes.
Other Opinions: Rav Poalim ibid allows riding a bike on Shabbos in an area with an Eiruv, although later Poskim write he retracted his ruling. [See Yaskil Avdi ibid]

May one ride roller blades?

Doing so has the same status as riding a bicycle in terms of being a mundane activity, and hence should not be done due to the holiness of Shabbos.

May one play in a sand box on Shabbos?[72]

Yes. However, one may not add liquid to the sand due to the kneading prohibition.

May one put together puzzles on Shabbos?[73]

- <u>Placing together word or number puzzles</u>: [Meaning that the individual pieces contain complete letters and numbers and do not form a letter or number when compiled]. So long as one does not strongly fasten the pieces to each other or to a background in a way that the puzzle sits firmly together, it is permitted to put it together. This applies whether it creates words or numbers.[74]

- <u>Placing together letter or picture puzzles</u>: If placing the pieces together creates new letters or pictures which did not exist individually, as is common by most puzzles, some Poskim[75] rule that it nevertheless has the same laws as a word puzzle mentioned above and may be put together so long as the pieces are not firmly attached.[76] Others[77] however rule that in such a case doing so is forbidden[78].

May one play chess?[79]

Yes. However, it is improper for one to spend his Shabbos day doing such activity.[80]

May one play scrabble?[81]

Yes. See "The Laws of Writing and Erasing" for the full analysis on this subject.

May one play Monopoly?

Yes.[82] However some Poskim[83] have discouraged doing so being it appears like gambling.

May one play dreidal?[84]

One may only play dreidal if it does not involve gambling, which refers to loss and gains.

May a child play with toys that make music or noise?

Some Poskim allow giving a child noise[85] making toys for the child to play with up until the age of 6.[86]

---

[72] SSH"K 16:4

[73] Piskeiy Teshuvos 340:16-footnote 51

[74] So rules Chayeh Adam and Ketzos Hashulchan 144:10 regarding cases brought there [to sew letters onto a peroches, that if they are weekly sewn they contain no writing prohibition]. So rules also Igros Moshe 1:135; Piskeiy Teshuvos 340:7 and 16; Beir Moshe 6:26; Avnei Neizer, brought in Ketzos Hashulchan 144 footnote 4, rules that placing letters near each other has no prohibition.

[75] Beir Moshe 6:26; Yesod Yeshurun 1:53; SSH"K 16:23

[76] As they hold that this is similar to closing a book with writing on its edges which is allowed. These Poskim similarly rule that one may place a torn page together to read it-See Halacha 8 Q&A there!

[77] Shalmeiy Yehuda 5:1; Seemingly Az Nidbaru 5:18 and Bris Olam regarding the prohibition in placing torn pages together would also agree that this is forbidden.

[78] As it is not similar to closing a book being that there the pages are bound together and is already considered to be very close.

[79] Minchas Yitzchak 1:33; Igros Moshe Yoreh Deah 3:15; See Halacha 1 above!

[80] The Igros Moshe ibid states that if losing the game will make one feel sad then it is forbidden from the letter of the law to play it on Shabbos.

[81] Beir Moshe 6:26

[82] Rav SZ"A in SSH"K 16 footnote 84; Beir Moshe 6:26

[83] SSH"K 16:32; Piskeiy Teshuvos 338:11

[84] SSH"K 16:32; Piskeiy Teshuvos 338:11

[85] In contrast to music, see next footnote.

[86] Beir Moshe 6:27; SSH"K 16:3. As the entire reason behind the noisemaking prohibition-in the opinion of M"B- is because of Uvdin Dechol, which is not so applicable by such toys. However according to Admur which rules the reason behind the prohibition is due to a decree one may

However according to Admur it is seemingly forbidden to allow a child who has reached the age of Chinuch to play with such objects even if the objects merely make noise and not music.[87] The age of Chinuch in this regard is defined as the age that the child can understand being told not to do something. Practically this is near the age of three.[88] Furthermore, according to Admur, even a child below the age of Chinuch, such as a mere infant, may not be given any toy which is designated for making music[89] or noise[90].

May one use a swing which is attached to a tree?[91]
If the swing is directly attached to the tree from above 3 Tefach from the ground it is forbidden to be used in all cases. If it is attached to a metal pole and the like which in turn is attached to the tree then it still remains forbidden to be used if doing so will cause the tree or its branches to shake in the process. If no part of the tree will shake in the process, then from the letter of the law it may be used.[92] however some Poskim[93] forbid its use entirely under the claim it is difficult to ascertain whether such action causes the tree to shake. If the swing is attached to the tree from below 3 Tefach to the ground, it may be used in all cases.

May one watch a game on a neighbor's television or go see a game in a stadium?[94]
Even if doing so involves no actual transgressions, it is forbidden being that it desecrates the spirit of Shabbos.

---

come to fix the vessel, then it would seemingly be forbidden. Seemingly according to all it would be forbidden to give the child music making toys as it is forbidden due to a Rabbinical decree according to all. [So also concludes Piskeiy Teshuvos 338 footnote 2]

[87] So seems to be the opinion of Admur, as the reason behind the prohibition of intentionally making noise is because one may come to fix the item. Hence this is a typical Rabbinical prohibition which applies to all children above the age of Chinuch. However, Tzaruch Iyun as noise making items are disputed if they are forbidden to be used even by adults and hence perhaps by children there is room to be more lenient.

[88] See Piskeiy Teshuvos 343

[89] Admur 301:21 regarding giving a child clothing with bells to wear. This ruling is based on the understanding of Chikrei Halachos 4 p. 54, and other alternative explanations of this ruling. However according to the explanation of Hearos Ubiurim 831 p. 79 so long as the adult has no intent for the child to make noise with the object, such as the objects can be used in a different way to entertain the child, then giving him the object is allowed.

[90] Tzaruch Iyun regarding noise making objects as bells can be defined as an item which makes music, as well as that noise making items is a dispute if forbidden even by an adult.

[91] Based on Beir Moshe 6:29; SSH"K 16:16; See "The Laws Relating to Plants and Trees"

[92] SSH"K 16:16

[93] Beir Moshe 6:29

[94] Biur Halacha 301:2 "Kol"

Game	Halachic status
Binoculars	Permitted
Blocks	Permitted[95]
Boggle	Forbidden
Bubbles	Permitted
Checkers	Permitted
Chess	Permitted
Dominos	Permitted
Etch-A-Sketch	Forbidden
Magna-Doodle	Forbidden
Marbles/Kugelach	Permitted
Monopoly	Permitted
Pick Up Sticks	Permitted
Scrabble	Permitted
Scrabble-Deluxe	Forbidden
Soccer	Forbidden[96]
Bowling	Dispute.[97]
Ping Pong	Permitted[98]
Play Dough	Forbidden

---

[95] Beir Moshe 6:25

[96] Due to decree of "Mashveh Gumos". 338:6; SSH"K 16:7. It is forbidden even to play on a concrete court as rules Ketzos Hashulchan 146:60

[97] According to the Ketzos Hashulchan this is forbidden even in one's home as it is a rolling game. However according to SSH"K it is allowed inside one's home.

[98] SSH"K 16:6

CHAPTER 10: LAWS RELATING TO PLANTS, TREES, AND GARDEN PRODUCE

1. Making use of trees on Shabbos:[1]

The Sages decreed against making any use of a tree on Shabbos due to worry that if this were to be allowed one may come to climb the tree and remove fruits, leaves, or branches from it. This decree applies equally to all trees, even to those which are barren and have no leaves or branches.[2]

The decree against making use of trees includes the following prohibited actions:

- Climbing a tree.
- Hanging on a tree branch.
- Leaning on a tree.
- Placing or removing objects from a tree or its branch.
- Tying items to a tree or its branch.

A. Climbing:[3]

One may not climb on a tree on Shabbos whether the tree is dry or damp.

Climbing up a tree before Shabbos:[4] One may not climb a tree from before Shabbos in order to remain on it throughout Shabbos.[5] If one climbed the tree from before Shabbos, and remained on it into Shabbos he may descend from it on Shabbos. [See footnote if he must descend immediately upon remembering[6]]. This applies even if one ascended the tree before Shabbos with intent to remain there on Shabbos, and had prior knowledge that being on the tree on Shabbos is forbidden.[7] It certainly applies if one ascended without prior knowledge of the prohibition involved in remaining there on Shabbos.[8]

If one climbed up a tree on Shabbos may he climb down: [9] If one climbed up a tree on Shabbos unknowing of the prohibition involved, it is permitted for him to descend on Shabbos.[10] If, however, one climbed the tree despite his knowledge of the prohibition, it is forbidden for him to descend from the tree on Shabbos, and he must rather remain there throughout Shabbos.[11]

B. Hanging on a tree:[12]

One may not hang on a tree.

---

[1] Admur 336:1

[2] As the Sages decided to make a guardrail for their decree, and hence forbid all trees from their use. [ibid]

[3] Admur 336:1

[4] Admur 336:2

[5] As sitting on the tree on Shabbos is itself considered making use of the tree, which is forbidden to be done. [ibid]

[6] Seemingly he must descend immediately upon remembering as it is forbidden to remain on the tree on Shabbos, as explained above. However, it requires further analysis why this was omitted from Admur, and on the contrary Admur gives no implication that one must descend at all. Perhaps the reason is because going down from the tree is also a prohibition and hence whether he decides to remain on the tree or descend he is doing a prohibition, and it is just that he is allowed to descend. However, this matter requires further analysis as remaining on the tree is seemingly a continuous prohibition while descending is a onetime action, hence why should it not be required for him to descend?

[7] There is a dispute regarding this matter brought in Admur: The first [Stam] opinion rules it is permitted to descend on Shabbos if one ascended before Shabbos, even if one did so with prior knowledge of the prohibition.

Other opinions however rule that in a case that one ascended *Bemeizid* before Shabbos with intent to remain there on Shabbos, [meaning he ascended with prior knowledge of the prohibition], then if he in truth remains on the tree into Shabbos, in such a case the Sages fined him to need to remain on the tree until the end of Shabbos. According to this opinion it was only permitted to descend from a tree which one ascended before Shabbos if one intended to descend before Shabbos, and inadvertently remained into Shabbos.

Practically, the final ruling is that regarding Rabbinical matters one is to follow the lenient opinion. [ibid]

[8] This applies according to all as explained in the previous footnote.

[9] Admur 336:2

[10] As although by climbing down the tree he is making use of it, nevertheless this was not prohibited as either way he will be making use of the tree, as if we require him to remain on the tree until after Shabbos, then he has made use of sitting on the tree on Shabbos. [ibid] And making use of a tree on Shabbos by sitting on it is likewise forbidden, therefore the Sages allowed him to descend even though he is making use of the tree by doing so. [336:3]

[11] This is due to a fine of the Sages. [ibid]

[12] Admur 336:1

C. Leaning on a tree:[13]

Ruling of Admur in SH"A: (One may not lean on a frail tree on Shabbos if doing so will cause it to shake. One may lean on a sturdy tree that will not shake as a result of one's leaning.[14])

Final ruling of Ketzos Hashulchan: The Ketzos Hashulchan[15] rules that practically, even for those which follow the rulings of Admur[16], it is forbidden to lean on any tree, whether sturdy or weak, to the point that if the tree were to be removed the person would fall. However, it is permitted to slightly lean on a [strong[17]] tree in a way that even if the tree were to fall one would remain standing.[18] Other Poskim[19] rule it is only permitted for a healthy person to lean on a healthy tree while a weak person or a weak tree is forbidden in leaning.[20]

D. Touching a tree:[21]

It is permitted to touch a tree so long as one does not cause it to shake in the process.[22]

E. Making use of a tree for one's objects:[23]

One may not use a tree for any purpose. Thus, it is forbidden to:

- Place an item on it.
- Remove an item from it.
- Tie an animal to it.

If one left an item on a tree from before Shabbos may he take it down on Shabbos?[24] If one left an item on a tree from before Shabbos it is forbidden for him to take it down on Shabbos.[25]

---

[13] Admur 336:1 and 21

Background:

Ruling of M"A and its explanation: The M"A 336:15 writes "to lean on a tree for a healthy is allowed while for a weak is not allowed" It is unclear from the M"A if the term healthy and weak refers to the tree or the person. Meaning is he ruling that if the tree is week it is forbidden to lean on it, or is he ruling that if a person is week, he may not lean on it". Admur [as well as Chayeh Adam] here rules like the former option, that if the tree is week it is forbidden due to it shaking while if the tree is healthy it is permitted. Admur [and Chayeh Adam] makes no differentiation regarding a healthy or week person, hence showing he understood the M"A to be referring to the tree and not to the person. However the Machatzis Hashekel [end of 336] and Peri Megadim A"A 336:15 learn like the latter that if the person is week it is forbidden while if the person is healthy it is permitted.

Question on Admur: The Igleiy Tal [brought in Ketzos Hashulchan 142 footnote 10] and Biur Halacha [336 "Umutar"] takes issue with the explanation of Admur and Chayeh Adam being that to lean on a tree is prohibited due to Tzedadin [using the sides of a tree] and hence what relevance is there whether the tree will shake or not, either way it is forbidden in use. They thus conclude that it is forbidden to lean even on a strong tree. The Ketzos Hashulchan [142 footnote 10] concludes based on these questions, that even Admur himself did not conclusively rule like the former option ,and hence placed the ruling in parentheses. He thus concludes to be stringent.

[14] The parentheses are in the original and were entered by Admur. The Sheiris Yehuda writes that all laws that were placed by Admur in parentheses were done so because they were in need of final review. Thus, as will be explained next the Ketzos Hashulchan 142 footnote 10 rules not to follow this ruling.

Other Opinions: As rules Admur so also rules Chayeh Adam. However the PM"G; Machatzis Hashekel; M"B and Igleiy Tal ibid rule it is forbidden to lean on any tree unless one he is merely touching it. The Ketzos Hashulchan ibid defines this as leaning slightly in a way that one would still remain standing even if the tree were to fall.

[15] 142 footnote 10

[16] Meaning that they should not follow the ruling of Admur in parentheses, as maters placed in parentheses are not considered a final Halachic ruling of Admur, and hence one is allowed to rule like other Poskim. [Ketzos Hashulchan ibid]

[17] However, on a weak tree it would remain forbidden due to causing it to shake, as explained in Admur and other Poskim. [so rules also Kaf Hachaim 336:90]

[18] The Ketzos Hashulchan defines the ruling of the Igleiy Tal and M"B that touching is not literal

[19] Kaf Hachaim 336:90

[20] The Kaf Hachaim ibid suspects for both explanations and is hence stringent to require both the person and the tree to be healthy.

[21] Admur 336:22

[22] As a tree is Muktzah and hence may not be moved. [ibid]

[23] Admur 336:1

[24] Admur 336:3

[25] As upon taking the item down one is using the tree, which is forbidden. If, however, the item were to remain on the tree until after Shabbos no prohibition would be done. Hence this case is not similar to a person who has climbed a tree from before Shabbos, as in such a case even making him remain on the tree involves a prohibition of using the tree, and hence there is no Halachic advantage of making the person remain there rather than descend. [Admur ibid]

Q&A
If one's Tallis got stuck on a tree may one remove it?[26]
Yes.

Question:
It was very windy this Shabbos and the wind blew my hat onto a tree. Is it permitted for me to take it down or is this prohibited due to the prohibition to make use of a tree on Shabbos?

Answer:
You should not remove it from the tree on Shabbos, unless you can do so very easily and casually without removing any leaves or branches and without leaning on the tree, and only if it is a case of great need such as you suspect that your hat may not be there after Shabbos, or you have no other hat to wear for Davening in Shul by Mincha and Maariv and will be embarrassed. Otherwise, you should leave it there till after Shabbos and then take it off.

The explanation: It is rabbinically forbidden to remove things from a tree on Shabbos just as it is forbidden to place things on the. Now, there are various reasons recorded behind the prohibition of removing it from the tree, and the final ruling follows that the reason is due to an essential use being made of the tree when one removes an item from it. This would imply that it would be prohibited to remove an item from the tree even if it fell onto the tree unintentionally. Nonetheless, in the case of great need there is room for leniency in the event that it fell on the tree unintentionally, due to the joining of all the other reasons mentioned which would imply that in such a case of the in the Poskim the decree does not apply.

Sources: See Admur 336:3; M"A 336:2; Rosh Shabbos 5; Elya Raba 514:26 [leans to rule like Rosh that there is no decree against removing; Makor Chaim 336 [decree does not apply if will not shake tree with hands when moving]; Shevet Halevi 7:44; 11:98; Shevet Hakehasi 4:99; Piskeiy Teshuvos 336:3 footnote 28

If a ball fell into a tree on Shabbos, may one take it down?[27]
No. It may not be taken down in any way.

F. May one place an item on a tree before Shabbos having it remain there into Shabbos?[28]
It is permitted to place a candle on a tree from before <u>Shabbos</u> with intent that it remains there into Shabbos being that the candle is Muktzah.[29] It is however forbidden to place a candle on a tree from before <u>Yom Tov</u> with intent that it remains there into Yom Tov, as on Yom Tov a candle is not Muktzah.[30] [Thus as a general rule all non-Muktzah items are forbidden to be placed on a tree from before Shabbos with intent that they remain there on Shabbos due to suspicion that one may come to take them down. The same applies on Yom Tov.[31]]

---

[26] Sheivet Haleivi 7:44
[27] Nitei Gavriel Yom Tov 42:5
[28] Admur 277:7; 514:16
[29] As since a candle is Muktzah there is no worry that one may come to take it down from the tree on Shabbos. ibid]
[30] Hence, we suspect one may come to take it down on Yom Tov and by doing so one makes use of the tree which is forbidden to be done whether on Shabbos or Yom Tov. [ibid]
[31] Ketzos Hashulchan 142 footnote 11 in name of Iglei Tal.

Summary:
It is forbidden to leave non-Muktzah objects on a tree over Shabbos. It is permitted to leave Muktzah items on a tree over Shabbos.

G. Making use of items which are attached to a tree:[32]

It is forbidden to make use of items which are in direct contact with a tree. Those items which are in contact with an item that is in direct contact with a tree, one may make use of that item[33] so long as that doing so will not inevitably cause the tree or its branches to shake.[34]

- *Example 1-Climbing a ladder:*

   One may not climb a ladder which is leaning on a tree[35], although one may climb the ladder if it is leaning on a nail which is attached to the tree.[36] Furthermore one may even initially lean this ladder on the nail on Shabbos.[37]

- *Example 2-Using a basket:*

   One may make use of a basket which is hanging on a nail which is knocked into the tree[38] if doing so will not inevitably cause the tree or its branches to shake.[39] Thus one may remove an item from within a widely opened basket [or enter an item into it[40]]. However, a narrowly opened basket which will cause the tree to shake upon removing, or entering an item into it, may not be

---

[32] Admur 336:20

[33] As only the use of the side of the tree was decreed against, while the use of "the sides of the side" were permitted. [Ibid]

[34] As if one causes it to shake he has made use of the tree itself which is forbidden. [ibid]

[35] As by doing so one is making use of the side of the tree which he is using as support. [ibid]

[36] As the nail is considered the side while the ladder is the side of the side which is allowed to be used. [ibid]

[37] This ruling of Admur is based on Michaber 336:13

Question on above ruling and Other Opinions: Tzaruch Iyun as for why it is allowed to lean a ladder onto a nail, is this not considered making use of the nail which is "sides", and it is forbidden to make use of sides on Shabbos? The M"B [336:60;62 in name of Achronim, Upashut] and Kaf Hachaim 336:85 both take issue with this ruling based on this question and conclude to reinterpret the ruling of the Michaber to rather read as follows "It is permitted to place a ladder on a nail on **Erev Shabbos** in order to climb on it on Shabbos". However, on Shabbos itself it is forbidden to place a ladder onto the nail. SSH"K 16:16 practically rules like their opinion that it is forbidden to place the ladder on the nail on Shabbos.

Question on "Other Opinions": However, it is very difficult to enter this explanation into either the wording of Admur or the Michaber and it is literally requiring rewriting their words. Admur writes "It is permitted to place the ladder on the nail and climb up" According to the new explanation why did he not just simply state "However if the ladder is leaning on a nail of the tree it is permitted to climb up" as is the wording of the first case in which he writes "if the ladder is leaning on the tree itself it is forbidden to climb it on Shabbos". If anything, the change of wording in the second case to "It is permitted to place a ladder on the nail" negates the explanation given above and hence is the reason why Admur wrote it this way so there be no misunderstanding in the Michaber. In the Michaber as well it is difficult to enter this explanation as he simply rules "it is forbidden to place the ladder on the tree itself while onto a nail is permitted". The Michaber here is not even discussing the idea of climbing the tree but simply of placing the ladder. Hence it appears that according to the Michaber and Admur, as well as all the other Poskim such as the Taz, M"A, Aruch Hashulchan which did not edit anything into the Michaber, it is clear they rule one may place the ladder onto the actual nail.

Explanation: As a possible explanation of why there is no prohibition involved in placing the ladder onto the nail, perhaps one can answer that placing a ladder onto the nail is not considered doing an actual use with the nail, which is the Tzedadin, as the actual use is when he climbs onto the ladder. Meaning the same way there is no prohibition in touching a tree as by doing so he has not done any use of the tree, so too there is no prohibition in leaning a ladder on a tree as until he climbs the tree, he has done absolutely no use of the tree, as the ladders only purpose and use is for climbing. This understanding can find support in the wording of the Michaber. He writes "One may not lean a ladder onto a tree **as when one climbs it** he us using the sides". The Michaber clearly writes that the prohibition is the climbing and not the actual leaning of the ladder. Meaning that only the climbing in the ladder is considered using the Tzedadin while the leaning is not. However according to this it remains to be understood why the Michaber wrote in the first place it is forbidden to lean the ladder on the tree if the prohibition is only the leaning? Perhaps this is the inference in the change of wording of Admur from the wording of the Michaber, Admur, unlike the Michaber, does not mention it is forbidden to lean the ladder on the tree on Shabbos, he rather simply states it is forbidden to climb a ladder that is leaning directly on a tree. Perhaps this change of wording is emphasizing the exact point brought above, that placing the ladder onto the tree is permitted as it has done no use, while only climbing is forbidden. [Note of Author: All this I have written not because I Chas Veshalom feel I understand the Shulchan Aruch better than the M"B and Kaf Hachaim but simply to defend the simple straightforward meaning of the Michaber and Admur, as well as all the other Poskim which never felt a need to explain or edit their words. What does however require further study is why Admur rules that removing the basket from the nail is considered using the side of the tree, as what actual use has been done by removing the basket. Vetzaruch Iyun.]

[38] As the nail is considered the side while the basket is the side of the side which is allowed to be used. [ibid]

[39] As if one causes it to shake, he has made use of the tree itself which is forbidden.

[40] Ketzos Hashulchan 142:7

used. In all cases one may not remove the basket from the nail as by doing so he is making use of the nail.[41] If the basket is hanging directly on the tree, such as on a branch, it is forbidden in use in all cases and hence one may not remove items from it or insert items into it.[42]

Q&A

May one lie on a hammock which is attached to a tree?[43]

If the hammock is directly attached to the tree in an area that is above 3 Tefach from the ground, the hammock is forbidden to be used in all cases.[44] If the hammock is not directly attached to the tree but is rather attached to a metal pole or nail and the like which is attached to the tree, then it still remains prohibited to be used if doing so will cause the tree or its branches to shake in the process. If, however, no part of the tree will shake in the process of using the hammock, then from the letter of the law it may be used.[45] However, some Poskim[46] forbid its use entirely under the claim it is difficult to ascertain whether such action causes the tree to shake. If the hammock is attached to the tree from below 3 Tefach to the ground, it may be used in all cases.[47]

May one use a swing which is attached to a tree?[48]

This maintains the same ruling as using a hammock. Hence:

If the swing is directly attached to the tree from above 3 Tefach from the ground it is forbidden to be used in all cases.[49] If it is attached to a metal pole and the like which is attached to the tree, then it still remains forbidden to be used if doing so will cause the tree or its branches to shake in the process. If no part of the tree will shake, then from the letter of the law it may be used.[50] However some Poskim[51] forbid its use entirely under the claim it is difficult to ascertain whether such action causes the tree to shake. vIf the swing is attached to the tree from below 3 Tefach to the ground, it may be used in all cases.

Compilation-May one lie on a swing or hammock which is attached to a tree on Shabbos?[52]

Background:[53] It is forbidden to make use of a tree, or of items which are being directly supported by a tree or its branches [that are above three Tefach-24 cm-from the ground[54]].[55] [Such an item is referred to in Halacha as Tzedadin.] However, one may make use of items that are not directly supported by a tree even though they are being supported by an item that is supported by the tree.[56] Thus, if an item is attached to a nail that was hammered into a tree, one may make a use of that item.[57] [Such an item is referred to in Halacha as Tzedei Tzedadin.] However, this is only permitted on condition that it will not

---

[41] And the nail is considered the side of the tree which is forbidden in use. [ibid]
[42] As the basket is considered the side of the tree which is forbidden in use. [ibid]
[43] Based on Beir Moshe 6:29; SSH"K 16:16
[44] As the hammock is considered "the sides" which is forbidden to be used as explained above.
[45] SSH"K 16:16
[46] Beir Moshe 6:29
[47] See below for the relevance of three Tefachim
[48] Based on Beir Moshe 6:29; SSH"K 16:16
[49] As the hammock is considered "the sides" which is forbidden to be sued as explained above.
[50] SSH"K 16:16
[51] Beir Moshe 6:29
[52] See Admur 336:20; Beir Moshe 6:29; SSH"K 16:16; Piskeiy Teshuvos 336:23
[53] Admur 336:1 regarding tree; 336:20 regarding Tzedadin; Michaber 336:1 and 13; Shabbos 154b-155a; Eiruvin 32b
[54] Admur 336:6
[55] The reason: As by doing so one is making use of the side of the tree which he is using as support. [Admur ibid; Michaber ibid; Rav Ashi in Shabbos ibid]
[56] The reason: As only the use of the side of the tree was decreed against, while the use of "the sides of the side" was permitted. [Admur ibid; Michaber ibid; Rav Ashi in Shabbos ibid]
[57] The reason: As the nail is considered the side while the ladder is the side of the side which is allowed to be used. [Admur ibid; Michaber ibid; Rav Ashi in Shabbos ibid]

inevitably cause the tree or its branches to shake, otherwise it is forbidden even though it is Tzidei Tzedadin.[58] [An item is considered to be directly supported by a tree even if it contains many parts and only its last piece is directly attached, while the remainder of it is supported by the attached part.[59] Thus, it is only considered Tzidei Tzedadin if it is attached to an item that has been fixed onto the tree, such as a nail.]

Directly attached to tree: Accordingly, if a hammock or swing is directly attached to a tree [in an area that is above three Tefach from the ground, which is almost always the case], the hammock is forbidden to be used. This applies even though the hammock or swing contains a hook, chain or rope which supports the hammock material, and only its chain or rope is directly attached to the tree.[60]

Indirectly attached to tree:[61] If the hammock or swing is not directly attached to the tree but is rather attached to a metal pole or nail which has been fixed onto the tree, then its permissibility depends on whether the tree or its branches shake during its use. If using it will cause the tree or its branches to shake in the process, then it is prohibited to be used even though it is indirectly attached. If, however, no part of the tree will shake in the process of using the hammock, then it may be used. [However, some Poskim[62] forbid its use entirely under the claim it is difficult to ascertain whether such action causes the tree to shake. If the hammock is attached to the tree from below three Tefach from the ground, it may be used in all cases.]

Attaching and detaching it to and from the tree:[63] It is forbidden to attach an item to a tree **even indirectly**, such as to hang it on an item that is being supported by the tree [i.e. a nail]. Thus, the hammock or swing must be set up before Shabbos on the protruding nail for one to be allowed to swing on it on Shabbos. Likewise, it is forbidden to remove an item from a tree even if it is only indirectly attached, such as if it is hanging on an item that is being supported by the tree [i.e. a nail]. Thus, the hammock or swing must be removed before Shabbos from the protruding nail if one does not want it there over Shabbos.

Summary:
It is forbidden to attach a hammock or swing to a tree, or to a nail that is fixed on a tree, on Shabbos. It is likewise forbidden to be removed. If it was attached before Shabbos, it may only be used on Shabbos if a) It is attached to a nail that is fixed on the tree, and not to the tree itself and b) The tree does not shake in the process of it being used.

---

[58] Admur ibid; M"A 336:15; Rav Papa 155a; M"B 336:63
The reason: As if one causes it to shake, he has made use of the tree itself, which is forbidden. [Admur ibid]
[59] See M"B 305:67; Piskeiy Teshuvos 336:23; Maor Hashabbos 2:28; Or Letziyon 2:38
[60] Piskeiy Teshuvos ibid footnote 186
[61] SSH"K 16:16
[62] Beir Moshe 6:29
[63] Admur 336:1 regarding a tree itself; 336:20 regarding removing an item from the basket [Vetzaruch Iyun regarding the allowance of Admur to lean the ladder on the nail which seems to contradict this notion; See Michaber 336:13; M"B 336:60; 62 in name of Achronim; Kaf Hachaim 336:85 that the intent is from before Shabbos]; SSH"K 16:16

H. Making use of tree roots:[64]

Roots of trees which protrude from the ground[65] are permitted to be used in their area that is within three Tefach[66] from the ground.[67] However the area of a root that is above three Tefach from the ground is considered like a tree and is forbidden to be used.[68] Roots which do not reach three Tefach from the ground are considered like the ground itself and are entirely permitted to be used. If the roots reach above three Tefach from ground from one direction while in other directions they are equal to ground then if in 2 areas they are equal to ground, one measures the three Tefach from that area of ground for the entire root. If, however, only one area is equal to ground then the entire root is forbidden in being used.[69]

> ➢ Moving the roots with one's hands:[70] In all cases it is forbidden to move the roots of a tree with one's hands due to the Muktzah prohibition.

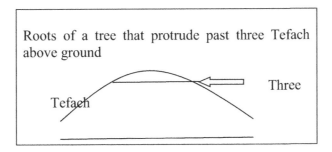

I. Making use of branches of a tree:[71]

Grow below three Tefach from the ground: All branches which grow on the bark within three Tefach[72] from the ground are allowed to be used.

Grow above three Tefach from the ground: All branches which grow on the bark above three Tefach[73] from the ground are prohibited from being used. However, if the branch bends downwards towards the

---

[64] Admur 336:5-6 and 8

Explanation of case: All parts of a tree which are within three Tefach from the ground are permitted in use just like the ground itself. At times trees grow roots which protrude above the ground. Sometimes these roots are very tall, and extend as high up as 24 cm. The question thus is asked what status do these roots have, are they considered like ground or like the tree. Hence Admur explains that the entire area of the root which is within three Tefach from the ground is permitted in use, while those areas of the root which are above three Tefach from the ground are forbidden in use.

[65] As is common by old trees. [ibid]

[66] 24 cm.

[67] As the entire area within three Tefach from the ground was never prohibited in use by the Sages. [336:6 regarding the trunk of a tree and so applies likewise to the root, as on the contrary the main Halacha of the Michaber 336:2 is going on the root and not the trunk or branches, and it is only added that it also applies to the branches.]

[68] As although by such roots the suspicion that one may come to remove a branch and the like is inapplicable, nevertheless the Sages did not make a differentiation in their decrees. [ibid]

[69] It requires further analyses as to the exact understanding of this Halacha in terms of the exact positioning of the root.

[70] Admur 336:4

[71] Admur 336:6

[72] 24 cm.

[73] 24 cm.

ground[74] then the area of the branch which reaches within three Tefach from the ground may be used[75], while the area of the branch which extends above three Tefach from the ground is forbidden to be used.

> Moving the branches with one's hands:[76] In all cases it is forbidden to move branches with one's hands due to the Muktzah prohibition.

J. Making use of the trunk of a tree:[77]
The trunks of all trees may be used up to three Tefach from the ground.[78]

K. Entering into a pit on Shabbos:[79]
It is permitted to descend into a pit, and ascend from a pit on Shabbos. This allowance applies irrelevant to the measurement of depth of the pit.[80]

Q&A
May one climb into a tree house on Shabbos?
No! If, however, the tree house is built in a way that it never makes direct contact with the tree, and is rather being supported by a second item which is supported by the tree, including the ladder[81], then it is allowed to be used so long as one does not shake the tree or the branches in the process.

May one make use of a tree which grows in a pot?[82]
If it is three Tefach tall, then one may not make use of it from three Tefach and above. Hence such a pot may not be moved even within one's house, as doing so is considered making a use of it.

Question:
I am Davening outside on Shabbos, may I rest my Siddur on a very low tree trunk which is the remnant of a tree that has been cut down?

Answer:
If the tree trunk is less than 24 cm from the ground, then you may do so.

The explanation: It is only forbidden to make use of a tree, or tree trunk, on Shabbos if it is more than 24 cm from the ground, and thus in the above case it is permitted being that it does not reach 24 cm from the ground. Likewise, regarding the law of not placing a Siddur on the floor seemingly this does not apply to a tree trunk being that it is not common to be stepped on, and hence there is no disrespect

---

[74]

[75] Now although the root of the branch grows above three Tefach from the ground which is a forbidden area of use, and this area of the branch too was once within this area of growth and hence forbidden, nevertheless upon it growing further and bending downwards it became permitted, as it is now considered like ground. As all which is less than three Tefach to the ground is considered like ground. [ibid]
[76] 336:4
[77] 336:6
[78] As the entire area within three Tefach from the ground was never prohibited by the Sages. [ibid]
[79] 336:1
[80] We do not decree that one may come to consciously remove earth from the pit upon his decent or ascent (and fix for himself steps and hence be liable for building) as a person is more careful to avoid doing these actions then he is in regards to avoiding removing leaves, fruits and branches off a tree. [ibid]
[81] As explained above in G!
[82] Az Nidbaru 1:14

in lying it there.

Sources: See Admur 336:6 regarding tree trunks and Rama Y.D. 282:7 regarding not placing Sefarim on the floor, and see Nosei Keilim there from which it is implied that it only applies to areas that one steps on.

2. Making use of plants and grass on Shabbos:[83]

It is permitted to make use of grass, plants, soft canes[84], weeds, vegetables[85] and any soft produce of the ground, even when they are still attached to the ground.[86] It is, however, forbidden to move any of the above items with one's hands being that all produce attached to the ground is Muktzah. Hence if one desires to make use of the above produce, he must beware not to move it with his hands [and is rather to move it with his body]. Hard canes[87] are forbidden to be made use of at all [from three Tefach and above from the ground[88]].[89] Likewise one may not make use of hard stalks of cabbage in the area above three Tefach from the ground.[90]

3. Walking on Grass:[91]

It is permitted to walk on grass on Shabbos, even barefoot, despite the fact that doing so may cause certain blades of grass to rip from the ground.[92]

Q&A

May one walk quickly on blades of grass?
Some Poskim[93] rule it is forbidden to walk quickly over long blades of grass.[94] Others[95] however rule there is no differentiation between long or short blades of grass or whether one is walking slow or fast[96], and rather it is permitted in all cases.

May one walk on stalks which break upon walking over them?[97]
No, as when walking on hard stalks it is inevitable to avoid breaking them.

If blades of grass, thorns and the like became stuck in one's shoes may one remove it?[98]
It is forbidden to remove the grass or thorns with one's hands.[99] One may however brush them off using his feet.

---

[83] Admur 336:4; 312:9
[84] Canes that are as soft as vegetables.
[85] Lit. Yerek. Vetzaruch Iyun as to what this refers.
[86] As the decree of the Sages was only against making use of trees and the like of hard produce of the ground, however regarding plants and the like no such Rabbinical decree is mentioned. [ibid]
[87] Hard canes are defined as any cane which has slightly hardened and is no longer as soft as vegetables, even if they are not as hard as a tree.
[88] As Admur explains in 336 5-6 that below three Tefach the Sages did not make their decree.
[89] Furthermore, by hard canes the Sages were more stringent than even trees themselves. [ibid] As is ruled in 409:3 that if one left his Eiruv on slightly hard canes the Eiruv is invalid.
[90] Admur 336:5
[91] Admur 336:8
[92] Such as if they get caught between his toes and get pulled out while walking. This is allowed being that one has no intent to rip out the grass [ibid], and it is not an inevitable occurrence. [so is evident from word "possible" written by Admur, and so writes Ketzos Hashulchan 142:11]
[93] M"B 336:25
[94] As doing so will inevitably cause blades to tear from the ground. [ibid]
[95] Ketzos Hashulchan 142 footnote 13
[96] As in all cases it is not inevitable that one will tear a blade from the ground.
[97] Ketzos Hashulchan 142 footnote 13
[98] Mishneh Berurah 336:24; Ketzos Hashulchan 142 footnote 13
[99] As they are Muktzah.

4. Smelling fruits, flowers and plants that are still attached to the ground:[100]

Fruits and vegetables: It is forbidden to smell any <u>edible</u> food which is still attached to the tree or ground due to a decree one may come to remove the fruit in order to eat it.[101]

> ➤ Example: It is forbidden to smell an Esrog or apple that is attached to a tree.

Plants, flowers and leaves: It is permitted to smell plants, flowers or leaves as there is no worry one may come to remove the plant from the ground or tree, being that they are inedible.[102] **See Summary for other Opinions!** [Nevertheless, it is forbidden to move the above items with one's hands, as explained above.]

> ➤ Example: It is permitted to smell a myrtle branch even while it is still attached to the tree.

5. Scenting branches and leaves that are detached from the ground:[103]

It is permitted to move scented branches and leaves [which have become detached from the ground before Shabbos].[104] One may even rub the branches and pluck off leaves [with his hands] in order to increase its scent.[105] [It is however forbidden to cut off pieces from the branch or leaf using a knife or other utensil.[106]]

Summary:

It is forbidden to smell edible ground produce that is attached to the ground, such as an Esrog. It is permitted to smell inedible ground produce even if it is still attached to the ground, such as a myrtle branch. [However, there are opinions[107] which rule the contrary, that edible foods such as an Esrog may be smelled while in-edibles such as myrtle may not be smelled. Practically some Poskim[108] rule one is to be stringent like both opinions and not smell any produce while still attached to the ground.]

Q&A

May one smell scented leaves of a pot plant?

Yes. [However according to those opinions mentioned above which are stringent against smelling all ground attached produce, then the ruling would be as follows: If the pot is on a surface of stone, metal, or glass, one may smell it. If it is on a surface of wood, then it may only be smelled if the pot does not contain breathing holes. If the pot is sitting on earth it is not to be smelled unless it does not contain holes and is made of metal or glass.[109]]

---

[100] Admur 336:16

[101] Although it is possible to eat the fruit without removing it, as one can take a bite from it while it is attached, nevertheless being that this is also forbidden, as there is no greater form of removal than this, therefore the decree is intact. Now although biting off a fruit attached to a tree is not a regular way of removing a fruit, as regularly a fruit is removed with one's hands and not his mouth, and hence one is Biblically exempt for doing so, nevertheless it is Rabbinically forbidden, as is nursing from an animal. [ibid] Regarding why this is not considered a decree upon a decree, this is because the main worry is that one may come to remove it with his hands, which is the normal way of removal, as he will forget that it is Shabbos. It is only *Derech Agav* that it is brought that eating while attached is forbidden. [Ketzos Hashulchan 142 footnote 1 in answer of the question of the Iglei Tal. Vetzaruch Iyun as the simple implication from Admur is that if not for the Rabbinical prohibition we would not suspect for the person removing it with his hands. Hence perhaps the explanation is as follows: The normal suspicion is one may come to remove it with his hands, however on this someone can ask, why would the Sages decree against a matter if there is a permitted way of accomplishing his request, such as here by eating it while attached. Hence Admur explains that this too is forbidden at least Rabinically, and since there is thus no permitted way of accomplishing the eating of the fruit the Sages applies their decree.]

[102] As the entire benefit of these items are their smell which one can benefit from while they are still attached. Hence there is no reason for one to need to remove it. [ibid]

[103] Michaber 323:5

[104] They are not Muktzah as one has not removed his mind from them. [M"B 322:15]

[105] As the area of the which is plucked off gives off a greater scent. [M"B 322:17]

[106] M"B 322:17; As if this were to be allowed one may come to do so to make a use out of the cut item, such as to use as a toothpick, and transgress the prohibition of Tikkun Keli. [ibid in name of Rashal. However, the Taz [322:3] rules one may cut it with a knife in order to smell.]

[107] Ran in name of Geonim, brought in Iglei Tal "Kotzer" 34

[108] Iglei Tal ibid; Ketzos Hashulchan 142 footnote 2.

The Mishneh Berurah [336:48] rules leniently and so rules Admur above.

[109] Ketzos Hashulchan 142 footnote 2

6. Are flowers in a vase Muktzah on Shabbos?[110]

Background: All items that do not contain a use are considered Muktzah Machams Gufo on Shabbos and may not be moved for any purpose in a regular fashion, neither for space, use or to save from damage.[111] Thus, ground products such as plants, flowers, grass, branches and twigs that are laying on the ground are Muktzah on Shabbos, whether they are attached or detached from the ground, plant or tree.[112] However, if one takes any of the above products before Shabbos and designates it for a use, it is no longer considered Muktzah and may be moved on Shabbos like any other non-Muktzah item.[113]

The law: Although flowers that are lying on the ground are Muktzah on Shabbos, flowers that have been gathered and prepared from before Shabbos to be used for decoration of one's home, are not Muktzah.[114] Accordingly, it is permitted without restriction to move a bouquet or vase of flowers on Shabbos. Likewise, on Shavuos, it is permitted to move the various flowers and plants [that are not in pots with earth] that have been placed around the house or Shul for decorative purposes.[115] For this reason, it is also permitted to lift and move a good scenting branch or leaf [i.e. myrtle, rosemary, mint, etc] that has been designated before Shabbos for smelling, and there is no Muktzah prohibition involved.

Plants in pots with earth: Plants or trees that grow within pots that contain earth do have Muktzah restrictions applicable to them, as will be discussed in a further Halacha!

Entering and removing the flower to and from the water vase: It is permitted to remove flowers from the water vase on Shabbos, however, certain restrictions apply regarding placing the flowers into the water vase, as will be explained in a future Halacha.

Summary:

Flowers in a vase are not Muktzah and may be moved without restriction.

---

7. Fruits which fell off a tree:[116]

All fruits which have fallen off a tree on Shabbos are forbidden to be eaten until after Shabbos[117] and are therefore Muktzah[118]. [Furthermore, even if there is doubt as to if the fruits fell on Shabbos or beforehand it is forbidden.[119]]

Q&A

Are vegetables which detached from the ground on Shabbos forbidden to be eaten?[120]

Yes. Hence, they are Muktzah.

---

[110] See Admur 336:18; 494:14; Rama 336:11; M"A 336:13; 494:5

[111] Admur 308:8; Michaber and Rama 308:7

[112] Admur 312:9; 336:4; M"A 312:6; See Peri Megadim 312 A"A 6

Other opinions: Some Poskim rule that all grass which is attached to the ground is not Muktzah. [Elya Raba and Tosefes Shabbos brought in Machatzis Hashekel 312:6; so rules also M"B 312:17; Shaar Hatziyon 336:42] According to this opinion Muktzah only applies to those things attached to the ground which had a decree of Shimush Gidulei Karka attached to it, such as fruits of a tree. However, grass and the like is not forbidden due to Gidulei Karka, as explained in 336, and it is therefore also not Muktzah. However, once the grass is detached it becomes Muktzah.

[113] Admur 308:50

[114] See Admur 336:18; 494:14; M"A 336:13; 494:5; Piskeiy Teshuvos 336:22

The reason: As they have been designated for a use from before Shabbos and thus have the status of a vessel. [Admur ibid]

[115] Admur 494:14; M"A 494:5

[116] Michaber 322:3

[117] The reason for this is due to a decree one may come to pluck a fruit from the tree on Shabbos. Alternatively, it is because the fruit is Muktzah as one did not have it in mind from before Shabbos. [M"B 322:7]

[118] Ketzos Hashulchan 146:23 from Peri Megadim, Upashut.

[119] M"B 322:5; brought in Ketzos Hashulchan 146:23

[120] M"B 322:6 in name of Peri Megadim

8. Watering plants and grass:[121]

One who waters seeds[122] in order so they grow is liable for the plowing and planting prohibition.[123] Therefore it is forbidden to pour liquid over grass, plants, [trees[124]] and the like.

May one wash his hands over grass, plants, or weeds? It is forbidden to wash one's hands over plants, grass and the like even if one has no intent to water the grass by doing so.[125] This prohibition applies by all plants, grass [and trees] whether owned by oneself, one's friend or public property.[126] [**Regarding watering plain earth see Q&A!**]

Eating outside on the lawn: For the above-mentioned reasons, when eating outside over a lawn which contains grass, plants or trees one must beware not to spill or pour water over it. Hence it is best not to eat at all over a lawn if one will be drinking or using water during the meal, as it is very difficult to avoid any spillage.

Urinating over grass: It is permitted to urinate on grass[127], however it is proper to refrain from doing so.[128]

Pouring juice over grass: It is permitted to pour wine and other juices over grass[129], however it is proper to beware from doing so.

Q&A

May one pour water over plain earth?[130]

There is no planting prohibition involved in pouring water over plain earth[131] unless one of the following apply:

1. The earth is designated to be plowed or seeded, in which case it is forbidden to water it due to the planting and plowing prohibition.[132]

2. There are trees within 15 Amos radius of the area in which case it is forbidden due to the planting prohibition.[133]

3. The water will flow onto plants, or grass in which case it is forbidden due to the planting prohibition.[134]

4. <u>The earth is loose</u>: It is forbidden to pour any liquid over loose earth due to the kneading prohibition.

---

[121] Admur 336:9

[122] Lit. Zeraim. Rashi Moed Katan 2b interprets this to mean pouring water over the roots of the plant.

[123] <u>The reason</u>: As the water makes the soil soft for planting, as is done by plowing, as well as the water is placed so the seeds grow, which is like planting. [ibid]

[124] Ketzos Hashulchan 142 footnote 18, Upashut.

[125] <u>The reason</u>: As nevertheless this matter is an inevitable occurrence. [ibid]

[126] However, in such a case that it is not owned by oneself, being that one has no intent at all to cause the plants to grow, it is merely a Rabbinical prohibition, as it is considered a Melacha Sheiyno Tzarich Legufa. [ibid]
<u>Other Opinions</u>: Many opinions rule as do Admur above that even on another's garden spilling water is forbidden. However, there are opinions which are lenient to allow spilling water in a garden which is not one's own and does not belong to a friend, and hence one has no interest in the benefits gained by watering the garden. The basis behind this dispute is whether we say a Pesik Reishei Delo Nicha Lei [which is not desired by the person] is even initially permitted or not. [M"B 336:27]
<u>A Public garden</u>: A public garden has the same status as personal property as all the garden visitors receive benefit from its growth. Hence according to all it would be forbidden to spill water in such a garden. [Az Nidbaru 6:37]

[127] As urine does not cause further growth of a plant, on the contrary it damages it. [ibid] Nevertheless this is not forbidden due to it being considered as if one is uprooting the plant as the plant has the ability to grow after the initial damage done by the urine. [Ketzos Hashulchan 142 footnote 19]

[128] So learns Ketzos Hashulchan 142:14 in Admur that the warning to beware from even pouring other liquids on grass included also urine.

[129] As only water has the ability to cause further growth of plants. However, juice, not only does it not cause further growth of a plant, on the contrary it damages it. [ibid]

[130] Ketzos Hashulchan 142:14

[131] Kaf Hachayim 336:27

[132] Shevisas Shabbos Zoreia 2; Ketzos Hashulchan 142 footnote 18; Kaf Hachayim 336:27

[133] Daas Torah 336:3, brought in Piskeiy Teshuvos 336:3

[134] Piskeiy Teshuvos 336 footnote 8

May one pour water over plain earth if it is near grass or plants?[135]

It is permitted to pour water on hard earth which is near plants or grass, even if the water within 24 cm. of the plant. It is forbidden to pour it if it is within 15 Amos of a tree. In all cases it is forbidden to pour water for plowing or planting purposes, or if the water will flow onto the plants or grass.

May one eat over bare earth that has no grass or plants?

Yes. However, one should distance himself fifteen Amos from any trees.

May one pour liquid or urinate onto earth?[136]

Loose earth:[137] Even if doing so does not contain a planting prohibition[138] doing so is forbidden due to the kneading prohibition.[139] [However, if there is no other area to urinate then one may be lenient to do so.[140]]

Hard earth:[141] It is permitted to pour water or urinate over hard earth if doing so does not contain a planting prohibition.

May one pour liquid or urinate onto Sand/Ash:[142]

It is forbidden to urinate or pour liquids over sand, ash and all items of the like. [Thus, children that have reached the age of Chinuch are to be prevnetd from palying with sand and water on Shabbos.[143]]

In a time of need: If there is no other area to urnate then one may be lenient to do so.[144]

May one pour liquid or urinate onto mud?[145]

Very liquidy mud: If the mud is very liquidly, like a mud puddle than this is allowed.

Thick mud: If the mud is still slightly thick, it is forbidden to be done due to the kneading prohibition.[146]

Hard and dry mud: Even if the mud is hard and dry it is forbidden to urinate on it, as the mud will soften due to the urine.[147]

Time of need: Some Poskim[148] rule that in a time of need one may urinate on the mud if the mud does not belong to him.[149]

---

[135] Daas Torah 336:3, brought in Piskeiy Teshuvos 336:3

[136] Ketzos Hashulchan 130:8

[137] M"A 321:19 regaridng mud; P"M 321 A"A 19; M"B 321:57; Ketzos Hashulchan ibid

[138] See Admur 336:9; The Laws of Shabbos Volume 3 "Plants trees and Garden produce" that urinating on earth is from the letter of the law not prohibited due to the sowing, and that earth which is not designated for sowing and is not near plants or trees does not contain the sowing prohibition even qwith water.

[139] The reason: This is Biblcially forbidden according to Rebbe Yehuda, and is Rabbinically forbiudden according to Rebbe Yossi. [ibid]

[140] Beis Meir brought in M"B 321:57; Implication of M"A ibid which motions the reader to Michaber 320:14 which brings a dispute if one may urinate on snow, and regarding that dispute Admur rules that in a time of need one may do so, and here too seemingly it is allowed as the main ruling is like Rebbe Yossi that there is no prohibition until one actually kneads the liquid. [See P"M 321 A"A 19]

[141] Ketzos Hashulchan ibid; Aruch Hashulchan 321:25; Chazon Ish 58:8

[142] P"M ibid; M"B ibid; Ketzos Hashulchan ibid

[143] SSH"K 16:4

[144] Beis Meir brought in M"B 321:57; Implication of M"A ibid which motions the reader to Michaber 320:14 which brings a dispute if one may urinate on snow, and regarding that dispute Admur rules that in a time of need one may do so, and here too seemingly it is allowed as the main ruling is like the Rambam in the opinion of Rebbe Yossi that there is no prohibition until one actually kneads the liquid, and that there is no prohibition by Eino Bar Gibul. [See P"M 321 A"A 19]

[145] Ketzos Hashulchan 130:8

The reason there is no allowoance due to the rulke of "Ewin Lash Acchar Lash": As the mud still requires more water for its kneading or the mud is hard and dried, hence entering into the Lash prohibition. [Ketzos Hashulchan ibid footnote 3; Shevisas Hashabbos Lash 6]

[146] The reason: This is Biblcially forbidden according to Rebbe Yehuda, and is Rabbinically forbiudden according to Rebbe Yossi. [ibid]

[147] Peri Megadim 321 A"A 19 leaves this matter in question being that the mud eventually melts due to the liquid; brought in M"B 321:57 and Shaareiy Tziyon 321:66

[148] M"B 321:57; Beis Meir brought in M"B ibid permits in all cases ina tikme of need

[149] The reason: As this is considered a Piseik Reisha Delo Nicha Lei on which one may be lenient in a time of need. [ibid] To note however that Admur rules stringently regarding Pesik Resihei Delo Nicha Lei even by a Rabbinical prohibition, as brought in 316:4 and 320:24]

May one spit onto plants, or grass?[150]
No.

May one spit onto plain earth?[151]
If the earth is hard it is permitted to do so. If the earth is soft then it is proper to avoid doing so[152] although there is much room to side that this is allowed.[153]

May one spit into a vessel or area which contains sand/dirt?[154]
It is proper to avoid doing so[155] although there is much room to side that this is allowed to be done[156], and so rule some Poskim[157].

May one cover liquid [such as urine] with sand/dirt?[158]
One may only do so with a large ratio of dirt/sand over water to the point that the mixture will not form a knead-able substance.

May one wash in a sink which has a drainage pipe that draws the water onto plants or seeded soil?
Some Poskim[159] rule doing so is allowed [even if the water will spill into one's own garden].[160] Others[161] rule doing so is forbidden even if it will spill onto plants that one does not own.[162]

May one pour a plant killing agent over plants on Shabbos?[163]
No.

May one water a pot plant that does not have any breathing holes?[164]
No.[165]

May one cover plants which are outside to protect them from rain?
Some Poskim[166] rule in a case of loss it is permitted to cover plants in protection of rain. Other Poskim[167] rule it is never allowed due to the planting prohibition.[168] According to all it may only be

---

[150] Shevisas Shabbos Zoreia 2

[151] Based on Ketzos Hashulchan 130:8

[152] As the Peri Megadim leaves this matter in question. According to the one opinion mentioned in 321:16 even entering liquid into a material constitutes kneading. The Peri Megadim leaves in question if even here this would be a problem being that by here he no intent to knead the material with his saliva, and it's a case of "Pisek Reshei Dilo Nicha Lei".

[153] So rules Ketzos Hashulchan [130:8 footnote 22] based on that a) spitting is an irregularity and thus only Rabbinical. B) The amount that can be mixed is less than the Biblical amount needed to transgress kneading. C) Naturally saliva does not sink into material but rather floats over it.

[154] Ketzos Hashulchan 130:8 footnote 22

[155] The Peri Megadim ibid [brought in M"B ibid] leaves this matter in question due to the following reason: According to the second opinion mentioned above, even entering liquid into a non-kneadabel material constitutes a Biblical kneading prohibition, and thus perhaps there is no room to permit the spitting. On the other hand perhaps in this case one can be leinity as he has no intent to knead the material with his saliva, and it's a case of "Pisek Reshei Dilo Nicha Lei". [P"M ibid]

[156] So rules Ketzos Hashulchan based on that a) spitting is an irregularity and thus only Rabbinical. B) The amount that can be mixed is less than the Biblical amount needed to transgress kneading. C) Naturally saliva does not sink into material but rather floats over it.

[157] Beis Meir, brought in M"B ibid

[158] Chayeh Adam; M"B 321:57; Ketzos Hashulchan 130:8

[159] SSH"K 12:18 in name of Rav SZ"A

[160] As the matter is a mere Grama as it is caused by a Koach Kocho, therefore one may be lenient when he has no intent to do so, even though it is occurring inevitably. [Rav SZ"A ibid]

[161] Az Nidbaru 4:17

[162] See above in footnote that some opinions rule it is permitted to even wash over plants that one does not own as he has no intent to do so and it is not of any benefit. Hence to be stringent even in a case of Grama is a double stringency. However so rules Az Nidbaru ibid that even in such a case it is forbidden.

[163] Ketzos Hashulchan 142 footnote 19

[164] Ketzos Hashulchan 142:2 in name of Peri Megadim; Shevisas Shabbos Zoreia 2.

[165] One who does so is Biblically exempt, although it is Rabbinically forbidden.

placed in a way that it does not touch the plants as explained in the laws of Muktzah.[169]

If rainwater has gathered over one's awning or Schach covering, may it be removed if it will subsequently cause the water to fall onto grass and the like?[170]
If the ground is already anyways very wet due to the rain, then one may be lenient to remove the covering, having the water fall on the ground. If, however, the ground is not very wet then it is forbidden to be done due to a possible planting prohibition.

Question:
We have an outdoor Minyan which takes place on grass and would like to know if it is permitted to spit on the grass such as during the prayer of Aleinu Leshabeiach?

Answer:
No, it is prohibited to spit on grass due to the planting prohibition. Thus, in such a case you should either find a different area to spit by Aleinu or not spit at all.

Sources: See Admur 336:9; Shevisas Shabbos Zoreia 2

9. Uprooting plants and other growths from their source:[171]
A. The general rule:
One who uproots any plant growth from its source is liable for the prohibition of "uprooting an item from its source of growth". One who uproots with an irregularity, such as using his teeth, is Biblically exempt, although doing so is Rabbinically forbidden.[172]

B. Case examples:
Removing the string like growths called Kishus off from thorns: It is forbidden to remove the string like growths called *Kishus*[173] from their source of growth.[174]
Removing moss and plant growth from vessels and objects: Moss and other plant growth which have grown on vessels or objects as a result of moisture are forbidden to be removed on Shabbos.[175]
Removing dried fruits from a tree:[176] Fruits which have dried while on a tree are nevertheless forbidden to be picked off the tree, and one who does so is liable for the uprooting prohibition.[177]
Moving a stone that has moss growth:[178] It is forbidden to lift a stone that contains moss growth in a way that it is lifted from the ground, as by doing so one temporarily limits its nurture from the ground which is similar to uprooting.

---

[166] Lev Chayim 3:69
[167] Sheivet Haleivi 4:36
[168] As preventing the flooding of the plants is considered an act of planting.
[169] 310:10 So rules the Ketzos Hashulchan 113 Halacha 2 like the first opinion in Admur.
[170] Piskeiy Teshuvos 626:6
[171] 336:11
[172] 336:16
[173] This refers to the thread like growths that come out of some thorns and thistles. [Rashi Shabbos 107b] The English equivalent to this is the *Humulos Lupulos* plant although it does not seem to fit this description.
[174] As although they are not attached to the ground, nevertheless by doing so one uproots the growth from its source which is the thorn. [ibid]
[175] These growths are considered similar to plants connected to the ground as this is the way these plants grow. Hence one who removes them from their area of growth is liable for uprooting an item from its source of growth. [ibid]
[176] 336:19
[177] This is despite that regarding the laws of impurity it is considered like it is detached, nevertheless regarding Shabbos they are Biblically considered attached. [ibid]
[178] Implied from 312:6 which only allows doing so for Kavod Habriyos.

C. Laws relating to Pot Plants:

Removing growths or seeds from a pot plant: It is forbidden to uproot any seeds or growth from a pot plant even if the pot contains no breathing holes, and is placed in one's attic.[179]

Moving a pot plant from one place to another:[180] It is forbidden to move a pot plant that contains a breathing hole from on top of a peg and place it directly on the earth[181] or from on the earth and place it onto a peg[182] [or to lift it from the earth and place it in another area of the earth[183]]. If the pot does not contain any holes then if its pot is made of earthenware or wood, it likewise may not be moved from a peg to the earth or vice versa.[184] [If however the pot does not have a breathing hole and is made of metal or glass, then it may be moved from one area to another.[185] If a pot that does not have a hole contains a plant which hovers over the earth, past the boundary of the pot, then the entire pot is considered as if it is attached to the ground and may not be moved just like a pot which has a hole.[186]]

Summary:

It is only permitted to move a pot from one area to another if all the following conditions are fulfilled:

1. The pot does not contain a breathing hole
2. The plant in the pot does not hover over the earth past the boundary of the pot.
3. The pot is made of metal or glass; not earthenware or wood
4. One is moving it to use its space or to use in a different area. However, one may not do so to save it from damage.[187]

Q&A

How large does the hole of a pot have to be for it to be considered a breathing hole?

Some Poskim[188] rule if the hole is 2 square cm. then it is large enough to be considered a breathing hole. Others[189] rule it is the amount of space for a small root to be able to protrude through the hole.

---

[179] In a case that the pot has no breathing holes doing so is only Rabbinically forbidden as a complete pod is not considered a normal place of planting and hence one is Biblically exempt if he removes from it seeds and plants. [Admur ibid] If the pot contains breathing holes, it is Biblically forbidden to uproot any growths from it as it is considered attached to the ground being that it nurtures from the ground through its hole which it is able to breathe the moisture of the ground. This applies even if the pod plant is sitting on pegs above ground, as nevertheless its breathing holes are able to nurture partially from the earth even through a distance. [336:12]

[180] 336:12

[181] By doing so one is not Biblically liable for the planting prohibition being that the pod was already able to breathe the moisture of the earth through its hole even while standing on the peg, and hence was already considered attached to the earth. Nevertheless, this is Rabinically forbidden being that it is similar to planting. [ibid]

[182] By doing so one is not Biblically liable for the uprooting of a plant prohibition being that the pod is still able to breathe the moisture of the earth through its hole even while standing on the peg, and hence it is still considered attached to the earth. Nevertheless, this is Rabinically forbidden being that it is similar to uprooting. [ibid]

[183] So is implied from Admur 312:6, and so brings Ketzos Hashulchan 142 footnote 5 in his conclusion of his analysis on this subject as a proof for it being forbidden. So rules Meiri.
Other Poskim: The Sheivisas Shabbos; Minchas Pitim and Tehila Ledavid 336:6 rule it is permitted.
[See Ketzos Hashulchan 142 footnote 5 for analysis of above]

[184] Background:
Ideally, a pod without a breathing hole is allowed to be uprooted from one area to another. However, Admur records a dispute regarding as to which type of pod this allowance refers to: The first [Stam-Rashi] opinion rules if the pod is made of wood, then if it contains no holes it is permitted to be moved from the pegs onto the ground or vice versa. However, if made of earthenware it may not be moved, as even if it does not contain a hole, it is considered as if it does being that earthenware is a breathable material, and hence the plants that are in it nurture from the ground through the earthenware. Other opinions [Rabbeinu Tam] however explain the opposite; if the pod is made of earthenware then it is allowed to be moved if it contains no holes. If however it is made of wood, then even if it does not contain holes nevertheless its plants are able to nurture from the ground through it. Practically Admur concludes one is to suspect for both opinions and hence beware from moving either an earthenware pod or wood pod even if they contain no holes. [ibid]

[185] Ketzos Hashulchan 142 footnote 5

[186] Ketzos Hashulchan ibid in name of Iglei Tal

[187] See Q&A below.

[188] Minchas Yitzchak 8:92

[189] M"B 336:42

What is the status if the pot only has a hole on its side and not its bottom?[190]

If the hole is opposite the earth contained within the pot the pot is considered to have a breathing hole.

May one move a pot plant within one's house?[191]

Yes. This applies even if the pot has a hole.[192] [If, however, the pot is on the porch and hovers over the earth, then it is forbidden to be moved.]

Is a pot plant considered Muktzah and thus even when allowed to be moved, it is only to be moved in ways permitted by Muktzah?

All pot plants which may be moved, as explained above, are considered MM"I and hence may only be moved to use their space or to use in a different area, and not to save from damage.[193] However there are Poskim[194] who rule they are completely Muktzah and may not be moved for any reason. This especially applies by expensive plant pots which are given a designated place and are not moved from there.[195] [However seemingly according to Admur even in such a case the pot would only be MM"I-See Volume 1 "The Laws of Muktzah".]

May one move a <u>tree</u> which grows in a pot in one's house?[196]

If the tree is three Tefach tall, then one may not make use of it from three Tefach and above. Hence such a pot may not be moved even within one's house, as doing so is considered making a use of it.

May one move a pot plant from on the earth or on a peg into one's home or vice versa?

It is only permitted to move a pot from inside to outside or vice versa if all the following conditions are fulfilled:

1. The pot does not contain a breathing hole.
2. The plant in the pot does not hover over the earth past the boundary of the pot.
3. The pot is made of metal or glass; not earthenware or wood.
4. One is not doing so in order to enhance the growth of the plant, such as to protect them from sun or rain.

May one move a pot plant from one area of the earth to another?[197]

No. However there are Poskim which rule that it is allowed.

May one move a pot that is sitting on a tray together with its tray?[198]

It is always permitted to move a pot together with its metal or glass tray even if the potd contains breathing holes as the tray blocks the pot from nurturing from the ground. It is however forbidden to lift the pot off from the tray as explained above regarding moving a pot from one area to another.

---

[190] M"B 336:42
[191] Bris Olam Kotzeir 15
[192] As the floors are well sealed and prevent the pod from nurturing from the ground.
[193] Shevisas Shabbos brought in Ketzos Hashulchan 142 footnote 5
[194] Kalkeles Shabbos Zoreia
[195] Az Nidbaru 1:15
[196] Az Nidbaru 1:14
[197] See above and footnote there.
[198] Ketzos Hashulchan 142 footnote 2 and 5

Q&A relating to pot plants growing in one's house:

May one open the window to allow the plants to breath fresh air, or for rain to fall on them?[199]

No.[200] [However one may open the window for other purposes even though this will consequently allow the plant to breathe new fresh air.[201]]

May one close the window to prevent the cold air from damaging the plants?[202]
No.

May one cover plants to protect them from the cold?[203]
No.

May one move the plants towards the sun in order for them to further grow?[204]
No.

Question:

Is it permitted on Shabbos for me to rest my Siddur on a pot plant? I have many pot plants in my yard sitting on the gate and they are a perfect height for me to rest my Siddur on when I Daven there on Shabbos. May I do so?

Answer:

Resting just on the actual pot without touching any of the plants: Is permitted.

Resting it on the actual plant: It depends on the type of plant, as well as the height of the plant, growing within the pot. If the plant has grown taller than 24 cm then you may not rest your Siddur on top of the area that is higher than 24 cm if the plant contains a hard stem which if bended will break. However, if the plant is less than 24 cm tall, or if the plant is soft and its stem is flexible and will not break when bent, then you may rest items on top of the actual plant, although making sure not to touch the plants with your actual fingers and hand, unless necessary for the sake of the resting of the item.

The explanation: There are two halachic issues with making contact with plants on Shabbos; 1) Muktzah 2) Making use of a tree. All plants that are attached to the ground are Muktzah on Shabbos, and thereby may not be moved with one's hands. However, not all plants contain the second prohibition of making a use with them in other ways [without moving them with your hands] and this depends on whether it is a tree, or bush with branches, or a plant with a hard cane in which case it is forbidden to make any use of it from 24 cm and higher, versus if it is a soft plant in which case it is permitted to make a use of it [without moving it with one's hands] even if it is taller than 24 cm. Even by trees and bushes with branches and plants with hard stems that cannot be bent without breaking, they are only prohibited in use from a height of 24 cm while below this height it is permitted to be used.

Now let's discuss pot plants: Regarding the second prohibition of making use of a tree, pot plants follow the same law, and hence one may not make use [i.e. rest a siddur] on any area of the plant that grows to a height of 24 cm if its stem is not flexible, [although it remains permitted to rest it simply on

---

[199] Ketzos Hashulchan 142 footnote 18 in name of Shevisas Shabbos
[200] As doing so causes them to grow.
[201] Har Tzevi 2:11 brought in Piskeiy Teshuvos 336:11
[202] Ketzos Hashulchan 142 footnote 18 in name of Shevisas Shabbos
[203] Ketzos Hashulchan 142 footnote 18 in name of Shevisas Shabbos
[204] Piskeiy Teshuvos 336:11

the pot itself without it touching any of the plants]. However, one may rest it on top of flexible plants, or areas of the plant that do not reach 24 cm, as even if we were to define pot plants as Muktzah [the first issue above], it is permitted to rest an object on top of a Muktzah item on Shabbos. Furthermore, a pot plant is not defined as actual Muktzah, but rather as a Keli Shemilachto Lissur [or even Heter], if the plant is less than a height of 24 cm or is flexible as explained above. Thus, in such a case, one may even bend the plant for the sake of resting one's Siddur on top of it as is the law by any Keli Shemichato Lissur that it may be moved for a use or for its space.

*Sources: **Regarding the prohibition of making use of trees/plants on Shabbos**: Admur 336:1, 4-6; 312:9; **Regarding the Muktzah status of plants attached to the ground**: Admur 312:9; 336:4; M"A 312:6; See Peri Megadim 312 A"A 6; See also: Elya Raba and Tosefes Shabbos brought in Machatzis Hashekel 312:6; so rules also M"B 312:17; Shaar Hatziyon 336:42; **Regarding Muktzah status of pot plants**: Admur 336:12; P"M 636:10; Tiferes Yisrael Kalkeles Shabbos Zoreia 1; Shevisas HaShabbos Kotzer 5 and 7; Shaar Hatziyon 336:38; Tehila Ledavid 636:6; **Regarding the allowance to rest an object on top of a Muktzah item when it is not for the sake of the Muktzah item see**: Admur 308:14; 310:10; Terumos Hadeshen 1:67; M"A 310:3; Taz 301:5; Ketzos Hashulchan 142 footnote 5; Minchas Shabbos 80:194; Az Nidbaru 1:15; Piskeiy Teshuvos 336:16 footnotes 123-125*

Question:
Does the prohibition against making use of a tree also apply against a pot plant?

Answer:
Yes, it follows the same exact law as a growth from the ground, and thus if the plant contains a hard stem which if bended will break, and the plant has grown taller than 24 cm, then you may not then you may not make use of any area of the plant that is higher than 24 cm, and also may not move the plant at all on Shabbos due to this reason.

The explanation: The entire reason that the sages decreed against making use of plants and trees on Shabbos is because one may come to uproot a part of it from the ground which is a biblical prohibition. Now, this biblical prohibition against breaking a piece from the ground applies also to pot plants that are defined as a Atzitz Nakuv and rabbinically apply to pot plants that are defined as Atzitz Sheiyno Nakuv. Thus, certainly the decree against making use of the plant would apply equally to a pot plant that is defined as an Atzitz Nakuv as there is no difference between it or a plant that grows in the ground regarding the reason for the decree. However, regarding a pot plant that is defined as Atzitz Sheiyno Nakuv is unclear as to whether this additional rabbinical decree of making use of the plant would also apply. Practically, one should be stringent, and thus we concluded above to follow all the laws regarding all types of pot plants without differentiation.

Sources: See Admur 336:1, 4-6; 11-12; Minchas Pitim of Maharam Arik 336:8 [questions whether it applies to pot plants defined as "Eino Nakuv" as perhaps it is considered a decree upon a decree and therefore should not apply]; Minchas Shabbos 80:194; Az Nidbaru 1:14; Piskeiy Teshuvos 336:1 and 16 [concludes to be stringent by all pot plants especially being that the definition of Eino Nakuv is not clear]

D. Removing garden produce that is insulated within earth:[205]
One who insulated vegetables or herbs within earth before Shabbos may remove them on Shabbos so long as they have not yet become rooted into the ground.[206] If the vegetable contains a leaf which is sticking out from the earth one may pull it out from the leaf. If it is completely insulated within the earth one may stick a knife into it in order to pull it out. [It is however forbidden to move the earth with one's hands due to the Muktzah prohibition.]

E. Picking fruits from a branch which has fallen:[207]
One may pick fruits off from a branch which has fallen from before Shabbos [and has become completely detached from the tree[208]]. If the branch fell on Shabbos it remains forbidden to pick fruit from it.
Picking leaves from a fallen branch:[209] One may not pick leaves off a branch in order to use the leaf for a certain purpose, due to the prohibition of "Tikkun Keli". This prohibition applies even if the branch is detached from the tree.

Q&A

May one remove dates from its stalk?[210]
Some Poskim[211] rule this is forbidden to be done even in order to eat right away.[212]

May one remove bananas, grapes and other fruits from their vine?[213]
One may do so immediately prior to eating. It is however forbidden to do so for later use.[214]

---

9. Throwing seeds and pits onto the ground:[215]
One is to beware from throwing seeds in an area where it rains[216] [or in an area that the earth is wet[217]] and can eventually cause the seed to grow. It is however permitted to throw them in an area that the seeds will certainly be destroyed prior to any chance of growth, such as in an area that people walk[218]. Likewise,

---

[205] Admur 336:13; 311:14

[206] This applies even if one placed them in the earth with intent to root and further grow. The reason for this is because so long as the item has not yet rooted it is not considered part of the ground. It is also not considered Muktzah as edible foods never become Muktzah even if one sets them aside. [311:14]

[207] Admur 336:14

[208] Peri Megadim M"Z 336:8 brought in Ketzos Hashulchan 142 footnote 12
From the letter of the law so long as the branch can no longer live, one may detach fruits from it even if it is still slightly attached. However, since people are not expert in this matter it is only permitted to do so if the branch has become completely detached. [ibid]

[209] Admur 314:11

[210] Ketzos Hashulchan 126:5

[211] Peri Megadim A"A 320

[212] This is forbidden due to the Mifarek prohibition, as it is the common way to remove the stalk of dates from the tree and then cut the dates off the stalks and send them to storage. This is exactly similar to threshing. Others however argue that threshing only applies to fruits which are concealed within their stalks, as are grains, and not by revealed fruits. [see Ketzos Hashulchan ibid footnote 9]

[213] Ketzos Hashulchan 126 footnote 10-11; Shabbos Kehalacha Vol. 2 p. 316

[214] Some Poskim [Peri Megadim A"A 320] rule that the "Dosh" "Threshing" prohibition applies equally to items which are removed from their stalk even if the fruits are revealed. Meaning that not only by concealed fruits such as legumes in their pods does the prohibition apply, but also by all foods which are attached to a stalk. Nevertheless, even according to them it is only forbidden when done in order to store, or eat later on, as is the form of Melacha of threshing that it is done for storage purposes. If however it is done to eat right away then it is allowed according to all, as this is not like Dash at all. Thus, one may remove bananas from their stalk, and grapes from their vines to eat right away. However, this is only by fruits which it is common to eat the food soon after removing it from its stalk. If, however it is common to store the fruits after removing them from their stalk then they have the same law as does removing dates, in which some rule it is forbidden even to do in order to eat right away due to the threshing prohibition. [see Ketzos Hashulchan ibid footnote 9-10]

[215] Admur 336:10

[216] Seemingly this includes all times, including the summer, in those areas which don't have rain in the summer, as perhaps the seed will last until the rain season and then be able to grow. In any event since it is not inevitable that the rain will come at a time that will allow the seed to grow, and it is hence not a pure prohibition to throw the seeds in such areas, but a mere hazard. [based on Ketzos Hashulchan 142 footnote 19]

[217] Based on explanation of M"B:Chayeh Adam in definition of "place of rain".

[218] As certainly in such an area the seeds will not grow and hence there contains no prohibition of planting. [ibid]

one who owns chickens may throw them the number of seeds that they will need for the next two days, as certainly these seeds will be eaten prior to any chance of growth.

10. Placing kernels in water on Shabbos:[219]

One who soaks wheat or barley and the like in water in order for it to grow is liable for the planting prohibition.[220] This applies even if one soaks only a single kernel. For this reason, it is forbidden to place kernels in water with intent to leave them there for enough time for them to be able to grow.[221] However it is permitted to place the kernels there for a short amount of time, such as to place barley within water for animals [which one owns[222]] for them to eat right away.[223]

Q&A

May one remove kernels that have begun to grow from within their water?[224]

No. One who does so is liable for the uprooting prohibition.

May one remove an avocado pit from water if it has begun to sprout?[225]

No.

May one plant seeds in the ground on Shabbos with intent to remove them prior to growing?

Some Poskim[226] rule it is a Biblical prohibition to plant seeds into the ground even if one removes them immediately after.[227]

Watering seeds to make Sprouts:[228]

Is Biblically forbidden to be done on Shabbos. The same applies that it is forbidden to remove the sprouts from the water on Shabbos.

---

[219] 336:17

[220] Doing so is a secondary prohibition under the planting Melacha. [ibid] Regarding if one is liable immediately upon entering the seed into the water, or only later on when it grows. The Magen Avraham 336:12 learns one is only liable when it begins to grow, which is approximately after a half a day. So is the implication of Admur ibid. However, there are Poskim which learn that one is liable immediately.

[221] Literally "For a long time" [Admur] Ketzos Hashulchan 142 footnote 14 explains this to mean for enough time for it to grow. The Magen Avraham however writes that it refers to a half a day.

[222] As otherwise it is forbidden to feed animals on Shabbos.

[223] Now even if some kernels will remain left over in the water, nevertheless one may place them there as it is not inevitable that these kernels will grow, as perhaps the animals will eat them beforehand. [ibid]

[224] Ketzos Hashulchan 142 footnote 14

[225] SSH"K 26 Footnote 9 in name of Rav SZ"A.

[226] Minchas Chinuch Mitzvah 298 p. 112

[227] As the liability is on the act of planting irrelevant of the results. [ibid] However see Admur 336:10 and 17 which implies that we go after the final growth and not after the beginning action.

[228] See Piskeiy Teshuvos 336:19

11. Placing flowers and plants into water on Shabbos:[229]

Branches [and flowers] which have been designated before Shabbos for a specific use in a way that they are no longer considered Muktzah[230], may be entered into a bucket or vase of water on Shabbos[231], if the water was placed into the vase or bucket from before Shabbos[232]. It is however forbidden to place water in a vase or bucket on Shabbos [or Yom Tov[233]] for the purpose of placing the branch in it.[234] Furthermore, if the branch contains flowers [which are not fully open] or buds it is forbidden to place them in water at all on Shabbos being that the moisture of the water causes the flowers to further open.[235]

Adding water to the vase: In all cases it is forbidden to add water to the vase on Shabbos.[236] However on Yom Tov it is permitted to add more water to the vase[237] [if the plants do not contain flowers or pellets]. [Some Poskim[238] however limit this allowance to add water on Yom Tov to only up until half of the current amount of water found in the vase. It is however forbidden even on Yom Tov to add more water than the vase originally contained.]

Switching the waters: It is forbidden to switch the waters of the vase/bucket in all cases, whether Shabbos or Yom Tov.[239]

➤ **Example-Placing flowers into a water vase**: Flowers which were designated to beautify the home, such as flowers bought for Shabbos, are not Muktzah and may be entered into water on Shabbos if the water was prepared from before Shabbos, and the flowers will not further open due to the water.

➤ **May one water his Lulav/Hadassim/Aravos on Yom Tov?**[240]
One may enter them into a vase with water, if the water was placed into the vase before Yom Tov. One may likewise add more water to the vase [if the amount will not exceed the original amount of water in the vase[241]].

Summary:
It is only permitted to enter plants and flowers into water on Shabbos if:
1. The plant has been designated before Shabbos for a use such as to beautify the home, and is

---

[229] Admur 336:18; Rama 336:11
[230] Being that the designation has given them a status of a vessel. [ibid; see also 494:14]
[231] Meaning not only may they be returned to a vase if they were removed from it on Shabbos, but one may even initially place the plant into the vase on Shabbos for the first time if it contained water from before Shabbos. [so is understood from Admur ibid, and so understands M"B (336:54 in Shaareiy Tziyon 48) to be the opinion of Admur, and so understands also Kaf Hachaim 336:75 to be the opinion of Admur. As rules Admur so rules also Peri Megadim A"A 336:13; Bechureiy Yaakov 654:2; and so leans the M"B in Shaareiy Tziyon to be lenient]
Other Opinions: Other Poskim [first opinion in M"B 336:54 in name of Chayeh Adam 11:3; Tosefes Shabbos 336:21; Kapos Temarim brought in Kaf Hachaim 336:75; 654:4 and so rules Kaf Hachaim himself] rule it is forbidden to place the branch into the vase for the first time on Shabbos and only if it was removed from the water on Shabbos may it be returned to it. Regarding placing the plant for the first time on Yom Tov it is allowed to be done as even the above Poskim were only stringent regarding Shabbos. [So rules Kaf Hachaim 654:4 and Kapos Temarim ibid]
[232] So is implied from Admur ibid that it has to be placed before Shabbos and so rules M"B 336:54 explicitly.
[233] Bechureiy Yaakov 654:2; Kaf Hachaim 336:79; In 336:18 Admur does not explicitly mention Yom Tov, although he also does not differentiate in this aspect.
[234] So is implied from Admur as stated above and so rules Kaf Hachaim 336:79. The reason for this is because one is troubling himself to "fix" the plant and it is thus similar to the prohibition of switching waters.
[235] Admur ibid; Rama 336:11
If, however, the flowers are already fully open, there is no prohibition to place them into water, as explained above.
Other Poskim: Some Poskim rule it is permitted to place roses and other flowers into the water as even if they open it is merely revealing that which was already concealed and only by grains and the like which actually root in water was it forbidden. [Kaf Hachaim 336:77]
[236] As it is forbidden to trouble oneself to fix a vessel. [ibid] Meaning watering the plants is like he is trying to fix them.
[237] Admur 654:1
In Admur here he records, "and Yom Tov" regarding the prohibition of adding water to the vase. However, in Lekutei Sichos 21 p. 385 the Rebbe notes that it is a printing error and really it should read "and change the water on Yom Tov". However, to add water is permitted on Yom Tov as is explained in 654:1
[238] Aruch Hashulchan 654:2
[239] As this switching of water involves a greater trouble than simply adding water, and is hence forbidden to be done even on Yom Tov. [Kaf Hachaim 654:4 in name of Peri Megadim]
[240] Admur 654:1
[241] Aruch Hashulchan 654:2

thus not Muktzah.

2. The plant does not contain flowers or pestles which will further open in the water.

3. The water had been placed in the bucket or vase from before Shabbos.

Q&A

May one sprinkle water onto detached flowers and plants?
This matter requires further analyses.[242]

May one move the flowers towards the sun in order that they open?[243]
No.

May one remove plants from the water on Shabbos?
Yes. This applies even to flowers. If, however, the plant stayed in the water long enough that it has begun rooting, then it is forbidden.

May one make a flower bouquet on Shabbos?
Some Poskim[244] rule it is forbidden to do so.[245] This is forbidden to be done even if one does not tie the flowers together and simply places them in the same vase.

12. Watering detached vegetables:[246]

Edible vegetables: It is permitted to water detached vegetables in order to prevent them from shriveling, as since these vegetables are fit to be eaten on Shabbos it is therefore allowed to water them just as it is [similarly] allowed to move them.

Inedible vegetables: However, if they are not fit to be eaten today [on Shabbos] in which case they are forbidden to be moved [because of Muktzah] it is [also] forbidden to water them.

---

[242] On the one hand it is forbidden to initially place water into a vase due to Tikkun Mana, and hence here too it should seemingly be forbidden. On the other hand perhaps, it only applies when placing water into a vase being it is a greater trouble than simply sprinkling it. To note that SSH"K 26 footnote 97 allows dripping water onto the Lulav and dry cloth in order to wet it, hence implying such a matter has no prohibition of Tikkun Maneh.

[243] Piskeiy Teshuvos 336:11

[244] Igros Moshe 4:73

[245] This is forbidden due to fixing a vessel, as the gathering of the different flowers to make a bouquet are considered making a nice vessel out of the flowers. [ibid] However see Ketzos Hashulchan 8 p. 92 which seems to imply that the only question involved in gathering the flowers together is the prohibition of Miameir. However, when done outside of the area of growth, such as in one's home, it is permitted. Hence implying doing so does not carry the Tikkun Keli prohibition. Furthermore, it requires further analysis on the essence of the logic to consider simply placing flowers near each other as Tikkun Keli. It does not appear at all like one is making a Keli. This is unlike a necklace which when one enters the beads it is clearly apparent as if one is making a Keli. Vetzaruch Iyun.

[246] Admur 321:6

CHAPTER 11: THE LAWS INVOLVED IN PERFORMING A BRIS ON SHABBOS

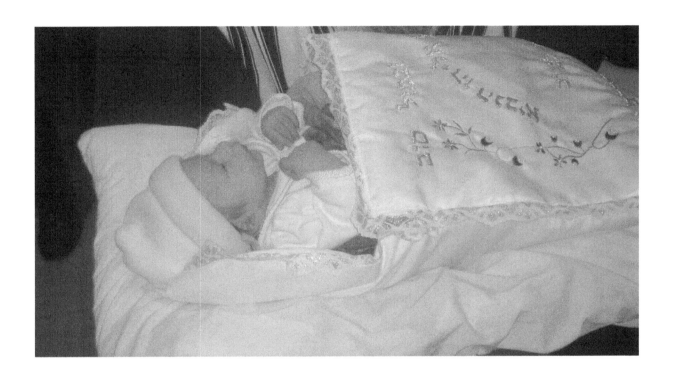

Based on: Shulchan Aruch Chapter 331;
Yoreh Deah Chapter 266

1. In what scenarios is a child to be circumcised on Shabbos?

The circumcision of an infant is to be performed on the eighth day after birth even if it falls on Shabbos.[1] If, however, it is past the child's eighth day and the child has still not been circumcised for whatever reason[2], then the circumcision may not be done on Shabbos.[3]

A child who was born during twilight:[4] A child who was born during *Bein Hashmashos*[5] of either Erev Shabbos or Motzaei Shabbos is not to be circumcised on Shabbos.[6] Even if the child stuck out[7] majority[8] of his head[9] during Bein Hashmashos, even though it was only fully removed after nightfall, nevertheless it is considered as if he was born during Bein Hashmashos and the circumcision may not be done on Shabbos. [**For this reason, special heed must be taken to verify the exact time the baby's head has protruded in case of a birth taking place near the time of Bein Hashmashos of Erev Shabbos or Shabbos!** Nevertheless, unless known otherwise[10], we do not assume the head came out much time prior to the body and we thus go in accordance to when the baby was taken out.[11] However other Poskim[12] rule it is always considered a doubt as to whether the head exited during Bein Hashmashos if she was in active labor during Bein Hashmashos and then gave birth at the beginning of the night.]

A premature baby:[13] A premature baby who is medically able to be circumcised on his eighth day, may be circumcised on Shabbos. If however the child's hair or nails are not fully developed and it is questionable whether the child was born in its eighth month, and certainly if one knows that it was born in the eighth

---

[1] Admur 331:1 As the verse states, "And on the eighth day circumcise his foreskin" The word "day" is expounded to include even Shabbos. [ibid]

[2] Such as the infant was ill and could not be circumcised on his eighth day. [ibid]

[3] Admur 331:4 The reason for this is because it is possible to circumcise the child after Shabbos without diminishing any fulfillment of the Mitzvah, as in any event it will not take place on its proper time whether it is done on Shabbos or after. [ibid] Meaning pushing it off one more day due to Shabbos does not lessen one's quality of performance of the Mitzvah once it is past the 8th day. For this reason, it must be delayed until after Shabbos.

[4] Admur 331:5

[5] Between sunset and nightfall. [Siddur as rules Geonim and so is the custom of all Jewry today; This ruling is in contrast to the ruling of Admur in the Shulchan Aruch in 331:5 and 261:5. Practically according to Admur in the Siddur Bein Hashmashos only begins a few minutes [between 3 and 5 minutes-see Kitzur Hilchos Shabbos Miluim p. 99] after the visual sunset. The start of Nightfall varies in each area. An expert Rav is to be contacted in cases of any doubt as to the Halachic definition of the time the child was born.]

The ruling of Admur in the SHU"A 331:5: In the Shulchan Aruch Admur rules like the opinion of Rabbeinu Tam [unlike the Yereim: Geonim] that Bein Hashmashos begins 15 minutes prior to nightfall, which in turn begins only 72:96 [depending on calculation of Mil in Admur] after sunset. Hence for up to 56.5-78 minutes after sunset it is still considered day for all purposes. Thus, if a child was born during this time on Erev Shabbos he is to be circumcised the next Friday. If he was born at this time on Shabbos he is to be circumcised on Shabbos. The reason we are not stringent like the opinion of the Yireim in this case to suspect that perhaps it is already after Shabbos when he was born is because no one in these provinces are accustomed like the Yireim regarding Melacha on Erev Shabbos, hence there is no need at all to be stringent here and push off the circumcision due to their opinion. [ibid; No mention of the opinion of the Geonim is made by Admur in his Shulchan Aruch. Now although in 251:5 Admur rules regarding one who accepted Shabbos before Plag Hamincha of Rabbeinu Tam, to be stringent like Yireim, perhaps there is it different as by one accepting Shabbos at that time he has shown that he suspects for the opinion of the Yireim. Alternatively, in that case there is nothing to lose by being stringent while here if one is stringent the Bris will be delayed from its proper time according to the main opinion.]

Other Poskim: The Shach [Yoreh Deah 266:11] brings the Maharahm Alshiker which rules to be stringent like the Geonim and push off the Bris if the child is born on Shabbos anytime between sunset and nightfall [of Rabbeinu Tam]. [This is unlike the ruling of Admur in the Siddur which rules completely like the Geonim that if born after nightfall of Geonim on Erev Shabbos, the Bris is to be done on Shabbos even though it is still Friday according to Rabbeinu Tam.] Birchei Yosef [brought in M"B 331:14] writes that the custom has spread like the Geonim in all Eretz Yisrael.

[6] As we do not override the Shabbos prohibitions if there is question as to whether the Mitzvah is to be performed that day. [ibid] As there is doubt as to whether Bein Hashmashos is part of the previous day or the coming day. Hence if born on Bein Hashmashos of Erev Shabbos the coming Shabbos is questionable whether it is the child's 8th day or 9th day. In the case the child was born on Bein Hashmashos of Motzaei Shabbos it is questionable if the coming Shabbos is the 7th or 8th day.

[7] See Piskeiy Teshuvos 331:6 for a discussion in Poskim on the exact definition of the head coming out. Is it defined as having come out once it exists the Prozdor to the Beis Hachitzon, or is it only considered to have come out when it enters to the actual air of the world. The custom is like the latter opinion. [Chasam Sofer Yoreh Deah 167; Sidrei Taharah 194:26; Piskeiy Teshuvah 266:8]

[8] It is disputed in Poskim as to how one is to measure the majority of the head. Is it the majority of the forehead, or the entire forehead. [see Piskeiy Teshuvos 331:6]

[9] Regarding a child which was born breached [leg first] then when majority of the body exits it is considered to have been born. Practically once the naval has come out majority of the body is considered to have exited. [see Piskeiy Teshuvos 331:6]

[10] Such as a case that the mother had difficulty pushing the child out.

[11] See Piskeiy Teshuvos 331:6 in name of Migdal Oaz [Yaavetz]

[12] Pischeiy Teshuvah 266:8

[13] Admur 330:8; 331:3

month, then it is better to abstain from circumcising this child on Shabbos.[14] [This applies even today, despite the fact that most premature babies of this kind will live to term.[15]] Nevertheless some are accustomed even in such a case to circumcise the child on Shabbos. If the child has fully developed hair and nails, or it does not but one knows for certain that it is a ninth- or seventh-month baby, then it is to be circumcised on Shabbos. [Practically, based on standard medical advice it is suggested to always wait until the 36-37th week prior to circumcising, even if the child is Halachicly allowed to be circumcised on Shabbos.[16]]

Androgenus:[17] An *Androgenus* is not to be circumcised on Shabbos even if it coincides with his 8th day.[18]

One who was born circumcised:[19] A child who was born circumcised[20] is not to be circumcised on Shabbos even if it coincides with his 8th day.[21]

Caesarean:[22] A child which was born Caesarean is not to be circumcised on Shabbos even if it coincides with his 8th day.[23]

Convert:[24] If an infant was converted by his mother prior to his 8th day he is not to be circumcised on Shabbos even if it coincides with his 8th day.[25]

Two foreskins or two Gidim:[26] A child born with two foreskins[27] or two complete sets of Gidim is not to be circumcised on Shabbos even if it coincides with his 8th day.[28]

Ben Mumar: A child born from a father who is an apostate Jew[29] is to be circumcised on Shabbos if it coincides with his 8th day, if the mother is not an apostate Jew.[30] [Likewise if the father is not an apostate while the mother is, the child is to be circumcised on Shabbos.[31]] If however both the mother and the father are apostate Jews it is disputed amongst Poskim whether one may circumcise the child on

---

[14] The Michaber Yoreh Deah 266:11 rules it is forbidden to circumcise an 8th month child who has not developed its hair and nails. This is brought as the first opinion in Admur in 330:8. The reason for this is because the child is Muktzah.

The Rama [ibid] however rules it is allowed to circumcise the child if there is doubt as to whether he was born in 7th or 8th month as perhaps he was born on the 7th and is considered a live child. However, if it is certain the child was born the 8th month then even according to the Rama the child is not to be circumcised. Practically the custom is to circumcise even in such a case as we do not know for certain when she became pregnant with the child. Nevertheless, Admur concludes as stated above that this is not to be done, even when it is a true doubt as to which month the child was born, as in a case of dispute it is better to act in a passive manner. [ibid]

[15] Minchas Yitzchak 4:123; Kinyan Torah 3:42; Chazon Ish Yoreh Deah 155 rule that today all premature babies, even in 8th month may have Shabbos desecrated on their behalf. Nevertheless, since there are medical issues involved in circumcising a child prematurely, practically we do not circumcise any premature child. [Piskeiy Teshuvos 331:4]

[16] Piskeiy Teshuvos 331:4; see Igros Moshe Yoreh Deah 2:121 that if a child is in an incubator, he is considered ill and cannot be circumcised until 7 days have passed after he is removed.

[17] Admur 331:6

An Androgenus is a person born with the both the male and female genitals.

[18] As there is doubt in the status of his gender [ibid] and we do not overrule the Shabbos prohibitions in a case of doubt. [331:5]

[19] Admur 331:6

[20] Which is defined as an unapparent foreskin, even if the foreskin is only undetectable when the child has an erection. [ibid]

[21] As although he is required to have blood dripped from his foreskin area, nevertheless since this is not a clear Biblical requirement it therefore does not overrule the Shabbos prohibitions. [ibid]

[22] Admur 331:6

[23] As there is doubt as to whether an infant born through Caesarean is required to be circumcised immediately, or on his 8th day. The reason for this is because the Torah juxtaposes the command of circumcision on the 8th day to a woman's impurity due to the birth, and since such a woman did not become impure due to the birth perhaps the obligation to circumcise on the 8th day does not apply. [ibid] [Background: The Gemara [Shabbos 135] suggests that a child born to a mother who did not become impure in the process is not required to be circumcised on the 8th day. Hence it does not override the Shabbos prohibitions.]

[24] Admur 331:6

[25] As there is doubt as to whether an infant which was converted is required to be circumcised immediately upon the conversion, or on his 8th day. The reason for this is because the Torah juxtaposes the command of circumcision on the 8th day to a woman's impurity due to the birth, and since such a woman did not become impure due to the birth perhaps the obligation to circumcise on the 8th day does not apply. [ibid]

[26] Admur 331:6

[27] Two foreskins, one over the other.

[28] As there is doubt as to whether an infant which was born with two foreskins is required to be circumcised on his 8th day, as the Torah states "Circumcise his foreskin" which refers to a single foreskin. Therefore, although such a child is to be circumcised on the 8th day due to doubt it nevertheless does not override the Shabbos prohibitions due to this mere doubt. [ibid]

[29] Known as a Mumar.

[30] Michaber Yoreh Deah 266:12

[31] Piskeiy Teshuvos 266:14

Shabbos.[32] [Practically, the custom is to circumcise all Jewish children on Shabbos if it coincides with their 8th day irrelevant of their parent's religious affiliation.[33]]

Mother Jewish, father not: It is disputed amongst Poskim[34] whether a child who was born from a gentile father may be circumcised on Shabbos even if it coincides with his 8th day.

Father Jewish, mother not:[35] A child whose mother is not Jewish is forbidden to be circumcised on Shabbos [even if it coincides with the child's 8th day and the father wants to convert him].

Mamzeir:[36] A Mamzeir is to be circumcised on Shabbos if it coincides with his 8th day.

Summary:
The following children may not be circumcised on Shabbos even if they were born the previous Shabbos:
1. A child born with C-Section.
2. A child born circumcised.
3. An Androgenus.
4. A child born with two foreskins.
5. A child born with two Gidim,
6. A child which converted after the birth, before the eighth day.
7. Father of child is not Jewish-dispute if may be circumcised.
8. Mother of child is not Jewish

Q&A

May one circumcise the child of an unorthodox couple on Shabbos if doing so will lead to unnecessary desecration of Shabbos?

Some Poskim[37] rule that one is to always go thru with a Bris on Shabbos even if this will cause others to desecrate Shabbos, as one may not delay such a great Mitzvah due to these reasons.[38]

Other Poskim[39] however rule that if one is certain that unnecessary Shabbos desecration will occur due to the circumcision, then it is to be delayed until the next day. If, however, due to one's refusal an unorthodox Mohel will be hired in one's place to perform the Bris on Shabbos, then he may agree to do so.[40] In any event [according to this latter opinion] one is to try to influence the parents to delay the Bris under different pretexts, such as the child is too yellow and reasons of the like.[41]

Must a Mohel agree to travel away from home to do a Shabbos Milah?

Some Poskim[42] rule the Mohel is obligated to travel to the area of the child in order to perform a Bris. Others[43] however rule there is no obligation to do so. This especially applies today that it is possible

---

[32] The Bedek Habayis rules that nevertheless the child may be circumcised on Shabbos while the Shach [266:9] Taz [266:16] rule it is forbidden to circumcise the child on Shabbos

[33] Mahrsham 2:156; Sheivet Haleivi 4:132

[34] Pischeiy Teshuvah Yoreh Deah 266:14 rules he is to be circumcised on Shabbos. Mahrahm Shik [Even Haezer 20] and Beis Yitzchak [Even Haezer 29:11] rule the child may not be circumcised on Shabbos as some Poskim hold he has the status of a gentile and needs conversion, as well as that he is probably no better than the child of a Mumar/Mumeres.

[35] Yoreh Deah 266:13

[36] Yoreh Deah Shach 266:17

[37] Minchas Yitzchak 3:35; Igros Moshe Yoreh Deah 1:156

[38] A) It is a mere Grama b) This can lead others to push off doing their Bris on time. C) Perhaps a non-religious person will do the Bris improperly.

[39] Mahrshag 2:24; Sheivet Haleivi 4:132 and 135

[40] See Minchas Yitzchak 3:35

[41] Brought in Piskeiy Teshuvos 331:1

[42] Mahrsham 1:209; Beis Yitzchak 42; Beis Shearim 120; Minchas Yitzchak 2:75

[43] Avnei Neizer 2:392; Chayeh Adam 68:19 leaves this matter in question

for the baby to come to the Mohel's area for Shabbos.[44] Likewise some Poskim[45] rule there is no obligation to do so for the child of a non-orthodox couple.

One who follows Rabbeinu Tam regarding Motzaei Shabbos, how is he to follow regarding a child born after sunset?[46]

He is to be stringent to consider it Bein Hashmashos from after sunset[47] until after nightfall of Rabbeinu Tam [approximately 65 minutes after sunset in Eretz Yisrael].[48]

If a child was born on Shabbos with use of a vacuum is he to be circumcised on his 8th day which coincides with Shabbos?[49]

Yes.

Is an IVF or AI baby to be circumcised on his 8th day which coincides with Shabbos?[50]

Some Poskim[51] leave this matter in question.[52]

---

2. Actions that may be performed for the child when a Bris is performed on Shabbos:[53]

- Periah[54]
- Metzitzah[55]
- <u>Medical treatment to the area</u>: One may place a bandage or poultice[56] on the area of circumcision.[57] Likewise all other medical treatments may be done to the area of circumcision.[58] Nevertheless initially one is required to prepare all the medical treatments before Shabbos [if their preparation involves transgressing Shabbos, even Rabbinically[59]]. Thus, all ointments which require preparation are to be prepared before Shabbos.[60] If one did not prepare the medicines before Shabbos then one may do so on Shabbos with an irregularity.[61] If one is unable to prepare the medicines on Shabbos using an irregularity[62] then it is forbidden to prepare them on Shabbos [even if doing so involves only a Rabbinical transgression[63]]. It is forbidden to prepare the

---

[44] SSH"K 42 footnote 245

[45] Minchas Yitzchak ibid

[46] Piskeiy Teshuvos 331:5

[47] As rule Geonim

[48] Minchas Elazar 1:23; Divrei Yoel 18; Igros Moshe 4:62; Sheivet Haleivi 1:49; 4:132; Beir Moshe 2:61

[49] Har Tzevi Yoreh Deah 248

[50] Har Tzevi Yoreh Deah 248

[51] Rav SZ"A brought in Piskeiy Teshuvos 331:7

[52] As this is not the natural way of becoming impregnated and the verse states "a woman when she <u>Tazria</u> and has a son…" regarding Milah on the 8th day.

[53] Admur 331:1

[54] As Periah is included within the Milah process. [ibid]

[55] It overrides the Shabbos prohibition [of causing wound] being that not doing so can lead to danger to the child. [ibid]

[56] This refers to a dressing or pad which has ointment smeared over it which is then placed on the wound

[57] Although applying a poultice was forbidden even in a case of illness that does not involve danger, here it is allowed as giving treatment to the area is considered to be a case of danger. [ibid]

[58] As the area that was circumcised can become lethally dangerous if not properly treated. [ibid]

[59] As one must even mix the oil and wine ointment together before Shabbos, even though doing so on Shabbos is a Rabbinical prohibition.

[60] For example, back in the day when they would place crushed cumin and wine mixed with oil on the area, then before Shabbos one would need to crush the cumin and mix the wine with oil. [ibid]

[61] Thus, is they forgot to crush the cumin before Shabbos they would be allowed on Shabbos to chew it until it is crushed. Similarly, if the wine/oil mixture was not prepared before Shabbos it would have to be placed separately, one after the other, onto the area in order to do it with an irregularity. However, one would not be allowed to mix it on Shabbos. [ibid] As for the reason why it is allowed to do so with an irregularity even before the circumcision, seemingly this is because a child has a status of a Choleh Sheiyn Bo Sakana towards which all Rabbinical prohibitions may be done with an irregularity.

[62] Such as one is unable to chew the cumin and must thus grind it in its normal fashion. [ibid]

[63] Admur 331:7. It may not be implied from Admur 331:1 which only mentions this Halacha with regards to grinding the cumin and not regarding mixing the oil that he holds that Rabbinical prohibitions may be done, as it is always permitted to do a Rabbinical prohibition with a Shinui for the sake of one who is bedridden, and a child has the status of one who is bedridden. Vetzaruch Iyun as prior to the Milah, the child does not need

medicine in such a case even if this will cause the circumcision to need to be delayed until the next day.[64] If, however, the child was already circumcised then all matters may be done to treat the child, even if they could have been done before Shabbos.[65]

- Removing pieces of the foreskin after the circumcision:[66] After the circumcision it is permitted, if necessary, to cut off any remaining pieces of the foreskin if those pieces refrain the Mitzvah from being fulfilled. However, those pieces of skin which do not refrain the Mitzvah's fulfillment, even though they are initially required to be removed, may not be cut on Shabbos once the Mohel has removed his hand from the area after the initial circumcision. Prior however to removing his hand from the area of circumcision it is permitted to fix and cut even these pieces of skin.

3. Machshireiy Milah/Transgressions involved in preparing for the circumcision:[67]
Only the act of circumcision itself overrides Shabbos, while all other matters which are done to prepare for the circumcision may not be done on Shabbos if they involve any Shabbos prohibition, even of Rabbinical nature.[68] Thus all the forbidden preparations for the circumcision must be done from before Shabbos. This includes:

- Sharpening the blade
- Bringing the knife to the area of the circumcision must be done before Shabbos if it involves passing an area in which carrying is forbidden, whether Biblically or Rabbinically.
- Preparation of medicines, as explained above.
- Chaluk[69]

If a person did not do the above before Shabbos: If a forbidden action was not taken care of from before Shabbos, it remains forbidden to do so on Shabbos even if doing so involves a mere Rabbinical prohibition[70], and even if this will cause the circumcision to be delayed until the next day.[71] This applies even if it was beyond one's control that the above actions were not fulfilled before Shabbos. Likewise, even if the necessary preparations were fulfilled before Shabbos but the items got lost [or damaged] and new one's are required it nevertheless remains forbidden.

Asking a gentile to do one of the forbidden preparations: One may ask a gentile to perform a Rabbinically forbidden action needed for the circumcision.[72] Furthermore, if absolutely necessary to the point that lack of doing so will require delaying the circumcision until the next day[73], one may even ask a gentile to perform a Biblically forbidden act needed for the circumcision.[74]

---

this treatment, so how can it be allowed to enter the child into this situation. In any event Admur states explicitly in 331:7 that Rabbinical prohibitions may not be done if they could have been done before Shabbos.

[64] As Mila preparations that involve Shabbos transgressions do not override the Shabbos prohibitions being that they could be done before Shabbos, and it is only the Mila itself which overrides. Now although if the treatments are not given they could jeopardize the child's life and hence indeed override Shabbos, nevertheless this is only after the fact. However initially it is forbidden to enter the child into this state of danger, hence allowing the treatment. Thus, it is forbidden to go through with the circumcision. [ibid]

[65] Although Admur writes this case to be referring to one who did prepare the ointment before Shabbos and after the circumcision it spilled, nevertheless obviously it is not coming to exclude a case that one transgressed and did not prepare the ointment before Shabbos, as it is a matter of life and death for the child.

[66] Admur 331:2

[67] Admur 331:7

[68] The reason for this is because since these acts can be performed before Shabbos there is no need for them to override Shabbos. [ibid]

[69] A Chaluk is a cloth which has a hole pierced in its middle to be garbed onto the child's Gid, which is then tightened around the Gid to prevent its skin from covering over the foreskin. Hence this hole may not be made on Shabbos. One may however tie a regular cloth around the Gid without making a hole. Likewise, one may carry it with an irregularity through a Rabbinical forbidden domain such as by wrapping it on his finger. [ibid]

[70] Such as to carry the knife or the infant through a courtyard which did not have Eiruv Chatzeiros done. [ibid]

[71] As the Sages upheld their decrees even when a Kareis penalty will ensue due to abiding by it. [ibid]

[72] As the Sages did not decree against Shvus Deshvus in a case which involves a Mitzvah. [ibid]

[73] Such as sharpening the knife, or to carry it through a public domain. [ibid]

[74] A dispute of this matter is recorded in Admur. Some opinions rule it is forbidden to ever ask a gentile to perform a Biblical prohibition even in the case of a Mitzvah. Others however rule that even Biblical prohibitions may be performed through a gentile for the sake of a Mitzvah. Practically although one may not rely on this latter opinion regarding a typical Mitzvah, nevertheless regarding Mila since it itself overrides Shabbos one may rely on their words regarding the prohibited preparations. [ibid]

Asking a gentile to carry the child to Shul:[75] It is disputed whether one may ask a gentile to carry the infant from his house to Shul if the area does not have an Eiruv.[76] Practically those which are lenient are to do as follows: The gentile is to take the child out from his house into the public domain. The child is then to be handed to a Jew which in turn hands it to another Jew within his 4 cubit radius and so on and so forth until the child reaches near the entrance of the Shul.[77] The gentile then takes the child and carries him into the Shul.

4. Bathing the infant:[78]

Today that it is no longer viewed as a medical necessity to bathe a circumcised child, it remains forbidden to do so to the child the same way as is forbidden for an adult. Hence only minority of his limbs may be bathed in hot water, and only if the water was heated before Shabbos.[79] Nevertheless if one sees that it is necessary to be done for medical reasons, and lack of doing so can endanger the child, then one may desecrate Shabbos for the infant just as is the law in all cases of danger.

5. Washing the baby with a wet cloth:

It is forbidden to soak a cloth into water in order to wash down the infant. Nevertheless, one may ask a gentile to do so.[80]

6. Is a Mila knife Muktzah on a Shabbos Bris?[81]

The Milah knife is Muktzah[82] and remains Muktzah even when there is a Bris on Shabbos. [83] It may therefore only be moved for the purpose of performing the Bris. After the Bris it remains forbidden to be moved for any purpose as is the law by all Muktzah objects. Nevertheless, it is not required to immediately place down the knife after the Mila and rather it may be brought by the Mohel to a safe area for it to be kept until after Shabbos. It is forbidden to wash the blood off the knife even while the knife is still in the Mohel's hand.[84]

Q&A

Is the foreskin Muktzah?[85]
The foreskin is considered Muktzah. Nevertheless, one may carry it to its destined place within the prepared earth.

---

[75] Admur 331:8

[76] As on the one hand the child can be circumcised at his home, and hence bringing the child to Shul involves no Mitzvah need for which the Sages allowed asking a gentile. This would apply even if the area is merely Rabbinically forbidden to carry in such as a courtyard without Eiruv Chatzeiros. Others however allow asking a gentile to bring the child to Shul [through a merely Rabbinically forbidden area of carrying] as circumcising in Shul will gather greater attendance which thereby beautifies G-d. [ibid]

[77] A Jew is not to carry the child from inside to outside or vice versa, even if another Jew will take the child from his hands before he puts the child down, as nevertheless a Rabbinical prohibition has been performed by this Jew, as he has performed Akirah or Hanacha. [ibid]

[78] Admur 331:11; Michaber 331:9; See also 616:1 regarding Yom Kippur

[79] Admur ibid see Volume 2 "The Laws of Bathing"]

[80] As all Melachas which occur unintentionally are permitted to be performed by a gentile even if they are inevitably done as a result of the action the gentile was asked to do. Thus, although the Melacha of whitening is performed when soaking a cloth in water, one may nevertheless ask the gentile to enter the cloth into the water as the gentile is not being asked to whiten the cloth but rather to soak it. [ibid]

[81] Admur 331:10

[82] It is defined as Muktzah Machmas Chisron Kis

[83] This follows the ruling of the Taz:Magen Avraham in 331 that even on a Shabbos Bris the knife is Muktzah. However, the Rama and Shach Yoreh Deah 266:2 rule that the knife is not Muktzah at all as something cannot be Muktzah for only part of Shabbos.
The M"B 310:15 rules that in a time of need, such as there is suspicion of robbery, one may rely on this lenient opinion to hide the knife even after one already placed it down. The Sheivet Haleivi [4:135] rules likewise saying that majority of Poskim are lenient.

[84] As one may only wash vessels on Shabbos if they have a Shabbos use. [323:6]

[85] Yoreh Deah Pischeiy Teshuvah 266:2

7. May one perform his first Bris on Shabbos?[86]

It is forbidden for one who has never circumcised before to perform a circumcision on Shabbos[87] [even if he is the father of the child[88]]. Similarly, one who has never before performed Periah is forbidden to perform it on Shabbos. It is permitted for the father to circumcise his son on Shabbos if he has done so once in the past.[89]

8. Having two people do the Milah and Periah:

It is disputed[90] whether one may have two people do the Milah and Periah, one person the Milah while the other the Periah, or if it all must be done by one person. [Practically the custom is to be lenient.[91] Some[92] rule that if the father of the child desires to do either the Milah or Periah and have another do the other part, then it is permitted according to all.[93]]

---

[86] Admur 331:13

[87] As he may come to perform it incorrectly and hence end up desecrating Shabbos for no need. [ibid]

[88] So is implied from Admur. However, there are Poskim which allow a father to do so even for the first time. [See Piskeiy Teshuvos 331:9]

[89] We do not claim that if another Mohel is available the father should not do so, due to that he is fixing his child which is Tikkun Keli [ibid] as in truth every Mohel is fixing the child and not just the father. [M"B 331:39]

[90] The Michaber [Yoreh Deah 266:14] rules it is forbidden to have two different people perform the Milah. The Rama however rules that doing so is permitted, although initially one is to be stringent. Many Poskim however argue on this conclusion, ruling that even initially one may have two different people perform the Milah/Periah, and so was the widespread custom in Poland. [M"B 331:36]

[91] M"B ibid

[92] Eretz Tzevi 63

[93] As the Mohel is the emissary of the father and it is hence as if only one person is doing the Milah/Periah. [ibid]

CHAPTER 12: LAWS WHICH RELATE TO THE DATE OF SHABBOS, INTERNATIONAL DATELINE, AND TIME ZONES

One who lost track of the weekdays

1. One who is lost in the desert or wilderness and has lost track of days, when does he keep Shabbos?[1]

One who has become lost in the wilderness or desert and has lost track of the days of the week is to count 7 days starting from the day which he lost track of Shabbos on[2], and sanctify Shabbos on that seventh day[3].

What is he to do on his seventh day: On the seventh day of one's count he is to say Kiddush and Havdala, and follow all the laws of Shabbos, including both the Biblical and Rabbinical laws[4]. However, it is permitted for him to continue traveling even many miles on his seventh day in order to enable him to leave the desert as soon as possible.

Not to do work on the other days: On all the other six days prior to one's scheduled seventh day, if one has food to eat it is forbidden for him to transgress any Biblical Shabbos prohibition, being that perhaps that day is in truth Shabbos[5]. However, one is allowed to transgress Rabbinical Shabbos prohibitions.[6]

Doing work to obtain food to eat: After one's food has run out, he may work each day, including his seventh day, so that he obtains enough food to eat for that day, even if doing so involves transgressing Biblical prohibitions.[7] However one may only perform prohibited work in order to obtain the minimum food he needs to survive that day and may thus not work for the next day's food. This applies even against working on his sixth day for the food of his seventh day.[8] Accordingly if one has enough bread to eat for that day, he may not cook any food that day.[9]

If one knows how many days, he has been traveling for but lost track of when he left?[10] If one knows he has been traveling for a certain number of days but is unsure the day he left, then on his eighth day he may do all weekday work, as for certain he did not leave on Shabbos and thus his eighth day must be a weekday. Similarly, every eighth day from when he left is a weekday and he may thus do all forms of work on that day.

Q&A

If one has been captured and no longer has track of which day is Shabbos what is he to do?[11]

He is to follow the same laws as one who is lost in the desert.

Is one to wear Tefillin on his seventh day?[12]

Yes[13], although not while Davening the Shabbos prayer. [Others[14] however rule that one is not to don Tefillin even during his supposed weekdays, due to possibility that it is Shabbos.[15] We do not rule like this opinion.[16]]

---

[1] Admur 344:1

For a story of Rav who got mixed up with day of Shabbos: See Sippurei Chassidim Vayakhel 1st story

[2] Literally "from the day where he became conscious of his forgetfulness". Meaning if he knows he was in the desert for at least seven days and he remembers losing track of the days three days ago then he begins counting from three days back as day one, and the seventh day from that counting is sanctified. [Mishneh Berurah 344:2 in name of Bach]

[3] This is Rabbinically required in order to prevent one from forgetting the existence of the sanctity of Shabbos which surpasses the other days of the week. [ibid]

[4] As although Safek Derabanan Lekula, nonetheless this seventh day of his counting was considered by the Sages like the second day of Yom Tov celebrated in the Diaspora which is likewise forbidden in even Rabbinical prohibitions. [ibid]

[5] And by a Biblical doubt one is to be stringent.

[6] As Safek Derabanan Lekula.

[7] As this is a matter of life and death.

[8] As perhaps really the sixth day is Shabbos and the seventh is Sunday.

[9] As he is no longer in a life-threatening situation. [Admur]

[10] Admur 344:2

[11] M"B 344:1

[12] M"B 344 in Biur Halacha "Afilu"

If one of the days is for certain a weekday, as explained above, then if he is able to work enough on this day to supply food for all the other days must he do so?[17]
Yes.

Q&A relating to changes in time zones

When does one keep Shabbos in Japan and New Zealand?[18]
One keeps Shabbos on the same day as the local community keeps Shabbos, which is on Saturday[19]. Some Poskim[20] however rule that one should in addition to keeping Shabbos on Saturday[21], be stringent to also not do any Melacha on Sunday. Others[22] rule that one is to act on both days as a weekday[23], with exception to that one may not do any Biblical Melacha on both days and that one is to say Kiddush only on Saturday. To note that Chabad of Japan keeps Shabbos only on Japan's Saturday.

In areas[24] which the daylight or night lasts for more than 24 hours, how is Shabbos calculated?[25]
Shabbos is calculated based on 24 hours and not based on daylight or night. One thus counts six days of 24 hours and sanctifies the seventh day as Shabbos. However there requires further analysis regarding the times of prayer.

May one who owns a business in a later time zone have the business open at the conclusion of Shabbos of his time zone?[26]
❖ Example: One lives in Israel and owns a business in the U.S.A.
No. the business may only open after Shabbos in its time zone has concluded.

---

[13] As one follows majority of the days which are weekdays, and although Shabbos is Kavua, nevertheless since there is a Biblical doubt one must be stringent.

[14] Zichron Yitzchak 31

[15] As wearing Tefillin on Shabbos transgresses a Biblical command, and it is better to transgress a Biblical command through Sheiv Veal Taseh than through Kum Veasei. [ibid] However, Tzaruch Iyun Gadol on this opinion as to avoid this problem one is simply to don the Tefillin with a stipulation "If it is Shabbos then I am wearing it as a clothing, if it is weekday, I am wearing it for its Mitzvah" as is ruled in 31:2 regarding Chol Hamoed.

[16] As explained in the previous footnote.

[17] M"B 344:11

[18] The International dateline refers to an imaginary line which cuts through the globe and separates between where on the globe the day begins and where the day ends. For secular legal terms the dateline runs through the Pacific between Alaska/Hawaii and Russia/Australia, and hence Russia/Australia is the first to start its day while Alaska and Hawai are the last. Thus, there is an almost 24 hour difference between those countries, even though they are not far in distance. There is a dispute amongst later Poskim regarding the Halachic positioning of the International dateline. Some Poskim [Chazon Ish] rule that Japan is west of the Dateline and thus is the last country to begin its day. Thus, while according to the legal dateline Japan is the first to begin the new weekday, according to Halacha it is the last. Thus, while according to the legal dateline Japan is beginning Saturday so to say, according to the Halachic dateline [according to the Chazon Ish] it is really beginning Friday, and thus Shabbos is really on its Sunday. Many other Poskim however argue with this opinion and rule that Japan is on the east of the dateline, as states the secular legal dateline and its Saturday is the correct day. Below we will discuss final rulings on this matter.

[19] Rebbe in Shaar Halacha Uminhag 2:220; Sheivet Haleivi 3:28 and 6:34 explains the importance of the fact that the custom always was to keep Shabbos on Saturday in Japan and thus one must keep Shabbos on that day for all matters, and G-d forbid to desecrate any part of it. However, the Sheivit Haleivi himself concludes that also on Sunday no Melacha should be done as will be brought next.

[20] Sheivet Haleivi 6:34; The Rav asking the question to the Sheivet Haleivi 3:28.

[21] In Sheivet Haleivi 3:28 the questioner writes that he would tell askers to put on Tefillin without a blessing on Shabbos. However, the Sheivet Haleivi negates this.

[22] Yisrael Vehazmanim 78

[23] Such as regarding prayer, Tefillin, Rabbinical Melacha.

[24] This can occur by areas near the North and South pole. It is most common in cities in Northern Finland, Norway; Russia; Canada; and Alaska. A common tourist city in which this occurs is the city of Longyyearbyen, Norway. During the summer months the sun never sets, and one thus does not experience night. During the winter months the sun never rises, and one thus never experiences day during those months.

[25] Shaareiy Teshuvah 344 in name of Mur Uketzia; Shaareiy Halacha Uminhag 1:134

[26] Piskeiy Teshuvos 344:2

In the above scenario may the business remain open on Erev Shabbos until Shabbos begins in its time zone, or must it close at the time the owner accepts Shabbos?
Some Poskim[27] rule that the business must close by the time the owner accepts Shabbos in his earlier time zone. Others[28] however rule that the business may remain open until Shabbos begins in its own time zone.

May one call or send a fax to an area of a later time zone if Shabbos has not yet ended there?
Many Poskim[29] rule that doing so is permitted, although there are Poskim[30] which are stringent against doing so.

May one send an e-mail to a person of a later time zone if Shabbos has not yet ended there?
Yes.

May one travel after Shabbos to a country that is in a later time zone?[31]
  ➤ Example: May one travel from Australia to California or from Israel to the U.S.A. immediately after Shabbos ends.
It is forbidden to initially travel to an area with a later time zone if he will be arriving at the time zone when it is still Shabbos there. If one went ahead and traveled there, he must keep the remaining hours of Shabbos in that country.

---

[27] Eretz Tzevi 44; Minchas Yitzchak 7:34; Betzeil Hachachma 3:125
[28] Chelkas Yaakov ???; Shraga Hameir 2:65
[29] Beir Moshe 6 Kuntrus Electricity 49; Chelkas Yaakov 3:106; Betzeil Hachachma 3:125
[30] See Piskeiy Teshuvos 344:2
[31] Piskeiy Teshuvos 344:2 in name of Betzeil Hachochmah 83
Such as traveling from New Zealand to Hawaii in which if one leaves right after Shabbos he will arrive on Shabbos in Hawaii.

Index

Index

Index

Index

Perspiring, 101
Physiotherapy, 238
Picture album, 317
Ping Pong, 374
Pit, 388
Planting, 400
Plants, 389
  Watering, 392
Play dough, 374
Pod plants, 396
Polishing, 38, 363
Polishing silverware, 363
Post-it notes, 317
Pregnancy test, 288
Push Ups, 238
Puzzles, 294, 377

R

Reading on Shabbos
  Billboards, 333
  Books, 328
  Bulletin board, 333
  Business documents, 321
  cook book, 333
  Descriptions under portraits and paintings, 326
  Engraved words, 322
  guest list, 321
  Homework, 329
  Mail, 324
  Manuscript, 329
  Mitzvah related matters, 323
  Muktzah, 331
  Names for Mishebeirach, 323
  Newspapers, 332
  Non-business documents, 321
  Peroches, 323
  Public related matters, 324
  Torah reading of next week, 330
Resuscitation machine, 170
Robbers, 186, 190
Roller blades, 377
Rubber stamps, 286
Running and Jumping, 373
Rust, 364

S

Safety pin, 314
Sakanas Nefashos, 161
Sandbox, 377
Scabs
  Removing scabs, 283
Scotch tape, 317
Scrabble, 292
Seeds, 400
Sefer Torah, 302
Sewing, 313
Sheital-Braiding, 281
Shining one's floor, 351
Shoetree, 121
Showering, 75
Siddur versus Shulchan Aruch, 11
Sink-unplugging, 366
Sleeping pills, 209
Smearing oil, 115
Smelling
  fruits and plants attached to ground, 390
  Plants detached from ground, 390
  Pod plant, 390
Snapping finger, 341
Snow, 376
Snow balls, 376
Snow men, 376
Soap, 37, 361
Soot of pots, 300
Spitting on grass, plants, 394
Splashing twigs and debris, 99
Sponges, 38, 362
Squeegee, 351
Squeezing hair, 95
Stalk of dates, 400
Stamps, 289
Staples, 314
Stay awake pills, 209
Steel wool, 362
Storage room, 367
Suicide, 169
Suspicios object, 191
Sweeping, 347
Swimming, 97
Swing, 378, 385

Index

SHULCHANARUCHHARAV.COM MEMBERS BENEFITS

Choose a subscription plan today and gain access to extra features, including access to our full Audio Shiurim database with over 1500 classes, original source sheets behind the laws, PDF downloads of articles, and much more!

Subscription level	Monthly Payment	Help support a Torah Institution	PDF download of article	10% off purchase of all titles	Access all audio Shiurim	Free copy of annual publication	Access Sources Database	Request Source Sheets	Access Courses
Silver	$18	YES	YES	YES	YES	✖	✖	✖	✖
Gold	$36	YES	YES	YES	YES	YES	✖	✖	✖
Platinum	$54	YES	YES	YES	YES	YES	YES	✖	✖
Sapphire	$100	YES	YES	YES	YES	YES	YES	Four monthly*	✖
Diamond	$150	YES	YES	YES	YES	YES	YES	Eight monthly*	One course per year

*Source sheet requests are dependent on their availability in our personal database

How to subscribe:

- See the following link: https://shulchanaruchharav.com/product/support-subscription/

Membership level Features

PDF downloads [starting from silver]:

- Our online articles on http://shulchanaruchharav.com/ contain a special PDF download option available to all site members and subscribers who are logged in. This allows you to be able to publish, and save or print, a PDF style format of the article for easier reading and for you to keep for your record.

- This feature is only available if you are logged into the website using your username and password. You will receive a username and password after your subscription. If you have lost your username or password, or never received one to begin with, then please contact us to receive it.

- Also, to note, the PDF feature is not available in all articles and it depends on its length. Due to technical limitations, the PDF feature cannot publish into a PDF, articles that have very long HTML pages and thus the above feature is limited only to the short articles which is the bulk of the articles on the website.

10% off all purchases [starting from silver]:

- All members and subscribers can receive a 10% discount on all their book purchases done through our website through entering the discount code in the shopping cart towards the end of the purchase.

- You will receive the code in your confirmation email after your subscription.

- Please save this code for all your future purchases. In case you forget it, you can always request it from us.

Access all our audio Shiurim [starting from silver]:

- Our exciting new feature which is now available for all members is access to our database of recorded Shiurim, which includes over 1,500 recorded classes. While many of the classes are already publicly available for free on our various outlets, such as our website, YouTube, Vimeo, and Podbean, there are many classes which have never been published and are available in our personal database which we are now extending access to all members. In addition, the classes are all organized under their specific topic and hence you will have a much easier time accessing them and searching for a specific Shiur. Likewise, you are able to download the entire library and listen to it at your leisure without Internet connection. These are benefits not available to the public through our already established outlets.

- The classes consist of all our previous Daily Halacha audios that have featured on the Daily Halacha email and Whatsapp for the past seven years, organized according to topic. They likewise include recordings of public classes that have been given over the years on various subjects, such as the weekly Parsha, Farbrengens, and other events. In addition, our entire Hebrew collection of classes on the laws of Shabbos is likewise available for those who are Hebrew friendly. There are also recordings for various courses that we have taught, such as the Shabbos kitchen, and Meat and Milk for women, and various Semicha courses that are likewise available.

- We will give you access to your email to the folder after your subscription is processed.

- If you choose to download the classes, or the entire folder, which you may, it is strictly for your own personal use and may not be shared with others. If others would like to benefit from it then they should either look for our free public options on the various outlets mentioned above, or become a member just like you.

- Subscribers must commit to remain a member for a full year to merit this benefit.

Free copy of our publications [starting from Gold]:
- All members and subscribers from **gold** level and above are sent a free copy of all new titles that are published in their year of membership.
- If you change your address, please update us right away and especially after a new publication is advertised so that we can send it to the correct address.

Access database of our sources [starting from Platinum]:
- All members and subscribers from **platinum** level and above will be given access to a special OneDrive folder that will hold a database of source sheets for various topics and Halachos.
- This new feature is without doubt one of our most prized and most beneficial for all those who are interested in further researching a given law or subject, without taking the time in searching for all the original sources. In this feature we give applicable members access to files which contain both full articles on various subjects, as well as original photocopies of many of the sources used to write the article.
- Mainly, this feature will include the photocopied sources behind the articles that feature in the daily Halacha. The source sheets will be archived in the relevant folder of their topic. Additional source sheets will also feature in this database, and with time this will become a very large database of source sheets with a photocopy of original sources.

- This feature is perfect for Rabbis, teachers, Magidei Shiurim, etc, for them to be able to prepare a class using the original sources, and even make photocopies to distribute to the participants.

Request source sheets [starting from Sapphire]:
- Members and subscribers from **sapphire** level and above will be able to request a limited amount of source sheets per month on topics that are not found in our database. For example, if a subscriber of sapphire level and above desires to do research on a certain topic, or give a class on a certain subject, and it is not already available in the above-mentioned database, then he may send us a request for sources on the subject, and based on availability in our private personal database, we will arrange it to be sent to the person requesting it.
- Providing source sheets for topics requested is dependent on current availability in our private database and the amount of time required to research the subject. We also reserve the right to reject providing sources on a certain subject based on our discretion. To note, that we already have over 25,000 source sheets in our private database on myriads of subjects that simply require restructuring to be made available upon request.
- The number of requests per month is limited to four monthly requests for a sapphire member and eight monthly requests for a diamond member.

Access courses [Diamond]:
- Members and subscribers from **diamond** level and above will be able to request free enrollment in one of our available courses.
- Members are limited to one course per year and must finish their previous course prior to choosing another course the next year.

Our other Sefarim available on shulchanaruchharav.com, Amazon.com and selected book stores

430

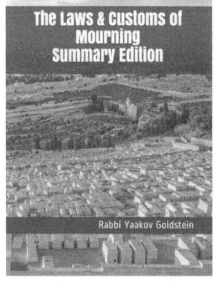

KEDUSHAS HABAYIS

A comprehensive guide on Siman Reish Mem

Rabbi Yaakov Goldstein

Topics in Practical Halacha Vol. 4

RABBI YAAKOV GOLDSTEIN

The Pesach Seder

Summary & Handbook

Rabbi Yaakov Goldstein

The Laws of Tefillin

Summary & Handbook

Rabbi Yaakov Goldstein

היה קורא פרק שני ברכות   יז.

ולא פריה ורביה ולא משא ומתן ולא קנאה ולא שנאה אלא תחרות אלא צדיקים יושבין ועטרותיהם
בראשיהם ונהנים מזיו השכינה שנאמר יויחזו את האלהים ויאכלו וישתו: גדולה הבטחה שהבטיחן
הקב״ה לנשים יותר מן האנשים שנא יונשים שאננות קומנה שמענה קולי בנות בוטחות האזנה אמרתי
א״ל רב לר׳ חייא נשים במאי זכיין יבאקרויי בנייהו לבי כנישתא ובאתנויי גברייהו בי רבנן ונטרין לגברייהו
עד דאתו מבי רבנן. כי הוו מפטרי רבנן מבי ר׳ אמי ואמרי לה מבי ר׳ חנינא אמרי ליה הכי עולמך תראה בחייך
ואחריתך לחיי העולם הבא ותקותך לדור דורים לבך יהגה תבונה פיך ידבר חכמות ולשונך ירחיש רננות
עפעפיך יישירו נגדך עיניך יאירו במאור תורה ופניך יזהירו כזוהר הרקיע שפתותיך יביעו דעת וכליותיך

Rav said to Rav Chiya

*"With what do women receive merit [of learning Torah]? Through escorting
their children to the Talmud Torah, and assisting their husbands in learning
Torah, and waiting for their husbands to return from the Beis Midrash"*

*This Sefer is dedicated to my dear wife whose continuous support and sharing of
joint goals in spreading Torah and Judaism have allowed this Sefer to become a
reality.*

*May Hashem grant her and our children much
success and blessing in all their endeavors*

שיינא שרה ליבא בת חיה ראשא
&
מושקא פריידא
שניאור זלמן
דבורה לאה
נחמה דינה
מנוחה רחל
חנה
שטערנא מרים
שלום דובער
חוה אסתר
בתשבע
יהודית שמחה

Made in United States
North Haven, CT
17 July 2022